D0916956

xi

# AMERICAN COMMUNES
## 1860–1960

SECTS AND CULTS IN AMERICA
BIBLIOGRAPHICAL GUIDES
(General Editor: J. Gordon Melton)
(VOL. 13)

GARLAND REFERENCE LIBRARY
OF SOCIAL SCIENCE
(VOL. 402)

# BIBLIOGRAPHIES ON SECTS AND CULTS IN AMERICA
## (General Editor: J. Gordon Melton)

# AMERICAN COMMUNES
## 1860–1960
### *A Bibliography*

Timothy Miller

GARLAND PUBLISHING, INC. • NEW YORK & LONDON
1990

Library of Congress Cataloging-in-Publication Data

Miller, Timothy, 1944–
   American communes, 1860–1960: a bibliography / Timothy Miller.
   p.  cm. — (Sects and cults in America. Bibliographical guides;
vol. 13) (Garland reference library of social science; vol. 402)
   ISBN 0–8240–8470–5 (alk. paper)
   1. Collective settlements—United States—History—Bibliography.
2. Collective settlements—United States—Bibliography. I. Title.
II. Series: Sects and cults in America. Bibliographical guides; v.
13. III. Series: Garland reference library of social science; v.
402.
Z7164.C69M54  1990
016.335'973—dc20                                                89–27481
                                                                     CIP

Printed on acid-free, 250-year-life paper
Manufactured in the United States of America

For Tamara

Who's been there

# Table of Contents

# Light from a Black Hole:
# An Introduction to
# American Communalism 1860-1960

American communalism is commonly believed to have been in near eclipse from the time of the Civil War until the emergence of the hippie communes in the late 1960s. The great communal societies and movements of the early years of the Republic—the Rappites, the Shakers, the Owenites, the Fourierists, the Oneida Community, and others—were in terminal decline, and no one, it seems, was taking their place. Perhaps there was a general decline in idealism; perhaps the industrialization of America displaced the cottage industries of the communes. In several movements celibacy took its inevitable toll by eliminating natural increase. For whatever reason, communalism drifted from the American picture. One seeking to confirm that view has to look no farther than most of the standard surveys of the history of American communalism; few of them devote much space to the supposedly dead century between 1860 and 1960. Occasionally a chapter is given over to one or another communal project, but even so a sense of any real vitality during that century is rarely conveyed.

Examples of that treatment of the period abound. Mark Holloway (his book is cited below as item 102) has surveyed American communalism to 1880, but only three of his 246 pages deal with anything after 1860; the chapter which contains that little bit is entitled "Utopia in Decline." Kenneth Rexroth devotes nine chapters of his book (item 1363) to American communal societies; the Hutterites rate one, but no one else after 1860 does. Donna Lawson (item 761) devotes one of her eleven chapters to Father Divine, but everything else in her book has origins prior to 1860. Everett Webber (item 168) devotes two of 20 chapters to the period, as does Victor

Calverton (item 39).    Peyton Richter (item 152) surveys the history of American communalism at some length, but hardly anything between 1860 and 1960 is mentioned.    Many other examples of the same sort of treatment of the period could be cited as well.    Few general studies of American communalism do it otherwise, in fact.

Relatively recently, however, that mistaken presumption of a lengthy dead spot in American communal history has been challenged.    One major salvo came in 1975 with Robert Fogarty's article "American Communes, 1865-1914" (cited in this volume as item 74).    In a relatively few pages Fogarty demolished the myth of a communal vacuum between the Civil War and World War I.    Although he did not delve deeply into the history of any specific communal group, he did provide an unusually broad survey of communal ventures large and small from that era.

Nearly a decade after Fogarty published his article, Michael Barkun, arguing that there was a cyclical pattern to the founding of communities (see item 31, below), concluded that there had been four major periods of "unusually intense communal activity" in the United States, and that two of the four had occurred in the usually downplayed years.    Barkun's four periods of greatest activity were the early 19th century, the very late 19th century, the Depression era, and the 1960s. Barkun counted 36 communities founded between 1894 and 1900, and 99 founded with New Deal government assistance between 1933 and 1937.    Although government-sponsored communalism was an innovation, and a fairly short-lived one, it did introduce thousands of families to "subsistence homesteads" influenced by earlier utopian settlements.    Moreover, other communities were founded in the Depression without government assistance.

Other works before and after Fogarty's and Barkun's have buttressed their claims.    Fortunately, several individuals surveyed the communities in existence at one time or another during the period in question, and their surveys demonstrated, almost without noticing it, that communalism was far from dead after 1860.    Ralph Albertson surveyed communes old and new in 1936 (item 27), as did W.A. Hinds in 1878 and 1908 (items 94 and 95).    Communities founded after 1860 dominate Ernest Wooster's 1924 survey (item 175), as they do Alexander Kent's in 1901 (item 117), and several others cited in the following pages.    More recently, others have written specialized surveys of communal life in the overlooked era, often focusing on a particular geographical area.    Two good examples of that type of contribution are Robert V. Hine's book *California's Utopian*

*Colonies* (item 98) and Charles P. LeWarne's doctoral dissertation which was abridged and published as *Utopias on Puget Sound* (item 124).

One wonders, in fact, how the presumption of a dead century ever developed. The most successful communal experiment in American history, apart from the Catholic religious orders, reached our shores during those years: the Hutterites, compromising a movement which, with one of the world's highest birth rates, has expanded about a hundredfold in just over a century. The Mormons founded a string of communal enterprises in Utah in the 1870s; secular socialists founded communities such as Llano del Rio and Ruskin which should be familiar to all but the most casual of students of American communal history.

This volume proceeds, then, on the assumption that the period from 1860 to 1960 amounts to a historical black hole—an object full of material but one from which light does not escape. Communalism there was, in abundance, but it has not been much noticed. That does not mean that communities founded after 1860 were the same as their more famous predecessors in size or type. On the whole, individual communes tended to be relatively small. Groups with many hundreds of residents in one location, as the Rappites and Amanans, for example, had among groups founded earlier, were rare, and where they existed they tended to be short-lived. Large movements with many separate communal locations, along the lines of the Shakers, were also rare, the Hutterites being the chief exception. The important point is that the post-1860 communes were numerous, running into the hundreds, and that in the aggregate they had a substantial membership.

The century between 1860 and 1960 was marked by waves of communalism, not by a hundred years of steady activity. The 1870s saw a burst of communalism, especially with the arrival of the Hutterites and the flowering of the United Order among the Mormons in Utah. In the 1880s many secular and religious colonies were founded, most notably the settlements of East European Jewish immigrants. The 1890s were important for secular communalism, especially among socialists who became disaffected with the prospects for success in the American political system and decided that utopian demonstrations of the socialist way on a small scale might be a fruitful new direction for the movement. There were other smaller bursts as well. The greatest lull came after World War I; if communalism had a relatively dormant period between 1860 and 1960, it was between the World Wars. A few stalwart souls, such as Arthur Morgan of Yellow Springs, Ohio, managed to keep the flame burning, but it was little more than a flicker. A flicker there was, though; Morgan helped found Celo in 1936, and the Macedonia Cooperative Community was begun the following year. Religious communities occasionally appeared in that era; Father Divine saw the glory days of his communal "heavens" in the 1930s, and the People of the Living God organized their commune in 1932, to name two. The Fellowship of Intentional Communities (FIC), intimately related to Morgan and his associates, gained energy in the 1940s and 1950s. Several new communities were founded after World War II with FIC cooperation. The movement gained more steam as the 1950s progressed, with the arrival of the Bruderhof in America and with the founding of communities with a new vision, such as Koinonia, Georgia, which sought to bring racial equality to the land of Jim Crow. Thus was the stage set for the new burst of communalism with the hippies in the late 1960s.

*Types of communities*

What were these communes like? They were diverse in philosophy, geography, and structure. One could easily construct a typology with dozens of categories for them. At the very least it is useful to distinguish between religious and secular communities, even if the line between those two types is not always distinct. Each of those categories may then be broken down into several subgroups. The most useful categorization of those subgroups, it seems to me, is by the principles, goals, and outlook of the various groups. Here follows a list of types of communities founded between 1860 and 1960, with examples of each type. Some communities are hard to categorize precisely, and many have characteristics which could place them in more than one place in the following list. Generally, though, these categories are provided as an orientation for the reader who wants to know what types of communes were founded between 1860 and 1960 and what the typical and important groups in each category were.

*A. Religious communities*
    1.  *Anabaptists.* The Anabaptists should head the list simply because of their record numbers. Most in this category are Hutterites, but there have been a few communal experiments among Mennonites (Reba Place, for example) and there is the special case of the Bruderhof, or Society of Brothers, a group founded in Germany in 1920 on Hutterite principles but independent of Hutterite historical connections. The Hutterites divided into three "leuts" upon arriving in North

America in the 1870s, and the leuts have remained separate, even to the point of eschewing intermarriage. Their similarities are much greater than their differences, however, and despite persecution and hardship they have prospered in their new homeland.

2. *Other committed, conservative Protestants.* A few deeply conservative Protestants have come to the conclusion that authentic biblical living cannot be done in isolation, that the people of God must pool their resources and their lives to make their most effective witness to the fallen world—indeed, that the Bible demands such a course. Such groups try to undertake extensive outreach programs, preaching their message as widely as possible. Groups such as Burning Bush, Shiloh Farms, Bethany Fellowship, and Pisgah Grande exemplify this communal type.

3. *Jews.* Second in number to the Anabaptists, probably, have been Jews who have formed rural communes. Most of the Jewish communities were founded in the 1880s following severe persecutions in Russia and Poland which led to massive emigration from those two nations to America. The emigrants were for the most part poor villagers, and, to put it bluntly, many of the American Jews who had prospered and were quite happy with a liberalized American Judaism were not anxious to join forces with these newcomers, who were largely poorly educated, often desperately poor, and usually Orthodox and observant in their Judaism. Although the American Jewish community as a whole helped its poorer siblings settle here, the fact that many were routed to rural communes had as much to do with the desire to see them steered away from existing Jewish centers as with helping them get on with their lives. The most attention has been given to the six communities of southern New Jersey, on the whole the most successful of the Jewish projects, but many colonies were also founded in Kansas and the Dakotas, with others scattered from Connecticut to California. Some of the immigrant colonies were secular in outlook (e.g., New Odessa, in Oregon), but they were the exception. A few Jewish communes were also founded apart from the wave of immigration; they also tended to be quite secular (although culturally still Jewish), as in the case of Sunrise, located at Alicia, Michigan. A special case which might be included here is that of the black Jews; the self-designated black Jewish communes in America have had no historical connection to Judaism, and have typically blended Jewish and Christian elements in their worship services. Two black Jewish communal groups included in this volume are the Church of God and Saints of Christ and the Temple of the

Gospel of the Kingdom.

4. *Mormons.* Communalism has been a Mormon theme since the early days of the Church of Jesus Christ of Latter Day Saints in the 1830s. The first teachings about community were announced at one of the early Mormon sites, Kirtland, Ohio. Some efforts to establish cooperative and communal structures were made a few years later in Independence, Missouri; the big push came in the 1870s after the Saints were well settled in Utah. Meanwhile, the communal theme played well among the Mormon dissidents, of whom there were (and are) always plenty. The sectarian Mormon leader James J. Strang, whose movement separated from the main body in the middle 1840s, established an important communal settlement on an island in Lake Michigan; even today new communal (and often polygamous) groups are still being established in remote locations in Utah and Arizona. Sectarian Mormon communal settlements may run into the hundreds.

5. *Theosophists.* Following the death of founder Helena Petrovna Blavatsky in 1891, the Theosophical Society began to split in several directions, and some of the resulting factions organized communal settlements. Probably the best known of them was the Universal Brotherhood at Point Loma, California, in what is now part of San Diego. Others included Krotona, which operated at Hollywood and later at Ojai, California, and the Temple of the People, located farther up the coast at Halcyon, California. Some other theosophical offshoots were communal as well.

6. *Adventists.* William Miller convinced thousands that Christ was going to return in 1844; when the Second Coming apparently failed to occur, the Millerites went in several directions. Some returned to their former churches, and some regrouped under Ellen White to form the Seventh-Day Adventists, but a few eventually formed communes of persons who believed that the Lord would surely come very soon and that they, the believers, should live a life of daily preparedness for the Second Coming. What better way to do that than in a communal setting, which, after all, had explicit biblical sanction as a way for Christians to live? Adonai Shomo and Celestia were among the Adventist communes of the late nineteenth century.

7. *The egalitarians and liberationists.* Protestant Christianity has a long tradition in America of holding that good faith will result in good works, and from that tradition have sprung social reform movements of all types, from antislavery societies to peace movements to prohibitionism. In some cases that reformist zeal has led to the founding of

members of a downtrodden race or class, and perhaps incidentally to show the rest of the world a new model for egalitarian living. The Women's Commonwealth, founded in Belton, Texas, was such a community which provided much improved status for its female members. Delta and Providence tried to provide improved lives through cooperative endeavor for impoverished southern blacks. Port Royal was a colony of freed slaves which operated during the Civil War. The Salvation Army opened three rural colonies for refugees from the teeming, fetid cities. More recently, groups such as Koinonia Farm in Georgia have worked hard to make racial equality a reality.

8. *Other Protestant social reformist communities.* After the Civil War the social gospel movement developed a particularly radical variety of Christian social reformist thought and action, arguing that true Christianity could not abide gross social sin. Some social gospelers founded colonies to act out their convictions; the best known was the Christian Commonwealth in Georgia. Willard was another. Many years later reform-minded communities were still being founded; the Church of the Savior and the Ecumenical Institute are two examples from the 1950s.

9. *Oriental groups.* Communalism rooted in Oriental religious traditions has been limited in America, especially prior to 1960, but a few hardy souls have undertaken such ventures. Among the projects were Buddhist and Vedanta communes.

10. *All the rest* are mainly the offspring of visionary founders not closely related to any major existing religious tradition. The history of American religion is replete with tales of visionaries and dreamers, and more than a few of them have commanded their followers to abandon their private lives and occupations for a communal alternative. In most cases these communities have been run almost exclusively on the charismatic energy of the founding leader, and rarely have they long survived the death or discrediting of the founder. Many communes of that type are included in this volume, among them the Lord's Farm, new Jerusalem, the Bride of Christ Church, the Koreshan Unity, Shalam, the Lemurian groups, Holy City, the Spirit Fruit Society, and Zion City. The Emissary communities probably belong in this group, although some would find their focus not sufficiently conventionally religious.

## II. Secular Communities

11. *Socialist communes.* Karl Marx derided communal societies as "utopian," but many socialists have concluded that the best way to have some sort of real socialism is to pursue

it in voluntary groups; such groups, they argue, can provide some of the benefits of socialism within a larger capitalistic society, and they can serve as examples which demonstrate the merits of socialism. In the late nineteenth century socialism was a growing movement in America, and among its many strands was a communal element, one which believed that the surest way to socialism was to found an independent little socialist society. Eugene V. Debs was one of those intrigued with the communal alternative in the 1890s, and was involved in the grandest of the communitarian socialist schemes of the era, the plans to socialize Washington. With Debs's support the Brotherhood of the Co-operative Commonwealth adopted, in 1896, a plan to found one "cooperative commonwealth," and then another, and another, so that before long the socialists would control a whole state. The plan ultimately failed, of course, but not before a socialist colony, Equality, had been planted. Other socialists pursued communalism at other times and places; Kaweah, near Visalia, California, was an important communal settlement which threatened to become a major success before the federal government took away its land. Ruskin, Tennessee, similarly appeared promising before internal squabbling destroyed it. Llano del Rio, California, and its successor Newllano, Louisiana, together comprised one of the longest-lived secular communes in American history.

    12. *Anarchist communities.* Anarchism and socialism were, despite some basic incompatibilities, closely intertwined in the late nineteenth century, and some Anarchists found communal living an attractive alternative to the capitalist world. The most famous of the anarchist experiments was Home, Washington. By definition an anarchist colony could not be coercive or highly centralized, but nevertheless a real sense of community developed at Home, which was a relatively stable and long-lived community. There were other less prominent examples of the genre as well; one of them, Ferrer Colony in New Jersey, operated an alternative school and survived for many years.

    13. *The single tax enclaves.* At the turn of the century the movement to implement Henry George's proposal of levying only one tax, on the unearthed increment of real estate values, had a wide following. As a political movement it never made much headway, despite a long and committed battle; finally some disciples decided that the best way to pursue the matter was through the founding of colonies which would demonstrate, roughly, the soundness of the theory. Since of course the colonies could not be in charge of all taxation of members, they restricted their activities to real estate.

Typically, the colony corporation held the land and rented it to members at a price which reflected only the basic value of the land, not its increased value as a result of improvements to it or of external activities which would tend to make it more valuable. Several of the single tax enclaves, as they were called, still exist in modified form today, including Fairhope, Alabama, the most prominent of them.

14. *The Fellowship of Intentional Communities groups.* After World War I only a few new communes of cooperative colonies were founded, and many of them had connections to Arthur Morgan and his associates in Yellow Springs, Ohio, who ran a sort of communal clearing house and support group in the Fellowship of Intentional Communities. Most of the FIC groups were small; they were often not entirely communal, but they generally met the standards used for inclusion in this volume. Celo, North Carolina; Macedonia Cooperative Community, Georgia; and the Vale, outside Yellow Springs, were among the FIC communities.

15. *Ethnic communities.* Immigrants were often intimidated by the new land they entered, especially when they couldn't speak its language, and in several cases banded into cooperative features. Among such communities covered here are the Bohemian Cooperative Farming Company, the Danish Colony, the various English communitarian settlements, the Italian-Swiss Colony, Modjeska's colony at Anaheim, Molokan communalism, and the Wayne Produce Association. Most of them were short lived, the most transitory lasting only for a matter of weeks. In some cases the immigrants found more attractive employment opportunities outside the community and moved away once they had made sufficient cultural adjustment to do so. Silkville, for example, was originally populated nearly exclusively with French nationals, but few of them stayed at the site very long.

16. *Special-purpose communities.* In some cases communalism was incidental to a particular task being undertaken. There were, for example, some artistic communal settlements, such as the Roycroft Shop, Rose Valley, and New Clairvaux. Gould Farm was established along communitarian lines as a residential center for educating and assisting the handicapped. The anarchist Ferrer Colony centered on its operation of the Modern School.

17. *The last gasp of Fourierism.* The American disciples of Charles Fourier had their heyday well before 1860; nearly all of the major Fourierist phalanxes were defunct by the late 1840s. Nevertheless, some clung to the vision, and at least two Fourierist communities were founded after 1860. One, Silkville,

never really got off the ground; it spent several years in development at the expense of its wealthy patron, but never achieved its communal goals. The other, Union, was a mix of Fourierism, prohibitionism, and western land development; although it prospered and birthed the city of Greeley, Colorado, it never managed to develop its Fourierist principles very far.

18. *Back to the land/opening the West.* The romantic ideal of rural self-sufficiency is a long-standing one, and frequently it has involved communal settlements. In California early in the twentieth century, the Little Landers experiments established one-acre plots for gardeners; they were economically independent, but the colonies had common buildings and they engaged in cooperative marketing of their produce. A bit later Ralph Borsodi began agitating for decentralization, urging city dwellers to move to small, relatively self-sufficient homesteads; a communitarian movement known as the School of Living emerged from his work. A variant of these small-scale back-to-the-land experiments occurred in several locations in developing frontier outposts. The Colorado Co-operative Company centered on a collectively built and owned irrigation ditch; the Southwestern Colony and St. Louis-Western Colony similarly were engaged in pioneering in Colorado, as was Union Colony. In Mexico, Americans founded the Topolobampo community, which was connected to a railroad scheme which would have provided eastern shippers with a Pacific outlet much closer to them than the Pacific ports in the United States. The railroad was not completed during the lifetime of the colony, however, and Topolobampo soon fell apart.

19. *The secular visionaries and utopians.* In several instances in American communal history, readers of a utopian novel have been so consumed by the vision they have seen that they set forth to recreate the Eden described in the book. Such were the Icarians, a group that came to the United States from France in the 1840s as well. The most prominent case was probably the Freeland movement, based on the German writer Theodor Hertzka's utopian novel Freiland. The novel was set in Africa, and thence an early party traveled to establish its ideal world, but the site proved less than hospitable and the vision was relocated in the United States. The most prominent Freeland outpost was in Washington, where Equality Colony was taken over by Freeland disciples. Another case of trying to bring fiction to life was Altruria, founded in northern California as a community inspired by William Dean Howells's novel *A Traveler to Altruria.* Other visionaries and utopians developed communites apart from such literary

inspiration. In Des Moines, Alfred Lawson founded the Des Moines University of Lawsonomy as a communal institution; in California, Mankind United made quite a stir in the 1930s and 1940s in its quest for a secular utopia.

## What is a commune?

Supreme Court Justice Potter Stewart once said that he found it virtually impossible to define pornography, but he knew it when he saw it. Intentional community is rather like that; it is usually easy to recognize, but it is hard to define precisely. There is an ideal, and extreme, type; a microsociety in which individuals, subscribing to a common philosophy, own nothing and the community holds title to all property, real and personal. Some groups approach that ideal; individual Hutterites, for example, actually own nothing beyond their immediate personal effects. Most would-be communes, however, are not so stringent. They allow at least small personal financial holdings or give members a small discretionary allowance. Some residential colonies allow ownership of cars and even of homes.

More important than a technically correct definition of communalism in the abstract is a working definition. Several guidelines directed the compilation of this bibliography. They were always flexible; in many cases I could not find enough information about a specific group to analyze its communality in detail, while in others the elements of community were present in unusual ways and combinations. My working definition came to take on three elements: geographical proximity, economic sharing, and a common vision. When a group exhibited those features and considered itself a commune or cooperative community, it was generally included here. Those which lacked one or more of the features were excluded. In cases of sparse information I often made the best guesses I could, but tried to err on the side of including marginal groups rather than excluding one which might actually qualify.

Geographical proximity means living in adjacent homes, if not in common buildings. Many communal enterprises have had unitary dwellings as an ideal; individual members receive rooms or apartments in large community-owned structures. Others, however, especially those whose population consists largely of families, provide or permit decentralized dwelling units. Some groups included here actually deeded out land to individual members; however, as a rule, in those cases the community members lived in adjacent small tracts, with some control over land use retained by the colony as a whole, and they retained a distinct sense of community life involving some shared land

and buildings, or a deliberately communitarian social life, or at least a common commitment to a set of goals and ideals. If the other standards were met, I included groups with such privatization of real estate. I tried, however, to exclude self-described communities which seemed to be little more than residential cooperatives. A New York apartment building can be a co-op, but it is not at all communal. Having like-minded people living on private pieces of ground in the same neighborhood was not enough for inclusion; there had to be some kind of central vision and economic sharing as well.

Some groups practice communal and private living in different situations, and judgment had to be made as to how important the communal element was in the overall life of the group. The Church of God and Saints of Christ, for example, long operated communally at its headquarters in Virginia, but its many other local congregations did not. It is included here since the commune was at the heart of things. Where communalism seemed more peripheral, some groups were not listed. The Moorish Science Temple, for example, operates two more or less communal "National Homes" where families can raise their own food and which will be available as sanctuaries when the prophesied destruction comes to American cities. The Homes today actually amount to little more than small retirement villages for believers. Since they are not large, not very fully communal, and not centrally important to Moorish Science beliefs or practices, I have not listed them here.

One rule for inclusion in this volume was that the community, or family of communities, had to have been founded or to have arrived in the United States between 1860 and 1960. That means, for example, that this volume attempts to be comprehensive with regard to the Hutterites; they have continued to found colonies since 1960, but their American origins are in the time period this volume covers. Some of the groups included here have origins prior to 1860 as movements, but did not establish communes until later. The religious movement which organized Celestia, for example, was founded in the 1850s, but the commune did not operate until 1863; thus it is listed.

One family of communities playing chronological havoc with my categories was the Latter Day Saints—the Mormons and their offshoots. The first dabbling of the Mormons in communitarianism came in the early 1830s in Kirtland, New York. Further efforts, somewhat feeble, toward establishing communitarian life were made soon thereafter in Independence, Missouri. However, nothing that could honestly be described as communal took very clear shape until 1874, when Brigham

Young began to advocate that United Order communities be founded in Utah. Thus the Mormons are included here rather than in the volume in this series covering the pre-1860 period.

But since entire communal families are to be housed in a single volume in this series, a major chronological leap had to be taken. Various persons and small groups began dropping out of Mormonism very early in the movement's history, and some of them adopted a communalism based on Mormon principles but outside the main church. Particularly during the struggle for the succession after the death of Joseph Smith in 1844 did splinter groups break away, several of them professing allegiance to the communal ideal which the Mormons had proclaimed but hardly practiced. James J. Strang organized a dissident Mormon community on Beaver Island in Lake Michigan in 1847, and other sectarian Saints initiated similar projects, as a perusal of the Mormon section of this volume will demonstrate. Because the only really important communal experiment within the main branch of Mormonism was founded after 1860, all of Mormon communalism is covered here, even that which was founded earlier.

With one exception, only groups which engaged in communalism in the United States have been included here. Doukhobors have been living in this country for some time, but to my knowledge their only communal settlements have been in Canada, and they are therefore not listed. The one exception to the guideline is Topolobampo, which operated in Mexico. It is included on the grounds that is was a distinctly American project, even though it was located on foreign soil. The colony in that case was tied to a railroad-building project; the colonists would dwell in a edenic city adjacent to a railroad terminus and port in the Pacific coast of Mexico.

Hutterites are, of course, included in the volume. Since the movement spans a large territory on both sides of the U.S.-Canadian border, and since its North America beginnings came in South Dakota, works on all of North American Hutterism were included in what I believe to be the most inclusive bibliography of North American Hutterites yet published. However, the extensive literature on the Hutterites in Europe prior to their migration to South Dakota is largely omitted. A few representative samples of such works are listed, plus all of those I could locate which had any bearing on later developments in America. The researcher who wants information on the early years of the Hutterites should consult the indices of the *Mennonite Quarterly Review* for such materials.

The largest family of communes of all has not been

included in this volume.    The Catholic religious orders are so
numerous and so well documented that they are easily merit a
volume of their own, and such a volume is projected as a later
one in this series.    Similarly the Catholic Worker, a
noncanonical Catholic community, has a volume of its own and
is therefore not listed here.

It is possible that some groups listed in this bibliography
never actually existed, or existed so marginally that they were
not real communities.    In several cases I located announcements
of new projects, and in some of them I could never locate
further material.    I have eliminated those which probably did
not exist, but have included some which, if they did actually
function, did so extremely briefly or perhaps with so few
members—as few as a single family—that they might not have
been eligible for inclusion had I had access to enough material
to make an informed judgement.    Thompson Colony in Kansas is
one such case. Enterprise, in Nebraska, is another.

Inevitably, this compilation is incomplete.    I have pursued
every lead I have encountered, but it quickly became apparent
that some materials would not be unearthed.    Many times I
located references to other works which could not be pursued,
usually because the citation was incomplete.    In late nineteenth
century materials, especially, there are abundant references to
things on the order of "Professor Kellogg's study of the
communal Adventists."    Without a full author or title citation,
such references were usually useless, although I tried to locate
the work in question and occasionally succeeded.    In many
other cases the citation was satisfactory, but I could not
confirm, independently, the actual existence of the work using
standard research tools.    Inevitably, I also encountered more
than a few citations which were simply incorrect.    When an
author cites a serial entitled *Publication of the Sociological
Society of America*, the bibliographer will not always figure out
that s/he means *Social Conflict: Papers of the American
Sociological Society*, to mention one actual citation which I did
manage to decipher.

In some cases I declined to pursue a source whose value
was not fairly clear, especially if the cost of obtaining the
source material in question was high.    When a dissertation, for
example, seemed likely to be useful, I usually ordered it
through interlibrary loan.    But some possible materials escaped
my scrutiny.    To pick a single example, William Lawrence
Smith's dissertation "Urban Communitarianism in the 1980s:
Seven Religious Communes in Chicago" (Notre Dame, 1984),
might contain useful information on Reba Place and the
Ecumenical Institute.    However, Notre Dame dissertations are

not available on interlibrary loan; the only way I could look at one first hand was to buy it on microfilm for $18, or in hard copy for more than that. Many works were of that nature, and I simply could pursue very few of them out of pocket. So Dr. Smith's dissertation is not cited, and any leads to additional resources it might have contained have not been tracked. I regret that many possibly useful documents could not be examined.

*Research collections*
Several archives and libraries contain important collections on historic North American communes. Most of them have manuscripts and other materials not listed in this volume. I have visited the following archives and can certify their importance:

*The American Jewish Archives.* Located in its own building on the campus of Hebrew Union College/Jewish Institute of Religion in Cincinnati, the AJA apparently has the best collection of material on Jewish communes in existence. The focus, naturally, is on the major wave of communitarian settlements of East European immigrants in the early 1880s. The AJA participates in the interlibrary loan system, so its materials are readily available.

*The Center for Communal Studies.* Located in the library of the University of Southern Indiana at Evansville, this center is a main locus of contemporary communal research. It has been instituted relatively recently and therefore is not enormous, but it has financial support from the university and is actively acquiring additional materials. It is already substantial and in time could be the most important single source of communal material.

*Community Service, Inc.* This organization, created by Arthur Morgan at Yellow Springs, Ohio, has operated as a support system for intentional communities for several decades. In the course of that work it has acquired a large quantity of material on communes, especially those with which it has been organizationally involved. When I visited CSI the material was principally in a bank of filing cabinets in a room near the organization's office; in due course it is to be transferred to nearby Antioch College for permanent preservation. It is by far the most important source of material on the period after World War I; it includes many community documents, including newsletters, which probably do not exist anywhere else.

*The East Wind collection.* The East Wind Community at Tecumseh, Missouri, has one of the better communal libraries in existence. Much of it focuses on the post-1960 period, but some earlier material is there as well.

*The Institute for the Study of American Religion.* ISAR is located in the library of the University of California at Santa Barbara. The collection has been privately gathered by J. Gordon Melton, general editor of this series of bibliographies, over the course of about a quarter century. At this writing it appears to be the largest single repository of communal material. Religious communities are emphasized, although there is a good deal of material on secular communities as well.

Unfortunately, I was not able to visit some other important repositories of material. Through correspondence and the perusal of other research material this list of other important communal collections has emerged:

*The Alternative Library* at Cornell University. Housed in Anabel Taylor Hall, the campus religious activities center, this collection is independent of the general library at Cornell. It contains substantial holdings on historical and contemporary communalism.

*The American Communities Collection.* This archive is a part of the Oneida Community Collection at the Syracuse University library. It contains the papers of William Alfred Hinds, the important chronicler of communes in the latter nineteenth and early twentieth centuries. This collection has manuscripts and other unduplicated material covering about 100 communities, the majority of them from the 1860-1960 period. For a list of communities covered by the collection, see the article by Mark F. Weimer (item 23, below).

*Bancroft Library: the Social Protest Project.* Among other things, this collection at the University of California at Berkeley has archival material on Community Service, Inc., and Koinonia Farm.

*State Historical Society of Wisconsin Library.* For nearly a century and a half this library has been gathering historical material which is by no means confined to Wisconsin. It has extensive book holdings and even more important runs of periodicals, many of them found nowhere else.

*Alternative Lifestyles*, by Jefferson Selth (item 19, below), has been my main source of information for the collections I was unable to visit. The book provides extensive descriptions of each collection, its holdings, and its accessibility. The collections covered by Selth include the Alternatives Library, The Bancroft Library, the Center for Communal Studies, Community Service, Inc., East Wind, and the State Historical Society of Wisconsin Library. Selth also lists several other collections of communal material; I have not included them here because it was not clear that they contained material from the century covered by this volume. The meticulous scholar is therefore referred to Selth for further information.

*Other sources of material*

This bibliography is as comprehensive as I could make it, but over the course of the research it became clear that it would take many more years to pursue every possible promising lead. Thus some materials are not represented in these pages. Some items which I believe exist simply could not be located through interlibrary loan in time for me to examine them.

Generally, I did not pursue materials in foreign languages. When I did come across them, I usually listed them if they seemed to contain information not available in English. I did not deliberately seek out any such works, however.

Newspaper articles about communal groups were generally avoided. Since a commune is a novelty in its own locality, communal projects are popular subjects of media attention. My experience has been that the local popular press is mixed in the accuracy and comprehensiveness with which it covers such projects. Quality ranges from excellent to terrible. In many cases newspaper accounts I came across were clearly sensationalistic and of dubious historical value. Thus I did not actively seek such accounts, although they exist in abundance. When I did come across a newspaper report, I listed it only if it seemed to contain information or provide a perspective which was not contained in the other literature on the group in question. State historical societies often have files of newspaper articles which existed within their borders.

As a rule, standard encyclopedias and other reference books aimed at broad audiences were not consulted. Many of them cover specific communities and movements briefly, but rarely do they have important material not readily available elsewhere. The researcher who wants a brief overview of a particular group or person can sometimes profit from examining such works; biographical sketches of major communal leaders can often be found in standard biographical dictionaries, for example.

Generally, I limited this bibliography to published materials. In many cases manuscript materials regarding communities have been preserved; those materials are often accessible through the National Union Catalog of Manuscript Collections. State historical societies and (especially) local libraries sometimes have manuscript collections not listed in the NUC.

Although I excluded a large body of potentially useful material, I also attempted to include a broader selection of materials than some would find necessary. Some works providing background information not immediately related to a particular community in question have been listed if they are potentially useful to some scholars. For example, material about Laurence Gronlund is included, even though not all of it is connected to any specific communal experiment; the point is that Gronlund inspired the Brotherhood of the Cooperative Commonwealth, and the movement and its main colony, Equality, cannot be fully understood without reference to him and his seminal ideas. Similarly an article by Ezekiel Lifschutz is listed (item 1495); it concerns a proposed Jewish colony which never actually opened. Nevertheless, the article does help complete the larger picture of Jewish colonization projects, and it does provide a faint sidelight on Woodbine, a colony which actually did exist. Such material is included here in the hope that some readers will find it useful.

It became clear to me during the course of the research that a wealth of material sits in various collections, public and private, which are not listed in any standard index. The extensive holdings of many state historical societies are often not fully listed in generally available national indices. Some have ongoing cataloging projects, so old manuscripts, for example, are continually being added to the National Union Catalog of Manuscript Collections. The scholar who is doing work on a particular community would be well advised to contact the relevant state historical society for further information. Incidentally, the lengthy standard histories (often multi-volume works) which exist for most states often have accounts of communal projects; I have not located or listed all such publications.

## Accessibility of listed materials

It is a commonplace among librarians that material which cannot be located does not exist. It has been my goal to list only materials which exist in the sense of being somehow accessible to the public. I have personally examined a large majority of the materials listed here; most of the rest are cited in a standard bibliographical or reference works whose listings have proved consistently reliable.

*Books and pamphlets*: Virtually all such titles in this bibliography are listed either in the National Union Catalog or on the computerized Ohio College Library Center system (OCLC); they should be available to anyone with access to interlibrary loan. In a few cases I found material not listed by the NUC or OCLC; I have tried to note its location in those cases. The largest single source I have encountered for such unlisted material has been the Institute for the Study of

American Religion.

*Dissertations and theses*: Dissertations listed in Dissertation Abstracts have been included in this bibliography. Some of them are available through interlibrary loan; some are not. There is no single index of master's theses, so references to them were difficult to verify. I have listed only theses I could examine personally or which are listed on OCLC. It is clear that there are many more theses concerning the communities covered by this volume but are hard to verify at a distance.

*Periodicals*: Cataloging for articles is much less comprehensive than that for books. In hundreds of cases I could not verify articles through standard indices and therefore had to order them through interlibrary loan. Most articles listed here I have seen personally, and they should be available through interlibrary loan. I also included some articles which I did not see but which were listed in *America: History and Life, the International Index* (and its successors, *Social Sciences and Humanities Index, Social Sciences Index*, and *Humanities Index*) or *Readers Guide*, all of which I found very reliable.

A loophole on proprietary periodicals: Many communities published their own periodicals. However, many of those publications were impossible to locate; they do not appear in the Union List of Serials or on computer databases to which I had access. The problem is complicated by the fact that house organs tend to undergo frequent changes in title, frequency of publication, location of publication, and the like. I thought them too important not to mention, since they will be of enormous interest to some researchers, so when I was convinced that a particular community periodical had indeed appeared at some time, even if I could not verify it I listed it (along with information on its dates and frequency of publication as I could gather) under "Community Periodicals" for the group in question. In many cases I believe that they exist at various state historical libraries or at public libraries near the site of a former community but have not been fully cataloged. In other cases they may exist only in private collections, or may have been destroyed entirely.

*Incomplete citations of articles*: In many cases I found only abbreviated references to useful works, and in some of those cases I could not complete the citation before I ordered the item through interlibrary loan. In dozens of cases correspondent libraries located materials on the basis of my incomplete citations, but when I received an item it often had no amplification of my original citation. Given the enormous volume and quality of service I received from the interlibrary loan system, I hesitated to ask for further spadework. What I can certify is that incomplete citations here provide enough information for the item to be borrowed through interlibrary loan.

*Terms and conventions used in this volume*

Each distinct communal group or movement has its own section in this bibliography. In addition there are two sections of other types of works: bibliographies, and works dealing with more than one community from the 1860-1960 period. Entries in the bibliographies section have been limited to works which are entirely or primarily bibliographical in nature; many articles and books cited in the remainder of this volume have bibliographies appended to textual material. As a general rule, works covering more than one community are listed in the section on multiple-community works as well as in the section covering each group involved, although in a few cases works dealing with only two groups are cited under the headings for the respective groups only.

Garland Publishing's standard practice is to assign each item listed a separate number, but not to assign it a second number when it is listed a second time. Instead, on second and subsequent reference it is marked by an asterisk. That system works well for most bibliographies, but presents some problems here. Since the index of this volume is by item number, not by page number, it is impossible to index the entries bearing only an asterisk. Thus the index would contain a reference to the first entry of a particular work, but not to subsequent entries. Since many items in this bibliography are listed more than once, the index is not comprehensive.

I have coped with this problem in part by assigning numbers to items as freely as possible. My rule has been to assign a number not only to each book and article, but to each identifiable section within a book or article when more than one community is covered. That is, if a work has separate sections on various communities, and the various sections are given titles or subtitles, each section is entered under its section title as if it were a separate article. The reader is then referred back to the section on multiple-community works for the full reference on the overall book or article. When, however, the work does not give each group a separately titled section, an asterisk is assigned to each entry after the first. That will present no problem for a reader looking for information on a particular group, since the entries with asterisks are in alphabetical order in each section of the bibliography.

It has been my goal to annotate the items listed in this bibliography. Generally, annotations have been provided for all items I have personally examined. In a relatively few cases I was provided with reliable information concerning the content of items I was not able to see; in those instances I provided brief annotations followed by the words "not seen." Usually, however, I did not attempt to annotate unseen material. The citations which are not annotated are those of items I have not seen and of whose content I am not certain, even though the title may provide strong clues.

Several phrases occur repeatedly in the bibliography. Here is an explanation of the more important ones:

"*Community Periodicals.*" Many communities published magazines or newspapers in which they represented themselves to the outside world. Items listed in this subsection are those which are official or semiofficial organs of the community, intended for either internal or external consumption. As I have noted above, this is the only category of material listed which I have not personally verified fully. I am satisfied that each periodical listed was actually published, but in a number of cases community periodicals underwent changes in title, frequency of publication, location of publication, and the like. Some entries may not reflect all such changes, since some permutations proved impossible to track.

"*Survey works.*" Some works are essentially dictionaries or catalogs of communes, providing brief references to many of them, but not yielding detailed information on any one or more. Such references are not repeated in full under the heading of each group covered; instead only an item number is given, referring the reader to the encyclopedic work listed in the section on works covering more than one communities. Where a work provides brief references to some communities and more substantial entries on others, the more substantial references are listed fully in the appropriate sections while the brief references are given the "survey works" treatment.

"*Not cited here.*" Many works I have listed are based on materials too extensive or too obscure for me to examine and cite separately. I have, for example, avoided pursuing information on local newspapers; some secondary works, however, cite newspaper articles extensively. Other works are based on research in primary materials concerning a particular community, materials which often exist in a single library and which I could not examine. In such cases I have ended the annotation by noting that the work in question contains specialized bibliographical references which will be of interest to those who want to pursue a particular group in detail.

"*Primary works.*" Items listed here are ones not attributed to any author and which are clearly published as documents officially representing the community's point of view. Unattributed items whose intent to speak for the community is not clear are listed as secondary works.

"*Works by the community leaders.*" This subsection lists only works by the most important leaders of the community, the founder(s) or a very few others with centrally important roles. All other work by members or supporters of the community are listed as secondary works.

The terms "commune," "community," and "colony" are used interchangeably.

*Acknowledgments*

Special funding for my travel to visit research collections and archives was provided by the Hall Center for the Humanities at the University of Kansas. Funding for the writing of this introduction was provided by the General Research Fund at the university. Expenses for photocopying, telephone calls, and other incidentals were partially borne by the Department of Religious Studies at the university. My chairpersons, Robert Shelton and Robert Minor, helped at several critical points to secure funding and clerical help.

I received help far beyond the call of duty from the library system at the University of Kansas. The departments I leaned on most heavily were reference, interlibrary loan, the Kansas collection, microforms, and circulation. In every case the librarians and their assistants were enormously helpful. Eleanor Symons, reference librarian and bibliographer, took a special interest in the project and provided continuous support. It is a privilege to work in a library with such a strong staff.

Members of the staffs of the various archives and research collections I visited also went out of their way to assist me. The staff at the American Jewish Archives, headed by Fannie Zelcer, not only supplied the materials I needed to see but provided many helpful suggestions about materials I had hitherto not known of. Donald Pitzer and Gina Walker of the Center for Communal Studies provided me access and skilled assistance there. At Community Service, Inc., excellent help was provided by Jane Morgan and Teresa Wilhelm Fallon. Gordon Melton, director of the Institute for the Study of American Religion and editor of this series, spent much valuable time with me in Santa Barbara and gave me direction without which the project would have been greatly poorer.

Most of the information on communities in by own backyard, the state of Kansas, was gathered at the Kansas State Historical Society library in Topeka, and I received consistently helpful service there.

Many members of the National Historic Communal Societies Association commented on the various drafts of the bibliography and provided suggestions and other help from time to time throughout the project. Those who took a special interest and provided important assistance included Philip Cook, H. Roger Grant, Lyell Henry, James E. Landing, Christina M. Lemieux, Lyman Tower Sargent, Virginia Warren, and Mark Weimer, among others.

Several scholars provided generous assistance from their own resources. Robert V. Hine of the University of California at Riverside graciously allowed me access to his files, thus providing me with much material I would not otherwise have discovered. John A. Hostetler, dean of scholars of the Anabaptists, provided me with material on the Hutterites I could not locate elsewhere. Wayne E. Warner provided information on communalism with Pentecostal connections, especially at Zion City.

Shelley Miller spent many lunch hours pursuing leads for me at the Library of Congress, and provided further help later at the University of Kansas libraries. Elly Wynia-Trey undertook a student research project which turned up previously unknown resources about communal Black Jews. Barney Hubert, doing graduate research on the Hutterites, provided me with many references I had not previously located. Christopher Magerl unearthed valuable new information on the Koreshan Unity. Larry Hoyle provided, once again, expert assistance in data processing. Pam Detrixhe and Paisley Hokanson also provided good computer support. Finer individuals one could never hope to work with. My family also deserves special thanks, putting up with dinner-table conversation about obscure details of communal history and accompanying me on several trips to communal sites and archives.

If this volume is well received, it is possible that a second edition may in time be issued. Readers are invited to send corrections, clarifications, and new citations to me at the following address:

Department of Religious Studies
University of Kansas
103 Smith Hall
Lawrence, Kansas 66045

# AMERICAN COMMUNES
## 1860–1960

SECTS AND CULTS IN AMERICA
BIBLIOGRAPHICAL GUIDES
(General Editor: J. Gordon Melton)
(VOL. 13)

GARLAND REFERENCE LIBRARY
OF SOCIAL SCIENCE
(VOL. 402)

# I. BIBLIOGRAPHICAL WORKS AND RESEARCH AIDS

Books and articles listed in this section are primarily bibliographical in nature. Many items listed in section II, below, also contain bibliographical information.

1.  Adams, Frederick B., Jr. *Radical Literature in America.* Stamford, Conn.: Overbrook Press, 1939. 66 pp.
    Contains an address focusing on pre-1860 American communitarianism and a checklist for an exhibition of radical literature including various late nineteenth century community-oriented labor publications and works by such communitarian founders and theoreticians as Longley, Bellamy, Hertzka, and Gronlund.

2.  Adams, Raymond. *Booklist of American Communities: A Collection of Books in the Library of Raymond Adams.* Chapel Hill: University of North Carolina English Department, 1935. Mimeographed.
    Contains 127 entries, including subentries, principally on pre-1860 communities, but also including other bibliographies, general works on communalism, utopian literature, and works on Topolobampo, Llano, and several miscellaneous small colonies.

3.  Bassett, T.D. Seymour, bibliographer; Donald Drew Egbert and Stow Persons, eds. *Socialism and American Life.* Princeton: Princeton University Press, 1952, v. 2, "Bibliography: Descriptive and Critical."
    A massive bibliography which includes much material on American communes in all time periods, including special material on education in communes and communal art and literature. Extensively indexed. Volume 1, chapters 4 and 5, includes much material on American communes, with many references to communes active in the 1860-1960 period.

1

4.    Bauer, Patricia M., ed. *Cooperative Colonies in California: A Bibliography Collected from Printed and Manuscript Material Located in Bancroft Library and Doe Memorial Library.* Berkeley: n.d. Typescript; also microfilmed. 26 pp.
      Given its grounding in a single library, this list is incomplete and sometimes seems random in its offerings. However, it has many good citations of newspaper articles, manuscripts, pamphlets, and other specialized materials not cited here.

5.    Bercaw, Louise O., A.M. Hannay, and Esther M. Calvin. *Bibliography on Land Settlement with Particular Reference to Small Holdings and Subsistence Homesteads.* United States Department of Agriculture Miscellaneous Publication no. 172. Washington: Government Printing Office, 1934. 492 pp.
      Provides bibliographic information on a number of collective agricultural settlements, including Fellowship Farm Association, the Little Landers, the Salvation Army Colonies, and others.

6.    Davis, Elizabeth Gould, compiler. *Bibliography on Cooperation in Agriculture, 1946-1953.* Library list no. 41, Supplement 1. Washington: U. S. Department of Agriculture, 1954. 21 pp.
      First supplement to the bibliography of Turner and Bell (item 22, below); contains 344 general and United States entries, in addition to entries on other countries. Focuses primarily on farmers' cooperatives, but contains some information on related matters, including cooperative communities.

7.    Fogarty, Robert S.    "Communal History in America." *Choice* 20 (June, 1973): 578-90. Reprinted in *American Studies: An International Newsletter* (supplement to *American Quarterly*) 12 (Winter, 1973): 3-21.
      A brief overview history of American communalism, with bibliographical citations for each major period and movement.

8.    Goldwater, Walter.    *Radical Periodicals in America,* 1890-1950.    New Haven: Yale University Library, 1966.    51 pp.
      An annotated bibliography which includes references to periodicals published by communes.

9. Herbert, Miranda C., and Barbara McNeil, eds. *Biography and Genealogy Master Index.* Detroit: Gale Research, 1975.
Multivolume work with supplements. Provides an index for hundreds of biographical dictionaries and related works, including references to biographical sketches of many communal leaders.

10. Jones, Helen Dudenbostel. *Communal Settlements in the United States: A Selected List of References* Washington: U.S. Library of Congress, General Reference and Bibliography Division, 1947. 74 pp., typescript.
Covers many pre-1860 communities plus Father Divine's Peace Mission Movement, the Hutterites, the Lord's Farm, Mormon communitarianism, Zion City, the Altruist Community, Fairhope, Llano, Ruskin, and the Woman's Commonwealth. Contains references to manuscripts, collections of clippings, and specialized works, including book dealers' catalogs not cited here.

11. Kubal, Gene J., compiler. *Cooperation in Agriculture, 1954-1964: A List of Selected References.* Library List no. 41, supplement 2. Washington: U.S. Department of Agriculture, 1966. 115 pp.
Second supplement to the work of Turner and Bell (item 22, below), with 918 entries on general and U.S. topics. Focuses primarily on farmers' cooperatives, but contains some references to related matters, including cooperative communities.

12. Library of Congress, Division of Bibliography. *List of References on Communistic Societies in the United States.* February 13, 1917. Typescript. 5 pp.
Contains 57 citations on American communalism; the important ones from the post-1860 period are cited here.

13. Mariampolski, Hyman. "Communes and Utopias, Past and Present." *Bulletin of Bibliography* 36 (1979): 119-27, 143.
Lists articles on communes from all historical periods, with special emphasis on the hippie era. Listed works on communes from the 1860-1960 period are also cited here.

14. Negley, Glenn R. *Utopia Collection of the Duke Univesity*

*Library*.    Durham,    N.C.:    Friends   of   the   Duke
University Library, 1965.
A  bibliography  of  utopian  books,  including  some  which
became   models   for   American   communes   such   as   Altruria
and Freeland.

15.    ———. *Utopian     Literature:     A     Bibliography*.    Lawrence,
Kansas: Regents Press of Kansas, 1977.
A  bibliography  of  utopian  literature,  mainly  novels,
plus   a   bibliography   of   works   influential   on   utopian
thinkers,    including    some    which    were    used    by
communitarians.

16.    Owings,   Loren   C.   *American   Communitarian   Tradition*,
1683-1940:  A  Guide  to  the  Sources  in  the  Library  of  the
University   of   California   at   Davis.       Davis:   University   of
California Library, 1971.  88 pp.
A  bibliography  covering  Altruria,  Arden,  Burley,  Cedar
Vale,   the   Christian   Commonwealth,   Equality,   Freeland
(Hertzka),   Home,   the   Hutterites,   Kaweah,   Llano,   the
Mormons,   Nevada   Colony,   Point   Loma,   Rugby,   Ruskin,
Shalam,   Social   Freedom,   Topolobampo,   the   Woman's
Commonwealth,   and   Zion   City,   plus   the   Bellamy   Nationalist
movement and many pre-1860 communities.

17.    Schlebecker,   John   T.    *Bibliography   of   Books   and   Pamphlets
on   the   History   of   Agriculture   in   the   United   States,
1607-1967*.    Santa   Barbara:   ABC-Clio   Press,   1969.      183
pp.
An  excellent  index  has  entries  on  communal  societies,
cooperation,   cooperatives,   and   several   different   specific
groups.    Generally,   the   communal   works   listed   are   also
cited here.

18.    Schwantes,   Carlos   A.    "Washington   State's   Pioneer   Labor-
Reform   Press:   A   Bibliographical   Essay   and   Annotated
Checklist."  *Pacific   Northwest   Quarterly*  71  (July,  1980):
112-26.
Provides  detailed  bibliographical  information  on  papers
published   at   several   colonies   in   Washington,   including
Burley,   Equality,   Freeland,   Home,   and   the   Puget   Sound
Cooperative   Colony.    Also   includes   information   on   several
publications   (not   cited   here)   only   loosely   related   to   a
particular colony.

19.    Selth,   Jefferson.    *Alternative   Lifestyles:   A   Guide   to*

*Research Collections on Intentional Communities, Nudism, and Sexual Freedom.* Westport, Connecticut: Greenwood, 1985.

Lists ten collections of research material on intentional communities, plus two collections of related materials. Some collections cited focus on the post-1960 period, while others span a wider time frame. The cited collections with relatively major holdings on the 1860-1960 period are the Social Protest Project at Bancroft Library, University of California, Berkeley; the archives of Community Service, Inc., Yellow Springs, Ohio; the Center for Communal Studies at the University of Southern Indiana, Evansville; and the State Historical Society of Wisconsin Library, Madison. This guide describes the nature of the collection's holdings, the place where the collection is housed, bibliographic access to the materials, and other such things. An important resource book for basic research on communities.

20. Solis, Miguel J. *American Utopias (1683-1900).* Bloomington, Indiana: author, 1984. 185 pp.

Provides brief descriptions and annotated bibliographies for selected American communal societies, including eighteen from the 1860-1960 period. The bibliographical citations are limited; most groups receive fewer than half a dozen.

21. Sweetland, James H. "Federal Sources for the Study of Collective Communities." *Government Publications Review* 7A (1980): 129-38.

Provides an overview of U.S. government documents and other sources (such as archives and libraries) dealing with communalism throughout American history.

22. Turner, Howard B., and Florence C. Bell, compilers. *Bibliography on Cooperation in Agriculture.* Library list no. 41. Washington: U. S. Department of Agriculture, 1948. 178 pp.

Focuses on farmers' cooperatives, but includes some listings covering agricultural cooperative communities.

23. Weimer, Mark F. "William A. Hinds *American Communities Collection.*" *Communal Societies* 7 (1987): 95-103.

Describes the extensive files, located at the Syracuse University Library, of William A. Hinds, author of *American Communities*, an important primary source for information on American communities before 1908 (cited below as items 94 and 95). Reproduces the questionnaire Hinds circulated among the communities; provides a list of the approximately 100 communities represented in the files, the majority of them founded after 1860.

24.    Zimand, Savel. *Modern Social Movements: Descriptive Summaries and Bibliographies.* New York: H.W. Wilson, 1921.
       Bibliographies of several social movements, including cooperatives, selected communes, and utopian socialism.

# II. THEORETICAL WORKS AND WORKS COVERING MORE THAN ONE COMMUNITY

25.    Abrams, Philip, and Andrew McCulloch, with Sheila Abrams and Pat Gore. *Communes, Sociology and Society.* Cambridge, England: Cambridge University Press, 1976.
       Sociological theory, methodology, and bibliography, principally dealing with recent communes, but including some material on the 1860-1960 period.

26.    Adams, Herbert B., ed. *History of Cooperation in the United States.* Baltimore: Johns Hopkins Studies in Historical and Political Science, v. 6, 1888.
       A survey of communes and cooperatives in the U.S., including material on Mormon communities, the Italian-Swiss Colony, and Kaweah. Emphasis is on cooperative business ventures.

27.    Albertson, Ralph. "Survey of Mutualistic Communities in America." *Iowa Journal of History and Politics* 34 (October, 1936): 375-444. Reprinted in book form, New York: AMS Press, 1973.
       A major research tool. Contains brief descriptions of American communes in all eras, together with analytical material and an index of communities and leading individuals involved with them. Thirty-one major communities founded after 1860 are featured in entries a paragraph long each; a survey of other less prominent

number of members of each. Of the latter groups, those listed by Albertson but not included in this bibliography are Askov, Christian Cooperative Association, Cooperative Subsistence Colony, Friedheim, Kinder Lou, Lystra, National Production Company, Niksur Cooperative Association, and Union Mills.

28. Alexander, Peter, and Roger Gill. *Utopias.* LaSalle, Illinois: Open Court Publishing Co., 1984. 218 pp.
Contains 17 essays on utopian topics, some touching on various communes. Many of the articles feature extensive bibliographies.

29. Bach, Marcus. *Strange Sects and Curious Cults.* New York: Dodd, Mead, 1961. 277 pp.
Provides characterizations of contemporary alternative religions, including the Father Divine movement and the Hutterites.

30. Baker, James H., ed. *History of Colorado.* Denver: Linderman, 1927. Three volumes.
Provides, in volumes 1 and 2, basic historical information and interpretations on the Chicago-Colorado Colony, the German Colonization Co., the Southwestern Colony, and Union Colony.

31. Barkun, Michael. "Communal Societies as Cyclical Phenomena," *Communal Societies* 4 (1984): 35-48.
Argues that two of the four major periods of intense communal activity in the United States occurred at the close of the nineteenth century and in the 1930's. Concludes that communal surges occurred in times in which millenarianism was popular in society.

32. Bassett, T.D. Seymour. "Quakers and Communitarianism." *Bulletin of Friends Historical Association* 43 (Autumn, 1954): 84-99.
Describes early Quaker interest in communitarianism and Quaker involvement in several nineteenth-century communities. Deals mainly with pre-1860 groups, but does mention Quaker or Quakerlike involvement in several later projects, including Macedonia, the Bruderhof, Bryn Gweled, Celo, Canterbury, Hidden Springs, Kingwood, and Tanguy Homesteads.

33. Bestor, Arthur Eugene. *Backwoods Utopias: The Sectarian*

*and Owenite Phases of Communitarian Socialism in America, 1663-1829.* Philadelphia: University of Pennsylvania Press, 1950.
A standard work dealing mainly with the period before 1860, but including a comprehensive bibliography of communes.

34.  Blackmar, Frank W., ed. *Kansas: A Cyclopedia of State History.* Chicago: Standard Publishing, 1912. 2 volumes.
Contains articles on Silkville and silk culture (v. 2, pp. 694-6) and Freedom Colony (v. 1, p. 686).

35.  Bliss, William D.P., ed. *New Encyclopedia of Social Reform.* New York: Funk and Wagnalls, 1908. 1321 pp.
Contains encyclopedia entries on the Altruist Community, the Brotherhood of the Cooperative Commonwealth, the Christian Commonwealth, the Colorado Cooperative Company, the Cooperative Brotherhood, Fairhope, Helicon Hall, Home Colony, the House of David, Jewish colonies, Kaweah, the Koreshan Unity, the Roycrofters, Ruskin, and the Straight Edge Settlement, plus a biographical item on Theodor Hertzka, who conceived Freeland.

36.  Bloesch, Donald G. *Wellsprings of Renewal: Promise in Christian Communal Life.* Grand Rapids: Eerdmans, 1974. 124 pp.
A wide-ranging survey of Christian communalism in all ages. Contains overview information on Koinonia Farm, Reba Place, Koinonia (Maryland), the Ecumenical Institute, and Bethany Fellowship, with references to other communes founded between 1860 and 1960. Contains an extensive bibliography.

37.  Bouvard, Marguerite. *Intentional Community Movement: Building a New Moral World.* Port Washington, N.Y.: Kennikat Press, 1975. 207 pp.
Provides articles or short features on the Bruderhof, the Fellowship of Intentional Communities, the Hutterites, Koinonia Farm, Reba Place, and the School of Living and Ralph Borsodi, plus a brief note on Celo and material on groups in other time periods.

38.  Bushee, Frederick A. "Communistic Societies in the United States." *Political Science Quarterly* 20 (1905): 625-64.

A survey of communes from colonial times to 1905, including good surveys of Ruskin, Equality, the Cooperative Brotherhood, and the Alcander Longley communes (notably the Altruist Community). Emphasizes communal problems and reasons for failure. Includes a useful checklist of American communes, including some obscure ones not listed in this bibliography.

39. Calverton, Victor. *Where Angels Dared to Tread*. New York: Bobbs-Merrill, 1941. 381 pp.
    Contains chapters on major American communal societies including Zion City and Father Divine's Peace Mission Movement; also contains briefer information on Commonwealth College and Llano.

40. Carroll, H. K. *Religious Forces of the United States*. New York: Charles Scribner's Sons, 1912.
    A survey work covering most American religious bodies, including the communal groups Adonai-Shomo, the Altruist Community, the Church Triumphant, and the Koreshan Unity.

41. Cavan, Ruth Shonle, and Man Singh Das, eds. *Communes: Historical and Contemporary*. New Delhi: Vikas Publishing House Pvt. Ltd., 1979. 359 pp.
    A survey of communities, including four chapters concerning the Hutterites.

42. Chianese, Robert L., ed. *Peaceable Kingdom: An Anthology of Utopian Writings*. New York: Harcourt Brace Jovanovich, 1971.
    Describes visions of the ideal society, often involving communitarianism, from the Bible to the Black Panthers.

43. Clark, Elmer T. *Small Sects in America*. New York and Nashville: Abingdon, 1949. 256 pp.
    Provides brief sketches of the Koreshan Unity, the Llano colonies, the Church of God and Saints of Christ, the House of David, Zion City, the Hutterites, and the Father Divine Peace Mission Movement.

44. *Communal Societies*. Annual journal of the National Historic Communal Societies Association, 1981-.

45. *Communal Studies Newsletter*. Published in the late 1970s at Temple University. Edited by John A. Hostetler.

46.  "Communes Report."    *Alternatives!*  no.  3  (1972):  34-48.
     Surveys  many  new  communes;  includes  a  two-page  report
     on Heathcote and half a page on Koinonia, Maryland.

47.  "Communism."   *New  International  Encyclopedia.*    New
     York: Dodd, Mead, 1914, v. 5, p. 677.
     Lists  several  post-1860  communal  societies;  recounts
     some  general  arguments  for  communal  living  and  analyzes
     the causes of failure of several communities.

48.  *Communiteer.*   Teaburyport,  New  City,  N.Y.    1942-?
     Newsletter  of  the  Rural  Cooperative  Community
     Conference,  a  group  promoting  rural  voluntary
     communities. At Community Service, Inc.

49.  *Community  of  Correspondence.*    Elletsville,  Indiana.
     1951-2. Monthly.
     Contains  letters  and  other  communications  among
     participants  and  others  interested  in  intentional
     communities. At Community Service, Inc.

50.  Conkin,  Paul  K.    *Two  Paths  to  Utopia:  The  Hutterites  and
     the  Llano  Colony.*    Lincoln:  University  of  Nebraska
     Press, 1964. 212 pp.
     Provides  comparative  histories  of  the  two  movements,
     including an unusually complete one of Llano.

51.  *Cooperative  Living.*    Poughkeepsie,  N.Y.    1949-56.
     Quarterly.    Published  by  the  Group  Farming  Research
     Institute.
     Important  periodical  on  intentional  communities,  with
     articles  and  statistical  information  on  many  then  current.
     A backfile is at Community Service, Inc.

52.  Curl,  John.    *History  of  Work  Cooperation  in  America.*
     Berkeley: Homeward Press, 1980. 58 pp.
     Provides  brief  (usually  one  paragraph  or  less)  sketches
     of  or  references  to  the  Brotherhood  of  the  Cooperative
     Commonwealth,  Burley,  the  Christian  Commonwealth,
     Equality,  Glennis,  Home,  Kaweah,  Llano,  Lopez  Island,
     Pisgah  Grande,  Puget  Sound  Cooperative  Company,  Ruskin,
     the single tax colonies, and the Theosophical communities.

53.  Destler,  Chester  M.    *American  Radicalism,  1865-1901:
     Essays  and  Documents.*    New  London,  Ct.:  Connecticut

College, 1946, pp. 20-3.
Describes the popularity, in the 1890s, of planning for cooperatives and communes in reaction to political setbacks experienced by labor and Populists.

54. "Directory of Intentional Communities." *Alternatives! Newsmagazine* 1 (1971): 42-6.
Contains a directory of communities operating in 1971, including, from the pre-1960 period, Bethany Fellowship, Camp Hill, Celo, the Children of Light, Heathcote, the Hutterites, Koinonia (Maryland), Koinonia Farm, May Valley Co-operative Community, the Order of Aaron of the Glendenningite Mormons, Peace Action Farm, People of the Living God, Reba Place, Tanguy Homesteads, United Cooperative Industries, and the Vale. *Alternatives Newsletter* and its successor, *Alternatives! Newsmagazine*, published at least four issues in the early 1970s.

55. Doig, Ivan, ed. *Utopian America: Dreams and Realities.* Rochelle Park, N.J.: Hayden Book Co., 1976.
Includes introductory material and reading selections on Port Royal, Kahweah, Helicon Hall, and Home along with selections from Utopian literature and a good bibliography.

56. Douglas, Dorothy W., and Katharine Du Pre Lumpkin. "Communistic Settlements." *Encyclopedia of the Social Sciences.* Edited by Edwin R.A. Seligman. New York: Macmillan, 1930, v. 4, pp. 95-102.
Survey of communities from the ancient world to the twentieth century, including brief descriptions of the Hutterites, Mormon communalism, Ferrer Colony, Ruskin, Llano, Topolobampo, and Fairhope. Contains a useful bibliography.

57. Durnbaugh, Donald F., ed. *Brethren Encyclopedia.* Philadelphia: Brethren Encyclopedia, Inc., 1983. Three volumes.
Contains useful articles on the Bruderhof, the Hutterites, and Reba Place, plus other communities founded prior to 1860 and after 1960.

58. Eaton, Joseph W. "Conceptual Theory of Cooperation." *American Journal of Sociology* 54 (September, 1948): 126-34.
Proposes a conceptual scheme for describing, comparing,

and manipulating cooperative processes. Makes passing reference to various communes and types of communes.

59. ———. *Exploring Tomorrow's Agriculture.* New York: Harper and Brothers, 1943. 255 pp.
Principally devoted to the Farm Security Administration cooperative farms project, providing data on those project settlements in regard to membership, goals, management, work life, and the like. Also contains information on Saline Valley Farms, Delta and Providence, the Macedonia Community, and the Hutterites, plus other groups outside the purview of this bibliography.

60. Egerton, John. *Visions of Utopia: Nashoba, Rugby, Ruskin, and the "New Communities" in Tennessee's Past.* Knoxville: University of Tennessee Press, 1977. 95 pp.
Contains histories of Rugby and Ruskin, along with information on communities from other periods. Well illustrated with photographs.

61. "Emigration Colonies." New York *Daily Tribune*, May 6, 1869, p. 3.
Reports that several new groups in New York are working to send urban workers to new colonies in the West. Mentioned are Excelsior Colony (Nebraska), Battleson Colony (preparing to settle in Missouri), and a German colony (intending to settle on 25,000 acres in Pennsylvania).

62. *Experimental Community Exchange.* New Haven, Connecticut. Semimonthly at first; later monthly. 1950-1. Published by Cooperative Community Builders.
Contains communications among persons interested in communes and cooperatives; includes news of specific groups and theoretical articles. At Community Service, Inc.

63. Fairfield, Dick. "Communes, U.S.A." *Modern Utopian* 5 (1971). 187 pp.
A report on a personal tour of American communes. This special issue of a magazine became the basis for Fairfield's book (item 64, below), although it differs from the book in many particulars. Surveys the Hutterites, the Bruderhof, Llano, the Nevada Colony, the Fellowship of Intentional Communities, the School of Living, Camphill, Koinonia Farm, and Gould Farm, plus many communities

founded after 1960.

64.    ———. [Richard Fairfield]    *Communes USA: A Personal Tour*. Baltimore: Penguin, 1972. 400 pp.
An expanded version of item 63, above.    Provides basic information on the Fellowship of Intentional Communities, the School of Living, Camphill Village, and Gould Farm, plus many later communes.    Includes a substantial bibliography.

65.    ———, ed.    *Utopia* U.S.A.    San Francisco: Alternatives Foundation, 1972. 231 pp.
Primarily focuses on hippie communes active at the time, but also contains articles on the Bruderhof and Koinonia Farm.

66.    Faris, Robert E.L.    *Social Disorganization*.    New York: Ronald Press, 1948; second edition, 1955.
Provides overviews of Father Divine's Peace Mission Movement, Kaweah, Mankind United, and the Theosophical communes.

67.    Federal Writers' Project.    *Colorado: A Guide to the Highest State*.    New York: Hastings House, 1941.
Provides historical information on the Colorado Cooperative Company and Union Colony.

68.    ———.    *Michigan: A Guide to the Wolverine State*.    New York: Oxford University Press, 1941.
Provides background information on the House of David, Ora Labora, the Strangite Mormons, and the Sunrise community.

69.    ———.    *New Washington: A Guide to the Evergreen State*.    Portland, Oregon: Binfords and Mort, 1941; revised edition, 1950.
Provides information on Equality and Home colonies.

70.    ———.    *Tennessee: A Guide to the State*.    New York: Viking, 1939.
Provides basic information on Rugby and Ruskin.

71.    Fellman, Michael.    *Unbounded Frame: Freedom and Community in Nineteenth Century American Utopianism*.    Westport, Connecticut: Greenwood, 1973.
A biographical study of utopian thought, with some

information on turn-of-the-century communal theorists.

72.    Felton,   Bruce,   and   Mark   Fowler.    *Felton   and   Fowler's*
       *Famous   Americans   You   Never   Knew   Existed.*    New   York:
       Stein and Day, 1979. 293 pp.
       Contains   sketches   of   the   lives   and   ideas   of   Cyrus   Teed
       (Koresh), Alfred Lawson, and Wilbur Glenn Voliva.

73.    Fitzgerald,   George   R.    *Communes:   Their   Goals,   Hopes,*
       *Problems.* New York: Paulist, 1971. 214 pp.
       A   survey   of   contemporary   communalism,   including   newer
       and   older   communities.    Contains   a   substantial
       bibliography.

74.    Fogarty,   Robert   S.    "American   Communes,   1865-1914."
       *Journal   of   American   Studies*   9   (August,   1975):   145-62.
       Lists   over   100   communes   founded   during   the   period
       covered;   argues   that   the   era   was   not   a   fallow   time   for
       commune-building,   as   others   have   suggested.    Discusses
       the   contributions   of   major   promoters   of   communalism   at
       the   beginning   of   the   era   (J.   H.   Noyes,   H.   Greeley,   Marie
       Howland)   and   provides   a   paragraph   or   more   of   information
       on   the   Woman's   Commonwealth,   the   Alcander   Longley
       communes,   Rugby,   Shalam,   Topolobampo,   the   Jewish
       agricultural   colonies,   the   Koreshan   Unity,   and   the
       Christian Commonwealth.

75.    ———.    *American   Utopianism.*    Itasca,   Illinois:   Peacock
       Publishers, 1972.
       A   collection   of   old   communal   documents,   some   primary,
       some   secondary,   including   statements   by   members   and
       supporters   of   communes   and   reports   on   communal   life
       made   by   visitors   to   various   communities.    Covers   all   of
       American   communal   history,   including   material   on   Altruria,
       Helicon   Hall,   the   Army   of   Industry,   Llano,   the
       twentieth-century   subsistence   farming   movement,   Sunrise,
       and Koinonia Farm.

76.    ———.    *Dictionary   of   American   Communal   and   Utopian*
       *History.*    Westport,   Connecticut:   Greenwood,   1980.    271
       pp.
       Contains,   in   two   sections,   dictionary   entries   averaging
       about   one   page   each   on   most   of   the   communities   covered
       in   this   bibliography   and   on   many   of   the   more   important
       communal   leaders.    Also   includes   Otohiko   Okugawa's
       "Annotated   List   of   Communal   and   Utopian   Societies,

1787-1919" (cited below as item 139). Contains an excellent bibliography.

77.    ———.    "Familistere:    Radical    Reform    Through Cooperative Enterprise."    Introduction to Porcupine edition of Marie Howland, *Papa's Own Girl (The Familistere)* (cited below as item 103).
Describes Marie Howland's work as publicist for Topolobampo and her later career at Fairhope.

78.    Fried, Albert.    *Socialism in America: From the Shakers to the Third International: A Documentary History.*    New York: Doubleday, 1970.
Contains documents from nearly a dozen American communes and communal theorists, along with other material on socialism; includes several important theorists of the late nineteenth century (Gronlund, Bellamy, Howells) and material on the Christian Commonwealth Colony.    Lucid introductions to the documents are provided as well.

79.    Garvin, Philip, and Julia Welch.    *Religious America.*    New York: McGraw-Hill, 1974.    189 pp.
A book of photo features on several small churches and other religious groups, including the Hutterites and Reba Place.

80.    Gide, Charles.    *Communist and Cooperative Colonies.*    New York: T.Y. Crowell, 1930.
Information on several modern communes, some American, but more located in Europe.

81.    Gladstone, Arthur.    "Cooperative Communities Today." *Cooperative Living* 6 (Spring, 1950): 13-4.
An introduction to a supplement to the *Research Guide to Cooperative Group Farming* (following item).

82.    ———.    "Cooperative Communities Today II: A Supplement to the Research Guide."    *Cooperative Living* 7 (Winter, 1955-6): 13-5.
Brief updates (one to two paragraphs each) on many contemporary communities, including the Catholic Worker Farms, Celo, the Essenes of Kosmon, the Glen Gardner Cooperative Community, Gould Farm, Hidden Springs, the Hutterites, Koinonia Farm, Macedonia, Quest, Red Banks Mutual Association, and Tuolumne Farms.

83.    ———.    "Cooperative    Communities    Today    III:    A
       Supplement  to  the  Research  Guide."    *Cooperative  Living*
       7 (Spring, 1956): 10- 1.
       Provides  basic  information  on  United  Cooperative
       Industries,   a   producers'   cooperative   moving   toward
       becoming  a  cooperative  community,  and  the  opening  of  the
       Woodcrest Bruderhof.

84.    Gorni, Yosef, Yaacov Oved, and Idit Paz, eds.    *Communal
       Life: An International Perspective.*    New Brunswick, N.J.:
       Transaction Books, 1987. 758 pp.
       Provides   general   and   theoretical   articles   on
       communalism,  plus  articles  with  specific  material  on  the
       Bruderhof, Ferrer, the Hutterites, Reba Place, and Sunrise.

85.    Grant,   H.   Roger.    "Missouri's   Utopian   Communities."
       *Missouri  Historical  Review*  66  (October,  1971):  20-48.
       Contains   material   on   early   Mormon   communalism   at
       Independence  and  Far  West,  Missouri,  and  on  the  Alcander
       Longley  communities,  as  well  as  information  on  colonies
       founded prior to 1860.

86.    ———.    "New    Communitarianism:    The    Case    of Three
       Intentional  Colonies,  1890-1905."    *Indiana  Social  Studies
       Quarterly* 30 (Spring, 1977), 59-71.
       Provides  basic  information  on  Freedom  Colony,  the
       Home  Employment  Cooperative  Company,  and  the  Colorado
       Cooperative  Company,  as  well  as  colonies  which  preceded
       or succeeded them. Well documented.

87.    ———.    "Western    Utopians    and  the  Farmers'  Railroad
       Movement,   1890-1900."    *North   Dakota   History*   46
       (Winter, 1979): 13-8.
       Describes  cooperative  railroad  plans  in  the  West  in  the
       late  19th  century,  showing  their  relation  to  communities
       such  as  Topolobampo  and  the  Colorado  Cooperative
       Company.

88.    Hafen,   LeRoy   R.,   ed.    *Colorado   and   Its   People.*    New
       York:  Lewis  Historical  Publishing  Co.,  1948,  v.  1,  pp.
       328-33.
       Provides  brief  historical  accounts  of  Union,  the  German
       Colonization Co., and the Chicago-Colorado Colony.

89.    Hall,  Frank.    *History  of  the  state  of  Colorado.*    Chicago:

Blakely Printing Co., 1899, v. 1, pp. 531-48.
Provides a good overview history of Union Colony, a shorter history of the Chicago-Colorado Colony, and a still shorter note on the German Colonization Co.

90. Hayden, Dolores. *Seven American Utopias: The Architecture of Communitarian Socialism*, 1790-1975. Cambridge, Massachusetts: Massachusetts Institute of Technology Press, 1976.
A heavily illustrated book on seven communes and families of communities, including Union Colony and Llano. Contains rich supportive materials, including useful introductory chapters, a chart comparing features of the communes discussed, an annotated bibliography, and many diagrams and maps.

91. Hedgepeth, William, and Dennis Stock (photographer). *Alternative: Communal Life in New America*. London: Collier-Macmillan, 1970.
A profusely illustrated book focusing principally on post-1960 hippie communes, but with some material on earlier communities, especially Koinonia Farm.

92. Hendricks, Robert J. *Bethel and Aurora: An Experiment in Communism as Practical Christianity*. New York: Press of the Pioneers, 1933. 324 pp.
Bethel and Aurora were founded before 1860, but information is appended on several other communities, including the Llano Colony. Especially useful is a list of then-active communes in the U.S. compiled by residents of the Co-operative Farm at Eugene, Oregon; the list includes about a dozen entries, most of which are for groups which have received little outside attention.

93. Hertzler, Joyce Oramel. *History of Utopian Thought*. New York: Macmillan, 1923. 321 pp.
Much material covered is pre-1860, but a section on "Social Anticipations" covers utopian thinkers whose ideas inspired and influenced communes founded late in the nineteenth century (Bellamy, Hertzka, Wells).

94. Hinds, William Alfred. *American Communities*. Oneida, New York: Office of the American Socialist, 1878. 175 pp.
A standard work on American communalism. Contains major articles on ten communities founded before 1860;

has a directory which lists seventeen Shaker villages and ten other communes. Also includes short notes on some eighteen other communities, most of them founded after 1860 and most of them not the recipients of much attention elsewhere. Some are not clearly identified; those which are include Adonai-Shomo, the Progressive Community (Cedar Vale, Kansas), Esperanza, Home (Michigan), an unidentified Alcander Longley community, Silkville, and Union. For most communities the reference is very brief, sometimes as little as a single sentence.

95.    ———. *American        Communities       and       Co-operative Colonies.* Chicago: Kerr, 1908. 608 pp.
    The third edition of the book listed at no. 94, above, but so much larger and so heavily revised that it deserves separate citation. Covers several major communities and families of communities, along with brief notes on some 42 others; those founded after 1860 include Adonai-Shomo, the Altruist Community of Alcander Longley, Celesta, the Christian Commonwealth Colony, the Colorado Co-operative Company, the Co-operative Brotherhood (Burley), Equality, Fairhope, Fellowship Farm Association, Helicon Hall, Home, the House of David, the Hutterites, the Koreshan Unity, the Lord's Farm, Modjeska's Colony, Point Loma, the Roycrofters, Ruskin, Shalam, the Spirit Fruit Society, the Straight Edge community, the Temple of the People, Topolobampo, and the Woman's Commonwealth.

96.    ———. "Communities    in    America."   *New   Encyclopedia   of Social Reform* (cited above as item 35), 264-5.
    Provides a discussion of the philosophy of communalism and a six-part typology of American communes. Contains one-paragraph characterizations of the most important American communal societies and a list of recently founded (turn of the century) communities.

97.    Hine, Robert V.   *California Utopianism: Contemplations of Eden.*   San Francisco: Boyd and Fraser, 1981.   95 pp.
    Describes many utopian visions in California, from literary utopianism to urban improvement schemes. Provides brief sketches of Altruria, the Army of Industry, Holy City, Kaweah, Little Landers, Llano del Rio, Mankind United, Modjeska's colony, Pisgah Grande, theosphical communalism (Krotona, Point Loma, and Temple of the People), and Winters Island.

98. ———. *California's Utopian Colonies.* San Marino, California: Huntington Library, 1953. 209 pp.
    Contains chapters on the Brotherhood of the New Life, the Theosophical communities, Kaweah, Altruria, and Llano del Rio, along with a chapter on ten smaller communes from the post-1860 era: the Army of Industry, Fellowship Farm, Holy City, Joyful, Little Landers, Modjeska's colony, the Mormons at San Bernardino, Pisgah Grande, Tuolumne Farms, and Winters Island. Includes an extensive bibliography.

99. ———. *Community on the American Frontier: Separate but Not Alone.* Norman: University of Oklahoma Press, 1980.
    Concerned in large part with rural cooperation in the West and ethnic settlements on the frontier, but also contains information on several communes, including Mormon United Order communities, Union Colony, the Colorado Cooperative Co., Kahweah, the Brotherhood of the Cooperative Commonwealth, and Home. Includes an extensive bibliography.

100. ———. "Naming of California's Utopias." *Western Folklore* 12 (April, 1953): 132-5.
    Discloses the origins of the names of the Theosophical communes of Point Loma, Krotona, and the Temple of the People, as well as Holy City, Kaweah, Llano, Altruria, Winters Island, and the Modjeska colony at Anaheim.

101. Holbrook, Stewart H. *Far Corner: A Personal View of the Pacific Northwest.* New York: Macmillan, 1952, pp. 145-59.
    Provides overview histories of the Puget Sound Cooperative Colony, Equality, the Cooperative Brotherhood (Burley), Freeland, and Home.

102. Holloway, Mark. *Heavens on Earth: Utopian Communities in America 1680-1880.* London: Turnstile Press, 1951. Repr., New York: Dover, 1966. 246 pp.
    Focuses primarily on pre-1860 communities, but the closing chapters include information on the Mormon community at Orderville and the Topolobampo colony, as well as brief mentions of several other late nineteenth century communities.

103. Howland, Marie. *Papa's Own Girl.* New York: J.P.

Jewett, 1873. Repr., Philadelphia: Porcupine, 1975, under the title *The Familistere*. 547 pp.
A utopian romance based on the author's experiences at a French commune begun in the late 1850s. Shortly after the publication of this book, Howland became the chief publicist for Topolobampo, and after that community closed moved to Fairhope, where she was the community librarian and a newspaper columnist.

104. Infield, Henrik F. *American Intentional Communities: Study on the Sociology of Cooperation.* Glen Gardner, N.J.: Glen Gardner Community Press, 1955. 118 pp.
Basic information on and sociological analysis of active communities, focused on the "Campanella Community" (a pseudonym for Koinonia Farm), the Macedonia Co-operative Community, and Gould Farm.

105. ———. *Cooperative Communities at Work.* New York: Dryden Press, 1945. 201 pp.
A brief history of American communalism, plus specific material on the Hutterites, the Jewish communes, Llano, Sunrise, and the FSA Farms, along with chapters on analysis and theory of communes.

106. ———. "Cooperative Community: A Note on a Potential New Field of Sociological Research." *American Sociological Review* 7 (December, 1942): 854-5.
A research note urging more scholars to study cooperative projects.

107. ———. *Sociology of Cooperation and the International Council for Related Research.* Glen Gardner, N.J.: Glen Gardner Community Press, 1955. 40 pp.
Contains an essay urging research into the sociology of cooperation, a report on the First General Assembly of the International Council for Research in the Sociology of Cooperation, and the constitution and bylaws of that council. Does not contain information on specific communities, but does address sociological and methodological questions and other matters related to the study of communes.

108. ———. *Utopia and Experiment: Essays in the Sociology of Cooperation.* New York: F.A. Praeger, 1955. 320 pp.
Provides information on several twentieth century

communal experiments, including Penn-Craft, Celo, Bass Lake Farm, Macedonia Cooperative Community, and the Hutterites, along with information on communal projects in other countries and largely statistical sociological data on communes.

109. Infield, Henrik F., and Joseph B. Meier, eds. *Cooperative Group Living.* New York: Henry Koosis and Co., 1950. 261 pp.
An international survey of communal and cooperative farms, along with essays on the sociology of cooperation. The U.S. material includes information on Macedonia, Saline Valley Farms, and the communal farms promoted by the Farm Security Administration from 1937 to 1939.

110. *Intentional Community.* Baltimore (issues 1-3); Berkeley thereafter. 1965-? Edited and published by Ben and Elaine Zablocki.
News and information about communities from persons living in them and interested outsiders. Copies of some issues are located at Community Service, Inc.

111. Jackson, Dave. *Coming Together.* Minneapolis: Bethany Fellowship, 1978.
Surveys and discusses many contemporary religious communes, including a few founded prior to 1960. Includes material on the Bruderhof and Bethany Fellowship. Jackson is a member of Reba Place. Much of his focus is theological. Appendix A contains "A Selected List of Christian Communities," most (but not all) founded after 1960.

112. Jackson, Dave, and Neta Jackson. *Living Together in a World Falling Apart.* Carol Stream, Illinois: Creation House, 1974.
Contains a description of the Jacksons' personal pilgrimage toward communal living. Describes five contemporary Christian communes, including Koinonia Farm, the Bruderhof, and Reba Place. Subsequent chapters cover such topics as organization, leadership, relationships, aging, children, problem-solving, work, and finances, with references to the above groups *passim*. Also contains a list of contemporary religious communes with a one-paragraph description of each.

113. Johnpoll, Bernard K., and Lillian Johnpoll. *Impossible*

Dream: The Rise and Demise of the American Left. Westport, Connecticut: Greenwood, 1981.
Provides basic information about Kaweah, focusing on the role of Burnette Haskell, its moving force. Provides a brief overview of the Christian Commonwealth Colony, emphasizing the problems which led to its demise.

114. Jones, Raymond Julius. *Comparative Study of Religious Cult Behavior Among Negroes with Special Reference to Emotional Group Conditioning Factors.* Washington, D.C.: Howard University Graduate School, 1939. 125 pp.
Provides several pieces of descriptive information on the Church of God and Saints of Christ and Father Divine's Peace Mission Movement, at one point comparing the two in their similar concern for the material as well as spiritual well-being of their members.

115. Kagan, Paul. *New World Utopias: A Photographic History of the Search for Community.* New York: Penguin, 1975. 191 pp.
Contains brief surveys of many communal groups; has major chapters on Theosophical communities, Kaweah, Holy City, Llano del Rio, and Pisgah Grande, as well as other groups outside the 1860-1960 time frame. Engagingly written and profusely illustrated.

116. Kanter, Rosabeth Moss, ed. *Communes: Creating and Managing the Collective Life.* New York: Harper and Row, 1973.
A collection of articles from scholarly journals and other sources, several of them referring to the 1860-1960 period, most frequently to the Hutterites. Specific pertinent articles are listed separately in this bibliography.

117. Kent, Alexander. "Cooperative Communities in the United States." *Bulletin of the Department of Labor* 6 (July, 1901): 563-646.
An important survey providing descriptions and historical material on 25 communities, including these from the 1860-1960 period: Altruist Community, Burley, Christian Commonwealth, the Colorado Cooperative Company, Commonwealth of Israel, Equality and the Brotherhood of the Cooperative Commonwealth, Freedom Colony, Home, the Home Employment Co., the Lord's Farm, Ruskin, Silkville, the Straight Edge Community, Willard Cooperative Colony, the Woman's Commonwealth,

and several smaller communes and collective industrial and commercial enterprises: the Association of Altruists, the Brotherhood Company, the Cooperative Association of America, the Cooperative Industrial College, the Industrial Brotherhood, and the Union Mills Company. Reproduces several documents, especially of the commercial and industrial projects.

118. Kramer, Wendell Barlow. "Criteria for the Intentioanl Community." Ph.D. dissertation, New York University, 1955. 279 pp.
    Provides a brief survey of communities (including Topolobampo and Llano) in American history; then focuses on communities currently operating. Determines that there were, in 1955, six "comprehensive communities" (the Hutterites, the Shakers, the Doukhobors, Koinonia Farm, Macedonia, and Tuolumne Farms) and eighteen "partially comprehensive communities." Of the latter, five are listed as housing cooperatives (Bryn Gweled Homesteads, Celo, Fellowship [Tanguy Homesteads], San Fernando Farm, Skyview Acres), five are characterized as involving cooperative farming (Saline Valley Farms, plus four Canadian cooperative farm associations), and eight are in neither category (Canterbury Community, Essenes of Kosmon, Gould Farm, Hidden Springs, Kingwood, Parishfield, Quest, the Vale). Also mentioned is the Bruderhof, not yet in the United States. Each of the groups is characterized in a few pages; subsequent chapters discuss characteristics of contemporary communities, their basic principles, factors related to their success or failure, and means for evaluating their potential for success. Also contains a bibliography and appendices.

119. Lauer, Jeanette C., and Robert H. Lauer. "Sex Roles in Nineteenth-Century American Communal Societies." *Communal Societies* 3 (1983): 16-28.
    Outlines the roles played by women in several nineteenth century communes, including Kaweah and Ruskin.

120. Lauer, Robert H., and Jeanette C. Lauer. *Spirit and the Flesh: Sex in Utopian Communities.* Metuchen, N.J.: Scarecrow Press, 1983.
    Discusses sexual attitudes and practices of celibate communes, those approving of traditional sexuality, and

those espousing nontraditional practices. Mentions briefly many of the communes in this volume, providing information in slightly greater depth on Cedar Vale, the House of David, the Alcander Longley communes, Ruskin, Spirit Fruit, and the Woman's Commonwealth.

121. Lears, T.J. Jackson. *No Place of Grace: Antimodernism and the Transformation of American Culture, 1880-1920.* New York: Pantheon, 1981, pp. 66-96.
Describes cooperative colonies founded in the early twentieth century as a part of the Arts and Crafts Movement, providing basic information on New Clairvaux and Rose Valley along with comments on the Roycrofters.

122. LeWarne, Charles P. "Communitarian Experiments in Western Washington, 1885-1915." Ph.D. dissertation, University of Washington, 1969. 595 pp.
The work from which the author's published book (item 124, below) was extracted. Covers Heaven Colony, the Christian Cooperative Colony, Washington Colony, the Puget Sound Cooperative Colony, Equality, Harmony, Freeland, Burley, Glennis, Home, and Lopez Island; also gives brief descriptions of communities in nearby British Columbia and of Soviet communes initiated by expatriate Washingtonians. Contains a thirty-page bibliography.

123. ———. "Labor and Communitarianism, 1880-1900." *Labor History* 16 (Summer, 1975): 393-407.
Focuses principally on the role of organized labor in several colonies, including Rugby, Ruskin, Altruria, the Christian Commonwealth Colony, the Llano colonies, Burley, Topolobampo, and the Puget Sound Cooperative Colony. Also describes the formation and brief life of the Brotherhood of the Cooperative Commonwealth. Chronicles the decline of labor involvement in communitarianism as the labor movement moved more firmly toward trade unionism and collective bargaining.

124. ———. *Utopias on Puget Sound, 1885-1915.* Seattle: University of Washington Press, 1975. 325 pp.
Contains major chapters on Burley, Equality, Freeland, Home, and the Puget Sound Cooperative Colony; also provides information on Glennis, Harmony Colony, Lopez Island, and Washington Colony. Heavily documented with many specialized, local, and manuscript references. Illustrated with photographs of the colonies and

reproductions of colony documents.

125. Liefmann, Robert. *Kommunistischen Gemeinden in Nordamerika.* Jena: Gustav Fischer, 1922. 95 pp.
Contains brief overviews of a number of communes operating around the turn of the century, including Adonai-Shomo, the Altruist Community, Burley, Celesta, the Colorado Co-operative Company, Equality, Kaweah, the Koreshan Unity, Point Loma, Ruskin, Shalam, and Zion City, plus a major chapter on the Hutterites and material on pre-1860 communes. Also includes information on leaders of major communities of the era. In German.

126. McWilliams, Carey. *Southern California Country.* New York: Duell, Sloan and Pearce, 1946. Repr., Freeport, New York: Books for Libraries Press, 1970. 387 pp.
Chapter 13, "The Purple Mother," covers various religious movements, including the Theosophical communities of Point Loma and Krotona, and Mankind United. Chapter 24, "The Politics of Utopia," provides an overview of Llano. The book also contains a brief account of the founding of Modjeska's colony.

127. Mathison, Richard. *Faiths, Cults and Sects of America: From Atheism to Zen.* Indianapolis: Bobbs-Merrill, 1960. 384 pp.
An anthology containing sketches of many communal movements, including the Strangite Mormons, Theosophical communalism, Mankind United, Father Divine's Peace Mission Movement, the Bride of Christ Church, the House of David, John Briggs and his Devouts, Holy City, and the WFLK Fountain of the World. Not documented.

128. Mayer, F.E. *Religious Bodies of America.* St. Louis: Concordia Publishing House, 1958.
Includes accounts of several communal movements, including the House of David, the Church of God and Saints of Christ, and the Christian Catholic Church in Zion (Zion City).

129. Meany, Edmond S. *History of the State of Washington.* New York: Macmillan, 1909. 406 pp.
Chapter 30, "Social Improvements," provides overviews of several colonies, including Washington Colony, Puget Sound Cooperative Colony, Home, Burley, and Equality/Freeland.

130. Melton, J. Gordon. *Encyclopedia of American Religions*, second edition. Detroit: Gale Research, 1987.
     Contains brief but informative entries on the Bruderhof, the Church of God and Saints of Christ, the Church of the Savior, the Colony, the Davidian Seventh-Day Adventists, the Emissary Communities, the Esoteric Fraternity, the House of David, the Hutterites, the Koreshan Unity, the Lemurian Fellowship, People of the Living God, Pisgah Grande, Reba Place, Shiloh Trust, the Temple of the People, the WFLK Fountain of the World, and the Latter Day Saints groups led by Bickerton, Cutler, Glendenning, Joseph, LeBaron, Strang, and Woolley. The first edition of this work covers many of the same groups.

131. *Mennonite Encyclopedia*. Scottdale, Pennsylvania: Mennonite Publishing House, 1956. Four volumes. Contains many articles on the Hutterites and the Bruderhof.

132. Mercer, John. *Communes: A Social History and Guide*. Dorchester, England: Prism Press, 1984.
     A wide-ranging survey of early utopian literature, monasticism, and European communitarianism, with material on American communes of the nineteenth and twentieth centuries, especially the Hutterites and the Bruderhof.

133. Miller, Ernest I. "Some Tennessee Utopias." M.A. thesis, University of Tennessee, 1941. 91 pp.
     Provides good survey accounts of the Bohemian Cooperative Farming Co., Rugby, and Ruskin, as well as other earlier communal ventures.

134. Moment, Gairdner B., and Otto F. Kraushaar, eds. *Utopias: The American Experience*. Metuchen, N.J.: Scarecrow Press, 1980.
     A collection of essays by various authors on topics such as "Women in Utopia: The Nineteenth-Century Experience," "Town Planning for the City of God," and "The Economics of Utopia." Notes and bibliographies at ends of essays provide numerous references.

135. Muncy, Raymond Lee. *Sex and Marriage in Utopian Communities: Nineteenth Century America*. Bloomington: Indiana University Press, 1973. 275 pp.
     Extensive coverage of communities founded both before

and after 1860, including the Hutterites, Ruskin, the Christian Commonwealth Colony, Kaweah, New Jerusalem, the Strangite Mormons, the Harmonial Vegetarian Society, the Koreshan Unity, and the Woman's Commonwealth. Filled with information of all types, focusing on sexual and marital ideas and practices.

136. Negley, Glenn, and J. Max Patrick, eds. *Quest for Utopia: An Anthology of Imaginary Societies.* New York: Henry Schumann, 1952.
Deals with utopian thought from all ages, including several authors (such as Bellamy and Hertzka) who inspired communes founded between 1860 and 1960.

137. *New Nation.* 1891-4. Edited by Edward Bellamy.
Contains scattered articles on late nineteenth century communities.

138. Nordhoff, Charles. *Communistic Societies of the United States.* New York: Harper and Brothers, 1875. Repr., New York: Dover, 1966. 439 pp.
Provides brief overviews of Cedar Vale, the Social Freedom Community, and Silkville, plus many communities founded before 1860.

139. Okugawa, Otohiko. "Annotated List of Communal and Utopian Societies, 1787-1919." Published as an appendix to Robert Fogarty, *Dictionary of American Communal and Utopian History* (cited above as item 76), 173-233.
Provides a brief paragraph each of basic information on most of the communities founded through 1919, including several not listed in this bibliography. (Most of those not listed here were either not very communal in their makeup, or very short lived, or not listed or described in any other generally available source.) Those communities listed by Okugawa but not given sections in this bibliography are the Bennett Co-operative Colony, the Bible Community, the Christian Corporation, Dawn Valcour, the Christian Social Association, Friedheim, Fruit Crest, the Israelites or New House of Israel, Kinder Lou, Lystra, Magnolia, the Mutual Aid Community, the Niksur Co-operative Association, the Southern Co-operative Association of Apalachicola, the Union Mill Co., and Warm Springs.

140. ———. "Intercommunal Relationships among Nineteenth-

Century Communal Societies in America." *Communal Societies* 3 (1983): 68-82.

Traces intercommunal migrations and relationships from the Shakers through the early twentieth century. Concludes that "failed" communes actually lived on in that their members often ended up in other communities. Contains many tables and diagrams.

141.  Orrmont, Arthur. *Love Cults and Faith Healers.* New York: Ballantine, 1961. 192 pp.

Provides chapter-length historical sketches of four movements and their leaders: the House of David, the Strangite Mormons, the WFLK Fountain of the World, and Zion City.

142.  Oved, Yaacov. *Two Hundred Years of American Communes.* New Brunswick, N.J.: Transaction Books, 1988. 500 pp.

Contains major chapters surveying the Christian Commonwealth Colony, the Hutterites, Kaweah, Llano, New Odessa, Ruskin, Sunrise, and the Washington state colonies (the Brotherhood of the Cooperative Commonwealth, Burley, Equality, and the Puget Sound Cooperative Colony); also contains chapters on several pre-1860 groups along with several chapters on general and theoretical topics. Generally covers ground already worked, but does so accurately and innovatively, often using sources previously little explored.

143.  Parrington, Vernon Louis, Jr. *American Dreams: A Study of American Utopias.* Providence: Brown University Press, 1947.

A wide-ranging monograph including a variety of material on utopian and communal thought from various eras.

144.  Pitzer, Donald E. "Collectivism, Community and Commitment: America's Religious Communal Utopias from the Shakers to Jonestown." *Utopias.* Edited by Peter Alexander and Roger Gill. London: Duckworth, 1984, pp. 119-35.

Provides a survey of communities beginning with the very earliest, dealing briefly with many groups, including Point Loma, Father Divine's Peace Mission, and the Hutterites. Contains a good bibliography.

145. Preston, John Hyde. "Collective Living." *Harper's Monthly Magazine* 176 (May, 1938): 603-14.
    Describes "Collectiva," a small pseudonymous communally-operated college. Argues that group housekeeping is economical; urges the foundation of communes and collectives in every city and town in America.

146. Quaife, Milo Milton. *Lake Michigan.* Indianapolis: Bobbs-Merrill, 1944.
    Contains "The King of Benton Harbor," the first serious and substantial work on the House of David. Also provides information on several communes in Wisconsin, most of them founded prior to 1860, including the Strangite Mormons.

147. Quill Pen Club, ed. *Rawhide and Orange Blossoms.* Santa Ana, California: Pioneer Press, 1967. 359 pp.
    Contains articles on Anaheim (Modjeska's Colony) and the Societas Fraternia by Maude Rubin and Fern Colman, respectively.

148. Quint, Howard H. *Forging of American Socialism.* Indianapolis: Bobbs-Merrill, 1964.
    Originally published in 1953. Provides an overview of the Christian Commonwealth Colony, a description of Ruskin emphasizing the role of J. A. Wayland, and an account of the Brotherhood of the Cooperative Commonwealth, including the founding, subsequent history, and goals of that organization, focusing especially on the controversy it raised among socialists.

149. Randolph, Vance. *Americans Who Thought They Were Gods: Colorful Messiahs and Little Christs.* Girard, Kansas: Haldeman-Julius Publications, 1943. 24 pp.
    Depicts several dissenting religious movements in two to four pages each, including the Strangite Mormons, New Jerusalem (Cyrus Spragg), Zion City, the House of David, and Father Divine.

150. Rhodes, Harold V. *Utopia in American Political Thought.* Tucson: University of Arizona Press, 1967. 115 pp.
    A survey of several American utopian theorists who influenced communalism, including, in the 1860-1960 period, Edward Bellamy and Henry George. Analyzes their reformist/utopian ideas and their actions in trying to

implement those ideas.

151.  Richardson, James T. "Data Frame for Commune Research." *Communal Studies Newsletter* 4 (March, 1977): 1-13.
      Provides a detailed outline for scholars to use when studying communities. Includes a substantial bibliography.

152.  Richter, Peyton E., ed. *Utopia/Dystopia?* Cambridge, Massachusetts: Schenkman Publishing Co., 1975.
      Contains only brief, passing references to communes founded between 1860 and 1960, but a good bibliography (pp. 143-151) lists a number of works dealing with that period in whole or in part.

153.  Roberts, Ron E. *The New Communes: Coming Together in America.* Englewood Cliffs, New Jersey: Prentice-Hall, 1971. 144 pp.
      Provides profiles of Reba Place, Koinonia Farm, and the Vale, plus later communes.

154.  Roemer, Kenneth. *Obsolete Necessity: America in Utopian Writings, 1888-1900.* Kent, Ohio: Kent State University Press, 1976, pp. 45-54.
      Characterizes the writings of Ralph Albertson and Alcander Longley as the works of utopian thinkers who actually tested their theories.

155.  Shenker, Barry. *Intentional Communities: Ideology and Alienation in Communal Societies.* London and Boston: Routledge and Kegan Paul, 1986. 283 pp.
      Provides a comparative study of the Hutterites, the kibbutzim of Israel, and the Richmond Fellowship, a British therapeutic community. Ends with a list of 69 conclusions about communal societies, finding that they are rooted in their respective cultures of origin rather than opposed to them; that they tend to emerge at times of great social stress; that they develop and change their goals over time; and so forth.

156.  Skinner, Charles M. *American Communes: Practical Socialism in the United States.* Brooklyn: Brooklyn Daily Eagle, 1901.
      Provides basic information on several American communities, including Ruskin Colony and Leclaire (Illinois). Apparently a compilation of a series of

newspaper articles.

157. Smith, Sam B. *Tennessee History: A Bibliography*.
Knoxville: University of Tennessee Press, 1974. 498 pp.
Contains bibliographies for Rugby and Ruskin.
Manuscript material listed is not cited here, although all
references to published work are.

158. Sparks, Edwin E. "Seeking Utopia in America."
*Chautauquan* 31 (May, 1900): 151-61.
Part of a longer series, this installment provides basic
information on a variety of religious and secular
communes. It begins with the earliest cooperative
ventures after the European settlement, and concludes
with brief mentions of Union Colony, Esperanza, and New
Odessa.

159. Stephan, Karen H., and G. Edward Stephan. "Religion and
the Survival of Utopian Communities." *Journal for the
Scientific Study of Religion* 12 (March, 1973): 89-100.
Finds that communes with a single religious faith tend
to survive longer than other kinds of communes do.
Includes a list of about 200 communities founded between
1776 and 1900.

160. Stone, Grace. "Tennessee: Social and Economic
Laboratory." *Sewanee Review* 46 (January, April, and
July, 1938): 36-44, 158- 66, 312-36.
The first portion of this extended article covers the
pre-1860 period; the second discusses Thomas Hughes and
Rugby; the third provides a good overview of Ruskin and
characterizes the veterans of that colony, as well as those
of Rugby, as believing years later that their colony
experiences had been largely positive and that in that
sense their colonies had not "failed."

161. Strachey, Ray, and Hannah Whitall Smith. *Group
Movements of the Past and Experiments in Guidance*.
London: Faber and Faber, 1934. Originally published
under the title *Religious Fanaticism*. London: Faber and
Gwyer, 1928.
Smith did research on sectarian and communal
movements in America in the early and middle nineteenth
century; Strachey, her gradddaughter, devoted half of this
book to Smith's writings and wrote the rest of it herself,
based on Smith's research. Strachey's half of the book

surveys many groups, including Adonai-Shomo, Cedar Vale, Celesta, the Church Triumphant, the House of David, the Koreshan Unity, the Lord's Farm, Modjeska's Colony, the Social Freedom Community, and the Woman's Commonwealth.

162. "Suggestion for Socialists." *Nation* 58 (February 8, 1894): 97-8.
    Urges small communitarian settlements as a practical way for socialists to improve their lives and put their ideas into practice.

163. Taylor, R. Bruce. "Communistic Societies of America." James Hastings, ed., *Encyclopaedia of Religion and Ethics.* Edited by James Hastings. New York: Charles Scribner's Sons, 1911, v. 3, pp. 780-787.
    Good, engaging accounts of several major communal experiments, including Ruskin and the Woman's Commonwealth as well as earlier communities. Also contains very brief references to the Altruist Community and the American Settlers' Cooperative. Includes a bibliography.

164. Thomas, John L. "Romantic Reform in America, 1815-1865." *American Quarterly* 17 (Winter, 1965): 656-81.
    Discusses social-reformist communes, focusing primarily on those founded prior to 1860, but including some later ones.

165. U.S. Department of Commerce, Bureau of the Census. *Religious Bodies.* Washington: U.S. Department of Commerce, 1906-36.
    At decennial intervals on four occasions (1906, 1916, 1926, 1936) the Bureau of the Census recorded detailed information about American religious bodies, comprising two large volumes each time (three volumes in 1936). Communal religious groups are listed with statistics and brief characterizations.

166. Veysey, Laurence. *Communal Experience: Anarchist and Mystical Communities in Twentieth-Century America.* Chicago: University of Chicago Press, 1973. 495 pp.
    Contains chapter-length studies of the Ferrer Colony and Vedanta communalism.

167. Wagner, Jon, ed. *Sex Roles in Contemporary American Communes*. Bloomington: Indiana University Press, 1982.
   Separate articles discuss sex roles in six communities, including the Mormon Glendenningites ("Levites") and the Shiloh Trust.

168. Webber, Everett. *Escape to Utopia: The Communal Movement in America*. New York: Hastings House, 1959. 444 pp.
   A survey of communes from colonial days to the twentieth century. Includes material on Adonai-Shomo, the House of David, the Koreshan Unity, the Strangite Mormons, New Jerusalem, and Zion City. Contains a bibliography.

169. Weeks, Vickie D. "Late Nineteenth Century Kansas Utopian Communities: The Value of Hostility in Commitment Development." Ph.D. dissertation, Kansas State University, 1980. 104 pp.
   Provides historical accounts of the Cedar Vale communities, the Danish colony, Esperanza, and Silkville, plus theoretical discussion.

170. Weisbrod, Carol. *Boundaries of Utopia*. New York: Pantheon, 1980.
   A discussion of legal problems various communal societies have encountered.

171. Whisenhunt, Donald. "Utopians, Communalism, and the Great Depression." *Communal Societies* 3 (1983): 101-10.
   Describes the efforts of James Cox, Henry McCowen, Maury Maverick, and Ralph Turton to found communal settlements as a solution to the nation's economic problems during the Depression.

172. Whitman, Alden, ed. *American Reformers*. New York: H.W. Wilson, 1985.
   Provides biographical sketches of several persons important in American communal history, including Laurence Gronlund (whose work inspired Equality) and Ernest B. Gaston (the guiding light of Fairhope).

173. Willard, James F., and Colin B. Goodykoontz, eds. *Experiments in Colorado Colonization, 1869-1872*. Boulder: University of Colorado, 1926. 483 pp.

A companion volume to Willard's work on the Union Colony at Greeley. Chiefly an anthology of primary communal documents, newspaper articles about specific communities, and other related materials. The colonies receiving the most attention are the German Colonization Company, the Chicago-Colorado Colony, the St. Louis-Western Colony, and the Southwestern Colony. Briefer sections cover Georgia Colony, Platville, and Fountain Colony, plus several other colonization projects, most of which appear not to have had cooperative or collective features.

174. Williams, Julia Elizabeth. "Analytical Tabulation of North American Utopian Communities by Type, Longevity and Location." Master's thesis, University of South Dakota, 1939.
    Divides communes into several categories: religious, Fourierist, Owenite, socialist-cooperative, Single Tax, and miscellaneous. 148 colonies and families of them (labelled "systems") are identified, encompassing 262 separate communities, 126 religious and 136 secular. Some 74 of those are listed as having been founded in the post-1860 period. A master table categorizes communes by type, longevity, and location; other tables compare those variables.

175. Wooster, Ernest S. *Communities of the Past and Present.* Newllano, Louisiana: Llano Cooperative Colony, 1924. 156 pp.
    A deceptively thin volume with a wealth of information on communes both prominent and obscure. Post-1860 communities discussed include the Woman's Commonwealth, Topolobampo, Ruskin, Christian Commonwealth, Equality, Colorado Cooperative Co., Adonai-Shomo, the Hutterites, Modjeska's Colony, Shalam, the Lord's Farm, the Nevada Colony, the Koreshan Unity, the House of David, Llano, the Army of Industry, Heaven City (Illinois), Ruskin (Georgia), and several foreign communes and domestic industrial cooperatives.

176. Yearley, Clifton K., Jr. *Britons in American Labor: A History of the Influence of United Kingdom Immigrants on American Labor, 1820-1914.* Johns Hopkins Studies in Historical and Political Science, 75th series. Baltimore: Johns Hopkins University Press, 1957.
    Part seven of this study, "Toward a Co-operative

Commonwealth" (pp. 266-302), traces the role of the British in various cooperative programs, including some which were communal (especially Rugby). Also includes information on cooperative and communal programs within the American labor movement, notably the Knights of Labor.

# III. ADONAI-SHOMO

Adonai-Shomo, or the Community of Fullerites (so called because they settled on the property of Leonard Fuller), represented a sectarian communal movement within Adventism. It was founded in 1861 at Petersham, Massachusetts, by Frederick T. Howland, and practiced community of goods and equality of men and women. It was principally agricultural in its endeavors. Its peak membership was around 30. The group eventually owned some 840 acres and a large communal dwelling. Eventually the community declined; the property was sold in 1897.

Some manuscript material on the community is located in the American Communities Collection at Syracuse University.

Survey works: Liefmann (item 25), 20-1; Okugawa (item 139), 201.

### Secondary works

177. Albertson, Ralph. "Adonai-Shomo." "Survey of Mutualistic Communities in America" (cited above as item 27), 390-1.
     Provides a brief overview of the history and life of the community.

*    Carroll, H.K. *Religious Forces of the United States* (cited above as item 40), 117.
     Provides a brief history and description of the movement.

178. Hinds, William Alfred. *American Communities* (cited above as item 94), 154.
     Provides a one-paragraph characterization of the colony.

179. ———. "Adonai-Shomo." *American Communities and Co-*

operative Colonies (cited above as item 95), 403-7. Provides a historical sketch of the colony.

\* Strachey, Ray, and Hannah Whitall Smith. *Group Movements of the Past and Experiments in Guidance* (cited above as item 161), 142-3.
Provides a summary history of the community, detailing its decline after a change in leadership.

\* Webber, Everett. *Escape to Utopia: The Communal Movement in America* (cited above as item 168), 312-3.
Provides a history of the Adventist movement, with a brief sketch of Adonai-Shomo.

180. Wooster, Ernest S. "Adonai-Shomo." *Communities of the Past and Present* (cited above as item 175), 63.
Provides a historical overview of the community.


# IV. ALTRURIA

Altruria was a community of Christian socialists led by Edward B. Payne, a Unitarian minister. It was inspired by the Altrurian novels of William Dean Howells. The colony was established in 1894 near Santa Rosa, California, on about 200 acres. It used no money, issuing labor checks for work performed. Financial problems, especially lack of capital, forced the colony to split into three smaller groups in 1895; that effectively brought things to an end.

A collection of documents from Altruria is at Bancroft Library at the University of California, Berkeley.

Survey work: Okugawa (item 139), 217.


*Community periodical*

181. *Altrurian: New Thoughts, New Motives, New Aims, New Deeds.* 1894-6. Weekly; later monthly.


*Works by a community leader*

182. Payne, Edward B. "Altruria." *American Magazine of Civics* 6 (February, 1895): 168-71.

Outlines the goals of the newly established colony: mutual good will; economic and social progress; diverse industries; democratic government; equal distribution of resources.

183. ———. "Socialists's Answer," in "What Shall Society Do to Be Saved?" (symposium). *Overland Monthly* 35 (June, 1900): 530-4.
A Christian socialist manifesto, emphasizing the importance of high idealism and working for better social conditions. A good look at Payne's thought, which was basic to Altruria.

## Secondary works

184. Albertson, Ralph. "Altruria." "Survey of Mutualistic Communities in America" (cited above as item 27), 414.
Attributes the failure of the colony to its spending too much on large buildings.

185. Crider, Gregory L. "Howells' Altruria: The Ambivalent Utopia." *Old Northwest* 1 (1975): 405-18.
Provides an analysis of Howells's Altrurian writings.

186. Fogarty, Robert S. "Altruria." *American Utopianism* (cited above as item 75), 109-13.
Brief introduction to the community, followed by a reprint of Swift, "Altruria in California" (item 193, below), 109-13.

187. ———. "Altruria" and "Payne, Edward Biron." *Dictionary of American Communal and Utopian History* (cited above as item 76), 127, 90-1.
Dictionary entries on Payne and the colony.

188. Hansot, Elisabeth. *Perfection and Progress: Two Modes of Utopian Thought.* Cambridge, Massachusetts: Massachusetts Institute of Technology Press, 1974, pp. 169-92.
Characterizes the Altruria created by Howells.

189. Hine, Robert V. "Altruria." *California's Utopian Colonies* (cited above as item 98), 101-13.
Provides the best general history of the colony.

190. Howells, William Dean. "Letters of an Altrurian

Traveller."    *Cosmopolitan*,   November   1893-September
1894 (11 installments).
A serial sequel to Howells's book *A Traveller from
Altruria* (item 192).

191. ———.            *Through the Eye of the Needle.*    New   York:
Harper and Brothers, 1907.
A sequel to *A Traveller from Altruria* (item 192), based
on the last six installments of "Letters of an Altrurian
Traveller" (item 190).

192. ———.            *Traveller from Altruria.*    New York: Harper and
Brothers, 1894.
A popular utopian romance which achieved widespread
popularity and inspired the California commune which took
its title for a name.

193. Swift, Morrison I.    "Altruria in California."    *Overland
Monthly* 29 (June, 1897): 643-5.
Provides a sympathetic overview of the founding, life,
and demise of the colony.

194. Walsh, Harry.    "Tolstoy and the Economic Novels of
William Dean Howells."    *Comparative Literature Studies*
14 (June, 1977): 143-65.
Locates the roots of Howells's Altrurian ideas in Tolstoy
and the romantic reformers of early nineteenth century
America.

# V. AMERICAN COLONY

This group grew from a prayer group meeting in the home
of Mr. and Mrs. Horatio E. Spafford in Chicago in the 1870s.
In 1882 the group moved to Jerusalem to prepare for the
Second Coming; much of the communal phase of the group
occurred there.    Eventually the community ran several small
industries, and had as many as 175 members in the 1890s.    It
was still in existence in 1907.

*Community Periodical*

195.  *Our Rest and Signs of the Times.*  1873-91.

*Secondary works*

196. Fogarty, Robert S. "Spafford, Horatio E." *Dictionary of American Communal and Utopian History* (cited above as item 76), 106-7.
Dictionary entry providing an overview of the colony's history.


# VI. AMERICAN WOMAN'S REPUBLIC

In 1908 Edward G. Lewis, a publisher of magazines aimed at a female audience, announced the formation of the American Woman's League. Members produced subscriptions for his magazines, and he repaid them by building chapter houses for local club chapters and doing other projects of interest to women, such as promoting woman's suffrage and attacking poor working conditions. A People's University at University City, Missouri, outside St. Louis, was created to offer courses to League members. In 1913 Atascadero, California, was founded as a cooperative colony for members of the group and as the seat of the American Woman's Republic, a would-be independent nation where women would have the vote they did not have in the U.S. The A.W.R. was modeled after the government of the United States; each state had a governor, members of the House and Senate, and other such officials. When women obtained the right to vote, the Republic folded.


*Community periodical*

197. *Woman's National Daily*. 1906-11.

198. *Woman's National Weekly*. 1911-6.


*Primary works*

199. *American Woman's League and the People's University*. University City, St. Louis, Missouri: n.p., 1910.

200. *Brief Prospectus of the American Woman's Republic*. University City, St. Louis, Missouri: n.p., [1912?]. 16 pp.

201. *Twenty Ambassadors and Their Escort: A Free Tour of Europe.* N.p., [1911]. 32 pp. Available in the microfilm series "History of Women," reel 941, no. 8380.
     Outlines the structure and membership requirements of the group; projects the plan for creating a cooperative colony. Includes a nine-item statement of purpose and describes various programs of the organization.

### *Work by a community leader*

202. Lewis, Edward G. "A University That Is a School, a City and a Nation." *World To-day* 19 (August, 1910): 823-30.
     Describes the coursework of the university, emphasizing the visual arts; describes the organization of the A.W.L. and its magazine-sales program. Illustrated with photographs.

### *Secondary works*

203. Fendelman, Earl. "Empire of Women." *American Heritage* 35 (August/September, 1984): 70-6.
     Provides basic biographical information on Lewis; depicts Lewis's business dealings and the development of the League and the Republic.

204. Meyer, Pauline. *Keep Your Face to the Sunshine: A Lost Chapter in the History of Woman Suffrage.* Edwardsville, Illinois: Alcott Press, 1980. 56 pp.
     Contains a history of the movement and descriptions and photographs of the many chapter houses.

# VII. ARMY OF INDUSTRY

In 1914 a group of socialists in Auburn, California, organized a colony in which 30 to 40 persons initially participated. Members had to certify upon joining that they owned no property and did not want to get rich. The group did some farming; some members took outside jobs for the common benefit. The group was small for most of its life, sometimes dropping to under a dozen active members. No one was turned away from the colony's doors, and it thus consistently lost money. It did not survive World War I.

Survey works: Albertson (item 27), 421; Okugawa (item 139), 232.

### Secondary works

205. Fogarty, Robert S. "Socialist Community." *American Utopianism* (cited above as item 75), 123.
     Brief introduction to the colony, followed by a reprint of Wooster, "Army of Industry" (item 206, below), pp. 123-7.

*    Hine, Robert V. *California's Utopian Colonies*(cited above as item 98), 149-53.
     Provides a general history of the community.

206. Wooster, Ernest S. "Army of Industry." *Communities of the Past and Present* (cited above as item 175), 133-7.
     Provides an overview history of the colony, quoting extensively from a community publication entitled "Let's Go."

# VIII. BASS LAKE FARM

In 1941 a Father Marston, an Episcopal priest, and two other pacifists founded this community on 80 acres which they purchased near Minneapolis. The other two founders rejected military service and were placed in a Civilian Public Service Camp. After the war they returned to the community; thereafter several others joined as well. However, the cold climate bothered some, and the members' lack of farming skills hurt the group severely. The group was disbanded following Marston's sudden death in 1946. Some members reportedly intended to join Celo.

### Secondary work

207. Infield, Henrik F. "American Folk School and the Bass Lake Farm." *Utopia and Experiment* (cited above as item 108), 81-2.
     Provides a report on the community based on author's

personal visit; the community was at the time apparently heading toward dissolution.

# IX.  BETHANY FELLOWSHIP

This group began in the early 1940s as a home Bible study group in Minneapolis.   In 1943 they purchased a church building, and in 1945 took up communalism.   The developed common dwellings and buildings for a Christian training institute.   Supported by various industrial enterprises, the community has a very active missionary program.

## *Community periodical*

208. *Message of the Cross.*     Minneapolis.     Ca.   1949-. Bimonthly.

## *Primary work*

209. *Bethany Fellowship Bible and Missionary Training Institute Catalog.* Minneapolis: Bethany Fellowship, n.d.
    A catalog of the school run by the Fellowship. Provides a brief history of the group and its statements of doctrine and purpose.   At the Institute for the Study of American Religion.

## *Secondary works*

\*      Bloesch, Donald G.    *Wellsprings of Renewal* (cited above as item 36), 83-4.
    Provides a brief overview of the community.

\*      Jackson, Dave.    *Coming Together* (cited above as item 111), 35.
    Provides basic information about the community.

# X.  BOHEMIAN COLONIES

Nineteenth-century Bohemian immigrants to the U.S. tended

to settle in cities, but the urge among them to recreate rural peasant life was often strong, and as a result of that there were at least two attempts to start rural Bohemian communities.

# X(A). BOHEMIAN COOPERATIVE FARMING COMPANY

The more substantial Bohemian colony was established near Mayland, Tennessee, in 1913. The 5,300-acre tract was wooded, and much hard work was expended clearing the land and planting corn and potatoes. The community was isolated, discouraging visitors, and tried to reproduce Bohemian village life with common storehouses and treasury. Bickering seems to have been present from the first, however, especially over the authoritarian rule of the group's president. It led to violence, even gunplay; the group split into two factions, then dissolved. The last families left the area in 1916.

Survey work: Okugawa (item 139), 231.

*Secondary works*

210. Miller, Ernest I. "Bohemian Cooperative Farming Company." "Some Tennessee Utopias" (cited above as item 133), 72-83.
A survey of the community's history and life, largely based on interviews with persons in the vicinity of Mayland.

# X(B). RYS

Predating the Bohemian Cooperative Farming Co. was the Rys colony in Virginia, founded in 1897. Several urban Bohemian families longing for Bohemian village life raised enough money to buy an old plantation, and thirteen of them moved to the land. The rest were to send money to help establish the colony, but little was forthcoming. The colony's economy was communal. Internal bickering led to disbanding later in 1897.

211.  Humpal-Zeman,  Josefa.  "Bohemian  Settlements  in  the
      United  States."  *Reports  of  the  Industrial  Commission  on
      Immigration.*  Washington:  Government  Printing  Office,
      1901, v. 15, pp. 507-10.
      Deals  primarily  with  Bohemian  immigration  more
      generally, but one section tells the story of Rys.

*     Miller,  Ernest  I.  "Some  Tennessee  Utopias"  (cited  above
      as item 133), 73.
      Provides  a  brief  characterization  of  Rys  as  a  prelude  to
      a  more  substantial  discussion  of  the  Bohemian  Cooperative
      Farming Co.

# XI. BOOKWALTER

   John  W.  Bookwalter,  a  wealthy  Springfield,  Ohio,
industrialist,  began  to  buy  land  in  Pawnee  County,  Nebraska,  in
1879.   By  1891  he  had  a  plan  to  establish  a  cooperative  or
communal  farmers'  village,  where,  on  the  European  model,
farmers  would  live  in  a  village  and  head  out  to  a  nearby
acreage  by  day  to  farm.   However,  economic  difficulties  and
war  in  the  1890s  made  planning  difficult,  and  the  project  never
achieved  its  aims  entirely,  although  many  participants  farmed
the land for some time. Bookwalter died in 1915.

*Works by community leaders*

212.  Bookwalter,  John  Wesley.  *If  Not  Silver,  What?*
      Springfield, Ohio: J.J. Little, 1896.
      A polemic for a silver monetary standard.

213.  ———.  *Rural  versus  Urban:  Their  Conflict  and  Its
      Causes.*  New York: Knickerbocker Press, 1910.  292 pp.
      A  history  of  rural  life,  arguing  for  rural  over  urban
      values.

*Secondary works*

214.  Fogarty,  Robert  S.  "Bookwalter,  John  Wesley."  *Dictionary
      of  American  Communal  and  Utopian  History*  (cited  above

as item 76), 15-6.
Biographical dictionary entry.

215. Gilman, Musetta. "Bookwalter, Agricultural Commune in Nebraska." *Nebraska History* 54 (Spring, 1973): 91-105.
A sketch of Bookwalter and his project by the daughter of a resident family.

# XII. BRIDE OF CHRIST CHURCH

Franz Edmond Creffield, a German immigrant, after being run out of Idaho, where he had gathered a largely female following, arrived in Portland, Oregon, in 1903. He soon joined the Salvation Army and was sent to work in Corvallis. Soon, however, he was promoting himself as a second Christ and quickly gathered as many as 100 followers, mainly women (some already married) who were convinced that they were brides of Christ. Reports of nudity and sex led to Creffield's being run out of town in 1904; he later returned and lived for a time in a shallow trench under a house. He was naked there, and subsisted on food smuggled to him by followers. He was finally located, removed, and jailed for adultery. Released from prison in 1906, he reconvened his group. Threatened by opponents, he fled from Oregon to Seattle, where he was shot down by a brother of two of his followers. His assassin was in turn shot by Maud Hurt Creffield, the prophet's legal wife, who soon thereafter died in jail.

*Secondary works*

216. Beam, Maurice. "Crazy After Women." *Cults of America.* New York: MacFadden-Bartell, 1964, pp. 35-58.
The most substantial piece on Creffield, covering his early life, his preaching in Idaho, and later developments in Oregon. Emphasizes his strong sex drive, female following, and sexual escapades. No documentation.

217. Holbrook, Stewart H. "Oregon's Secret Love Cult." *American Mercury* 40 (February, 1937), 167-74.
A basic account of Creffield's career.

218. Mathison, Richard. "Franz Creffield: Naked Reformer." *Faiths, Cults and Sects of America: From Atheism to*

*Zen* (cited above as item 127), 301-5.
Provides an overview history of Creffield and his movement.

219.  Pintarich, Dick.    "Gospel According to Edmond Creffield."
      *Oregon Magazine*, March, 1983, pp. 44-6.
      Provides an overview history of Creffield and his movement. Illustrated.

220.  Pintarich, Dick, and J. Kingston Pierce.    "Strange Saga of
      Oregon's Other Guru."    *Oregonian* (Portland), January 7,
      1986, pp. C1-C2.
      A basic journalistic account of Creffield and his followers. Illustrated. Similar to item 219, above.


# XIII.  BRIGGS AND HIS DEVOUTS

In 1920 John Briggs embezzled $97,000 from a bank where he worked and used it to start an isolated commune for his followers in the desert in Coconino County, Arizona. Briggs taught polyandry, that each woman should have nine husbands; some of the men in the colony had nine wives as well. The group lasted seven months, scattering when a member left to report the others to the authorities, causing the rest to flee in fear.


*Secondary work*

221.  Mathison, Richard.    "John Briggs: Southwest Messiah."
      *Faiths, Cults and Sects of America: From Atheism to
      Zen* (cited above as item 127), 317-23.
      Provides an overview of the movement.


# XIV.  THE BRUDERHOF (HUTTERIAN SOCIETY
# OF BROTHERS)

The Society of Brothers was founded in 1920 in Sannerz, Hesse, Germany, by Eberhard Arnold (1883-1935), who sought to imitate the original Hutterites but at the time did not know that the Hutterites still existed.    After learning that the

Hutterites were living in North America, he journeyed there in 1930 and spent about a year traveling among them; they ordained him a Hutterite minister. Persecution which accompanied the rise of Hitler caused the band to move to Liechtenstein, where Arnold died unexpectedly. In 1936 they fled to England to escape military service under Hitler, but anti-German hostility in England led most of them to emigrate to Paraguay in 1941. There their population reached 700. Problems in rural Paraguay led them to found the first American Bruderhof, called Woodcrest, in 1954 in New York State. Soon two other communities were opened in Pennsylvania and Connecticut, and later another in New York. The movement has experienced slow growth and economic prosperity since then.

The Society is alphabetized here instead of under "Hutterian Society of Brothers," the group's formal name, in order distinguish it from the original Hutterites.

The *Mennonite Encyclopedia* (cited above as item 131) contains several articles on the Bruderhof which are not cited here. See, particularly, entries on "Arnold, Eberhard" (v. 1, pp. 162-4) and "Society of Brothers" (v. 4, pp. 1126-7).

## Community periodicals

222. *Open Door.*
    A Bruderhof periodical published in the 1950s in Paraguay.

223. *Plough.* Rifton, N.Y. 1953-. Published "several times a year."

## Primary works: Plough publications

This list contains most of the books published by the Plough Publishing House, the Bruderhof press, including the extensive works of Eberhard Arnold and members of his family. However, it does not include the many children's books published by Plough, or the majority of Plough pamphlets. It does include works written by the Arnolds and published by other publishers than Plough.

224. Arnold, Annemarie. *Youth Movement to Bruderhof: Letters and Diaries of Annemarie Arnold (nee Waechter), 1926-1932.* Rifton, N.Y.: Plough, 1986. 256 pp.

48                                                    *The Bruderhof*

225.  Arnold, Eberhard.    *Children's Education in Community:*
      *the Basis of Bruderhof Education.*    Rifton, N.Y.: Plough,
      1976.  55 pp.
      Selections from the writings of Arnold on the methods,
      theory, and content of Bruderhof education.

226.  ———.    *Early Anabaptists.*    Rifton, N.Y.:    Plough, 1984.
      64 pp.
      Describes the beginnings of the Radical Reformation.

227.  ———.    *Early Christians after the Death of the*
      *Apostles.* Rifton, N.Y.: Plough, 1970.  484 pp.
      An anthology of early Christian writings, with a lengthy
      introduction by Arnold.

228.  ———.    *Eberhard Arnold: A Testimony of Church*
      *Community from His Life and Writings.*    Rifton, N.Y.:
      Plough, 1964.  107 pp.
      Selections from Arnold's writings and lectures.    Contains
      a biographical essay by Emmy Arnold and letters
      reminiscing about Eberhard Arnold written by his friends.

229.  ———.    *Else von Hollander.*    Rifton, N.Y.:    Plough, 1973.
      128 pp.
      The story of a faithful disciple, Emmy Arnold's sister
      and one of the original founders of the Bruderhof.

230.  ———.    *Foundation and Orders of Sannerz and the*
      *Rhoen Bruderhof.* Rifton, N.Y.: Plough, 1976.

231.  ———.    *God's Revolution: The Witness of Eberhard*
      *Arnold.*    Edited by the Hutterian Brethren and John
      Howard Yoder.    New York: Paulist Press, 1984.    232 pp.
      Selections from Arnold's writings on discipleship.

232.  ———.    *History of the Baptizers Movement.*    Rifton,
      N.Y.: Plough, 1969.

*     ———.    *Hutterian Brethren*    (cited below as item 1063).
      This book, mainly about the Hutterites, has appendices
      which include documentation of the Hutterian ordination
      of Eberhard Arnold and a brief discussion of the
      Bruderhof and its relationship to the Hutterites.

233.  ———.    *Inner Land: A Guide into the Heart and Soul of*
      *the Bible.* Rifton, N.Y.: Plough, 1976.  588 pp.

A five-volume series; also available in a single-volume edition. Titles of individual volumes: *The Inner Life*; *The Struggle of Conscience*; *The Experience of God and His Peace*; *Light and Fire and the Holy Spirit*; *The Living Word*.

234. ———. *Love and Marriage in the Spirit.* Rifton, N.Y.: Plough, 1965.
Devotional talks and essays on love and marriage. Includes a glossary on Bruderhof life and history.

235. ———. *Peace of God.* Rifton, N.Y.: Plough, 1940.

236. ———. *Salt and Light: Talks and Writings on the Sermon on the Mount.* Rifton, N.Y.: Plough, 1967. 344 pp.

237. ———. "Spirit of the Risen Lord." *Mennonite Life* 24 (July, 1969): 142-3.
A meditation on the resurrection and how it needs to work in the life of the believer.

238. ———. *War: A Call to the Inner Land.* New York: Paulist Press, 1986. 135 pp.

239. ———. *Why We Live in Community.* Rifton, N.Y.: Plough, 1967.
A manifesto arguing that community is an inescapable part of the Christian faith.

240. Arnold, Eberhard, and Emmy Arnold. *Seeking for the Kingdom of God: Origins of the Bruderhof Communities.* Rifton, N.Y.: Plough, 1974. 304 pp.

241. Arnold, Eberhard, Emmy Arnold, and Heini Arnold. *Heavens Are Opened.* Rifton, N.Y.: Plough, 1974. 192 pp.

242. Arnold, Eberhard, Emmy Arnold, Christoph Blumhardt, and Alfred Delp. *When the Time Was Fulfilled: On Advent and Christmas.* Rifton, N.Y.: Plough, 1965. 256 pp.
Talks and writings on Advent and Christmas.

243. Arnold, Eberhard C.H. "Eberhard Arnold, 1883-1935: A Short Biography." *Mennonite Quarterly Review* 25 (July, 1951): 219.

Provides basic biographical information on the founder of the Bruderhof; emphasizes the affiliation with the Hutterites which was effected in 1931.

244. ———. "Education for Altruism in the Society of Brothers in Paraguay." *Forms and Techniques of Altruistic and Spiritual Growth.* Edited by Pitirim A. Sorokin. Boston: Beacon, 1954, pp. 293-307.
Discusses the philosophy of the Bruderhof, the basic attitudes needed on the part of a member (responsiblity plus humility are the key ones), the methods of educating persons for altruistic behavior, and the necessity of a strong faith as the inescapable basis for an altruistic community.

245. Arnold, Emmy, ed. *Inner Words for Every Day of the Year.* Rifton, N.Y.: Plough, 1963. 185 pp.
A book in almanac form containing daily thoughts from the writings of Eberhard Arnold and others.

246. Arnold, Emmy. *Torches Together.* Rifton, N.Y.: Plough, 1964. 240 pp.
An account of the early days of the Bruderhof in Germany.

247. Arnold, Heini. *Freedom from Sinful Thoughts: Christ Alone Breaks the Curse.* Rifton, N.Y.: Plough, 1973. 136 pp.

248. ———. "Hutterian Society of Brothers." *Brethren Encyclopedia* (cited above as item 57), v. 1, pp. 639-41.
Provides an overview history of the movement, emphasizing relations between the Bruderhof and the Hutterites.

249. ———. *In the Image of God: Marriage and Chastity in Christian Life.* Rifton, N.Y.: Plough, 1977. 184 pp.

250. ———. *May Thy Light Shine: Prayers for All Ages.* Rifton, N.Y.: Plough, 1986. 230 pp.

251. ———. *Stories about Francis of Assisi.* Rifton, New York: Plough, 1979. 14 pp.

252. Arnold, Heini, and Annemarie Arnold. *Living in Community: A Way to True Brotherhood.* Rifton, N.Y.:

Plough, 1974. 18 pp.
Contains a description of the faith of the Bruderhof and the way in which that faith is expressed in daily life. Illustrated with photographs of the three American Bruderhofs and former Bruderhofs in Europe.

253. ———. *Purity of Childhood.* Rifton, N.Y.: Plough, 1974. 9 pp.

254. Barth, Karl. *Action in Waiting.* Rifton, N.Y.: Plough, n.d. 80 pp.
An essay on the work of Christoph Blumhardt (d. 1919), whose life the Bruderhof found inspirational. Includes the text of Blumhardt's "Joy in the Lord."

255. *Behold That Star.* Rifton, N.Y.: Plough, 1966. 368 pp.

256. Blumhardt, Christoph. *Evening Prayers for Every Day of the Year.* Rifton, N.Y.: Plough, 1971. 252 pp.
Contains prayers keyed to days of the year.

257. ———. *Lift Thine Eyes: Evening Prayers.* Rifton, N.Y.: Plough, 1988.

258. Blumhardt, Johann C., and Christoph F. Blumhardt. *Now Is Eternity.* Rifton, N.Y. Plough, 1976. 37 pp.

259. ———. *Thoughts about Children.* Rifton, N.Y.: Plough, 1980. 58 pp.

260. Clement, Jane T. *Secret Flower.* Rifton, N.Y.: Woodcrest Service Committee, 1961. 62 pp.

261. Fletcher, Stanley. *Hour and Its Challenge.* Rifton, N.Y.: Plough, 1961. 12 pp.

262. Hindley, Sydney. *Work and Life at the Bruderhof in Paraguay.* Burwarton, Bridgnorth, Shropshire: Wheathill Bruderhof, 1943. 24 pp.

263. Hutterian Brethren, editors. *Brothers Unite: An Account of the Uniting of Eberhard Arnold and the Rhoen Bruderhof with the Hutterian Church.* Ulster Park, N.Y.: Plough, 1988. 384 pp.

264. ———. *Gospel in Dostoyevsky: Selections from His*

*Works*. Rifton, N.Y.: Plough, 1988.

265. ———. *Straight Word to Kids and Parents: Help for Teen Problems*. Rifton, N.Y.: Plough, 1987. 153 pp.

266. Lejeune, R. *Christoph Blumhardt and His Message*. Rifton, N.Y.: Plough, 1963. 240 pp.
A biography and nineteen sermons of Blumhardt.

267. *Share in the Joy of Singing! Youthful Songs for Hiking, Working, Freedom, and Praise*. Rifton, N.Y.: Plough, 1974.

268. Society of Brothers, eds. *Behold That Star: A Christmas Anthology*. Rifton, N.Y.: Plough, 1966.

269. ———. *Children in Community*. Rifton, N.Y.: Plough, 1963, 1974. 184 pp.
A photographic essay on the children of the Bruderhof.

270. "Statement of Belief." *Plough* no. 19 (May/June, 1988): 12-3.
A basic theological declaration for the community, consisting in large part of a statement made by Eberhard Arnold in 1935.

271. *Ten Years of Community Living: The Wheathill Bruderhof, 1942-1952*. Bromdon, England: Plough, 1952.
An account of the history, ideas, and communitarian convictions of the British branch of the Bruderhof. Includes "A Brief Statement of Our Belief in Relation to Community Life."

### Secondary works

272. Armytage, W.H.G. "Wheathill Bruderhof, 1942-58." *American Journal of Economics and Sociology* 18 (April, 1959): 285-94.
Provides a synopsis of the history of the Bruderhof into the early 1950s, emphasizing the English phases of the movement's existence.

273. Blumhardt, Johann C., and Christoph F. Blumhardt. *Thy Kingdom Come: A Blumhardt Reader*. Edited by Vernard Eller. Grand Rapids: Eerdmans, 1980. 179 pp.

274. Bouvard, Marguerite. "Society of Brothers." *Intentional Community Movement* (cited above as item 37), 44-55.
Surveys the movement from its beginnings in Germany through its settlement in the U.S., focusing on its economic structure, child rearing, organizational structure, and social control mechanisms.

275. "Bruderhof Communities." *Intentional Communities: 1959 Yearbook of Intentional Communities* (cited below as item 807), 17-8.
Contains a brief introduction to the history and life of the Bruderhof.

276. Cody, Morrill. "Refuge in the Chaco." *Inter-American* 2 (July, 1943): 10-3.
Primarily concerns Mennonite settlements in Paraguay, but refers briefly to the Bruderhof settlement, depicting it as thriving, with working agricultural and industrial operations and 334 members.

\*     Conkin, Paul K. *Two Paths to Utopia*: The Hutterites and the Llano Colony (cited above as item 50), 95-8.
Traces the uneven course of relations between the Hutterites and the Bruderhof.

277. Eggers, Ulrich. *Community for Life*. Scottdale, Pennsylvania: Herald, 1988. 198 pp.
A narrative of Eggers's visit to the Woodcrest Bruderhof. Not seen.

278. ———. *Gemeinschaf—Lebenslanglich*. Scottdale, Pennsylvania: Herald, 1988. 200 pp.
The German original of *Community for Life* (item 277, above). Not seen.

279. Eller, Vernard. "Who Are These Blumhardt Characters Anyhow?" *Christian Century* 86 (October 8, 1969): 1274-8.
Describes the work of the two Blumhardts (father and son) who started a discipled-living experiment which strongly influenced Eberhard Arnold.

280. Fairfield, Dick. "Bruderhof Movement." "Communes U.S.A." (cited above as item 63), 37.
Provides a brief sketch of the Bruderhof.

281. Freier, Koka. "Housewarming at the Woodcrest Bruderhof." *Cooperative Living* 6 (Fall, 1954): 4-5.
A visit to Woodcrest at its founding, describing its new property and its people.

282. French, David, and Elena French. *Working Communally: Patterns and Possibilities.* New York: Russell Sage Foundation, 1975, pp. 172-7.
Contains descriptive material on the Bruderhof plus information on several pre-1860 and post-1960 communes.

283. Friedmann, Robert. "Fifty Years Society of Brothers (1920-1970): Their Story and Their Books." *Mennonite Life* 25 (October, 1970): 159-64.
Provides a historical sketch of the Bruderhof and a history of the Bruderhof publishing program, arguing that the community's publications are seen as essential to its proclamation of the Gospel.

284. ———. "Living in a Society of Brothers." *Fellowship* 31 (July, 1965). Reprinted as "Society of Brothers." *Utopia*, U.S.A. (cited above item 65), 32-5.
A favorable, descriptive article on the three American Bruderhofs, characterizing the history, leadership, life, and crises of the community.

\* Gladstone, Arthur. "Cooperative Communities Today III" (cited above as item 83), 10-11.
Notes the opening of the first American Bruderhof at Woodcrest (Rifton, New York).

285. Hall, Francis. "Pitfalls of Intentional Community." *Christian Century* 80 (August 14, 1963): 1000-2.
Argues that intentional communities are unstable because they magnify human weakness and sin as well as good values; that when they are stable, they are authoritarian; that they succeed only when their corporate lives are incidental to their work. The author had left the Bruderhof when this article was written.

286. ———. "Revival of Christian Community." *Christian Century* 74 (October 30, 1957): 1283-5.
Provides an overview of the history, economy, life, and theology of the Bruderhof. The author was a member of the Bruderhof (in Paraguay) when this article was written.

287. Hazelton, Philip. "Trailing the Founders: On Being a Second-Generation Bruder." *This Magazine Is About Schools* 4 (Spring, 1970): 11-41; (Summer, 1970): 54-78.
A two-part interview reflecting on a Bruderhof upbringing, growing up in the second generation of a movement in which the founders were regarded as spiritual giants.

288. "Hutterian Brethren at Primavera." *Mennonite Life* 5 (January, 1950): 34-6.
Describes the migration of the Bruderhof to Paraguay and colony life in that country. Includes a description of the conversion process used by the group. Well illustrated with photographs.

289. Ineson, George. *Community Journey.* London: Catholic Book Club, 1956, pp. 25-6.
Characterizes the operations of the Bruderhof in Wiltshire in 1937-8.

* Jackson, Dave. *Coming Together* (cited above as item 111), 21-3.
An overview of the history and life of the Bruderhof.

* Jackson, Dave, and Neta Jackson. *Living Together in a World Falling Apart* (cited above as item 112), 33-6.
Contains basic information on Bruderhof life.

290. Johnson, Martin. "Strengthening the Brotherly Spirit." *Bulletin of the International Communal Studies Association* no. 3 (Spring, 1988): 7-8.
Provides an appreciation of a visit by several members of the Society of Brothers to Yad Mordechai and several other kibbutzim in Israel. The visit ran from October, 1987, to March, 1988.

291. Kramer, Wendell B. "Bruderhof Communities." "Criteria for the Intentional Community" (cited above as item 118), 57-61.
Provides an overview of the movement.

292. Marchant, Will. "Bruderhof Communities." *Cooperative Living* 3 (Winter, 1951-2): 13-15.
Marchant, a member of the Bruderhof, describes the history and current organization of the Bruderhof at Primavera, Paraguay.

293. ———. "Bruderhof Communities—II." *Cooperative Living* 3 (Spring, 1952):4-6.
    Describes the founding and building of the Bruderhof at Primavera, Paraguay, and outlines the development of the three community units there. Continuation of item 292, above.

294. ———. "Bruderhof Communities—III. *Cooperative Living* 4 (Fall, 1952): 8-11.
    Describes education and the arts at the Primavera, Paraguay, Bruderhof communities. Also provides some basic Bruderhof philosophy, including a statement of why the members have chosen to live in community and why the whole world should do so.

295. Marshall, Joseph. "Bruderhof: Society of Brothers." *Communitarian* no. 1 (March-April, 1972): 18-22.
    Describes community work life, especially as related to the principal community business (Community Playthings) and other topics about Bruderhof life such as religion and personal possessions.

296. Meier, Hans. *Dissolution of the Rhoen Bruderhof in Retrospect*. Rifton, N.Y.: Plough, 1974.

297. ———. "Roundtable of Oldtimers." *Communal Life: An International Perspective* (cited above as item 84), 744-8.
    Describes the author's early communal experiences, beginning with a Swiss group which merged with the Bruderhof; recounts the experience of the Bruderhof under the Nazis; epitomizes the spiritual life of the community.

298. ———. "Spiritual Sources of the Society of Brothers." *Communal Life: An International Perspective* (cited above as item 84), 91-7.
    Describes the religious and spiritual principles undergirding the Bruderhof. Characterizes the community's sense of mission as a living witness of a society of peace and justice. Provides a brief overview history of the Hutterites and Bruderhof.

299. Melton, J. Gordon. "Society of Brothers." *Encyclopedia of American Religion* (cited above as item 130), 502-3.
    Provides a brief overview of the group.

\*   Mercer, John.   *Communes:   A   Social   History   and   Guide*
     (cited above as item 132), 68-71.
     Describes   the   Bruderhof   within   a   sweeping   survey   of
     communalism and utopianism.

300.  Miller,   Glen   R.   "Hutterites   in   England."   *Proceedings   of
      the   Fifth   Annual   Conference   on   Mennonite   Cultural
      Problems* (cited below as item 1356): 67-9.
      Provides   a   sketch   of   the   English   Bruderhof   community
      based on a visit in 1944.

301.  Morse,   Flo.   *Yankee   Communes:   Another   American   Way*.
      New   York:   Harcourt   Brace   Jovanovich,   1971,   pp.   149-78.
      Presents   a   history   of   the   Bruderhof   and   a   depiction   of
      life at Woodcrest. Illustrated with photographs.

302.  "Open   Door   of   the   Bruderhof   Community."   *Cooperative
      Living* 5 (Fall, 1953): 5-7.
      A   statement   of   the   process   by   which   the   Bruderhof
      members   chose   to   live   communally,   and   an   exposition   of
      the   community's   belief   that   common   living   is   the   solution
      to the problems of the world.

303.  Peck,   Robert   N.   "Ex-Member's   View   of   the   Bruderhof
      Communities   from   1948-1961."   *Utopian   Studies*   I.
      Edited   by   Gorman   Beauchamp,   Kenneth   Roemer,   and
      Nicholas   D.   Smith.   Lanham,   Maryland:   University   Press
      of America, 1987, pp. 111-22.
      Provides   a   detailed   description   of   the   process   of   joining
      the   community   during   its   years   in   Paraguay;   describes   the
      internal   crisis   in   the   years   following   1959,   in   which   the
      author   saw   the   formerly   broad-minded   community
      transformed   into   a   closed-minded,   fearful   one.   The   author
      was a member of the Bruderhof for thirteen years.

304.  "Pen-Ultimate:   Something   Long   Forgotten."   *Christian
      Century* 81 (September 16, 1964): 1159.
      Describes   the   toy-making   and   publishing   enterprises   of
      the   Bruderhof;   argues   that   the   community   reminds   one   of
      the Book of Acts.

305.  Peters,   Victor   John.   "History   of   the   Hutterian   Brethren,
      1528-1958."   Ph.D.   dissertation,   University   of
      Goettingen, 1960, pp. 170-9.
      Describes   relations   between   the   Bruderhof   and   the
      Hutterites;   characterizes   the   divisions   among   the

Hutterites over the question of recognizing the
Bruderhof's request for recognition as a legitimate
Hutterite group.

306. Riley, Marvin P.    *Hutterite Brethren: An Annotated
     Bibliography with Special Reference to South Dakota
     Hutterite Colonies* (cited below as item 1366), 170-3.
     Short section on "Affiliated Colonies" provides a brief
     bibliography of the Bruderhof, including references to
     several articles in the Mennonite Encyclopedia.

307. Saxby, Trevor J.    *Pilgrims of a Common Life.*    Scottdale,
     Pennsylvania: Herald, 1987, pp. 152-4.
     Provides a brief historical sketch of the Bruderhof in a
     book about Christian groups practicing community of
     property.

308. Smith, Willard H.    "Hutterites in Paraguay."    *Proceedings
     of the Fifth Annual Conference on Mennonite Cultural
     Problems* (cited below as item 1356), 71-5.
     Provides a sketch of the Bruderhof community in
     Paraguay based on a visit there in the 1940s.

309. "Society of Brothers."    *Time* 70 (July 29, 1957): 48.
     Sketches the Bruderhof's history and ideals on the
     occasion of its moving into its Pennsylvania Bruderhof,
     a former resort hotel.

310. Sorokin, Pitirim A.    "Techniques of Contemporary Free
     Brotherhoods."    *Ways of Power and Love.*    Boston:
     Beacon, 1954, pp. 441-55.
     Characterizes the Bruderhof in Paraguay, using a
     Bruderhof document entitled *Toward Community Living in
     Our Time* and an eyewitness report extensively.    Also
     quotes part of the Eaton-Weil-Kaplan study of the mental
     health of the Hutterites (item 1141); concludes that both
     groups are similar to monastic orders.

311. Thompson, Barbara R.    "Challenge of True Brotherhood."
     *Christianity Today*, March 15, 1985, 22-7.
     Contains a history of the Bruderhof, information on the
     movement's current status (1200 members in the U.S. and
     England are reported), an account of its ideas and goals,
     and a long series of questions and answers with members,
     the answers providing a good statement of the Bruderhof's
     goals. Illustrated.

312. Tillson, David Stanley. "Pacifist Community in Peacetime:
An Introductory Description of the Woodcrest Bruderhof
at Rifton, New York." D.S.S. Dissertation, Syracuse
University, 1958. 371 pp.
Contains one of the earliest descriptions of the
Bruderhof. The study is based on 49 days of field work
and a review of Bruderhof historical documents. Covers
demographics, meetings, organization, goals and ideals,
religious ideas and practices, and daily life.

313. Whitney, Norman. *Experiments in Community.*
Wallingford, Pennsylvania: Pendle Hill, 1966, pp. 29-33.
Describes the commitment, feeling of peoplehood, and
sense of sacrifice which hold the community together.

314. Whitworth, John M. "Bruderhof in England: A Chapter in
the History of a Utopian Sect." *Sociological Yearbook
of Religion in Britain* 4 (London: SCM Press, 1971):
84-101.
Relates the early history of the Bruderhof, dwelling on
the movement's years in England since the late 1930s.
Examines the internal conflicts which beset the group in
the late 1950s and early 1960s.

315. ———. "Contemporary Utopian Sect—The Society of
Brothers (or Bruderhof)." *God's Blueprints: A
Sociological Study of Three Utopian Sects.* London:
Routledge and Kegan Paul, 1975, pp. 167-241, 247-8.
Discusses the Arnolds and their early striving for
community; follows the history of the Bruderhof through
its settlement in the U.S. Contains information on
organizational structure, social control, worship, economic
life, social composition, relations with the outside world,
relations with the Hutterites, evangelism, and attitudes
toward the state. Appendix 4 contains a chronology of
the Bruderhof from the birth of Eberhard Arnold in 1883
to 1970. Contains a bibliography.

316. Wright, N. Pelham. "Utopia in Paraguay." *Americas* 4
(March, 1952): 9-12, 31.
An admiring account of the Bruderhof communities in
Paraguay based on a three-day visit. Depicts a thriving
movement. Well illustrated with photographs.

317. Zablocki, Benjamin David. "Christians Because It Works:
A Study of Bruderhof Communitarianism." Ph.D.

dissertation, Johns Hopkins University, 1967. 470 pp.

318.    Zablocki,  Benjamin.    *Joyful   Community*.    Baltimore:
        Penguin, 1971. 362 pp.
        The  standard  and  most  complete  monograph  on  the
        Bruderhof;  contains  information  on  the  community's
        history,  theology,  social  practices,  social  control
        mechanisms,  industries  and  economic  structure,  and
        organizational structure.

# XV.  BRYN GWELED HOMESTEADS

Bryn  Gweled  was  founded  as  a  housing  cooperative  with
larger  goals  than  usual,  seeking  to  avoid  real  estate
speculation,  to  maintain  community  control  of  the  land
involved,  and  to  share  community  facilities  and  activities.    It
was founded in 1939 northeast of Philadelphia.

*Secondary works*

319.    "Bryn  Gweled  Homesteads."  *1959  Yearbook  of  the
        Fellowship  of  Intentional  Communities*  (cited  below  as
        item 807), 30-1.
        Provides a brief description of the project.

320.    Kramer, Wendell B.    "Bryn Gweled Homesteads."    "Criteria
        for  the  Intentional  Community"  (cited  above  as  item
        118), 74-6.
        Provides basic information on the project.

# XVI.  BUDDHIST COMMUNITARIANISM

Dwight  Goddard  (1861-1939)  was  the  promoter  of  what
turned  out  to  ba  a  very  limited  experiment  in  Buddhist
monasticism  in  America.    Trained  as  a  mechanical  engineer,  he
enrolled  in  seminary  and  after  graduation  became  a  Baptist
missionary  to  China.    There  he  became  interested  in  Eastern
religions  and  converted  to  Zen,  which  he  promoted  upon
returning  to  the  United  States.    He  published  various
translations  from  the  Chinese,  returning  to  China  to  make
pilgrimages  to  monasteries  and  to  Japan  to  study  Zen  with  D.T.

Suzuki.

*Works by the community leader*

321. Goddard, Dwight. *Buddhist Bible: The Favorite Scriptures of the Zen Sect.* Thetford, Vermont: n.p., 1932. 316 pp. Revised and enlarged edition, New York: E. P. Dutton, 1938. 677 pp.
An anthology of important Zen documents.

322. ———. *Followers of Buddha: An American Brotherhood.* Santa Barbara: J. F. Rowney Press, 1934. 35 pp.
A prospectus for a Buddhist community for men. Includes materials on Buddha's life and teachings and his prescriptions for living, together with the author's proposals for the community, which was to be located in Santa Barbara, with a summer retreat in Thetford, Vermont.

323. ———. *Vision of Christian and Buddhist Fellowship in the Search for Light and Reality.* Los Gatos, California: author, 1924. 16 pp.

*Secondary work*

324. Starry, David. "Dwight Goddard—the Yankee Buddhist." *Zen Notes* 27 (July, 1980), unpaginated. Published by the First Zen Institute of America.
Provides a biography of Goddard, tracing his career from his days as an engineer through those he spent as a missionary in China through his conversion to Zen and his subsequent promotion of Buddhist monasticism in America.

# XVII. BURLEY: THE CO-OPERATIVE BROTHERHOOD

Burley grew out of socialist agitation in the 1890s. The Brotherhood of the Co-operative Commonwealth and the Social Democracy of America joined forces to form the Co-operative Brotherhood, which set out to found a colony. The first settlers arrived at the chosen site on the southern part of

Puget Sound in 1898; Cyrus Field Willard was the most
important of several leaders. For several years the colony
maintained a population of about 120. The main industry was a
sawmill; the colony also made cigars and farmed. There was a
strong social life, and various religious groups were active.
The colony gradually stagnated after a decentralizing
reorganization in 1905 and was dissolved by court order in
1913.

Some manuscript material on the community is in the
American Communities Collection at Syracuse University.

Survey works: Curl (item 52), 35; Liefmann (item 125), 22;
Okugawa (item 139), 222.

## Community periodicals

325. *Co-operator*. 1898-1906. Weekly.

326. *Soundview*. 1902-8. Independent monthly published by
    L.E. Rader.

## Work by a community leader

327. Willard, Cyrus Field. "As It Is To-day." *Industrial
    Freedom*, November 12, 1898, supplement, p. 2.
    Provides a sketch of the founding and development of
    the Cooperative Brotherhood and of the founding of
    Burley Colony.

## Secondary works

328. Albertson, Ralph. "Cooperative Brotherhood." "Survey of
    Mutualistic Communities in America" (cited above as
    item 27), 416.
    A brief sketch of Burley's history.

*    Bushee, Frederick A. "Communistic Societies in the
    United States" (cited above as item 38), 637-9, 656.
    Provides an overview of the community's history and
    activity, with specific information on the financial
    problems which led to its downfall.

329. Copeland, W.E. "Cooperative Brotherhood." *Arena* 28

(October, 1902): 403-5.
Highly upbeat article written at the colony makes it out to be thriving and possessed of a great future.

330. ———. "Co-operative Brotherhood and Its Colony." *Independent* 55 (February 5, 1903): 317-23.
Highly upbeat account of the history and life of the first of many projected colonies sponsored by the Co-operative Brotherhood. Describes community industries and work life, demographics, and economics as the community begins its fifth year.

331. Ellis, A.B. "Cooperative Brotherhood." *New Encyclopedia of Social Reform* (cited above as item 35), 307-8.
Provides an overview history of the colony, including its founding and its reorganzation in 1905.

332. Fogarty, Robert S. "Borland, Wilfred," "Cooperative Brotherhood" and "Hinton, Richard J." *Dictionary of American Communal and Utopian History* (cited above as item 76), 16-7, 136, and 51-2, respectively.
Dictionary entries providing a basic overview of the movement.

333. Hinds, William A. "Co-operative Brotherhood Colony of Burley, Washington." *American Communities and Co-operative Colonies* (cited above as item 95), 536-43.
Provides a history of the Cooperative Brotherhood; reproduces the rules of the colony; traces the group's movement away from cooperative principles.

334. Holbrook, Stewart H. *Far Corner* (cited above as item 101), 151-3.
Describes the community, its industries, and its gradual decline.

335. Kent, Alexander. "Cooperative Brotherhood." "Cooperative Communities in the United States (cited above as item 117), 618- 21.
Describes the organization of the colony and its social and economic life. Includes a balance sheet as of June 30, 1900.

336. LeWarne, Charles P. "Burley Colony: Brotherhood on Henderson Bay." "Communitarian Experiments in Western Washington, 1885-1915" (cited above as item

122), 313-46.
Provides a comprehensive history of the colony. An
earlier version of a chapter from the author's published
book (following item).

337. ———. "Burley Colony: Brotherhood on Henderson Bay."
*Utopias on Puget Sound* (cited above as item 124),
129-67.
The basic monograph on the colony, covering events
that led to its founding, the life of the colony, its
decline, and its dissolution. Well documented, including
references to specialized local and manuscript sources.

\* Meany, Edmond S. *History of the State of Washington*
(cited above as item 129), 323-4.
Describes the organization of the Brotherhood, the plan
for many colonies, the selection of the Burley site, and
the status of the colony in 1908.

338. Oved, Yaacov. "Cooperative Brotherhood at Burley." *Two
Hundred Years of American Communes* (cited above as
item 142), 267- 72.
Describes the founding and development of the colony,
the important role played by the *Co-Operator*, and the
division of property and dissolution of the colony.

339. Solis, Miguel J. "Burley Colony." *American Utopias* (cited
above as item 20), 35.
Contains a brief description of the colony plus one
bibliographical entry.

# XVIII. BURNING BUSH

The Burning Bush colony was founded by dissident
Methodists interested in Holiness ideas and practices; a
headquarters for the group, formally known as the Metropolitan
Church Association, was established in Waukesha, Wisconsin.
Several communal church settlements were founded in Virginia,
West Virginia, New Orleans, and Texas, the latter apparently
being the most important. The land for it was purchased in
1912 and in 1913 some 375 members arrived at the site near
Bullard, Texas. The group owned 1,520 acres and operated a
large farm, a sawmill, and a cannery. They had a common
treasury, a common storehouse, and common dining facilities.

The community was disbanded in 1919 due to financial problems.

Survey work: Okugawa (item 139), 231.

*Secondary works*

340. Fogarty, Robert S. "Burning Bush." *Dictionary of American Communal and Utopian History* (cited above as item 76), 133-4.
Provides an overview history of the group.

341. Smyrl, Edwin. "Burning Bush." *Southwestern Historical Quarterly* 50 (January, 1947): 335-43.
Provides a history of the group based on interviews and local public records.

# XIX. BYRDCLIFFE

Ralph Radcliffe Whitehead made several attempts at starting communal artists' colonies. The most successful of them was Byrdcliffe, near Woodstock, New York. There he purchased about 1000 acres for $10,000 in 1902 and opened a colony which was subsidized by his personal wealth. The property was gradually sold off following his death in 1929.

*Secondary work*

342. Edwards, Robert. "Utopias of Ralph Radcliffe Whitehead." *Antiques* 127 (January, 1985): 260-76.
Sketches the history of Whitehead's attempts at artists' communes. Heavily illustrated with photographs of buildings and of pieces of art produced at Byrdcliffe.

# XX. CANTERBURY COMMUNITY

This community was founded adjacent to Canterbury Shaker Village, from which the land and a building were purchased, 14 miles north of Concord, New Hampshire, in 1951. The Quaker-oriented community had three families about 1953.

343.  Kramer, Wendell B.    "Canterbury    Community."    "Criteria
      for the Intentional Community" (cited above as item
      118), 88-9.
      Describes the early development of the community.


# XXI.  CEDAR VALE, KANSAS: PROGRESSIVE, INVESTIGATING, CEDAR VALE COMMUNITIES

After leaving Alcander Longley's Reunion colony in Missouri, William Frey, his family, and three others staked claims near Cedar Vale in southern Kansas in 1871.    After several months of work they had a communal dwelling and had started farming. New members were soon attracted, although the communal population never exceeded a dozen.    A constitution was adopted in 1872.    Life was monotonous and hard; food and shelter were always scarce.    Suddenly, in 1875, Frey and his family left the community without explanation and founded the Investigating Community next door.    It was never much of a community, however; the largest group of prospective members, arriving in 1875, under the leadership of Alexander K. Malikov and Nikolai V. Chaikovsky, decided not to join and instead founded the Cedar Vale Community four files away.    Soon the two newer communities merged, but morale declined and the merged commune broke up in 1877.    The Progressive Community broke up either in that year or in 1878.    The Frey family remained at Cedar Vale through the summer of 1879, then joined the Positivist Commune at Clermont, Iowa, and finally, in 1883, moved to Oregon where Frey became the focal point of the New Odessa community.

The correspondence of William Frey and Leo Tolstoy is at the New York Public Library in the Slavonic Section.    The papers of William Frey are at the New York Public Library in the Manuscript Section.

Survey works: Hinds (item 94), 154-5; Okugawa (item 139), 204, 207.

344.  *Progressive Communist.*    1875.    Monthly.    Published by the
      Progressive Community.    Issue no. 1 (January) includes

the community's "Preamble and Constitution," p. 8.

345. *Social Investigator*. 1875. Monthly.
Published by the Investigating Community. Published as the two middle pages of the *Progressive Communist*, issues 7-10, July-October, 1875.

### Works by community leaders

346. Frey, William. *On Religion*. London: n.p., 1888. 22 pp.

347. ———. "Our Past." *Progressive Communist* nos. 2-4, 6 (1875).
A history of the community's early days.

348. ———. *Religion of Humanity*. London: W. Reeves, 1894. 45 pp.

349. ———. *Testament of William Frey*. London, n.p., 1889. 7 pp.

350. ———. *Under What Conditions Positivism Can Successfully Compete with Socialism*. London: n.p., 1885. 26 pp.

351. ———. *Vegetarianism in Connection with the Religion of Humanity*. [London? W. Frey and brothers, 1887?]

### Secondary works

352. Albertson, Ralph. "Progressive Community." "Survey of Mutualistic Communities in America" (cited above as item 27), 411-2.
Provides a brief note on the community.

353. Aldanov, Mark. "Russian Commune in Kansas." *Russian Review* 4 (Autumn, 1944): 30-44.
Focuses on the leaders of the Cedar Vale groups (William Frey, Alexander K. Malikov, and Nikolai V. Chaikovsky) more than the communities themselves.

354. Christman, Henry M. "Kansas Commune." *Kansas Magazine* (no volume or number) 1952: 92-3.
Concerns the work of Frey, Chaikovsky, and Malikov,

especially concentrating on Chaikovsky's later activism in support of the Kerensky government in Russia.

355. Fogarty, Robert S. "Frey, William." *Dictionary of American Communal and Utopian History* (cited above as item 76), 37-8.
Biographical dictionary entry.

356. Hecht, David. "America: The 'Sullen Stepmother.'" *Russian Radicals Look to America, 1825-1894.* Cambridge: Harvard University Press, 1947, pp. 196-216. Tells the story of Frey's original settlement on the land and that of the arrival of Chaikovsky and associates.

357. "Hit Oil in Kansas." Topeka *State Journal,* May 17, 1919. An interview with Chaikovsky, now President of the North Russian Republic, about his memories of the community. Suggests that the group discovered oil on the property without knowing it.

*   Lauer, Robert H., and Jeanette C. Lauer. *Spirit and the Flesh* (cited above as item 120), 44-5.
Provides an account of the hardships endured in daily life by members of the Progressive Community.

358. Maher, John Patrick. "Exposition of the *Progressive Communist.*" M.S. thesis, University of Kansas, 1974. 253 pp.
Characterizes the Russian socialism which influenced the founders of the Progressive Community; provides a survey history of the three Cedar Vale colonies; gives a detailed exposition of the content of the community newspaper.

359. Nordhoff, Charles. "Cedar Vale Community." *Communistic Societies of the United States* (cited above as item 138), 353-6.
Provides a brief sketch of the community and reproduces its constitution.

360. Solis, Miguel J. "Progressive Community." *American Utopias* (cited above as item 20), 145.
Provides a brief description of the colony plus one bibliographical entry.

*   Strachey, Ray, and Hannah Whitall Smith. *Group Movements of the Past and Experiments in Guidance*

(cited above as item 161), 85.
Contains a brief characterization of the Cedar Vale Community, noting that much individual freedom was allowed.

361. Titov, A. A. *Nikolai Vassilevich Chaikovskii.* Paris: n.p., 1929.
A massive biography of Chaikovskii. In Russian.

362. Weeks, Vickie D. "Cedarvale." "Late Nineteenth Century Kansas Utopian Communities" (cited above as item 169), 49-61.
Characterizes William and Mary Frey and other members of the communities; describes the successive creation of the three communities; portrays their relations with their neighbors as mixed.

363. Yarmolinsky, Avraham. *A Russian's American Dream.* Lawrence: University of Kansas Press, 1965. 147 pp.
A biography of William Frey, the central figure in the communities at Cedar Vale. Provides the most complete extant history of the communities.

# XXII. CELESTIA

This community of Adventists was founded in 1863 in Sullivan County, Pennsylvania, on about 600 acres of mountaintop land which Peter Armstrong, the community's founder, had earlier settled and cleared. Armstrong, believing that God's children should consecrate all their possessions to the lord, eventually deeded the land to God and refused to pay taxed on it. Officials subsequently sold the land and Armstrong's sheep to satisfy the tax bill. Armstrong hoped to gather at Celestia the 144,000 persons he believed necessary to usher in the millennium, and planned a great city for them. The community never had more than 20 members, but its periodical reached a circulation of 3,000. In many accounts the Community is called "Celesta," but the research of D. Wayne Bender (see item 366, below) demonstrates that the original spelling was "Celestia."
Some manuscript material on Celestia is located in the American Communities Collection at Syracuse University.

Survey works: Liefmann (item 125), 21; Okugawa (item 139),

202.

### Community periodical

364. *Day Star of Zion and Banner of Life.* 1864, 1880.
     Monthly. Published for a few issues in each of those
     years.

### Secondary works

365. Albertson, Ralph. "Celesta." "Survey of Mutualistic
     Communities in America" (cited above as item 27), 389.
     Provides a brief sketch of the community, dating its
     founding at 1852.

366. Bender, Donald Wayne. *From Wilderness to Wilderness*:
     Celestia. Dushore, Pennsylvania: Sullivan Review, 1980.
     57 pp.
     Characterizes Armstrong's involvement in the Adventist
     movement, his purchase and development of the property,
     the deeding of the property to God, and the problems and
     decline of the community. Provides a bibliography with
     references to many specialized and localized sources not
     cited here. Illustrated with photographs, maps, and
     reproductions of primary documents.

367. Fogarty, Robert S. "Armstrong, Peter." *Dictionary of
     American Communal and Utopian History* (cited above as
     item 76), 8.
     Biographical dictionary entry giving an outline of the
     colony's history.

368. Hinds, William A. "Celesta." *American Communities and
     Co-operative Colonies* (cited above as item 95),
     397-403.
     Provides a historical sketch focusing on the personality
     of Armstrong.

369. Ingham, Thomas J. *History of Sullivan County,
     Pennsylvania.* Chicago: Lewis Publishing Co., 1899, pp.
     49-50.
     Details Armstrong's deeding of his property to God and
     the ensuing forced sale of it for back taxes; describes an
     incident in which the community petitioned the legislature

to be regarded as "peaceable aliens" and "exiles" rather than citizens of Pennsylvania.

* Strachey, Ray, and Hannah Whitall Smith. *Group Movements of the Past and Experiments in Guidance* (cited above as item 161), 86-7.
  Emphasizes the differences of opinion within the Second Adventist movement and how they touched Celestia.

370. Wood, T. Kenneth. "Celesta." *Now and Then* (Muncy, Pa.) 4 (1936): 17-27.
  Provides biographical information on Armstrong and a rather sketchy history of the colony, based largely on the memories of a contemporary of Armstrong's and on information provided by one of Armstrong's grandsons. Reproduces the text of the deed by which Armstrong donated the land to God.

371. Wooster, Ernest S. "Celesta Second Adventists." *Communities of the Past and Present* (cited above as item 175), 62- 3.
  Provides a brief overview history of the community.

# XXIII. CELO

Celo was founded in 1936 when its wealthy patron, William Regnery of Chicago, communicated to Arthur Morgan his desire to endow some project of substantial social value. Morgan suggested that he underwrite the establishment of an intentional community, which he readily did. 1250 acres were selected in a mountain valley in the southwest corner of North Carolina. Several families, many of them pacifists, settled there.

A typewritten manuscript containing information on the founding of Celo as recorded by Arthur and Griscom Morgan is in the archives at Community Service, Inc.

## Community periodical

372. *Celo Community Newsletter.* Issues were published in the 1960s.

*Secondary works*

\*      Bouvard, Marguerite.  *International Community Movement*
       (cited above as item 37), 126.
       Provides a note about the Arthur Morgan School at
       Celo.

373.   "Celo Community: *Intentional Communities: 1959 Yearbook
       of the Fellowship of Intentional Communities* (cited
       below as item 807), 28-30.
       Provides a brief but comprehensive overview of the
       philosophy and projects of Celo.

374.   Federal Writers' Project.  *North Carolina Guide.*  Edited
       by Blackwell P. Robinson.  Chapel Hill: University of
       North Carolina Press, 1955, p. 559.
       Describes the community as consisting of about 20
       families, living and working on 1,200 communally owned
       acres (although individual homes were privately owned).

\*      Gladstone, Arthur.  "Cooperative Communities Today II"
       (cited above as item 82), 13.
       Describes the community, providing information about
       housing, the cooperative nursery school, and the summer
       program.  Reports a community population of 74 (over
       half of them children) as of March, 1954.

375.   Hicks, George L.  "Utopian Communities and Social
       Networks."  *Aware of Utopia.*  Edited by David Plath.
       Urbana: University of Illinois Press, 1971, pp. 135-50.
       Describes the history and life of "Banner," a
       pseudonymous secular utopian community which in reality
       must be Celo.  Focuses on the community's pacifist
       politics and its relationships with other like-minded
       groups.

376.   Infield, Henrik.  *Utopia and Experiment* (cited above as
       item 108), 74.
       A brief report on the current status of the community.

377.   Kramer, Wendell B.  "Celo Community, Inc."  "Criteria for
       the Intentional Community" (cited above as item 118),
       76-7.
       Provides an outline history of Celo.

\*      Phillips, Jack.  *Dictionary of Some Persons Planning to*

*Live in Small Communities* (cited below as item 836), 30.
Contains a brief description of Celo, focusing on its
cooperative store and its cooperative program.

378. Preston, John Hyde.     "Collective Living."     *Harper's*  176
     (May, 1938): 603-14.
     A reflection on the strengths of communal living after a
     five-month stay at "Collectiva" (a pseudonym for Celo,
     apparently) in the North Carolina mountains.    Emphasizes
     the economic advantages and possibilities for social
     intimacy in communal living.

# XXIV.  CHICAGO-COLORADO COLONY

The Chicago *Tribune* supported this colony, modeled on
Union Colony, which was supported by the New York *Tribune*.
Organized in Chicago, it was settled in 1871 on 55,000 acres at
Longmont, Colorado.    It was reported to have 350 to 400
residents in May, 1871.    The communal features of the
settlement disappeared when the irrigation projects were
completed.

Survey work: Okugawa (item 139), 204.

### Secondary works

*   Baker, James H., ed.    *History of Colorado* (cited above as
    item 30), v. 2, pp. 450-1.
    Provides an overview history of the colony, noting its
    rapid growth.

*   Hafen, Leroy R., ed.    *Colorado and Its People* (cited above
    as item 88), v. 1, pp. 331-3.
    Provides a brief historical sketch of the colony.

*   Hall, Frank.    *History of the State of Colorado* (cited
    above as item 89), v. 1, pp. 546-8.
    Provides a historical overview of the colony.

379. Willard, James F., and Colin B. Goodykoontz, eds.
     "Chicago-Colorado Colony."    *Experiments in Colorado
     Colonization, 1869-1872* (cited above as item 173),
     135-330.

Provides the main documents of the colony.

# XXV. CHRISTIAN COMMONWEALTH COLONY

Founded in 1896 by a group of Christians committed to radical social change in the social gospel era, the Christian Commonwealth colony was located on 1000 acres 12 miles east of Columbus, Georgia. Ralph Albertson was the chief founder. The colony was free and open to all, and some 300 persons lived there at one time or another. The industrial base included a sawmill, a print shop, and a towel weaving factory, and a large agricultural operation. Freeloaders and malcontents were always present in large numbers, and the colony lived in grinding poverty. A typhoid epidemic in 1900 finally brought it to an end.

Some manuscript material on the Christian Commonwealth Colony is in the American Communities Collection at Syracuse University.

Survey works: Curl (item 52), 36; Okugawa (item 139), 220.

### Community periodical

380. *Social Gospel.* 1896-1900. Monthly.
       "The Christian          Commonwealth" was a regular feature, with two or more articles on the colony in every issue.

### Primary work

381. *Christian Commonwealth Colony.   To All Who Pray "Thy Kingdom Come . . . " Greeting.* [Commonwealth, Georgia: Christian Commonwealth, 1896]. 4 pp.

### Works by community leaders

382. Albertson, Ralph. Autobiography. New York: 1936. An untitled typescript, never published. Described in Davis, *A Fearful Innocence* (cited below as item 674), pp. xiii and 241.

383. ———. "Christian Commonwealth." Unpublished man-uscript.

Probably the most complete history of the colony. For description, see Davis, *A Fearful Innocence* (cited below as item 674), pp. xiii and 241.

384. ———. "Christian Commonwealth." *Kingdom*, April 2, 1897.
Announces the opening of the community, describing its goals and its work so far.

385. ———. "Christian Commonwealth." *Social Gospel* 3 (February, 1898): 15-6.
A manifesto on the need to overcome selfishness and private property.

386. ———. "Christian Commonwealth Colony." "Survey of Mutualistic Communities in America" (cited above as item 27), 415-6.
A positive overview and assessment of the colony by its founder.

387. ———. "Christian Commonwealth in Georgia." *Georgia Historical Quarterly* 29 (June, 1945): 125-42.
A very personal account of the colony's history. Describes the colony's origins, its industries, its primitive living conditions, its relations with neighbors, the typhoid epidemic, and its dissolution. Especially useful for biographical sketches of the colony's leaders. Reproduces the covenant signed by all members.

388. ———. "Christianizing Property." *Twentieth Century* 18 (May 22, 1897): 10-1.
An argument for the socialization of property as the rule of Christ.

389. ———. "Common Property." *Kingdom*, September 11, 1896.
A historical and theological argument for holding property in common; presages the Christian Commonwealth Colony.

390. ———. "Commonwealth Sermon." *Social Gospel* no. 27 (April, 1900): 25-8.
A sermon on Christian idealism preached at the colony schoolhouse on March 4, 1900.

391. ———. *Little Jeremiads.* Lewiston, Maine: Cooperative

Press, 1903.

392. ————. *Little    Preachments.*    Lewiston,    Maine:    Cooperative Press, 1903.

393. ————. "New Evangelism." *Kingdom*, November 27, 1896.
Urges the preaching of a gospel of giving rather than
one of getting.

394. ————. "Passion That Left the Ground." Unpublished
manuscript novel based on the history of the Christian
Commonwealth Colony.
Cited by Dombrowski (item 404, below), 195. Not seen.

395. ————. "Social Incarnation." *Kingdom*, October 16,
1896.
Portrays unselfish communalism as the harbinger of the
millennium.

396. ————. *Social Incarnation: Studies in the Faith of
Practice.* 36 pp. Commonwealth, Georgia: Christian
Commonwealth, 1898.

397. Gibson, George Howard. "Christian Commonwealth
Economics." *Industrial Freedom*, June 25, 1898, p. 2.
Describes the organization of labor at the colony,
noting the absence of labor accounts and wages. Predicts
that the colony will expand to other locations.

398. ————. "Communism Again." *Kingdom* 8 (January 17,
1896): 643.
An argument, from a member of the new colony, that
religious communes will succeed where secular ones have
failed.


*Secondary works*

399. Addams, Jane. *Twenty Years at Hull-House.* New York:
Macmillan, 1910, pp. 277-9.
Describes a visit to the colony in which she found 60
residents; notes that paupers did not linger at the colony
because life was better at the poorhouse. The account is
largely admiring of the conscientious living the author
observed.

400. Bliss, W.D.P.    "Christian Commonwealth."    *New Encyclopedia of Social Reform* (cited above as item 35), 198.
    Provides a succinct history of the community.

401. Bolster, Paul D.    "Christian Socialism Comes to Georgia: The Christian Commonwealth Colony."    *Georgia Review* 26 (Spring, 1972): 60-70.
    Interprets the ideology of the community; presents an analysis of the group's demise.

402. "Brotherhood Organization."    *Social Gospel* 1 (February, 1898): 21-3.
    Describes the new colony's physical plant, agriculture, and common life.    Three following articles (pp.23-8) provide more details.

403. "Christian Commonwealth."    *Social Gospel* 1 (February, 1898): 15-6.
    A manifesto on the need to overcome selfishness and private property.

*    Davis, Frances.    *Fearful Innocence* (cited below as item 674), 17-19.
    Provides personal information about Albertson at the time of the Christian Commonwealth Colony experiment, including the story of his son who died there at the age of seven months of cold and starvation and his divorce soon afterwards.

404. Dombrowski, James.    *Early Days of Christian Socialism in America.*    New York: Columbia University Press, 1936. Repr., New York: Octagon Books (Farrar, Straus and Giroux), 1966, pp. 132- 70.
    The most complete extant account of the colony's history and life, discussing the motivations of the founders, the process of founding the colony, its goals, its activities, its demise, and its place in the social gospel movement.

405. Fish, John O.    "Christian Commonwealth Colony: A Georgia Experiment, 1896-1900."    *Georgia Historical Quarterly* 57 (Summer, 1973): 213-26.
    Describes the social gospel era and the founding of the colony, the colony's industries and school, and its problems and demise.    Concludes that despite its problems

and lack of long-term success, the colony exposed thousands to social gospel thinking and helped undergird the Progressive Movement.

\*       Fogarty, Robert S.   "American Communes, 1865-1914" (cited above as item 74), 161.
Provides a two-paragraph overview of the colony.

406. ———.   "Albertson, Ralph," "Christian Commonwealth Colony," and "Gibson, George Howard." *Dictionary of American Communal and Utopian History* (cited above as item 76), 5-6, 134-5, and 39-40, respectively. Dictionary entries providing basic information on the colony.

407. Fried, Albert.   "Christian Commonwealth." *Socialism in America* (cited above as item 78), 341-2, 355-61. Provides a brief historical sketch and reproduces a community document exploring the group's goals.

408. Gabriel, Ralph Henry.   *Course of American Democratic Thought.* New York: Ronald Press Co., 1940, pp. 322-4. Describes the communal ideas of Ralph Albertson, the founding of the colony, its organizational structure, its economic and labor system, its total communism and democracy, and problems which led to its demise.

409. Hinds, William Alfred.   "Christian Commonwealth." *American Communities and Co-operative Colonies* (cited above as item 95), 522-30. Provides a sympathetic history of the colony; quotes extensively from the pamphlet *Commonwealth Details*.

\*       Johnpoll, Bernard K., and Lillian Johnpoll. *Impossible Dream: The Rise and Demise of the American Left* (cited above as item 113), 242-3. Provides an overview of the history of the colony, emphasizing the problems which destroyed it.

410. Kent, Alexander.   "Christian Commonwealth."   "Cooperative Communities in the United States" (cited above as item 117), 612- 6. Provides an overview of the colony's history. Quotes from the colony's constitution on the goals its founders set for it, and then quotes Albertson further on the same topic.

* Muncy, Raymond Lee. *Sex and Marriage in Utopian Communities* (cited above as item 135), 119-20.
Provides basic information on the colony, emphasizing its traditional, monogamous sexual attitudes.

411. Oved, Yaacov. "Christian Commonwealth in Georgia." *Two Hundred Years of American Communes* (cited above as item 142), 275-83.
Characterizes the ideas of George Herron as the driving force behind the colony; describes the publication of the *Social Gospel*, the colony's economy and facilities, and the internal tensions and decline of the colony.

* Quint, Howard H. *Forging of American Socialism* (cited above as item 148), 131-2.
Contains a brief history of the colony. The balance of chapter 4, "The Christian Socialist Crusade," (pp. 103-41), contains material which bears on the colony and its principal activists.

412. Walker, Samuel. "George Howard Gibson, Christian Socialist Among the Populists." *Nebraska History* 55 (Winter, 1974): 553- 72.
Characterizes Gibson's work as a Populist agitator and publisher, his move toward communalism and cooperative business, his founding of the Christian Corporation in Nebraska (which, with 23 families involved, owned 1360 acres, but lasted only a short time), and his departure to Georgia to help found the Christian Commonwealth in 1896. Illustrated with photographs, a cartoon, and a newspaper page. Documentation includes references to specialized material not cited here.

* Weisbrod, Carol. *Boundaries of Utopia* (cited above as item 170), 117-8.
Contains a discussion of the social and legal problems the colony faced when dealing with a hostile ex-member.

413. White, Ronald C., and C. Howard Hopkins. *Social Gospel: Religion and Reform in Changing America.* Philadelphia: Temple University Press, 1976, pp. 176-7.
Quotes part of the manifesto of the colony as taken from its periodical, *The Social Gospel*. A note on *The Social Gospel* itself is on pp. 151-2.

414. Wooster, Ernest S. "Christian Commonwealth."

*Communities of the Past and Present* (cited above as item 175), 46.
Provides a brief overview of the colony's history and practices, focusing on its decline, which Wooster blames on the group's open-door policy.

# XXVI. CHRISTIAN COOPERATIVE COLONY

In the 1890s three members of the Progressive Brethren Church (S.J. Harrison, H.M. Lichty, and Christian Rowland) had dreams of a cooperative Christian colony; in 1898 they bought a defunct townsite and hotel at Sunnyside, Washington. Land in the colony was sold to settlers, but the deeds contained a forfeiture clause: if prohibitions of alcohol, gambling, and prostitution were violated, the land reverted to the company. There were other moral rules as well. After the heyday of the colony the restrictions were dropped and Sunnyside developed into a conventional town.

### Secondary works

\*      LeWarne, Charles Pierce. "Communitarian Experiments in Western Washington, 1885-1915" (cited above as item 122), 21.
Provides a brief sketch of the colony based on Sheller's account (following item).

415.   Sheller, Roscoe C. *Courage and Water: A Story of Yakima Valley's Sunnyside.* Portland, Oregon: Binfords and Mort, 1952, 23-7.
Provides a sketch of the settlement of the colony and its development into a town.

# XXVII. CHURCH OF GOD AND SAINTS OF CHRIST

The Church of God and Saints of Christ, a black Jewish group, was founded in 1896 by William S. Crowdy in Lawrence, Kansas. The headquarters church, founded in the Belleville neighborhood of Portsmouth, Virginia, early in the twentieth century, functioned communally until the World War II era; the hundreds of local churches elsewhere did not. The group owned over 1,000 acres of land near Portsmouth (now within the city limits of Suffolk), supporting itself by farming and operating small industries. The group believes blacks to be the descendents of the ten lost tribes of Israel and observes Jewish as well as Christian rituals. It claimed 38,000 members in 1970.

## Community periodical

416. *Weekly Prophet.*

## Secondary works

417. Armao, Rosemary, and Greg Schneider. "'Black Jews' Step Out of the Shadows." *Virginian-Pilot* (Norfolk), April 1, 1988, pp. 1, 6-7.
   Summarizes the history of the church, concentrating on its development in Belleville; provides an account of a typical worship service; surveys the recent move toward development of church property in Belleville, including new housing for members as well as commercial development.

418. Clark, Elmer T. "Church of God and Saints of Christ." *Small Sects in America* (cited above as item 43), 151-3.
   An account of the group based on a personal visit to its headquarters. Lists the "Seven Keys" of the group's faith.

*   Jones, Raymond Julius. *Comparative Study of Religious Cult Behavior Among Negroes with Special Reference to Emotional Group Conditioning Factors* (cited above as item 114), 5, 20, 100-4, and *passim.*
   Provides an eyewitness account of a Sabbath service at the church in Washington, D.C.; describes distinctive dress and spiritual claims employed by the church; compares the movement to that of Father Divine in its concern with the material as well as spiritual needs of its members.

419. Landis, Benson Y., ed. *Yearbook of American Churches.* New York: National Council of Churches, 1952, pp. 29-30.
   Provides a directory listing reporting 204 congregations

and 34,710 members for the denomination. Some other editions of this annual title provide information on the group, although often in less detail.

420. Mayer, F.E.   *Religious Bodies of America* (cited above as item 128), 523.
     Describes Crowdy's "Seven Keys" which undergirded his theology.

421. Melton, J. Gordon.   "Church of God and Saints of Christ." *Encyclopedia of American Religions* (cited above as item 130), 674.
     Outlines the history, doctrine, and organization of the group.

422. "Strange Sect of Negroes."   Kansas City *Star*, March 28, 1909, p. 5A.
     A feature story based on a reporter's visit to a Sabbath service.

423. Tinney, James S.   "Black Jews: A House Divided." *Christianity Today* 18 (December 7, 1973): 52-3.
     Outlines the current condition of the church and describes its distinctive practices.

424. Wynia-Trey, Elly.   "Church of God and Saints of Christ: A Black Judeo-Christian Movement Founded in Lawrence, Kansas in 1896."   Honors thesis, University of Kansas, 1989. 132 pp.
     A comprehensive history of the group.   At the Institute for the Study of American Religion.

# XXVIII.  CHURCH OF THE LIVING GOD

Frank Sandford was a Baptist preacher who claimed to have received a revelation at a revival in 1893 and established a colony in Durham, Maine, which eventually numbered 300 members.   After 1900 repeated controversies struck the group, and it disbanded in 1920.   The strangest episode was one in which Sandford and many of his followers undertook a missionary voyage on a sailing ship and refused to put into port for provisions, even though passengers starved to death, because Sandford said it was contrary to God's will.   Sandford was subsequently convicted of manslaughter.

*Secondary works*

425. Abram, Victor P. *Restoration of All Things.* Amherst, New Hampshire: Kingdom Press, 1962. 149 pp.

426. Fogarty, Robert S. "Sandford, Frank." *Dictionary of American Communal and Utopian History* (cited above as item 76), 102-3.
     Biographical dictionary entry which provides a basic overview of the community.

427. White, Arnold L. "Tragic Voyage of the Shiloh Schooner 'Coronet.'" *Down East*, May, 1974, pp. 54-7, 72-6.
     Recounts the bizarre tale of the missionary cruise which led to starvation for members of the group. Illustrated with photographs, including two of Shiloh Temple, the headquarters of the movement.

# XXIX. CHURCH OF THE SAVIOR

The Church of the Savior was founded in Washington, D.C., in 1946 by Gordon Cosby, a former Baptist. The church is organized in several subcommunities which are committed to outreach work to the poor and oppressed.

*Community periodical*

428. *Wellspring.*

*Works by community leaders*

429. Cosby, Gordon, *Handbook for Mission Groups.* Waco, Texas: Word Books, 1975. 179 pp.

430. O'Connor, Elizabeth. *Call to Commitment.* New York: Harper and Row, 1963.
     Provides considerable information on the church, including its history, ideas, programs, and projects. Illustrated.

431. ———. *Journey Inward, Journey Outward.* New York: Harper and Row, 1968.

The journey inward is that of self-discovery; outward is servanthood. The book tells much of the story of the Church of the savior, covering its ideas, programs, maintenance of community, worship life, and children's programs.

432. ———. *New Community.* New York: Harper and Row, 1976. 121 pp.
An essay pointing the way toward good communal relations through personal caring and inner transformation. Illustrated with photographs.

*Secondary work*

433. Melton, J. Gordon. "Church of the Savior." *Encyclopedia of American Religions* (cited above as item 130), 498. Provides a brief overview of the community.

# XXX. CHURCH TRIUMPHANT

A Mrs. Beckman was the founder of this movement. She claimed she was the mother of Christ in his second incarnation, but when she pointed to a young German, G.J. Schweinfurth, as her spiritual son, the "Messiah of the New Dispensation," many were skeptical. Dissension arose within the group, but Schweinfurth managed to keep several local groups of followers for two or three decades, into the early twentieth century. "Mt. Zion," the communal center, was a large house near Rockford, Illinois, where Schweinfurth and his disciples lived. At the peak of the movement in about 1880, it reportedly had 300 to 400 followers.

*Secondary works*

\*   Carroll, H.K. *Religious Forces of the United States* (cited above as item 40), 105-6.
Describes the rise of Schweinfurth in the group and the life of the community at Mt. Zion.

\*   Strachey, Ray, and Hannah Whitall Smith. *Group Movements of the Past and Experiments in Guidance* (cited above as item 161), 146.

Provides an overview of the movement, emphasizing the disputes over the naming of Schweinfurth as the second Christ.

# XXXI. THE COLONY

This group was founded in 1940 by Brother John Korenchan and eighteen followers in Seattle; it soon moved to Burnt Ranch, California, where it developed an agricultural economy. Mystical in outlook, it had 16 members in 1984.

*Secondary work*

434. Melton, J. Gordon. "Colony." *Encyclopedia of American Religions* (cited above as item 130), 498-9.
Provides a brief sketch of the group.

# XXXII. COLORADO CO-OPERATIVE COMPANY

To some extent, the Colorado Cooperative Company may be regarded as a successor to Topolobampo. Several persons gathered in Denver after Topolobampo's demise, hoping to found a new community. After some searching, colony scouts found Tabeguache Park in southwestern Colorado. The first settlers arrived in the fall of 1894 and began to file land claims. They built their first town, Pinon, soon thereafter. Essential to the success of the project was the completion of an irrigation ditch 13 miles long. It took a decade, but the ditch was finally finished. Once that job had been completed, the community focused on improving its primitive living conditions and began to construct the new town of Nucla. The town gradually turned into a noncommunal rural settlement; most of the Company's common holdings were transferred to private ownership in 1906. The Colorado Cooperative Company survived as a cooperative of water users who depended on the irrigation ditch.

Some manuscript material on the community is in the American Communities Collection at Syracuse University.

Survey works: Liefmann (item 125), 22; Okugawa (item 139), 218.

435. *Altrurian*.     Denver,    Naturita,    Nucla.     1895-?.     Monthly,
     1895-8; weekly, 1898-.
     The first issue contained the community's manifesto.


*Secondary works*

436. Albertson,    Ralph.     "Colorado    Co-operative    Colony."
     "Survey  of  Mutualistic  Communities  in  America"  (cited
     above as item 27), 412-3.
     Provides a brief sketch of the history of the colony.

437. "Cooperative    Colony-Builders."     *Out West*   19   (July,   1903):
     108-14.
     Describes   the   aftermath   of   the   failure   of   Topolobampo,
     when  many  refugees  from  that  colony  gathered  at  Denver
     and  organized  a  new  colony  in  1894.     Claims  that  the
     colony's future is bright. Illustrated.

*    Federal    Writers'    Project.     *Colorado:   A   Guide   to   the
     Highest State* (cited above as item 67), 421.
     Describes   the   cooperative   past   of   Nucla,   including   an
     account of the digging of the ditch.

438. Fogarty,   Robert   S.     "Colorado   Cooperative   Company"   and
     "Gallatin,   E.L."   *Dictionary   of   American   Communal   and
     Utopian   History*   (cited   above   as   item   76),   135-6   and
     38-9, respectively.
     Dictionary   entries   providing   basic   information   on   the
     group.

439. Gallatin,   E.L.     *What   Life   Has   Taught   Me*.     Denver:   John
     Frederic, 1900, pp. 51-195.
     Provides   a   detailed,   nearly   month-by-month   account   of
     the  life  of  the  colony  by  one  of  its  members,  with
     frequent  discursions  relating  the  author's  ideas  about
     cooperation  and  other  topics.     The  account  is  partisan  and
     personal,  lambasting  many  colony  participants  for  their
     greed  or  other  sins.     The  author  also  comments  briefly
     (pp.  142-51)  on  other  colonies  of  the  day,  including
     Ruskin and Equality.

440. Grant,   H.   Roger.     "Blueprints   for   Co-Operative   Colonies:
     The   Labor   Exchange   and   the   Colorado   Cooperative

Company." *Journal of the West* 13 (July, 1974): 74-82. Provides an overview history of the colony; compares it to the Labor Exchange, showing that both were depression-era altruistic plans to help people in need.

* Grant, H. Roger. "New Communitarianism" (cited above as item 86), 67-69.
Provides a good summary overview of the colony.

441. Hinds, William Alfred. "Colorado Co-operative Company." *American Communities and Co-operative Colonies* (cited above as item 95), 500-4.
Provides a description of the colony and details of the ditch project.

* Hine, Robert V. *Community on the American Frontier* (cited above as item 99), 221-4.
Contains a brief characterization of the community. Illustrated with a photograph of Main Street, Nucla.

442. Julihu, C.E. "Pinon—A New Brook Farm of the West." *National Magazine* 11 (October, 1899): 29-34.
The earliest account of the colony available; the author states that he had trouble gathering information because the members were adverse to publicity. Describes the physical facilities, the organization of the colony, and its daily life. Illustrated with photographs.

443. Kent, Alexander. "Colorado Cooperative Company." "Cooperative Communities in the United States" (cited above as item 117), 624-6.
Discusses the organization of the community and the financing of the ditch project. Provides a community financial statement from mid-1900.

444. Logan, F.B. "Colorado Cooperative Company." *New Encyclopedia of Social Reform* (cited above as item 35), 253.
Provides a brief description of the community, focusing on the landholdings and economic arrangements of the group.

445. Mercer, Duane D. "Colorado Co-operative Company, 1894-1904." *Colorado Magazine* 44 (Fall, 1967): 293-306.
The most extensive scholarly work on the colony. Describes the founding of the colony, membership and

stock ownership, the construction of the irrigation ditch and problems associated with it, internal disputes, colony social life, and the decline of communal spirit which followed the completion of the ditch.

446. Peterson, Ellen Z. "Origin of the Town of Nucla." *Colorado Magazine* 26 (October, 1949): 252-8.
Describes the beginnings of the colony, the hard living conditions there, and internal colony problems of the ditch-digging years. Illustrated with photographs. Much of the content of this article closely resembles parts of the author's book (item 447).

447. ————. *Spell of the Tabeguache.* Denver: Sage Books, 1957. 60 pp.
A personal memoir, comprising a history of the colony containing many names and other specifics.

448. Rockwell, Wilson. *Uncompahgre Country.* Denver: Sage Books, 1965, pp. 166-74.
Describes the origin of the colony and the beginning of work on the ditch, tells of the establishment of Pinon, provides an anecdotal slice of colony life, and discusses the gradual transition to a private economy. Well illustrated with photographs.

449. Wooster, Ernest S. "Colorado Co-operative Community." *Communities of the Past and Present* (cited above as item 175), 61- 2.
Provides a historical sketch of the community, including information taken from a letter written by a former member.

# XXXIII. COMMONWEALTH COLLEGE

Commonwealth College, a radical, communal educational institution which paid no salaries, was established at Newllano, Louisiana, in 1923 as a training school for labor leaders. Confrontations with Newllano management led to a move to Mena, Arkansas, where rural land was cheap, in 1924. In 1931 the moderate socialists in charge were ousted by a more radical element, including several Communist Party members. In 1935 the State of Arkansas tried to close the college. However, sectarian strife followed the Communist takeover, and by 1938 the college was in serious decline. It was closed in 1940; the property was sold to satisfy a fine stemming from a court judgment that the college was subversive.

The Commonwealth College Papers are located at the University of Arkansas in Fayetteville.

## Community periodicals

450. *Commoner.* 1938-40.

451. *Commonwealth College Fortnightly.* 1925-38.

452. *Windsor Quarterly.* 1934-5. Literary magazine published by the college.

## Secondary works

453. Black, Henry. "Library Service on No Budget at All." *Library Journal* 59 (October 1, 1934): 746-7.
Describes the methods by which research and library service were conducted in the bare-bones college library.

\* Calverton, Victor. *Where Angels Dared to Tread* (cited above as item 39), 362-3.
Provides a brief sketch of the project.

454. Cobb, William H. "Commonwealth College: A History." M.A. thesis, University of Arkansas, 1960. 267 pp.

455. ———. "Commonwealth College Comes to Arkansas, 1923-1925." *Arkansas Historical Quarterly* 23 (Summer, 1964): 99-122.
Provides details of the founding of the college, the controversy between Newllano and Commonwealth, and the land purchase in Arkansas. Illustrated with photographs.

456. ———. "From Utopian Isolation to Radical Activism: Commonwealth College." *Arkansas Historical Quarterly* 32 (Summer, 1973): 132-47.
Describes the freewheeling ways of the college and recounts its daily schedule; charts the college's move into more serious radicalism. Illustrated; documented largely from primary sources not cited here.

457. ———. "State Legislature and the 'Reds': Arkansas's

General Assembly v. Commonwealth College, 1935-1937."
*Arkansas Historical Quarterly* 45 (1986): 3-18.
Chronicles the crusade of some anticommunist state
legislators against the college.

458.  Cobb, William H., and Donald H. Grubbs.    "Arkansas'
      Commonwealth College and the Southern Tenant
      Farmers' Union."    *Arkansas Historical Quarterly* 25
      (Winter, 1966): 293-311.
      Describes the founding of the college, the move to
      Arkansas, the radical takeover, and demise of the college.
      Illustrated with photographs.

459.  "Commonwealth College Library, Arkansas."    *Library
      Journal* 57 (July, 1932): 631.
      Describes the library facilities and the improvements
      which are planned.    Illustrated with a photograph of the
      library building.

460.  Cunningham, William.    "Commonwealth College—An
      Educational Mutant."    *World Tomorrow* 12 (December,
      1929): 503-5.
      Depicts the goals of and daily life at the college.
      Portrays it as a promising mutant in a world dominated by
      huge, ineffective educational dinosaurs.

461.  ———.    "Commonwealth College: Learning and Earning."
      *Bulletin of the American Association of University
      Professors* 15 (February, 1929): 157-9.
      Argues that the lack of structure and conventional goals
      at the college has freed students to do real learning, and
      that because they work four hours per day to help
      support themselves and the school, they value what they
      get.

462.  Federal Writers' Project.    *Arkansas: A Guide to the State.*
      New York: Hastings House, 1941, pp. 319-20.
      Provides a characterization of the history of the
      college, especially of its conflicts with its neighbors and
      with the Arkansas legislature.

463.  Koch, Raymond, and Charlotte Koch.    *Educational
      Commune: The Story of Commonwealth College.*    New
      York: Schocken, 1972.
      Monograph covering the history and problems of the
      college. No bibliography.

464. Peterson, Ralph. "Utopian Afternoon: Post Mortem on Commonwealth College." *Labor Today* 2 (April, 1942): 17-20.
     Provides a historical sketch of the college, a characterization of life there, and a description of the campus. Tells of an article on the college in *Liberty* in 1936 which led college president Lucien Koch to sue the magazine for libel, obtaining a $5,000 settlement.

465. Sandler, Mark. "Workers Must Read: The Commonwealth College Library, 1925-1940." *Journal of Library History, Philosophy and Comparative Librarianship* 20 (Winter, 1985): 46-69.
     Chronicles the development of the Commonwealth College Library from the construction of its building through the sale of its collection at auction. The college developed strong collections on labor and politics with virtually no budget. Extensively documented.

# XXXIV. COMMONWEALTH OF ISRAEL

A group of Baptists organized this communal society in 1899 in Mason County, Texas. 900 acres were held in common; the community's economy centered on farming. Dissolution occurred in 1902.

Survey work: Okugawa (item 139), 224.

### *Secondary works*

466. Albertson, Ralph. "Commonwealth of Israel." "Survey of Mutualistic Communities in America" (cited above as item 27), 393.
     Furnishes a one-paragraph note on the colony.

467. Kent, Alexander. "Commonwealth of Israel." "Cooperative Communities in the United States" (cited above as item 117), 634.
     Provides a one-paragraph description of the colony.

# XXXV.  CO-OPERATIVE FARM

The Co-operative Farm was founded in 1951 near Eugene,
Oregon, on 185 acres.   It practiced pooling of income, with all
sharing.   There were nine original members; by 1933 that
number had reached 14, although there was a serious decline
later that year.

*Community periodical*

468.  *Bulletin.*

*Secondary work*

\*       Hendricks, Robert J.   *Bethel and Aurora* (cited above as
          item 92), 266-71.
          Provides a basic description of the project, an ongoing
          experiment at the time of writing.   Also provides a short
          list of similar communities operating about 1933.

# XXXVI.  DANISH COLONY (HAYS, KANSAS)

A group of Danish socialists leaving their country under
duress in the mid-1870s began to plan a communal venture in
North America.   In 1877, under the leadership of Louis Pio and
others, they acquired land near Hays under the homestead act;
individuals owned title to the land, but they agreed to consider
it common property.   The project commenced with hard
work--digging wells, plowing land, erecting the first log
cabin—but friction set in quickly.   Economic difficulties and
dissatisfaction with the high prairie swiftly followed, and the
18 colonists soon ate their cow and horses.   The colony was
abandoned six weeks after its founding and the assets were
sold and divided among the members.

Survey work: Okugawa (item 139), 208.

*Secondary works*

469.  Christensen, Thomas Peter.   "Danish Settlements in

Kansas." *Collections of the Kansas State Historical Society* 17 (1926-8): 300-5.
Provides an overview history of the colony and briefly describes the later careers of its leaders. Based on Danish-language sources.

470. Fogarty, Robert S. "Pio, Louis Albert Francois." *Dictionary of American Communal and Utopian History* (cited above as item 76), 93-4.
Biographical dictionary entry.

\* Hine, Robert V. *Community on the American Frontier* (cited above as item 99), 224-5.
Provides a historical sketch of the colony, emphasizing its endemic intellectual disputes.

471. Miller, Kenneth E. "Danish Socialism and the Kansas Prairie." *Kansas Historical Quarterly* 38 (Summer, 1972): 156-68.
The basic monograph on the colony.

472. Thompson, Vance. "Organized Thrift." *Cosmopolitan* 29 (August, 1900): 319-25.
Provides a biography of Louis Pio and a personality sketch of him in old age; contains scattered references to his communal ideas and involvements, mainly European. Contains a brief and inaccurate apparent reference to the Kansas colony; useful mainly for material on Pio.

473. Weeks, Vickie D. "Danish Colony." "Late Nineteenth Century Kansas Utopian Communities" (cited above as item 169): 64- 9.
Sketches the life of Pio; characterizes the founding and brief life of the colony. Information derived mainly from article by Miller (item 471).

# XXXVII. DAVIDIAN SEVENTH-DAY ADVENTISTS

Victor T. Houteff founded one of the many Adventist splinter groups in the 1930s and opened a colony, the Mount Carmel Center, near Waco, Texas, in 1935. At its peak it had 125 members. An eschatological prophecy by Houteff's widow failed in 1959, and the Davidians splintered. One important group reorganized and settled near Exeter, Missouri.

474.  *Symbolic Code.* Exeter, Missouri.

475.  *Timely-Truth Educator.* Exeter, Missouri.


*Secondary works*

476.  Melton, J. Gordon.   "Branch SDA's" and "Davidian
      Seventh-Day Adventists Association."   *Encyclopedia of
      American Religions* (cited above as item 130), 432-3.
      Provides a historical sketch and current characterization
      of the Davidians.


# XXXVIII. DELTA AND PROVIDENCE

In 1936 several religious leaders, including Sherwood Eddy,
Reinhold Niebuhr, and Bishop William Scarlett of St. Louis
undertook to help black tenant farmers in dire economic
straits.   They purchased 2,138 acres in near Hillhouse, Mississippi, and set up Delta Cooperative Farm, an interracial
community farming and sawmill operation involving 24 families.
Later a second tract of 2,888 acres was purchased near Cruger,
Mississippi.   Marked improvements in health care and economic
life resulted.   Both experiments lasted several years; Providence
Farm was hurt when white racist pressure drove two of the
founders from the community in 1955.


*Secondary works*

477.  Daniels, Jonathan.   *A Southerner Discovers the South.*
      New York: Macmillan, 1938, pp. 148-55.
      Provides an account of the author's visit to Delta; he
      finds it a worthy project run by energetic people, but
      argues that it prospers because of subsidies from liberal
      Yankees and probably could not make its own way.

478.  Eaton, Joseph.   "Delta and Providence Co-operative
      Farms."   *Exploring Tomorrow's Agriculture* (cited above
      as item 59), 198- 204.
      Tells the basic story of the land purchase and progress
      at the communities.

479. Eddy, Sherwood. "Delta Cooperative's First Year."
   *Christian Century* 54 (February 3, 1937): 139-40.
   Details the founding of the colony and its guiding
   principles. Argues that it is doing well, that its members
   are making money, and that black and white races are
   working together. Discloses that plans are well advanced
   for a second cooperative farm.

480. "Self-Help for Sharecroppers." *Literary Digest* 121 (April
   11, 1936): 16.
   Outlines plans for the new Delta project; says that 20
   families have been involved so far. Illustrated with
   photographs.

481. Taylor, Alva W. "Sherwood Eddy Launches a New
   Enterprise." *Christian Century* 53 (April 22, 1936):
   607-8.
   Provides a brief description of Delta in its early stages.

# XXXIX. ECUMENICAL INSTITUTE

The Ecumenical Institute was organized in Evanston, Illinois,
in 1957 as a conference center. A few years later it was
transformed under the leadership of Joseph Mathews into a sort
of Protestant religious order featuring communal living and
economic arrangements. The group saw itself as experimental,
seeking new approaches to religion, discipline, and social
reform. The headquarters was moved to Chicago and inner-city
work and social activism was stressed. 350 members were
reported in 1972.

*Community periodicals*

482. *Ecumenical Institute.* Also called *Newsletter.* 1964-?

483. *I.e.* 1964-?

484. *Image: Journal of the Ecumenical Institute.* 1963-70?

485. *Wedge.* In publication in 1970.

*Secondary works*

486.  Blair, William C.    "Re-evaluating the Ecumenical Institute."
      *Christian Century* 89 (November 15, 1972): 1159-60.
      Defends the group against criticisms leveled by Robert
      Seymour (item 495, below), arguing that members are
      simply rejecting blandness in favor of committed living.
      The article is followed by several letters to the editor
      praising or criticizing the Institute.

*     Bloesch, Donald G.    *Wellsprings of Renewal* (cited above
      as item 36), 93-4.
      Provides brief general information on the community.

487.  Brown, Harold O.J.    "Plumbing the Abyss."    *Christianity
      Today* 17 (December 8, 1972): 46-7.
      Provides a historical sketch of the group, trying to
      convey basic facts in the light of recent articles which
      have attacked it variously as radically revolutionary and
      inflexibly fundamentalist.

488.  "Church Funds for Revolution?"    *Christianity Today* 12
      (April 26, 1968): 27-8.
      An editorial finding much vitality in the Ecumenical
      Institute, but finally condemning it for its insufficiently
      evangelical outlook.

489.  Horn, J.A.    "Ecumenical Institute of Chicago: A New
      Sect? A Bibliography." Manuscript, 3 pp.
      Provides several references to articles in specialized
      periodicals not cited here.    At the Institute for the Study
      of American Religion.

490.  "Laboratory for the Future."    *Time*, March 17, 1967, p. 79.
      Describes the Institute favorably as an interfaith
      monastery centered on work, study, and prayer, an
      iconoclastic and experimental movement combining
      religious commitment with serious work on urban
      problems.

491.  Liebrecht, Walter.    "Ecumenical Institute, Evanston."
      *Religion in Life* 31 (Winter, 1961-2): 41-8.
      Outlines the founding of the Institute; characterizes its
      work as seeking greater religious commitment and
      Christian unity.    Describes programs and conferences
      currently being conducted.

492.  McNally, Arthur.    "Religion for a One-Story Universe."

*Sign* 47 (January, 1968): 30-9.
Describes the founding and life of the colony and criticizes its theology for being insufficiently Christocentric.

493. Petersen, William J., and Robert T. Coote. "Mr. Jones, Meet the Ecumenical Institute." *Eternity* 24 (March, 1973): 34-6, 72, 74-5.
Describes the founding and metamorphosis of the group from a somewhat negative, conservative Christian perspective.

494. Rose, Stephen C. "Ecumenical Institute: Ode to a Dying Church." *Christianity and Crisis* 28 (November 11, 1968): 263-70.
Characterizes the author's participation in an Ecumenical Institute course; provides a sketch of Joseph Mathews, the driving force behind the group. Supplies an ambivalent review of the role and function of the Institute.

495. Seymour, Robert E. "Prepackaged Religion." *Christian Century* 89 (September 20, 1972): 922-3, 926.
Accuses the Institute's leadership of being narrow-minded, intense zealots.

# XL. EGLINTON

Twelve English families gathered in New York in 1882 to found a colony in the West. Some settled in Taney County, Missouri; the rest, not satisfied with that location, went on to Texas. Those who stayed bought land near Taney City and opened a cotton and tobacco farm. The group seems not to have lasted very long as a colony, although several members stayed in the area.

*Secondary work*

496. Stout, Roy E. "Eglinton Colony in Missouri, 1882." *White River Historical Society Quarterly* 2 (Summer/Fall, 1967): 1-3.
Provides a brief sketch of the colony and discussion of what happened to descendants of the founders. Illustrated

with a photograph and a woodcut.

# XLI.  EMISSARY COMMUNITIES

The seed of the Emissary Communities (Emissaries of Divine Light) was planted in 1932, when Lloyd Meeker attracted a number of seekers with his lectures on the potential of humankind.   He met Martin Cecil in 1939, and the two began to move toward developing a community.   The principal settlements which emerged were Sunrise Ranch, near Loveland, Colorado, and 100 Mile House, British Columbia.   Other smaller centers were subsequently opened.   In 1987 the movement counted 12 communal locations and approximately 155 other meeting locations in 23 countries. The Emissary communities are involved in modern technology, hydroponic farming, and transportation via their private jet.   They also sponsor seminars and retreats for the general publc.

## *Community periodicals*

497.  *Business Dynamics*.  In publication in 1988.

498.  *Eden Valley News*.     Annual publication of Sunrise Ranch, Colorado.

499.  *Emissary*. 1975-.
      Monthly journal of the Emissary movement, containing fiction, nonfiction, poetry, photography, cartoons, interviews, and news briefs.   Some issues have a topical focus (e.g., an undated 1979 issue contains 26 articles on music).

500.  *Healing Currents*.  In publication in 1988.

501.  *Integrity*.   Newsletter published at 100 Mile Lodge. Stresses traditional social values.

502.  *Integrity International*.  In publication in 1983.

503.  *JTS World*.   Loveland, Colorado.   In publication in the 1970s and 1980s. Bimonthly.
      Children's periodical.   JTS stands for Junior Training School program.

504. *News Light.* Newsletter for members.

505. *Northern Light.* Annual publication of 100 Mile House.

506. *Ontological Thought.* Ca. 1969-? Monthly.

507. *Renaissance Educator.* In publication in 1988.

508. *Renaissance Woman.* In publication in 1988.

### Primary works

509. Aumra. *As of a Trumpet.* Loveland, Colorado: Eden Valley Press, 1968. 79 pp.
Tract on spiritual and personal growth.

510. *Divine Design.* Loveland, Colorado: Emissaries of Divine Light, n.d. 7 pp.

511. Uranda. *Seven Steps to the Temple of Light.* Loveland, Colorado: Emissaries of Divine Light, 1936. Third edition, 1958. 28 pp.

### Works by community leaders

512. Cecil, Martin. *Being Where You Are.* New Canaan, Connecticut: Keats Publishing, 1974. 204 pp.
Transcribed lectures constituting a guide to dealing with the problems of life.

513. ———. *Fountain of Life.* Loveland, Colorado: Emissaries of Divine Light, n.d. 18 pp.

514. ———. *Look Up.* Loveland, Colorado: Universal Institute of Applied Ontology, n.d. 17 pp.

515. ———. *On Eagle's Wings.* New York: Two Continents Publishing Group, 1977. 186 pp.
An introduction to the ideas of the Emissary movement. Transcribed lectures.

516. ———. *Question of Belief.* Loveland, Colorado: Emissaries of Divine Light, 1955. 12 pp.

517. ———. *Reincarnation?* Loveland,    Colorado:    Emissaries
     of Divine Light, n.d.  18 pp.

518. ———. *Trap.* Loveland,  Colorado:  Universal  Institute  of
     Applied Ontology, n.d.  16 pp.

519. ———. War in Heaven. Loveland,  Colorado:  Universal
     Institute of Applied Ontology, n.d.  20 pp.

### *Secondary works*

520. Cecil, Michael.  "100 Mile Lodge." *Communities* no. 16
     (September/October, 1975): 47.
     Provides an overview description of the community and
     its philosophy.

521. ———. *100 Mile Lodge: Agreement in Action.* Loveland:
     Eden Valley Press, Inc., 1975.  Transcript of a lecture
     on basic Emissary principles.

522. Christenberry, Dan.  "Oakwood Farm of the Emissaries of
     Divine  Light  and  the  Art  of  Living  Seminar."
     *Community Service Newsletter* 36 (May/June, 1988):  1-3.
     Provides impressions of the Emissary movement based
     largely on the author's attendance at an Emissary seminar
     at Oakwood Farm, an Emissary community located near
     Muncie, Indiana.

523. Cummings, Michael S.  "Democratic Procedure and
     Community in Utopia." *Alternative Futures* 3 (Fall,
     1980): 35-57.
     Discusses structure, power, and decision making in
     several communes, including Sunrise Ranch, the principal
     Emissary community.

524. Giglio, Nick.  "Sunrise Ranch and the International
     Emissary Community." *Communities* no. 71-2 (combined
     issue) (Summer/Fall, 1986): 46-8.
     A brief statement of philosophy and current Emissary
     events by a member of the community.  Illustrated.

525. Melton, J. Gordon.  "Emissaries of Divine Light."
     *Encyclopedia of American Religions* (cited above as item
     130), 576- 7.
     Provides a brief sketch of the history and ideas of the

Emissary movement.

526. Pittman, PenDell. "Sunrise Ranch: Adventures with Technology." *Communities* no. 67 (Summer, 1985): 12-14. Describes Sunrisc Ranch and the Emissary communities. Emphasizes major building projects and the use of high technology.

527. *Spirit of Sunrise.* London: Mitre Press, 1979. 192 pp. Talks by seven members of the Emissary movement, on such topics as renewing your human experience, finding fulfillment and meaning, and getting past misery and frustration and working toward a new consciousness.

528. Thatcher, Dave. "100 Mile Lodge—Emissaries of Divine Light." *Communities* no. 36 (January-February, 1979): 39-41. Provides the best single overview history of the community, its businesses, and its ideas.

# XLII. ENGLISH COLONIES

In the late nineteenth century, a number of landed families of England thought that their sons could settle in enclaves in America and prosper while preserving the traditions of British life. Several English colonies attracted hundreds of young Englishmen on that basis, but the relatively hard life of rural America appealed to few of them, and most drifted away from the settlements. The economic arrangements at the colonies varied; some were substantially communal, while many were simply centers of English culture which allowed young men a happy alternative to traditional British life. Those covered here are the ones which had to least some substantial level of communal or cooperative features.

*Works covering more than one colony (secondary)*

529. Berthoff, Rowland Tappan. *British Immigrants in Industrial America, 1790-1950,* pp. 114-6. Cambridge, Mass.: Harvard University Press, 1953. Provides brief sketches of the English colonies of Lemars (Iowa) and Rugby (Tennessee).

530. Howes, Cecil. "This Month in Kansas History." *Kansas Teacher* 5 (April, 1943): 30-2.
     A summary sketch of several colonies in Kansas, including Wakefield, Victoria, and Runnymeade.

531. Shepperson, Wilbur Stanley. *British Emigration to North America*. Minneapolis: University of Minnesota Press, 1957, pp. 99-104.
     Sketches communitarian emigration plans, focusing more heavily on the English than the American end.

532. ———. *Emigration and Disenchantment*. Norman University of Oklahoma Press, 1965, pp. 113-6.
     Contains brief information on several English cooperative colonies, including Rugby, Runnymede, and Wakefield, with brief mentions of the Welsh Colony, Powis Colony, and Llewellyn Castle, all in Kansas.

533. Waldron, Nell Blythe. "Colonization in Kansas from 1861 to 1890." Ph.D. dissertation, Northwestern University, 1932, pp. 53-70.
     Sketches the history of the English colonies of Wakefield and Runnymede.

# XLII(A). LEMARS

In the late 1870s, William and Frederick Close purchased 3,000 acres of Iowa farmland, a holding which they rapidly expanded until it reached 300,000 acres in 1881. Plots of land at the LeMars colony were then sold to wealthy English buyers who moved there. The managers oversaw the building of houses and barns and exercised broad powers over the community.

## Secondary works

\* Berthoff, Rowland Tappan. *British Immigrants in Industrial America, 1790-1950* (cited above as item 529), 115-6.
     Provides a brief sketch of the colony.

534. Van der Zee, Jacob. *British in Iowa*. Iowa City: State Historical Society of Iowa, 1922, pp. 129-40.

Discusses the founding and life of the colony.

# XLII(B). LLEWELLYN CASTLE

About 1870 the London Colonization Society purchased a section of Kansas farmland and had an eight-room house built on it. "Llewellyn Castle" was a communal dwelling for English settlers who came there to farm. The project soon failed.

*Secondary Work*

535. Bristow, John T. *Memory's Storehouse Unlocked.* Wetmore, Kansas, and Fresno, California: n.p., 1948, pp. 192-214.
Two chapters of this book discuss the colony and its relations with other local settlers.

# XLII(C). RUGBY

Founded in 1880, Rugby was the most prominent and successful of the English colonies, perhaps because its founder was the most famous: Thomas Hughes, author of the phenomenal best seller, *Tom Brown's School Days.* Hughes was deeply interested in utopian settlements throughout his life, and long hoped to open one in England. Circumstances forced him to undertake his experiment in the United States, and he threw himself into Rugby, in Eastern Tennessee, which he hoped would eventually become a perfect example of "Christian Communism." He purchased 35,000 acres, erected several buildings and then opened the colony to young Englishmen, who lived largely on money sent them from home. Most did not work and lived lives of decadent luxury. The laziness of some colonists helped prevent the effort from cohering; a typhoid epidemic hastened the demise of the project.

Four collections of correspondence explain much of the origin and history of Rugby: the Howell correspondence, at Bishopsgate Institute, London; the Mundella correspondence, Sheffield University Library; the Gladstone papers, in the manuscripts room, British Museum; and the Ripon papers, also in the manuscripts room, British Museum. Other original manuscripts survive in the library at Rugby, which is still in operation.

Survey work: Okugawa (139), 209.

## Community periodicals

536. *Plateau Gazette and East Tennessee News.* 1883-4.
     Weekly. Continuation of *The Rugbeian.*

537. *Rugbeian.* 1881-3. Monthly at first, then weekly.

538. *Rugby Gazette and East Tennessee News. 1884-1890.
     Weekly. Continuation of Plateau Gazette and East
     Tennessee News.*

539. *Rugby News.*


## Works of the community leader

540. Hughes, Thomas.    "Co-operation."    *Library Magazine* 6
     (December, 1880): 389-97.
     An address given at Cooper Union, New York, November
     5, 1880.    Hughes's optimistic statement of his principles
     and his prediction of a glowing future for cooperative
     projects.    Hughes provides some information on the
     beginnings of his new colony in Tennessee.

541. ———. *Foundations:    A    Study    in    the    Ethics    and
     Economics of the Co-operative Movement.*    Manchester:
     The Co-operative Union, Ltd., 1916.
     A revision of *A Manual for Co-operators* (item 547); the
     revision was made by A. Stoddart and W. Clayton.

542. ———. *G.T.T.—Gone to Texas.* London:    Macmillan,
     1884.
     A collection of letters by English boys during the Rugby
     period.

543. ———. "Rubgy, Tennessee." *Macmillan's Magazine* 43
     (February, 1881): 310-5.
     A chapter from Hughes's book of the same title.
     Provides information to young British men who were
     encouraged to settle at Rugby.

544. ———. *Rugby, Tennessee.* London: Macmillan, 1881.
     168 pp.
     Gives Hughes's account of the colony, from its origins

as a proposed solution to overcrowding in England through the early days of the colony's existence. Describes the search for a site for the colony and the erection of the original buildings.

545. ———. *Vacation Rambles.* New York: Macmillan, 1895, pp. 181-260.
A travel book in the form of letters. Much of the material on Rugby in reproduced from the author's *Rugby*, Tennessee (item 544, above).

546. Hughes, Thomas, and Edward V. Neale. *Co-operative Faith and Practice.* Manchester: Co-operative Union, Ltd., n.d. 15 pp.
A manifesto for communalism.

547. ———. *Manual for Co-operators.* London: Macmillan and Co., 1881.
A manifesto on the moral basis and practical application of various kinds of cooperation, chiefly consumer cooperative organizations.

*Secondary works*

548. Altstetter, Mabel Flick. "Thomas Hughes in America." *Peabody Journal of Education* 15 (July, 1937): 92-100.
Provides a historical sketch of the colony. Describes the acquisition and cataloging of the colony library.

549. Armytage, W.H.G. "New Light on the English Background of Thomas Hughes' Rugby Colony in East Tennessee." *East Tennessee Historical Society Publications* 21 (1949): 69-84.
Provides a chronicle of the life of Thomas Hughes, from his activism among the British Christian Socialists through his stint in Parliament to the founding of the colony in 1880.

550. ———. "Public School Paradise." *Queen's Quarterly* 57 (Winter, 1950-1): 530-6.
Describes the founding of the Board of Aid to Land Ownership, the erection of buildings at the Rugby site, the colony's early success, and its demise amid dissolution and disease.

\*      Berthoff, Rowland Tappan. *British Immigrants in
       Industrial America, 1790-1950* (cited above as item 529),
       114-5.
       Provides a historical sketch of the founding of the
       colony, its subsequent decline, and the modest revival it
       enjoyed in 1886.

551.   Bertz, Eduard. *Sabinergut.* Berlin: Verein der
       Buecherfreunde, 1901. 484 pp.
       A novel about Rugby by the first librarian there. In
       German. Not seen.

552.   Board of Aid to Land Ownership, London. *Rugby
       Handbook of the English-American Colony on the
       Plateau of the Cumberland Mountains, in East
       Tennessee.* Cincinnati: n.p., 1885? 32 pp.

553.   ———. *Rugby, Morgan County, Tennessee, Settlement
       Founded October 5th, 1880, by the Board of Aid to Land
       Ownership (Limited) of London, England.* Cincinnati:
       Robert Clarke and Co., 1880. 24 pp.

554.   DeBruyn, John R. "Letters to Octavius Wilkinson: Tom
       Hughes' Lost Uncle." *Princeton University Library
       Chronicle* 34 (Autumn, 1972): 33-52.
       Provides an exposition of Hughes's letters to an uncle.
       Many of the letters were written from Rugby and provide
       Hughes's candid view of daily life and problems at the
       colony. The letters on which the article is based are
       housed at the Princeton University library.

555.   ———. "Thomas Hughes on Eduard Bertz." *Notes and
       Queries* new series 23 [continuous series, v. 221]
       (September, 1976): 405-6.
       Consists of a brief note on a Hughes letter about Bertz,
       a young German scholar who organized the Thomas Hughes
       Library at Rugby.

556.   Egerton, John. "Rugby: The 'New Jerusalem' of Thomas
       Hughes." *Visions of Utopia* (cited above as item 60),
       36-63.
       Provides an informal history of the colony. Illustrated.

\*      Federal Writers' Project. *Tennessee: A Guide to the State*
       (cited above as item 70), 360-1.
       Outlines Hughes's goals, the British features of life at

Rugby, and the buildings still in use in the late 1930s.

\*     Fogarty, Robert S. "American Communes, 1865-1914" (cited above as item 74), 154.
Contains a long paragraph giving a succinct overview of the history of Rugby.

557. ———. "Hughes, Thomas," and "Rugby Colony." *Dictionary of American Communal and Utopian History* (cited above as item 76), 56-7 and 160-1.
Dictionary entries which provide basic information on the colony.

558. Hamer, Marguerite B. "Correspondence of Thomas Hughes Concerning His Tennessee Rugby." *North Carolina Historical Review* 21 (July, 1944): 203-14.
An edited collection of Hughes's correspondence on the colony from its planning stages to the end of the experiment.

559. ———. "Thomas Hughes and His American Rugby." *North Carolina Historical Review* 5 (October, 1928): 390-412. Also appears in Hamer's *Cameos of the South* (Chicago: Winston, 1940).
Describes the life of Hughes, the selection of the colony site and purchase of land, the development of the colony, leisure and aesthetic life there, and the colony buildings and businesses. Contains a lengthy analysis of the causes of the failure of the colony. Heavily documented with references to local and specialized articles not cited here.

560. Hughes, William Hastings. "True Story of Rugby." Boston *Evening Transcript*, December 2, 1905, part 3, p. 10. Also published as pamphlet, edited by John R. DeBruyn; Jackson, Tennessee: n.p., [1970?].
Debunks some long-standing rumors about the colony (such as that the colony owned 100,000 acres, when it actually owned only about 35,000) and provides a brief history of the experiment, focusing especially on the period before the colony's settlement.

561. Jones, Audrey. "Rugby in Tennessee." *Tennessee Folklore Society Bulletin* 14 (June, 1948): 23-6.

562. Lasswell, Lynda. *Rugby: A Brave Failure, a Brave Success.* Rugby: Rugby Restoration Press, 1975. 34 pp. Part of

a series entitled "Rugby Perspectives." Illustrated.

563. Little, John E.   *Thomas Hughes, 1822-1896.*   Uffington,
     England: author, 1972, pp. 18-21.
     Describes Hughes's goals for the colony, emphasizing his
     desire to eliminate competition and to promote a spirit of
     cooperation.   Provides a sketch of the site selection
     process, the decline of the colony, and the disposition of
     the property.

564. Mack, Edward C., and W.H.G. Armytage.   *Thomas Hughes:
     The Life of the Author of Tom Brown's School Days.*
     London: Ernest Benn, Ltd., 1952, chapter 14.
     Tells of Hughes's motives and plans, the building of the
     colony, and the colony's early success, along with its
     problems, such as unwillingness of some colonists to work
     and a typhoid epidemic which killed 17 settlers.   Heavily
     documented from primary sources.

565. McClary, Ben Harris, ed.   "Not for the Moment Only:
     Eduard Bertz to Mary Percival, February 18, 1886."
     *Tennessee Historical Quarterly* 24 (Spring, 1965): 54-62.
     Reproduces a letter from Rugby's first librarian to his
     successor concerning collecting books and preparing the
     library for use.

566. Maloney, John.   "Town of Cultured Ghosts."   *Holiday* 4
     (October, 1948): 81, 83-4, 86-92.
     Provides a historical sketch of the colony; describes the
     surviving buildings and the residents as of 1948.
     Illustrated with photographs of both old and recent
     vintage.

567. Mathews, John Joseph.   *Life and Death of an Oilman: The
     Career of E.W. Marland.*   Norman: University of
     Oklahoma Press, 1951, pp. 10-4.
     Provides a description of the colony and of Marland's
     education at the Arnold School there; the school tried to
     imitate the English Rugby.

568. Miller, Ernest I.   *English Settlement at Rugby, Tennessee.*
     Rural Research Series no. 128.   Knoxville: University of
     Tennessee Agricultural Experiment Station, 1941.   37 pp.
     Describes the background of the creation of the colony,
     site selection and purchase, the geology of the site, the
     types of persons who settled there, the organization of

the colony, the crops and industries of the colony, and the colony's access to markets; provides an analysis of the colony's decline. Contains a map of Rugby and another of the surrounding area.

569. ———. "English Settlement at Rugby." *Some Tennessee Utopias* (cited above as item 133), 27-57.
    Contains a history of the community, a discussion of the choice and nature of the site, characterizations of the settlers, the agricultural program, the community's industries, and its decline. Bibliography lists many specialized items, some of which are not cited here.

570. Minton, Lee R. "Rugby, Tennessee." Nineteenth Century 7 (Winter/Spring, 1981-2): 43-6.
    Provides a brief history of Rugby and a description of the contemporary town. Illustrated with photographs and an engraving of Rugby buildings, plus a photograph of a group of colonists.

571. Montgomery, James Elmer. "Two Resettlement Communities on the Cumberland Plateau: An Introductory Study of Recent Utopian Reform." M.A. thesis, Vanderbilt University, 1941. 113 pp.

572. "New Rugby." *Harper's Weekly* 24 (October 16 and November 6, 1880): 665-6 and 709-10.
    The first of the two articles provides a highly upbeat and optimistic description of the colony's history and organization; the second focuses on overcrowding and other problems in England which led to widespread emigration. Published just after the opening of the colony. Well illustrated.

573. Owsley, Harriet C. "Rugby Papers: A Bibliographic Note." *Tennessee Historical Quarterly* 27 (Fall, 1968): 225-8.
    An overview of correspondence and other manuscripts retained at Rugby and copied for storage at the Tennessee State Library and Archives.

574. Shelley, Henry C. "Book Table: The Centenary of Thomas Hughes." *Outlook* 133 (February 7, 1923): 275-6.
    A sketch of Hughes's life and literary work; notes that he left a relatively small estate, having lost most of his fortune in the colony experiment.

\*      Shepperson,  Wilbur  Stanley.  *Emigration  and  Disenchantment* (cited above as item 532), 115.
       Mentions  and  briefly  describes  Rugby  while  arguing  that the  British  colonies  were  not  necessarily  "Edens  of America," as they were often characterized to the English.

575.   Solis,  Miguel  J.   "Rugby  Colony."  *American  Utopianism* (cited above as item 20), 146-7.
       Provides  a  brief  description  of  the  colony  plus  two bibliographical entries.

576.   Stagg,  Brian  L.   "America's  Rugby."  *Historic  Preservation* 19 (April-June, 1967): 76-9.
       Describes  the  process  of  preserving  and  restoring  the Rugby  land  and  buildings.   Illustrated  with  photographs  of Rugby buildings.

577.   ———.   *Distant   Eden:   Tennessee's   Rugby   Colony.* Rugby, Tennessee: Paylor Publications, 1973. 34 pp.
       Contains  a  history  of  the  colony  plus  a  guide  to  the historic site. Illustrated with photographs and maps.

578.   ———.   "Tennessee's   Rugby   Colony."   *Tennessee Historical Quarterly* 27 (Fall, 1968): 209-24.
       Provides  a  biographical  sketch  of  Hughes  and  a  history of  the  colony  from  its  origins  to  its  aftermath. Illustrated with photographs.

579.   Stone,  Grace.   "New  Agrarianism  in  Tennessee:  Thomas Hughes."   "Tennessee:  Social  and  Economic  Laboratory" (cited above as item 160), 160-6.
       Provides  a  brief  survey  of  Thomas  Hughes  and  the Rugby  project,  based  primarily  on  the  published  works  of Hughes.

580.   Stott,  Kathleen  Brook.   "Rugby,  Tennessee:  An  Attempted Utopia."   M.A.  thesis,  University  of  Missouri,  1938.   136 pp.
       Surveys  conditions  in  England  which  led  to  the  founding of  American  colonies,  the  ideas  of  Hughes,  the development  of  Rugby,  life  at  the  colony,  and  its  decline. Documented  from  letters,  manuscripts,  popular  press articles, and colony publications.

581.   "'Tom  Brown'  in  Tennessee."  *Harper's  Weekly* 24 (September 18, 1880): 595.

A note on the opening of the colony, describing the facilities built and the goals of the community.

582. "Trees." *Time* 34 (December 25, 1939): 9.
Describes the battle currently raging over a lumberman's cutting of the old pine trees at Rugby, which local residents saw as a desecration of history.

583. Walton, Sarah L. *Memories of Rugby Colony*. Rugby: n.p., 1952. 15 pp.

584. ———. "Rugby in America." *Georgia Review* 10 (October, 1956): 394-403.
An appreciative historical sketch, emphasizing the enthusiasm of Hughes and his commitment to human community. Illustrated with photographs of three Rugby buildings.

585. Wichman, Patricia Guion. *Christ Church Episcopal, Rugby, Tennessee: A Short History*. Rugby: n.p., 1959. 47 pp.

586. ———. *Rugby: A Great Man's Dream*. Rugby: Hughes Library, 1963. 43 pp.

587. Worth, George J. *Thomas Hughes*. Boston: Twayne, 1984, pp. 81-91.
Describes Hughes's efforts to finance and build the colony; focuses more on Hughes's writings on Rugby than on the actual community.

588. Young, Arthur C., ed. *Letters of George Gissing to Eduard Bertz, 1887-1903*. New Brunswick: Rutgers University Press, 1961. 337 pp.
Contains scattered references to Bertz's years at the colony and to his novel about Rugby, *Das Sabinergut* (item 551, above).

# XLII(D). RUNNYMEDE

Runnymede was founded in Harper County, Kansas, in 1885 or early 1886. It had a glorious heyday, with a three-story hotel, stores, a population of over 500, and service by two stage lines. But it was short lived; the breakup was the result of the Panic of 1893, poor crop yields, and the unfortunate burning death of an intoxicated Englishman. Parents of the fun-loving colonists learned of the dissolute behavior which characterized the colony and ordered their sons home.

## *Secondary works*

589. Kramer, Lulu Sue. "Runnymede, Kansas." *Kansas Magazine* (no volume or number) 1955: 95-7.
    A recounting of Runnymede vignettes by a descendant of a resident.

590. "Lost Town of Runnymede, Kas., Where Merry English Gentlemen Played at Farming." *Kansas City Star*, September 7, 1924.
    An informative feature story based on the memories of older persons who remembered the colony. Illustrated with pictures of those who shared their memories.

591. Miller, Nyle H., ed. "English Runnymede in Kansas." *Kansas Historical Quarterly* 41 (Spring, 1975): 22-62; (Summer, 1975): 183-224.
    Provides extensive information about the colony by presenting many newspaper stories on the project.

592. Seton, Charles. "Reminiscences of Runnymede." *Kansas Historical Collections* 12 (1911-2): 467-9.
    Describes the young British settlers as having had a good time—while the brief project lasted. Reprinted from the Kansas City *Star*.

\*    Shepperson, Wilbur Stanley. *Emigration and Disenchantment* (cited above as item 532), 114.
    Provides a brief historical overview, focusing on the causes of the failure of the colony.

# XLII(E). WAKEFIELD

Wakefield, Kansas, was founded in the late 1860s as a cooperative community. The cooperative features disappeared fairly quickly, and Wakefield became a conventional town.

*Secondary works*

593. Chapman, William J. "Wakefield Colony." *Kansas State Historical Collections* 10 (1907-8): 485-533.
Describes the project as one which originally intended to be a cooperative, but instead quickly became simply a neighborhood of Britons operating private farms. Illustrated with maps.

594. Curl, Thelma Jean. "Promotional Efforts of the Kansas Pacific and Santa Fe to Settle Kansas." M.A. thesis, University of Kansas, 1960, pp. 171-2.
Provides a brief description of the colony.

\* Shepperson, Wilbur Stanley. *Emigration and Disenchantment* (cited above as item 532), 116.
Provides a brief history of the settlement, focusing principally on the American career of its founder, the Rev. Richard Wake.

# XLIII. ENTERPRISE COMMUNITY

The Enterprise Community existed in Long Lane, Missouri, from about 1872 to 1877.

*Secondary work*

\* Grant, H. Roger. "New Communitarianism" (cited above as item 86), 65-6.
Provides a brief overview of the community.

# XLIV. EQUALITY

In the mid-1890s the Brotherhood of the Co-operative Commonwealth, a socialist organization headquartered in Maine and endorsed by the emerging socialist leader Eugene V. Debs, proposed spreading socialism by starting a chain of cooperative or communal colonies. The first goal of the group was to socialize the state of Washington. Equality was the first (and only, if one discounts Harmony) colony to materialize from the scheme. It was founded under the leadership of G.E. Pelton in 1897; the site was his farm near Bellingham, comprising 620 acres. The name of the colony was the title of Edward Bellamy's latest book; the first building on the site was called

Fort Bellamy.    Although the colony attracted cranks and loafers, it was reasonably successful for several years.    In 1904 Alexander Horr arrived, spreading the doctrines proposed by Theodor Hertzka in his novel *Freeland*.    By the end of that year the colony had been renamed "Freeland" and its constitution revised; many anarchists arrived and joined in 1905, and the colony drifted toward anarchy and dissolution by early 1906.    A disastrous fire hastened the end; the last of the property was sold in early 1907.

Some material on the colony is in the American Communities Collection at Syracuse University.

The papers of Harry E.G. Ault, a colony leader and sometime colony periodical publisher, are at the University of Washington library.

Survey works: Curl (item 52), 35; Liefmann (item 125), 22; Okugawa (item 139), 221.


*Community periodicals*

595.   *Industrial Freedom*.    1898-1902.    Weekly/monthly.    Later
       called *Freedom*.

596.   *Young Socialist*.  1899-1902.
       Monthly magazine for children.


*Secondary works about Equality colony*

597.   Albertson, Ralph.    "Brotherhood of the Cooperative
       Commonwealth."    "Survey of Mutualistic Communities in
       America" (cited above as item 27), 415.
       Provides a brief overview of the history and life of the
       community, including the transition to the Freeland
       scheme.

598.   Burn, June.    "Puget Soundings: A Strange Chapter in Puget
       Sound History."    *Puget Sounder*, August 9, 1935, pp. 1,
       7.
       An informal history spiced with anecdotes about the
       colony.

*      Bushee, Frederick A.    "Communistic Societies in the
       United States" (cited above as item 38), 635-7.
       Provides a good, concise account of the history of the

community, including the move to embrace the ideas of Theodor Hertzka, which led to the reorganization and renaming of the colony.

599. Caldwell, Worth W. "Equality Colony." *Sunset* 52 (February, 1924): 27-9.
Provides an excellent overview of the colony's story. Estimates peak membership at 5,000. Illustrated with photographs of old colony buildings and of one former member still living in the area.

\* Federal Writers' Project. *New Washington: A Guide to the Evergreen State* (cited above as item 69), 524.
Characterizes the village of Freeland which survived after the demise of the colony.

600. Halladay, H.W. "Equality Colony: A Brief History Showing Our Objects and Present Condition--Cooperative Colonies Are Not All Failures." *Industrial Freedom*, n.s. no. 9, November 1, 1901, pp. 1, 4.
Details the founding of the Brotherhood of the Cooperative Commonwealth, site selection, the opening and rapid population of the colony, the development of industries there, the government of the colony, and the struggle for good roads and rail service.

601. Hinds, William Alfred. "Brotherhood Co-operative Commonwealth of Equality." *American Communities and Co-operative Colonies* (cited above as item 95), 531-5.
Provides a history of the Brotherhood of the Cooperative Commonwealth; describes the growth of Equality and the division over the ideas of Horr.

\* Hine, Robert V. *Separate but Not Alone: Community on the American Frontier* (cited above as item 99), 226.
Provides a brief sketch of colony history and life.

\* Holbrook, Stewart H. *Far Corner* (cited above as item 101), 149-51.
Describes the optimistic beginnings of the colony, its problems, especially those with freeloaders, and its decline.

602. LeWarne, Charles Pierce. "Equality Colony: The Plan to Socialize a State." "Communitarian Experiments in Western Washington, 1885-1915" (cited above as item

122), 127-267.

The most complete history of the colony available. Extensively documented, including references to local and specialized materials not cited here.

603. ———. "Equality Colony: The Plan to Socialize a State." *Utopias on Puget Sound* (cited above as item 124), 55-113.

An abridged version of a chapter from the author's dissertation (item 602). Contains thorough documentation.

604. ———. "Equality Colony: The Plan to Socialize Washington." *Pacific Northwest Quarterly* 59 (July, 1968): 137-46.

Provides an overview history of the Brotherhood of the Cooperative Commonwealth and sketches the history of the colony from early planning through the end. Meticulously documented, with references to many local and specialized publications not cited here. Illustrated with photographs.

* Meany, Edmond S. *History of the State of Washington* (cited above as item 129), 324.

A brief note focusing primarily on the demise of the colony.

605. Oved, Yaacov. "Equality." *Two Hundred Years of American Communes* (cited above as item 142), 262-7.

Describes the founding and development of the colony, problems in its relations with the BCC, and its conflicts and decline.

606. Solis, Miguel J. "Equality." *American Utopias* (cited above as item 20), 49.

Contains a brief description of the colony plus two bibliographical entries.

607. Tyner, Paul. "Under the Rose: 'Bellamy Colonies.'" *Arena* 21 (April, 1899): 528-9.

Argues that "Bellamy colonies," such as Equality, founded in response to Edward Bellamy's ideas, don't reflect Bellamy's actual thinking.

608. Wooster, Ernest S. "Brotherhood Co-operative Community of Equality." *Communities of the Past and Present* (cited above as item 175), 47-9.

Sketches the history of the colony; reproduces statements former members made concerning problems in the group.

## *Works on the Freeland/Hertzka phase of the colony*

609. Bliss, W.D.P. "Hertzka, Theodore." *New Encyclopedia of Social Reform* (cited above as item 35), 571.
Provides a brief biographical sketch of Hertzka, with passing reference to the colony.

610. Fogarty, Robert S. "Horr, Alexander." *Dictionary of American Communal and Utopian History* (cited above as item 76), 53-4.
Biographical dictionary entry.

611. "Freeland Colony Scheme." *All the Year Round* 75 (July 21, 1894): 65-9.
Tells of the expedition to establish Freeland in Africa, but notes the fact that all of the suitable land in Kenya is occupied, and in any event has less than fertile soil. Concludes, therefore, that the project is unlikely to succeed.

612. *"Freiland."* *Nation* 50 (1890): 323-4.
A review of Hertzka's new book; the review finds the town unrealistic and lacking common sense.

613. Gray, Donald J., and Allan H. Orrick. "Hertzka: Freeland." *Designs of Famous Utopias.* New York: Holt, Rinehart and Winston, 1959, pp. 31-41.
Reproduces key excerpts from Hertzka's original book.

614. Guempel, C. Godfrey. "Possible Solution of the Social Question." *Westminster Review* 138 (1892): 270-85.
Provides an outline of Hertzka's ideas, quoting frequently from his first Freeland book (item 617). Describes the current effort to establish an actual Freeland colony.

615. Hertzka, Theodor. *Eine Reise Nach Freiland.* Leipzig: Philipp Reclam jun., [1893].
Hertzka's second utopian work on his mythical Freeland; these books were the inspiration for the commune. In German.

616. ———. *Freeland: A Social Anticipation.* London: Chatto and Windus, 1891; New York: Appleton, 1891.
English translation of Hertzka's first Freeland romance (item 617).

617. ———. *Freiland: Ein Sociales Zukunftsbild.* Leipzig: Duncker and Humblot, 1890. 677 pp.
The first of Hertzka's Freeland utopian novels. Describes a society formed by European communitarians in East Africa in which self-governing production associations are formed by workers and members receive shares of profits according to their respective contributions. In German.

618. ———. *Trip to Freeland.* Bow, Washington: Freeland Colony, [1905].
The colony's version of Hertzka's Freeland writings.

619. ———. *Visit to Freeland, or, The New Paradise Regained.* London: W. Reeves, 1894.
The English translation of the second of Hertzka's Freeland books (item 615).

*      Hertzler, Joyce Oramel. *History of Utopian Thought* (cited above as item 93), 236-44.
Recounts the basic plot of Hertzka's *Freeland* (items 615 and 616, above), giving the story of the settlement of Freeland and the fundamental laws governing the utopia. Also tells of the sensation which arose in response to the publication, in 1890, of the first *Freeland* book, resulting in the creation of nearly 1000 local Freeland societies in Austria and Germany, as well as an ill-fated attempt to form a Freeland colony in British East Africa in 1893.

620. Horr, Alexander. *Fabian Anarchism: A Fragmentary Exposition of Mutualism, Communism and Freeland.* San Francisco: Freeland Printing and Publishing Co., 1911. 30 pp.

621. ———. *Freeland Movement.* New York: Freeland Printing, 1904. 14 pp.

622. Jenks, Jeremiah W. *"Freiland." Political Science Quarterly* 5 (1890): 706-8.
Review of Hertzka's first book. Concludes that it is not a good novel, and that Hertzka's reformist views

reflect too optimistic a view of human nature.

623. Negley, Glenn, and J. Max Patrick, eds. "Freeland."
    *Quest for Utopia: An Anthology of Imaginary Societies*
    (cited above as item 136), 108-35.
    Provides an appraisal of Hertzka's philosophy and an
    account of the great interest it generated at the time it
    was published; reproduces an excerpt from Hertzka's
    Freeland writings.

624. Salmon, Edward. "Side-Lights on Socialism: Experiments
    by Colonisation." *Fortnightly Review* 63 (1895): 260-6.
    An exposition of Hertzka's ideas, along with an account
    of the expedition which went to Africa, unsuccessfully, to
    select a site for the acting out of the book. Wishes the
    experimenters well, but concludes that their chances for
    success are small.

625. "Sociology, Politics, Voyages and Travels." *Westminster
    Review* 136 (1891): 442-3.
    A review of Hertzka's first book. Provides a synopsis
    of the novel, emphasizing the individualism which is
    central to the scheme. Passes no judgment on the book,
    but provides a brief, cogent summary of its principal
    ideas.

626. Udny, Ernest. *Dr. Hertzka's Freeland Colony.* *The
    Freeland Colony.* (Co-operation in East Africa.)
    Preface by Theodor Hertzka. Philadelphia: American
    Freeland Association, 1894.

627. Urban, Sylvanus. "Socialistic Paradise." *Gentlemen's
    Magazine* 272 (January, 1892): 108.
    Reviews Hertzka's first book and describes the attempt
    now under way to make the theory a reality. Wishes the
    experimenters well, but argues that all will not go as well
    for them as things do in the book.

### Works on the Brotherhood of the Cooperative Commonwealth

The Brotherhood of the Cooperative Commonwealth was
organized in 1894; it was headquartered in Maine. The aim was
grand: all socialists should be united into a single brotherhood,
and that brotherhood should found colonies of socialists. The

plan called for the movement to focus on a single state until the state had become the nation's first socialist outpost. Washington state was chosen for the beginning of the effort, and Equality was thus established. Equality survived for several years, although little was heard of the Brotherhood after 1898.

Survey work: Curl (item 52), 34-5.

628. Baker, Ray S. "Debs Cooperative Commonwealth." *Outlook* 56 (July 3, 1897): 538-40.
Describes the new plan by Eugene V. Debs to form colonies and take over the government of one or more states.

629. Bliss, W.D.P. "Brotherhood of the Cooperative Commonwealth." *New Encyclopedia of Social Reform* (cited above as item 35), 133.
Provides a brief sketch of the movement.

630. Brommel, Bernard J. "Debs's Cooperative Commonwealth Plan for Workers." *Labor History* 12 (Fall, 1971), 560-9.
Describes the devisiveness of the Debs colonization plan among socialists and unionists. Argues that Debs's failure to follow through on his plan kept the movement from being successful. Documented with contemporary newspaper articles and union publications not cited here.

631. "By-Laws Governing Colonies of the B.C.C." *Industrial Freedom*, June 25, 1898, p. 4.
Reproduces the thirty articles of bylaws, which emphasized membership requirements, finances, and the time-check system for compensating workers.

632. Fogarty, Robert S. "Gronlund, Laurence," and "Lermond, Norman Wallace." *Dictionary of American Communal and Utopian History* (cited above as item 76), 43-4, 68-9.
Biographical dictionary entry.

633. Fried, Albert. *Socialism in America* (cited above as item 78), 256-60.
Discusses the life and works of Laurence Gronlund and his book, *Co-operative Commonwealth* (item 635).

634. Gemorah, Solomon. "Laurence Gronlund—Utopian or Reformer? *Science and Society* (Fall-Winter, 1969) 33:

446-58.
Provides a biographical sketch of Gronlund and outlines his ideas about the cooperative commonwealth.

635. Gronlund, Laurence. *Co-operative Commonwealth.* Boston: Lee and Shepard, 1884.
Something of a programmatic manifesto depicting a glorious future for communitarian socialism and answering some typical objections to this kind of idealism. Discusses democracy, sexual equality, the administration of justice, education, moral behavior, and the like in a communal society of the future. Led directly to the founding of the Brotherhood of the Co-operative Commonwealth; also influenced other communitarian socialists.

636. ———. "Our Destiny." *Nationalist* 2 (1890): issues 4-6 (special section, paginated separately at the end of each issue) and issues 7-8, pp. 239-62 and 305-28; and 3 (1890): issues 1-2, pp. 55-72 and 123-44.
A series setting forth Gronlund's basic ideas for the cooperative commonwealth movement. Focuses on the moral foundations of the movement.

637. Kent, Alexander. "Brotherhood of the Cooperative Commonwealth." "Cooperative Communities in the United States" (cited above as item 117), 617-8.
Provides a brief characterization of the goals of the Brotherhood and tells of the founding of Equality, providing a brief overview of the colony and its members.

638. McInerney, Peter. "Gronlund, Laurence." *American Reformers* (cited above as item 172), 383-4.
Summarizes the theories presented by Gronlund in *Co-operative Commonwealth* and provides a sketch of his life.

639. Oved, Yaacov. "Settlement Policy of the Socialist Parties." *Two Hundred Years of American Communes* (cited above as item 142), 258-62.
Provides an overview history of the BCC, the Social Democracy of America, and their merger, generally covering the years 1895 through 1898.

640. Pelten [sic; should be "Pelton"], G.E. "Historical Sketch of B.C.C." *Industrial Freedom*, November 12, 1898,

supplement.
Describes the organization of the Brotherhood, the search for a colony site, and the purchase and financing of the site of Equality.

641. Quint, Howard H. "Communitarians' Last Stand." *Forging of American Socialism* (cited above as item 148), 280-318.
Describes the controversy among socialists over communes generally and the Brotherhood plan specifically.

642. "Unsound Cooperative Scheme." *Outlook* 56 (July 3, 1897), 527-8.
Editorial arguing that the Debs Cooperative Commonwealth plan will not work.

643. Ware, Norman J. "Cooperation." *Labor Movement in the United States, 1860-1895: A Study in Democracy.* New York: D. Appleton and Co., 1929, pp. 320-33.
This chapter focuses on cooperative communities and cooperative stores within the labor movement, and particularly those of the Knights of Labor.

# XLV. ESOTERIC FRATERNITY

Hiram Erastus Butler founded this organization in the 1870s in Boston. After several trips to India he proposed a method of synthesizing Eastern and Western thought, and promoted his ideas as a scientific approach to life. He soon published *Solar Biology*, his magnum opus. Told by "the spirit" to move to California in the late 1880s, the movement purchased 500 acres near Applegate and operated businesses and a successful publishing operation. At its peak the movement claimed 2,000 members worldwide, but only a few lived at the California commune. The movement preached celibacy and promised immortality, or, failing that, resurrection. When Butler died in 1916, the movement owned 11 buildings, including a 26-room main house. After years of stagnation, a new member moved in around 1971. The other resident members were mainly aged. In 1973, one of the aged members was shot to death while working in the community garden; the crime went unsolved. Some older members accused the new, younger member of taking over the property for his own benefit.
Some material on the community is in the American

Communities Collection at Syracuse University.

*Community periodical*

644. *Esoteric: A Magazine of Practical Esoteric Thought.*
Monthly. 1887-? At times entitled *Esoteric Christian.*

*Primary works*

The works in this section are located at the Institute for
the Study of American Religion.

645. *Bible Review.* Applegate, California: Esoteric Fraternity.
Seventeen volumes.
On growth and spiritual regeneration.

646. *Chimaera.* Applegate, California: Esoteric Fraternity, n.d.
Advises that one should not be deceived by carnal
desires.

647. *Monkey Glands or Conservation.* Applegate, California:
Esoteric Fraternity, n.d.
On retaining bodily fluids.

648. *Planetary Influences.* Applegate, California: Esoteric
Fraternity, n.d.

649. *Practical Methods to Insure Success.* Applegate,
California: Esoteric Fraternity, n.d.
Instructions for those starting out on the esoteric path.

650. *Remission of Sins.* Applegate, California: Esoteric
Fraternity, n.d.
On the law of karma.

651. *Revised Esoteric.* Applegate, California: Esoteric
Publishing Co., 1895.
Revised, abridged version of the first four volumes of
*Esoteric.*

652. *Sweets.* Applegate, California: Esoteric Fraternity, n.d.
Poems and other inspirational writings.

Works by community leaders

653. Butler, Hiram Erastus. *Everlasting Covenant.* Applegate,
California: Esoteric Fraternity, n.d.
A new interpretation of the Ten Commandments.

654. ———. *Goal of Life, or Science and Revelation.*
Applegate, California: Esoteric Fraternity, 1908.
A description of pathways for achieving blessings in
life.

655. ———. *Narrow Way of Attainment.* Applegate, California: Esoteric Fraternity, n.d.
Lectures providing instructions for high spiritual
attainment.

656. ———. *Purpose in the Creation of the World.* Applegate, California: Esoteric Fraternity, n.d.
A discussion of the purpose of the creation, as revealed
by the Bible and nature.

657. ———. *Seven Creative Principles.* Applegate, California:
Esoteric Fraternity, 1950.
A series of lectures on natural principles which affect
human beings. Reprint.

658. ———. *Solar Biology.* Boston: Esoteric Publishing Co.,
1887.
A treatise on the influence of the sun and planets on
persons, along with specific advice for living.

659. ———. *Special Instructions for Women.* Applegate, California: Esoteric Fraternity, 1942.
Discusses natural forces and one's role in relation to
them.

660. ———. *Useful Instructions for a Successful Life.*
Applegate, California: Esoteric Fraternity, n.d.
A sequel to *Practical Methods to Insure Success* (item
649).

661. ———. *Way of Holiness.* Applegate, California: Esoteric
Fraternity, n.d.

662. Penn, Enoch. *Endless Life.* Applegate, California: Esoteric
Publishing Co., 1930. 128 pp.

On true immortality.

663. ———. *Order of Melchisedek.* Applegate, California: Esoteric Fraternity, 1926. Fourth edition, 1961.
A description of the esoteric path to priesthood in this order, of which Jesus was reportedly high priest.

*Secondary works*

664. Bronstein, Phil. "Mystical Society Has Become a Mystery." San Francisco *Sunday Examiner and Chronicle*, March 8, 1981, pp. 1B, 8B.
Tells of criminal acts, conspiracies, and lawsuits related to the Esoteric Fraternity. Also contains some useful historical information.

665. Hillinger, Charles. "Sex Is a No-No in This Fraternity." Los Angeles *Times*, August 13, 1980, pp. 3, 23. Reprinted in other newspapers via Los Angeles Times News Service.
An interview with Fred Peterson, a relatively new member of the Fraternity. Discusses the founding and early history of the movement under Butler's leadership. Illustrated with pictures of Peterson and the group's cemetery.

666. Kerning, J. *Esoteric Education.* Applegate, California: Esoteric Fraternity, n.d.

667. Melton, J. Gordon. "Esoteric Fraternity." *Encyclopedia of American Religions* (cited above as item 130), 499. Provides a brief historical sketch of the organization.

# XLVI. ESPERANZA

This colony was organized in late 1877 at Urbana, Kansas; its chief leader was N.T. Romaine. Its members mainly came from an existing colony at Buffalo, Missouri. It lasted less than a year.

Survey works: Albertson (item 27), p. 419; Hinds (item 94), 155; Okugawa (item 139), 207-8.

### Community periodical

668.  *Star of Hope*. 1878. Monthly.

### Secondary works

669.  Curl, H.G.    "Left Hand Pitch."    Chanute (Kansas) *Tribune*,
      November 27, 1953.
      A brief feature article on the communal site, based on
      other newspaper reports on the colonies.

670.  Douthit, Katrina S. Adams.    "Shortlived Experiment:
      Esperanza Colony at Urbana."    *Kanhistique* 6 (August,
      1980): 5.
      Describes the origins and founding of the colony.

671.  Graves, William Whites.    "Communism in Neosho County."
      *History of Neosho County*.    St. Paul, Kansas: Journal
      Press, 1949, v. I, pp. 513-22.
      Tells the story of the founding and development of the
      community through the departure of the Romaine and
      other leaders.

672.  ———.    "Communist Leaders Once   Started   Colony   for
      Followers  in  Urbana."    Chanute  (Kansas)  *Tribune*,
      January 5, 1946.
      A brief account of the colony's history drawn from
      Graves's research on the history of Neosho County.

673.  Weeks, Vickie D.    "Esperanza."    *Late Nineteenth Century
      Kansas Utopian Communities* (cited above as item 169),
      61-4.
      Sketches the history of the community; tells of its goals
      (especially that of showing others the value of communal
      living); notes that little is known of the community's
      dissolution.

# XLVII. THE FARM (WEST NEWBURY,
# MASSACHUSETTS)

Ralph and Hazel Albertson, he the former principal member
of the Christian Commonwealth Colony, purchased an old house

and small acreage in 1909. The small commune became a center for visiting intellectuals; both Walter Lippman and Lincoln Steffens were among the frequent visitors. Never large or prosperous, the project lasted for at least three generations.

## Secondary work

674. Davis, Frances. *Fearful Innocence.* Kent, Ohio: Kent State University Press, 1981. 253 pp.
Tells the story of Albertson's founding of the farm a few years after the demise of the Christian Commonwealth Colony. As of 1981, a third generation was keeping the place alive.

# XLVIII. THE FARM SECURITY ADMINISTRATION (FSA) FARMS

During the Depression the federal government became involved in promoting subsistence farming as a way of coping with hard times. In several cases the government promoted cooperative group farming settlements; at least 25 such more or less communitarian projects were organized between 1937 and 1939 by the Farm Security Administration as a means of providing a realistic chance of survival through agriculture to indigent farmers. These farms were part of a larger effort on the part of a variety of New Deal agencies (including the FSA's predecessor, the Resettlement Administration) to establish cooperative agricultural and industrial villages, resulting in nearly a hundred such settlements.

## Secondary works

675. Baldwin, Sidney. *Poverty and Politics: The Rise and Decline of the Farm Security Administration.* Chapel Hill: University of North Carolina Press, 1968. 438 pp.
Provides a detailed history of the FSA from the beginning of the New Deal through the stormy demise of the agency and after. Extensively documented with footnotes, but contains no separate bibliography.

676. Conkin, Paul. *Tomorrow a New World: The New Deal*

*Community Program*.    Ithaca: Cornell University Press, 1959. 350 pp.
A monograph on New Deal community building, including FSA and Resettlement Administration projects in building communities and cooperatives.    An appendix lists and categorizes all of the New Deal communities, both agricultural and industrial.

\*      Daniels, Jonathan.    *Southerner Discovers the South* (cited above as item 477), 142-8.
Provides an account of the author's visit to Dyess Colony in Arkansas, which he contends has provided no answers to rural poverty despite its nice appearance.

677.   Eaton, Joseph W.    "Co-operative Farms of the Farm Security Administration."    *Exploring Tomorrow's Agriculture* (cited above as item 59), 63-191.
Summarizes the philosophy of the FSA Farms project and provides specific data on the various settlements, including demographics, management arrangements, and work life.

\*      Gladstone, Arthur.    "Cooperative Communities Today II" (cited above as item 82), 15.
Describes the situation, in 1955, of the Red Banks Mutual Association, the only FSA farm which survived the government liquidation of the project.    It was founded in 1938 in Maxton, North Carolina.    As of April, 1955, it had 70 members, 40 of whom were children.

678.   Glick, Philip M.    "Federal Subsistence Homesteads Program."    *Yale Law Journal* 44 (1935): 1324-79.
Describes the role of the federal government in creating subsistence homestead communities.    Discusses problems which the program encountered.

679.   Holley, Donald.    "Negro in the New Deal Resettlement Program."    *Agricultural History* 45 (July, 1971): 179-93.
Finds that the FSA provided hope and help to blacks in its programs, even though it had to move cautiously in the South.

680.   ———.    "Old and New Worlds in the New Deal Resettlement Program: Two Louisiana Projects."    *Louisiana History* 11 (Spring, 1970): 137-65.
Contrasts Crew Lake, a Resettlement Administration/FSA

project with individual ownership (but also with some cooperative features) with Terrebone, a more thoroughly collective farming project. Finds that both provided uplift to poor tenant farmers.

681. ———. "Trouble in Paradise: Dyess Colony and Arkansas Politics." *Arkansas Historical Quarterly* 32 (Autumn, 1973): 203-216.
Sketches the history of the colony, focusing on the conflicts it had with many Arkansas politicians.

682. ———. *Uncle Sam's Farmers: The New Deal Communities in the Lower Mississippi Valley.* Champaign: University of Illinois Press, 1975. 312 pp.
Provides a history of New Deal resettlement communities (with varying levels of cooperative features) in Arkansas, Louisiana, and Mississippi. An appendix lists the communities in the three states. A bibliographic essay lists many specialized resources not cited here.

683. Infield, Henrik. "F.S.A. Cooperative Corporation Farms." *Cooperative Communities at Work* (cited above as item 105), 63-84.
Provides statement of the objectives of the project, membership in the settlements, special problems associated with government projects, and other problems, such as outbreaks of disease. A useful table of basic data on the settlements is located on p. 65.

684. Infield, Henrick F., and Joseph B. Maier, eds. "FSA Cooperative Farms." *Cooperative Group Living* (cited above as item 109), 5-12.
Provides information on the scope of the project, demographics, locations of settlements, work agreements, and organizational structures of settlements, as well as on opposition to the project and its subsequent liquidation by Congress in 1943. Includes a list of the 25 farms.

685. Lord, Russell, and Paul H. Johnstone, eds. *A Place on Earth: A Critical Appraisal of Subsistence Homesteads.* Washington: Bureau of Agricultural Economics, United States Department of Agriculture, 1942. 202 pp.
A study of nine of the subsistence homestead communities organized by the government. Provides a history of various such projects, including some run by the government and some operated by private and

charitable groups. Finds that the government projects had serious shortcomings due to the larger economic ills of the society during the Depression and due to the desire of many participants for a more private, less restrictive way of life.

686. Maddox, James G.    "Farm Security Administration."    Ph.D. dissertation, Harvard University, 1950.

687. Mehlman, Michael Harris.    "Resettlement Administration and the Problems of Tenant Farmers in Arkansas, 1935-1936."    Ph.D. dissertation, New York University, 1970. 311 pp.

688. Sternsher, Bernard.    *Rexford Tugwell and the New Deal.* New Brunswick, N.J.: Rutgers University Press, 1964. Provides a detailed examination of Tugwell's role in the New Deal, including his work as head of the Resettlement Administration.

689. Tugwell, Rexford G.    "Cooperation and Resettlement." *Current History* 45 (February, 1937): 71-6. Discusses various types of agricultural cooperation; describes the FSA communities, the attack on them by Congress, and the attempts of some of them to survive without governmental backing. A government administrator, Tugwell was a major proponent of the communities.

690. ———.    "Resettlement Idea."    *Agricultural History* 33 (October, 1959): 159-64. Describes the goals of the Resettlement Administration, the problems it experienced, and the hope for helping poor people which underlay it.

691. Warner, George A.    *Greenbelt: The Cooperative Community.* New York: Exposition Press, 1954. 232 pp. A history of Greenbelt, Maryland, a Resettlement Administration community, by a resident and official of it.

692. Wilson, M.L.    "Place of Subsistence Homesteads in Our National Economy."    *Journal of Farm Economics* 16 (January, 1934): 73-84.    Followed (pp. 84-7) by further comments by Carle C. Zimmerman. Wilson describes the potential of the new subsistence homesteads program to improve the lives of some of the

rural poor. Zimmerman sees growth of subsistence homesteads as likely in the near future.

# XLIX. FATHER DIVINE'S PEACE MISSION MOVEMENT

Father Divine is generally supposed to have originally been known as George Baker, who was preaching a distinctive gospel in Georgia by 1913 and who came to local prominence in Sayville, New York, in 1919. Major fame came with a 1931 trial for breach of the peace; the harsh judge died unexpectedly three days after sentencing Divine, and Divine commented, "I hated to do it." In depression Harlem, the Peace Mission Movement provided religion and social services to poor members of all races. Its best known activities were munificent banquets, presided over by Father Divine. Members were celibate and lived communally in dormitories called "heavens." After Father Divine's death in 1965, his widow, Mother Divine, assumed the leadership of the movement.

The major New York newspapers covered Father Divine, for the most part unfavorably, for years. *Time* and *Newsweek* also provided numerous articles on the movement. The black press in several major cities, including Baltimore, New York, Chicago, and Pittsburgh, provided major coverage over many years.

### Community periodicals

693. *New Day*. 1936-. Weekly.

694. *New York News*. Weekly newspaper.

695. *Spoken Word*. 1934-7. Semiweekly/weekly.

696. *World Herald*. Semiweekly.

### Primary works

697. *Rosebuds', Lily-buds', Crusaders' Creeds*. No imprint.
The Rosebuds were the female youth group; the Crusaders, the male youth group; and the Lily-buds, the senior female group. These creeds have members promise

to be pure in thought and deed; the booklet is a handbook of right thinking and behavior. At the Institute for the Study of American Religion.

698. *Father Divine's Universal Peace Mission Movement: Some of Its Tenets.* Pamphlet, no imprint. 4 pp.
Provides a concise statement of the beliefs of the movement. At the Institute for the Study of American Religion.

## Works by community leaders

699. [Divine, Father.] *Father Divine's Sermon Before the Verdict at Mineola, Long Island, New York.* Philadelphia: New Day Publishing Co., [1932]. 32 pp. Father Divine discusses his beliefs and goals.

700. ———. "Realness of God, to you-wards." *Afro-American Religious History: A Documentary Witness.* Edited by Milton C. Sernett. Durham, N.C.: Duke University Press, 1985, 404-12.
Reproduces a 1936 speech by Father Divine from the *New Day*; provides a testimony of members' faith in the divinity and good works of Father Divine.

701. Divine, Mrs. M.J. (Mother Divine). *Peace Mission Movement.* Philadelphia: Imperial Press, 1982. 191 pp. An official explanation of the structure, beliefs, and practices of the movement. Reproduces several documents important to the history of the movement. Illustrated with photographs.

## Secondary works

702. Alexander, Jack. "All Father's Chillun Got Heavens." *Saturday Evening Post* 212 (November 18, 1939): 8-9, 64, 66, 69-70, 72, 75.
An unusually thorough journalistic examination of Father Divine and his followers, real estate purchases, finances, banquets, language, businesses, and claims to divinity. Illustrated with photographs.

703. Bach, Marcus. "Father Divine." *Strange Sects and Curious Cults* (cited above as item 29), 125-39.

Characterizes the movement's property holdings, banquets, and members, focusing especially on the attitudes of followers toward Father Divine.

704. ———. "Kingdoms of Father Divine." *They Have Found a Faith*. Indianapolis: Bobbs-Merrill, 1946, pp. 162-88.
Provides a first-person account of encounters with Father Divine.

705. Barnes, R.P. "'Blessings Flowing Free': The Father Divine Peace Mission Movement in Harlem, New York City, 1932-1941." D.Phil. dissertation, University of York (U.K.), 1979.
Finds that the group's teachings did not support the movement's venture into pressure group politics, and that the move into politics thus helped lead to the group's decline. Not seen.

706. Bender, Lauretta, and M.A. Spaulding. "Behavior Problems in Children from the Homes of Followers of Father Divine." *Journal of Nervous and Mental Diseases* 91 (April, 1940): 460-72.
Provides some background on Father Divine plus discussions of several case studies in which parents had diverted their attention to Father Divine and neglected their children. There was no single reaction to the situation shared by all the children, the authors find.

707. Bender, Lauretta, and Zuleika Yarrell. "Psychoses Among Followers of Father Divine." *Journal of Nervous and Mental Diseases* 87 (1938): 419-49.
Provides general information on Father Divine, plus case histories of some of his followers who ended up in mental hospitals. Authors conclude that the participation of persons in the movement contributed to their problems, but blame other factors, such as their race, equally, finally determining that the teaching of the movement seemed to precipitate mental problems in only part of the cases.

708. Boaz, Ruth. "My Thirty Years with Father Divine." *Ebony* 20 (May, 1965): 88-98.
Describes the author's personal odyssey in the movement, emphasizing Father Divine's sexual transgressions, amassing of money donated by members, and final physical deterioration. Illustrated with

photographs.

709. Bowden, Henry Warner. "Divine, Father." *Dictionary of American Religious Biography.* Westport, Connecticut: Greenwood, 1977, pp. 128-9.
Biographical dictionary entry.

710. Braden, Charles S. *These Also Believe: A Study of Modern American Cults and Minority Religious Movements.* New York: Macmillan, 1949, pp. 1-77.
Provides a fair and perceptive account of the movement, covering its history, organization, social ideals, economy, religious ideas, and roots in other movements.

711. Brussel, James A. "Father Divine, Holy Precipitator of Psychosis." *American Journal of Psychiatry* 92 (July, 1935): 215-223.
Provides a general description of the movement and presents three case studies of members who were mentally ill, concluding that the weak seek Father Divine for protection and that their association with him aggravates their problems, whereas they could have been cured easily with standard psychiatric treatment.

712. Buehrer, Edwin T. "Divine's Prestige Wanes as Disciples Protest." *Christian Century* 54 (January 6, 1937): 30.
Notes that little is known about the finances of the Peace Mission movement, and asserts that some disciples are beginning to feel betrayed. Predicts that Father Divine's influence will soon begin to decline.

713. ———. "Father Divine Also Loses Prestige." *Christian Century* 53 (November 18, 1936): 1534.
Father Divine had told his followers not to vote in the 1936 general election, and some thought that 50,000 persons might thus stay away from the polls. Since turnout was only 2,000 lower than expected, author concludes that Father Divine's influence is waning.

714. ———. "Harlem's God." *Christian Century* 52 (December 11, 1935): 1590-3.
Contains a description of a visit to a Divinite "Heaven," including one of the movement's famous banquets. An analysis of Father Divine's appeal is ventured: he has sex appeal to women, and he appeals to the desire of all his followers for equality, brotherhood, and material

abundance. Author finds it all "wonderful," as Divinites claim, but also finally "truly tragic."

715. Burnham, Kenneth E. "Father Divine: A Case Study of Charismatic Leadership." Ph.D. dissertation, University of Pennsylvania, 1963. 222 pp.

716. ———. "Father Divine and the Peace Mission." *Black Apostles: Afro-American Clergy Confront the Twentieth Century.* Edited by Randall K. Burkett and Richard Newman. Boston: G.K. Hall, 1978, pp. 25-47.
Describes the origin and growth of the movement (focusing on the mysterious early years), Father Divine's theology and charismatic leadership, and the movement's economic base and social patterns.

717. ———. *God Comes to America: Father Divine and the Peace Mission Movement.* Boston: Lambeth Press, 1979.
Provides a general history of the movement. Gives a summary of the Peace Mission Tenets, pp. 125ff.

718. Calverton, Victor. "Father Divine: Black Kingdom Come." *Where Angels Dared to Tread* (cited above as item 39), 328-43.
Provides basic information on the history and life of the movement, focusing especially on the famous banquets and the distinctive words and phrases used by Father Divine and his followers.

719. Cantril, Hadley. *Psychology of Social Movements.* New York: Wiley, 1941, pp. 123-43.
Argues that the Peace Mission Movement succeeded because it met the perceived needs of its members.

720. Cantril, Hadley, and Muzafer Sherif. "Kingdom of Father Divine." *Journal of Abnormal and Social Psychology* 33 (April, 1938): 147-67.
Discusses Father Divine's banquets, the philosophy of the movement, the diversity of its members, the relations of the movement with the outside world, and possible reasons why persons join, concluding that the movement helps fulfill converts' desires to achieve economic security, give themselves a sense of meaning, raise their social status, and find God.

721. Clark, Elmer T. "Father Divine's Peace Mission." *Small*

*Sects in America* (cited above as item 43), 124-7. Provides a historical sketch emphasizing the legal problems of Father Divine and some of his followers.

722. Crumb, C.B., Jr.    "Father Divine."    *American Speech* 15 (October, 1940): 327.
Provides a list of unusual and conventional pronunciations used by Father Divine.

723. "Cults: A Deity Derepersonifitized."    *Time*, September 17, 1965, p. 41.
Provides a good overview of the movement from a more sympathetic viewpoint than one might expect.

724. Davie, Maurice R.    *Negroes in American Society*.    New York: McGraw-Hill, 1949, pp. 184-5.
Finds that Father Divine's "megalomania" stems from his bitter experiences as a child.

725. Davis, Grady Demus.    "Psychological Investigation of Motivational Needs and Their Gratification in the Father Divine Movement."    Ph.D. dissertation, Boston University, 1953.

726. Denlinger, Sutherland.    "Heaven Is in Harlem."    *Forum* 95 (April, 1936): 211-8.
Provides a sketch of the movement, with emphasis on the early work at Sayville; quotes several members' testimonies to Father Divine's great power.

727. "Divine Judgment."    *Literary Digest* 123 (May 1, 1937): 6-7.
A news story on conflict in the movement, especially focusing on the defection of Faithful Mary.

728. "Election Officials Irk Father Divine Cultists."    *Christian Century* 52 (August 14, 1935): 1043.
Father Divine's followers have been trying to register to vote under their movement names, such as "Wonderful Wisdom," "Truth Delight," and "Pearly Rest." This article reports on their decision to seek a writ of mandamus to force the New York Board of Elections to register them thus.

729. Erickson, Keith V.    "Black Messiah: The Father Divine Peace Mission Movement."    *Quarterly Journal of Speech*

63 (December, 1977): 428-38.

Examines Father Divine's rhetoric and its ability to convince thousands that he was God. Based primarily on published accounts of Father Divine's pronouncements, especially in the *New Day*.

730. Faithful Mary (Mary Rozier). *God, He's Just a Natural Man*. New York: Gailliard Press, 1937. 112 pp.

Faithful Mary, for some years Father Divine's chief assistant, defected from the movement in 1936 and wrote this bitter expose. However, she recanted and rejoined the movement the next year; this account, written during her absence, is regarded as of dubious reliability. Not seen.

731. Faris, Robert E.L. "Movement of Father Divine." *Social Disorganization* (cited above as item 66), 419-24 (second edition, pp. 584-9).

Finds that the success of the movement came from Father Divine's raising of his followers' self-esteem and his provision for them of a sense of close association with God.

732. "Father Divine." *Commonwealth* 26 (May 7, 1937): 46.

Recounts alleged abuses (e.g., child labor) found in the Peace Mission Movement.

733. "Father Divine, Cult Leader, Dies; Disciples Considered Him God." New York *Times*, September 11, 1965, pp. 1, 12. Obituary.

Describes Father Divine and the movement; provides a summary of theories about Divine's actual identity. Reproduces several examples of Divine's rhetoric. Illustrated with photographs of two of the movement's mansions and of Father and Mother Divine.

734. "Father Divine Enters Politics." *Christian Century* 53 (October 7, 1936): 1334.

A news item on the founding of the International Righteous Government movement, led by Father Divine.

735. "'Father' Divine in Court Again." *Christian Century* 52 (March 13, 1935): 346.

Brief note indicating that Father Divine is the object of a legal proceeding; the situation is not specified.

736. "Father Divine Purchases 'The Promised Land.'" *Christian Century* 53 (April 15, 1936): 579.
Reports Father Divine's purchase of a farm of over 500 acres, including a hotel. The farm is to produce food for the Harlem "Heavens."

737. "Father Divine's Flock Stays Home When He Issues Order Not to Vote." New York *Times*, November 4, 1936, p. 12.
Describes Father Divine's plan to keep his followers from the polls on the grounds that no party has accepted his plan for righteous government.

738. Fauset, Arthur Huff. *Black Gods of the Metropolis.* Philadelphia: University of Pennsylvania Press, 1944, pp. 52-67.
Provides an extended portrait of a member, known as Sing Happy; tells of origins of the movement, as well as its organization, membership, finances, publications, beliefs, worship practices, and lifestyle regulations.

739. Fischer, Miles Mark. "Organized Religion and the Cults." *Afro-American Religious History: A Documentary Witness* (cited above as item 700), 390-8. Originally published in *Crisis* 44 (January, 1937): 8-10, 29-30.
Argues that several important black movements, including that of Father Divine, were of much greater significance than was generally assumed in the 1930s, and suggests that Father Divine's movement be included in the next (1936) American religious census. Appears to have been written in 1935.

740. Flynn, John T. "Other People's Money." *New Republic* 91 (May 26, 1937): 73-4.
Finds that Father Divine is making major progress toward general respectability.

741. Fogarty, Robert S. "Divine, Father." *Dictionary of American Communal and Utopian History* (cited above as item 76), 31-2.
Biographical dictionary entry.

742. Frazier, E. Franklin. *Negro Church in America.* New York: Schocken, 1974, pp. 57-61.
Provides a survey of the movement, focusing on the centrality of the person of Father Divine to the movement

and the absence of racial prejudice in it.

743 Freedman, Alix M. "His Widow Keeps Flickering Flame of Father Divine." *Wall Street Journal*, May 8, 1985, pp. 1, 25.

A journalist's survey of the dwindling movement led by Mother Divine, touching on its few remaining elements of more glorious times.

744. Garrison, W.E. "Security at Any Price." *Christian Century* 70 (November 11, 1953): 1297-8.

Reviews Harris's book on Father Divine (item 746), generally deprecating the movement in the process.

745. Harkness, Georgia. "Father Divine's Righteous Government." *Christian Century* 82 (October 13, 1965): 1259-61.

A reflection on the occasion of the death of Father Divine. Contains recollections of the author's visit to a Father Divine rally and banquet in 1936; concludes that the movement has most of the elements of Christianity and of other religions.

746. Harris, Sara. *Father Divine*. New York: Macmillan, 1971. 377 pp. Originally published in 1953.

One of the earliest substantial books on the movement, based on the author's personal observations and interviews with Father Divine in the early 1950s. Offers an intimate view of the movement, but tends toward sarcasm and sensationalism.

747. Hoshor, John. *God in a Rolls Royce: The Rise of Father Divine: Madman, Menace, or Messiah*. New York: Hillman-Curl, Inc., 1936.

A somewhat anecdotal and racially biased history of Father Divine and the Peace Mission Movement. Contains good basic information, including a list of Peace Mission operational sites (47 in New York state, 110 elsewhere). Illustrated. No footnotes or other documentation provided.

748. Howell, Clarence. "Father Divine: Another View." *Christian Century* 53 (October 7, 1936): 1332-3.

A letter to the editor protesting the article of Frank S. Mead (item 771, below), arguing that Father Divine does far more good than harm.

749. Howland, Arthur H. "Talks with Father Divine." *Everyday Psychology and Inspiration* 1 (December, 1934, and January, 1935): 15, 36, 38.

750. Jamison, A. Leland. "Religions on the Christian Perimeter." *Shaping of American Religion.* Edited by James W. Smith and A. Leland Jamison. Princeton: Princeton University Press, 1961, pp. 162-231; see especially pp. 228-9.
Analyzes Father Divine's movement as unusual in that it is an indigenous black religious movement and one which emphasizes the here and now rather than pie in the sky. Concludes that it must meet needs which other American religions fail to satisfy.

\*    Jones, Raymond Julius. *Comparative Study of Religious Cult Behavior among Negroes with Special Reference to Emotional Group Conditioning Factors* (cited above as item 114), 19-20, 36-7, and *passim.*
Emphasizes the movement's concern for the material well-being of its members; describes Father Divine's special appeal to the poor.

751. Kelley, Hubert. "Heaven Inc." *American Magazine* 121 (January, 1936): 40-1, 106-8.
A sketch of the movement based in part on the author's personal observations. Illustrated with photographs.

752. Kephart, William M. "Father Divine Movement." *Extraordinary Groups: The Sociology of Unconventional Life-Styles.* New York: St. Martin's Press, 1976 (second edition, 1982), 107-58 (second edition, pp. 243-82).
Provides a lucid overview of the movement's history and practices and an analysis of the role of Father Divine in it.

753. Lanyon, Walter C. *Behold the Man!.* London: L.N. Fowler, [1933]. 224 pp.
Lanyon was a follower of Father Divine; this and the following titles are expositions of Divine's thought, although explicit references to Father Divine are fairly rare. Some later editions of Lanyon's books omit the explicit references to Father Divine.

754. ———. *Eyes of the Blind.* London: L.N. Fowler,

[1932]. 222 pp.
The final chapter of the book (pp. 205-222) in the original edition describes, sympathetically, Father Divine and his work. That chapter has been deleted from later editions.

755. ———. *Impressions of a Nomad.* New York: T. Gaus' Sons, 1930. 256 pp.

756. ———. *It Is Wonderful.* London: E.K. Reader, [193-?]. 228 pp.

757. ———. *Laughter of God.* London: L.N. Fowler, [1935]. 220 pp.

758. ———. *London Notes and Lectures.* London: L.N. Fowler, [1934]. 214 pp.

759. ———. *Out of the Clouds.* London: L.N. Fowler, [1934]. 256 pp.

760. Larsen, Egon. *Strange Sects and Cults.* New York: Hart, 1971, pp. 55-63.
Provides an overview of the history and practices of the group, based largely on Sara Harris's *Father Divine* (item 746, above).

761. Lawson, Donna. *Brothers and Sisters All Over This Land.* New York: Praeger, 1972, pp. 124-36.
Provides an overview of the Peace Mission Movement.

762. Levick, Lionel. "Father Divine Is God." *Forum* 92 (October, 1934): 217-21.
An eclectic sampling of the movement, expressing ignorance about its size, source of funds, and appeal. Illustrated with drawings.

763. LeWarne, Charles P. "Vendovi Island: Father Divine's 'Peaceful Paradise of the Pacific.'" *Pacific Northwest Quarterly* 75 (January, 1984): 2-12.
Vendovi, a 200-acre island off Bellingham, Washington, was active as a retreat center for the Peace Mission Movement for several years in the 1930s. A year-round staff of movement members lived there communally. This article is the basic account of Vendovi. Illustrated with photographs, a map, and an engraving.

764. Lincoln, C. Eric, and Lawrence H. Mamiya. "Daddy Jones and Father Divine: The Cult as Political Religion." *Religion in Life* 49 (Spring, 1980): 6-23.
   Provides a comparison of the Jim Jones and Father Divine movements, citing similarities and differences.

765. McKay, Claude. "Father Divine's Rebel Angel." *American Mercury* 51 (September, 1940): 73-80.
   Tells the story of the defection and return to the movement of Faithful Mary, Father Divine's second in command.

766. ———. *Harlem, Negro Metropolis.* New York: Dutton, 1940, pp. 32-72.
   Characterizes Father Divine's early work at Sayville, the growth of the movement, the testimonies of his followers, his political power, and the departure and return of Faithful Mary. Speculates on the movement's prospects for the future.

767. ———. "There Goes God! The Story of Father Divine and His Angels." *Nation* 140 (February 6, 1935): 151-3.
   An account of the movement as it was emerging into national prominence, based on personal observations and an interview with Father Divine.

768. McKelway, St. Clair, and A.J. Liebling. "Who Is This King of Glory?" *New Yorker*, June 13, 20, 27, 1936, pp. 21-34, 22-32, and 22-36, respectively.
   A comprehensive look at Father Divine, including a well researched account of his early life, a description of the finances of the movement, and accounts of daily life in the movement, its business empire, and its legal problems. One of the more substantial pieces on the movement.

769. Martin, Walter R. "Reign of Father Divine." *Kingdom of the Cults.* Minneapolis: Bethany Fellowship, 1965, pp. 213-21.
   A debunking overview of the movement written from a strongly evangelical Protestant viewpoint.

770. Mathison, Richard. "Father Divine." *Faiths, Cults and Sects of America: From Atheism to Zen* (cited above as item 127), 235-39.
   Provides a sketch of the movement, focusing on Father Divine's speeches and the movement's feasts and

distinctive terminology.

771.  Mead, Frank S.    "God in Harlem."    *Christian Century* 53
      (August 26, 1936): 1133-5.
      Contains an account of a Father Divine banquet and the
      entertainment it featured, a description of Divine's
      colorful language, and unflattering characterizations of
      Divine and his followers.

772.  Mitchison, Naomi.    "Epiphany of Harlem."    *New Statesman
      and Nation* series 2, volume 9 (June 29, 1935): 961-2.
      An observer's report on a Father Divine banquet.

773.  Moon, Henry Lee.    "Thank You, Father So Sweet."    *New
      Republic* 88 (September 16, 1936): 147-50.
      Finds Father Divine unimpressive, but nevertheless
      firmly in control of the sentiments of his followers.

774.  Moseley, Joel Rufus.    *Manifest Victory*.    New York: Harper
      and Brothers, 1941, pp. 106-9.
      Recounts Moseley's visit with Father Divine when Divine
      was locally a sensation for calling himself "God" while in
      jail in Valdosta, Georgia.    Describes Moseley's later trip
      to visit Father Divine in Harlem, where he was received
      warmly.

775.  "New Mrs. Divine."    *Life* 21 (August 19, 1946): 38.
      Announces the marriage of Father Divine to "Sweet
      Angel" (Edna Ritchings). Illustrated with a photograph.

776.  Ottley, Roi.    *"New World A-Coming": Inside Black America*.
      Boston: Houghton Mifflin, 1943, pp. 82-99.
      Depicts Depression-era Harlem, conveying a good sense
      of the conditions which helped spur the rise of Father
      Divine's movement.    Also provides a sense of the
      atmosphere of the movement, especially in the "heavens."

777.  Parker, Robert Allerton.    *Incredible Messiah: The
      Deification of Father Divine*.    Boston: Little, Brown,
      1937. 323 pp.
      The first major book-length study of Father Divine and
      his movement.    Covers the origins of Father Divine/
      George Baker, the building of the movement, its setting,
      the love feasts, daily life, the content of Father Divine's
      message, the movement's finances, its political activities,
      its legal problems, and the like.    Some of the information

comes from contemporary interviews with persons important to the history of the movement.

778. Pearson, Fred Lamar, Jr., and Joseph Aaron Tomberlin. "John Doe, Alias God: A Note on Father Divine's Georgia Career." *Georgia Historical Quarterly* 60 (Spring, 1976): 43-8.
Traces Father Divine's early career, especially in his gaining of his first substantial following in Valdosta, Georgia, in the early 20th century.

779. "People." *Review of Reviews* 95 (June, 1937): 23-4.
Describes the arrest of Father Divine for assault, which came from a scuffle in front of the main heaven on 115th St.

780. Posten, Tom. "Shepherd of Fantasties." *Saturday Review of Literature* 36 (November 14, 1953): 19.
A generally favorable review of Harris's book on Father Divine (item 746, above).

781. Powell, Oliver G. "Divine and Lung Power." *Forum* 92 (November, 1934): x-xi.
A letter to the editor in response to Levick (item 762, above), trying to explain the appeal of the movement, something about which Levick expressed bewilderment.

782. "Prophet and a Divine Meet." *Life* 35 (September 28, 1953): 103-4, 106.
An account of a meeting of Father Divine and Prophet Jones, leader of a small religious movement in Detroit. Heavily illustrated with photographs.

783. Randolph, Richard V. *God Is on Earth Today!* Los Angeles: Society of the Sacred Seven, 1952. 146 pp.
Testimony by a fervent disciple. Not seen.

784. Randolph, Vance. "Black God of Harlem." *Americans Who Thought They Were Gods* (cited above as item 149), 21-4.
Tells the story of the growth of the Peace Mission Movement, focusing on its material success.

785. Rasky, Frank. "Harlem's Religious Zealots." *Tomorrow* 9 (November, 1949): 11-7.
Focuses mainly on post-Father Divine religious

movements in Harlem, but provides some information on Father Divine's operations in Harlem after his move to Philadelphia.

786. Schroeder, Theodore. "'Living God' Incarnate." *Psychoanalytic Review* 19 (January, 1932): 36-45.
Details the psychological progress of "Lany Jency" of the "Church of the Living God," apparently a fictionalized version of the Peace Mission Movement.

787. Stewart, Ollie. "Father Divine Is God." *Scribner's Commentator* 8 (June, 1940): 20-6.
An overview history of the movement and a survey of its current holdings, especially in real estate.

788. Streator, George. "Father Divine: An Economic and Social Analysis of a Movement Often in the Headlines." *Commonweal* 31 (December 15, 1939): 176-8.
Takes contemporary publications to task for their frequent ridiculing of Father Divine. Argues that mainline religious commentators to the contrary, Father Divine has fostered good relations between the sexes and races and has done economic good for his followers, housing them, feeding them, and enabling them to work together to support themselves.

789. ———. Review of Parker's *Incredible Messiah*. *Opportunity* 15 (October, 1937): 314.
Finds Parker's analysis superficial.

790. Thomason, John W., Jr. "Father Divine's Afflatus." *American Mercury* 39 (December, 1936): 500-5.
Reviews Hosher's book (item 747), providing some historical information on the movement in the context of other black religious movements of the early twentieth century.

791. Vellinga, Mrs. M.C. *Unmasking of Mr. Divine*. Los Angeles: author, 1936.
An attack on Father Divine from an evangelical Christian viewpoint. At the Institute for the Study of American Religion.

792. Warmsley, V. Review of Hoshor's *God in a Rolls-Royce*. *Crisis* 43 (November, 1936): 348-9.
Takes Hoshor to task for his racist assumptions and

rash conclusions.

793. Washington, Joseph J., Jr. *Black Sects and Cults.* Garden City, New York: Anchor/Doubleday, 1972, pp. 117-27 plus other scattered references.
Finds the central meaning of the Father Divine movement to lie in its speaking to the black ethos of empowerment.

794. Weinberg, Arthur, and Lila Weinberg. "Father Divine: Peace." *Passport to Utopia.* New York: Quadrangle, 1968, pp. 284-95.
Provides a brief overview of the movement; reproduces the text of the Platform of Father Divine's Peace Mission Movement, 1936.

795. Weisbrot, Robert. *Father Divine and the Struggle for Racial Equality.* Urbana: University of Illinois Press, 1983. 241 pp.
A biography of Father Divine, emphasizing his work to help poor blacks during the Depression and to achieve racial equality in America. Contains an excellent bibliographical essay. Illustrated with photographs.

796. Williams, Chancellor. *Have You Been to the River?* New York: Exposition Press, 1952. 256 pp.
A fictional look at black religious leaders, including Father Divine. Not seen.

797. Young, Bradford. "Father Divine Acquitted." *Christian Century* 54 (June 2, 1937): 721.
Reports that Father Divine has been acquitted of assault in a case stemming from "a fracas in one of his 'heavens.'"

798. Zwick, Stephen E. *Father Divine Peace Mission Movement.* B.A. senior thesis, Princeton University, 1971. 283 pp.

# L. FELLOWSHIP FARM ASSOCIATION

In 1908 a group of 40 persons under the leadership of George Elmer Littlefield pooled their savings of about $1000 and purchased 70 acres near Westwood, Massachusetts. Each member received the use of an acre; the 30 common acres were cultivated collectively. The community was still alive and well several years later.

Survey works: Albertson (item 27), 421; Okagawa (item 139), 228.

*Secondary works*

799. Geddes, A.S. "Living from an Acre." *Technical World*, July, 1912, pp. 574-7.
Provides an overview history of the project, depicting a thriving community in 1912. Illustrated with photographs of homes on the Farm.

800. Hinds, William Alfred. "Fellowship Farm Association." *American Communities and Co-operative Colonies* (cited above as item 95), 588-90.
Describes the origin and goals of the group; quotes Littlefield on the group's approach to cooperative socialism.

# LI. FELLOWSHIP FARMS

Kate Buck organized the Los Angeles Fellowship Farms Co. in 1912 on 75 acres near Puente, California, in the Los Angeles area. She enlisted George Littlefield, the leader of the earlier unsuccessful Fellowship Farm colony in Massachusetts to help her. Twelve families moved in during the winter of 1912-3. Each colonist got one acre of land; membership reached 50 to 60. The plots were too small to sustain persons, however, and the colony disintegrated in the 1920s.

Survey work: Okugawa (139), 230.

*Secondary work*

\* Hine, Robert V. *California's Utopian Colonies* (cited above as item 95), 148-9.
Provides a brief history of the colony and an analysis of its eventual demise.

# LII. FELLOWSHIP OF INTENTIONAL COMMUNITIES

The Fellowship of Intentional Communities was not itself a commune, but for some years in the middle twentieth century was a support organization for several of the most prominent communes in those years. Member communes included the Bruderhof, Celo, Glen Gardner, Gould Farm, Hidden Springs, Koinonia Farm, Macedonia, the May Valley Cooperative, Quest, Tanguy Homesteads, and Tuolumne Cooperative Farms. The most stable of the members was the Bruderhof, and when that organization withdrew from the FIC, the FIC collapsed. Publications focusing on the FIC have much to do with the communal history covered by this bibliography, and thus are included here.

The FIC was closely related to Community Service, Inc., which for many years provided services, including loans, to intentional communities, and at this writing continues to promote community in various ways. CSI headquarters is in Yellow Springs, Ohio; it was founded by Arthur Morgan in 1940. His son Griscom Morgan later played an active role in CSI leadership.

### *Periodicals serving FIC communities*

801.  *Communiteer.*
      Newsletter of the Rural Cooperative Community Conference, New York City.

802.  *Community Comments.*
      Newsletter of Community Service, Inc., for many years. Continued *Community Service News*; was continued by *Community Service Newsletter*. It concluded publication with volume 23, 1975. Volume numbers are continuous through all three publications.

803.  *Community Fellowship Newsletter.* 1958-?
      Publication of the Community Fellowship of Yellow Springs, Ohio. Contains information on communal problems and situations currently being experienced.

804.  *Community Service News.*    1943-?    The first periodical of Community Service, Inc.

805. *Community Service Newsletter.* 1975-.
The third title of the periodical publication of Community Service, Inc.

806. *Fellowship of Intentional Communities Newsletter.* Rifton, N.Y. 1951-?
Published by the Woodcrest Bruderhof. Provided FIC member communities with news about each other and about other experiments in community.

*Primary works*

807. *Intentional Communities: 1959 Yearbook of the Fellowship of Intentional Communities.* Yellow Springs, Ohio: Fellowship of Intentional Communities, 1959. 43 pages, mimeographed.
Provides a summary of the basic concepts and principles of the FIC, explaining its commitment to intentional community. Also contains other articles and reprints of interest to community members. Contains a directory of FIC member and other communities, including the Bruderhof, Bryn Gweled Homesteads, Celo, Glen Gardner, Gould Farm, the House of David, Koinonia Farm, May Valley, the Order of Aaron (Glendenningite Mormons), Tanguy Homesteads, Tuolumne Cooperative Farm, and the Vale, along with several other foreign and minor domestic communities not listed in this biography. At Community Service, Inc.

808. *Intentional Community Handbook.* Yellow Springs, Ohio: Community Fellowship (c/o Community Service, Inc.), 1971. Revised edition, 1974. Unpaginated.
A compendium of information on successful intentional communities, providing data on existing communities and reflective and theoretical articles on contemporary communitarianism. Contains an annotated directory of communities and a list of literature available from CSI.

*Works by a community leader*

809. Morgan, Arthur E. *Nowhere was Somewhere: How History Makes Utopias and How Utopias Make History.* Chapel Hill: University of North Carolina Press, 1946.
A treatise on utopian thought and myths.

810. ———. *Philosophy of Edward Bellany.* New York: King's Crown Press, 1945. 96 pp.

*Pamphlets by Arthur E. Morgan and Griscom Morgan,*
*published by Community Service, Inc. (copies*
*at Community Service, Inc., and in the Arthur Morgan*
*Papers at Antioch College)*

811. Morgan, Arthur. *Bottom-Up Democracy.* 1964. 64 pp.

812. ———. *Community, a Universal in Human Society.*

813. ———. *Community of the Future and the Future of Community.*

814. ———. *Great Community.* 1946. 20 pp.

815. ———. *Industries for Small Communities.*

816. ———. *It Can Be Done.*

817. ———. *It Can Be Done in Economic Life.*

818. ———. *It Can Be Done in Education.*

819. ——— *It Can Be Done in Home and Community.*

820. ———. *Plagiarism in Utopia.* 1944. 33 pp.

821. ———. *Threefold Economic Balance.*

822. Morgan, Arthur, and Griscom Morgan, eds. *Heritage of Community.* 1956; revised edition, 1971. 64 pp.

823. Morgan, Griscom. *Community's Need for an Economy.*

824. ———. *Economics of Non-Inflationary Full Employment.*

825. ———. Future of the Heritage.

826. ———. *Vitality and Civilization.* 1947. 32 pp.

827. ———. *World View of the Galilean.* 1948. 22 pp.

*Secondary works*

828. Bouvard, Marguerite. "Community of Communities." *Intentional Community Movement* (cited above as item 317), 125-7.
Explains the workings of the FIC and of the Homer Morris Fund, which made loans to communes.

829. Fairfield, Dick. "Yellow Springs and Homer Morris." "Communes U.S.A." (cited above as item 63), 41, 47.
Provides a sketch of the FIC focusing on Arthur and Griscom Morgan and the Homer Morris Fund (set up to help communities with special needs).

830. ——— [Richard Fairfield]. "Morgans of Yellow Springs" and "Homer L. Morris Fund: A Little Help to Friends." *Communes USA: A Personal Tour* (cited above as item 64): 20-4.
Profiles the FIC, Griscom Morgan, and the Homer L. Morris Fund, which was set up to provide short-term loans to communities in emergencies.

831. "Fellowship of Intentional Communities." *American Utopianism* (cited above as item 75), 151-3. Reprinted from *Intentional Communities* (cited above as item 807).

832. Fogarty, Robert S. "Intentional Communities." *American Utopianism* (cited above as item 75), 150-1.
Introduction to the FIC and its member communities, followed by "Fellowship of Intentional Communities" (cited above as item 834), 151-3.

833. Kahoe, Walter. *Arthur Morgan: A Biography and Memoir.* Moylan, Pennsylvania: Whimsie Press, 1977. 180 pp.

834. Morgan, Jane. "History of Community Service." *Community Service Newsletter* 36 (July/August, 1988): 4-5.
Provides a historical sketch of CSI, quoting liberally from the writings of Arthur Morgan on the purpose it intended to serve.

835. Morgan, Lucy Griscom. *Finding His World: The Story of Arthur E. Morgan.* Yellow Springs, Ohio: Kahoe and Co., 1928. 108 pp.
A biography of Morgan's early years by his wife. The

majority of the text is taken from Morgan's diaries and notes.

836. Phillips, Jack.   *Directory of Some Persons Planning to Live in Small Communities.*   Yellow Springs, Ohio: Community Service, Inc., 1946. 32 pp.
    A directory of persons sympathetic to intentional communities, with an appendix discussing towns with relatively high numbers of persons interested in communities and another appendix providing brief, introductory material on Celo and Penn-Craft, as well as directory listings for other communities.


# LIII.  FERRER COLONY

In 1910 a group of New York anarchists founded the Francisco Ferrer Association, named after a recently executed Spanish anarchist, hoping in part to test Ferrer's libertarian educational theories.   In 1915 they opened a colony on 143 acres at Stelton, New Jersey, centered on the Ferrer Modern School.   There were individual homestead landholdings in the colony, but common property as well, especially the schoolgrounds.   In 1922 the colony had 80 to 90 houses and over 200 residents.   The sudden establishment of Camp Kilmer immediately adjacent to the colony during World War II hastened the colony's demise.

Survey work: Okugawa (item 139), 232.


*Community periodicals*

837. *Modern School.* 1912-21.

838. *Mother Earth.* New York.
    The colonists were closely linked to this anarchist magazine, although it was not a colony organ.


*Secondary works*

839. Avrich, Paul.   *Modern School Movement.*   Princeton: Princeton University Press, 1980. 447 pp.
    Provides a history of the Modern School at Ferrer, plus

spinoff school colonies in other locations (especially Mohegan Colony in New York state). Includes character sketches of some of the main participants in Ferrer and an account of the colony's decline and aftermath.

840. Bercovici, Rion. "Radical Childhood." *Scribner's Magazine* 92 (August, 1932): 102-6.
Supplies a brief memoir of the Modern School; spiced with anecdotes about Will Durant during his term as principal.

841. Brown, William Thurston. *Education for Constructive Democracy*. New York: Graphic Press, 1918. 34 pp.

842. ―――. *Most Important Educational Experiment in America*. Stelton, New Jersey: Ferrer Colony, n.d. 32 pp.
Presents the author's philosophy of education, a diatribe against the public schools, a critique of other educational alternatives, the philosophy of the Modern School, and a plea for contributions. Brown was a principal of the school.

843. ―――. *What Socialism Means as a Philosophy and as a Movement*. Portland, Oregon: Modern School, n.d. 32 pp.
Critiques capitalist society and predicts that a socialist revolution is coming.

* Cohen, Joseph J. *In Quest of Heaven* (cited below as item 2706), 25-6.
Contains a brief discussion of history and goals of the colony. Cohen was a major force in the founding of Ferrer.

844. Cohen, Joseph J., and Alexis C. Ferm. *Modern School of Stelton: A Sketch*. Stelton: The Modern School Association of New Jersey, 1925. 122 pp. Illustrated.

* Douglas, Dorothy W., and Katharine Du Pre Lumpkin. "Communistic Settlements" (cited above as item 56), 100.
Mentions Ferrer as an example of a relatively long-lived anarchistic colony.

845. Durant, Will. *Transition*. New York: Simon and Schuster, 1927, pp. 184-99.

Recalls the author's taking up and performance of the job of principal of the Modern School.

846. Ferm, Alexis. "Modern School at Stelton." *Freedom* (New York) n.s., v. 2 (March, 1934): 3.
Describes current conditions at the school, emphasizing that the Modern School wants children to grow as individuals.

847. ———. "Report of the Stelton Modern School." *Freedom* (New York) n.s., v. 2 (February, 1934): 6-7.
Provides an anecdotal account of daily life at the school, arguing that an unstructured curriculum with a heavy arts and crafts emphasis teaches children better than a structured one does with desk learning.

848. Ferrer, Francisco. *Origin and Ideals of the Modern School.* New York and London: Putnam's, 1913.  147 pp.
The English language edition of Ferrer's educational manifesto which inspired the Modern School.

849. "Ferrer Modern School." *Freedom* (New York) n.s., v. 2 (June, 1934): 5.
Urges supporters to send contributions to help the school and colony ride out a financial crisis brought on by the depression.

850. Fogarty, Robert S. "Abbott, Leonard," "Ferm, Elizabeth Byrne," "Ferrer Colony," and "Kelly, Harry." *Dictionary of American Communal and Utopian History* (cited above as item 76), pp. 3-4, 36-7, 140-1, 61-2.
Dictionary entries which provide basic information on the project.

851. Liptzin, Stanley. "Modern School of Stelton, New Jersey: A Libertarian Educational Experiment Examined." Ed.D. dissertation, Rutgers University, 1976.  332 pp.

852. "Nineteenth Anniversary of the Modern School, Stelton, New Jersey." *Freedom* n.s., v. 1 (June, 1933): 8.
Describes the state of the school, listing its personnel and characterizing its plans for the coming year. A Sidebar encourages parents to send their children there, emphasizing the bargain price of $7 per week for tuition and board.

\*    Oved, Yaacov. "Sunrise and Anarchist Communities" (cited below as item 2717), 314-5.
Provides a brief sketch of the colony and school.

853.   Perlin, Terry M. "Anarchism in New Jersey: The Ferrer Colony in Stelton." *New Jersey History* 89 (Fall, 1971): 133-48.
Provides an overview of the history of the colony in the context of the New York anarchism from which it grew. Finds the colony to have been successful both in longevity and in devotion to its principles. Well illustrated with photographs.

854.   Pitzer, Donald E. "Patterns of Education in American Communal Societies." *Communal Life: An International Perspective* (cited above as item 84), 278-88.
Describes the Modern School, under Elizabeth and Alexis Ferm, as a radical educational experiment, one which brought order out of the near-total anarchy in the school when they arrived.

855.   Shor, Francis. "Cultural Identity and Americanization: The Life History of a Jewish Anarchist." *Biography* 9 (Fall, 1986): 324-46.
Provides a biographical sketch of Joseph Cohen, including accounts of his involvement in Ferrer and Sunrise.

856.   Veysey, Laurence. "Ferrer Colony and Modern School of Stelton, New Jersey." *Communal Experience* (cited above as item 166), 77-177.
Provides a detailed account of the founding of the Francisco Ferrer Association, the opening of the colony, the conduct of the Modern School, and the colony's decline. Extensively footnoted with references to primary sources not cited here.

857.   Zigrosser, Carl. *Modern School.* Stelton, New Jersey: Ferrer Colony, n.d. 21 pp.

# LIV. FREEDOM COLONY

Freedom colony was founded at Fulton, Bourbon County, Kansas, by persons who had been involved in the Labor

Exchange, which had been operated by G.B. De Bernardi.
Several members wanted to start a colony; De Bernardi fiercely
resisted that course, so the members left his project and
founded the colony on their own.    It consisted of 60 acres and
several residential and industrial buildings.    It operated from
1898 to 1905.    The industries included farming and a sawmill;
an attempt to mine coal never was successful.    Two years after
its founding it had about 40 members.    The best known member
was Carl Browne, an artist from Berkeley, California, who had
been a leader of the Coxey's Army march on Washington.    At
Freedom Colony he constructed a meditation platform in a tree
and there, after considerable observation of crows, conceived,
before the Wright brothers, a plan for an airplane.    Several
models were built, but no full-size prototype emerged.    Browne
also ran for Congress as a Populist while at the colony.
Although the colony attracted numerous loafers, it experienced
several good years before a mysterious arson fire destroyed
most of the buildings and with them the morale of the
settlement.
    Some material on the colony is in the American Communities
Collection at Syracuse University.

Survey work: Okugawa (item 139), 221.


*Community periodical*

858.  *Progressive Thought and Dawn of Equity.*    1897?-1903.
       Various versions of the paper began prior to 1897 and
       ran as late as perhaps 1914, but under other auspices than
       those of the colony.


*Secondary works*

859.  Albertson, Ralph.    "Freedom Colony."    "Survey of
       Mutualistic Communities in America" (cited above as
       item 27), 416.
       Provides a brief overview of the colony.

860.  Blackmar, Frank W., ed.    "Freedom Colony."    *Kansas: A
       Cyclopedia of State History* (cited above as item 34), v.
       1, p. 686.
       Describes the founding of the colony and its industries;
       quotes from the "objects of the colony" on communal
       goals.

861.  "Browne in a New Role."    Topeka *Daily Capital*, August
      11,  1900. p. 3.
      Provides a profile of Carl Browne, who at this time was
      giving a series of public talks on socialism at Fort Scott,
      Kansas.    Also contains a description of Browne's flying
      machine.

862.  Delavan, Wayne.    "Bourbon Co. Once Had Experiment in
      Socialism in a Colony near Fulton."    Fort Scott *Tribune*,
      May 30, 1912, historical section, p. 12.
      Provides basic information about the colony and
      especially about Carl Browne.

863.  ———.    "Freedom Colony, a Kansas Brook Farm."    *Kansas
      Magazine* (1949): 51-4.
      Describes the founding of the colony, the role of
      Browne in Coxey's Army, life at Freedom Colony, and
      Browne's airplane.    Tells of the latter years of the
      colony, when several of the more able colonists left and
      when hostility from neighbors became more intense.    The
      article is based largely on interviews (conducted in 1941
      and 1947) conducted with persons who knew the colony
      and its residents.

*     Douthit, Katrina S. Adams.    "Shortlived Experiment:
      Esperanza Colony at Urbana" (cited above as item 670),
      5.
      Contains a brief note about Freedom Colony.

*     Grant, H. Roger.    "New Communitarianism" (cited above as
      item 86), 62-4.
      Provides an overview history of the colony, tracing its
      founding to the Labor Exchange and describing the fire
      which brought it to an end.

864.  Grant, H. Roger.    "Portrait of a Workers' Utopia: The
      Labor Exchange and the Freedom, Kan., Colony."
      *Kansas Historical Quarterly* 43 (Spring, 1977): 56-66.
      Describes the origins of Freedom colony in the Labor
      Exchange, the establishment of the colony, the role played
      by Carl Browne and his flying machine, and the colony-
      ending fire in 1905.

865.  Kent, Alexander.    "Freedom Colony."    "Cooperative
      Communities in the United States (cited above as item
      117), 639.

Provides a brief overview of the colony's industries and social organization.

866. "Socialist Colony." Fort Scott *Weekly Tribune*, August 17, 1899.
Describes the colony after two years of operation, focusing on its industries and its "labor exchange" which used scrip instead of money.

867. Stead, William T. "Coxeyism." *Review of Reviews*, American Edition, 10 (July, 1894): 47-59.
Provides a character sketch of Browne, whose concern for matters spiritual is emphasized.

868. "Will Lead New Army." Kansas City *Times*, May 28, 1899, p. 8.
Describes Browne's plan to spearhead a new march on Washington. Reproduces the text of a recent interview with Browne. Illustrated with a line drawing of Browne.

# LV.  FREELAND

In 1898 James Gleason began to acquire land on Whidby (now usually spelled "Whidbey") Island in Puget Sound. He was ready to dispose of much of it when disenchanted Equality socialists looked to relocate. In late 1899 George Washington Daniels and others organized the Free Land Association. It promoted the Rochdale plan; its economy focused on the cooperative ownership of a single store. The location was very isolated; gradually the colony evolved into a settlement of socialist-minded individuals. Note: this colony is not to be confused with its nearby contemporary, also called Freeland, which was the successor to Equality.

The Freeland Co-operative Association papers and other Freeland documents are in the University of Washington library.

Some material on Freeland is in the American Communities Collection at Syracuse University.

Survey work: Okugawa (item 139), 225.

*Community periodical*

869. *Whidby Islander.* 1900-3. Monthly.

*Secondary works*

870. Albertson, Ralph. "Freeland Association." "Survey of Mutualistic Communities in America" (cited above as item 27), 417.
Provides a brief note on the colony.

\* Holbrook, Stewart H. *Far Corner* (cited above as item 101), 153-5.
Outlines the philosophy of the colony and describes its decline.

871. LeWarne, Charles P. "Freeland: The Rochdale Town." *Utopias on Puget Sound* (cited above as item 124), 114-28.
Provides a history of the colony based on a chapter in the author's dissertation (following item).

872. ———. "Harmony and Freeland: The Hop Field Utopia and the Rochdale Town." "Communitarian Experiments in Western Washington, 1885-1915" (cited above as item 122), 279-312.
Provides the most comprehensive history of the colony available. Thoroughly documented; includes many references to specialized and local materials not cited here.

# LVI. GERMAN COLONIZATION COMPANY

Carl Wulsten of Chicago organized this colony in 1869 as a means of getting poor Germans out of their wretched urban environment. In February, 1870, 300 persons left Chicago for the colony site near Canon City, which they named "Colfax," after the Vice President of the U.S. The settlers had pledged to pool all labor and capital and work together for five years. However, problems quickly arose: land title problems were never solved, there was internal dissension, and the looming winter caused many to leave. The burning of the colony store was the final straw; the colony collapsed before the end of the year.

Survey work: Okugawa (item 139), 203.

### Secondary works

\*     Baker, James H., ed.   *History of Colorado* (cited above as item 30), v. 2, pp. 443-8.
        Provides an overview history of the colony, concluding that Wulsten's poor leadership was a major cause of its failure.

873.  Fogarty, Robert S.   "German Colonization Company." *Dictionary of American Communal and Utopian History* (cited above as item 76), 142.
        Provides a brief history of the colony.

\*     Hafen, LeRoy R., ed.   *Colorado and Its People* (cited above as item 88), v. 1, pp. 329-30.
        Provides a brief note on the history of the colony.

\*     Hall, Frank.   *History of the State of Colorado* (cited above as item 89), v. 1, p. 542.
        Characterizes the organization, settlement, and problems experienced by the colony.

874.  Solis, Miguel J.   "German Colonization Co." *American Utopias* (cited above as item 20), 52.
        Contains a brief description of the project plus one bibliographical entry.

875.  *Southern Colorado: Historical and Descriptive of Fremont and Custer Counties with Their Principal Towns.*  Canon City, Colorado: Binckley and Hartwell, 1879, pp. 98-108.
        Provides a historical sketch of the colony; reproduces Wulsten's essay "El Mojada, Or the Wet Mountain Valley," in which he argues that although the colony did not last long, several survivors of it eventually prospered as individual farmers in the vicinity.

876.  Willard, James F., and Colin B. Goodykoontz, eds. "German Colonization Company." *Experiments in Colorado Colonization, 1869-1872* (cited above as item 173), 27-133.
        Provides basic documents of and newspaper accounts about the colony.

# LVII. GLEN GARDNER COOPERATIVE COMMUNITY

This pacifist community at Glen Gardner, New Jersey, founded in 1947, operated a publishing house, raised gardens and livestock, and cared for preschool children. The land, known as "St. Francis Acres," was understood to be owned by God. The group provided housing and common meals. In February, 1955, it had 18 members, 9 of them children.

### Secondary works

* Gladstone, Arthur. "Cooperative Communities Today II" (cited above as item 82), 14.
  Provides basic information about the community.

877. "Glen Gardner." *Intentional Communities: 1959 Yearbook of the Fellowship of Intentional Communities* (cited above as item 807), 22-4.
  Provides an overview of the life and industries of the community. Reproduces the "Terms of Trusteeship," the group's bylaws.

# LVIII. GLENMORE

Thomas Davidson, an English reformer of the late nineteenth century, founded the Fellowship of the New Life in 1882 to promote his ideals. From that group arose two communal-living experiments. In the late 1880s Davidson acquired a tract of land in the Adirondacks and there founded Glenmore, a colony for the pursuit of the "Cultural Sciences." After his death the colony became a center, principally active in summer, for the Ethical Culture movement. In the early 1890s the London group also founded a group living experiment, Fellowship House, although the American and English communities were run separately.

### Secondary work

878. Smith, Warren Sylvester. *London Heretics, 1870-1914.*

London: Constable, 1967, pp. 131-41.
Tells the story of the Fellowship of the New Life,
including a brief account of the establishment of its
American community.

# LIX.  GLENNIS COOPERATIVE INDUSTRIAL COMPANY

Glennis was founded 17 miles south of Tacoma, Washington,
on the 160 acre homestead of Oliver Verity in 1894.    At its
peak it had nearly 30 members, a school, a dairy, a blacksmith
shop, a cigar factory, and a post office.     However, its rules
and regulations were very restrictive, and a lack of confidence
in the leadership set in.     Verity and others withdrew to try
again, founding Home colony.

Survey works: Curl (item 52), 35; Okugawa (item 139), 203.

### Secondary works

\*      LeWarne,  Charles  P.     "Communitarian  Experiments  in
       Western  Washington,  1885-1915"  (cited  above  as  item
       122), 347-8.
       Provides  a  brief  sketch  of  the  colony  and  the
       restrictiveness which led to its dissolution.

\*      LeWarne,  Charles  P.     *Utopias  on  Puget  Sound*  (cited  above
       as item 124), 168-9.
       Provides a historical sketch of the colony.

# LX.  GOULD FARM

Located  in  Great  Barrington,  Massachusetts,  Gould  Farm  was
a  service  community  specializing  in  mental  and  physical
rehabilitation.     It  was  founded  in  1913  by  William  Gould  and
occupied  550  acres.     In  addition  to  a  central  building,  it  had
several  cabins  and  farm  buildings.     The  normal  patient  load  was
50  to  100.     A  relatively  small  resident  community  served  the
patients.     In  recent  years  its  self-image  has  been  less  and  less
that of an intentional community.

Survey works: Fairfield (item 63), 161; Fairfield (item 64), 345.

## Community periodical

879. *Gould Farm News.* Volume 43, no. 2, was published in 1976.

## Primary work

880. *Gould Farm Hails 55th Year.* Great Barrington, Massachusetts: [Gould Farm, 1968]. Gould Farm's annual report for 1967-8.

## Secondary works

881. Adams, James Luther. "Notes on the Study of Gould Farm." *Cooperative Living* 7 (Winter, 1955-6): 8-10.
An appreciative appraisal of the current status of the farm. Describes Gould Farm as a community of faith currently going through self- renewal.

* Bouvard, Marguerite. *Intentional Community Movement* (cited above as item 37), 100.
Contains a brief note on the status of Gould Farm in the 1970s.

* Gladstone, Arthur. "Cooperative Communities Today II" (cited above as item 82), 14.
Describes Gould Farm in 1954, counting 39 permanent members (2 of them children).

882. "Gould Farm." *Intentional Communities: 1959 Yearbook of the Fellowship of Intentional Communities* (cited above as item 807), 19-20.
Provides a brief introduction to the history and work of the community.

883. Infield, Henrik. "Gould Farm: A Therapeutic Cooperative Community." *American Intentional Communities* (cited above as item 104), 73-109.
Describes the history, activities, and physical plant of Gould Farm; provides the results of sociological testing

conducted there.

884. ———. "Gould Farm, a Therapeutic Cooperative
     Community." *Cooperative Living* 6 (Spring, 1955): 1-13.
     Describes the community not long after its fortieth
     birthday. Praises the success of Gould Farm in treating
     the mentally ill.

\*    *Intentional Community Handbook* (cited above as item
     808), unpaginated.
     Provides a brief description of Gould Farm and its work.

885. Kramer, Wendell B. "Gould Farm." "Criteria for the
     Intentional Community" (cited above as item 118), 90-2.
     Characterizes Gould Farm as a lively spiritual
     community.

# LXI. HARMONIAL VEGETARIAN SOCIETY

This society of anarchists which was founded in 1860 in
Benton County, Arkansas, may have had as many as 54
members, including children. It espoused vegetarianism and,
reportedly, renounced marriage, choosing mates for members by
lot. A large building served as home for members and a
hospital for the area. The founder-leader was J.E. Spencer.
He fled for his life when neighbors attacked the settlement in
1861; soon thereafter Confederate soldiers arrived and took
over the community buildings, including a community house, a
general store, a bath house, and a print shop, thus severely
damaging the life of the community. The buildings burned
around the close of the war; the property was sold and the
proceeds divided among members.

*Community periodical*

886. *Theocrat.* 1860-1.

*Secondary works*

\*    Muncy, Raymond Lee. *Sex and Marriage in Utopian
     Communities* (cited above as item 135), 206.
     Provides a brief sketch of Spencer and his community,

including its dispersion at the approach of Confederate soldiers.

887. Seamster, Alvin. "Harmonial Vegetarian Society." *Benton County Pioneer* (Siloam Springs: Benton County Historical Society, 1962), v. 8, pp. 12-4.
Provides a good overview account of the society.

# LXII. HARMONY (WASHINGTON)

Harmony attempted to become the second colony of the Brotherhood of the Cooperative Commonwealth, which had helped found Equality. It was located on 620 acres on the upper Cowlita river in Washington; its economic base was to be agricultural, especially the cultivation of hops. However, the BCC poured its support into Equality, and Harmony never prospered. It was dissolved at the end of its first summer, in 1899. The principal leaders were S.M. Dunn and A.T. McDonald.

## *Secondary works*

* LeWarne, Charles Pierce. "Harmony and Freeland: The Hop Field Utopia and the Rochdale Town" (cited above as item 872), 269-78.
Provides a historical sketch of the colony, focusing on its inability to attract support.

* LeWarne, Charles P. *Utopias on Puget Sound* (cited above as item 124), 71.
Provides a brief note on the ill-fated colony.

# LXIII. HEAVEN CITY

Heaven City was founded by Albert J. Moore, originally of Chicago, near Harvard, Illinois, on 130 acres in 1923. Moore prophesied depression, strikes, devastating world war, and other calamities, all to be followed by a "new dawn" which his community presaged. Strict behavioral rules accompanied Moore's distinctive religious precepts.

888. Fogarty, Robert S. "Heaven City." *Dictionary of American Communal and Utopian History* (cited above as item 76), 143.
     Dictionary entry on the community.

889. Wooster, Ernest S. "Heaven Everywhere." *Communities of the Past and Present* (cited above as item 175), 143.
     Provides a brief history of the community.

# LXIV. HEAVEN COLONY

William W. Davies, a Mormon convert who was known as a mystic and a person of deep spirituality, joined the sectarian Morrisite Mormons in Utah sometime after arriving in Utah in 1855. After Morris's death, he followed his visions which led him, his family, and some 40 followers to Walla Walla, where they purchased 80 acres in 1867. When Davies's son Arthur was born in 1868, the father announced that he was the reincarnated Jesus. Another son, born the next year, was said to be the spirit of God the Father made manifest. The communal settlement lasted until 1880, when both boys died of diphtheria within a week. Later that year the colony dissolved amid lawsuits and dissension.

Some manuscript material on the colony is in the American Communities Collection at Syracuse University.

Survey work: Okugawa (item 139), 203.

\*    Beadle, John Hanson. *Life in Utah; or, Mysteries and Crimes of Mormonism* (cited below as item 2071), 427-8.
     Provides a brief note on Davis and his designation of his son as Jesus.

890. Blankenship, Russell. "Walla Walla Jesus." *And There Were Men.* New York: Knopf, 1942, 79-94.
     Provides the best account of the community from the arrival of Davies in the U.S. to the aftermath of the dissolution of the colony.

891. Fogarty, Robert S. "Davies, William W." *Dictionary of American Communal and Utopian History* (cited above as item 76), 29.
Biographical dictionary entry.

\* LeWarne, Charles Pierce. "Communitarian Experiments in Western Washington, 1885-1915" (cited above as item 122), 19-20.
Provides a brief sketch of the colony, largely based on Blankenship's work (item 890, above).

# LXV. HELICON HALL

Upton Sinclair founded Helicon Hall in 1906 at Englewood, New Jersey, purchasing 15 acres and a large building from a former boys' school with money he had earned from sales of *The Jungle.* One of the main purposes of the colony was to demonstrate the efficiencies of shared housekeeping. A disastrous fire in March, 1907, only six months into the experiment, ended it all.
Some material on Helicon Hall is in the American Communities Collection at Syracuse University.

Survey works: Albertson (item 27), 420-1; Okugawa (item 139), 228.

### Works of the community leader

892. Sinclair, Upton. *Autobiography of Upton Sinclair.* New York: Harcourt, Brace, 1962, pp. 126-36.
Sinclair's story of his motivation and his plan, the purchase of the property, the special programs for children at Helicon Hall, and the disastrous fire.

893. ———. *Co-Op: A Novel of Living Together.* New York: Farrar and Rinehart, 1936.
Extends Sinclair's ideas and experiences concerning communal living in fictional form. The novel's "San Sebastian Self-Help Exchange" is based on Helicon Hall.

894. ———. "Co-operative Home." *Industrial Republic.* New York: Doubleday, Page and Co., 1907, pp. 259-84.
Presents the philosophy of the Helicon Hall project,

arguing that group living is cheaper and more efficient than independent living and that cooperative housekeeping makes good sense. Reports on the experiment in progress, focusing on physical facilities and the organizational structure of the group. A last paragraph tells of the fatal fire, which occurred after the rest of the chapter had been written.

895. ———. "Helicon Hall." *New Encyclopedia of Social Reform* (cited above as item 35), 569-70.
Describes the founding and life of Helicon Hall, emphasizing its focus on cooperative distribution, not cooperative production, and its striving to minimize domestic labor.

896. ———. "Home Colony." *Independent* 60 (June 14, 1906): 1401-8. Repr. as "Home Colony: A Prospectus." New York: Jungle Publishing Co., 1906.
Outlines building plans and living options for Sinclair's new colony, which would be Helicon Hall.

897. ———. "Home Colony: Six Months After." *Independent* 62 (February 7, 1907): 306-13.
Sinclair's retrospective recounting of the story of Helicon Hall.

898. ———. "New Helicon Hall." *Independent* 67 (September 9, 1909): 580-2.
Proposes that a new experiment be undertaken along the lines of the former Helicon Hall colony.

## Secondary works

899. Dell, Floyd. *Upton Sinclair: A Study in Social Protest.* New York: George H. Doran, 1927, pp. 121-4.
This biographical study of Sinclair contains an account of the founding of and life at Helicon Hall.

900. Doig, Ivan, ed. "Dream Lived Briefly at Helicon Hall." *Utopian America: Dreams and Realities* (cited above as item 55), 72-6.
Provides a brief introduction to the community and an excerpt from the *Autobiography of Upton Sinclair* (item 892, above).

901. Fogarty, Robert S. "Helicon Hall." *American Utopianism* (cited above as item 75), 114.
     A one-paragraph summary of the Helicon Hall story, followed by "Upton Sinclair's Account," reprinted from *Autobiography of Upton Sinclair* (pp. 114-22).

902. ———. "Helicon Hall Colony" and "Sinclair, Upton." *Dictionary of American Communal and Utopian History* (cited above as item 76), 144 and 103, respectively.
     Dictionary entries providing an overview of the colony.

903. Gilman, Charlotte Perkins. "Beauty of a Block." *Independent* 57 (July 14, 1904): 67-72.
     Proposes a unified plan for community living on New York City blocks. Includes diagrams and illustrations as well as a discussion of the proposal. Gilman's ideas about cooperative housekeeping were among the basic propositions Sinclair proposed to test in daily life at Helicon Hall, and this much-noted article was especially important in propelling Sinclair to purchase the property and inaugurate the experiment.

904. Gottesman, Ronald. "Upton Sinclair: An Annotated Bibliographical Catalogue, 1894-1932." Ph.D. Dissertation, Indiana University, 1964. 420 pp.
     Provides a narrative of the early career of Sinclair, followed by a lengthy bibliography of Sinclair's pamphlets, leaflets, and broadsides, as well as his books and articles. Contains basic bibliographical information on Helicon Hall.

905. Harris, Mrs. L.H. "Upton Sinclair and Helicon Hall." *Independent* 62 (March 28, 1907): 711-13.
     Describes Sinclair's inspiration for Helicon Hall through his reading of Charlotte Perkins Gilman's 1904 article on urban community living (item 903, above), and provides an upbeat account of life at Helicon Hall from the perspective of a visitor.

906. Harris, Leon. *Upton Sinclair, American Rebel.* New York: Thomas Y. Crowell, 1975.
     Contains a critical account of the founding and development of Helicon Hall, including the story of the fire which ended the experiment prematurely.

907. Hinds, William Alfred. "Helicon Home Colony." *American Communities and Co-operative Colonies* (cited above as

item 95), 581-7.
Describes Sinclair's aims and goals, quoting extensively
from some of his written statements about the colony.

908.   Kaplan,   Lawrence.     "Utopia   During   the   Progressive   Era:
       The   Helicon   Home   Colony,   1906-1907."     *American   Studies*
       25 (Fall, 1984): 59-73.
       A   narrative   of   the   history   of   Helicon   Hall   which   pays
       special   attention   to   the   founders'   goal   of   freeing   women
       from   household   drudgery   and   providing   for   the   full
       equality   of   women   and   men   in   daily   life   at   the   commune.
       Shows   how   the   founders   of   Helicon   Hall   tried   to
       implement   the   liberationist   ideas   of   Charlotte   Perkins
       Gilman,   even   though   Gilman   specifically   denounced
       cooperative   housekeeping   as   a   path   to   liberation   from
       household   toil.     Well   documented,   including   many   citations
       from contemporary newspaper accounts of the experiment.

# LXVI.  HIAWATHA VILLAGE

Abraham   Byers,   an   itinerant   evangelist,   together   with
members   of   his   family,   homesteaded   several   adjoining   claims
thirteen   miles   north   of   Manistique   in   Michigan's   Upper
Peninsula   in   1882.     They   were   influenced   by   Walter   Thomas
Mills's   *The   Product-Sharing   Village*   (item   911,   below),   a   tract
advocating   cooperative   communities,   and   gave   him   a   chance   to
try   out   his   communitarian   ideas,   which   he   did.     The   colony   was
founded   in   1893;   the   members   of   the   Hiawatha   Village
Association   deeded   their   land   (totalling   about   1,000   acres)   to
the   corporation   and   built   a   village   of   colony   homes   and
industrial   and   community   buildings.     Labor   was   paid   for   in   time
credits.     Dissent   and   competitiveness   set   in,   however,   leading
to   violence   in   one   case.     Many   left   the   community   in   the   fall
of   1895   and   it   soon   disbanded.     The   population   of   the   colony
was   recorded   as   fifteen   families   in   the   winter   of   1895-6   after
several families had already departed.

Survey work: Okugawa (item 139), 216.

*Community periodical*

909.   *Industrial Christian.*
       Apparently published for most of the life of the colony.

*Works by a community leader*

910. Mills, Walter Thomas. "Hiawatha Colony." Escanaba (Michigan) *Daily Press*, December 16, 1931, p. 5.
Mills's own story of how he got involved in the project and why he later left it; mainly deals with his life before and after colony days.

911. ———. *Product-Sharing Village*. Oak Park, Illinois: Civic Letters Co., 1894. 63 pp.
Provides a critique of the current economic system; proposes replacing it with worker-owned industrial villages.

912. ———. *Struggle for Existence*. Chicago: International School of Social Economy, 1904. 640 pp.
Mills's socialist manifesto, written after his experience at Hiawatha. Contains brief notes on Ruskin and Kaweah regarding the hostility of the court system toward communal experiments.

*Secondary works*

913. Anderson, Olive M. *Utopia in Upper Michigan: The Story of a Cooperative Village*. Marquette: Northern Michigan University, 1982. 67 pp.
Provides the only major extant history of the community. Contains a bibliography.

914. Byers, Charlotte R. "History of Hiawatha Colony Venture Written by One of Members." Escanaba (Michigan) *Daily Press*, December 10-13 and 15, 1931.
Describes the founding of the colony; contains colonists' reminiscences of moving there in 1895; provides anecdotes of colony life and of the rise of discontent which led to dissolution. The author was a daughter of one of the founders of the community.

915. Byers, David C. "Utopia in Upper Michigan." *Michigan Alumnus Quarterly Review*, March, 1957, pp. 168-74.
Provides a good overview history of the colony from the original homesteading of the land through the dissolution of the group. Describes community life, industries, persons prominent in the community, and the details of the terminal conflict. The author was the son of

      Abraham Byers. Illustrated with line drawings of community leaders.

916. Fogarty, Robert S. "Byers, Abraham S." *Dictionary of American Communal and Utopian History* (cited above as item 76), 20-1.
Biographical dictionary entry.

917. Solis, Miguel J. "Hiawatha Village Association." *American Utopias* (cited above as item 20), 71-2.
Provides a brief description of the community plus one bibliographical entry.

# LXVII. HIDDEN SPRINGS

    Hidden Springs was founded in 1953 at Neshanic Station, New Jersey, to encourage cooperation and spiritual development. It provided housing for members, who practiced common gardening and farming. One meal per week was eaten communally; worship services were held each Sunday. In April, 1954, it had 12 members, one of them a child.

*Community periodical*

918. *From Hidden Springs.* No imprint; late 1940s?

*Secondary works*

\*    Gladstone, Arthur. "Cooperative Communities Today II" (cited above as item 82), 14.
Provides information on the community as of 1954.

919. Kramer, Wendell B. "Hidden Springs." "Criteria for the Intentional Community" (cited above as item 118), 92-3.
Characterizes Hidden Springs as a loose, somewhat diverse community.

# LXVIII. HOLY CITY

    The Perfect Christian Divine Way (PCDW) was founded in

1909 by William Riker, a San Francisco street preacher. The most notable feature of his teachings was KKK-style white racism. In 1918 Riker purchased land in the Santa Cruz Mountains and, with 30 followers, began to build a community. Celibacy was practiced, and the colony gradually dwindled over several decades.

Several miscellaneous shorter writings of Riker not included here are listed in the National Union Catalog and in the catalogs of the New York Public and Bancroft (Berkeley) libraries under Riker and under the Holy City Brotherhood. The Holy City bibliography provided by Paul Kagan in his *New World Utopias* (cited above as item 115) provides references to several other Riker works I was unable to verify.

Survey work: Okugawa (item 139), 233.

### Works of the community leader

920. [Riker, William E.] *Heart and Blood Government.* Holy City: [Riker/Holy City], 1960.
A plan for a perfect world government.

921. ———. *Light of the World.* True Solution Book. [Holy City, California: n.p., 1974?] 19 pp.

922. ———. *Perfect Government.* [Holy City: n.p., 1942?] 32 pp.

923. ———. *Sooner or Later You Will Accept and Apply William E. Riker's Perfect Solution for the Capital and Labor Problem.* [Holy City: n.p., 1947?] 2 pp.

924. ———. *White Race is Supreme.* Holy City: n.p., [1942?]. 37 pp.

### Secondary works

925. Allard, Charles J. "'Father' William E. Riker and His Holy City." M.A. thesis, California State University, San Jose, 1968. 102 pp.

926. Britton, Dennis. "Change in Religion—Not in Philosophy." San Jose *Mercury*, July 29, 1966, p. 25.
Describes Riker's conversion to Catholicism late in life.

927. "Famed 'Father Riker' of Holy City Is Dead."   San Jose
     *Mercury*, December 5, 1969, p. 36.
     Tells of Riker's death at 96; provides a retrospective
     look at the colony.

928. Flinn, John.   "When Weird 'Holy City' Featured Piety,
     Petroleum and Peep Shows."   San Francisco *Examiner*,
     January 7, 1985, pp. B1, B6.
     A retrospective feature article on the history and life
     of the community.

929. Fogarty, Robert S.   "Riker, William E."   *Dictionary of
     American Communal and Utopian History* (cited above as
     item 76), 98-9.
     Biographical dictionary entry.

930. Hansen, Ken.   "Holy City 'Faithful' Carry on."   San Jose
     *Mercury*, December 28, 1956.
     Recounts the reminiscing of the last eight disciples of
     the movement.

*    Hine, Robert V.   *California's Utopian Colonies* (cited
     above as item 98), 154-7.
     Provides a good summary of the history and ideas of
     Riker and Holy City.

931. "Holy City Brotherhood."   *Fortnight* (March 2, 1955).   At
     the Institute for the Study of American Religion.

932. "Holy City, Mountain Landmark, Soon to Vanish into
     History."   San Jose *Mercury-News*, May 22, 1960, p. 21.
     With bulldozers approaching, the end of the remnants of
     the colony is at hand.

933. Kagan, Paul.   "Holy City."   *New World Utopias* (cited
     above as item 115), 102-17.
     Heavily illustrated history of Holy City.

934. Mathison, Richard.   "Holy City."   *Faiths, Cults and Sects
     of America: From Atheism to Zen* (cited above as item
     127), 334-7.
     Provides an overview history of the movement.

935. Peyton, Wes.   "'Holy City' Is a Tattered Monument to
     Eccentricity."   San Jose *Mercury*, January 2, 1980, p.
     11B.

936. Plate, Harry. "Riker: From Mechanic to . . ." *California Today* (August 30, 1970): 7-19.

# LXIX. HOME

Home, a colony devoted to anarchism, was founded at Joe's Bay on Puget Sound in 1897 by Oliver Verity and other members of the nearby Glennis colony near Tacoma who withdrew from that community in 1896. Home survived two years with no formal organization, but one became necessary, and the Mutual Home Association was organized in 1898. Two acres of ground were allotted to each member, and most did fairly well at self-support through gardening and the raising of livestock. Liberty Hall, the building which contained the school and social center, was built by volunteer labor. The colony had cooperative stores and a rich cultural life. Eccentric behavior was tolerated, although later the colony was deeply divided when some members filed criminal complaints against others who engaged in nude swimming. Many members were vegetarians and teetotalers. Home suffered considerable persecution from neighbors scared of anarchism; with the decline of anarchism's popularity at the time of World War I, the colony declined and gradually evolved into a fairly conventional rural town. Formal dissolution, by court order, came in 1919. Membership estimates vary widely, from under 100 to 5000; around 200 seems likely. Some original members still lived at the site decades later; reunions continued in Southern California at least into the 1950s.

The Washington State Historical Society (Tacoma) holds a large collection of Home papers and photographs. Some material on Home is in the American Communities Collection at Syracuse University. A scrapbook of Home materials is located at the Gig Harbor Historical Society. The papers of Jay Fox, for a time the newspaper editor at Home, are housed at the Crosby Library, Gonzaga University, Spokane.

Survey works: Curl (item 52), 35-6; Okugawa (item 139), 223.

*Community periodicals*

937. *Agitator.* 1910-2. Semimonthly.
According to the Union List of Serials, the *Agitator's* successor was the *Syndicalist*, but the latter paper was

apparently not published at Home.

938. *Clothed with the Sun.* 1902.
     Advocated nudism; suppressed.

939. *Demonstrator.* 1903-8. Monthly/weekly.
     Successor to *Discontent*, initiated after its predecessor
     was banned by the post office.

940. *Discontent*, "Mother of Progress." 1898-1902. Weekly.

941. *New Era.* 1897. Monthly. Edited by Oliver Verity.


*Secondary works*

942. Albertson, Ralph. "Mutual Home Association." "Survey of
     Mutualistic Communities in America" (cited above as
     item 27), 417.
     Provides a brief sketch of the colony.

943. Bliss, W.D.P. "Home Colony." *New Encyclopedia of Social
     Reform* (cited above as item 35), 574-5.
     Provides an overview history of the colony.

944. Burns, William J. *Masked War: The Story of a Peril That
     Threatened the United States by the Man Who
     Uncovered the Dynamite Conspirators and Sent Them to
     Jail.* New York: George H. Doran, 1913, pp. 64-91.
     Describes Burns's detective agency's search for the
     anarchists suspected of bombing the Los Angeles Times
     building, a search which sent several agents to Home,
     where the suspects had earlier stayed. Told in
     unintentionally comical, cloak-and-dagger style; perspective
     is staunchly opposed to Home and its residents.

945. Doig, Ivan, ed. "Nudes versus Prudes: *The Agitator
     Agitates a Prosecutor.*" *Utopian America: Dreams and
     Realities* (cited above as item 55), 77-82.
     Provides a brief introduction to the colony and
     reproduces several articles from the *Agitator* and the
     *Syndicalist*.

*    Federal Writers' Project. *New Washington: A Guide to the
     Evergreen State* (cited above as item 00), 570-1.

Provides a brief introduction to the colony and reproduces several articles from the *Agitator* and the *Syndicalist*.

\* Fcdcral Writcrs' Projcct. *New Washington: A Guide to the Evergreen State* (cited above as item 69), 570-1. Provides a historical sketch of Home and the conflicts which surrounded it; depicts the village of Home which survived.

946. Fogarty, Robert S. "Home Colony, or Mutual Home Association" and "Morton, James Ferdinand." *Dictionary of American Communal and Utopian History* (cited above as item 76), 144-5 and 78, respectively. Dictionary entries providing basic information on the colony.

947. Gaskine, J.W. "Anarchists at Home, Washington." *Independent* 68 (April 28, 1910): 914-22. Describes the physical setting of the colony; provides descriptions of some of its residents; describes changes the colony has undergone since its founding. Reproduces a manifesto by founder Oliver Verity. Illustrated with photographs, including a panoramic photo of the colony from the bay.

948. Goldman, Emma. "Donald Vose: The Accursed." *Mother Earth* 10 (January, 1916): 353-7. On an 1898 visit to Home, Goldman visited her old friend Gertie Vose. Years later, Goldman helped Vose's son David, providing him with room and board. It turned out that Vose was then gathering information to betray two of her radical friends; this article stridently denounces Vose, who utterly failed to live up to the promise of his Home upbringing.

949. Hinds, William Alfred. "Mutual Home Association." *American Communities and Co-operative Colonies* (cited above as item 95), 544-7. Provides a sketch of the current condition of the colony, quoting from *Discontent* and from the colony's articles of incorporation.

\* Hine, Robert V. *Community on the American Frontier* (cited above as item 99), 226-30. Provides a colorful picture of the diversity at Home.

Includes a photograph of a colony picnic about 1898.

950. Holbrook, Stewart. "Anarchists at Home." *American Scholar* 15 (Autumn, 1946): 425-38.
Tells the story of Home in straightforward, readable fashion. Not documented.

951. ———. "Brook Farm, Wild West Style." *American Mercury* 57 (August, 1943): 216-23.
Provides an informal historical sketch of the colony, describing colony visitors, cultural life, publications which offended the colony's neighbors, and the unorthodox ideas and behavior of some residents.

*        ———. *Far Corner* (cited above as item 101), 155-8.
Describes the founding of the colony, its periodicals, the rumors of free love and orgies which hounded it, and the aftermath of its heyday.

952. Kent, Alexander. "Mutual Home Association." "Cooperative Communities in the United States" (cited above as item 117), 636-7.
Describes the community's founding, social and economic life, and emphasis on individual freedom. Quotes, from the Articles of Incorporation passages on colony goals.

953. Lang, Lucy Robins. *Tomorrow Is Beautiful.* New York: Macmillan, 1948, pp. 48-52.
Provides an account of a season lived at Home, with personal sketches of some of the more colorful residents. Discusses the differences between the founders and their children.

954. LeWarne, Charles P. "Anarchist Colony at Home, Washington, 1901-1902." *Arizona and the West* 14 (Summer, 1972): 155-68.
Provides a brief history of the colony, focusing on the persecution Home suffered at the hands of anti-anarchist activists in the vicinity.

955. ———. "Home: Nest of Anarchy or Haven of Individualism?" "Communitarian Experiments in Western Washington, 1885-1915" (cited above as item 122), 347-530.
The most comprehensive history of the colony, and the basis for the chapter on Home in the author's published book (following item). Heavily documented with

references to specialized and local materials not cited here.

956. ————. "Home: Nest of Anarchy or Haven of Individualism?" *Utopias on Puget Sound* (cited above as item 124), 168-226.
A slightly shorter version of LeWarne's dissertation chapter (item 122, above). Heavily documented with specialized and local sources, many of them not cited here.

\* Meany, Edmond S. *History of the State of Washington* (cited above as item 129), 321-3.
Describes the anarchist principles of the colony, its buildings, and the role of the Mutual Home Association as a landholding company, not a colony ruling body.

957. Morgan, Murray. *Last Wilderness.* Seattle: University of Washington Press, 1955, pp. 101-21.
Provides a historical sketch of the colony, discussing the Home periodicals, cultural life, espousal of free love, disputes over nude bathing, anti-anarchist sentiment in the area, and the trial of Jay Fox, a Home editor, for advocating disrespect for the law.

\* Oved, Yaacov. "Sunrise and Anarchist Communities" (cited below as item 2717), 313-4.
Focuses on the community's periodicals and the internal and external problems the settlers encountered.

958. Slosson, E.E. "Experiment in Anarchy." *Independent* 55 (April 2, 1903): 779-85.
Describes the founding of the colony, the rationale for dividing the land into two-acre homesteads, the buildings on the site; contrasts the nearby colonies of Equality and Burley with Home. Illustrated.

959. "Some Disadvantages of Anarchism." *Independent* 54 (December 25, 1902): 3103-4.
Criticizes Home and anarchism in general, arguing from anecdotes about Home that the high ideals of anarchists often do not work out in daily life.

# LXX. HOME EMPLOYMENT
# CO-OPERATIVE COMPANY

William H. Bennett, after withdrawing from Alcander
Longley's Friendship Community in 1872, established the
short-lived Enterprise Community in 1873; in 1894, he purchased
land in Long Lane, Missouri, to start a new community modeled
on Ruskin.    The Home Employment Co-operative Company had
several cottage industries, including a broom factory, a flour
mill, a barber shop, a blacksmith shop, a shingle mill, and a
cannery, plus a farm.    The population of the community never
exceeded 30.    Its end came about gradually; it was defunct by
1906 or earlier.

Some material on the colony is in the American Communities
Collection at Syracuse University.

Survey work: Okugawa (item 139), 218-9.


*Secondary works*

960.  Albertson, Ralph.    "Home Employment Co-operative
      Company."    "Survey of Mutualistic Communities in
      America" (cited above as item 27), 417.
      Provides a brief overview of the community.


*     Grant, H. Roger.    "New Communitarianism: The Case of
      Three Intentional Colonies, 1890-1905." (cited above as
      item 86), 65-6.
      Provides basic information on the community, describing
      its origins and its goals.


961.  ———.    "New Communitarianism: William H. Bennett and
      the Home Employment Co-operative Company, 1894-
      1905."    *Bulletin of the Missouri Historical Society* 33
      (October, 1976): 18-26.
      Describes Bennett's earlier participation in Alcander
      Longley's Friendship Community; provides an overview
      history of the Home Employment community.    Illustrated
      with photographs and a map.


962.  Kent, Alexander.    "Home Employment Company."
      "Cooperative Communities in the United States (cited
      above as item 117), 634.

Provides a brief overview of the community and its industries.

# LXXI. HOUSE OF DAVID

In 1903 Benjamin Purnell founded the Israelite House of David (the first word in the title was often not used) at Benton Harbor, Michigan. The movement was Southcottian, one of several descended from the teachings of the British visionary Joanna Southcott. By 1907 the group had over 700 members; by 1922, 900. It was best known to the general public for its barnstorming baseball teams featuring players who never cut their hair or beards. In 1922 Purnell was charged with rape and fled. He was located in 1926 and tried on mulitple charges in 1927, but died soon thereafter. Following his death the movement broke into two factions, both still active in Benton Harbor. One faction, known as the Israelite House of David as Re-organized by Mary Purnell, or City of David, was led for many years by Purnell's widow Mary Purnell. The other faction, led by Judge H.T. Dewhirst, retained the original community's real estate and enjoyed great prosperity for many years. The following listing of primary works combines publications of the original group and both subsequent factions.

Some material on the community is in the American Communities Collection at Syracuse University.

Survey work: Okugawa (item 139), 227.

## Community periodicals

963. *New Shiloh Messenger.* Monthly.

964. *Shiloh's Messenger of Wisdom.* 1905-. Monthly.

## Primary works

965. *Beautiful Mantle of Shiloh Immanuel.* Benton Harbor: Israelite House of David, n.d. 29 pp.

966. *Book of Dialogues.* Benton Harbor: Israelite House of David, 1912-? Multiple volumes.

967. *Book of Henoch, the Prophet, Literally Translated from*

*the Ethiopic.*   Benton Harbor: Israelite House of David, 1912.

968. *Book of Wisdom: the Flying Roll.*   Benton Harbor: Israelite House of David, n.d.  Seven volumes.

969. *Cain's Wife—and Her Address.*  Benton Harbor: n.p., n.d.

970. *Dark and Bright Side of Man and Woman.*   Benton Harbor: n.p., [1931].  16 pp.

971. *Debate References: Earth and Sun.*   [Benton Harbor: Israelite House of David, ca. 1905].  6 pp.

972. *Elocution.*   [Benton Harbor: Israelite House of David, ca. 1914].  8 pp.

973. *Gabriel's Vision.*   Benton Harbor: Israelite House of David, n.d.  30 pp.

974. *House of David Song Book.*   [Benton Harbor: Israelite House of David, n.d.]  33 pp.

975. *Ingathering and Restoration of Israel at the City of David.*   Benton Harbor: Israelite House of David, n.d.   4 pp.  Theological tract.

976. *Mary's Story of the Separation.*

977. *Preacher's Reference Book.*   [Benton Harbor: Israelite House of David, ca. 1910].  22 pp.

978. *Prove All Things, Hold Fast to the Good.*   Benton Harbor: [Israelite House of David, ca. 1906].  80 pp.

979. *Rolling Ball of Fire* (vv. 1-6, 1915-25).

980. *Royal Seed—Jesus' Vision.*  Benton Harbor: n.p., 1947.

981. *Shiloh's Wisdom, the Flying Roll.*   Benton Harbor: n.p., [1933-4?]  Three volumes.

982. *Star of Bethlehem, the Living Roll of Life.*   Benton Harbor: Mary and Benjamin, 1903.  Two volumes.  The group's first publication after its founding.

983. *Subject Texts to the Rolling Balls of Fire no. 1, References on Earth, Sun, Moon, Stars, etc., from Scriptures, Enoch and Jasher.* [Benton Harbor: Israelite House of David, ca. 1916]. 48 pp.

984. *Subject Texts to the Rolling Ball of Fire no. 2, a Few References from Jasher, Apocrypha and Scriptures.* [Benton Harbor: Israelite House of David, ca. 1910]. 48 pp.

985. *Subject Texts to Seventh Book of Wisdom and Images and Likenesses.* [Benton Harbor: Israelite House of David, ca. 1912].

986. *True Light the Word of God, Addressed to the Twelve Tribes of Israel Scattered Abroad.* [Benton Harbor: Israelite House of David, ca. 1918]. 35 pp.

987. *Vegetarian Cook Book.* Benton Harbor: n.p., 1915. 133 pp.

988. *Washington's Vision.* Benton Harbor: Israelite House of David as Re-organized by Mary Purnell, n.d. 29 pp.

989. *What Is the Soul?* Benton Harbor: House of David, n.d. 15 pp.

990. *What? Where? When? Why? and How? of the House of David: A Book of Remembrance!* Benton Harbor: House of David, 1931. 32 pp.
Answers the title questions, explaining what the group considers itself to be, describing Purnell's travels, recalling important dates in the movement, and giving a rationale for its organization. Focuses on the life and interests of Purnell.

991. *Where Did Cain Get His Wife?* Benton Harbor: [Israelite House of David], n.d. 15 pp.

*Works by community leaders*

992. Purnell, Benjamin. *Benjamin's Last Writing.* Benton Harbor: Israelite House of David, 1927. 16 pp.

993. ———. *Brief Points of Benjamin's Travels.* Benton

Harbor: House of David, 1926. 30 pp.

994. ———. *Eden's Paradisical Liberty: Prohibition (?)-Temperance (?).* Benton Harbor: House of David, 1915. 33 pp.

995. ———. *Key to the House of David.* Benton Harbor: House of David, 1927. 32 pp.

996. ———. *Little Book in the Hand of the Angel.* Benton Harbor: Israelite House of David, 1927. 32 pp.

997. ———. *Patriotic Songs.* Benton Harbor: Israelite House of David, 1918. 11 pp.

998. ———. *Poetry by Benjamin. Book II.* Benton Harbor: Israelite House of David, [1917?]. 44 pp.

999. ———. *Rules and Regulations for the Kingdom of God's Sake.* [Benton Harbor: Israelite House of David, ca. 1910.] 32 pp.
A compilation of many specific rules governing personal behavior and transaction of the community's business. Liberally sprinkled with biblical quotations.

1000. ———. *Seven Baskets of Fragments: Briefs from Benjamin's Discourses!* Benton Harbor: Israelite House of David, [ca. 1907- ?]. Four volumes.

1001. ———. *Sword of the Spirit of the House of David.* [Benton Harbor: Israelite House of David, ca. 1905]. 55 pp.

1002. ———. *Testimony of Benjamin (including Benjamin's Manuscript Notes) Given in Open Court in the Trial of the State of Michigan vs. House of David.* Benton Harbor: House of David, [1928?]. 73 pp.

1003. ———. *Views of the House of David.* [Benton Harbor: n.p., 1936?] 36 pp.
Chiefly illustrations.

1004. Purnell, Mary. *Book of Heaven.* Fifth volume in the *Comforter series.*

1005. ———. *Book of Paradise.* Sixth volume in the *Com-*

*forter* series.

1006. ———. *Comforter.* Four volumes.

1007. ———. *First Rudiments of Israel's Faith.* Benton Harbor: Israelite House of David, n.d. 30 pp. Theological and doctrinal tract.

1008. ———. *Mary and Benjamin's Travels.* 33 pp. Benton Harbor: Israelite House of David, n.d.
Recounts travels undertaken by the Purnells for the spreading of the faith. Contains on pp. 20-32, "Radio Talks by Sister Mary," transcripts of two radio programs on WKZO, Berrien Springs, Michigan. The first program transcript (February 1, 1931) tells of the schism in the movement. The second (March 1, 1931) announces that the ingathering is in progress at the new House of David.

1009. ———. *Preachers' Book: The Last Message of Life to Israel, Who Are Scattered Abroad.* Benton Harabor: Israelite House of David, n.d. 28 pp. Theological tract.

1010. ———. *Questions and the Ingathering of Israel.* Benton Harbor: Israelite House of David, n.d. 32 pp. Theological tract. Pp. 27-31 contain "Scriptural Questions of Interest," a list of questions which can be answered by House of David publications.

1011. ———. *Soul.* Benton Harbor: Israelite House of David, n.d. 16 pp.
A tract on the nature of the soul. Page 16 contains two poems opposing the use of alcohol and tobacco.

### Secondary works

1012. Albertson, Ralph. "House of David." "Survey of Mutualistic Communities in America" (cited above as item 27), 393.
Provides a very brief sketch of the community.

1013. Baldwin, R.A. *Jezreelites: The Rise and Fall of a Remarkable Prophetic Movement.* Orphington, Kent: Lambarde Press, 1962. 112 pp.

Provides a general history of the Jezreelites, primarily focusing on their activity in England, but describing their work in America, including the career of the Purnells.

1014. Balleine, George R. *Past Finding Out*. New York: Macmillan, 1956.
A history of the Joanna Southcott movement and its successors, including, on pp. 114-24, the House of David. Contains a table, on p. 147, showing all the Southcottian sects, indicating the lineage of the House of David and all the other groups.

1015. Bliss, W.D.P. "House of David." *New Encyclopedia of Social Reform* (cited above as item 35), 581.
Describes the theological claims of the movement and provides an inventory of its buildings and industries.

1016. Clark, Elmer T. "House of David." *Small Sects in America* (cited above as item 43), 153-4.
Provides a brief account of the movement's history and theology, plus an overview of Purnell's sex scandal.

1017. "Fall of the House of David." *Independent* 120 (January 7, 1928): 3-4.
Rejoices in the prospect that this "spurious religious order" is about to fail. Provides a brief outline of the claims of Benjamin Purnell and the history of the movement.

*      Federal Writers' Project. *Michigan: A Guide to the Wolverine State* (cited above as item 68), 207-9.
Describes the history and tenets of the movement, focusing on the downfall and death of Purnell; describes the division of the colony after Purnell's death, subsequent daily life in each colony, and their major collective impact on the economy of Benton Harbor. Also contains (on p. 605) a note on the virtual penal colony maintained by the House of David on High Island in Lake Michigan from 1912 to 1928.

1018. Ferguson, Charles W. *New Books of Revelations*. Garden City, N.Y.: Doubleday, Doran, 1930, pp. 49-62.
Provides a history of the Southcottians and the House of David; emphasizes Purnell's sexual transgressions and legal problems.

1019. Fogarty, Robert S. "Purnell, Benjamin." *Dictionary of American Communal and Utopian History* (cited above as item 76), 96-7.
Biographical dictionary entry.

1020. ———. *Righteous Remnant: The House of David.* Kent, Ohio: Kent State University Press, 1981. 195 pp.
The basic monograph on the movement, covering historical predecessors of the movement, scrapes with the law, especially over Purnell's womanizing, and the trial of Purnell. Includes a House of David theological document and bibliography on the movement, including some specialized items not listed here. Illustrated with photographs.

1021. Hinds, William Alfred. "House of David." *American Communities and Co-operative Colonies* (cited above as item 95), 563-76.
Provides an overview of the community based on a personal visit and on question-and-answer sessions with community leaders; quotes Ben and Mary Purnell on the theology of the group. Illustrated with photographs.

1022. "House of David." *Intentional Communities: 1959 Yearbook of the Fellowship of Intentional Communities* (cited above as item 807), 16.
Contains a brief overview of the movement.

* Lauer, Robert H., and Jeanette C. Lauer. *Spirit and the Flesh* (cited above as item 120), 65.
Provides an overview of the Purnell sex scandal.

1023. Mathison, Richard. "Ben Purnell and the House of David." *Faiths, Cults and Sects of America: From Atheism to Zen* (cited above as item 127), 306-16.
Sketches the history of the Southcottians, the rise of Purnell, and the blooming of the House of David.

1024. Mayer, F.E. "House of David." *Religious Bodies of America* (cited above as item 128), 446-7.
Contains a one-page description of the colony, including its basic history and the story of the scandal of the 1920s.

1025. Melton, J. Gordon. "Israelite House of David" and "Israelite House of David as Reorganized by Mary

Purnell."    *Encyclopedia of American Religions* (cited
above as item 130), 457-9.
Sketches the history and ideas of the movement, with
a separate note on Mary Purnell's faction.

1026.  Orrmont, Arthur.    "Benjamin Franklin Purnell: The
       Monarch of Benton Harbor."    *Love Cults and Faith
       Healers* (cited above as item 141), 91-110.
       Provides a history of Purnell and the movement,
focusing on sexual scandals and Purnell's arrest and trial.

1027.  Pender, James.    *History of Benton Harbor and Tales of
       Village Days.*    Chicago: Braun, 1915, pp. 107-9.
       Describes the very earliest "Flying Roller" preaching
and evangelism in Benton Harbor; largely based on a
hostile newspaper account.

1028.  Quaife, Milo.    "King of Benton Harbor."    *Lake Michigan*
       (cited above as item 146), 262-78.
       The earliest academically serious and substantial work
on the movement.

1029.  Randolph, Vance.    "Younger Brother of Jesus."
       *Americans Who Thought They Were Gods* (cited above
       as item 149), 11-14.
       Describes Purnell's early days, the baseball team, the
litigation against Purnell, his arrest and death, and the
schism after his death.

1030.  Rosentreter, Roger L.    "House of David: Hoax or
       Heaven?"    *Michigan History* 63 (1979): 29-39.
       Chronicles the activities of Southcott believers in
America, the development of the colony at Benton
Harbor, the arrest and trial of King Ben, and the
factions that developed after his death.    Finds the
movement successful and full of accomplishments, despite
the weaknesses of its founder.    Illustrated with
photographs.

1031.  Sterling, Anthony.    *King of the Harem Heaven: The
       Amazing True Story of a Daring Charlatan Who Ran A
       Virgin Love Cult in America.*    Derby, Connecticut:
       Monarch Books, 1960.  159 pp.

*      Strachey, Ray, and Hannah Whithall Smith.  *Group
       Movements of the Past and Experiments in Guidance*

(cited above as item 161), 148-50.
A brief history of the origins, rise, and decline of the movement.

1032. Thorpe, Francis. *Crown of Thorns: House of David Victory and Legal Troubles Reviewed.* Benton Harbor: Israelite House of David, 1929. 174 pp.
Tells the story of the split in the House of David after Purnell's death, and argues that the schism fulfilled prophecy.

1033. Waldron, Webb. "House of David." *We Explore the Great Lakes.* New York: Century, 1923, pp. 256-72.
Provides an account of an overnight visit to the colony, describing the group's amusement park and other facilities and recounting conversations with group leaders.

1034. Webber, Everett. "King Ben." *Escape to Utopia* (cited above as item 168), 348-53.
Provides an overview of the colony, focusing on Purnell's excesses.

1035. Wooster, Ernest S. "House of David." *Communities of the Past and Present* (cited above as item 175), 115-7.
Characterizes the beliefs of the community, its unusual practices, and its economy.

# LXXII. THE HUTTERITES

The Hutterites, named for one of their early leaders, Jakob Hutter, were radical Anabaptists who adopted community of goods in 1528. They were often persecuted in their early centuries, although there were also periods of freedom and toleration. In 1770 they settled in the Ukraine under an arrangement which guaranteed them special privileges, especially exemption from military service; when conscription was imposed in 1871, they prepared to move again. Communal living had been abandoned in 1819, but just before the move from the Russian Empire a religious revival among the Hutterites had seen some of their members re-establish it. Immigration to the United States began in 1874. The Hutterites came in three groups, and the three have remained distinct since, the Dariusleut, Lehrerleut, and Schmiedeleut.

They all settled in South Dakota initially, but when persecution set in during World War I, most moved to Canada. South Dakota welcomed the Hutterites back in the 1930s, and several colonies returned. Today the rapidly growing movement has colonies in several states and in all of the prairie provinces in Canada. They use modern agricultural technology, but try to retain old lifeways and to remain relatively isolated from the outside world.

Much has been published on the early Hutterites in Europe. Only a few selected articles on early history have been cited here. Some bibliographic works on the Hutterites list more articles on the European period; see especially Robert Friedmann, "Comprehensive Review of Research on the Hutterites 1880-1905" (item 1165, below).

The *Mennonite Encyclopedia* (item 131) contains many articles on the Hutterites; only a few of the more important ones are cited here.

Some materials on the Hutterites are located in the American Communities Collection at Syracuse University.

Survey work: Okugawa (item 139), 205-6, 208-9, 213-6, 226-31.


## Primary works

1036. *Chronicle of the Hutterian Brethren*, v. I. Rifton, N.Y.: Plough, 1987. 887 pp. Translated and edited by the Hutterian Brethren (i.e., the Bruderhof).
An English translation of the Hutterites' manuscript book of the movement's early history. A new introduction traces the survival of old Hutterite documents.

1037. *Constitution of the Hutterian Brethren Church and Rules as to Community of Property*. Winnipeg: E.A. Fletcher, 1950.
Codifies traditional observances. This constitution was composed to comply with governmental requirements for organizations.

1038. *Hutterian Brethren of America*. Lethbridge, Alberta: [Hutterian Brethren of North America], 1968. 24 pp.

1039. *Hutterian Brethren of Montana*. Augusta, Montana: n.p., n.d.
A statement composed by Hutterites in Montana in an

attempt to dispel false information about them. Contains information on their beliefs, church, baptismal oath, nomenclature, history, schools, stands of voting and citizenship, taxes, peace, and community life, and their answers to criticism of them and their way of life. At the Institute for the Study of American Religion.

*Works by community leaders*

Included in this section are a few works of some of the key leaders in early Hutterite history, plus those of Paul S. Gross, the most prominent contemporary spokesperson for the Hutterites.

1040. Ehrenpreis, Andreas. *Epistle Concerning Communal Life (1650).* Rifton, N.Y.: Plough, 1960. 30 pp. Introduction by Robert Friedmann. Also published in *Mennonite Quarterly Review* 34 (October, 1960): 249-74.

1041. Ehrenpreis, Andreas, and Claus Felbinger. *Brotherly Community: the Highest Command of Love.* Rifton, N.Y.: Plough, 1978. 150 pp. Presents two early Anabaptist documents on community.

1042. Gross, Paul S. *Hutterian Brethren.* Pincher Creek, Alberta: n.p., 1980. 38 pp. An informal, anecdotal history of the Pincher Creek colony from 1926 to 1980.

1043. ———. *Hutterite Way: The Inside Story of the Life, Customs, Religion and Tradition of the Hutterites.* Saskatoon: Freeman Publishing Co., 1965. A book rich in flavor as well as information: Gross is a Hutterite minister. Contains basic Hutterite history, with special attention paid to the differences between Hutterites and other Anabaptists. Provides information on Hutterite farming, order and authority, education, courtship, origins of the three leuts, pacifism, dress, food and drink, and other topics. Discusses opposition to Hutterite expansion in Canada and reflects on the impact of technology of Hutterite life. Contains a bibliography which includes unusual items not cited here.

1044. ———. "On the Trails of Our Anabaptist Forefathers, Summer 1968." *Mennonite Quarterly Review* 44

(January, 1970): 85-99.
A report on a trip to Hutterite homelands in Germany,
Switzerland, Austria, Slovakia, Hungary, and Roumania.
Illustrated with photographs of buildings significant to
Hutterite history and woodcuts of sixteenth century
Hutterites and of one of their buildings.

1045. ———. "Robert Friedmann and the Hutterites."
*Mennonite Quarterly Review* 48 (April, 1974): 192-7.
Traces the scholarly career of Friedmann and his
relations with the Hutterites.

1046. ———. *Who Are the Hutterites?* Scottdale, Pennsylvania: Mennonite Publishing House, 1959. 16 pp.

1047. Hutter, Jakob. *Brotherly Faithfulness: Epistles from a
Time of Persecution.* Rifton, N.Y.: Plough, 1979. 250
pp.
Nine letters written by the movement's namesake.

1048. ———. *Jakob Hutter's Last Epistle to the Church in
Moravia (1534).* Rifton, N.Y.: Plough, 1960. Edited
with an introduction by Robert Friedmann. Also
published in *Mennonite Quarterly Review* 34 (January,
1960): 37-47.

1049. Rideman, Peter. *Account of Our Religion, Doctrine and
Faith.* Rifton, N.Y.: Plough, 1950. 304 pp. Later
published under the title *Confession of Faith.*
Translated by Kathleen Hasenburg.
This historical treatise is regarded by the Hutterites as
the definitive statement of their faith and practice. The
author's name is sometimes spelled "Riedemann," the
proper German orthography.

1050. Waldner, Johannes. *Klein-Geschichtsbuch der
Hutterischen Brueder.* Philadelphia: Carl Schurz
Memorial Foundation, 1947. Edited by A.J.F.
Zieglschmid. In German.

1051. Walpot, Peter. *True Surrender and Christian Community
of Goods.* Rifton, N.Y.: Plough, 1957. 48 pp.
Translated by Kathleen Hasenberg. Also published,
with an introduction by Robert Friedmann, in
*Mennonite Quarterly Review* 31 (January, 1957): 22-62.
An early Hutterite document.

*Secondary works*

1052.  Alberta, Province of. *Report of the Hutterite Investigation Committee.* Edmonton: Government of Alberta, 1959. Mimeographed.
Includes the text of the Communal Property Act, by which the provincial government restricted Hutterite land purchases.

1053.  ———. *Report on Communal Property, 1972.* Edmonton: Select Committee of the Alberta Assembly, 1972.

1054.  "Alberta Eases Regulations on Hutterite Communities." *Financial Post* 54 (April 2, 1960): 10.

1055.  "Alberta's Hutterites Score a Significant Win in Court." *Financial Post* 61 (May 27, 1967): 8.

1056.  Albertson, Ralph. "The Hutterian (or Hutterische Brueder) Communities." "Survey of Mutualistic Communities in America" (cited above as item 27), 391.
Provides a brief overview of American Hutterite history through the World War I departure to Canada.

1057.  Allard, William Albert. "Hutterites, Plain People of the West." *National Geographic* 138 (July, 1970): 98-125.
Illustrated survey of Hutterite life focused on Spring Creek Colony, Montana.

1058.  Anderson, James Russell. "Pentecost Preaching of Acts 2—An Aspect of Hutterite Theology". Ph.D. dissertation, Southern Baptist Theological Seminary, 1971. 646 pp. in two volumes.

1059.  Apsler, Alfred. "Hutterites." *Communes Through the Ages: The Search for Utopia.* New York: Julian Messner, 1974, pp. 64- 78.
Provides an overview of the Hutterites, with emphasis on the mechanisms that make communal living work.

1060.  Argus, Orient, and B.H. Hardenbrook. "Hutterische Society Home." *South Dakotan* 6 (July, 1903): 11-3.
Contains Argus's description of "the Russian or Dunkard Colony at Elm Springs" and Hardenbrook's account of a visit to Wolf Creek colony, where he was surprised by the Hutterites' progressiveness and openness.

1061.  Arndt, Karl J.R.  *George Rapp's Successors and Material Heirs, 1847-1916.*  Rutherford, N.J.: Fairleigh Dickinson University Press, 1971, pp. 129-38.
Provides details on loans the Hutterites received from the Harmonists from 1875 until 1887, when the Harmonists decided that the Hutterites were not good business managers.  Describes the 1884 offer of Harmonist land in Pennsylvania to the Hutterites and the brief effort at Hutterite settlement there.

1062.  ———.  "Harmonists and the Hutterians."  *American-German Review* 10 (August, 1944): 24-7.
Summarizes the correspondence between the two groups in the 1870s; describes the temporary settlement of Hutterites on Harmonist land in Pennsylvania and the unsuccessful effort of the Harmonists to make the Hutterites their heirs.  Illustrated with photographs of the Harmonist granary at Economy, Pennsylvania.

1063.  Arnold, Eberhard.  *Hutterian Brethren.*  Ashton Keynes, Wiltshire, England: Plough, 1940.  45 pp.
Arnold planned to write an authoritative history of the Hutterites, but died before it could be completed.  This book contains a preliminary essay on Hutterite history plus four appendices, including a list of Hutterite colonies active in 1940 and information about cooperation between the Hutterites and the Bruderhof.

1064.  "Austrian Anabaptists in America."  *American Review of Reviews* 38 (August, 1908): 243-4.
Marvels at the rapid growth and prosperity of the Hutterites in America.

1065.  Bach, Marcus.  *Dream Gate.*  Indianapolis: Bobbs-Merrill, 1949.
A novel about the Hutterites, focusing on the temptations the outside world offers to a Hutterite boy.

1066.  ———.  *Faith and My Friends.*  Indianapolis: Bobbs-Merrill, 1951, pp. 109-50.
Provides the author's informal and personal reminiscences about his years of contact with Hutterites, especially recounting his conversations with John J. Maendel, a Hutterite, and characterizing his testimony before a legislative committee in Manitoba which was considering restrictions on Hutterite land purchases.

1067. ———. "Hutterites." *Strange Sects and Curious Cults* (cited above as item 29), 235-50.
Surveys Hutterite history and life, focusing on the inroads of the modern world on the movement.

1068. Baden, John A. "Management of Social Stability: A Political Ethnography of the Hutterites of North America." Ph.D. dissertation, Indiana University, 1967. 205 pp.

1069. Baden, John A., and Mary Anna Hovey-Baden. "Education, Employability and Role Taking Among North American Hutterites." *Conference on Child Socialization*. Edited by John A. Hostetler. Washington: Department of Health, Education and Welfare, 1969, pp. 235-51.
Provides a role-theory explanation of the high rate of returning to the colony found among young Hutterite males who leave.

1070. Baer, Hans A. "Effect of Technological Innovation on Hutterite Culture." *Plains Anthropologist* 21 (August, 1976): 187-97.
Argues that a tension exists between Hutterite cultural traditionalism and the use of modern technology. Based on a stay in a colony.

1071. Baer, Hans A., and Lawrence A. Kratz. "Hutterites: Communitarians for 350 Years." *Communities* no. 39 (August-September, 1979): 7-11.
A survey of Hutterite life by an anthropologist. Illustrated.

1072. Bainton, Roland. "Frontier Community." *Mennonite Life* 9 (January, 1954): 34-41.
Presents early Hutterite history, noting situations in which modern Hutterites have deviated from the practices of the earlier generations, as in supporting outside missionary activity. Illustrated with photographs of Hutterite ceramics.

1073. Barkin, David, and John W. Bennett. "Kibbutz and Colony: Collective Economies and the Outside World." *Comparative Studies in Society and History* 14 (January, 1972): 456-83.

Provides a detailed comparison of kibbutzim and Hutterite colonies, emphasizing the changes the two institutions have made in response to the encroachments of the modern world.

1074. Barnett, Don C., and Lowry R. Knight. *Hutterite People.* Saskatoon: Western Extension College Educational Publishers, 1977. 70 pp.

1075. Barrass, Georgeen. "Hutterites—the Peaceful People." *Canadian Collector* 11 (January-February, 1976): 77-9.

1076. Baum, Patricia. "Plain People of the West." *Another Way of Life: The Story of Communal Living.* New York: Putman's, 1973, pp. 105-22.
Provides an overview of Hutterite life.

1077. Baum, Ruth Elizabeth. "Ethnohistory of Law: The Hutterite Case." Ph.D. dissertation, State University of New York at Albany, 1977. 444 pp.
Describes the internal legal system of the Hutterites. Not seen.

1078. Bender, Harold S. "Chronological Bibliography of the Writings of Robert Friedmann." *Mennonite Quarterly Review* 35 (July, 1961): 243-7.
Provides a listing of Friedmann's works in German and English; most of his work focused on the European origins of Anabaptism.

1079. Bennett, John W. "Change and Transition in Hutterian Society." *Western Canada Past and Present.* Edited by Anthony W. Rasporich. Toronto: McClelland and Stewart West, 1975, pp. 120-32.
Outlines the Hutterites' rising standard of living, liberalization of lifestyle (especially among the Dariusleut), and wider external contacts. Predicts that these trends will continue in the future, although change will not be drastic. Predicts that nonhutterite farmers will see them more and more as a good alternative to individual farming and big agribusiness.

1080. ———. "Communal Brethren of the Great Plains." *Trans-Action* 4 (December, 1966): 42-7.
Provides an overview of Hutterite history, government, and life, emphasizing the sternness of the rules but the

unwritten flexibility which allows for some individual freedom.

1081. ———. "Frames of Reference for the Study of Hutterian Society." *International Review of Modern Sociology* 6 (Spring, 1976): 23-39. Reprinted in *Communes: Historical and Contemporary* (cited above as item 41), 25-43.
Proposes six theoretical approaches to the study of Hutterite society, e.g., "Hutterian agriculture as a resource-conservationist system."

1082. ———. *Hutterian Brethren*. Stanford: Stanford University Press, 1967.
This study of six Hutterite colonies in Saskatchewan contains information on their environment, history, relations with the outside world, marriage and family, organization, economics, work, social control, and reaction to technological change. Contains an extensive bibliography, illustrations, and many tables and diagrams.

1083. ———. "Hutterian Colony: A Traditional Voluntary Agrarian Commune with Large Economic Scale." *Cooperative and Commune: Group Farming in the Economic Development of Agriculture*. Madison: University of Wisconsin Press, 1977, pp. 65-88.
Argues that the Hutterites represent the most purely communal society currently active, and suggests that agrarian planners study the Hutterite model more closely for the benefit of noncommunal farmers. Includes two diagrams.

1084. ———. "Hutterites: A Communal Seat" [sic, although "Sect" is clearly meant]. *Minority Canadians: volume 2, Immigrant Groups*, pp. 15-32. Edited by Jean Leonard Elliott. Reprinted from *Plains Peoples: Adaptive Strategy and Agrarian Life in the Great Plains*. By John W. Bennett. Chicago: Aldine, 1969. (Apparently a variant title for item 1085, below).
Provides information on Hutterite history, religion, and culture, focusing on "Jasper," an anonymous colony. Has a useful chart on Hutterite organization.

1085. ———. *Northern Plainsmen*. Chicago: Aldine, 1969, pp. 246-75).
Describes the first settlements of Hutterites in the

"Jasper" area in the 1950s. Portrays their adaptation to a harsh farming climate which many earlier settlers had abandoned. Discusses their relations with others in the area. An abridgment of this chapter is in *Religion in Canadian Society* (Toronto: Macmillan of Canada, 1976), 256-67.

1086. ————. "Social Theory and the Social Order of the Hutterian Community." *Mennonite Quarterly Review* 51 (October, 1977): 292-307.
Outlines the techniques used by Hutterites to maintain internal discipline in the face of a multitude of inducements to deviation. Finds that belief, not commitment, is at the root of Hutterite life.

1087. Bleibtreu, Herman K. "Marriage and Residence Patterns in a Genetic Isolate." Ph.D. dissertation, Harvard University, 1964.

1088. Boldt, Edward D. "Acquiescence and Conventionality in a Communal Society." *Journal of Cross-Cultural Psychology* 7 (March, 1976): 21-36.
Finds that Hutterites are only marginally more acquiescent to the expectations of the group than nonhutterites are.

1089. ————. "Conformity and Deviance: The Hutterites of Alberta." M.A. thesis, University of Alberta, 1966. 94 pp.

1090. ————. "Conventionality and Acquiescence in a Communal Society." Ph.D. dissertation, University of Alberta, 1969. 286 pp.
Argues that acquiescence to group pressure is no more significant in Hutterite society than in society as a whole; therefore, acquiescence to the group is not a means for controlling deviance among the Hutterites.

1091. ————. "Death of Hutterite Culture: An Alternative Interpretation." *Phylon* 41 (December, 1980): 390-5.
A rejoinder to Frideres (item 1159); argues that liberalization of the old rules, rather than external pressures, is the biggest threat to Hutterite culture.

1092. ————. "Plain People: Notes on Their Continuity and Change." *Canadian Ethnic Studies* 11 (1979): 17-28.

1093. ———. "Recent Development of a Unique Population: The Hutterites of North America." *Prairie Forum* 8 (Fall, 1983): 235- 40.
Finds that the traditionally phenomenal rate of growth of the Hutterite population has slowed. The argument is supported with charts and tables.

1094. ———. "Structural Tightness, Autonomy, and Observability: An Analysis of Hutterite Conformity and Orderliness." *Canadian Journal of Sociology* 3 (Summer, 1978): 349-63.
Argues that "structural tightness" and the resultant restriction of individual autonomy has more to do with Hutterite conformity than internalized group norms or desire for approval of others do.

1095. Boldt, Edward D., and Lance W. Roberts. "Decline of Hutterite Population Growth: Causes and Consequences —A Comment." *Canadian Ethnic Studies* 3 (1980): 111.
A comment on an article of Karl Peter (item 1329, below). Says that not enough social scientific work has been done on the implications and consequences of rapid growth on Hutterite continuity.

* Bouvard, Marguerite. *Intentional Community Movement* (cited above as item 37), 43.
Brief note about the Hutterites emphasizes the steadfast, sealed-off-from-the-world nature of Hutterite life.

1096. Brednich, Rolf W. *Bible and the Plough: The Lives of a Hutterite Minister and a Mennonite Farmer.* Ottawa: National Museums of Canada, 1981. 141 pp.
Contains a biographical sketch of Michael S. Stahl, minister at Riverview Colony near Saskatoon, in an interview format, plus commentary by the author. Illustrated with photographs.

1097. Byfield, Link, and Andy Ogle. "Harnessing the Hutterites." *Alberta Report* 10 (January 31, 1983): 32.

1098. Caldwell, Mark Stuart. "Ideological and Institutional Reflections of the Benedictine Ideal in Sixteenth Century Hutterites: A Study in Ecclesiastical Ecology." Th.D. dissertation, Southern Baptist Theological Seminary, 1970. 257 pp.

1099.  Canadian Mental Health Association, Saskatchewan
       Division.  *Hutterites and Saskatchewan: A Study of
       Inter-Group Relations.*  [Regina]: n.p., 1953.  132 pp.
       Provides an overview of Hutterite life and a
       comparative study of Maple Creek and Shaunavon
       colonies.  Concludes that since Hutterites can be
       recognized readily as "different," they are subject to
       being made scapegoats and being the victims of
       misinformed rumors.

1100.  "Canadians Resist Sect's Expansion."  New York *Times,*
       September 29, 1957, p. 54.

1101.  "Can't Buy Land in Alberta; Hutterites Eye Washington."
       *Financial Post* 50 (June 16, 1956): 39.

1102.  Clark, Bertha W.  "Huterian Communities."  *Journal of
       Political Economy* 32 (1924): 357-74 and 468-86.
       One of the earliest published pieces of research on the
       Hutterites.  Describes the Hutterite colonies (then 26 in
       number) in terms of physical layout, work life, and
       educational system.  Isolates seven principles as central
       to Hutterism: adult baptism, the Lord's supper as a
       memorial only, abstaining from worldly activities,
       supporting a Christian ministry, nonresistance, abstinence
       from oath-taking, and rejecting all punishment other than
       the Ban.

1103.  Clark, Bertha W., as edited by Clifton H. Jones.
       "'Huterisch People': A View from the 1920s."  *South
       Dakota History* 7 (Winter, 1976): 1-14.
       Contains two manuscripts edited into one; they consist
       of observations made by Clark as she was working among
       the Hutterites for the YWCA.  Includes many anecdotes.
       Illustrated with photographs.

1104.  Clark, Bertha W.  "Turners of the Other Cheek."  *Survey*
       47 (December 31, 1921): 519-24.
       Conveys information gathered from Clark's work among
       the Hutterites.  Characterizes Hutterite history, daily
       life, worship, and pacifism.  Speculates about the future
       of the Hutterites in the face of encroachment by modern
       culture. Illustrated with line drawings.

1105.  Clark, Elmer T.  "Hutterian Brethren."  *Small Sects in
       America* (cited above as item 43), 192-3.

Provides a brief and somewhat inaccurate sketch of Hutterite history through the World War I era.

1106. Clark, Peter Gordon. "Dynasty Formation in the Communal Society of the Hutterites." Ph.D. dissertation, University of British Columbia, 1974. Abstract in *Mennonite Quarterly Review* 53 (January, 1979): 80.

1107. ———. "Leadership Succession Among the Hutterites." *Canadian Review of Sociology and Anthropology* 14 (August, 1977): 294-302.
Analyzes political leadership mobility patterns in sample colonies, arguing that inequality of opportunity to achieve leadership occurs when colony population growth exceeds the increase in the number of leadership positions.

1108. Clasen, Claus-Peter. *Anabaptism: A Social History, 1528-1618*. Ithaca: Cornell University Press, 1972, pp. 210-97.
Focuses on early Hutterite history in Europe.

1109. Cobb, Douglas S. "Jamesville Bruderhof: A Hutterian Agricultural Colony." *Journal of the West* 9 (January, 1970): 60-77.
Provides an overview history of the Hutterites and a discussion of new colony formation; focusing on the Jamesville, South Dakota, colony, describes land use, farming operations, industries, and other such matters.

1110. Cohen, Lori. "Hutterite Justice." *Alberta Report* 12 (March 18, 1985): 27.
Describes a criminal case in which a judge discharged a young Hutterite thief on the grounds that colony discipline would adequately discourage him from committing further crimes.

1111. Conkin, Paul K. "Brethren Known as Hutterites." *Two Paths to Utopia: The Hutterites and the Llano Colony* (cited above as item 50), 3-100.
Provides a history of the Hutterites in Europe and North America, emphasizing conflicts Hutterites have had with governments in the United States and Canada.

1112. Converse, T.A. "Hutterite Midwifery." *American Journal*

*of Obstetrics and Gynecology* 116 (July 1, 1973): 719-25.
Finds that infant and maternal mortality rates are about the same for Hutterites and nonhutterites, despite the Hutterites' adherence to traditional midwifery. Contains statistical tables and a bar graph.

1113. Cook, Robert C. "North American Hutterites: A Study in Human Multiplication." *Population Bulletin* 10 (December, 1954): 97-107.
Reports that 443 Hutterites immigrated between 1874 and 1877, and that by 1950 their numbers had grown to 8000. If they maintain the birth and death rates they have exhibited, they should reach 70,000 by the year 2000 and 500,000 by 2050. The Hutterite population was at the time of the study growing more rapidly than that of any country in the world. Discusses reasons for the high fertility rate and speculates that the group will eventually encounter declining prosperity because of its birth rate, or will experience acculturation and assimilation, which would lower the growth rate.

1114. Cooperstock, Henry. "Co-operative Farming as a Variant Social Pattern." *Canadian Society: Sociological Perspectives*. Edited by B.R. Blishen et al. New York: Free Press of Glencoe, 1961, pp. 256-74.
A comparative study of the cooperative farms of Saskatchewan, the Hutterite colonies, and the kibbutzim of Israel.

1115. Crow, James F., and Arthur P. Mange. "Measurement of Inbreeding from the Frequency of Marriages Between Persons of the Same Surname." *Eugenics Quarterly* 12 (December, 1965): 199-203.
Studies the probability of inbreeding among Hutterites, assuming that common last names may indicate common ancestry.

1116. Crysdale, Stewart, and Jean-Paul Montminy. *Religion in Canada: Annotated Inventory of Scientific Studies of Religion (1945-1972)*. Downsview, Ontario: York University Press, 1974. 189 pp.
Annotated bibliography on Canadian religion, with several references to works on Hutterites. Part 1 (pp. 3-73) covers works in French; part 2 (pp. 75-177) covers works in English.

1117. Davis, Morris, and Joseph F. Krauter. *Other Canadians: Profiles of Six Minorities.* Toronto: Methuen, 1971, pp. 87-101.
Describes colony life, the Hutterite settlements in Canada since 1899, restrictive provincial legislation, and Hutterite education.

1118. Decker, Hans. *God's Salvation Plan and a Brief History of the Hutterite People.* Hawley, Minnesota: Spring Prairie Printing, 1988.
A Hutterite minister's statement about the purpose of life. Available from the author at Wolf Creek Colony, South Dakota.

1119. ———. *What Is to Be Gained or Lost.* Olivet, S.D.: author, n.d. 8 pp.
A theological treatise on the purpose of human life on earth. Copies are available from the author, a minister at Wolf Creek colony.

1120. Deets, Lee Emerson. *Hutterites: A Study in Social Cohesion.* Gettysburg: Times Publishing Co., 1939. Repr., Philadelphia: Porcupine Press, 1975. 64 pp.
Emphasizes the methods which make the movement cohere. Footnotes provide some early Hutterite bibliography. A new epilogue appears in the reprinted edition.

1121. ———. "Origins of Conflict in the Hutterische Communities." *Social Conflict: Papers of the American Sociological Society* 25, part 2 (1931): 125-35.
Finds the Hutterites to be virtually free of internal conflict, but sees potential conflict beteween the family and the community; also suggests that external relations may lead to internal conflict, by, for example, introducing the desire for money.

1122. ———. "What Can We Learn from the Hutterites Regarding the Potentialities of Human Nature for Lasting Peace?" *Human Nature and Enduring Peace.* Edited by Gardner Murphy. Boston: Houghton Mifflin, 1945, 341-7.
Argues that the Hutterites see peace not simply as the absence of war, but as a permanent way of living.

1123. Diener, Paul. "Ecology or Evolution? The Hutterite

Case."    *American    Ethnologist*  1  (November,  1974):
601-18.
Finds  that  an  evolutionary  approach  is  more  useful
than  an  an  ecological  approach  in  the  anthropological
evaluation of Hutterites.

1124.  *Dominion   Law   Reports*  (Canada).      Second   series,  v.  59
(1967): 723-36.
Reports  a  1966  court  finding  denying  any  right  to  a
share  of  colony  assets  to  members  of  Interlake  Colony
(Manitoba)  who  had  been  expelled  for  being  baptized  into
the  Radio  Church  of  God  (later  Worldwide  Church  of
God).

1125.  Douglas,   Dorothy   W.,   and   Katharine   Du   Pre   Lumpkin.
"Communistic  Settlements"  (cited  above  as  item  56),  96.
Stresses the totality of Hutterite communalism.

1126.  Drache,   Arthur.     "'Hutterite   Provision'   Solves   Knotty
Problem   of   Fair   Play."    *Financial   Post*  71  (April  16,
1977): 17.

1127.  Duerksen,   Jacob   A.,   and   John   F.   Schmidt.      "Passenger
Ship   Lists   in   the   National   Archives."    *Mennonite
Quarterly Review* 42 (July, 1968): 219-24.
Provides  a  catalog  of  the  lists  of  ship  passengers,
available  from  the  National  Archives,  which  brought
Hutterites  and  Mennonites  to  America  in  the  last  quarter
of the nineteenth century.

1128.  Durnbaugh,   Donald   F.     "Hutterian   Brethren."    *Brethren
Encyclopedia*  (cited  above  as  item  57),  v.  l,  p.  639.
Provides  a  brief  article  on  the  Hutterites  focusing  on
their history.

1129.  Easton,   Carol.    "Touch   of   Innocence."    *Westways*  68
(December, 1976): 27-9, 60.
Depicts  Hutterite  life  as  a  tranquil  anachronism.
Illustrated with photographs.

1130.  Eaton,   Joseph   W.    "Adolescence   in   a   Communal   Society."
*Mental Hygiene* 48 (January, 1964): 66-73.
Argues  that  Hutterites  pass  through  adolescence  with
fewer  anxieties  than  other  youth,  probably  because  their
futures  are  more  certain.    Provides  a  useful  list  of  the
frequency of violation of Hutterite mores.

1131. ———. "Art of Aging and Dying." *Gerontologist* 4 (June, 1964): 94-100, 103, 112.
Describes the Hutterite manner of aging and dying "in a framework of realism and serenity." Characterizes the Hutterite practice of gradually entering retirement over many years, the prestige of older persons in the community, the lack of social isolation of older persons, and the sense of joy which surrounds death.

1132. ———. "Canada's Scapegoats." *Nation* 169 (September 10, 1949): 253-4.
Editorial that discusses prejudice against the Hutterites in Canada, especially Alberta, in light of the Communal Property Act of 1947, Albertan provincial legislation worded to apply only to the Hutterites. Argues that Canada's real problems are derived from other sources, and that the Hutterites have been made scapegoats.

1133. ———. "Controlled Acculturation: A Survival Technique of the Hutterites." *American Sociological Review* 17 (June, 1952): 331-40.
Depicts the slow but sure adaptation of the Hutterites to modern life, arguing that the movement does accept cultural innovations before the pressure for them becomes so great that it threatens group cohesiveness.

1134. ———. "Folk Obstetrics and Pediatrics Meet the M.D.: A Case Study of Social Anthropology and Medicine." *Patients, Physicians and Illness.* Edited by E. Gartly Jaco. Glencoe, Illinois: Free Press, 1958, 207-21. (Article not included in later editions of the book.)
Examines Hutterite prenatal care, childbirth, and infant care, concluding that cultural practices and expectations have an important impact on health, and that pediatric medicine is therefore an art as well as a science.

1135. ———. "Folk Psychiatry." *New Society: The Social Science Weekly* (London) no. 48 (August 29, 1963): 9-11.
Argues that Hutterites are effective in treating mental illness by using a combination of secular and religious therapeutic tools.

1136. ———. "'Hutterische Gemein.'" *Exploring Tomorrow's Agriculture* (cited above as item 59), 218-30.
Provides an overview of an "unexplored anthropological

gold mine."

1137. Eaton, Joseph W., and Albert J. Mayer. *Man's Capacity to Reproduce: The Demography of a Unique Population.* Glencoe, Illinois: Free Press, 1954. Reprinted from *Human Biology* 25 (1954), where it was titled "The Social Biology of Very High Fertility Among the Hutterites."
Concludes that the Hutterites have had a steady increase in population for 80 years and analyzes the causes of that increase (birth control is disavowed; children are valued; nearly all group members marry).

1138. Eaton, Joseph W., and Robert J. Weil. *Culture and Mental Disorders: A Comparative Study of the Hutterites and Other Populations.* Glencoe, Illinois: Free Press, 1955.
Concludes that Hutterite life is not free of mental illness, as some had presumed, but that mentally ill Hutterites have, because of their supportive communities, a better chance than others do of being cured.

1139. ————. "Mental Health of the Hutterites." *Scientific American* 189 (December, 1953): 31-7.
Finds the Hutterites by and large mentally healthy and well adjusted; concludes that culture has a large influence in shaping personality and mental health. Illustrated.

1140. ————. "Psychotherapeutic Principles in Social Research—an Interdisciplinary Study of the Hutterites." *Psychiatry* 14 (November, 1951): 439-54.
Probes interdisciplinary methods for studying the Hutterites; the authors are a psychiatrist and a social scientist. Provides good tips on field research among the Hutterites, including suggestions for gaining cooperation for research.

1141. Eaton, Joseph W., Robert J. Weil, and Bert Kaplan. "Hutterite Mental Health Study." *Mennonite Quarterly Review* 25 (January, 1951), 47-65.

1142. Edgerton, Jay. "Hutterite Brotherhood." *Introduction to Social Science.* Edited by Arthur Naftalin et al. Chicago: Lippincott, 1953, book 3, pp. 317-8. Originally published in the Minneapolis *Tribune.*

Finds that Hutterite happiness is rooted in the religion's otherworldliness.

1143. Ediger, Marlow. "Other Minorities: Old Order Amish and Hutterites." *Social Studies* 68 (July/August, 1977): 172-3.
An outline for secondary school teachers for teaching academic units on the Amish and Hutterites.

1144. Erasmus, Charles J. *In Search of the Common Good.* New York: Free Press, 1977, pp. 162-5.
Argues that Hutterite branching has kept the movement from becoming too wealthy and therefore has assisted communal longevity by keeping the most important source of corruption at bay.

1145. Evans, Simon M. "Dispersal of Hutterite Colonies in Alberta, 1918-1971: The Spatial Expression of Cultural Identity." M.A. thesis, University of Calgary, 1973. 220 pp.
Finds that branching helps preserve Hutterite cultural identity by insuring equality and controlling colony size. Identifies major variables in the Hutterite settlement pattern, contrasting external controls (such as legislative restrictions) with constraints imposed by the Hutterites themselves. Contains many maps, tables, and charts; bibliography includes manuscript and other material not cited here.

1146. ———. "Some Developments in the Diffusion Patterns of Hutterite Colonies." *Canadian Geographer* 29 (Winter, 1985): 328-38.
Describes the diffusion patterns of the three Leuts; depicts their responses to the repeal of the Alberta Communal Property Act in 1973, finding that some geographic infilling had taken place since then.

1147. ———. "Spatial Bias in the Incidence of Nativism— Opposition to Hutterite Expansion in Alberta." *Canadian Ethnic Studies* 6 (1974): 1-16.
Finds that tension and hostility concerning the Hutterites decreases as the Hutterites become more familiar fixtures of a locality, that a spirit of accomodation usually prevails with the passage of time.

1148. ———. "Spatial Expression of Cultural Identity: the

Hutterites in Alberta." *Kootenay Collection of Research Studies in Geography.* Occasional Papers in Geography, B. C. Geographic Series no. 18. Vancouver: Tantalus Research Ltd., 1974, pp. 9-20.
Documents the growth of the Hutterite population and describes the process of branching out to create new colonies. Includes several maps, graphs, charts, and tables which help illustrate the findings.

1149. Everitt, John. "Social Space and Group Life-Styles in Rural Manitoba." *Canadian Geographer* 24 (Fall, 1980): 237-54.
Finds that Hutterites and nonhutterites have different senses of space, from small "familial" space to larger "recreational" space. Illustrated with maps and diagrams.

1150. Faber, James. "Prolific People." *New York Times Magazine*, April 17, 1955, pp. 36, 39.
Provides a characterization of Hutterite life in light of recent studies of their fertility and their good mental health.

1151. Fairfield, Dick. "Forest River Community." "Communes U.S.A." (cited above as item 63), 35-6.
Provides a brief sketch of a small Hutterite colony.

1152. Falk, Robert D. "Hutterian Communism and Its Backgrounds." M.A. thesis, University of Colorado, 1931. 107 pp.
Provides basic information on early Hutterite history, the migration to America, Hutterite ideas and documents, faith and practice, community life (including a detailed description of the buildings and grounds of one colony), organization, work, education, family life, and relations with the outside world. Contains a detailed bibliography.

1153. "Fencing Match Due in Alberta on Hutterites?" *Financial Post* 53 (November 21, 1959): 30.

1154. Fischer, Hans. *Jacob Huter: Leben, Froemmigkeit, Briefe.* Newton, Kansas: Mennonite Publication Office, 1956.
A sympathetic life of the founder of Hutterism. In German.

1155. Fitzgerald, James A. "Hutterische Colony of Bon Homme." *South Dakota Education Association Journal* 3

(1928): 509-10.
Provides an overview of the colony site, Hutterite religion, daily life, education, health and sanitation, and economics.

1156. Flint, David. *Hutterites: A Study in Prejudice.* Toronto: Oxford University Press, 1975.
Provides an overview of Hutterite life and history; focuses on conflicts Hutterites have had with other Canadians and economic problems which have faced the colonies. Well illustrated with glossary, bibliography, and study questions.

1157. Fogarty, Robert S. "Hutterites." *Dictionary of American Communal and Utopian History* (cited above as item 76), 145-6.
Provides an overview of the movement.

1158. Fretz, J. Winfield. "Evaluation of the Hutterian Way of Life from the Sociological Point of View." *Proceedings of the Fifth Annual Conference on Mennonite Cultural Problems* (cited below as item 1356): 89-93.
Argues that the family and the church are less important among the Hutterites than among Mennonites and others, that the community is the sole important social organization for Hutterites. Also includes a brief response by Robert Friedmann.

1159. Frideres, James S. "Death of Hutterite Culture." *Phylon* 33 (Fall, 1972): 260-5.
Warns that certain provincial government policies will destroy Hutterite ethnic separateness.

1160. ———. "Termination or Migration: The Hutterites—A Case Study." *Canadian Ethnic Studies* 3 (June, 1971): 17-24.
Provides a history of anti-Hutterite sentiment in Alberta and other provinces, and of laws enacted to control Hutterite expansion. Argues that the Canadian provincial governments persecuting the Hutterites are in the process of killing Hutterite culture.

1161. Friedmann, Robert. "Anabaptist Research in Progress." *Mennonite Quarterly Review* 39 (January, 1965): 68-72.
Reports on the many projects Friedmann has in the works, most of them on the Hutterites.

1162. ———. "Bibliography of Works in the English Language Dealing with the Hutterite Communities." *Mennonite Quarterly Review* 32 (July, 1958): 237-8.
A brief bibliography of works which would handle most introductory questions about the Hutterites.

1163. ———. "Christian Communism of the Hutterite Brethren." *Archiv fuer Reformationsgeschichte* 46 (December, 1955): 196-209. Reprinted, slightly revised, in *The Recovery of the Anabaptist Vision*. Edited by Guy F. Hershberger. Scottdale, Pennsylvania: Herald Press, 1957, 83-90.
Analyzes the unique "theocratic communism" of the Hutterites, with information on its development and the philosophy behind it.

1164. ———. "Christian Love in Action: the Hutterites." *Mennonite Life* 1 (July, 1946): 38-43.
Discusses the early history of the Hutterites in Europe, the early Hutterite historical writings, and the journey to America. Also contains a note on the Bruderhof movement. Well illustrated, including several pictures of early Hutterite ceramics, for which the group was once well known.

1165. ———. "Comprehensive Review of Research on the Hutterites 1880-1950." *Mennonite Quarterly Review* 24 (October, 1950): 353-63.
Traces European scholarship on the Hutterites, including work on the earliest manuscript sources. Includes references to many items not cited here.

1166. ———. "Economic Aspects of Early Hutterite Life." *Mennonite Quarterly Review* 29 (1956): 259-66.

1167. ———. "Fate of the Hutterites in Europe." *Proceedings of the Fifth Annual Conference on Mennonite Cultural Problems* (cited below as item 1356): 61-5.
Outlines the situation of the Habaner, descendants of Hutterites in Slovakia who converted to Catholicism under pressure in the late nineteenth century.

1168. ———. "Hutterian Pottery or Haban Fayences." *Mennonite Life* 13 (October, 1958): 147-52, 182.
Provides a history of early Hutterite ceramic making plus a guide for locating pieces now in museums. Well

illustrated with photographs.

1169. ———. "Hutterite Census for 1969: Hutterite Growth in One Century, 1874-1969." *Mennonite Quarterly Review* 44 (January, 1970): 100-5.
Reports the results of a census superintended by Hutterite preacher Paul Gross. Contains many tables of information on the 17,000 Hutterites counted, a phenomenal increase during the 95 years of North American Hutterism.

1170. ———. "Hutterite Physicians and Barber-Surgeons." *Mennonite Quarterly Review* 27 (April, 1953): 128-36.
Describes Hutterite medical expertise in the early days of the movement.

1171. ———. *Hutterite Studies.* Goshen, Indiana: Mennonite Historical Society, 1961. Edited by Harold S. Bender.
Includes various of Friedmann's essays published in honor of his 70th birthday. Contains a bibliography of Friedman's writings.

1172. ———. "Hutterite Worship and Preaching." *Mennonite Quarterly Review* 40 (January, 1966): 5-26.
Surveys historical and contemporary worship practices, including holiday, wedding, and baptismal services. Based on the author's articles on the Hutterites in the *Mennonite Encyclopedia* (item 131, above).

1173. ———, ed. "Hutterites Revisit European Homesteads: Excerpts from the Travel Diary of David Hofer." *Mennonite Quarterly Review* 33 (October, 1959): 305-22, 346.
A portion of an account of a visit of two Hutterite elders to the Bruderhof (Society of Brothers) in Liechtenstein in 1937. Together the Hutterites and Bruderhof leaders went to visit old Hutterite sites in Czechoslovakia.

1174. ———. *Mennonite Piety Through the Centuries: Its Genius and Its Literature.* Goshen, Indiana: Mennonite Historical Society, 1949, pp. 51-4. Number 7 in the series Studies in Anabaptist and Mennonite History.
Describes contacts between Hutterites and Moravians between 1717 and 1811, showing that the two groups developed genuine affection for each other but that their

differences in theological outlook were too great to permit an enduring, close relationship.

1175. ———. "More About Habaner Pottery." *Mennonite Life* 14 (July, 1959): 129-30.
Provides details about Hutterite pottery supplementing those provided in the author's earlier article, item 1168.

1176. ———. "Notes and News Concerning Hutterites." *Mennonite Quarterly Review* 44 (January, 1970): 125-7.
Provides notes on forthcoming studies of the Hutterites, exhibitions of Hutterite artifacts, and Hutterite studies in Japan.

1177. ———. "Of Hutterite Books." *Mennonite Life* 7 (April, 1952): 81-2.
An account of the author's search in Europe for old Hutterite documents.

1178. ———. "Recent Hutterite Studies." *Mennonite Quarterly Review* 42 (October, 1968): 318-22.
An essay review of recent studies of the Hutterites.

1179. ———. "Re-Establishment of Communal Life Among the Hutterites in Russia." *Mennonite Quarterly Review* 39 (April, 1965): 147-52.
Details the Hutterite's return to communal living shortly before their migration to America. Reproduces Michael Waldner's account of the change back to community and the vision which led him to inaugurate it, as related by his son. Waldner was the blacksmith, "Schmied-Michel," for whom the Schmiedeleut branch of Hutterism is named.

1180. ———. "Report on Haban Pottery." *Mennonite Quarterly Review* 37 (July, 1963): 195-202.
Describes the pottery made by early Hutterites.

1181. Garvin, Philip, and Julia Welch. *Religious America* (cited above as item 79), 86-97.
Provides a brief history of the Hutterites and a view of Hutterite life based on visits to colonies. Heavily illustrated.

1182. Giffen, Dorothy. "Hutterites and Civil Liberties." *Canadian Forum* 27 (June, 1947): 55-7.

Defends the Hutterites against land-purchase restrictions being directed at them, arguing that there is no basis for infringing on Hutterite civil liberties. Provides a sketch of the existing and proposed laws restricting Hutterite land purchases in Alberta and Manitoba.

\* Gladstone, Arthur. "Cooperative Communities Today II" (cited above as item 82), 14.
Provides recent (as of 1955) information on the Hutterites.

1183. Goerz, H. "Day with the Hutterites." *Mennonite Life* 8 (January, 1953): 14-6.
Provides an hour-by-hour account of the Hutterite day, with separate trackings of weekdays and Sundays. Illustrated with photographs.

1184. Goldscheider, Calvin, and Peter R. Uhlenberg. "Minority Group Status and Fertility." *American Journal of Sociology* 74 (January, 1969): 361-72.
Argues that high fertility rates in certain subcultures, such as the Hutterites, must be understood as social behavior or social process, that traditional explanations based on social and economic characteristics of the group are inadequate. Contains several statistical tables.

1185. Goodhope, Nanna. "Must the Hutterites Flee Again?" *Christian Century* 57 (November 13, 1940): 1415-7.
Describes the hostility toward and sabotage of the Hutterites in South Dakota at the time of World War I, and speculates that they may have to move again with another war impending.

1186. Gross, Leonard. *Golden Years of the Hutterites, 1565-1578.* Scottdale, Pennsylvania: Herald, 1980. 264 pp.
A study of the second generation of the Hutterites.

1187. ———. "Symposium on the Hutterian Brethren." *Mennonite Quarterly Review* 55 (October, 1981): 384-5.
Describes a symposium on the Hutterites which took place in Germany in 1981; lists the papers presented at the conference.

1188. "Happy Hutterites." *Scientific American* 184 (June,

1951): 36, 38.
Discusses the study, currently in progress, of Eaton,
Weil, and Kaplan (item 1141, above) of the mental health
of the Hutterites.

1189. "Hard Times Face Fruitful Hutterites." *Life* 45 (August
25, 1958): 33-8.
A photo feature at the time of a new South Dakota
law forbidding further Hutterite land purchases.

1190. Harder, D.E. "Hutterian Church." M.A. thesis, Bethel
College (North Newton, Kansas), 1930. 117 pp.
Provides an overview history of the Hutterites from
their earliest times to the aftermath of World War I.
Contains short chapters on major leaders such as Peter
Riedemann and Andreas Ehrenpreis. Provides brief
histories and descriptions of the 28 existing colonies.
Provides statistical data on the nine Manitoba colonies.
Contains an account of the Hutterites who went to
Pennsylvania at the bidding of the Harmonists, only to
return to South Dakota.

1191. Hartzog, Sandra Hitchens. "Population Genetic Studies of
a Human Isolate, the Hutterites of North America."
Ph.D. dissertation, University of Massachusetts, 1971.
186 pp.

1192. "Have Hutterites Run Out of Cheeks?" *Financial Post* 57
(August 10, 1963): 19.

1193. Heath, Richard. "Living in Community." *Contemporary
Review* 70 (1896): 247-61.
A study of Hutterism in Moravia with overtones for
the movement in North America. Traces the Hutterites'
increasing material prosperity, which led to self-
interest, which finally killed Hutterite communalism in
Moravia, the author argues.

1194. Heiken, Diane Ellen Bray. "Hutterites: A Comparative
Analysis of Viability." Ph.D. dissertation, University of
California at Santa Barbara, 1978. 429 pp.
Finds that the more closely a colony adheres to
traditional doctrines and rules, the less subject to
breakdown it is. Not seen.

1195. Heimann, Franz. "Hutterite Doctrine of Church and

Common Life: A Study of Peter Ridemann's Confession of Faith of 1540." *Mennonite Quarterly Review* 26 (January and April, 1952): 22-47, 142-60.
A study of this classic Hutterite document.

1196. Hinds, William Alfred. "Bruderhof Communities." *American Communities and Co-operative Colonies* (cited above as item 95), 412-21.
Provides a brief overview of the Hutterites, quoting extensively from Hutterite documents.

1197. Hoeppner, K., and J. Gill. *Communal Property in Alberta.* Edmonton: Alberta Land Use Forum, 1974; "prepared by the Office of the Special Advisory Committee on Communal Property and Land Use." 19 pp.
Surveys Hutterite land ownership in 1974 and provides statistics on the rate of Hutterite population growth.

1198. Hofer, Jacob M. "Historical Background of the Hutterite Colonies, 1528-1946." *Proceedings of the Fifth Annual Conference on Mennonite Cultural Problems* (cited below as item 1356), 25-43.
Provides an overview history, spiced with anecdotes, of the Hutterites' from the group's origins to World War II.

1199. ———. "Hutterian Communism." M.A. thesis, University of Chicago Divinity School. 1928. 50 pp.

1200. Hofer, John S. *History of the Hutterites.* Elie, Manitoba: Hutterian Educational Committee, 1982. 108 pp.
A textbook for use in Hutterite schools. Not seen.

1201. Hofer, Joshua. *Japanese Hutterites: A Visit to Owa Community.* Elie, Manitoba: James Valley Book Center, 1985. 100 pp.

1202. Hofer, Peter. *Hutterian Brethren and Their Beliefs.* Starbuck, Manitoba: Hutterian Brethren of Manitoba, 1955. "Approved by the Committee of Elders." Discusses Hutterite beliefs and rebuts misconceptions about beliefs and communal life.

1203. Holtzman, Jerome J. "Inquiry into the Hutterian German Dialect." M.A. thesis, University of South Dakota, 1960. 60 pp.

1204.  Holzach, Michael.    "Christian Communists of Canada."
       *Geo* 1 (November, 1979): 126-54.
       A lavishly illustrated feature story on the Hutterites.

1205.  ———.    *Vergessene Volk*.    Hamburg:   Hoffmann   und
       Campe, 1980. 277 pp.
       Tells the story of Holzach's year-long stay at a colony
       in Alberta. Illustrated with photographs. Not seen.

1206.  "Homes for the Hutterites."    *Time* 49 (February 10, 1947):
       40.
       Describes the conflict over Hutterite expansion in
       Alberta.

1207.  Horsch, John.    *Hutterian Brethren, 1528-1931: A Story of
       Martyrdom and Loyalty*.    Cayley, Alberta: Macmillan
       Colony/Herald Press,  1974.    Originally published in
       1931; also repr., New York: Garland, 1971.    168 pp.
       Provides a detailed early history of the Hutterites, a
       brief account of their sojourn in Russia, and a detailed
       examination of Hutterite faith and ideals.    Includes a
       bibliography of books, manuscripts, and articles, most of
       them in German.

1208.  Hostetler, John A.    "Amish and Hutterite Socialization:
       Social Structure and Contrasting Modes of Adaptation
       to Public Schooling."    *Conference on Child
       Socialization*.    Edited by John A. Hostetler.
       Washington: Department of Health, Education and
       Welfare, 1969, pp. 283-308.
       Finds the existence of an indigenous educational system
       to be essential to the survival of any "little society" set
       apart from the social mainstream.

1209.  ———.    "Bibliography of English Language Materials on
       the Hutterian Brethren."    *Mennonite Quarterly Review*
       44 (January, 1970): 106-13.
       Most entries are cited here; the last section includes
       references to government documents and other
       unpublished materials not cited here.

1210.  ———.    "Communal Property Act of Alberta."    *Univers-
       ity of Toronto Law Journal* 14 (1961): 125-8.
       Outlines the provisions of the act; defends the
       Hutterites as good, if unconventional, citizens of Canada.

1211. ———. *Education and Marginality in the Communal Society of the Hutterites.* University Park, Pennsylvania: Pennsylvania State University Department of Sociology and Anthropology Research Report, Project No. 1683, 1965. 263 pp.
Reports findings that Hutterite moral indoctrination has several important bases, including belief in an omnipotent God and that communal living is the will of God; provides a detailed discussion of Hutterite socialization processes. Also includes some material on defection from the group. Contains extensive appendices with documents, charts, and maps. Includes an extensive bibliography.

1212. ———. *Hutterians in Perspective.* [Edmonton: University of Alberta, 1960]. 24 pp.
Defends the Hutterites against prejudice being exhibited toward them in Alberta. Contains a ten-page bibliography, including many items not cited here, especially regarding early Hutterite life in Europe.

1213. ———. *Hutterite Life.* Scottdale, Pennsylvania: Herald, 1965. 39 pp.
Contains an overview of Hutterite colony life; a section on "Art and Humor" quotes several Hutterite proverbs and witticisms. Illustrated with photographs.

1214. ———. "Hutterite Separatism and Public Tolerance." *Canadian Forum* 41 (April, 1961): 11-13. Reprinted, slightly revised, in *Social Problems: A Canadian Profile.* Edited by Richard Laskin. Toronto: McGraw-Hill of Canada Ltd., 1964, pp. 164-72.
Provides basic information on the Hutterites and debunks some myths, such as the assertion that they are the same group as the Doukhobors.

1215. ———. "Hutterite Socialization Study." *Mennonite Quarterly Review* 37 (July, 1963): 239-42.
An outline of the author's design for a study of Hutterite education, seeking to find out how Hutterites prepare their children for community living. (See item 1211 for the results of the study.)

1216. ———. *Hutterite Society.* Baltimore: Johns Hopkins University Press, 1974. 403 pp.
The *magnum opus* on the Hutterites. Major sections

cover history, contemporary social and cultural organization, and the problems and techniques of survival. Sixteen appendices cover Hutterite history, reproduce historic Hutterite documents, provide rules and other matters related to colony life, and supply a list of colonies and a chart of their branching. Well illustrated. Contains an extensive bibliography.

1217. ———. "Hutterites." *Harvard Encyclopedia of American Ethnic Groups*. Edited by Stephan Thernstrom. Cambridge, Massachusetts: Belknap Press, 1980. Provides a brief overview of Hutterite history and life.

1218. ———. "Hutterites: The Christian Bruderhof." *Communitarian Societies*. New York: Holt, Rinehart and Winston, 1974, pp. 34-46. Includes a bibliography.

1219. ———. "Socialization and Adaptations to Public Schooling Among The Hutterian Brethren and the Old Order Amish." *Sociological Quarterly* 11 (Spring, 1970): 194-205. Finds that maintaining an indigenous educational system is crucial to the survival of these two groups.

1220. ———. "Total Socialization: Modern Hutterite Educational Practices." *Mennonite Quarterly Review* 44 (January, 1970): 72-84. An abridgment of Hostetler and Huntington, "Communal Socialization Patterns in Hutterite Society" (item 1222, below).

1221. Hostetler, John A., Leonard Gross, and Elizabeth Bender, editors. *Selected Hutterian Documents in Translation, 1524-1564*. Philadelphia: Communal Studies Center, Temple University Press, 1975. 160 pp.

1222. Hostetler, John A., and Gertrude Enders Huntington. "Communal Socialization Patterns in Hutterite Society." *Ethnology* 7 (October, 1968): 331-55. Outlines Hutterite socialization practices and patterns through eight identified stages of life, finding several practices which the authors label "unique"; concludes that every Hutterite is subservient to the colony at each stage of life. Illustrated.

1223. ———. *Hutterites in North America.* New York: Holt, Rinehart and Winston, 1967. 119 pp.
Designed as a college textbook, this illustrated volume provides an excellent introduction to Hutterite life. An expanded "Fieldwork edition" (141 pp.) was published in 1980, with an extra chapter on field research in a communal society.

1224. Hostetler, John A., and Calvin Redekop. "Education and Assimilation in Three Ethnic Groups." *Alberta Journal of Educational Research* 8 (December, 1962): 189-203. Also published as "Education and Boundary Maintenance in Three Ethnic Groups." *Review of Religious Research* 5 (Winter, 1964): 80-91.
A study of the Old Order Amish, Old Colony Mennonites, and Hutterites in their efforts to maintain an otherworldly orientation; concludes that the ability to control the educational process is one of the most effective ways to survive as a group.

1225. Howard, Joseph Kinsey. "Hutterites: Puzzle for Patriots." *Pacific Spectator* 2 (Winter, 1948): 30-41.
Characterizes as a dilemma for democracy the Hutterite practice of withdrawing from the "world" and therefore refusing to assume the obligations of citizenship.

1226. ———. "Variability in Family Lines vs. Population Variability." *Annals of the New York Academy of Sciences* 134 (February 28, 1966): 624-31.
Describes variations in body measurements among Hutterites, concluding that there is as much variation in measurements among Hutterites as there is in the general population.

1227. Howells, William White. *Hutterite Differences in Body Measurements.* Cambridge, Massachusetts: Peabody Museum, 1970.
A technical publication with detailed anthropological data.

1228. Hubert, Barney. "Socialization and Education of Mentally and Physically Handicapped Individuals among the South Dakota Hutterites." M.A. project paper, School of Education, University of Kansas, 1988. 92 pp.
Provides case studies of handicapped individuals among the Hutterites. Suggests strategies for Hutterites and

English school teachers to use to improve care and treatment of these persons. Copy at the Institute for the Study of American Religion.

1229. Huenemann, Mark W. "Hutterite Education as a Threat to Survival." *South Dakota History* 7 (Winter, 1976): 15-27.
Argues that impending changes in state educational requirements, such as mandatory high school attendance, pose a serious threat to traditional Hutterite life. Illustrated with photographs.

1230. Huntington, Gertrude Enders. "Children of the Hutterites." *Natural History* 90 (February, 1981): 34-47.
Discusses Hutterite child rearing, focusing on processes which help conform children to the community. Also contains other observations on Hutterite life and thought. Heavily illustrated with color photographs.

1231. ———. "Freedom and the Hutterite Communal Family Pattern." *Proceedings of the Fifteenth Conference on Mennonite Educational and Cultural Problems*. North Newton, Kansas: Mennonite Press, 1965, pp. 88-111.
Contrasts Hutterite child rearing with child-rearing practices in the larger society at various points in Hutterite history. Describes in some detail the life cycle of a Hutterite child and adolescent, until and including the time of marriage.

1232. Huntington, Gertrude Enders, and John A. Hostetler. "A Note on Nursing Practices in an American Isolate with a High Birth Rate." *Population Studies* 19 (March, 1966): 321-4.
Analyzes certain specific practices (such as eating a high-protein diet) which help explain the short interval between births among Hutterite women.

1233. Hutterite Centennial Steering Committee. *History of the Hutterite Mennonites*. Freeman, South Dakota: Pine Hill Press, 1974. 172 pp.

1234. ———. *Hutterite Roots*. Freeman, South Dakota: Pine Hill Press, 1985. 127 pp.

1235. "Hutterite Hazard of In-breeding: A University of Alberta Scientist Documents the Genetics of a Colony One Man

Bred." *Alberta Report* 8 (August 21, 1981): 41.

1236. "Hutterite Land Fight Goes to Supreme Court of Canada." *Financial Post* 61 (January 28, 1967): 4.

1237. "Hutterite Problem." *Saturday Night* 63 (March 27, 1948): 5.

1238. "Hutterite Program: A Final Report." Government of Saskatchewan document, 1958.
Discusses Hutterite relations with the contemporary world.

1239. "Hutterites." *Newsweek* 34 (September 12, 1949): 74.
Discusses the work of Marcus Bach in studying the Hutterites and then writing his novel, *The Dream Gate* (item 1065, above), about them.

1240. "Hutterites: Alberta's Christian Communists." *Canadian Heritage*, April 2, 1980, p. 41.

1241. "Hutterites Could Outfox Ottawa's Tax Collectors." *Financial Post* 54 (December 31, 1960): 12.

1242. "Hutterites Get Okay to Expand." *Financial Post* 54 (August 6, 1960): 15.

1243. "Hutterites in Alberta Go to Supreme Court." *Financial Post* 61 (May 20, 1967): 17.

1244. "Hutterites Leave Manitoba for South Dakota." *Financial Post* 43 (April 9, 1949): 22.

1245. "Hutterites Maintain Old Traditions Despite Inroads of the Modern World." *Michigan Christian Advocate* (November 24, 1977): 13-14.
Focuses on pressures from "the world," and the Hutterites' way of resisting them. Adapted from a feature article in the Minneapolis *Tribune*.

1246. "Hutterites Pay Up." *Alberta Report* 8 (April 17, 1981): 30.

1247. Infield, Henrik. "Hutterites." *Cooperative Communities at Work* (cited above as item 105), 20-36.
Provides an overview of the Hutterites, with a

discussion of the advantages and disadvantages of the Hutterite system. Contains several tables of data.

1248. ———. "Hutterische Gemein'." *Utopia and Experiment* (cited above as item 108), 82-90.
Provides a brief history of the Hutterites and presents information gathered on a visit to a colony.

1249. Jager, Edward Charles. "Anabaptists' Resistance to Modernization: A Study in the Sociology of Religious Ideas." Ph.D. dissertation, New School for Social Research, 1984. 282 pp.

1250. Janzen, Rod A. *Perceptions of the South Dakota Hutterites in the 1980s.* Freeman, South Dakota: Freeman Publishing Co., 1984.
A reprint in book form of seven newspaper feature articles which originally appeared in the Freeman *Courier.*

1251. ———. *Terry Miller: The Pacifist Politician: From Hutterite Colony to State Capitol.* Freeman, S.D.: Pine Hill Press, 1985. 141 pp.

1252. Janzen, William. "Limits of Liberty in Canada: The Experience of the Mennonites, Hutterites, and Doukhobors." Ph.D. dissertation, Carleton University, 1981.

1253. Johnson, Kirk. "Idealists with a Knack for Being Prosperous." New York *Times,* November 25, 1987, p. A14.
Describes the plans of the Wolf Creek Colony for dealing with prosperity; presents an interview with a mature woman who left a South Dakota Hutterite colony and moved to Sioux Falls.

1254. Kaplan, Bert, and Thomas F.A. Plaut. *Personality in a Communal Society: An Analysis of the Mental Health of the Hutterites.* Lawrence, Kansas: University of Kansas Publications, Social Science Studies, 1956.
Analyzes a study of Hutterite mental health, outlining the procedures for the study and discussing its findings. Concludes that various forms of psychopathology are present among the Hutterites, but that they give rise to few symptoms.

1255. Kells, Edna. "Hutterite Commune." *Macleans*, March 15, 1937, pp. 50-4.
Describes a visit to Standoff Colony; depicts Hutterite life and economics, concluding that Hutterites are prosperous and independent. Illustrated with drawings.

1256. Kephart, William M. "Hutterites." *Extraordinary Groups: The Sociology of Unconventional Life-Styles* (cited above as item 752, 243-82 (second edition, 279-317).
Makes a lucid presentation of the history of the Hutterites, their way of life, and their religion.

1257. Kerstan, Reinhold J. "Hutterites: A Radical Christian Alternative." *Fides et Historia* 5 (1973): 62-7.
Contrasts Hutterite cultural traditionalism with the movement's modern farming practices.

1258. Khoshkish, A. "Decision-Making within a Communal Setting: A Case Study on Hutterite Colonies." *International Review of Modern Sociology* 6 (Spring, 1976): 41-55. Reprinted in *Communes: Historical and Contemporary* (cited above as item 41), 44-60.
Discusses the ways in which Hutterites maintain a balance between valuing the distinctions of individual persons and maintaining communal cohesion.

1259. Klassen, Peter James. *Economics of Anabaptism, 1525-1560.* The Hague: Mouton, 1964. 523 pp.
Chapters 3 and 4 and an appendix present early Hutterite economic thinking. Contains an extensive bibliography on early Anabaptism.

1260. Kloberdanz, Timothy J. "Gift from the Heart: Laura Ingalls Wilder and the Germans from Russia." *Heritage Review* 16 (May, 1986): 3-10.
Describes details of Wilder's encounter with the Hutterites of Jamesville Colony (described in her book, item 1455, below); fills in details about Hutterite customs not found in Wilder's original account.

1261. Knill, William Douglas. "Hutterian Education: A Descriptive Study Based on the Hutterian Colonies within Warner County No. 5, Alberta, Canada." M.A. thesis, Montana State University, 1958. 203 pp.
Contains a readable summary of Hutterite history and beliefs, a history of Hutterite education from the earliest

days, a history of the Hutterite schools of Alberta, a
discussion of the cultural interaction caused by the
presence of a state school on colony property, and a
study of Hutterite achievement in colony public schools,
finding that the students studied exceeded the national
norm for grade 4 but dropped below it in grades 5 and 6.
Contains many tables and charts and several documents
covering agreements between school officials of Alberta
and the Hutterites. The author was a teacher on a
Hutterite colony for a year.

1262. ————. "Hutterites: Cultural Transmission in a Closed
Society." *Alberta Historical Review* 16 (Summer, 1968):
1-10.
Argues that colony education is the institution which
contributes the most to sustaining Hutterite continuity
and stability. Provides a history of Hutterite education;
illustrates the ways in which the educational system
teaches communal ideas and practices. Credits the
Hutterites with the invention of the kindergarten.

1263. Knoll, Wilma I. "History of the Hutterites of South
Dakota." M.A. thesis, University of South Dakota,
1963. 74 pp.
Covers early history in Europe, later history in South
Dakota, community life and relationships, and implications
of a collective economy. Sources are standard secondary
accounts, popular journalism, and interviews.

1264. Kramer, Wendell B. "Hutterian Brothers." "Criteria for
the Intentional Community" (cited above as item 118),
50-7.
Provides a brief outline of Hutterite history and colony
life.

1265. Krauter, Joseph Francis. "Civil Liberties and the
Canadian Minorities." Ph.D. dissertation, University of
Illinois, 1968. 227 pp.

1266. Krisztinkovich, Maria H. "Historical Hungary as
Background for Hutterite Needlework in Canada."
*Hungarian Studies Review* 8 (1981): 11-23.

1267. Kurczynski, Thaddeus. "Studies of Genetic Drift in a
Human Isolate." Ph.D. dissertation, Case Western
Reserve University, 1969. 135 pp.

1268. Laatsch, William G. "Hutterite Colonization in Alberta." *Journal of Geography* 70 (September, 1971): 347-59. Shows that the Communal Property Act has resulted in the scattering of new Hutterite colonies but has increased overall Hutterite cohesiveness, since the Hutterites have strengthened their formal overall church organization to oversee the scattered colonies. Notes that the Act has worked hardship on farmers who have trouble selling their land, since the Hutterites, formerly good prospective buyers, can no longer make land purchases in certain areas. Documentation includes references to several Alberta government documents and interviews with government officials.

1269. Laing, L.M. "Declining Fertility in a Religious Isolate: The Hutterite Population of Alberta, Canada, 1951-1971." *Human Biology* 52 (May, 1980): 288-310. Finds, on the basis of 1971 Canadian census data, that the Hutterite birth rate declined from 45.9 per thousand in 1950 to 38.4 per thousand in 1971. Estimates that Hutterites get married at older ages than they once did and that more women are unmarried than was previously the case. Finds that the Hutterite rate of increase declined from 41.5 per thousand in 1950 to 35.5 per thousand in 1971.

1270. Lang, Hartmut, and Ruth Goehlen. "Completed Fertility of the Hutterites: A Revision." *Current Anthropology* 26 (June, 1985): 395. Finds that the completed family size of the Hutterites was erroneously calculated by Eaton and Mayer (item 1137, above) as averaging 10.4 children; the real rate, re-evaluating the original data, should be 8.97 children.

1271. Laurendeau, Andre. "On lui impose l'enfer, qui est de ne pas participer a la vie des autres." *Le Magazine Maclean* 4 (October, 1964): 96.

1272. Lee, Richard V., and Richard S. Buker, Jr. "Congenital Heart Disease Among the Hutterite Brethren." *New England Journal of Medicine* 280 (1969): 1061-2. Examines the high incidence of heart disease in one Hutterite family.

1273. Lee, S.C. *Social Cohesion in a Utopian Community: A Pilot Study of the Hutterite Colonies in South Dakota.*

Final progress report submitted to the National Institute of Mental Health, n.p., 1965. 47 pp.

1274. Lee, S.C., and Audrey Brattrud. "Marriage under a Monastic Mode of Life: A Preliminary Report on the Hutterite Family in South Dakota." *Journal of Marriage and the Family* 29 (August, 1967): 512-20. Finds that the Hutterites have a special kind of marriage, one which revolves around colony life rather than centering on a nuclear home. After a discussion of entering adulthood, courting, marriage, and reproduction, concludes that the Hutterites must suppress the conjugal family because its rise is tantamount to the rise of individualism, which poses a severe danger to group solidarity.

1275. Leibbrandt, Georg. "Emigration of the German Mennonites from Russia to the United States and Canada in 1873-1880." *Mennonite Quarterly Review* 6 (1932): 205-26, and 7 (1933): 5-41. Provides a basic history of the Anabaptists in Russia, the problems they encountered which moved many of them to leave, the search for land in North America, and a detailed account of the arrangements for the migration and the migration itself.

1276. Lewis, Russell E. "Comparison of Old Order Amish and Hutterian Brethren Family Systems and Community Integration." M.A. thesis, Michigan State University, 1972. 96 pp.

1277. ———. "Controlled Acculturation Revisited: An Examination of Differential Acculturation and Assimilation between the Hutterian Brethren and the Old Order Amish." *International Review of Modern Sociology* 6 (Spring, 1976): 75-83. Reprinted in *Communes: Historical and Contemporary* (cited above as item 41), 82-91. Concludes that Eaton's concept of controlled acculturation (see item 1133, above) helps explain differing rates of cultural change, but that more variables must be considered to achieve a full understanding of cultural change itself.

1278. *Lieder der Hutterischen Brueder, Gesangbuch....* Scottdale, Pennsylvania: Mennonitisches Verlagshaus,

1914. Hutterite songbook. In German.

1279. Liefmann, Robert. "Huterischen Bruederschaften." *Kommunistischen Gemeinden in Nordamerika* (cited above as item 125), 60-82.
Provides a historical survey of the Hutterites, emphasizing the ups and downs of the fortunes of the group over the centuries. The main focus is European Hutterite history. In German.

1280. Light, Charles E., Jr. "Case Notes: Status of South Dakota Communal Corporations." *South Dakota Law Review* 4 (Spring, 1959): 157-62.
Provides an interpretation of a South Dakota Supreme Court decision upholding the right of Spink Colony to buy 80 acres of land it had once rented, even though state law forbade the expansion of Hutterite operations.

1281. Loomis, Charles P. *Rural Sociology: The Strategy of Change.* Englewood Cliffs, New Jersey: Prentice-Hall, 1957, 161- 5.
Discusses the social structures and processes of the Hutterites as described by Joseph Eaton in *Exploring Tomorrow's Agriculture* (item 59).

1282. Loserth, Johann. "Decline and Revival of the Hutterites." *Mennonite Quarterly Review* 4 (April, 1930): 93-112.
Presents the work of the hitherto unknown historian of the Hutterites Johannes Waldner, focusing on his recounting of persecutions and the Hutterite response to them in the eighteenth century.

1283. Ludeman, W.W., and J.R. McAnelly. "Intelligence of Colony People." *Journal of Educational Psychology* 21 (November, 1930): 612-15.
Finds that the low scores of Hutterite children on IQ tests come from cultural isolation rather than limited intellectual ability.

1284. McConnell, Gail. "Hutterites: An Interview with Michael Entz." *Visions of the New Jerusalem: Religious Settlements on the Prairies.* Edited by Benjamin G. Smillie. Edmonton: NeWest Press, 1983, pp. 165-76.
Roughly half of the article is a statement by Entz, a leader of the Waldeck Colony, of the basic tenets and history of Hutterism and an argument that the Hutterite

life offers important advantages. The remainder is a
picture of Hutterite history and life based partly on
Entz's comments. Illustrated with photographs and a map
of Canadian Hutterite colonies.

1285. MacDonald, Robert J. "Hutterite Education in Alberta: A
Test Case in Assimilation, 1920-1970." *Canadian Ethnic
Studies* 8 (1976): 9-21. Also published in *Western
Canada: Past and Present* (Calgary: McClelland and
Stewart West, 1975): 133-49.
Tells of attempts by Canadians to assimilate the
Hutterites, especially by forcing their children to attend
schools off the colony. Concludes that attempts at
forcing assimilation have failed, and that the government
has largely given up the effort. Heavily documented;
includes many references to technical and legal
documents of various Canadian governmental units not
cited here.

1286. McGrath, W.R. *Why We Wear Plain Clothes*. Minerva,
Ohio: author, 1984. 44 pp.

1287. Mackie, Marlene Marie. "Accuracy of Folk Knowledge
Concerning Alberta Indians, Hutterites, and Ukranians:
An Available Data Stereotype Validation Technique."
Ph.D. dissertation, University of Alberta, 1971. 493 pp.
Tests the accuracy of prevailing stereotypes about
certain minorities, concluding that the majority of them
are accurate. A sociological study with many tables and
statistical analyses.

1288. ———. "Defection from Hutterite Colonies."
*Socialization and Values in Canadian Society*. Edited
by Robert M. Pike and Elia Zureik. Toronto:
McClelland and Stewart, 1975, volume 2, pp. 291-316.
Summarizes and highlights interviews with many
defectors from Hutterite colonies, outlining the
interviewees' reasons for leaving and their success in
adapting to the outside world.

1289. ———. "Ethnic Stereotypes and Prejudice—Alberta
Indians, Hutterites and Ukrainians." *Canadian Ethnic
Studies* 6 (1974): 39-52.
Finds that stereotypes of these Albertan ethnic groups
tend to be fairly accurate, that stereotypes and prejudice
are not the same thing.

1290. ———. "Outsiders' Perceptions of the Hutterites." *Mennonite Quarterly Review* 50 (January, 1976): 58-65. Summarizes the author's findings in her dissertation (item 1287, above).

1291. McKinley, Marilyn. "Attacking the Hutterites." *Alberta Report* 11 (December 24, 1984): 32. Reports on a controversy in Vulcan County, Alberta, over the local school board's operation of five Hutterite schools.

1292. ———. "Beware the Hutterites! Claresholmers Organize to Battle Communitarian Growth." *Alberta Report* 10 (December 20, 1982): 39.

1293. McKusick, Victor A., and David L. Rimoin. "General Tom Thumb and Other Midgets." *Scientific American* 217 (July, 1967): 103-110. Discusses the genetic factors in a certain syndrome causing some persons, including six Hutterites, to become midgets. Illustrated with a Hutterite genealogical diagram and a photograph of some of the Hutterite midgets.

1294. Mange, Arthur P. "Growth and Inbreeding of a Human Isolate." *Human Biology* 36 (May, 1964): 104-33. Concludes that the physical effects of Hutterite inbreeding vary with the degree of inbreeding.

1295. ———. "Population Structure of a Human Isolate." Ph.D. dissertation, University of Wisconsin, 1963. 103 pp.

1296. "Manitoba Hutterite Bill Hits Snag in Legislation." *Financial Post* 54 (March 19, 1960): 31.

1297. "Manitoba Hutterites Cry 'Peace' with Municipalities." *Financial Post* 51 (May 18, 1957): 34.

1298. "Manitoba Seeks to Curb Minority." *Christian Century* 64 (May 14, 1947): 628. News story reporting the campaign in the Manitoba legislature to stop Hutterite acquisition of farmland.

1299. Mann, George Adolf. "Functional Autonomy Among English School Teachers in the Hutterite Colonies of

Southern Alberta: A Study of Social Control." Ph.D. dissertation, University of Colorado, 1974.
Analyzes social control and social interaction of the teachers in Hutterite colonies. Concludes that the teachers with greater functional autonomy tend to be innovative in style and to conform less to Hutterite expectations than other teachers do.

1300. Martens, Helen. "Hutterite Songs: The Origins and Aural Transmission of Their Melodies from the Sixteenth Century." Ph.D. dissertation, Columbia University, 1968. 297 pp.
Provides an overview history of the Hutterites; describes the role of music in Hutterite life; discloses the origins of Hutterite music. Contains many excerpts from songs. Finds that after 400 years, Hutterite melodies are remarkably nearly unchanged.

1301. Martin, Alice Opaskar. "Recurrent Founder Effect in a Human Isolate: Historical and Genetic Consequences." Ph.D. dissertation, Case Western Reserve University, 1969. 101 pp.

1302. Mather, G.B. "Hutterites." *Christian Century* 78 (January 25, 1961): 125.
News item detailing a recent ruling that Canadian Hutterite colonies would have to start paying income tax.

1303. Melland, John Francis. "Changes in Hutterite House Types: The Material Expression of the Contradiction Between 'Being-on-the-Colony' and 'Being-in-the-World.'" Ph.D. dissertation, Louisiana State University, 1985. 310 pp.
Describes the Hutterites' shift toward more modern and more private housing. Not seen.

1304. Melnyk, George. *Search for Community: From Utopia to a Co-operative Society.* Montreal and Buffalo: Black Rose, 1985, pp. 93-7.
Provides an overview of the Hutterites, comparing them to other communal movements in other countries.

1305. Melton, J. Gordon. "Hutterian Brethren." *Encyclopedia of American Religions* (cited above as item 130), 499-501.
Contains brief sketches of each of the three branches

of Hutterism.

1306.   Mendel, J.J.   *History of Freeman from 1870 to 1958.*
        Freeman, S.D.: Pine Hill Printery, 1958, p. 1.
        Contains brief references to the settling of Wolf Creek
        Colony, detailing the original location of the colony and
        its move to a site with water power where the colonists
        could locate a mill.

1307.   ———.   *History   of   the   Hutterite   People   of   East
        Freeman,   Silver   Lake   and   West   Freeman   from   1528   to
        1961.*   North   Newton,   Kansas:   Bethel   College   Historical
        Library, 1962. 301 pp.

*       *Mennonite   Encyclopedia*   (cited   above   as   item   131).
        Contains,   in   volumes   2   and   3,   articles   by   Robert
        Friedmann   entitled   "Education,   Hutterite,"   "   Hutterian
        Brethren,"   "Hutterite   Missioners,"   "Hutterite   Family
        Names,"   and   "Marriage,   Hutterite   Practices,"   plus   an
        article   by   Johann   Loserth   entitled   "Hutter,   Jakob,"   as
        well   as   other   articles   on   specific   topics   concerning
        Hutterite life and history.

*       Mercer,   John.   *Communes:   A   Social   History   and   Guide*
        (cited above as item 132), 38-9.
        Provides a brief description of the Hutterites.

1308.   Meryman,   Richard   S.,   Jr.   "Hard   Time   Faces   Fruitful
        Hutterites."   *Life*   45   (August   25,   1958):   33-4,   37-8.
        Photographs   of   the   Spink   colony   during   a   period   of
        controversy about Hutterite land purchases.

1309.   ———.   "South   Dakota's   Christian   Martyrs."   *Harper's*
        217 (December, 1958): 72-9.
        Describes   a   visit   to   Spink   Colony,   South   Dakota,   at   a
        time   when   South   Dakota   had   banned   any   new   Hutterite
        land   purchases.   Provides   a   sympathetic   account   of
        Hutterite   life   and   thought;   quotes   the   colony   minister   at
        length.

1310.   Miller,   Tarrel   R.   *Dakotans.*   Stickney,   S.D.:   Argus
        Printers, 1964. 141 pp.
        Chapter   4   (pp.   48-70)   provides   a   synopsis   of   Hutterite
        history   and   characterizes   Hutterite   life   on   the   basis   of
        the   author's   visits   to   Tschetter   Colony.   Appendix
        contains   a   list   of   South   Dakota   Hutterite   colonies.

Illustrated with photographs of the Tschetter and Wolf Creek colonies.

1311.  Miller, Terrill R.  *Hutterites: A Story of Christian Loyalty*.  Freeman, S.D.: Pine Hill Press, 1975.  20 pp.
Apparently Terrill and Tarrel Miller are the same person, although the variant spellings coexist on OCLC.

1312.  Miller, Timothy.  "Families within a Family: Spiritual Values of Hutterites and Unificationists."  *Family and the Unification Church*.  Edited by Gene G. James.  New York: Rose of Sharon Press, 1983, pp. 53-65.
Argues that Hutterites value families, but that the needs of the community sometimes supersede those of the family.

1313.  Mitchell, W.O.  "People Who Don't Want Equality."  *MacLean's* 78 (July 3, 1965): 9-12, 33-8.
Notes that despite Hutterite disinclination to become involved in civil life, the movement has sued to abrogate the Communal Property Act of Alberta.  Describes ways in which the Hutterites are subtly changing and modernizing their way of life.  Illustrated with photographs.

1314.  Morgan, Kenneth.  "Mortality Changes in the Hutterian Brethren of Alberta and Saskatchewan, Canada."  *Human Biology* 55 (February, 1983): 89-99.
Finds, on the basis of Canadian vital statistics records, that in recent years infant mortality has declined substantially and female longevity has increased, probably because of the advent of lower fertility rates.

1315.  Morgan, Kenneth, and T. Mary Holmes.  "Population Structure of a Religious Isolate: The Dariusleut Hutterites of Alberta."  *Current Developments in Anthropological Genetics*.  Edited by Michael H. Crawford and James H. Mielke.  New York: Plenum Press, 1982, vol. 2, pp. 429-48.
Finds that there is considerable genetic diversity among the Dariusleut Hutterites studied.  Contains numerous charts and tables of information.

1316.  Morgan, Kenneth, T. Mary Holmes, Michael Grace, Sam Kemel, and Diane Robson.  "Patterns of Cancer in Geographic and Endogamous Subdivisions of the

Hutterite Brethren of Canada." *American Journal of Physical Anthropology* 62 (September, 1980): 3-10. Finds that Hutterite cancer rates are below those of the general population. Contains several tables of data.

\* Muncy, Raymond Lee. *Sex and Marriage in Utopian Communities* (cited above as item 135), 102-5.
Describes Hutterite marriages in terms of customs, ceremonial practices, their relation to community life, and theology.

1317. Obeng-Quaidoo, Isaac. "Hutterite Land Expansion and the Canadian Press." Ph.D. dissertation, University of Minnesota, 1977. 242 pp.
Finds that newspaper reportage (in the years 1940 to 1973) of interactions between Hutterites and nonhutterites in Alberta and Saskatchewan gradually became more favorable to Hutterites. Not seen.

1318. O'Brien, Elizabeth. "Population Structure and Genetic Variability among Forty-Four Hutterite Colonies." Ph.D. dissertation, Northwestern University, 1986. 175 pp.

1319. Olsen, Carolyn Lee. "Demography of New Colony Formation in a Human Isolate: Analysis and History." Ph.D. dissertation, University of Michigan. 1976. 298 pp.

1320. Orr, Fay, and Stephen Weatherbe. "Scapegoating the Hutterites." *Alberta Report* 11 (April 9, 1984): 36.

1321. Oved, Yaacov. "Hutterites: A Bridge between Past and Present." *Two Hundred Years of American Communes* (cited above as item 142), 333-65.
About half the article summarizes the European history of the Hutterites; the balance covers their settlement in South Dakota, their relations with the Harmony Society and Amana, their problems during World War I, their recent enormous growth, and their relations with the Bruderhof and other twentieth century communitarians.

1322. Palmer, Howard. "Hutterite Land Expansion Controversy in Alberta." *Western Canadian Journal of Anthropology* (July, 1971): 18-46.
Discusses the coming of the Hutterites to Canada,

reactions to the immigration, the introduction of
restrictive land-ownership legislation at the time of
World War II, further controversy in the 1950s and 1960s,
and Hutterite reaction to the actions taken against them.
Documentation includes accounts from the popular press,
field research, and government documents, most of which
are not cited here.

1323.   ———. *Land of the Second Chance.*      Lethbridge,
Alberta: Lethbridge Herald, 1972, pp. 39-53.
Provides a survey of Hutterite history and distinctive
practices, the movement's entrance into Alberta from
South Dakota, the hostility and restrictions the
Hutterites have encountered in Canada, the group's
values, economic life, and group solidarity.      Contains a
substantial bibliography.

1324.   ———.   "Nativism and Ethnic Tolerance in Alberta:
1920-1972." Ph.D. dissertation, York University, 1974.

1325.   "People of Jacob Hutter."      Minneapolis *Tribune* (October
16, 1977).
Discusses the problem of encroachment by the "world"
and the Hutterites' response to it, the movement's
history, colony branching, persons who leave a colony,
the role of women, and the prospects for the movement.

1326.   Peter, Karl A.   "Certainty of Salvation: Ritualization of
Religion and Economic Rationality Among the
Hutterites."   *Comparative Studies in Society and
History* 25 (April, 1983): 222-40.      Reprinted in
*Dynamics of Hutterite Society* (cited below as item
1330), 24-44.
Finds that Hutterite dynamism stems from having small,
democratic colonies, kinship, absence of a large
bureaucracy, and legitimate economic goals.      Argues that
attainment of salvation has, for Hutterites, changed from
a spiritual phenomenon speaking through the individual
conscience to participation in the Hutterite community.

1327.   ———.   "Childhood and Adolescent Socialization among
the Hutterites."   *Childhood and Adolescency in Canada.*
Edited by K. Ishwaran.      Scarborough, Ontario:
McGraw-Hill Ryerson, 1979, pp. 344-65.      Also in Peter's
book, *Dynamics of Hutterite Society* (cited below as
item 1330), 83-102.

Describes Hutterite socialization from birth through early adulthood.

1328. ———. "Death of Hutterite Culture: A Rejoinder." *Phylon* 40 (June, 1979): 189-94.
A rejoinder to Frideres (item 1159, above). Argues that the main threats to Hutterite culture are internal rather than the result of government pressure.

1329. ———. "Decline of Hutterite Population Growth." *Canadian Ethnic Studies* 12 (1980): 97-110. Reprinted in *Dynamics of Hutterite Society* (cited below as item 1130), 152-70.
Finds that Hutterite population growth dropped, between about 1965 and 1980, from 4.12% per year to 2.91% per year, or perhaps even below that. Argues that the Hutterites seem to be marrying later than they formerly did.

1330. ———. *Dynamics of Hutterite Society: An Analytical Approach.* Edmonton: University of Alberta Press, 1987. 232 pp.
A collection of the author's articles (some coauthored) on Hutterite religion, history, social relations, demographics, and change in outlook.

1331. ———. "Dynamics of Open Social Systems." *Social Process and Institution: The Canadian Case.* Edited by James E. Gallagher and Ronald D. Lambert. Toronto: Holt, Rinehart and Winston, 1971, pp. 164-72.
Explores relations within Hutterite society and between Hutterite and the larger society; finds that the Hutterites are interdependent with the larger society in economic matters, yet manage to stay separate in their private life.

1332. ———. "Factors of Social Change and Social Dynamics in the Communal Settlements of Hutterites: 1527-1967." Ph.D. dissertation, University of Alberta, 1968.

1333. ———. "Hutterite Family." *Canadian Family.* Edited by K. Ishwaran. Toronto: Holt, Rinehart and Winston, 1971, pp. 248-62. Also in Peter's *Dynamics of Hutterite Society* (item 1330), 61-82.
Describes Hutterite child rearing and socialization, coming of age, marriage, and husband-wife relations.

1334. ———. "Hutterite Problem in Alberta." *Social Problems: A Canadian Profile*. Edited by Richard Laskin. Toronto: McGraw-Hill Company of Canada, 1964. Originally a series of four articles in the Edmonton *Journal*, August 20-September 10, 1963.
Argues that the Hutterites make a real contribution to the economic and cultural life of Alberta, and therefore should not be restricted in the purchase of land.

1335. ———. "Hutterites: Values, Status, and Organizational Systems." *Variables* (University of Alberta) 2 (February, 1963): 55-9, and 3 (February, 1964): 7-8.
Part 1 describes the allocations of goods and work, arguing that the allocation system provides spiritual satisfaction; says that lines of authority are defined by sex, age, marital status, and baptism. Part 2 argues that persecution actually aids the internal mechanisms the Hutterites have developed to separate themselves from the larger society.

1336. ———. "Instability of the Community of Goods in the Social History of the Hutterites." *Western Canada Past and Present*. Edited by Anthony W. Rasporich. Toronto: McClelland and Stewart West, 1975, pp. 99-119.
Outlines the history of Hutterite community of goods, showing that communalism and private family life have alternated throughout Hutterite history, but argues that the current round of community of goods is especially stable and should last for several more generations.

1337. ———. "Problems in the Family, Community and Culture of the Hutterites." *Canadian Families: Ethnic Variations*. Edited by K. Ishwaran. Toronto: McGraw-Hill Ryerson Ltd., 1980, pp. 221-36. Also in the author's *Dynamics of Hutterite Society* (cited above as item 1330), 103-21.
Argues that Hutterite life seems idyllic not because there is no competition or strain, but because problems are well managed and kept hidden from outsiders.

1338. ———. "Toward a Demographic Theory of Hutterite Population Growth." *Variables* (University of Alberta) 5 (Spring, 1966): 28-37. Reprinted in *Dynamics of Hutterite Society* (cited above as item 1330), 135-51.
Argues that the branching process causes colonies to

oscillate between "old" and "young" stages, with young ones working more efficiently, since when colonies get large, leadership roles are harder to come by, leading members to be dissatisfied with their roles in the community.

1339. Peter, Karl, Edward D. Boldt, Ian Whitaker, and Lance W. Roberts. "Dynamics of Religious Defection Among Hutterites." *Journal for the Scientific Study of Religion* 21 (December, 1982): 327-37. Reprinted in *Dynamics of Hutterite Society* (cited above as item 1330), 45-58, under the chapter title, "Contemporary Dynamics of Religious Defection."
Finds increasing defection from Hutterite colonies as a result of members' conversions to evangelical Protestantism; finds individualization and privitization creeping into Hutterite life.

1340. Peter, Karl, and Franziska Peter, eds. *Gemein Ordnungen (1651-1873)*. [Reardan, Washington: Espanola Gemeinde, 1980]. 132 pp.

1341. Peter, Karl, and Ian Whitaker. "Acquisition of Personal Property Among Hutterites and Its Social Dimensions." *Anthropologica* n.s. 23 (1981): 145-55. Reprinted in *Dynamics of Hutterite Society* (cited above as item 1330), 173-83, under the chapter title, "Changing Attitudes and Practices Regarding the Acquisition of Property."
States that there has been a slight but real move toward allowance of private property among Hutterites, as in the case of household furniture; argues that this shift reflects changes in Hutterite society.

1342. ———. "Changing Roles of Hutterite Women." *Prairie Forum* 7 (Fall, 1982): 267-77. Reprinted in *Dynamics of Hutterite Society* (cited above as item 1330), 197-207.
Finds that the increase in the status of women in the larger society has tended to improve the status of women and to alter their lifestyles in Hutterite colonies, although the formal decision-making structure remains thoroughly male-dominated.

1343. ———. "Hutterite Economy: Recent Changes and Their Social Correlations." *Anthropos* 78 (1983): 535-46. Reprinted in *Dynamics of Hutterite Society* (cited

above as item 1330), 184-96.
Describes Hutterite ways of coping with technological
change and bureaucratic regulations which have made
some of their old methods of farming obsolete.

1344. ———. "Hutterite Perceptions of Psychophysiological
Characteristics." *Journal of Social and Biological
Structures* 7 (January, 1984): 1-8. Reprinted in
*Dynamics of Hutterite Society* (cited above as item
1330), 122-32.
Argues that the Hutterites display a high degree of
psychological uniformity due to the selective processes
that led to the group's appearance in history.

1345. Peters, Victor. *All Things Common: The Hutterian Way
of Life*. Minneapolis: University of Minnesota Press,
1965. 233 pp.
Provides a history of the Hutterites, information about
daily life, and information on Hutterite relations with the
outside world. Appendices reproduce the Constitution of
the Hutterian Brethren Church, a memoir by a young
woman who grew up in a colony, and a list of colonies
as of 1964. Illustrated with photographs.

*         ———. "History of the Hutterian Brethren, 1528-1958"
(cited above as item 305).
Covers, at approximately equal length, Hutterite history
before and after the migration to North America.
Separate major chapters treat U.S. and Canadian history.
Includes information on the relations between the
Hutterites and the Bruderhof movement. Extensively
documented; appendices reproduce several documents
important to the study of Hutterites.

1346. ———. "Hutterians: History and Communal Organization
of a Rural Group." *Historical Essays on the Prairie
Provinces*. Edited by Donald Swainson. Toronto:
McClelland and Stewart, 1970.
A historical and contemporary overview of the
Hutterites.

1347. ———. "Hutterians: History and Communal Organization
of a Rural Group in Manitoba." *Historical and
Scientific Society of Manitoba Papers, 1960-61* (1964
series, vol. 3): 6-14.

1348. ———. "Process of Colony Division Among the Hutterians: A Case Study." *International Review of Modern Sociology* 6 (Spring, 1976): 57-64. Reprinted in *Communes: Historical and Contemporary* (cited above as item 41), 61-9.

1349. Peterson, Hans J. "Hilldale: A Montana Hutterite Colony in Transition." *Rocky Mountain Social Science Journal* 7 (April, 1970): 1-7.
Sketches the history of the Hutterites in Montana; describes the efforts of legislators to restrict Hutterite land purchases; provides a look at the Hilldale colony, based on visits.

1350. Pickering, W.S.F. "Hutterites and Problems of Persistence and Social Controls in Religious Communities." *Archives de Sciences Sociales des Religions* 44 (July-September, 1977): 75-92.
Describes Hutterite control mechanisms and compares them to those of Catholic religious communities.

1351. Pitt, Edwin L. "Hutterian Brethren in Alberta." M.A. thesis, University of Alberta, 1949. 156 pp.
Provides an overview of Hutterite history, faith, organization, education, health, and colony life. Contains information on Hutterite growth and expansion in Alberta, and summarizes and analyzes the controversy over the Hutterites in western Canada. Appendix reproduces the 12 Hutterite Articles of Faith and the Baptismal Vow.

1352. "Practical Wisdom: Hutterites Sell Out for Richer Pastures." *Alberta Report* 8 (May 8, 1981): 46-7.

1353. Pratt, William F. "Anabaptist Explosion." *Natural History* 78 (February, 1969): 8-23.
A popularized adaptation of "Pockets of High Fertility in the U.S." (item 1376, below). Illustrated with photographs.

1354. Price, Edward T. "Demography of the Hutterites in North America." *Geographical Review* 45 (October, 1955): 573-4.
Provides a brief digest of Eaton and Mayer's study, *Man's Capacity to Reproduce* (item 1187, above).

1355. Priestley, David T.    "Study of Selected Factors Related to
      Attitudes Toward the Hutterites of South Dakota."
      M.S. thesis, South Dakota State College of Agriculture
      and Mechanic Arts, 1959. 117 pp.
      A sociological study of hostility toward the Hutterites.
      Finds that attitudes toward Hutterites have little or
      nothing to do with such things as frequency of contact
      with Hutterites and accurate knowledge about them.

1356. *Proceedings of the Fifth Annual Conference on Mennonite
      Cultural Problems.*    Berne, Indiana: Berne Witness, 1946.
      96 pp.
      The majority of the articles in this volume of the
      series deal with the Hutterites; individual articles are
      listed separately by author in this bibliography.

1357. "Promised Land." *Time* 68 (August 13, 1956): 24, 26.
      A story of Paul Gross, a Hutterite minister, and the
      Pincer Creek Colony, with pictures of Gross and the
      colony.

1358. Radtke, Hans D.    *Hutterites in Montana: An Economic
      Description.*    Bozeman: Montana Agricultural
      Experiment Station (bulletin 641), 1971.    58 pp.
      Provides a detailed economic picture of the Hutterite
      colonies of Montana, with charts providing gross income
      by crop and product, details of colony expenditures,
      profits, land ownership, marketing, purchases, and taxes
      paid, with a detailed comparison of taxes paid by
      Hutterites and those paid by their nonhutterite neighbors.

1359. Rankin, Diane M.    "Folklore and Ethnicity: 400 Years of
      Hutterite Hymnsinging." *Journal of the American
      Historical Society of Germans from Russia* 4 (Fall,
      1981): 26-8.
      Describes Hutterite music and the role it plays in
      defining the Hutterites as a people.

1360. Redekop, Calvin, and William Shaffir.    "Communal
      Organization and Secular Education: Hutterite and
      Hassidic Comparisons." *Communal Life: An
      International Perspective* (cited above as item 84),
      342-57.
      Describes the process by which the Hutterites, Reba
      Place, and two Hasidic groups comply with the
      requirement of the state that they educate to their

children. Characterizes the similarities and differences in the organizational structures of the Hutterites and Reba Place. Notes differences between Hutterite and Reba Place educational systems, the major one being that Reba Place primarily relies on the public schools.

1361. *Report of the Legislative Committee Regarding the Land Sales Prohibition Act, 1944, as amended.* [Edmonton, 1947?]. 15 pp.
Provides a sketch of Hutterite life and lists recommendations for restrictions on Hutterite land purchases (such as limiting each purchase to 6400 acres and requiring each new colony not to be within 40 miles of an existing colony). The proposed amendments would liberalize the 1944 law, which flatly outlawed the sale or lease of land to Hutterites.

1362. Ressler, Martin E. "American Continuance of European Origins in Mennonite, Hutterite, and Amish Music Functions." *Pennsylvania Mennonite Heritage* 9 (1986): 6-10.
Tracks the hymnody of the major Anabaptist groups from its European origins through its current status in America.

1363. Rexroth, Kenneth. *Communalism: From Its Origins to the Twentieth Century.* New York: Seabury, 1974, pp. 121-132 and 273-287.
Traces the early history of the Hutterites, the Russsian years, and Hutterite development in America; argues that elasticity in government is a major secret of Hutterite success.

1364. Riley, Marvin P. "Communal Farmers: The Hutterite Brethren." *South Dakota Farm and Home Research* 8 (1957-7): 5-11. Published by the Agricultural Experiment Station, South Dakota State College.
Provides a brief account of Hutterite history, early settlement in South Dakota, the movement of the Hutterites to Canada and back to South Dakota, and Hutterite beliefs.

1365. ———. "Farmers' Attitudes toward the Hutterite Brethren: A Study in Intergroup Relations." Ph.D. dissertation, University of Missouri, 1968. 241 pp.
Provides a sociological analysis of the attitudes of

neighboring farmers toward the Hutterites. Finds that attitudes change with certain variables (e.g., religious preference, agreement with Hutterite values) but not with others (e.g., various measures of contact with or knowledge of the Hutterites).

1366. ———. *Hutterite Brethren: An Annotated Bibliography with Special Reference to South Dakota Hutterite Colonies.* Brookings: South Dakota State University Experiment Station, Rural Sociology Department, 1965. Agriculture Experiment Station Bulletin 529. 188 pp.
One of the most comprehensive bibliographies of the Hutterites. Emphasizes Hutterites in South Dakota. Divided into 16 sections; topics range from "Religious Beliefs and Practices" to "Socialization and Education" to "Funeral and Burial Customs." Contains references to manuscripts and other specialized materials not cited here, including many articles from local newspapers and magazines. Also contains references to many legal documents.

1367. ———. *Hutterites and Their Agriculture: 100 Years in South Dakota.* Brookings: South Dakota Agricultural Experiment Station, South Dakota State University, 1980. Bulletin no. 669. 22 pp.
Provides an overview history of the Hutterites and a survey of their expansion in South Dakota. Summarizes Hutterite beliefs and principles. Supplies statistics on South Dakota colonies and their agricultural operations, and provides a relatively detailed description of the branching process. Illustrated with photographs.

1368. Riley, Marvin P., and Darryll R. Johnson. *South Dakota's Hutterite Colonies, 1874-1969.* Brookings: South Dakota State University Agricultural Experiment Station, 1970. Bulletin no. 565. 38 pp.
An update of Riley and Stewart, *Hutterites* (item 1370, below), with added information on Hutterite education and a case study of the newly founded Poinsett Colony. Illustrated with many pictures of Poinsett.

1369. Riley, Marvin P., and David T. Priestly. "Agriculture on South Dakota's Communal Farms." *South Dakota Farm and Home Research* 10 (1959): 12-6.
Provides statistics on the South Dakota Hutterites from a 1957 survey. Furnishes an overview of Hutterite

philosophy, work, and farming operations, examining especially the agricultural economics of the colonies. Illustrated with photographs.

1370. Riley, Marvin P., and James R. Stewart. *Hutterites: South Dakota's Communal Farmers.* Brookings: South Dakota State University Agricultural Experiment Station, 1966. Bulletin 530. 32 pp.
Covers Hutterite history, beliefs and principles, agriculture (including an analysis of Hutterite livestock and crop operations), and the Hutterite censuses of 1957 and 1964. Documents changes in the direction of the Hutterite agricultural economy, as in the shift from raising sheep to poultry. Contains a list of South Dakota colonies. Heavily illustrated.

1371. Robertson, Heather. *Grass Roots.* Toronto: James Lewis and Samuel, 1973, pp. 160-4.
Provides an account of a visit to Miami Colony, Manitoba. The essay deals primarily with the personality of the colony boss and with the prejudice exhibited toward the Hutterites by their neighbors.

1372. Romaine, Edward. "Alberta's Hutterites Pull Surprise—in Court." *Financial Post* 59 (March 6, 1965): 16.

1373. ———. "Hutterite Growth Heads for Showdown." *Financial Post* 59 (February 13, 1965): 36.

1374. ———. "Hutterite Row May End in Supreme Court of Canada." *Financial Post* 59 (November 27, 1965): 32. Concerns the Alberta Communal Property Act. Not seen.

1375. ———. "Hutterites in Alberta Await Critical Decision." *Financial Post* 59 (October 16, 1965): 36.

1376. Rountzounis, John, Betsy Cohen, and Arlene Joy. "Pockets of High Fertility in the United States." *Population Bulletin* 24 (November, 1968): 25-55. Provides statistical information on the fertility rates of the Hutterites and Amish, plus general historical and current information on the Hutterites. Concludes that the Hutterites have the highest fertility of any identifiable group in the United States.

1377. Rozen, Frieda Schoenberg.   "Role of Women in Communal Societies: The Kibbutz and the Hutterite Colony." *Communal Life: An International Perspective* (cited above as item 84), 614-21.
Characterizes the role of women, especially in their work, at Hutterite colonies.   Finds that marriage comes at a later average age among Hutterites than it did a generation ago, leading to a lower birth rate.   The author speculates that with smaller families, Hutterite women may have more leisure and will be less satisfied than they are now with the roles they play in the community.

1378. Runzo, Jean.   "Hutterite Communal Discipline, 1529-1565." *Archiv fuer Reformationsgeschichte* 71 (1980): 160-79.
Finds that discipline played an important role in early Hutterite communities, but concludes that the nature of that discipline is largely unknown.   Based on some thirty cases reported in the Hutterite Chronicle.

1379. Ryan, John.   *Agricultural Economy of Manitoba Hutterite Colonies.*   Toronto: McClelland and Stewart, 1977.   306 pp.

1380. ———.   "Agricultural Operations of Manitoba Hutterite Colonies." Ph.D. dissertation, McGill University, 1973.

1381. ———.   "Hutterite Settlements in Rural Manitoba." *Pressures of Rural Change in Canada.*   Edited by Michael F. Bruce and Michael J. Troughton. Downsview, Ontario: York University Geographical Monographs (no. 14), 1984, pp. 94-111.
Provides an overview of Hutterite history, a statistically oriented survey of Hutterite agriculture, a portrait of life at a typical colony, and an explanation of the Hutterites' long survival.   Illustrated with several maps.

1382. Sanders, Douglas E.   "Hutterites: A Case Study in Minority Rights." *Canadian Bar Review* 42 (May, 1964): 225-42.
Summarizes the sentiments of some rural Canadians against the Hutterites.   Provides a history of legislation restricting Hutterite expansion and discusses possible constitutional weaknesses of the Communal Property Act of Alberta.   Suggests less coercive ways of dealing with

provincial sentiments against the Hutterites and easing bitterness—for example, promoting dialogue between Hutterites and nonhutterites.

1383. Santow, Gigi. *Simulation Approach to the Study of Human Fertility.* Leiden and Boston: Martinus Nighoff Social Sciences Division, 1978. (Publications of the Netherlands Interuniversity Demographic Institute and the Population and Family Study Centre, v. 5). 215 pp.

1384. "Saskatchewan Pact Avoids Clustering." *Financial Post* 57 (August 10, 1963): 19.

1385. Sawka, Patricia. "Hutterite Way of Life." *Canadian Geographical Journal* 77 (October, 1968): 127-31.
An overview of Hutterite life; much information gathered from personal investigation. Illustrated with photographs.

\* Saxby, Trevor J. *Pilgrims of a Common Life* (cited above as item 307), 108-16.
Provides a historical sketch of the Hutterites as one of many historic Christian groups practicing community of property.

1386. Scheer, Herfried. "Hutterian German Dialect: A Study in Sociolinguistic Assimilation and Differentiation." *Mennonite Quarterly Review* 54 (July, 1980): 229-43.
Analyzes language differences among the three Hutterite leuts; speculates that the lack of interaction among them will lead to three separate subdialects.

1387. ———. "Research on the Hutterian German Dialect." *Canadian Ethnic Studies* 1 (December, 1969): 13-20.
Describes the author's research into the meanings and origins of unusual words in the Hutterite dialect.

1388. ———. "Studien zum Wortschatz der Mundart der Hutterischen Brueder. A Lexicological Analysis of the Hutterian German Dialect." Ph.D. dissertation, McGill University, 1972.

1389. Schilling, Arnold J. "Analysis of Hutterian Hymn Melodies." M.A. thesis, University of South Dakota, 1965. 105 pp.

1390. Schlaback, Theron, ed., *"An Account,* by Jakob Waldner: Diary of a Conscientious Objector in World War I." *Mennonite Quarterly Review* 48 (January, 1974): 73-111. A prison diary, translated from the German, with an introduction providing background information on Waldner.

1391. Schludermann, Shirin, and Eduard Schludermann. "Adolescent Perception of Parent Behavior (CRPBI) in Hutterite Communal Society." *Journal of Psychology* 79 (1971): 29-39. Finds that Hutterite adolescents' perception of parental behavior could be described in terms of acceptance vs. rejection, psychological control vs. psychological autonomy, and firm controls vs. lax controls.

1392. ———. "Adolescents' Perception of Themselves and Adults in Hutterite Communal Society." *Journal of Psychology* 78 (1971): 39-48. Concludes that Hutterite girls tend to rate both adults and teenagers more favorably than Hutterite boys do.

1393. ———. "Developmental Study of Role Perception Among Hutterite Adolescents." *Journal of Psychology* 72 (1969): 243-6. Finds that Hutterite adolescents, like Hutterite children, have difficulty in recognizing social roles.

1394. ———. "Factoral Analysis of Semantic Structures in Hutterite Adults." *Journal of Psychology* 73 (1969): 267-73. Finds that Hutterite adults, unlike Hutterite children, understand social role differentiation.

1395. ———. "Maternal Child Rearing Attitudes in Hutterite Communal Society." *Journal of Psychology* 79 (1971): 169-77. Finds that there are few differences in parental attitudes among Hutterite mothers according to age: both young and old mothers tend to accept traditional Hutterite values.

1396. ———. "Paternal Attitudes in Hutterite Communal Society." *Journal of Psychology* 79 (1971): 41-8. Finds that both young and old Hutterite fathers had authoritarian attitudes toward child rearing.

1397. ———. "Scale Checking Style as a Function of Age and Sex in Indian and Hutterite Children." *Journal of Psychology* 72 (1969): 253-61.
Finds that checking style on a rating scale does not vary by sex of the child responding among the Hutterites.

1398. ———. "Social Role Perception of Children in Hutterite Communal Society." *Journal of Psychology* 72 (1969): 183-8.
Finds that Hutterite children have difficulty recognizing differences in social roles.

1399. Schmidt, John. "Hutterites Have a Commune That Works." *Canada and the World* 37 (November, 1971): 6-7.

1400. Schwieder, Dorothy A. "Frontier Brethren: The Hutterite Experience in the American West." *Montana* 28 (January, 1978): 2-15.
Surveys Hutterite life, focusing on the Hutterite experience in settling the untamed frontier. Heavily illustrated with photographs.

1401. ———. "Utopia in the Midwest: The Old Order Amish and the Hutterites." *Palimpsest* 54 (May/June, 1973): 9-23.
Characterizes early Hutterite history, the migration to Dakota, and the attempt to retain old ways in a changing world. Illustrated with photographs.

1402. Serl, Vernon C. *Final Report on the Saskatchewan Hutterite Program.* Regina: Government of Saskatchewan, 1958. 39 pp.

1403. ———. "Stability and Change in Hutterite Society." Ph.D. dissertation, University of Oregon, 1964. 174 pp.
Surveys Hutterite society generally, then looks at one colony, telling of relations with other colonies and with the outside world, describing differences in sex roles in colony life, and analyzing Hutterite persistence. Includes charts and a bibliography.

1404. Shelly, Paul R. "Implications of the Hutterian Way of Life for Other Mennonite Groups." *Proceedings of the Fifth Annual Conference on Mennonite Cultural Problems* (cited above as item 1356), 83-7.

Summarizes a panel discussion on the lessons the Hutterites had for Mennonites, such as the need to carry out beliefs in daily life, the necessity of maintaining a disciplined church fellowship, and the importance of holding fast to basic beliefs.

*       Shenker, Barry. *Intentional Communities: Ideology and Alienation in Communal Societies* (cited above as item 155), passim.

Outlines early Hutterite history, Hutterite ideology, changes in Hutterite life over the years, colony education, the role of the individual, and social control mechanisms.

1405.   Sheps, Mindel C. "Analysis of Reproductive Patterns in an American Isolate." *Population Studies* 19 (July, 1965): 65-80.

Argues that high Hutterite fertility stems from the relatively brief post-partum period of reduced fecundability Hutterite women seem to experience.

1406.   Siegel, Bernard J. "High Anxiety Levels and Cultural Integration: Notes on a Psycho-Cultural Hypothesis." *Social Forces* 34 (October, 1955): 42-8.

Studies the strong social centralization and control of Hopi, ghetto Jewish, and Hutterite societies. Concludes that members of these tightly integrated groups have high levels of anxiety, and that such high levels are encouraged as a way of maintaining group cohesiveness.

1407.   Simpson-Housley, Paul. "Hutterian Religious Ideology, Environmental Perception, and Attitudes Toward Agriculture." *Journal of Geography* 77 (April/May, 1978): 145-8.

Describes ways in which Hutterite religious ideology influences members' attitudes toward farming and the agricultural environment. Illustrated.

1408.   Simpson-Housley, Paul, and Robert J. Moore. "Initial Investigation of Work and Beliefs in Internal-External Reinforcement Responsibility in Hutterite Children." *Prairie Forum* 7 (Fall, 1982): 279-87.

Finds that Hutterite children in Saskatchewan have more positive attitudes toward work than other children do.

1409. Smith, C. Henry. *Coming of the Russian Mennonites: An Episode in the Settling of the Last Frontier, 1874-1884.* Berne, Indiana: Mennonite Book Concern, 1927, pp. 277-82.
Tells the story of four young Hutterite men who were court martialed for resistance to military duty during World War I, constituting a narrative reminiscent of Reformation-era martyr tales.

1410. Smith, Robert T. *Cult and Occult.* Minneapolis: Winston, 1973, pp. 101-4.
Provides a brief sketch of the Hutterites through the eyes of a young man returning to live in his colony after deserting it for the outside world.

1411. Smucker, Donovan E. *Sociology of Canadian Mennonites, Hutterites and Amish: A Bibliography with Annotations.* Waterloo, Ontario: Wilfrid Laurier University Press, 1977, pp. 131-87.
An excellent annotated bibliography. Major items listed are cited here, but many shorter items and some theses are not. Cites books, articles, and theses.

1412. Sommer, J.L. "Hutterite Medicine and Physicians in Moravia in the 16th Century and After." *Mennonite Quarterly Review* 27 (April, 1953): 111-27.

1413. South Dakota State Legislative Research Council. *Hutterite Education.* Pierre: Legislative Research Council, 1973. 24 pp.
Surveys Hutterite attitudes toward public education and legal issues concerning education and the Hutterites. Reproduces excerpts from T. Miller, "Hutterites: A Story of Christian Loyalty" (item 1311, above).

1414. Spiteri, Edward. *Hutterites: The Hutterite Diamond Jubilee.* Calgary: Glenbow-Alberta Institute, 1978. 72 pp., mainly photographs.

1415. Staebler, Edna. "Lord Will Take Care of Us." *Macleans,* March 15, 1952, pp. 14-5, 42, 44-6.
A feature story based on a week's stay at Old Elm Springs colony, Alberta. Recounts many conversations with Hutterites, especially children. Illustrated with photographs.

1416.  Steele, C. Frank. "Canada's Hutterite Settlements."
       *Canadian Geographic Journal* 22 (June, 1941): 308-14.
       Provides an overview of Hutterite life, emphasizing the
       appeal it provides for its participants. Heavily
       illustrated, with photographs of children predominating.

1417.  Steinberg, Arthur G., Herman K. Bleibtreu, Thaddeus W.
       Kurczynski, Alice O. Martin, and Elizabeth M.
       Kurczynski. "Genetic Studies on an Inbred Human
       Isolate." *Proceedings of the Third International
       Congress of Human Genetics* (1967): 267-89.
       A technical study of genetics and genetic drift among
       the Hutterites.

1418.  Stephenson, Peter Hayford. "Dying of the Old Man and a
       Putting On of the New: The Cybernetics of Ritual
       Metanoia in the Life of the Hutterite Commune."
       Ph.D. dissertation, University of Toronto, 1978. 301
       pp.

1419.  ———. "'He Died Too Quick!' The Process of Dying in
       a Hutterian Colony." *Omega* 14 (1983-4): 127-33.
       Describes the way in which a drawn-out death plays an
       important social role in Hutterite life. Provides a list of
       recommendations for medical professionals for treating
       Hutterites with terminal illnesses.

1420.  ———. "Hutterite Belief in Evil Eye: Beyond Paranoia
       and Towards a General Theory of *Invidia*." *Culture,
       Medicine and Pyschiatry* 3 (September, 1979): 247-65.
       Finds that Hutterite fear of the "evil eye" is grounded
       in the movement's fear of envy.

1421.  ———. "'Like a Violet Unseen'—The Apotheosis of
       Absence in Hutterite Life." *Canadian Review of
       Sociology and Anthropology* 15 (1978): 433-42.
       Finds paradoxical and not readily explainable certain
       parts of Hutterite unspoken communication; finds that
       Hutterites imbue unseen and unheard phenomena with
       meaning.

1422.  Sturdevant, Lori. "People of Jacob Hutter." *Picture*
       magazine, Sunday supplement of the Minneapolis
       *Tribune*, October 16, 1977, pp. 4-47.
       An in-depth account of life at the Wolf Creek Colony,
       South Dakota, based primarily on interviews with

members. Heavily illustrated.

1423. "Supreme Court Hearing Ahead in Hutterite Case."
*Financial Post* 60 (June 11, 1966): 36.
Concerns Alberta Communal Property Act. Not seen.

1424. Swan, John. "400-Year-Old Commune." *Atlantic Monthly*
230 (November, 1972): 90-100.
A sympathetic account of Hutterite life by a visiting
New Yorker.

1425. Tanaka, Hiroshi. "Albertan Gift to Asia: Hutterites in
Japan." *Canadian Geographic* 98 (April/May, 1979):
70-3.
A group of Japanese Protestants began living
communally in the 1950s; after learning of the Hutterites
in 1970, they visited them in Canada and adopted
traditional Hutterite dress and other ways. North
American Hutterites have, in turn, provided financial
assistance to their Japanese counterparts. This article
provides a history of the Japanese group and a
description of its life. Illustrated with photographs.

1426. Teichroew, Allan. "Hutterite Mill of Bon Homme Colony:
An Architectural Documentary." *Mennonite Life* 39
(1984): 9-12.
Describes the history and layout of this old mill.
Heavily illustrated with photographs.

1427. Tennant, David. "Anabaptist Theologies of Childhood and
Education." *Baptist Quarterly* no. 31 (July, 1985):
118-36.
Outlines early Hutterite educational and communal
childrearing practices. Finds that Anabaptist education's
primary purpose is the promotion of acculturation.

1428. Thielman, George C. "Hutterites in Contemporary
Society." *Mennonite Life* 25 (January, 1970): 42-6.
Outlines differences between Mennonites and
Hutterites; describes Canadian opposition to Hutterite
expansion.

1429. Thijssen, Paula, and Paul S. Gross. *Christian Community:
The Outcome of Christian Belief.* Bromdon, England:
Plough, 1954. 10 pp. Reprinted from *Plough*, Autumn,
1954.

1430.  Thomas,  Kenneth  Charles.  *Survey  of  the  Hutterite
       Groups  in  Montana  and  Canada.*  M.A.  thesis,  Montana
       State University, 1949. 83 pp.
       Provides  a  sketch  of  Hutterite  history  and  life,  with
       special  attention  to  Montana.    Describes  opposition  to
       Hutterite  settlement  in  Montana  in  the  late  1940s  based
       on  the  non-Hutterites'  fear  of  communism,  antipathy
       toward  pacifism,  and  general  prejudice.    Bibliography  lists
       many  specialized  and  local  references,  plus  interview  and
       manuscript sources for the study.

1431.  Thomas,  Norman.   "Hutterian  Brethren."   *South  Dakota
       Historical Collections* 25 (1950): 265-90.
       Provides  an  overview  of  Hutterite  life  and  history,
       with  a  detailed  account  of  the  persecution  in  South
       Dakota  at  the  time  of  World  War  I.    Illustrated  with
       photography  and  maps;  also  contains  tables  of  Hutterite
       statistics and general information.

1432.  Thomlinson,  Ralph.  *Population  Dynamics:  Causes  and
       Consequences  of  World  Demographic  Change.*  New
       York: Random House, 1965, pp. 157-64.
       Provides  statistical  information  on  Hutterite  fertility
       rates  and  discusses  methods  of  analyzing  population
       statistics.

1433.  Thompson,  William  Paul.   "Hutterite  Community:  Artefact
       [sic]  Ark—An  Historical  Study  of  the  Architecture  and
       Planning of a Communal Society." 317 pp.
       Shows  how  the  colonies'  architecture  helps  them
       function as "arks," havens in a corrupt world.

1434.  ———.  "Hutterite  Community:  Its  Reflex  in  Arch-
       itectural  and  Settlement  Patterns."  *Canadian  Ethnic
       Studies* 16 (1984): 53- 72.

1435.  Thorkelson,  William  L.   "Dakota  Hutterites  Cry
       'Persecution.'"  *Christian  Century*  72  (April  17,  1955):
       517.
       Characterizes  Hutterites'  objections  to  a  new  law
       forbidding their expansion in South Dakota.

1436.  Tietze,  Christopher.   "Reproductive  Span  and  Rate  of
       Reproduction  among  Hutterite  Women."  *Fertility  and
       Sterility* 8 (January-February, 1957): 89-97.
       Finds  wide  variation  in  reproductive  span  and  also  in

rate of reproduction among Hutterite women.

1437. "Trouble for the Hutterites." *Christian Life* 17 (June, 1955): 32-3.
Describes Hutterite life in light of the recent enactment of a law in South Dakota banning creation of new colonies.

1438. Tschetter, Paul. "Diary of Paul Tschetter, 1873." *Mennonite Quarterly Review* 5 (1931): 112-27, 198-220.
Tschetter was one of the Hutterite delegates sent from Russia to find a place to settle in the United States; this diary covers that scouting trip.

1439. Tschetter, Peter S. *Hutterian Brethren of Yesterday and Today*. Minburn, Alberta: author, 1966.
A history and guide to Hutterite life authorized by the Mixburn Colony Hutterites. Mixburn Colony is located near Minburn, Alberta.

1440. Turner, Wallace. "Hutterite Farm Groups Facing Inquiry by Montana Legislature." New York *Times*, June 2, 1963, p. 79.
Provides an overview of the conflict in Montana which led the legislature to study legislation restricting Hutterite land purchases.

1441. ———. "Hutterites During World War I." *Mennonite Life* 24 (July, 1969): 130-7.
Tracks the fate of Hutterites drafted and sent to prison for refusing duty; describes cases of mistreatment, including torture under which two died. Also describes actions taken by civilians against the Hutterites during the war.

1442. ———. "Mennonites in South Dakota." M.A. thesis, University of South Dakota, 1933. 77 pp.

1443. ———. "Mennonites of South Dakota." *Mennonite Life* 5 (July, 1950): II-IV, 33.
Mainly describes the growth of the Mennonite population in the Freeman area, but includes notes on the interactions of Mennonites and Hutterites in the vicinity. Illustrated with photographs taken at the Jamesville Colony.

1444. ———. "Mennonites in South Dakota." *South Dakota Historical Review* 2 (July, 1937): 147-70.
Primarily a history of the Mennonites in South Dakota; special attention is paid to distinguishing Mennonites from Hutterites.

1445. ———. "What About the Hutterites?" *Christian Century* 76 (July 8, 1959): 801-3.
Recounts Hutterite migrations in North America, from South Dakota to Canada and back again. Defends the Hutterites against the charge that they are swallowing up all of Canada's farmland in the prairie provinces, arguing that other farmers use three to four times as much land per capita as the Hutterites do, and noting that much protest against Hutterite land purchases is based on simple prejudice against things such as distinctiveness in clothing.

1446. Vana, Lucille Ripley. "Maintenance of Genetic Polymorphism in an Inbred Human Isolate." Ph.D. dissertation, Case Western Reserve University, 1974. 178 pp.

1447. Waldner, Marie. "Present Day Social Customs and Culture Patterns of the Hutterites in North America." *Proceedings of the Fifth Annual Conference on Mennonite Cultural Problems* (cited above as item 1356), 45-59.
Describes colony life and concludes that encroachment by the outside world is a serious threat to the Hutterite way.

1448. Waltner, Elma. "South Dakota's Hutterite Colonies." *Travel* 105 (May, 1956): 26-30.
A popular account of Hutterite life. Illustrated with photographs.

1449. Waltner, Emil J. *Banished for Faith.* Freeman, South Dakota: Pine Hill Press, 1968. 219 pp.

1450. Weeks, John Arthur. "Genetics of Fertility in a Human Isolate." M.S. thesis, Case Western Reserve University, 1977. 72 pp.

1451. Whalen, William J. *Minority Religions in America.* Staten Island, N.Y.: Alba House, 1972, pp. 69-76.

Provides an overview sketch of the movement. Also contains a brief note on the Bruderhof.

1452. "What Was Said in Court about Hutterite Beliefs." *Financial Post* 59 (October 16, 1965): 36.

1453. "Why Hutterites Changed Line and Went to Court." *Financial Post* 59 (August 14, 1965): 10.

1454. Wild, Geoffrey. "Comenius, Education, and the Hutterite Anabaptists: I. Hutterite Education," and "II. A *Prima Facie* Case?" *Journal of Christian Education* (Papers) 63 (November, 1978): 22-33; and 66 (December, 1979): 25-38.

1455. Wilder, Laura Ingalls. *On the Way Home.* New York: Harper and Row, 1962, pp. 20-3.
Tells of an encounter the Wilder family had with Hutterites at Jamesville Colony, S.D. Describes the colony site and characterizes the people as generous and friendly.

1456. Willms, A.M. "Brethren Known as Hutterians." *Canadian Journal of Economics and Political Science* 24 (August, 1958): 391-405.
Provides an account of the Hutterite move from South Dakota to Canada at the time of World War I. Advocates better relations between Hutterites and other Canadians. Well documented, including many references to manuscript materials.

1457. Wilson, Bryan R. "Migrating Sects." *British Journal of Sociology* 18 (September, 1967): 303-17.

1458. Wipf, Joseph A. "Phonetics of the Hutterite Dialect." M.A. thesis, University of Colorado, 1966. 111 pp.

1459. Wolkan, Rudolf, ed. *Geschicht-buch der Hutterischen Brueder, hrsg. von den Hutterischen Bruedern in Amerika.* Macleod, Alberta: Standoff Colony, 1923. In German.

1460. Wooster, Ernest S. "Bruederhoff Communities." *Communities of the Past and Present* (cited above as item 175), 64.
Provides a brief characterization of the Hutterites;

Wooster speculates that they may no longer exist, since he has been unable to establish contact with them.

1461. Wurz, John K. *Hutterian Brethren of America.* Lethbridge, Alberta: Hutterian Brethren of North America, 1968. 24 pp.

1462. Yackulic, George A. "Hutterites' Problem." *Saturday Night* 67 (September 6, 1952): 30.

1463. Young, Gertrude S. "Mennonites in South Dakota." *South Dakota Historical Collections* 10 (1920): 470-506. A history of the Mennonites, their settlement in South Dakota, controversies about them, and efforts by the state to restrict Mennonites and Hutterites. Includes much information about the Hutterites, who are essentially regarded as one of several groups of Mennonites. Refutes the apparently common myth that the Hutterites are the only "Mennonites" in South Dakota. Documentation includes references to local newspaper articles, reports of state agencies, court records, and manuscript documents from various colonies.

1464. ———. "Record Concerning Mennonite Immigration, 1873." *American Historical Review* 29 (April, 1924): 518-22. Describes the scouting trip made by Russian Anabaptists in 1873 seeking locations for settlement. Reproduces a portion of the diary of Paul Tschetter made on that trip, characterizing the questions the scouting team asked of President Grant and reproducing the reply made by Grant's representative.

1465. Zepp, Fred R. "Communal Colonies: Why Neighbors Wince When Hutterites Move In." *National Observer*, October 21, 1963, p. 13. Describes existing and pending legislation in various states and provinces restricting Hutterite expansion, providing the arguments of those who would restrict the Hutterites and the Hutterite response to their critics.

1466. ———. "Religious Freedom for *Everybody*?" *Christian Herald*, November, 1963, pp. 14-9, 22, 117-8. Describes discrimination against Hutterites in various states and provicnes, along with controversies surrounding other religious minorities. Leaves unresolved the question of just how eccentric religious behavior can be and still be tolerated.

1467. Zieglschmid, A.J.F., ed. *Aelteste Chronik der Hutterischecn Brueder, Ein Sprachdenkmal aus Fruehneuhochdeutscher Zeit.* Ithaca, New York: Cayuga Press, 1943.

1468. ———. "Hutterites on the American Continent." *American-German Review* 8 (February, 1942): 20-4.
    Compares contemporary Hutterite life with that of the distant past, finding that little has changed, even in the style of buildings Hutterites build. Illustrated with photographs taken at Bon Homme colony, South Dakota.

1469. ———. "Must the Hutterites Leave Canada?" *Christian Century* 64 (October 22, 1947): 1269-71.
    Describes anti-Hutterite legislation in Alberta; provides a passionate defense of the Hutterites, arguing that they have been discriminated against unfairly and refuting the argument that the Hutterites will overrun all of Alberta's agricultural land.

1470. Zwarun, Suzanne. "Tussle Over Taxes." *Maclean's* 93 (January 14, 1980): 8.
    Provides an update on court battles over the Dariusleut Hutterites' refusal to pay income tax on the grounds that it is a war tax.

1471. ———. "When Money Talks: The Silent Side of Pacifism." *Maclean's* 91 (December 25, 1978): 21-2.
    Describes a court battle over Dariusleut Hutterites' refusal to pay income tax on the grounds that it is a war tax.

# LXXIII. THE INDUSTRIAL BROTHERHOOD

N.W. Lermond established this group at Thomaston, Maine, at the turn of the century with the goal of establishing cooperative industries, stores, colonies, and great cities. His original goal was to get a million members to pledge $100 million in capital toward the plan, but he attracted little support.

Some material on the Brotherhood is in the American

Communities Collection at Syracuse University.

*Community periodical*

1472.  *Humanity*.

*Secondary works*

\*      Bushee, Frederick A.   "Communistic Societies in the
        United States" (cited above as item 38), 639.
        Contains an overview of the movement.

1473.   Kent, Alexander.   "Industrial Brotherhood."   "Cooperative
        Communities in the United States (cited above as item
        117), 621-3.
        Provides information on the goals and organization of
        the movement.   Reproduces two pledges taken by
        members.

# LXXIV. ITALIAN-SWISS COLONY

About 1880 Andrea Sbarboro hit upon a plan to bring
prosperity to unemployed Italian immigrants in San Francisco.
In 1881 he purchased a 1500 acre sheep ranch at Asti, near
Cloverdale, California, starting a cooperative grape farm and
later a winery.   Dormitories were built on the site, but the
workers eventually resisted the cooperative plan which required
them to invest in the project, preferring straight pay.
Nevertheless, a worker-oriented benefits system continued to
operate for many years.

*Secondary Works*

1474.   Dondero, C.   "Asti, Sonoma County."   *Out West* 17
        (August, 1902): 253-66.
        Describes the origin of the colony, its finances, its
        recruitment of workers, problems encountered with the
        cooperative system, economic difficulties, and the
        evolution of the colony into a private business
        enterprise. Illustrated.

1475. Gumina, Deanna Paoli. "Andrea Sbarboro, Founder of the Italian Swiss Colony Wine Company." *Italian Americana* 2 (1975): 1-17.
Provides an overview history of the project and biography of Sbarboro.

1476. Shinn, Charles Howard. "Italian-Swiss Agricultural Colony." *History of Cooperation in the United States* (cited above as item 26), 449-59.
Provides a basic history of the colony and reproduces its bylaws.

# LXXV. JEWISH AGRICULTURAL COLONIES

Am Olam was an Eastern European Jewish organization which promoted collective agricultural settlements for Jews settling in the United States. In the 1880s it inspired some 26 colonies, mostly in the Midwest and West: they were located in Kansas, New Jersey, Louisiana, South Dakota, Michigan, Colorado, and Oregon. The failure of these colonies was not utterly discouraging; later the Baron de Hirsch fund was established to help finance such colonies, and other organizations were established to help found more Jewish communes and cooperative ventures.

The Am Olam leadership in America was seriously devoted to communal endeavors, but total community of goods and labor did not exist everywhere. In some colonies there was substantial economic sharing, while in others the community consisted essentially of Jewish families living in proximity.

Some miscellaneous correspondence and manuscript material concerning Jewish communalism survives. One repository of such material is the American Jewish Archives, located on the campus of Hebrew Union College-Jewish Institute of Religion in Cincinnati. The collection there also contains many photographs. On the same campus, in the HUC-JIR library, is the American Jewish Periodical Center, which holds many newspapers and magazines which contain articles on colonization. The American Jewish Historical Society in Waltham, Massachusetts, houses the extensive archives of the Baron de Hirsch Fund.

Only deliberately Jewish communities are listed in this section. Other communities which merely happened to have large numbers of Jews (such as Sunrise, Michigan) are listed separately.

*Periodicals not related to a specific colony*

1477. *American Israelite.*
This periodical is the source with the most material on
the Jewish communes during the most important period of
their existence, the late nineteenth century. It was, in
effect, the official organ of the Hebrew Union
Agricultural Society, one of several organizations
encouraging communal activity.

1478. *Jewish Farmer.* 1891-2.
Monthly farm journal in Yiddish, published by the
Jewish Agricultural Society. Another periodical by the
same name was founded in May, 1908, and was still being
published in 1912.

*Primary works covering more than one colony*

1479. *Annual Report of the Jewish Agricultural Society.* New
York: by the society.
Contains a year-by-year discussion of the situation of
Jewish farmers, many of them involved in the communitarian experiments. Has statistical data and information on special circumstances, such as problems with
crops and marketing.

1480. Jewish Colonization Association. *Memorandum and
Articles of Association of the Jewish Colonization
Association.* London: Waterlow and Sons, Ltd., 1891.
16 pp.
The basic documents of the British based organization
founded by Baron de Hirsch which promoted colonization
of European and Asian Jews in America.

*Secondary works covering more than one colony*

1481. Binder, Rudolph M. "Jewish Colonies." *New Encyclopedia of Social Reform* (cited above as item 35),
559-61. Provides a history of Jewish rural colonization
in Russia, Palestine, Argentina, Canada, and the United
States. Supplies a useful table of information on
American Jewish colonies.

1482. Bogen, Boris D. *Jewish Philanthropy in the United*

*States.* New York: Macmillan, 1917, pp. 17-31. Provides a brief summary of the purpose and activities of the Baron de Hirsch Fund and related colonization organizations. Chapter 9, "Back to the Soil Movement" (pp. 125-37), describes various efforts to promote agricultural communes and provides a brief history of the Woodbine colony.

1483. Brandes, Joseph. *Immigrants to Freedom: Jewish Communities in Rural New Jersey since 1882.* Philadelphia: University of Pennsylvania Press, 1971. 424 pp.
A comprehensive history of the New Jersey colonies, perhaps the most important group of Jewish agricultural communes; also contains information on Jewish colonization more generally. Describes the conditions in Europe which led the colonists to emigrate. Contains several useful statistical appendices and an extensive bibliography, including references to many specialized sources not cited here.

1484. Davidson, Gabriel. "Colonies, Agricultural: United States." *Universal Jewish Encyclopedia.* New York: Universal Jewish Encyclopedia, Inc., 1941, v. 3, pp. 294-7. Provides a brief account of Russian Jewish immigration, plus sketches of Sicily Island, the New Jersy colonies, New Odessa, Cremieux, Painted Woods, Cotopaxi, the Kansas colonies, Palestine, Ellicott City (as "Endicott City), the Arkansas colony, and Sunrise, plus mentions of others.

1485. ———. *Our Jewish Farmers and the Story of the Jewish Agricultural Society.* New York: L.B. Fischer, 1943. 280 pp.
A narrative history of the Jewish Agricultural Society and its efforts to help Jewish farmers, whether communal or not. "Supplement: Jewish Colonization in the U.S. in the Nineteenth Century," pp. 194-273, is especially useful for the communal projects. Contains information on colonies in Louisiana, Arkansas, South Dakota, Kansas, Oregon, Michigan, and New Jersey.

* Fogarty, Robert S. "American Communes, 1865-1914" (cited above as item 74), 157-8. Contains three paragraphs embodying the central history of the Jewish communal effort.

1486.  Geffen, Joel S.    "Jewish Agricultural Colonies as Reported
       in the Pages of the Russian Hebrew Press, *Ha-Melitz*
       and *Ha-Yom*:    Annotated Documentary."    *American
       Jewish  Historical  Quarterly*  60  (1970-71):  355-82.
       Provides information on how the American communal
       farming projects (most frequently involving Russian
       immigrants) were reported in Russia.    Special attention
       given to Sicily Island, Alliance, Vineland, and Winnipeg
       colonies.

1487.  Goering, Violet, and Orlando J. Goering.    "Agricultural
       Communes of the *Am Olam*."    *Communal Societies* 4
       (1984): 74-86.
       Describes the pogroms in Russia leading to the
       exodus of the Jews who ended up the the colonies;
       provides overview histories of Sicily Island, Cremieux,
       Bethlehem Yehudah, and New Odessa, and argues that Am
       Olam fulfilled some of its goals, despite the failure of
       the colonies.

1488.  Goldman, Julius.    *Report on the Colonization of Russian
       Refugees in the West.*    New York: Evening Post Job
       Printing Office, 1882. 35 pp.
       Report to the Hebrew Emigrant Aid Society of the
       United States.    Discusses possible locations and support
       needed for settling Jewish immigrants in the West.

1489.  Herscher, Uri D.    *Jewish Agricultural Utopias in America,
       1880-1910.*    Detroit: Wayne State University Press,
       1981. 197 pp.
       Provides a history of the Jewish communal movement.
       Colonies covered in some detail include Sicily Island, New
       Odessa, Cremieux, Bethlehem, Am Olam Group Settlement,
       Cotopaxi, Palestine, Painted Woods, Iola, Chananel,
       Alliance, and Woodbine.    Also includes information on
       earlier communes, Russian and American historical
       background to the colonies, the causes of failure of most
       of them, and a summary evaluation of the concept.
       Includes a substantial bibliography.    Illustrated with
       photographs.

*      Infield, Henrik F.    *Cooperative Communities at Work*
       (cited above as item 105), 14-6.
       Provides a brief overview of the Jewish colonies; a
       table provides information on location, lifespan, size,
       leadership, and source of support for 20 colonies.

1490. *Jews in American Agriculture: The History of Farming by Jews in the United States.* N.p.: Jewish Agricultural Society, Inc., 1954, pp. 23-35.
Discusses various communal agricultural projects. Illustrated.

1491. Katz, Nancy H. "Jewish Agricultural Colonies in the United States." M.A. thesis, Southern Methodist University, 1964.

1492. Kirsch, William. *Jew and the Land.* Madison: Office of the Secretary of the American Association for Agricultural Legislation, University of Wisconsin, 1920. 45 pp.

1493. Lee, Samuel J. *Moses of the New World: The Work of Baron de Hirsch.* New York: Thomas Yoseloff, 1970. 313 pp.
A biography of de Hirsch, containing information on his critical support of Jewish colonization in America through the Baron de Hirsch Fund. Chapter 18 covers the North American colonies and features a brief chronicle of the major colony sites (pp. 277-8).

1494. Levine, Herman J., and Benjamin Miller. *American Jewish Farmer in Changing Times.* New York: Jewish Agricultural Society, 1966. 100 pp.
Constitutes an updating of Gabriel Davidson, *Our Jewish Farmers* (item 1485), focusing on the more recent, noncommunal, era, but referring frequently (especially on pp. 7-12) to the colonies of the past.

1495. Lifschutz, Ezekiel. "Jacob Gordin's Proposal to Establish an Agricultural Colony." *American Jewish Historical Quarterly* 56 (December, 1966): 151-62. Reprinted in *Jewish Experience in America.* New York: KTAV Publishing House, 1969, v. 4, pp. 253-61.
Describes Gordin's unsuccessful attempt to establish a separatist Jewish colony in the 1890s, including a proposal that his followers settle as an isolated unit at Woodbine.

1496. Menes, Abraham. "*Am Olyom* Movement." *YIVO Annual of Jewish Social Science* 4 (1949): 9-33.
Discusses the ideology of Am Olam (as it is usually transliterated), covering its vision of a new economic

order, a return to the land, the ideal of manual labor, and how socialists dominated the movement in America. Tells of the origins of Am Olam in the Ukraine, its early activities in America, and three of its colonies (Sicily Island, Bethlehem Jehudah, and New Odessa).

1497. Osofsky, Gilbert. "Hebrew Emigrant Aid Society of the United States (1881-1883)." *Publication of the American Jewish Historical Society* 49 (March, 1960): 173-87.
Describes attempts at resettlement of Russian Jews. Briefly discusses Sicily Island, Cotopaxi, Vineland, and Beersheba, but is more concerned with the overall work of the Society than with individual projects.

1498. Price, George M. "Russian Jews in America," second installment. *Publication of the American Jewish Historical Society* 48 (December, 1958): 78-133. Translated by Leo Shpall. Reprinted in *The Jewish Experience in America.* Edited by Abraham J. Karp. New York: KTAV Publishing House, 1969, v. 4, pp. 300-55.
Provides basic information about forces and organizations (such as Am Olam) working toward colonization, and provides concise accounts of Sicily Island, the South Dakota colonies, Painted Woods, the Kansas colonies, New Odessa, and three South Jersey colonies (Alliance, Carmel, and Rosenhayn). Concludes with other material concerning the Baron de Hirsch Fund and the situation of the Russian immigrants of the early 1880s. Provides a useful chart comparing nine major colonies by number of families and life span.

1499. Reizenstein, Milton. "Agricultural Colonies in the United States." *Jewish Encyclopedia.* Edited by Isidore Singer. New York and London: Funk and Wagnalls, 1901, v. 1, pp. 256-62.
Brief but informative sketches of all the major Jewish colonies, including Sicily Island, Cremieux, Bethlehem-Yehudah, Cotopaxi, New Odessa, Painted Woods, Montefiore (Kansas), Lasker, Beersheba, Hebron, Gilead, Touro, Leeser, Palestine, Washington, Waterview, Chesterfield, Colchester, Monteville, Alliance, Carmel, Rosenhayn, Woodbine, Estelleville, and Montefiore (New Jersey). Includes three photographs of Woodbine.

1500. Robinson, Leonard G. "Agricultural Activities of the Jews in America." *American Jewish Year Book 5673.* Edited by Herbert Friedenwald. Philadelphia: Jewish Publication Society of America, 1912, pp. 21-108. Describes the exodus of Jews from Russia following the pogrom of 1881 and provides an overview of many colonies, including Sicily Island, Cremieux, Cotopaxi, New Odessa, and colonies in North Dakota, Kansas, and New Jersey; also describes several organizations promoting colonization.

1501. Rutman, H. David. *Beginnings of the Jewish Agricultural Movement in America.* Manuscript at American Jewish Archives. 9 pp. Deals with the roots of colonization in Europe and Russia, the earliest American colonies, and other parallel efforts, notably in Argentina.

1502. Ruxin, Robert H. "Jewish Farmer and the Small-Town Jewish Community: Schoharie County, New York." *American Jewish Archives* 29 (April, 1977): 3-21. Focuses primarily on one noncommunal Jewish farming situation, but includes a survey history of Jewish agricultural communes as well. Illustrated.

1503. Shpall, Leo. "Jewish Agricultural Colonies in the United States." *Agricultural History* 24 (July, 1950): 120-46. Explores the earliest roots of Jewish agricultural settlement, beginning with propagandizing in the late 18th and early 19th centuries. Describes the first actual attempts at the creation of agricultural communities in the 1830s, and then focuses on the greater efforts made after 1860. Provides brief characterizations of many of the more important colonies throughout the United States, concluding its chronological survey with Palestine colony (Michigan) in 1891. Well documented with many references to ephemeral periodicals in various languages.

1504. Singer, Richard E. *American Jew in Agriculture, Past History and Present Condition.* Prize essay, 1941, in manuscript at American Jewish Archives. Also on microfilm. V. 1, 358 pp. plus map plates; v. 2, pp. 359-707. The single most comprehensive work on Jewish agriculture, especially communal projects. About two-thirds of the paper focuses on the era of Russian immigration, 1880-1914, covering various aid societies as well as colonies in Massachusetts, New Jersey, the District of Columbia, Arkansas, Louisiana, Texas, Virginia, Maryland, Indiana, Illinois, Michigan, Wisconsin, North Dakota, South Dakota, Kansas, Nebraska, Colorado, Utah, Wyoming, Oregon, and California.    Singer's articles on the various colonies are listed separately below under the appropriate headings.    The essay also reproduces some important documents, such as the constitutions of some of the colonization assistance societies.    Contains a very substantial bibliography, including references to primary sources, government documents, ephemeral materials and periodicals, many of which are not cited here.

1505.   Wice, David H.    "Jewish Farmer in America."    *Hebrew Union College Monthly*, January, 1931, pp. 14-5.
Provides a brief survey of Jewish agricultural colonies from Ararat (1820) through the New Jersey settlements. Gives brief descriptions of agricultural training schools for Jews and of the Jewish Agricultural Society.    Argues that agriculture is the key to the revitalization of Jews and Judaism.

# LXXV(A).  ARKANSAS: AM OLAM GROUP SETTLEMENT

A colony was founded in Arkansas, between Little Rock and Memphis, in 1883, with an initial membership of 150. Never formally named, the community was given land and secured a contract with a lumber company to make barrel staves.    However, the climate was too hot for the settlers, and floods, storms, snakes, and malaria helped drive them all out by September of the year of the founding.    Many members went on to join the new Cremieux colony in South Dakota.    (Singer [item 1504, p. 322] mentions another Arkansas colony called Des Arc, but provides little information on it.)

Secondary works

1506.   Davidson, Gabriel.    "Pioneers in the Land of Cotton." *Our Jewish Farmers and the Story of the Jewish*

*Agricultural Society* (cited above as item 1485), 208-13. Provides a historical overview of the colony.

1507. Davidson, Gabriel, and Edward Goodwin. "Arkansas Colonization Episode." *Jewish Tribune* 95 (July 12, 1929): 2, 9.
Tells the history of the colony largely as a tale of woes—a difficult industrial base, too hot a climate, insects, and disease.

1508. Herscher, Uri. "Am Olam Group Settlement, Arkansas." *Jewish Agricultural Utopias* (cited above as item 1489), 52-5.
Sketches the history of the colony.

* Price, George M. "Russian Jews in America" (cited above as item 1498), 87.
Provides a brief account of the history of the colony, focusing on the malaria epidemic which hastened its demise.

1509. Singer, Richard E. "Newport." *American Jew in Agriculture* (cited above as item 1504), 321-2.
Describes the founding and early reports of success of the colony, as well as its decline. Also contains a brief reference to another colony in Arkansas, founded nearby about the same time, which failed largely due to the infertility of its farmland.

# LXXV(B). CALIFORNIA: PLACER COUNTY

According to Richard Singer, a colony was founded six miles from Lincoln in 1909. Small parcels of land were given or sold to settlers, who then farmed them cooperatively, principally planting orange trees. Norton Stern has described two other colonies, near Orangevale (which, located about 20 miles from Lincoln, may be the colony Singer also describes) and Porterville. The Orangevale colony was founded by David Lubin and Harris Weinstock on land they owned 15 miles east of Sacramento; ten Russian Jewish families were settled there in 1891. Accounts vary regarding the end of the colony. The Porterville colony resulted from the philanthropy of Philip N. Lilienthal; Jewish farmers were settled on land his company owned in the south San Joaquin Valley in 1891. The colony died about 1896.

*Secondary works*

1510.  Singer, Richard E.    "Placer County."    *American Jew in*
       *Agriculture* (cited above as item 1504), 543-4.
       Provides a brief overview of the colony.

1511.  Stern, Norton B.    "Orangevale and Porterville, California,
       Jewish  Farm  Colonies."    *Western  States  Jewish*
       *Historical  Quarterly*  10  (January,  1978):  159-67.
       Provides sketches of the two colonies.

# LXXV(C).  COLORADO: COTOPAXI

The  Cotopaxi  colony  was  founded  in  Fremont  County,
Colorado, in 1882.   It consisted of a site (reports of whose size
vary  from  500  to  3,220  acres;  it  was  probably  expanded  through
the  homesteading  of  additional  acreage  after  the  original
landholding  had  been  secured)  about  100  miles  southwest  of
Denver  in  the  Arkansas  River  valley.    The  ten  to  twenty
families  which  settled  there  proved  inexpert  at  farming,  and  in
any  event  the  land  was  not  suited  for  agriculture.    The
high-country  winter  caused  terrible  suffering  for  the
ill-prepared  colonists.    Cotopaxi  was  abandoned  in  1883,  when
Jewish  agencies  helped  move  the  colonists  elsewhere.    Singer
(item  1504,  pp.  508-9)  mentions  the  preparation  of  land  for  a
colony  at  Atwood  in  1896,  but  finds  no  record  of  further
activity.

*Secondary works*

1512.  Herscher, Uri.    "Cotopaxi, Colorado."    *Jewish  Agricultural*
       *Utopias* (cited above as item 1489), 55-61.
       Provides a historical sketch of the colony.

1513.  Roberts,  Dorothy.    "Jewish  Colony  at  Cotopaxi."    *Colorado*
       *Magazine* 18 (July, 1941): 124-31.
       Provides  a  list  of  settlers,  a  summary  of  the  goals  of
       the  colony,  and  a  description  of  the  severe  hardships
       which afflicted the settlers.

1514.  Satt, Flora Jane.    "Cotopaxi Colony."    M.A.  thesis,
        University of Colorado, 1950.

1515.  Schwartz, Julius.    *Hebrew  Emigrant  Aid  Society  Report:*
        *Report  on  the  Colony  of  Russian  Refugees  at  Cotopaxi,*
        *Colorado.*    New  York:  Hebrew  Emigrant  Aid  Society,
        1882.
        At the Harvard University library.

1516.  Singer,  Richard  E.    "Cotopaxi."    *American  Jew  in*
        *Agriculture* (cited above as item 1504), 493-507.
        Outlines  the  history  of  the  colony;  quotes  much
        primary source material.

# LXXV(D). CONNECTICUT: CHESTERFIELD

Chesterfield  was  founded  by  the  Baron  de  Hirsch  fund  in
1892;  it  had  a  brief  life  as  a  cooperative  colony  and  soon
became  a  roadside  hamlet.    28  families  were  reported  to  be
living there soon after the founding of the colony.

*Secondary works*

1517.  Federal  Writers'  Project.    *American  Guide  Series:*
        Connecticut.    Boston:  Houghton  Mifflin,  1938,  p.  447.
        Locates  the  site  of  Chesterfield  and  provides  a  note
        about its founding.

1518.  Singer,  Richard  E.    "Chesterfield."    *American  Jew  in*
        *Agriculture*  (cited  above  as  item  1504),  206-18.
        Provides a historical sketch of the colony.

# LXXV(E). DISTRICT OF COLUMBIA:
# WASHINGTON COLONY

Founded  in  1883  when  fifteen  Jewish  families  puchased  the
land  for  it.    For  a  time  it  was  successful,  with  a  working  dairy
farm  for  its  economic  backbone.    However,  a  need  for  outside
support  developed  after  about  a  year,  and  when  it  did  not
materialize,  the  settlers  moved  back  to  the  cities  whence  they

came.

*Secondary work*

1519. Singer, Richard E. "District of Columbia." *American Jew in Agriculture* (cited above as item 1504), 319-20. Provides an overview history of the project.

# LXXV(F). ILLINOIS: FLORA

Flora was begun after a St. Louis group had purchased 800 acres for $48,000. At first the colonists tried cooperative farming, but when that did not succeed, they subdivided the land. Financial problems ensued, and the farmers gradually drifted away.

*Secondary work*

1520. Singer, Richard E. "Flora." *American Jew in Agriculture* (cited above as item 1504), 349-50.
Provides a sketch of the rise and decline of the colony.

# LXXV(G). THE KANSAS COLONIES

There were eight Jewish colonies founded in Kansas, making it one of the most active states for Jewish colonization. Most of the communities were located on the arid high plains and lasted only a short time.

*Secondary works on the Kansas colonies in general*

*     Davidson, Gabriel. "Jewish Covered Wagon." *Jewish Criterion* 29 (January 29, 1932): 2. Reprinted in *Our Jewish Farmers* (cited above as item 1485), 221-5.
Provides an overview history of seven Jewish colonies in Kansas: Moses Montefiore, Hebron, Gilead, Touro, Leeser, Beersheba, and Lasker. Relates their rise to the decline of the colony in Arkansas.

1521. Harris, Lloyd David. *Sod Jerusalems: Jewish Agricultural Communities in Frontier Kansas.* Topeka: author, 1984. 185 pp. A bound manuscript at the Kansas State Historical Society.
Describes the crisis in Russia and the American response to it; provides extensively documented histories of the colonies of Wyandotte, Beersheba, Montefiore, Lasker, Hebron, Gilead, Touro, and Leeser.

\*      Price, George M. "Russian Jews in America" (cited above as item 1498), 87.
Supplies a brief note on Montefiore, Lasker, and Beersheba colonies and their problems.

1522. Sapinsley, Elbert L. "Jewish Agricultural Colonies in the West: the Kansas Example." *Western States Jewish Historical Quarterly* 3 (April, 1971): 157-69.
Discusses the European origins of Am Olam and similar organizations, and the seven Kansas colonies Am Olam inspired or initiated. Discusses the motives for founding the colonies and the problems they experienced. Focuses especially on Beersheba, providing a good account of that colony. Well documented. An apparently earlier version of the paper, entitled "Moshavot That Missed: The Attempts to Establish Jewish Agricultural Colonies in Kansas: Beer Sheba as a Prime Example of the Effort," (1968), is on file at the American Jewish Archives.

# LXXV(H). BEERSHEBA

Beersheba was the first and most successful of the eight Jewish agricultural colonies in Kansas. It was founded in 1882, located 22 miles northeast of Cimarron, and populated with Russian Jewish immigrants. Many of the colonists ended up as shopkeepers in town rather than farmers.

Survey work: Okugawa (item 139), 211.

### Primary work

1523. Davis, Charles K. Diary. Manuscript at American Jewish Archives.
Consists of Davis's diary from July 26 through August

11, 1882, when he headed a group traveling from
Cincinnati to Beersheba.


*Secondary works*

1524.  "Colony in Kansas—1882." *American Jewish Archives* 17
       (November, 1965): 114-39.
       Reproduces the diary of Charles K. Davis on the
       settling of Beersheba; reproduces reports to the Hebrew
       Union Agricultural Society by M.H. Marks; includes
       "Humble Plea for a Russian Colony" by Isaac M. Wise.

1525.  Federal Writers' Project. *Kansas, A Guide to the
       Sunflower State.* New York: Viking, 1939, p. 387.
       Provides directions to the site of Beersheba and gives
       an overview of the project.

1526.  Feld, Lipman Goldman. "New Light on the Lost Jewish
       Colony of Beersheba, Kansas, 1882-1886." *American
       Jewish Historical Quarterly* 60 (1970-71): 159-68.
       Purports to correct errors made by earlier researchers
       working on Beersheba, notably the allegation that the
       colony failed because of lack of rain. Maintains that the
       actual problems involved leadership, poor planning, and
       most importantly poor relations with the colony's
       sponsor, the Hebrew Union Agricultural Society in
       Cincinnati. Much of the documentation refers to
       contemporary periodicals.

1527.  Harris, L. David. "Lest We Forget Beersheba." *Wichitan*
       3 (February, 1981): 48-51, 60-63.
       Tells the story of Beersheba and follows the later
       history of its site. Illustrated with several photographs,
       the majority picturing the few crumbling ruins from the
       colony (the colony school building, the graveyard).

*      ———. *Sod Jerusalems* (cited above as item 1521),
       40-88.
       Offers an excellent history of the colony.

1528.  Myers, A.J. "Long Time Resident of Lane County Writes
       of Early History of Ravanna." Dighton (Kansas)
       *Herald*, February 18, 1953, p. 4.
       An anecdotal, vernacular history consisting of memories
       of seventy years earlier provided by a man who had been

fourteen years old when Beersheba was settled.

1529. Norman, H.C.   *History of Hodgeman County, Kansas.*
Kinsley, Kansas: author, 1941, p. 2.
Contains a very brief history of Beersheba.

1530. Rudin, A. James.   "Beersheba, Kansas: God's Pure Air on
Government Land."   *Kansas Historical Quarterly* 34
(Autumn, 1968): 282-98.
Describes the new Russian immigration, Isaac Mayer
Wise's commitment to the Beersheba colony, the founding
and life of the colony, and its dissolution and an analysis
of its failure.

1531. Singer, Richard E.   "Beersheba."   *American Jew in
Agriculture* (cited above as item 1504), 453-70.
A detailed history of the colony, showing that it did
quite well in its first year, but that a dispute with its
sponsors in Cincinnati led to the colony's loss of its
farm implements, an insuperable blow.   Heavily
documented, primarily referring to accounts in the
*American Israelite.*

# LXXV(I).  GILEAD

Gilead was founded in March, 1886, near the existing
Lasker Colony.   The colonists were 20 families of Romanian
Jews.   The colony was never prosperous, and it soon failed.

### Secondary works

\*   Harris, Lloyd David.   *Sod Jerusalems* (cited above as item
1521), 103-23.
Provides a history of Hebron and Gilead.

1532. Singer, Richard E.   "Gilead."   *American Jew in
Agriculture* (cited above as item 1504), 481.
Provides a brief sketch of Gilead.

# LXXV(J).  HEBRON

Hebron was founded in Barber Co., Kansas, in 1882. The colonists were assisted by the Montefiore Agricultural Society of New York. 80 families participated; they lived, at first, in dugouts on hillsides. The colony had a better water supply than most other Kansas colonies did, and perhaps because of that Hebron survived longer than most. It was still alive in 1887, and apparently died soon thereafter.

### Secondary works

\*       Harris, Lloyd David.  *Sod Jerusalems* (cited above as item 1521), 103-23.
         Provides a history of Hebron and Gilead.

1533.  Singer, Richard E.  "Hebron."  *American Jew in Agriculture* (cited above as item 1504), 484-5.
         Provides an overview history of Hebron.

# LXXV(K).  LASKER

Lasker was founded by persons who had been involved in the ill-fated Arkansas colony. The Arkansas company split, some heading for Kansas to establish a new colony, the rest returning to New York to be able to provide financial help. The pioneering group hunted for land, stopping from sheer exhaustion in Commanche County, Kansas. A large sod house was the first building. Water proved difficult to come by and financial problems loomed quickly. A drought the second year sealed the fate of the colony. The few lingering colonists had left by 1889.

### Secondary works

\*       Harris, Lloyd David.  *Sod Jerusalems* (cited above as item 1521), 92-102.
         Provides a survey of the colony's history.

1534.  Singer, Richard E.  "Lasker."  *American Jew in Agriculture* (cited above as item 1504), 471-81.

Provides a relatively detailed and well documented history of Lasker.

# LXXV(L).  LEESER

Leeser was founded in Finney County in 1886.  The settlers were Russian emigrants.  The colony encountered problems similar to those of nearby Touro, and had only a brief existence.

## Secondary works

\*     Harris, Lloyd David.  *Sod Jerusalems* (cited above as item 1521), 124-33.
Provides a history of Touro and Leeser.

1535.  Singer, Richard E.    "Leeser."    *American Jew in Agriculture* (cited above as item 1504), 483.
Provides a brief history of the colony.

# LXXV(M).  MOSES MONTEFIORE

Moses Montefiore colony was founded in March, 1885, largely through the efforts of Michael Heilprin.  Its location is uncertain, but it was probably in Ford County.  It was settled by fifteen young families, but various problems, notably a lack of water, soon led to its abandonment.  Some of the members moved on to the Alliance, New Jersey, colony; others stayed in Kansas and moved to Lasker.

## Secondary works

\*     Harris, Lloyd David.  *Sod Jerusalems* (cited above as item 1521), 89-92.
Provides an overview of the colony.

1536.  Singer, Richard E.   "Moses Montefiore."   American Jew in Agriculture (cited above as item 1504), 485-7.
Provides an overview history of the colony.

# LXXV(N).  TOURO

Touro was settled on March 20, 1886, by twelve Russian Jewish families in Finney County, Kansas.  Nine days later a devasting blizzard hit, delaying building and planting.  The summer was dry, and despite hard work by the colonists, the colony soon failed.


Secondary works

\*        Harris, Lloyd David.  *Sod Jerusalems* (cited above as item
          1521), 124-33.
          Provides a history of Touro and Leeser.

1537.   Singer, Richard E.  "Touro."  *American Jew in Agriculture*
          (cited above as item 1504), 482-3.
          Provides an outline history of the colony.


# LXXV(O).  WYANDOTTE

The Wyandotte agricultural colony was founded in the winter of 1881-82 to provide a settlement for Russian Jews. The site was a tract of government land in Wyandotte County, Kansas; assistance was provided by the nearby Temple B'nai Jehudah in Kansas City, Missouri.  B.S. Flersheim and Nathan Lorie were the organizers of the project.  The colony failed before the end of the winter of 1882-83.


*Secondary works*

1538.   Adler, Frank J.  *Roots in a Moving Stream: The*
          *Centennial History of Congregation B'nai Jehudah of*
          *Kansas City, 1870-1970.*  Kansas City: Congregation
          B'nai Jehudah, 1972, p. 49.
          Provides a brief history of the colony.

\*        Harris, Lloyd David.  *Sod Jerusalems* (cited above as item
          1521), 39.
          Provides a brief historical note on the colony.

# LXXV(P). LOUISIANA: SICILY ISLAND

In 1881 a group of colonists acquired a tract of land (some sources say 2,800 acres; some say 5,000) on Sicily Island, Lousiana, 350 to 400 miles upriver (about 160 air miles) from New Orleans. At least 125 persons participated in the project. The place was swampy and remote; despite an investment of hard work, life there was a disaster. There were rattlesnakes, mosquitoes, and malaria, as well as problems with neighbors. Drinking water was in short supply. The summer heat was oppressive, and the lack of a synagogue hurt morale. A disastrous flood in the spring of 1882 brought the colony to an end.

Correspondence to and from Sicily Island has been collected at the American Jewish Archives.

Survey work: Okugawa (item 139), 210.

### *Secondary works*

1539. Davidson, Gabriel, and Edward Goodwin. "Chalutzim in the Land of Cotton." *Jewish Tribune* 95 (September 27, 1929): 2, 15. Reprinted as "Pioneers in the Land of Cotton." *Our Jewish Farmers* (cited above as item 1495), 204-8.
Describes the purchase and settlement of the colony's land, the communal economic arrangements, social life in the colony, and the problems the colonists encountered.

1540. Fogarty, Robert S. "Rosenthal, Herman" and "Sicily Island Colony." *Dictionary of American Communal and Utopian History* (cited above as item 76), 101-2, 164. Dictionary entries providing an overview of Sicily Island. Rosenthal was later a member of Woodbine.

1541. Heller, Max. *Jubilee Souvenir of Temple Sinai, 1872-1922.* New Orleans: American Printing Co., 1922, pp. 67-71. Details the organizational steps taken to found the colony; describes the settlement and the problems which soon afflicted it. Well documented; contains many specific names, dates, and statistics.

1542. Herscher, Uri. "Sicily Island, Louisiana." *Jewish Agricultural Utopias* (cited above as item 1489), 32-7.

Provides a basic history of the colony.

*       Menes, Abraham. "*Am Olyom* Movement" (cited above as item 1496), 23-4.
Discusses the origins, financing, ideas, and abrupt end of the colony.

1543. Menken, J. Stanwood. *Report on the Formation of the First Russian Jewish Colony in the United States at Catahoula Parish, Louisiana.* New York: Thalmessinger, 1982. 18 pp.

*       Price, George M. "Russian Jews in America" (cited above as item 1498), 83-5.
A brief account of the history of Sicily Island, focusing on the dismal location of the colony.

1544. Shpall, Leo. "Jewish Agricultural Colony in Louisiana." *Louisiana Historical Quarterly* 20 (1937): 821-31.
Describes the problems of the Russian immigrants in general; tells of the efforts of New Orleans Jews to help mitigate the problems of the immigrants and details the donation of land for the colony. Cites several original letters and documents regarding the founding of the colony; provides a copy of the colony's constitution.

1545. ———. *Jews in Louisiana.* New Orleans: Steeg Printing and Publishing, 1936, pp. 13-5.
Contains a description of the origins of the experiment and quote from a letter from colony leader Herman Rosenthal giving a catalog of work done, a list of problems and grievances, and a description of the fatal flood.

1546. Singer, Richard E. "Sicily Island." *American Jew in Agriculture* (cited above as item 1504), 325-35.
Provides statistical information on the land purchase and the settlers. Describes problems the colony experienced, culminating in the devastating flood. Provides a synopsis of the colony's constitution.

# LXXV(Q). MARYLAND: BALTIMORE AREA

700 acres of rural Maryland land were purchased in 1882

for settlement by nine Russian families totalling 90 souls. Despite the establishment of a successful woodcutting business, the colony failed to stay afloat very long.

*Secondary work*

1547. Singer, Richard E. "Colony in the Baltimore Area." *American Jew in Agriculture* (cited above as item 1504), 342-3.
Provides an overview of the colony.

# LXXV(R). MARYLAND: ELLICOTT CITY

25 persons settled this 351-acre tract ten miles from Baltimore in 1902. Although some financial problems dogged the settlement in its early days, several families stayed on as private farmers and ended up doing fairly well.

*Secondary work*

1548. Singer, Richard E. "Ellicott City." *American Jew in Agriculture* (cited above as item 1504), 343-4.
Provides an outline history of the colony.

# LXXV(S). MASSACHUSETTS: MONTEVILLE

This colony was founded in 1908 at Sandisfield; little information on it seems to be available. In 1937 it was reported to have 20 or more families apparently living in proximity but not in an organized community.

*Secondary works*

1549. Federal Writers' Project. *Massachusetts, a Guide to Its Places and People.* Boston: Houghton Mifflin, 1937, p. 600.
Provides directions to Monteville, the cluster of Jewish homes still in existence.

1550.  Singer, Richard E.  "Sandisfield."  *American Jew in Agriculture* (cited above as item 1504), 240-1.
       Tells of the existence of the colony and the paucity of information on it.

# LXXV(T).  MICHIGAN: CARP LAKE

Lazarus Silberman, a Chicago banker, became interested in helping Russian immigrants and purchased 300 acres for a group settlement in 1882, promising to provide more land when the success of the colony had been demonstrated.  Thirteen families totalling 100 persons settled there, but Silberman soon withdrew his support and the colony closed.

*Secondary work*

1551.  Singer, Richard E.  "Carp Lake."  *American Jew in Agriculture* (cited above as item 1504), 350-3.
       Outlines the brief history of the colony.

# LXXV(U).  MICHIGAN: PALESTINE

Palestine Colony was located near Bad Axe, Michigan.  It was founded by Russian Jewish immigrants, led by Herman Lewenberg, who bought up a section of land in 1891.  70 residents were reported in 1895.  The colony never quite achieved financial stability, and soon fell behind in its debt payments.  Eventually disintegration set in.  It was dissolved in 1900, although some former colonists remained in the area until around 1920.

*Secondary works*

1552.  Davidson, Gabriel.  "Palestine Colony in Michigan—An Adventure in Colonization."  *Publications of the American Jewish Historical Society* 29 (1925): 61-74.  Reprinted in *Our Jewish Farmers* (cited above as item 1485), 234-49.
       Provides a good basic history of the colony.

1553. Herscher, Uri. "Palestine, Michigan." *Jewish Agricultural Utopias* (cited above as item 1489), 61-70.
Provides an overview history of the colony.

1554. Rudin, A. James. "Bad Axe, Michigan: An Experiment in Jewish Agricultural Settlement." *Michigan History* 56 (Summer, 1972): 119-30.
Provides an overview history of the colony and its major supporters; analyzes the reasons for its demise. Illustrated.

1555. Singer, Richard E. "Palestine." *American Jew in Agriculture* (cited above as item 1504), 359-74.
Outlines the basic history of the colony, largely using information gathered by Davidson (item 1485, above).

# LXXV(V). NEBRASKA: LINCOLN COUNTY

21 families of Russian pogrom refugees settled in Lincoln County on 500 acres which they purchased, with much help from Morris Cohn of Canon City, for $5 per acre. There seems to be no further record of the colony.

*Secondary work*

1556. Singer, Richard E. "Lincoln County." *American Jew in Agriculture* (cited above as item 1504), 489-90.
Provides a sketchy history of the founding of the colony.

# LXXV(W). NEVADA: OCCIDENTAL COLONY

In June, 1897, some 25 Russian Jewish families were settled on a 5500-acre ranch in the Smith Valley, Nevada. Their supposed benefactors, however, turned out to be manipulators more than friends; colony problems were compounded by agricultural inexperience and water shortages. The property was sold to settle colony debts in 1898.

*Secondary work*

1557. Stern, Norton B., and William M. Kramer. "American Zion
      in Nevada: The Rise and Fall of an Agricultural
      Colony." *Western States Jewish Historical Quarterly* 13
      (January, 1981): 130-4. Provides a basic history of the
      colony.
      Documentation is drawn largely from local and
      specialized sources not cited here.


# LXXV(X). THE NEW JERSEY COLONIES

Southern New Jersey was the scene of a major Jewish
communal enterprise. By 1920 these colonies were the only
survivors of the colony mania of the 1880s. They gradually
turned toward private economic life, and in that modified form
some of them still survive.

The Jewish periodical with the most contemporary coverage
of the South Jersey colonies was the *Menorah.*


### Secondary works covering more than one colony

*        Brandes, Joseph. *Immigrants to Freedom* (cited above as
         item 1483).
         Provides a comprehensive history of the South Jersey
         colonies, including many tables of statistical information.
         Also includes information on minor colonies not listed in
         this bibliography. A map on p. 35 shows sixteen Jewish
         colonies in South Jersey, some of which apparently did
         not have major communal or cooperative features:
         Alliance, Brotmanville, Carmel, Cedarville, Centre Grove,
         Centreton, Cumberland, Fairton, Garton Road, Norma,
         North Vineland, Rosenhayn, Six Points, Union Grove,
         Woodbine, and Woodruff.

1558. Federal Writers' Project. *New Jersey: A Guide to its
      Present and Past.* New York: Hastings House, 1939, p.
      660.
      Mentions the colonies of Norma, Brotmanville, Alliance,
      Rosenhayn, and Carmel, describing the economy and
      buildings of the area after the first generation of
      colonists had passed from the scene.

1559. Goldstein, Philip Reuben. *Social Aspects of the Jewish
      Colonies of South Jersey.* New York: League Printing

Co., 1921. 74 pp.
Provides a survey of the status of the New Jersey colonies in 1919, presenting detailed statistics and other information on all of them in both tabular and prose format. Includes an extensive primary and secondary bibliography.

1560. "Jewish Farmers." *American Review of Reviews* 37 (May, 1908): 617-8.
Provides current information about the colonies, including acreage and financial data. Depicts Alliance, Norma, Brotmanville, Carmel, Rosenhayn, and Woodbine as doing well.

1561. Lipman, Jacob G. "Eastern States." *Russian Jew in the United States.* Edited by Charles S. Bernheimer. Philadelphia: Winston, 1905, pp. 376-91.
Provides a history and description of the New Jersey colonies, covering agricultural conditions and operations as well as religious and social life. Also contains information on Jewish farmers in New England. A companion article (pp. 392-403) characterizes noncommunal Jewish farming in the West.

1562. Norman, Theodore. *Outstretched Arm: A History of the Jewish Colonization Association.* London: Routledge and Kegan Paul, 1985. 326 pp.
Briefly characterizes the work of the Jewish Colonization Association and the Baron de Hirsch Fund in New Jersey, including some efforts to aid Jewish chicken farmers as late as the 1950s.

\* Price, George M. "Russian Jews in America" (cited above as item 1498), 92-7.
Tells the story of Alliance colony and its economy, providing five statistical tables. Provides a brief account of the history and status of Carmel as of 1889. Describes Rosenhayn colony in 1889, providing statistics on membership and property owned.

1563. Robinson, Leonard G. "Agricultural Activities of the Jews in America." *Our Jewish Farmers* (cited above as item 1485), 249-55.
Provides an overview of several of the New Jersey colonies, including Alliance, Rosenhayn, Carmel, Garton Road, Six Points, and Woodbine. Not the same as item

1500, above, despite similar authorship and title.

1564. Singer, Richard E. "South Jersey Colonies" and "Woodbine." *American Jew in Agriculture* (cited above as item 1504), 599-611.
Focuses on the history of the colonies after 1914. Singer is the most important source for historical material on several minor colonies not listed below, including Garton Road (pp. 295-7), May's Landing (pp. 310-1), Millville (p. 299), Montefiore (p. 310), Six Points (pp. 280-1), and Woodstown (pp. 281-2).

1565. Stainsby, William, ed. *Jewish Colonies of South Jersey: Historical Sketch of Their Establishment and Growth.* Camden: Bureau of Statistics of New Jersey, 1901. 28 pp.
Provides a chronicle of the Jewish colonization effort in New Jersey, its most fertile locus, when several colonies were still active. Begins with Alliance, the first New Jersey colony, in 1882, and covers Rosenhayn, Woodbine, and Carmel, as well as several smaller, mostly already defunct, projects. Concludes that the colonies started by Jewish charities have generally done quite well, while those started by private speculators have failed.

1566. *Yoval: A Symposium upon the First Fifty Years of the Jewish Farming Colonies of Alliance, Norma and Brotmanville, New Jersey.* N.p.: Committee on Arrangements, 1932. 47 pp.
A collection of memoirs gathered from original settlers and others who had been there for many years. Contains various lists and statistical tables on the three colonies covered. Illustrated with photographs of early colony life.

# LXXV(Y). ALLIANCE

Alliance Colony was named for the Alliance Israelite Universelle, the organization whose funding made the colony possible. It was located in Salem County, New Jersey, and was the first of the South Jersey colonies. It was founded in May, 1882, and consisted of 150 acres of common land and 66 farms of 15 acres each. Each family was to be charged $300 for its

15 acres, to be paid over 33 years interest-free. The agricultural project was never prosperous; industries were soon introduced into the community, and prosperity ensued. By 1889 it had 529 members. Eventually the holdings were all divided for private ownership.

Survey work: Okugawa (item 139), 211.

### Secondary works

1567. Brandes, Joseph. "Alliance: 'Pioneer of All Jewish Colonies in America.'" *Immigrants to Freedom* (cited above as item 1483), 55-60 and *passim*.
   Provides a good outline history plus other information on the colony.

1568. Herscher, Uri. "Alliance." *Jewish Agricultural Utopias* (cited above as item 1489), 73-84.
   Provides a history of the Alliance colony from its founding through its period of prosperity to its breakup into noncommunal farms.

1569. Mounier, Louis. "Glimpses of Jewish Life in the Colonies of Southern New Jersey." *Vineland Historical Magazine*, April, 1965, pp. 477-85.
   Focuses on the courtship and marriage of an Alliance couple, Jacob Sobleman and Leah Levinson.

\*    Price, George M. "Russian Jews in America" (cited above as item 1498), 92-8.
   Tells the story of the development of the colony and its economy; provides five statistical tables.

1570. Reis, J.C. "History of the Alliance Colony." *Menorah* 42 (1906-7): 167-73.
   An overview history of the early years of the colony.

1571. Singer, Richard E. "Alliance." *American Jew in Agriculture* (cited above as item 1504), 261-80.
   An overview history of Alliance, with emphasis on the colony's history and its industries. Reports 891 residents (165 families) by 1905. Well documented.

1572. Solomons, Adolphus S. "Alliance: The First Successful Jewish Colony in America." *Menorah* 5 (1888): 179-87.

Discusses the founding of the Hebrew Emigrant Aid Society, the purchase of land for the colony, and the settlement and development of the colony. Contains specific information about the financing of the project.

# LXXV(Z). BROTMANVILLE

Located near Alliance, Brotmanville had a similar history to that of its neighbor colony. Its outside support was always smaller, so the colony never achieved great prominence. Eventually it became a largely industrial district.

*Secondary works*

1573. *American Jewish Yearbook, 5673* (Philadelphia: Jewish Publication Society, 1912): 82-90.
   Contains a good overview history of the colony.

*       Brandes, Joseph. *Immigrants to Freedom* (cited above as item 1483), 66-7 plus other scattered references.
   Provides a historical sketch of the colony.

1574. Singer, Richard E. "Brotmanville and Millville." *American Jew in Agriculture* (cited above as item 1504), 299.
   Provides a brief sketch of the colony.

# LXXV(AA). CARMEL

Carmel was founded in 1882 under the leadership of Michael Heilprin, a native of Russian Poland who had been in the United States since 1856. The first group of settlers soon left; they had not been able to secure much outside help, since most available resources were being directed toward nearby Alliance. However, more settlers soon arrived, and by 1888 the colony was well established. By 1889 it had 286 inhabitants and owned 848 acres with many buildings. A shirt factory became an important industry, and eventually industries dominated the local economy.

1575. Brandes, Joseph. "Carmel." *Immigrants to Freedom* (cited above as item 1483), 61-5 plus other scattered references.
Provides an engaging, somewhat anecdotal historical sketch.

* Price, George M. "Russian Jews in America" (cited above as item 1498), 97-8.
Provides a brief account of the history and status of the colony as of 1889.

1576. Singer, Richard E. "Carmel." *American Jew in Agriculture* (cited above as item 1503), 289-95.
Provides a good summary history of the colony.

# LXXV(BB). NORMA

Founded in the early 1880s, this colony was from the beginning more industrial than agricultural. A vest factory was the economic mainstay, and there were other smaller industries. Farming was limited.

*Secondary works*

* Brandes, Joseph. *Immigrants to Freedom* (cited above as item 1483), 65-6 plus other scattered references.
Provides a sketch of the development of the colony.

1577. Singer, Richard E. "Norma." *American Jew in Agriculture* (cited above as item 1504), 288-9.
Provides basic information about the colony.

# LXXV(CC). ROSENHAYN

Rosenhayn was originally a colony of Seventh Day Baptists. The original colonists, while approaching the site, saw a large field of roses, and named their nearby colony "field of roses" in German. By 1880 the colony was failing, and in 1882 the first Jews settled there. Outside support was minimal, and many returned to the cities, but a new and better financed colonization effort was launched in 1887. By 1889 there were 270 Russian Jews living there; in all they owned 1,912 acres and had a mixed economy dependent on farming and industry.

Survey work: Okugawa (item 139), 211.

*Secondary works*

1578. Brandes, Joseph. "Rosenhayn." *Immigrants to Freedom* (cited above as item 1483), 60-1 plus other scattered references.
Provides an outline history of the colony.

* Price, George M. "Russian Jews in America" (cited above as item 1498), 98.
Provides an account of the situation of the colony as of 1889, with statistics on membership and property owned.

1579. Singer, Richard E. "Rosenhayn." *American Jew in Agriculture* (cited above as item 1504), 282-8.
Provides a general account of the colony.

# LXXV(DD). WOODBINE

Woodbine was one of the most successful of the Jewish colonies in New Jersey. The 5,300-acre site was purchased in 1891; 800 acres were reserved for the town, with 15-acre farms assigned to members and pasture land beyond. The layout was sometimes characterized as imitative of an English medieval village. Although there were some problems from the beginning, industries were established after 1893 and the community prospered. Locks, clothing, bricks, and machine tools were manufactured there; the agricultural enterprise continued to produce fruits and vegetables. Gradually Woodbine became less communal, and eventually became a community of private homes.

*Community periodical*

1580. *Woodbine Blast*. 1909-? Yiddish newspaper operated at Woodbine by Harry J. Moss.

Woodbine by Harry J. Moss.

*Secondary works*

1581. Blaustein, David.    "First Self-Governed Jewish Community
Since the Fall of Jerusalem."    *Circle* 2 (1907): 138-40.
Provides a glowing description of Woodbine, portraying
it as prosperous and idyllic.    Illustrated with
photographs.

\*       Bogen, Boris D.    *Jewish Philanthropy in the United
States* (cited above as item 1482), 130-3.
Provides a brief overview history of the early days of
Woodbine.

1582. Brandes, Joseph.    "Woodbine."    *Immigrants to Freedom*
(cited above as item 1483), 69-72 plus other scattered
references.
Sketches the development of the colony and of the
Baron de Hirsch Agricultural School there.

1583. DeFeo, Lawrence Joseph.    "Transformation of a
Community: A History of the Development and
Education of Woodbine."    Ed.D. Dissertation, Rutgers
University, 1979.

1584. Herscher, Uri.    "Woodbine."    *Jewish Agricultural Utopias*
(cited above as item 1489), 84-107.
Provides a history of the colony.    Illustrated with
photographs.

1585. "Jewish Colony at Woodbine, New Jersey."    *Leslie's
Weekly* 74 (April 7, 1892): 168-9.
Describes the 63 Russian families in the project, the
grants from the Baron de Hirsch Fund which established
it, and the farming and factory enterprises.

1586. Joseph, Samuel.    *History of the Baron de Hirsch Fund:
The Americanization of the Jewish Immigrant.*
Philadelphia: Baron de Hirsch Fund, 1935.    Repr.,
Fairfield, New Jersey: Augustus M. Kelley, 1978.
Contains a comprehensive history of Woodbine (pp.
48-115), with information on the preliminary planning for
the colony, site selection, industries, the Agricultural
School, internal problems, and community life.    Also

contains a history of the Jewish Agricultural Society (pp. 116-83) which makes some references to other New Jersey colonies.

1587. Ludins, David G. "Memories of Woodbine: 1891-1894." *Jewish Frontier*, June, 1960, pp. 7-15.
    Describes the author's Russian childhood and migration to America and work clearing land at Woodbine. Provides informal and personal sketches of some of the persons involved in building the colony. Describes conflicts between the Baron de Hirsch Fund and some of the settlers.

1588. Sabsovich, Hirsch Leib. *Woodbine Settlement of the Baron de Hirsch Fund.* Woodbine: n.p., n.d. 4 pp.
    Provides a characterization of the colony shortly after the turn of the century, discussing industries, housing, religion, education, agriculture, and social life. The author was superintendent of the project; the pamphlet is accordingly upbeat.

1589. Singer, Richard E. "Woodbine." *American Jew in Agriculture* (cited above as item 1504), 300-10, 606-7.
    Provides an early history of Woodbine, together with an update made some decades later. Singer also has, on pp. 657-70, a history of the Woodbine Agricultural School, which he judges a failure.

# LXXV(EE). THE NORTH DAKOTA COLONIES

Two or three colonies appear to have been founded in North Dakota. No single article on the North Dakota colonies deals with both Chananel and Devils Lake, leading one to suspect that the two (both said to have been in Ramsey County) were the same. However, their reported founding dates are different.

*Secondary work covering more than one colony*

1590. Kirk, Marvin Steward. "Study of the Jews' Contribution to Land Settlement and Land Credit with Special Reference to North Dakota." M.S. thesis, North Dakota State College of Agriculture and Mechanic Arts, 1926.

51 pp.
Describes American Jewish colonies, focusing on the work of the Jewish Agricultural Society; provides detailed information of Jewish farming in North Dakota, both communal and private.

# LXXV(FF). CHANANEL

Chananel was founded about 1887 in Ramsey County, North Dakota. The weather immediately presented the colony with major problems, and it was soon dissolved. However, several families survived as individual farmers and some were prospering by 1897. It is not clear how long they stayed in the area.

*Secondary work*

1591. Herscher, Uri. "Chananel, North Dakota." *Jewish Agricultural Utopias* (cited above as item 1489), 71-2. Provides a brief sketch of the colony based on an 1897 letter to the *American Hebrew.*

# LXXV(GG). DEVILS LAKE

This colony was established, with help from the Baron de Hirsch Fund, about 1882; 22 persons were reported living there at the end of that year. Poverty and hardship marked the early years, but the community gradually grew stronger, although details for many years after the founding are lacking. Privatization set in early, and by the mid-1920s most of the families had drifted away.

*Secondary works*

1592. Plaut, W. Gunther. "Jewish Colonies at Painted Woods and Devils Lake." *North Dakota History* 32 (January, 1965): 59-70. Reprinted from *Jews in Minnesota* (New York: American Jewish Historical Society, 1959). Provides an overview of the history of the colony.

1593. Schwartz, Lois Fields. "Early Jewish Agricultural
      Colonies in North Dakota." *North Dakota History* 32
      (October, 1965): 217-32.
      Provides an overview of the colony; much of the
      information provided comes from Plaut (item 1592, above)
      and from reminiscences of colonists.

1594. Singer, Richard E. "Devil's Lake." *American Jew in
      Agriculture* (cited above as item 1504), 419-26.
      Provides a good historical overview of the colony.

# LXXV(HH). PAINTED WOODS

   Painted Woods was located near Bismarck, North Dakota,
and was active between 1882 and 1887. Judah Wechsler, a
rabbi in St. Paul, Minnesota, was instrumental in its founding.
One to two dozen families, all Russian immigrants, settled there
initially. They built log houses and grew successful crops at
first; in 1883 their prospects were good enough that more
settlers came, more than doubling the number in the original
company. In 1884, however, the colony was devastated by a
prairie fire, and in 1885 a major drought sealed its fate. By
the spring of 1886, only a handful were left. A few stayed on,
farming privately; after 1901, there was something of a revival
of things with new Jewish families homesteading in the
immediate area.

Survey work: Okugawa (item 139), 211.

*Secondary works*

1595. Herscher, Uri. "Painted Woods and Iola, North Dakota."
      *Jewish Agricultural Utopias* (cited above as item 1489),
      70-1.
      Provides a brief history of Painted Woods and of Iola,
      an area in North Dakota with many Jewish farmers
      (noncommunal).

*      Plaut, W. Gunther. "Jewish Colonies at Painted Woods
       and Devils Lake (cited above as item 1592), 59-66.
       Provides a good overview history of Painted Woods.

*      Price, George M. "Russian Jews in America" (cited above

as item 1498), 87.
Gives a one-paragraph history of the colony, focusing on the severe weather and isolated location it endured.

* Schwartz, Lois Fields. "Early Jewish Agricultural Colonies in North Dakota" (cited above as item 1593), 217-32.
Provides an overview history of the colony, leaning heavily on the work of Plaut (item 1592, above).

1596. Singer, Richard E. "Painted Woods." *American Jew in Agriculture* (cited above as item 1504), 409-19. Historical sketch of the founding and life of the colony.

# LXXV(II). OREGON: NEW ODESSA

Russian Jews interested in colonization came to the United States under the auspices of Am Olam in 1881 and 1882 and organized themselves into a communal household called "The Commune" on Pell Street in New York. They founded New Odessa in 1882 on a 760-acre tract about 250 miles south of Portland in Douglas County, Oregon. By the spring of 1883 it had 40 to 50 members; it peaked at about 65. Marxist in spirit, the colony practiced thorough community of goods. William Frey, formerly of the colonies at Cedar Vale, Kansas, was the leading spirit at New Odessa, and eventually became the focal point of a division in the ranks. Vegetarianism was one of the divisive issues. Some members departed, and a fire also took its toll. By 1885 the last colonists had departed. Some of them returned to New York and lived communally for four or five years on Suffolk Street, where they operated, communally, a steam laundry.

Correspondence regarding New Odessa has been collected at the American Jewish Archives.

The works of William Frey are listed in this bibliography at the Cedar Vale heading.

Survey works: Albertson (item 27), 419; Okugawa (item 139), 212.

*Secondary works*

1597. Abdill, George B. "New Odessa: Douglas County's Russian Communal Colony." *Umpqua Trapper* 1 (Winter, 1965): 10-14; and 2 (Spring, 1966): 16-21.
Describes the colonists' flight from persecution in Russia, the details of the land purchase, improvements to the property, social life, and the colony's breakup; also contains notes on the later careers of some former colonists.

1598. Blumenthal, Helen E. "New Odessa Colony of Oregon, 1882-1886." *Western States Jewish Historical Quarterly* 14 (July, 1982): 321-32.
Provides a good narrative history of the colony and follow-up information on the subsequent lives of some of its members. Documentation includes references to specialized and local sources not cited here.

1599. ———. "New Odessa 1882-1887: United We Stand, Divided We Fall." M.A. thesis, Portland State University, 1975. 98 pp.
A history of New Odessa providing Russian historical background, information on the development of the site, the saga of Frey, and information on the later lives of participants. Appendix includes a list of members and financial records. Documentation includes some references to local and specialized sources.

1600. ———. "Pioneer Jewish History: 'New Odessa.'" *Historical Scribe* (Portland, Oregon; Summer, 1977): 1-2.
Provides an overview history of the colony, detailing the land purchase, life at the community, and the final breakup.

1601. Cahan, Abraham. *Education of Abraham Cahan.* Philadelphia: Jewish Publication Society of America, 1969. 450 pp.
Describes, at several scattered points, William Frey's early espousal of utopian socialism, his life and ideas in his New York years, the role of Michael Heilprin in supporting New Odessa, and the problems which led to the dissolution of the community. Also contains several brief references to Frey's stay at Cedar Vale.

1602. Davidson, Gabriel, and Edward A. Goodwin. "Unique Agricultural Colony." *Reflex* 2 (May, 1928): 80-6. Reprinted in *Our Jewish Farmers* (cited above as item

1495), 226-33.
Characterizes the original move toward community in New York, the trip to Oregon, the early prosperity of the colony, the development of bickering, and the return of some colonists to New York.

1603. Fogarty, Robert S.   "Heilprin, Michael" and "New Odessa Community."   *Dictionary of American Communal and Utopian History* (cited above as item 76), 49-50, 154-5.
Dictionary entries providing basic information on New Odessa and one of its leaders.

1604. Herscher, Uri.   "New Odessa, Oregon."   *Jewish Agricultural Utopias* (cited above as item 1489), 37-48.
Provides a good overview history of the colony. Illustrated with photographs.

1605. Levin, Nora.   *While Messiah Tarried: Jewish Socialist Movements, 1871-1917.*   New York: Schocken, 1977, pp. 49-53.
Provides biographical information on Michael Heilprin; describes the founding of New Odessa, the arrival of and role played by William Frey, and the demise of the colony.

*       Menes, Abraham.   *"Am Olyam* Movement" (cited above as item 1496), 28-33.
Discusses the settlement, life, and decline of the community.   Provides accounts of colony life from letters written from New Odessa.

1606. Moskowitz, Henry.   "Paul Kaplan: An East Side Portrait." *Outlook* 118 (January 16, 1918): 108-9.
Characterizes Kaplan's role as a founder of New Odessa; depicts his later life as a physician on the Lower East Side.

1607. Oved, Yaacov.   "New Odessa: A Jewish Commune of the Am Olam Group."   *Two Hundred Years of American Communes* (cited above as item 142), 223-31.
Describes the development of Am Olam in Odessa, the colonists' search for support in New York, the development and life of the Oregon colony, and an analysis of its eventual failure.   Based in large part on Hebrew-language sources.

\*      Price, George M.   "Russian Jews in America" (cited above
      as item 1498), 89-92.
      Supplies a brief history of the colony, describing the
      manner in which the colonists arrived there and telling
      of the problems which led to the colony's disintegration.

1608.  Rosenthal, Herman.   "Chronicles of the Communist
      Settlement Known by the Name 'New Odessa.'"
      Translated by Gary P. Zola. Typescript. 31 pp.
      At American Jewish Archives.

1609.  Singer, Richard E.   "New Odessa." *American Jew in
      Agriculture* (cited above as item 1504), 535-8.
      Provides a good basic history of the colony.

1610.  Solis, Miguel J.   "New Odessa Community." *American
      Utopias* (cited above as item 20), 139-40.
      Provides a brief description of the community plus
      three bibliographical entries.

1611.  "Wedding Among the Communistic Jews in Oregon."
      *Overland Monthly* 6 (second series) (December, 1885):
      606-11.
      Provides a description of living conditions at Odessa,
      which the author regards as "wretched." Also provides a
      brief history of the colony beginning with the departure
      of its members from Russia.

# LXXV(JJ).  SOUTH CAROLINA: HAPPYVILLE

Happyville was settled in South Carolina at the behest of
public officials who were looking for European immigrants to
farm and otherwise work to enhance the economic development
of the South.   A group of New York Jews, headed by Charles
Weintraub, were looking for a happy, quiet home, and they
were persuaded to move to a 2200 acre site which was located
for them.   They arrived in the fall of 1905.   Ten families were
the initial contingent; fifteen more persons soon joined them.
The population in all averaged about 50.   Terrible weather
marked their first summer, but they worked hard and that fall
opened a saw mill, grist mill, and cotton gin, all powered by
water on the property.   A schism developed late in 1907, and
Weintraub was expelled from the colony.   Financial problems
led to the closing and sale of the colony in 1908; Weintraub

and some associates bought the property and tried to open a new colony, but were unsuccessful.

*Secondary work*

1612. Shankman, Arnold. "Happyville, the Forgotten Colony." *American Jewish Archives* 30 (1978): 3-19.
Provides a history of the colony. Illustrated.

# LXXV(KK). THE SOUTH DAKOTA COLONIES

Two important colonies were founded in South Dakota. In addition there were at least two small, less successful experiments.

*Secondary works on South Dakota colonies in general*

1613. Goering, Violet, and Orlando J. Goering. "Jewish Farmers in South Dakota—the Am Olam." *South Dakota History* 12 (Winter, 1982): 232-47.
Tells of the founding and goals of the Am Olam, and describes the founding, economic arrangements, cultural life, problems, and dissolution of Bethlehem Yehudah and Cremieux.

* Price, George M. "Russian Jews in America" (cited above as item 1498), 85-6.
Tells the story of the founding and the problems of Cremieux and Bethlehem-Jehudah.

# LXXV(LL). ADLER AND MENDELSOHN

These two short-lived colonies were founded in Davison County, South Dakota, in 1882. The settlers faced great hardships; the land was unsuited for pioneer settlements, and the colonies were inadequately capitalized. Both were abandoned within a year.

*Secondary work*

1614.  Singer, Richard E.  *American Jew in Agriculture* (cited
       above as item 1504), 442.
       Provides a brief historical sketch of the colonies.


# LXXV(MM).  BETHLEHEM-JEHUDAH

Founded about 1884 near the Cremieux Colony in South
Dakota.   It was intended to be one of the more radically
communal settlements, with a fully collective economy and full
equality of men and women.   However, the colony succumbed to
strife, discontent, and natural disasters by 1885.

Survey work: Okugawa (item 139), 212.


*Secondary works*

1615.  Herscher, Uri.   "Bethlehem-Jehudah, South Dakota."
       *Jewish Agricultural Utopias* (cited above as item 1489),
       52.
       Provides an overview history of the community.

*       Menes, Abraham.   "*Am Olyom* Movement" (cited above as
        item 1496), 25-8.
        Discusses the ideas and problems of the community.
        Reproduces part of the community's constitution.

1616.  Silber, Jacques.   "Jewish Colonization in the United
       States:   Saul Sokolofsky on Bethlehem-Yehudah, South
       Dakota." 1980. Photocopy of manuscript. 13 pp.
       An exposition of Sokolofsky's published writings on
       Jewish colonization.   Appendix 2 reproduces "Statutes of
       the Colony of Bethlehem-Yehudah," a list of nine rules
       on government, work, and the like.   At American Jewish
       Archives.

1617.  Singer, Richard E.   "Bethlehem Yehudah." *American Jew
       in Agriculture* (cited above as item 1504), 441.
       Provides a synopsis of the history of the colony.

# LXXV(NN). CREMIEUX

In the wake of the breakup of the Sicily Island colony in Louisiana, Herman Rosenthal led an effort to start another colony. In 1882 the first two families arrived at Mitchell, South Dakota, to begin anew; soon the colony numbered about 200. It was named for Adolphe Cremieux, president of the Alliance Israelite Universelle. Colonists took out homestead claims totalling some 15 square miles. The colony prospered with good first-year crops, but hail, fire, and drought ruined the next two years' crops, by the end of which time most of the settlers had left. The colony was dissolved in 1885; the last settlers left in 1889.

Survey work: Okugawa (item 139), 211.

### Secondary works

* Davidson, Gabriel, and Edward A. Goodwin. "Epic of the Prairies." *Detroit Jewish Chronicle*, January 29, 1932, pp. 1, 6-7. Repr., *Our Jewish Farmers* (cited above as item 1485), 213-21.
Provides a historical sketch of the colony.

1618. Herscher, Uri. "Cremieux, South Dakota." *Jewish Agricultural Utopias* (cited above as item 1489), 48-52.
Provides an overview of the colony.

* Singer, Richard E. *American Jew in Agriculture* (cited above as item 1504), 439-41.
Describes the colony and its problems.

# LXXV(OO). TEXAS: TYLER

The Tyler colony was founded in 1904 on 220 acres purchased by the Jewish Agricultural and Industrial Aid Society. Five families settled the site initially. In 1905, however, a malaria epidemic struck, and the settlers left, warning other Jews not to try to settle in unhealthy Tyler.

*Secondary work*

1619. Singer, Richard E.    "Tyler."    *American Jew in Agriculture*
(cited above as item 1504), 336-7.
Provides a brief history of the colony.

# LXXV(PP).  UTAH: CLARION

Clarion was founded in 1910 by a group of 150 persons
interested in the back-to-the-soil movement.    They formed a
formal organization and in August, 1911, they purchased 6,085
acres in the Sevier Valley in Sanpete County, Utah, near the
towns of Axtell and Gunnison.    Benjamin Brown was the
principal leader.    The plan was to have 200 families settle
there initially and 800 more move in later.    By November, 1912,
25 persons were at the site.    However, the colony soon failed
due to financial problems, lack of farming experience,
inadequate water for irrigation, poor leadership, and poor
planning.

*Secondary works*

1620. Cooley, Everett L.    "Clarion, Utah: Jewish Colony in
'Zion.'"    *Utah Historical Quarterly* 36 (Spring, 1968):
113-31.
Provides a history of the colony and details the
financial problems which led to its failure.    Illustrated
with photographs.

1621. Freund, Charles J.    "Jewish Farm Colony at Clarion,
Utah."    *Improvement Era* 16 (January, 1913): 248-53.
Contains a history of the young colony plus an account
of a visit made by the author.    Illustrated with
photographs.

1622. Silverman, B.D.    "Short History of Clarion the Jewish
Colony in the State of Utah."    Manuscript (n.p., n.d.)
in the American Jewish Archives.  104 pp.
A personalized history of the colony, in which the
author was a participant, from the first organizational
meeting in a hall over a saloon in South Philadelphia
through the abandonment of the colony, with a brief
epilogue on what happened to the site in later years.

1623. Singer, Richard E.    "Clarion."    *American Jew in*

*Agriculture* (cited above as item 1504), 511-21.
Provides a good summary history of the colony.

# LXXV(QQ). VIRGINIA

Three colonies existed in Virginia, one known as Middlesex Settlement, in Middlesex County; another unnamed, in the Richmond area; and a third, also unnamed, at Waterview on the Rappahannock. Little is known about them.

### Secondary work

1624. Singer, Richard E. "Richmond Area, Henrico County" and "Middlesex County: Middlesex Settlement." *American Jew in Agriculture* (cited above as item 1504), 338-401. Provides basic information on the colonies.

# LXXV(RR). WISCONSIN: ARPIN

The village of Arpin was founded 150 miles northwest of Milwaukee by a lumber company about 1894. When the company abandoned the area around 1904, the town was made available to a Jewish colonization project. The colony population fluctuated between six and fifteen families, reaching its highest point in 1906. It gradually disintegrated in the 1920s.

### Secondary works

1625. Singer, Richard E. "Arpin." *American Jew in Agriculture* (cited above as item 1504), 376-95.
Provides a fairly comprehensive history and analysis of Arpin.

1626. Swichkow, Louis J. "Jewish Colony of Arpin, Wisconsin." *American Jewish Historical Quarterly* 54 (1964-65): 82-91.
A basic history of the colony.

# LXXV(SS).  WYOMING: LARAMIE COUNTY

This colony was founded in 1907; it was to be agricultural, but the needed irrigation was not available.   The colony was made up of city dwellers who had tired of urban life, but they were not ready for the hard existence of the desert.

### Secondary work

1627. Singer, Richard E.   "Laramie County."   *American Jew in Agriculture* (cited above as item 1504), 522-7.
   Provides a brief history of the colony.   Singer also mentions (pp. 527-8) an ambitious plan to settle hundreds of Jewish families from Chicago in Platte County, but there are no records to show that the settlement was even begun.

# LXXVI.  JOYFUL

In the early 1880s Isaac and Sara Rumford became activists for the "Edenic Diet," which involved no meat or cooking.   In January, 1884, they announced the opening of a colony based on their ideas in Kern County, California.   It attracted only about half a dozen members.

Survey work: Okugawa (item 139), 213.

### Community publication

1628. *Joyful News Co-operator*.  1884.

### Secondary works

*   Hine, Robert V.   *California's Utopian Colonies* (cited above as item 98), 140-2.
   Provides a historical sketch of the colony and of the ideas of the Rumfords

*   ———.   *Community on the American Frontier* (cited above as item 99), 220.

Provides a very brief characterization of the colony, emphasizing its unusual diet.

# LXXVII. KAWEAH COOPERATIVE COMMONWEALTH

The Kaweah Cooperative Commonwealth, whose chief founder was Burnette G. Haskell, was based on the ideas of Laurence Gronlund (see item 635, above). The decision to found a colony was made in 1884; in 1885 a group of colonists moved to the Sierra Nevada and filed 45 claims on adjoining tracts of land. By 1886 the colony was operating on a cooperative basis. By 1890 several businesses were operating, and the colonists had built, with prodigious labor, a road into their domain. Success seemed assured. However, in 1890 Congress pre-empted the land by creating Sequoia National Park; the government refused to compensate the settlers, calling their claims invalid and some of their activity on the land (especially cutting government-owned trees) illegal. Extremely hostile press coverage further soured former supporters of the colony.

The Bancroft Library of the University of California at Berkeley has several collections of papers important to the study of Kaweah: the Haskell Family Papers, the James John Martin File, and the Kaweah Colony Papers. Material on Kaweah is also found in the American Communities Collection at Syracuse University. Still other material is located in the Kaweah Colony File, Historical Library, Tulare County Free Library, Visalia, California.

Survey works: Albertson (item 27), 420; Curl (item 52), 30; Liefmann (item 125), 22; Okugawa (item 139), 213-4.

### Community periodicals

1629. *Commonwealth*. San Francisco. 1888-9. Weekly. Edited by Burnette G. Haskell.

1630. *Kaweah Commonwealth*. Kaweah. 1890-2. Weekly; later monthly.

## Primary works

1631. *Commonwealth at Last Established.* San Francisco: Kaweah Co-operative Colony Executive Committee, 1888. 36 pp.

1632. *Kaweah, a Co-operative Commonwealth.* San Francisco: Burnette G. Haskell, 1887. 16 pp.

1633. Kaweah Co-operative Colony Co., San Francisco Committee. *Crisis.* [San Francisco: n.p., 1887.] 24 pp. Provides transcripts of meetings trying to resolve community problems. Includes list of members of the company as of November 3, 1887.

1634. *Pen Picture of the Kaweah Co-Operative Colony Co.* San Francisco: B.G. Haskell, 1889. 32 pp. Also published as a supplement to *Commonwealth,* April 24, 1889. Characterizes the goals and philosophy of the colony; tells how to join; provides a description of the Kaweah area and an explanation of the colony's time-check system. Contains the Deed of Settlement, Kaweah's constitution.

1635. *Persecution of Kaweah: Story of a Great Injustice.* New York: Eastern Group of the Kaweah Co-operative Colony, 1891.

1636. *Treasurer's Financial Statement of Cash Receipts and Disbursements from the Origin of Kaweah Co-operative Colony Co., Limited, to May 1st, 1891.* San Francisco: n.p., 1891.

## Works by a community leader

1637. Haskell, Burnette G. "Kaweah: How and Why the Colony Died." *Out West* 17 (September, 1902): 300-22. A revised version of an article published in the San Francisco *Examiner,* November 29, 1891.
Haskell was the colony's president. Provides a history of the colony, an analysis of its problems, and the story of its demise. Well illustrated.

1638. ———. "Plan of Action." *Nationalist* 2 (December, 1889): 30-2.

Proposes that socialists take power by winning the next election in San Francisco and set up socialized utilities and businesses. The article is not about Kaweah, but it provides a good look at Haskell's ideas which underlay the colony.

## Secondary works

1639. Berland, Oscar. "Giant Forest's Reservation: The Legend and the Mystery." *Sierra Club Bulletin* 47 (December, 1962): 68- 82.
Tells the story of Kaweah Colony as it relates to the history of Sequoia National Park. Focuses on the complicated dealings of the government and the Southern Pacific Railroad in suddenly establishing the park and invalidating the colony's land claims.

1640. Bliss, W.D.P. "Kaweah." *New Encyclopedia of Social Reform* (cited above as item 35), 669-70.
Argues that the federal government unfairly usurped the lands the Kaweah colonists were entitled to.

1641. Challacombe, J.R. "Utopian Trail to the Big Trees." *Westways* (August, 1967): 24-7, 62-3.
Tells the history of the colony, emphasizing the difficulty of building the road to the big trees.

1642. Cross, Ira B. *History of the Labor Movement in California.* Berkeley: University of California Press, 1935, pp. 156-65.
Provides basic information on Burnette G. Haskell, the founder of Kaweah, and the International Workingmen's Association. Kaweah is mentioned only in passing, but the information on Haskell constitutes useful background material for study of the colony.

\*      Destler, Chester M. *American Radicalism, 1865-1901: Essays and Documents* (cited above as item 53), 79-104.
Reproduces a Burnette Haskell manifesto for the union of radical forces in America.

1643. Doig, Ivan, ed. "Socialism Under the Redwoods." *Utopian America: Dreams and Realities* (cited above as item 55), 65-71.
Provides a brief introduction to Kaweah and an excerpt

from Robert V. Hine, *California's Utopian Colonies* (item 98, above).

\*       Faris, Robert E.L.   *Social Disorganization* (cited above as item 66), second edition, pp. 574-6.
Provides a brief sketch of the colony; reproduces the statement of principles which was printed on Kaweah membership cards.

1644.   Federal Writers' Project.   *California: A Guide to the Golden State.*   New York: Hastings House, 1939, pp. 447, 657.
Includes a brief note on the founding of the colony, describing its precise location, and an outline of legal problems over title to the land, focusing on conflicts in the local area as well as in Congress.

1645.   Fogarty, Robert S.   "Haskell, Burnette" and "Kaweah Co-operative Commonwealth."   *Dictionary of American Communal and Utopian History* (cited above as item 76), 47, 148-9.
Dictionary entries providing basic information on the colony.

1646.   "Forest Reservations in California."   U.S. Senate *Reports.* 52d Congress, Second Session, v. 1, no. 1248, February 2, 1893. 82 pp.
Presents the finds of a Senate investigation into the Kaweah settlement.   Includes Kaweah's case as argued by its attorney, Henry C. Dillon; reproduces letters and statements of J.J. Martin, the colony secretary, along with various legal and congressional documents and statements; reproduces the colony pamphlet, *The Persecution of Kaweah* (item 1635, above).

1647.   Hine, Robert V.   "California Utopia: 1885-1890." *Huntington Library Quarterly* 11 (August, 1948): 387-405.
An earlier version of Hine's chapter on Kaweah in his book (see item 1635, below).

1648.   ———.   "Kaweah Co-operative Commonwealth."   *California's Utopian Colonies* (cited above as item 98), 78-100.
This chapter on Kaweah is probably the best monograph on the project; it covers the filing of land

claims, Haskell's plans for Kaweah, the colony's economic system, daily life, and the end of the experiment and Haskell's reaction to it.

\* ———. *Community on the American Frontier* (cited above as item 99), 225-6.
Provides a brief characterization of the colony, emphasizing its sense of being persecuted.

\* Johnpoll, Bernard K., and Lillian Johnpoll. *Impossible Dream: The Rise and Demise of the American Left* (cited above as item 113), 192-5.
Provides a brief history of Kaweah, emphasizing the role of Haskell.

1649. Jones, William Carey. "Kaweah Experiment in Co-Operation." *Quarterly Journal of Economics* 6 (October, 1891): 47-75.
Describes the origins of the colony, its organizational structure, procedures for admitting members, the work-credit system used instead of money, and the controversy with the government. Describes a diverse group of 150 persons living and working at the site at the time of writing.

1650. Kagan, Paul. "Kaweah Co-operative Commonwealth." *New World Utopias* (cited above as item 115), 84-101.
A heavily illustrated history of Kaweah.

1651. Kennedy, Dane. "Kaweah Colony." Senior honors thesis, University of California, Berkeley, 1973. 67 pp.
Provides a history of the colony, sketches of the leading personalities involved in it, and some analysis of community problems.

1652. Lewis, Ruth R. "Kaweah, an Experiment in Co-operative Colonization." *Pacific Historical Review* 17 (November, 1948): 429-41.
A summary of the author's University of California master's thesis on the topic. Covers the ideas of Laurence Gronlund which undergirded the colony, the land claims and problems with them, innovative social policies such as the eight-hour day and minimum wage, the rise of dissension in the colony, and the pre-emption of the land by the government and the subsequent trial of the colony's trustees.

1653. ———. "Rise and Fall of Kaweah: An Experiment in
    Cooperative Colonization, 1884-1892." M.A. thesis,
    University of California, Berkeley, 1942.
    Noncirculating and not available for photocopying.

1654. Mackie, Gerry. "Kaweah." *Communities* no. 34
    (September/October, 1978): 4-5.
    Provides a basic account of the community, based on
    the material in Hine, *California's Utopian Colonies* (item
    98, above).

1655. McWilliams, Carey. *Factories in the Fields: The Story of
    Migratory Farm Labor in California.* Boston: Little,
    Brown, 1939, pp. 39-47.
    Provides a history of the colony describing it as
    having had much promise; contrasts the sanctioning by
    the courts of land thefts from the public domain by the
    rich with the harassment of the poor, peaceful,
    productive Kaweans, arguing that the colony's
    self-avowed socialism was the cause of its badgering by
    the authorities.

1656. Martin, J.J. "Co-operative Commonwealth: The Kaweah
    Colony." *Nationalist* 1 (1889): 204-8.
    Provides an upbeat account of Kaweah's early days,
    predicting that the colony will survive and prosper.
    Focuses on the favorable natural environment of the
    colony in terms of climate and natural resources.

*    Muncy, Raymond Lee. *Sex and Marriage in Utopian
    Communities* (cited above as item 135), 120-1.
    Gives a description of marital life at Kaweah: families
    were encouraged; divorce was permitted; a formal system
    existed for deciding which partner could remain at the
    colony following a divorce.

1657. Oved, Yaacov. "Kaweah Cooperative Colony in
    California." *Two Hundred Years of American
    Communes* (cited above as item 142), 233-46.
    Provides basic biographical information on Haskell, a
    history of the development of the colony, a description
    of the colony's economic arrangements, internal disputes,
    and the government action which destroyed Kaweah.
    Based largely on articles from the colony's own
    periodicals.

1658. Philpot, Hamlet. "Kaweah." *Spectator* 68 (February 13, 1892): 235-6.
Corrects mistakes in the magazine's article on Kaweah the previous week (item 1663, below).

1659. Purdy, Will. *Kaweah: an Epic of the Old Colony.* Visalia, California: Tulare County Historical Society, [1959]. 16 pp.
Tells the story of the colony in the form of a narrative poem of rhymed couplets. A foreword contains a sketch of Purdy's life; his parents had moved to Kaweah when he was 11.

1660. Russell, Frances Theresa. *Touring Utopia.* New York: Dial, 1932, pp. 263-4.
Describes Haskell's disgust with the many loafers and malcontents in the colony.

1661. "Settlers on Forest Reservations in California." *U.S. Congressional Record*, 52d Congress, 2d Session, v. 24, part 2 (1893): 1466-75.
Records the Senate debate on paying settlers for their good-faith improvements on land claimed for Sequoia National Park, and reproduces at length a report by a clerk in the General Land Office which claims that beneath the veneer of a cooperative colony, a few crafty persons were actually trying to acquire much timberland for speculation.

1662. Shinn, Charles Howard. "Kaweah: A Cooperative Commonwealth." *History of Cooperation in the United States* (cited above as item 26), 464-75.
Provides basic information on the colony in an upbeat, optimistic tone. Describes the origin of the colony, and tells how land was acquired virtually free through the filing of adjacent homestead claims. Contains the basic statement of purpose promulgated by the colony, along with its bylaws.

1663. "Story of Kaweah." *Spectator* (London) 68 (February 6, 1892): 194-6.
Summarizes a recent article by Haskell on the history of the colony, detailing the ideas behind the colony and the problem it had with persons who wouldn't work hard. Accuses Kaweah of failing because it ignored human nature.

# LXXVIII. KINGWOOD

Kingwood was a Quaker community founded in 1949 near Frenchtown, New Jersey. It functioned as a religious retreat center and had nine resident members in 1953. At the end of that year it closed when most of its members left to join the Woodcrest Bruderhof.

## *Community periodical*

1664. *Seeker*. 1961-?.

## *Secondary work*

1665. Kramer, Wendell B. "Kingwood." "Criteria for the Intentional Community (cited above as item 118), 93-5.
Describes the community's origin, purpose and pooling of money.

# LXXIX. KOINONIA (Maryland)

This community was founded in 1951 as a Christian spiritual growth center located in the Greenspring Valley north of Baltimore. It has permanent participants, long-term guests, and short-term visitors on retreats and educational programs.

## *Community periodicals*

1666. *Koinonia*. Monthly. In publication in the late 1970s.

1667. *Koinonia Coworkers Newsletter*. In publication in the early 1960s.

1668. *Koinonia Magazine*. In publication in the late 1960s.
Contained articles on diverse subjects.

## *Primary work*

1669. *Koinonia*. Baltimore: Koinonia, n.d. 16 pp.

An introduction to the community. Contains a listings of available community programs. At the Institute for the Study of American Religion.

*Secondary works*

\* Bloesch, Donald G. *Wellsprings of Renewal* (cited above as item 36), 84.
Provides a brief look at the life of the community.

\* "Communes Report" (cited above as item 46), 44.
Provides a brief report on Koinonia.

1670. Davis, Nancy M. "Feeding the Communal Spirit." Washington *Post*, January 31, 1980, p. E1.
On cooking and diet at Koinonia.

1671. Green, Clifford J. "Ambiguities of Community: A Koinonia Experience." *Utopias: The American Experience* (cited above as item 134), 179-193.
Contains a description and history of the community, along with information about daily life and critical issues faced by the community.

1672. Harding, Glenn. "Background and Historical Notes on Koinonia Foundation." 1977. 8 pp. Mimeographed.
An account of the history of the community by its director from 1951 to 1968. At the Institute for the Study of American Religion.

1673. Kernan, Michael. "Centering on Community and Harmony." Washington *Post*, December 1, 1975, pp. B1-B2.

# LXXX. KOINONIA FARM (Georgia)

In 1942 Clarence Jordan founded an interracial community near Americus, Georgia, to promote communal values and to combat rural southern poverty. Koinonia Partners, as they are called, are given help in the form of homes and tools; products are marketed cooperatively, and profits go to a common fund. In the 1950s, during the civil rights movement's heyday, the community was the object of racist violence. However, it

survived that violence as well as Jordan's death in 1969.
The *Christian Century* has followed Koinonia Farm off and
on over the years, often by running short news items.  Those
items are accessible through the magazine's semiannual index.

### Community periodicals

1674.  *Koinonia Community Newsletter.*  Irregularly issued in the
1950s.  Mimeographed.

1675.  *Koinonia Newsletter.*  In publication in the early 1980s.
Quarterly.

1676.  *Koinonia Partners.*  In publication in the 1970s.
Quarterly.

### Primary work

1677.  *Koinonia Partners.*  Americus, Georgia: Koinonia Partners,
n.d. 16 pp.
A pamphlet providing basic information on the
community's ideas, farming activities, economy, children,
housing, and industries.  At the Institute for the Study
of American Religion.

### Works by community leaders

1678.  Jordan, Clarence.  *Letters to the Georgia Convention
(Galatians) and to the Alabaster African Church,
Smithville, Alabama (Philippians) in the Koinonia
"Cotton Patch" Version.*  Americus, Georgia: Koinonia
Farm, 1964.  19 pp.
One of the original pamphlets containing the original
editions of Jordan's translations of books of the New
Testament.

1679.  ———. *Letter to the Christians in Atlanta, or First
Corinthians in the Koinonia "Cotton Patch" Version.*
Americus, Georgia: Koinonia Farm, 1968.  28 pp.
Another booklet in the series of original New
Testament translations.

1680.  ———.  "Ordeal by Bullets."  *Liberation* 2 (May, 1957):

8-10, 19.
Provides the founder's story of the ideas, practices, and history of the community.

1681. ———. *Second Letter to the Christians in Atlanta, or Second Corinthians in the Koinonia "Cotton Patch" Version.* Americus, Georgia: Koinonia Farm, 1968. 19 pp.
Another booklet in the series of original New Testament translations.

1682. ———. *Substance of Faith and Other Cotton Patch Sermons by Clarence Jordan.* Edited by Dallas Lee. New York: Association Press, 1972.
A collection of sermons chosen to illustrate Jordan's basic ideas. Contains an introduction by Lee on Jordan and his way of creating community.

1683. ———. *To God's People in Washington: The Koinonia "Cotton Patch" Version of Romans.* Americus, Georgia: Koinonia Farm, 1968.
Another booklet in the series of original New Testament translations.

1684. Jordan, Clarence, and Bill Lane (Doulos). *Cotton Patch Parables of Liberation.* Scottdale, Pennsylvania: Herald Press, 1976. 154 pp.
An earthy retelling of parables, with commentary.

### Secondary works

\* Bloesch, Donald G. *Wellsprings of Renewal* (cited above as item 36), 78-81.
Provides a brief account of life at Koinonia Farm.

1685. Bouvard, Marguerite. "Koinonia Partners." *Intentional Community Movement* (cited above as item 37), 56-67.
Discusses the founding of Koinonia Farm by Jordan and the goals it announced at the time; provides historical discussion of community, including heated opposition to it from the Ku Klux Klan; the 1968 reorganization which pulled the community from the threat of immediate demise; the farm's economy and industries; and its basic goal of reconciliation. A good general account of the project.

1686.  Byron,  Dora.    "Koinonia  Revisited."    *Nation*  184  (March
        16, 1957): 226-8.
        Describes  the  current  violence  against  the  community,
        emphasizing  the  attitudes  of  whites  in  the  surrounding
        area.

1687.  "Clarence  Jordan."    *Christian  Century*  86  (November  12,
        1969): 1442-3.
        A eulogy for Jordan.

1688.  Egerton,  John.    "People's  Houses:  South  Georgia:
        Koinonia."    *Southern  Exposure*  8  (Spring,  1980):  42-3.
        Describes  the  Koinonia  housing  program,  which  is
        producing houses for the poor at $20,000 each.

1689.  "Embattled  Fellowship  Farm."    *Time*  68  (September  17,
        1956): 79-80.
        News story about the bombings at Koinonia.

1690.  "Farm  in  Georgia."    *Nation*  183  (September  22,  1956):
        237-8.
        Reproduces  a  statement  composed  by  Koinonia  members
        concerning  violence  directed  at  them;  provides  grim
        details  of  the  persecution,  but  exhibits  a  spirit  of  hope
        nevertheless.

1691.  Fey,  Harold  E.    "Creative  Church  in  Georgia."    *Christian
        Century* 74 (March 6, 1957): 285-7.
        Describes  the  author's  visit  to  Koinonia  Farm,  where
        he  observed  people  working  hard  despite  violence  aimed
        at  the  community  by  its  neighbors.    Concludes  that
        persecution will strengthen the community.

1692.  Fogarty,  Robert  S.    "Jordan,  Clarence."    *Dictionary  of
        American  Communal  and  Utopian  History*  (cited  above
        as item 76), 60.
        Biographical dictionary entry.

1693.  ———.    "Koinonia  Community."    *American      Utopianism*
        (cited above as item 75), 145.
        Introduction  to  the  community,  followed  by  "History
        and Persecution" (item 1694, below).

*       Gladstone,  Arthur.    "Cooperative  Communities  Today  II"
        (cited above as item 82), 14-15.
        Provides  an  account  of  the  recent  status  of  the

community; reports that in January, 1955, there were 40 members, including 24 children.

* Hedgepeth, William, and Dennis Stock. *Alternative* (cited above as item 91), 175-81.
   Provides description of the physical farm, biographical information on founder Clarence Jordan, and accounts of run-ins with local segregationists.

1694. "History and Persecution." *American Utopianism* (cited above as item 75), 145-9. Originally published in *Intentional Communities* (item 807, above).

1695. Howard, Walden. "Legacy of Clarence Jordan." *Faith at Work* 30 (April, 1970): 15-18.
   A transcript of Jordan's last outside interview, in which he describes the founding of Koinonia, assesses American Christianity, and discusses ways of implementing one's ideals.

1696. Infield, Henrik. "Campanella Community: A Study in Experimental Religion." *American Intentional Communities* (cited above as item 104), 17-37.
   Provides description (from visits by author) and sociological analysis of a community which is pseudonymously referred to as "Campanella," but which surely is Koinonia Farm.

1697. ———. "Campanella Community: A Study in Experimental Religion." *Cooperative Living* 4 (Fall, 1952): 1-8.
   Reports the results of a study of Koinonia, using a fictitious name for the community. The study, based on answers members provided to questionnaires, concludes that the community is composed of persons with an unusually deep commitment to the project. Similar to item 1696, above.

1698. Jackson, Dave, and Neta Jackson. "Koinonia Partners." *Living Together in a World Falling Apart* (cited above as item 112), 24-8.
   Provides an overview of life at the community.

1699. Jones, Ashton. "Koinonia Means Community." *Utopia U.S.A.* (cited above as item 65), 39.
   A description of the community by one of its members.

1700. "Koinonia Community." *Intentional Communities: The 1959 Yearbook of the Fellowship of Intentional Communities* (cited above as item 807), 24-7.
       Contains a description of the community in its early days.

1701. Kowinski, Martin. Untitled article in *Utopia U.S.A.* (cited above as item 65), 40-1.
       Discusses the community's history, farming operation, industries, housing, and other topics.

1702. Kramer, Wendell B. "Koinonia Farm." "Criteria for the Intentional Community" (cited above as item 118), 67-8.
       Provides a brief summary of Koinonia Farm's goals and methods for achieving them.

1703. Lane, Bill. *Radical Church.* Americus, Georgia: Koinonia Partners, 1972.
       Contains two essays challenging to Christians to return to serious servanthood.

1704. Lee, Dallas. *Cotton Patch Evidence.* New York: Harper and Row, 1971. 240 pp.
       A sympathetic history of Koinonia, from the early life of Clarence Jordan through the aftermath of his death.

1705. Lee, Robert. "The Crisis at Koinonia." *Christian Century* 73 (November 7, 1956): 1290-1.
       Describes violence against the community—gunfire, dynamite blasts, vandalism—and economic pressure being exerted by local whites. Expresses doubt that the community can survive the onslaught.

1706. Lipman, Eugene J. "Report on a Siege." *Christian Century* 76 (February 25, 1959): 233-5.
       Describes the ongoing harassment of the community and Koinonia's understated, even serene, response to it.

1707. Reich, Kenneth. "Utopian Farm Prospers in Rural Georgia." Los Angeles *Times*, February 27, 1972.
       An account of the state of Koinonia on its 30th birthday, after the death of Jordan, emphasizing the history and philosophy of the community.

1708. Roberts, Ron E. "Koinonia Farm." *New Communes: Coming Together in America* (cited above as item 153):

69-71.
Provides a brief history of Koinonia Farm, information about Jordan, and sketches the goals and ideals of the community.

1709. Snider, Philip Joel. *"Cotton Patch" Gospel: The Proclamation of Clarence Jordan.* Lanham, Maryland: University Press of America, 1985. 112 pp.
Published version of the author's doctoral dissertation. (Ph.D., Southern Baptist Theological Seminary, 1984, 194 pp.)

# LXXXI. KORESHAN UNITY

Cyrus Teed (1839-1908), known as "Koresh" (said to be the Hebraicized version of "Cyrus"), founded his first community at Moravia, N.Y., in 1880. It moved to Chicago in 1886. By the end of the decade there was a substantial communal home there, as well as a large publishing house. In the winter of 1893-4 Teed visited Estero; the first group left Chicago to move there in 1894, and the final members arrived in 1903. The community was celibate, although an auxiliary order of married persons was established. The best known Koreshan doctrine was that the earth is hollow and we live on the inside of it.

Teed's death in 1908 was discouraging, but many loyal members stayed on, expecting his resurrection. One count taken in 1912 found 205 members at Estero and elsewhere. However, one group of dissidents, the "Order of Theocracy," left Estero in 1910 and settled in Fort Myers, where the group lived communally. Its publications are listed below.

Some material on the community is in the American Communities Collection at Syracuse University.

Survey works: Liefmann (item 125), 23; Okugawa (item 134), 214-5, 218, 229.

*Community periodicals*

1710. *American Eagle.* Estero. 1906-49 and 1965-. Weekly.
Founded to promote the Koreshan cause against local opponents of the movement; eventually became a journal of tropical horticulture.

1711.  *Flaming Sword.*    Chicago,    1889-1903;    Estero,    1904-49.
       Variously monthly or weekly.

1712.  *Guiding Star.* 1886-9. Monthly.

1713.  *Herald.* 1879.

1714.  *Herald of the New Covenant.* 1880-?

1715.  *Plowshare and Pruning Hook.*    San Francisco,  1891-4;
       Chicago, 1894-5.
       Primarily concerned with expounding Teed's economic
       philosophy.

1716.  *Pruning Hook.* San Francisco. 1891.

1717.  *Salvator and Scientist.* Allegheny, Pennsylvania. 1895-6.


### Works by community leaders

    Most of these works were written by Teed, although his
authorship is not always attributed.    Items in this section not
listed in the National Union Catalog or on OCLC are generally
at the Institute for the Study of American Religion.    This is
not an exhaustive list of Koreshan publications; see the
specialized works on the movement, especially the theses, for
more detailed bibliographies.

1718.  *Alchemical Laboratory of the Brain.*    Chicago: Eta Co.,
       n.d.
       A treatise on the chemistry of the brain.

1719.  *Astronomical Hypotheses.*

1720.  *Cardinal Points of Koreshanity.*

1721.  *Celibacy.*

1722.  *Co-operation.* Washington, D.C.: n.p., 1909. 24 pp.

1723.  *Covenant of Life.*

1724.  *Emanuel Swedenborg—His Mission.*    Chicago:    Guiding
       Star Publishing House, 1895. 32 pp.

1725. *Fundamental Principles and Covenant Defined.*

1726. *Fundamentals of Koreshan Universology.* Estero: Guiding Star, 1927.

1727. *Geolineur Foreshortening.*

1728. *Great Red Dragon; or, the Flaming Devil of the Orient.* Estero: Guiding Star, 1909.

1729. *Identification of Israel.*

1730. *Immortal Manhood: The Laws and Processes of Its Attainment in the Flesh.* Chicago: Guiding Star, 1902.

1731. *Joseph, a Dramatization from Biblical History in Seven Acts.* Estero: n.p., 1904.

1732. *Judgment (A Discussion of the Sex Question).*

1733. *Koreshan Daily Graces.* Estero: [Koreshan Unity Press], 1900.

1734. *Koreshan Integral Cosmogony.*

1735. *Koreshan Science and Its Application to Life.* Chicago: Guiding Star, 1896.

1736. *Koreshan Unity: Communistic and Co-operative Gathering of the People.* Chicago: Guiding Star, 1895.

1737. *Koreshan Unity, Co-operative: The Solution of Industrial Problems.* Estero: Guiding Star, 1907.

1738. *Koreshan Unity: General Information Concerning Membership and Its Obligations, by Koresh.* Estero: Guiding Star, n.d. 20 pp.

1739. *Law of God.*

1740. *Mission of the Lord.*

1741. *Mnemonics, or the Science of Memory.*

1742. *More Literal Exposition of the Decalogue.*

1743.  *Mystery of the Gentiles.*  Estero: Guiding Star, 1926. 153 pp.

1744.  *Proclamation.*

1745.  *Reincarnation, or, the Resurrection of the Dead.* Chicago: Guiding Star, 1896.  44 pp.

1746.  *Science of the Decalogue.*  N.p.: Guiding Star, 1896.

1747.  *Shephard* [sic] *of Israel: The Lord Comes Through the Posterity of Joseph.*  N.p.: Guiding Star, 1896.

1748.  Teed, Cyrus R. (Koresh), and U.G. Morrow.  *Cellular Cosmogony, or, The Earth a Concave Sphere.*  Estero: Guiding Star, 1905.  Repr., Philadelphia: Porcupine Press, 1975.
       Provides Teed's own statement of his philosophy and his "proofs" of the concavity of the earth.  The reprinted edition contains a historical essay by Robert S. Fogarty.

1749.  Teed, Cyrus R. (Koresh), and J. Augustus Weimar.  *Koreshanity, the New Age Religion.*  *Miami, Florida: Koreshan Foundation, 1971.*  Edited by Elizabeth G. Bartosch for the Koreshan Foundation.
       Provides four articles on the religious aspects of the Koreshan system by the movement's founder and a close associate.  The articles present an argument that Teed was divinely chosen as a spiritual leader, the Koreshan doctrine of reincarnation, the Koreshan interpretation of the Ten Commandments, and an outline of Koreshan theology.

1750.  *Unsolved Problems of Astronomy.*

1751.  *Unsolved Problems of Chemistry.*

1752.  *What Is Koreshanity?*

1753.  *Where is the Lord?*

*Publications of the Order of Theocracy*
*(Fort Myers, Florida)*

1754.  *Double-Edged Sword.* Fort Myers. Ca. 1910. Periodical.

1755.  *Appearance of the Man of Sin.* Tract.

1756.  *Celibacy.* Tract.

1757.  *Elijah the Prophet—Koresh.* Tract.

1758.  *Personality and Humanity of Deity.* Tract.

*Secondary works*

1759.  Albertson, Ralph.  "Koreshans."  "Survey of Mutualistic Communities in America" (cited above as item 27), 393. Provides a brief sketch of the community.

1760.  Anderson, Kenneth Edwin.  *American Eagle*: A Unique Florida Weekly Newspaper."  M.A. thesis, University of Florida, 1970.
Provides an overview history of the Koreshan Unity and the founding of the *American Eagle* in response to local prejudice against the movement.  Tells of the early, highly political content of the paper and its shifting to horticultural coverage after about 1920.  Covers the cessation of publication of the paper in 1949 and its revival in 1965 by Hedwig Michel, then President of the Koreshan Unity.  Bibliography includes references to many local newspaper and magazine articles.

1761.  Andrews, Allen H.  *Yank Pioneer in Florida.* Jacksonville: Douglas Printing Co., Inc., 1950. 515 pp.
Andrews went to Florida with the original Koreshan contingent and helped hack the colony out of the jungle. His book contains descriptions of the group's scientific experiments trying to prove the concavity of the earth, and tells the story of the founding and demise of the *American Eagle*, the Koreshan paper specializing in tropical plant lore which Andrews edited for 42 years.

1762.  Arndt, Karl J.R.  "Koreshanity, Topolobampo, Olombia, and the Harmonist Millions."  *Western Pennsylvania History Magazine* 56 (January, 1973): 71-86.
Describes the efforts of three later movements to get their hands on the millions of dollars belonging to the nearly defunct Harmonists.  The Olombia Commonwealth

was not a commune, but a cure-all scheme for the ills of
the world led by Dr. William H. Von Swartwout.
Illustrated with graphics from Olombian literature.

1763. Beater, Jack.   *Trilogy of South Florida Tales.*   Fort
Myers: author, 1965, part 2, pp. 65-8.
Provides a personal, first-person account of the
author's experiences when he lived near the Koreshan
Unity in 1920 and of his scattered encounters with them
throughout his life.

1764. Berry Richard S.   "Koreshan Unity: An Economic History
of a Communistic Experiment in Florida."   M.A. thesis,
University of Florida, 1928.

1765. Bliss, W.D.P.   "Koreshan Unity." *New Encyclopedia of
Social Reform* (cited above as item 35), 673.
Provides a history of the community and describes its
industries.

1766. Carmer, Carl.   "Great Alchemist at Utica." *Dark Trees to
the Wind.*   New York: David McKay, 1949, pp. 260-89.
This chapter is a well-written account of the story of
Teed and the founding and development of the Koreshan
Unity.   List of sources at end of book provides a good
bibliography on Teed and the movement.

*        Carroll, H.K.   *Religious Forces of the United States*
(cited above as item 40), 117-8.
Briefly characterizes the movement, emphasizing the
members' hope of avoiding death.

1767. Clark, Elmer T.   "Church Triumphant." *Small Sects in
America* (cited above as item 43), 147-50.
Provides a brief history of the group, emphasizing the
hollow-earth theory.

1768. D'Agostino, Ruth.   "Koreshans." *Florida Cruise.*   Edited
by Norman Alan Hill.   Baltimore: George W. King, 1945,
pp. 340-6.
Describes the Koreshan buildings and grounds; provides
sketches of and anecdotes about several persons, mainly
Koreshans, living at Estero.

1769. Damkohler, E.E.   *Estero, Florida, 1882: Memoirs of the
First Settler.*   Ft. Myers Beach, Florida: Island Press,

1967. 32 pp.
Damkohler was the person who gave the Koreshans their colony site. Not seen.

1770. "Do We Live Inside of the Earth?" Louisville *Courier-Journal*, August 1, 1897.
Several papers carried similar feature stories at about this time, when the Koreshans in Florida were carrying out extensive experiments to prove their hollow-earth theory.

1771. "Earth a Hollow Globe—A New and Startling Cosmogony," Louisville *Courier-Journal*, May 2, 1897.

1772. Evans, Frederick M. *Shakers and Koreshans Uniting.* Mt. Lebanon, N.Y.: n.p., 1892. 8 pp.

1773. Federal Writers' Project. *Florida: A Guide to the Southernmost State.* New York: Oxford University Press, 1939, pp. 400-1.
Describes the buildings, publications, and teachings of the group; notes that they grow fine citrus and truck vegetable crops.

1774. Felton, Bruce, and Mark Fowler. "Cyrus Teed." *Felton and Fowler's Famous Americans You Never Knew Existed* (cited above as item 72), 249-51.
Describes Teed's hollow-earth ideas; characterizes the development of the commune in Chicago and then in Florida.

1775. Fine, Howard D. "Koreshan Unity: The Chicago Years of a Utopian Community." *Journal of the Illinois State Historical Society* 68 (June, 1975): 213-27.
Contains material on the early life of Teed, the development of the movement in Chicago, and the move to Florida. Ilustrated with photographs and Koreshan graphics.

1776. Flynn, Stephen J. *Florida: Land of Fortune.* Washington: Luce, 1962, pp. 115-6.
Provides a brief sketch of the history of the group and of the cellular cosmogony. Consistently misspells the name of the group "Khoreshan."

* Fogarty, Robert S. "American Communes, 1865-1914"

(cited above as item 74), 158-9.
Contains three paragraphs outlining the history of the
Koreshan movement.

1777. ———. "Teed, Cyrus Read." [sic] *Dictionary of*
*American Communal and Utopian History* (cited above
as item 76), 110-1.
Biographical dictionary entry.

1778. ———. "We Live on the Inside." Introduction to 1975
reprint of Teed, *Cellular Cosmogony* (item 1748, above).
Provides a good overview of the life of Teed, the
development of his following, and the building of the
community at Estero.

1779. Fritz, Florence. *Unknown Florida.* Coral Gables:
University of Miami Press, 1963. 213 pp.
Scattered paragraphs provide information on Teed's
correspondence with Gustave Damkohler, leading to the
latter's gift of land and the Koreshans' moving to
Florida; local political controversies involving the
Koreshans; the disastrous 1921 hurricane; the decline of
the movement; and the deeding of the land to the State
of Florida as a park.

1780. Gadd, Laurence D. "Hollow Earth." *Second Book of the*
*Strange.* New York: World Almanac Publications, 1981,
pp. 236-8.
Provides a history of the hollow-earth idea beginning
with its first proclamation by Sir Edmund Halley.
Describes Teed's refinements of the theory and the
interest in Teed's version which arose in Nazi Germany,
where the admiralty once tried to take pictures of the
British fleet by aiming cameras upward.

1781. Gardner, Martin. "Flat and Hollow." *Fads and Fallacies*
*in the Name of Science.* New York: Dover, 1957, pp.
16-27.
Provides a discussion of hollow-earth theories,
including an account of Koreshan cosmology and
anecdotes about communal life in Estero. Also includes a
discussion of the flat-earth ideas of Wilbur Voliva of
Zion City.

1782. Herbert, Glendon M., and I.S.K. Reeves. *Koreshan Unity*
*Settlement, 1894-1977.* Winter Park, Florida: Architects

Design Group of Florida, 1977. 171 pp.
A planning document for the restoration of the colony's buildings and grounds. Contains a biography of Teed, an outline of the Koreshan Universology, a history and description of the Koreshan organization, and an account of the movement's decline. Includes a photographic survey of the grounds, industries, and many buildings of the colony, and detailed proposals for its restoration. Based in part on interviews with Hedwig Michel, the last full-membership Koreshan. Heavily illustrated with photographs, maps, and diagrams.

1783. Hinds, William Alfred. "Koreshans." *American Communities and Co-operative Colonies* (cited above as item 95), 471-85.
Provides an overview of the community with extensive quotes from members and visitors. Contains a list of Koreshan literature.

1784. Kitch, Sally L. "Body of Her Own: Female Celibacy in Three Nineteenth-Century American Utopian Communities." Ph.D. dissertation, Emory University, 1984. 319 pp.
Argues that the choice of celibacy by the Shakers, Koreshans, and Woman's Commonwealth came from an effort to reverse the established symbol system of the family and enabled women to reach higher spiritual, economic, and political status.

1785. "Koresh I Is Dead." New York *Times*, December 25, 1908, p. 7.
A brief notice of Teed's death; announces that Victoria Graftia [sic] has taken over the leadership of the group.

1786. Lamoreaux, Leroy. *Early Days on Estero Island*. Ft. Myers Beach, Florida: Estero Island Publishers, 1967. 32 pp.

1787. Landing, James E. "Cyrus R. Teed, Koreshanity and Cellular Cosmogony." *Communal Societies* 1 (Autumn, 1981): 1-17.
Documents the early development of the movement and traces its development through the Chicago years to the aftermath of the founder's death.

1788. Ley, Willy. "For Your Information: The Hollow Earth."

*Galaxy* 11 (March, 1956): 71-81.
Discusses various hollow-earth theories, including the Teed-Morrow version (as elaborated by Charles E. Neupert). Illustrated with drawings.

1789. Mackle, Elliott. "Cyrus Teed and the Lee County Elections of 1906." *Florida Historical Quarterly* 57 (July, 1978): 1-18.
Documents the Koreshans' contesting of a local election in 1906, an episode occasionally marked by violence.

1790. ———. "Koreshan Unity in Florida, 1894-1910." M.A. thesis, University of Miami, 1971. 172 pp.
Provides a biography of Teed and the story of the founding of the Koreshan Unity; the early days in Florida; the prime of the movement in the early years of the twentieth century; the decline after Teed's death in 1908; and the ongoing presence of the Koreshans in Estero since then. Contains a thorough bibliography, much of it from Koreshan and other primary sources.

1791. Markett, Beth. "Koreshan Park Awaits Restoration Funds." Fort Myers *News-Press*, March 11, 1985, pp. 1B-2B.
Describes the Koreshan buildings, most of them still in good condition, as the site awaits funds for their restoration.

1792. Melton, J. Gordon. "Koreshan Unity." *Encyclopedia of American Religions* (cited above as item 130), 501.
Provides an outline of the cellular cosmogony and a historical sketch of the group.

1793. McCullers, Jeff. *New Jerusalem.* [Ft. Myers: Ft. Myers *News-Press*, 1986]. [21] pp.
A heavily illustrated brief history of the group and summary of Teed's key ideas.

1794. Michel, Hedwig. *Gift to the People.* Estero: n.p., 1961. 7 pp.
Contains a biographical sketch of Teed, a brief history of the movement, and an account of the transfer to the property at Estero to the State of Florida. Illustrated.

* Muncy, Raymond Lee. *Sex and Marriage in Utopian*

*Communities* (cited above as item 135), 33-4.
Provides a brief overview history of the movement.

1795. Powell, Kathleen. "Koreshans Look to Hopeful Future."
*Fort Meyers News-Press*, October 23, 1974, pp. 1D, 5D.
A newspaper feature article on the movement in its
latter days.

1796. "Proof That We Live Inside of the Globe." Chicago
*Times-Herald*, July 25, 1897, part 3, p. 25.

1797. Rahn, Claude J. "Some Brief Phases of Koreshan
Universology." *American Eagle*, March, 1967, 7.
A historical and philosophical memoir of the movement.

1798. Rainard, R. Lyn. "Conflict Inside the Earth: The
Koreshan Unity in Lee County." *Tampa Bay History* 3
(1981): 5-16.
Provides a sketch of the work of Teed in Chicago;
characterizes the relations of the Koreshans and their
neighbors in Florida, especially in Fort Myers, as cordial
until 1906, when Teed challenged the local political
bosses. Documentation includes many references to local
periodicals and documents not cited here. Illustrated
with photographs.

1799. Sinclair, Upton. *Profits of Religion*. Pasadena: author,
1918, pp. 248-50.
Provides a brief, skeptical look at Teed's distinctive
ideas and terminology.

1800. Smith, Warren. *Hidden Secrets of the Hollow Earth*.
New York: Kensington Publishing, 1976.

*      Strachey, Ray, and Hannah Whitall Smith. *Group
Movements of the Past and Experiments in Guidance*
(cited above as item 161), 146-8.
A history of the Koreshan Unity, principally before the
death of Koresh; emphasizes the role of Victoria Gratia.

1801. "Sure He Is the Prophet Cyrus." New York *Times*,
August 10, 1884, p. 1.
Reports that a disillusioned patient has charged that
Teed got money from her by claiming to be the prophet
Cyrus predicted in Isaiah 14:12.

1802. Webber, Everett. "Koresh." *Escape to Utopia* (cited above as item 168), 353-9.
      Describes the movement as a personality cult of a vain leader.

1803. Wooster, Ernest S. "Koreshan Unity." *Communities of the Past and Present* (cited above as item 175), 100-5.
      Sketches the history of the colony and describes the cellular cosmogony theory. Provides quotes from former members and especially from colony literature to explain the cosmogony and the nature and organization of the colony.

# LXXXII. LAWSONIAN: THE DES MOINES UNIVERSITY OF LAWSONOMY

Alfred W. Lawson (1869-1954) was a minor-league baseball pitcher and manager who became an early aviation enthusiast, at one point designing an airliner. An economic reformer during the Depression, he became convinced that he could save humanity by teaching Lawsonomy, a complex reformulation of much of human learning, including new approaches to physics and physiology. In August, 1943, he purchased the six buildings and fourteen acres of the abandoned Des Moines University. His students lived there communally, trying to achieve self-sufficiency by growing garden crops on nearby lots. They lived a highly organized daily routine, largely separated from the surrounding city. In 1954 the community was dissolved and the property sold; Lawson died two weeks later.

No book or journal article has been published to date on the Des Moines University of Lawsonomy.

Alfred W. Lawson published many books beyond those listed here. The National Union Catalog provides additional citations.

*Works by the community leader*

1804. Lawson, Alfred W. *Born Again.* New York and Philadelphia: Wox, Conrad Co., 1904. 287 pp.
      A utopian fantasy with ideas which Lawson many years later tried to work out at the Des Moines University of Lawsonomy.

1805. ———. *Creation.* Philadelphia: Arnold and Co., 1931. 99 pp.

1806. ———. *Lawsonian Religion.* Detroit: Humanity Benefactor Foundation, 1949. 255 pp.
Outlines Lawson's religious principles; contains, on pp. 179-96, a manifesto for the Des Moines University of Lawsonomy with many photographs of the campus.

1807. ———. *Lawsonomy.* Detroit: Humanity Publishing Company, 1935-39. Three volumes. Lawson's *magnum opus.* The three volumes are titled *Lawsonomy, Mentality,* and *Almighty.*

### Secondary works

1808. Blair, William M. "Big Profit Denied on Surplus Sales." New York *Times,* March 6, 1952, p. 12.
Describes a controversy which erupted when the University of Lawsonomy sold, at a large profit, machine tools which it had purchased very cheaply from the federal government. See also follow articles on March 7 (p. 29), March 8 (p. 7), March 9 (p. 95), and March 20 (p. 21).

1809. Felton, Bruce, and Mark Fowler. "Alfred William Lawson." *Felton and Fowler's Famous Americans You Never Knew Existed* (cited above as item 72), 237-9.
Outlines the theories involved in Lawsonomy; describes the operations of the University of Lawsonomy.

1810. Gardner, Martin. "Zig-Zag-and-Swirl." *Fads and Fallacies in the Name of Science.* New York: Dover, 1957, pp. 69-79.
Provides an outline of Lawson's ideas, a biographical sketch, and a description of the Des Moines University of Lawsonomy.

1811. Jonas, Peter. "Alfred William Lawson: Aviator, Inventor, and Depression Radical." *Old Northwest* 9 (Summer, 1983): 157-73.
Provides a brief note on the University of Lawsonomy, explaining its policies and practices, on pp. 169-70.

1812. "Lawsonomy Cult Sells University." New York *Times,*

November 21, 1954, p. 81.
Tells of the sale of the campus; reports Lawson as vague about the future of the teaching of his ideas.

1813.   "Zigzag and Swirl." *Time*, March 24, 1952, p. 49.
Depicts the school's curriculum as primarily the memorizing of Lawson's many books; describes current controversy about the college.

# LXXXIII. LECLAIRE

Leclaire, founded in 1890, was an industrial town in Illinois in which most residents were employed by a firm which made plumbing supplies and mantels.   The firm, founded in 1890 by Nelson O. Nelson, provided unusually good working conditions and free schools, among other things, to workers; although the business was privately held, it engaged in extensive profit-sharing with workers.   The town had many cooperative facilities: a library, a clubhouse, an auditorium, recreational facilities, and other amenities.

Some material on Leclaire is in the American Communities Collection at Syracuse University.

1814.   Bliss, W.D.P.   "Leclaire."   *New Encyclopedia of Social Reform* (cited above as item 35), 706.
Provides a description of Leclair, emphasizing its democratic atmosphere and cooperative facilities.

1815.   Fogarty, Robert S.   "Nelson, Nelson O."   *Dictionary of American Communal and Utopian History* (cited above as item 76), 79-80.
Biographical dictionary entry.

1816.   Skinner, Charles M.   "Co-Operation at Leclaire."
*American Communes* (cited above as item 156), 28-31.
Describes the business and social life of the town. Illustrated with photographs.

# LXXXIV(A). LEMURIAN GROUPS: LEMURIAN FELLOWSHIP

The myth of Lemuria, a lost continent which is the Pacific counterpart of Atlantis, dates to the 1890s. Robert D. Stelle took up the concept and founded the Lemurian Fellowship in 1936 in Chicago. After several moves it ended up on 260 acres near Ramona, California in 1941. There are several buildings on the property and a correspondence school is operated from the site. The Fellowship subscribes to various spiritual principles, including reincarnation and karma, and devotes itself to building a new civilization on earth. Since Stelle's death in 1952 the group has been governed by a board of directors.

## Community periodical

1817. *Lemurian Viewpoint.* 1962?-?

## Primary works

1818. *Be It Resolved.* Milwaukee: Lemurian Press, 1940.
Lectures delivered at the national Lemurian conference, 1940. Constitutes a manifesto of fundamental Lemurian ideas.

1819. *Education and Morals.* Milwaukee: Lemurian Press, 1939.
An introduction to Lemurian thought.

1820. *Into the Sun.* Ramona, California: Lemurian Fellowship, 1973.
An introduction to Lemurian philosophy; also provides glimpses of the Master Plan for the advancement of believers.

1821. *Lemuria the Magnificent.* N.p.: Lemurian Fellowship, 1937.
An exposition of the group's ideas about Lemuria and the method by which it will be recovered and the new Lemurian empire established.

1822. *Phylos the Thibetan: An Earth Dweller's Return.* Milwaukee: Lemurian Press, 1940.

Purported historical and theoretical account of Atlantis and Mu.

*Secondary works*

1823. de la Torre, T. *Psycho-Physical Regeneration Rejuvenation and Longevity* [sic]. Milwaukee: Lemurian Press, 1938.
Discusses Lemurian ideas about health and longevity.

1824. Hillinger, Charles. "Mystery Cult Claims Wisdom of Mu." Los Angeles *Times*, July 31, 1977.

1825. Stelle, Robert D. *Sun Rises*. Ramona, California: Lemurian Fellowship, 1952. 443 pp.
Purported history of a society which existed 78,000 years ago.

*Secondary work*

1826. Melton, J. Gordon. "Lemurian Fellowship." *Encyclopedia of American Religions* (cited above as item 130), 600-1.
Outlines the beliefs of the group.

# LXXXIV(B). LEMURIAN GROUPS: STELLE

In 1963 Richard Kieninger broke with the Lemurian Fellowship and formed the Stelle Group. In that year he also published *The Ultimate Frontier* under the pseudonym Eklal Kueshana, outlining the content of his messages from spiritual beings. In 1966 he and his followers formed the Lemuria Builders to promote their ideas, and in 1973 they moved their headquarters from Chicago to Stelle, Illinois, a community based on Kieninger's ideas. A second location was opened at Adelphi, Texas, in 1976, in part because of differences which had developed between Kieninger and others at Stelle. In 1982 Stelle was opened to nonmembers of the Stelle Group. The Stelle Group in its various manifestations is repudiated by the Lemurian Fellowship.

## Community periodicals

1827. *Placeholder.* Ca. 1982-. Bimonthly. Stelle Group newsletter.

1828. *Lemuria Builder.* 1966-71.
Newsletter.

1829. *Personal Preparedness.* 1981-. Ten times per year. Stelle Group newsletter. Focuses on survivalism, providing tips on surviving a major world economic collapse on other long-term emergency.

1830. *Stelle Group Letter.* 1982-.
Newsletter. Also includes news of the movement's newer branch in Adelphi, Texas.

1831. *Stelle Letter.* 1972-1982.
Newsletter.

## Primary works

1832. *Adelphi Organization.* Garland, Texas: Adelphi Organization, 1976. 7 pp.
A prospectus for the new Stelle splinter operation in Texas; tells of the movement's history, ideas, and goals, and provides information on joining.

1833. *Bylaws of the Stelle Community Association. 1982.* Typescript.
At the Institute for the Study of American Religion.

1834. *Introduction to the Stelle Group.* Stelle: Stelle Group, 1981. 12 pp.
Provides information on the group's history, philosophy, and social goals. Later edition (Quinlan, Texas: The Stelle Group, 1983; 13 pp.) provides information on the history and philosophy of both the Stelle and Adelphi communities.

1835. *Lemuria Builders.* Chicago: Lemuria Builders, 1968. 16 pp.
Covers the background, history, and activities of the Stelle Group, and provides information on joining. Contains the group's constitution and bylaws.

1836. *Stelle: A City for Tomorrow.* Chicago: Stelle Group,

1965; revised edition, 1970. 12 pp.
Provides basic information about the Stelle group and a prospectus for the new model city.

1837. *Stelle—City of Tomorrow.*    Stelle: Stelle Group, 1965 (plus later editions). 20 pp.
Outlines the Stelle philosophy and provides other basic information about the movement.

1838. *Stelle Credit System: An Economic Model for the New Order.* Stelle: Stelle Group, 1977. 10 pp.
A treatise on Stelle economics, both theoretical and concrete, with examples. Stelle at this writing was moving toward a modified communal economic system, one it hoped would be imitated elsewhere.

### Work by a community leader

1839. Kieninger, Richard. *Observations.*    Stelle: Stelle Group, 1971.
19 essays from *Lemuria Builder.*

1840. ———. *Observations II. Stelle: Stelle Group, 1974.*
24 essays originally published in *Lemuria Builder.*

1841. ———.    *Observations* III.    Stelle:    Stelle    Group,    1974. 78 pp.

1842. ———. *Observations* IV. Stelle: Stelle Group, 1979.
25 essays originally published in *Stelle Letter.*

1843. ——— (Writing under the name of Eklal Kueshana). *Ultimate Frontier.* Chicago: Stelle Group, 1963.
The basic text of the Stelle Group. Purports to bring to light the messages of ancient brotherhoods.

### Secondary works

1844. Betterton, Charles, and Linda Guinn.    "Stelle: Dawn of a New Age City." *Communities* no. 63 (Summer, 1984): 9-13.
Describes Stelle's demography, its self-development program, its educational system, and its plans for surviving impending disaster.

1845.  Dorfman, Ron.    "Preparing for the End of the World."
       Chicago *Reader*, September 25, 1981, pp. 1, 28-35.
       A lengthy feature article on the Stelle Group.
       Illustrated.

1846.  McCabe, Michael.    "'End Is Near'—And They Get Ready."
       Chicago *Tribune*, January 12, 1979, pp. 1, 4.
       Feature article.

1847.  Melton, J. Gordon.    "Stelle Group."    *Encyclopedia of
       American Religions* (cited above as item 130), 603-4.
       Provides an overview of the group's ideas and activity.

1848.  Plous, F.K., Jr.    "Kingdom in a Cornfield: Is This 2001?"
       *Midwest* magazine (Chicago *Sun-Times*), February 24,
       1974, pp. 30-33.
       Newspaper feature article; heavily illustrated.

# LXXXV.  LITTLE LANDERS

William E. Smythe established the first Little Landers
colony in San Ysidro, Calfornia, in 1909.    The underlying
concept was that a person could eke out a living on one acre.
By 1912 the colony had 116 families, 300 persons in all, most
of them gardening their acre plots and enjoying an active
community educational and social life.    By 1916 several other
similar colonies had been opened elsewhere in California.
However, a flood devastated the original colony in 1916, and it
never recovered fully.    Some settlers were unable to make a
living from one acre and left the colony.    None of the other
colonies achieved notable success.

Survey works: Okugawa (item 139), 228-9.

*Community periodical*

1849.  *Little Lands in America*.    1916-8.    Monthly.    Published by
       William E. Smythe.

*Works by the community leader*

1850.  Smythe, William E.    *City Homes on Country Lanes*.    New

York: Macmillian, 1921. Repr., New York: Arno Press, 1974. 270 pp.
A manifesto for the "garden city," giving Smythe's vision of the Little Landers.

1851. ———. "For a Nation of Little Landers." *Proceedings of the Nineteenth National Irrigation Congress* 19 (1912): 176-80.
Reproduces a conference speech from the 1911 annual meeting in which Smythe says that he was influenced by the works of Bolton Hall, the single taxer who founded Free Acres, and provides a manifesto for Little Landers operations, arguing that such a scheme would be a panacea for the nation's problems.

1852. ———. *Homelanders of America.* Washington, D.C.: Homelander System, 1921. 13 pp.

1853. ———. "Quest of the Fortunate Life." *West Coast* 13 (June, 1913): 3-8.
Outlines Smythe's ideas about small cooperative farming; provides a historical sketch of the Little Landers project at San Ysidro, with characterizations of several of the colonists and an anecdotal sketch of life at the colony. Illustrated with photographs.

1854. ———. "Real Utopias in the Arid West." *Atlantic Monthly* 79 (May, 1897): 599-609.
Argues that small landholdings have a glorious economic future.

1855. ———. "Remarks by William E. Smythe." *Transactions of the Commonwealth Club of California* 11 (December, 1916): 425-6.
Smythe defends his concept that a family can eke out a living, if not become wealthy, on a small plot of land. Criticism of that concept had been leveled by a Commonwealth Club report (see "Data of Land Settlement," *ibid.*, p. 382).

1856. ———. *Twentieth Century Colony.* Chicago: author, 1895. 36 pp.

1857. ———. *"World's Fair" Colony, 1915, Little Landers, Hayward Heath.* San Francisco: Society of the Little Lands, 1915. 26 pp.

Secondary works

1858. Anderson, Henry S. "Little Landers Colonies: A Unique Agricultural Experiment in California." *Agricultural History* 5 (October, 1931): 139-50.
Provides an overview sketch of the history of the San Ysidro colony. Reproduces Smythe's creed, "The Hope of the Little Lands." Also provides sketches of the less successful Los Terrenitos (near Los Angeles) and Hayward Heath (near Hayward) colonies. Concludes that microagriculture make less sense than farming a larger area.

1859. Clark, A.W. *Little Landers: Social Survey of San Ysidro, California, the Mother Colony.* San Francisco: Modern Homestead Association, 1914. 32 pp.

1860. Cowan, John L. "Hope of the Little Landers." *World's Work* 23 (November, 1911): 96-100.
Describes the theory underlying the project; depicts life at the San Ysidro colony, emphasizing that it had all the advantages of both town and country.

1861. Fogarty, Robert S. "Little Landers Colony" and "Smythe, William Ellsworth." *Dictionary of American Communal and Utopian History* (cited above as item 76), 151 and 106, respectively.
Dictionary entries providing an overview of the Little Landers project.

* Hine, Robert V. *California's Utopian Colonies* (cited above as item 98), 144-8.
Provides a basic history of the project and an analysis of its shortcomings.

1862. Lee, Lawrence B. "Little Landers Colony of San Ysidro." *Journal of San Diego History* 21 (1975): 26-51.
The comprehensive history of the main colony. Describes Smythe's life as a San Diego civic leader, the development and life of the colony, and its gradual decline after the 1916 flood. Illustrated with photographs. Heavily documented with references to many specialized and local works not cited here.

1863. Lindsay, Forbes. "Little Land Movement." *Lippincott's* 90 (November, 1912): 619-22.

Argues for a return to subsistence farming, pointing to the Little Landers colony as proof that the concept works.

1863. Poeton, Josiah. "Story of the Little Landers." *Little Farms Magazine* 1 (October, 1911): 6, 22.
Describes Smythe's thinking which led to the project, portraying it as having been influenced by Bolton Hall, the founder of the single tax colony of Free Acres; argues that the Little Landers will bring great benefits to society. Illustrated with photographs.

1865. Pourade, Richard F. *History of San Diego: Gold in the Sun.* San Diego: Union-Tribune Publishing Co., 1965, v. 5, pp. 110-1, 177, 208, 210-2, 217.
Recounts the founding and early life of the San Ysidro colony; provides an account of the flood. Illustrated with photographs of the flood. Bibliography includes citations of manuscript materials not cited here.

# LXXXVI. LLANO DEL RIO AND NEWLLANO

Job Harriman, a prominent socialist attorney and politician, became disillusioned after losing a race for mayor of Los Angeles and founded the Llano del Rio colony, located some 45 miles north of Los Angeles, in 1914. Lack of rights to irrigation water soon doomed the colony, and internal strife also caused serious problems. In 1918 a decision was made to move to a company town in Louisiana which had recently been abandoned by a lumber company and which was available cheaply. Newllano remained poor throughout its life, but it enjoyed an active social life and managed to survive for some two decades, until it succumbed to its ongoing financial crisis and was liquidated in 1938.

An oral history project on Llano was undertaken in the late 1960s at the University of California at Los Angeles; information thus gained is available through the University of California library system. The Walter Millsap papers, which deal principally with Llano, are in the library at the University of California at Riverside. Archival materials, including many interviews with Newllano colonists, are located at the Louisiana State University library at Baton Rouge. Other archival materials are in the library at Northwestern State College, Louisiana. Some material on Newllano is in the American

Communities Collection at Syracuse University. The Wilson Collection of Newllano Colony Papers in located in the University of Arkansas library at Fayetteville. The minutes of the Board of Commissioners of the Llano Colony are in the Huntington Library, San Marino, California. The Job Harriman Collection is also located there, as are other primary documents. Some correspondence with Job Harriman is located in the Morris Hillquit Collection at the Wisconsin State Historical Library.

Survey work: Curl (item 52), 40; Okugawa (item 139), 231-3.

## Community periodicals

The catalog of the Bancroft Library (University of California, Berkeley) is a good source on the Llano periodicals.

1866. *Colony News and Colony Co-operator.* Newllano. 1918-22.

1867. *Industrial Democrat.* Newllano. 1932.

1868. *Internationalist.* Llano. 1913-8.

1869. *Llano Colonist.* Llano, 1916-9; Newllano, 1921-1937. Weekly.

1870. *Voice of the Unemployed.* Newllano. 1933.

1871. *Western Comrade.* Los Angeles and Llano. 1913-8. Monthly.

## Primary works

1872. *Detailed Information about the Llano Co-operative Colony.* Newllano, Louisiana: Llano Co-operative Press, July, 1932. 34 pp.

1873. *Gateway to Freedom: Co-operation in Action.* Llano: Colony Press Department, 1915; Leesville, Louisiana: Llano Co-operative Colony, 1924. 36 pp. An earlier version was published in *Western Comrade* 2 (June, 1914): 6-9, 24-5.
The manifesto of the colony.

1874. *Llano del Rio Colony, Cooperation in Action.* Los Angeles: Colony Press Department, 1914. 32 pp.

1875. *Llano Viewbook.* Llano, California: Llano Publications, 1917. 20 pp.

## Works by the community leader

1876. Harriman, Job. "Letter of Job Harriman—Founder." *American Utopianism* (cited above as item 75), 128-32.

1877. ———. "Llano—Community of Ideals." *Western Comrade* 5 (March, 1917): 8-9, 25.

## Secondary works

1878. Albertson, Ralph. "Llano Cooperative Colony and Newllano Cooperative Colony." "Survey of Mutualistic Communities in America" (cited above as item 27), 418. Provides a brief historical overview of the Llano movement.

1879. Brinsmade, Herman H. "Four Dollars a Day and Utopia." *Illustrated World* 24 (December, 1915): 523-4. An optimistic appraisal of the colony's potential, arguing that Llano is avoiding the problems of the more idealistic and credulous ventures of the past.

1880. Brown, Bob (Robert C). *Can We Co-Operate?* Pleasant Plains, New York: Roving Eye Press, 1940. Satirizes in scathing terms the anarchy the author saw at Newllano.

*       Calverton, Victor. *Where Angels Dared to Tread* (cited above as item 39), 364-6. Describes the founding of Llano and tells of the colony's struggle to survive.

1881. Clark, Elmer T. "Llano Colonies." *Small Sects in America* (cited above as item 43), 150-1. Provides a brief and somewhat inaccurate historical sketch of the Llano movement; also contains a note on a nearby satellite colony called the Christian Commonwealth.

1882. Clifton, Archie Roy. "History of the Communistic Colony Llano del Rio." Historical Society of Southern California *Annual Publications* 11 (1918): 80-90.
Discusses the site and use of the land, schools, social life, and organization of the colony. Includes a description of the colony from personal observation. Describes the growing internal dissent in 1915-6.

1883. ———. "Study of Llano del Rio Community in the Light of Earlier Experiments in Practical Socialism." M.A. thesis, University of Southern California, 1918.

1884. "Communities of the Past: New Llano." *Cooperative Living* 2 (Spring, 1951): 11-2.
Focuses on problems the community had with self-government.

1885. Conkin, Paul K. "Llano del Rio." *Two Paths to Utopia: The Hutterites and the Llano Colony* (cited above as item 50), 103-85.
One of the best surveys of Llano, recounting its history, government, daily life, and problems.

1886. Dequer, John. "Llano del Rio." *Western Comrade* 3 (December, 1915): 15, 25-6.
Argues that Llano is a corporation "conducted on business principles," not socialism.

1887. Dermody, Michael E., and Robert V. Hine. "California's Socialist Utopias." *Communities* no. 68 (Winter, 1985): 55-8.
Discusses California communities generally and then focuses specifically on Llano, describing its founding, its daily life, its educational system, its social life, and the special role played in the community by Walter Millsap.

* Douglas, Dorothy W., and Katharine Du Pre Lumpkin. "Communistic Settlements" (cited above as item 56), 100.
Contains a brief note on the colony.

1888. Fairfield, Dick. "Llano Cooperative Colony." "Communes U.S.A." (cited above as item 63), 38, 40.
Provides an overview of Llano, explaining strengths and weaknesses of the community.

1889. Fogarty, Robert S. "Eggleston, C.V." and "Harriman, Job." *Dictionary of American Communal and Utopian History* (cited above as item 76), 35, 45-6. Biographical dictionary entries.

1890. Fogarty, Robert S. "Llano Cooperative Colony." *American Utopianism* (cited above as item 75), 128.
An introduction to "Letter of Job Harriman—Founder" (item 1876, above), a primary Llano document written in 1924.

1891. Gleeser, Carl Henry. "Llano Movement." *Religions and Philosophies in the United States of America.* Edited by Julius A. Weber. Los Angeles: Wetzel Publishing Co., 1931, pp. 305-11.
Contains a statement of the aims and goals of the movement. Contains a copy of the Llano Pledge and a statement by George T. Pickett, the manager of Llano for many years. Gleeser was the editor of the *Llano Colonist.*

1892. Hanna, Hugh S. "Llano del Rio Cooperative Colony." U.S. Bureau of Labor Statistics *Monthly Review* 2 (January, 1916): 19-23.
Describes the California colony, emphasizing its industries, physical facilities, and organization.

1893. Hayden, Dolores. "Feminism and Eclecticism." *Seven American Utopias* (cited above as item 90), 288-317.
A survey of the history and life of the colony, with special attention paid to its artistic endeavors, and especially its architecture. Well illustrated with photographs and maps. Endnotes contain several references to manuscript materials and articles in the *Western Comrade* and *Llano Colonist* not listed here.

*        Hendricks, Robert J. *Bethel and Aurora: An Experiment in Communism as Practical Christianity* (cited above as item 92), 259-266, 271-2.
Provides an extended description of the Llano Colony, then still functioning. Shares recent correspondence of author with officials at the colony.

1894. Hine, Robert V. "Llano del Rio." *California's Utopian Colonies* (cited above as item 98), 114-31.
Provides good background on Harriman plus a history

of the colony, describing its economy, agricultural operations, organization, and politics.

1895. Hoffman, Abe. "Look at Llano: Experiment in Economic Socialism." *California Historical Society Quarterly* 40 (September, 1961): 214-36.
Provides an overview history of the California years of Llano. Contains important information about the rapid decline of the California colony after the majority moved to Louisiana. Contains references to manuscripts, newspaper articles, and interviews not cited here. Illustrated with two photographs.

1896. Huxley, Aldous. "Ozymandias, the Utopia That Failed." *Tomorrow and Tomorrow and Tomorrow and Other Essays.* New York: Harper and Brothers, 1956, pp. 84-102. Reprinted in *California Historical Quarterly* 51 (Summer, 1972): 119-30.
Provides some history of Llano, along with reflections on community dynamics and on the transient nature of life.

1897. Infield, Henrik. "New Llano." *Cooperative Communities at Work* (cited above as item 105), 37-52.
Discusses the goals, demography, principles, and pay system at Llano, along with the problems the colony faced at various times.

1898. Kagan, Paul. "Llano del Rio." *New World Utopias* (cited above as item 115), 118-37.
Heavily illustrated history of Llano del Rio in California.

1899. ———. "Portrait of a California Utopia." *California Historical Quarterly* 51 (Summer, 1972): 131-54.
Similar to the chapter on Llano in the author's book, *New World Utopias* (item 115, above). Heavily illustrated.

1900. "Llano Co-operative Colony." U.S. Bureau of Labor Statistics *Monthly Review* 32 (May, 1931): 101-9.
Describes the 1927 lawsuit by a former member trying to force the colony into receivership. Provides a current analysis of the colony, including membership requirements, government, living conditions, industries, and financial condition. Includes two balance sheets

from 1920 and 1930.

1901.  McDonald,  A.  James.  *Llano  Co-operative  Colony  and What It Taught.* Leesville, Louisiana: author, 1950.
An  informative  overview  of  the  colony  written  by  a member;  includes  several  basic  documents  of  the community.

1902.  McWilliams,  Carey.  "Bread  and  Hyacinths."  *Southern California  Country* (cited  above  as  item  126),  284-7.
Describes  Job  Harriman's  background,  the  founding  and growth  of  the  colony,  and  the  chronic  water  shortage which forced the move to Louisiana in 1917.

1903.  Marple,  Albert.  "Community  Farming  Proves  Profitable." *Craftsman* 30 (1915): 98-9.
An  account  of  a  successful  Southern  California community,  focusing  on  the  cobblestone  buildings constructed  of  rock  found  on  the  site.  The  community  is not  named,  but  the  building  pictured  in  the  article's  one illustration appears to be at Llano.

1904.  Mellon,  Knox.  "Job  Harriman  and  Llano  del  Rio:  The Chimerical  Quest  for  a  Secular  Utopia."  *Communal Societies* 5 (1985): 194-206.
Describes  Harriman's  interest  in  Altruria,  which  helped him  form  his  communal  ideals;  probes  the  contradiction between  socialist  theory  and  human  nature  which  led  to conflicts  at  Llano;  analyzes  Harriman's  personality  and leadership  abilities,  as  well  as  conflicts  at  the  colony over his leadership role.

1905.  ———.  (William  Knox  Mellon,  Jr.)  *Job  Harriman:  The Early  and  Middle  Years.*  Ph.D.  dissertation,  Claremont Graduate School, 1972.
Argues  that  Harriman  was  a  major  reformer  and  a neglected  figure  in  history.  Focuses  primarily  on Harriman's  early  career  through  his  mayoral  campaign  in Los  Angeles  in  1911.  It  was  after  losing  that  election that  Harriman's  thoughts  turned  increasingly  toward colonization.

1906.  Morris,  James  K.  "Outpost  of  the  Cooperative Commonwealth:  The  History  of  the  Llano  Del  Rio Colony  in  Gila,  New  Mexico,  1932-1935."  *New  Mexico Historical Review* 56 (April, 1981): 177-95.

Tells of the founding of this Llano outpost in 1932 in a 19th century hacienda. This location was to be home to 1000 colonists, one of a chain of colonies stretching across the country; its actual peak population in 1934 was 50. Article concludes that the decision to buy another property was the worst single action in the history of Llano, and did much to destroy the main colony, which already had deep financial problems.

1907. Murrah, Bill. "Llano Cooperative Colony, Louisiana." *Southern Exposure* 1 (Winter, 1974): 88-104.
Locates the origins of Llano in a perceived increasing oppressiveness of the new industrial society; provides an overview history of the colony, and describes its problems and strengths. Quotes extensively from former colonists and their neighbors.

1908. Oved, Yaacov. "Llano del Rio: A Socialist Commune in California and Louisiana." *Two Hundred Years of American Communes* (cited above as item 142), 285-310.
Characterizes Harriman and the founding of the colony, the development of Llano in California, the social and cultural life and internal friction of the colony there, the move to Louisiana, continuing conflicts over leadership and other matters, and the decline of the colony and sale of the property.

1909. Singleton, Allen. "Newllano Library Materials in Russell Library, Northwestern State College." *Louisiana Studies* 2 (Summer, 1963): 84-90.
Describes the Russell Library's recent acquisition of a major portion of the Newllano colony library; describes the collection and attempts to categorize its diverse holdings.

1910. Taylor, Alva W. "Llano Colony Reorganized." *Christian Century* 53 (April 22, 1936): 608.
Tells of one of the colony's several reorganizations; expresses confidence that problems have finally been ironed out.

1911. ———. "No Poverty in Llano Colony." *Christian Century* 50 (April 26, 1933): 571.
An upbeat report which depicts a thriving Llano colony.

1912. "United Communities." Hearing before Subcommittee, Committee on Agriculture and Forestry, U.S. Senate, 73d Congress, First Session, May 10, 1933. Washington: Government Printing Office, 1933.   47 pp.
A transcript of a hearing on S.1142, a bill to establish colonies to provide work for the unemployed.   Provides the text of the bill and testimony in favor of it by George T. Pickett, the manager of Llano, and other Llano supporters.   Also contains the text of the Llano pamphlet "Detailed Information about the Llano Cooperative Colony."

1913. Wilson, Henry Edward.   "History of the Llano Co-operative Colony."   M.A. thesis, Louisiana State University, 1951. 210 pp.

1914. Wooster, Ernest S.   "Llano Co-operative Colony." *Communities of the Past and Present* (cited above as item 175), 117-133.
A member's account of Llano's life and history. Includes a copy of the Llano "Declaration of Principles."

1915. ———.   "Bread and Hyacinths." *Sunset*, August, 1924, pp. 21-3, 59-60.
Second part of series (see item 1918, below).

1916. ———.   "Colonists Win Through." *Sunset*, September, 1924, pp. 30-3, 75-80.
Third part of series (see item 1918, below).

1917. ———.   "Inside a Cooperative Colony: An American Experiment with Wageless Work." *Nation* 117 (October 10, 1923): 378-80.
Portrays the colony as not wealthy, but working steadily toward better times.   Argues that the ideals practiced by the colonists constituted a "churchless religion."

1918. ———.   "They Shared Equally." *Sunset*, July, 1924, pp. 21-3, 80-2.
First of three parts of a series describing the history and life of the colony.   The articles are largely upbeat, although colony problems are discussed at several points. Wooster was a long-time member of the colony; these articles are an important historical resource.

1919. Young, Sid. *Crisis in Llano Colony, 1935-1936.* Los

Angeles: author, 1936. 93 pp.
A lengthy account of a major fracas within the colony; the author is a staunch supporter of George T. Pickett, the manager of the colony whose leadership is being attacked.

# LXXXVII. THE ALCANDER LONGLEY COMMUNITIES

Alcander Longley was the inveterate founder of many short-lived communes, mainly small ones, and publisher of communitarian periodicals. Here follow the names, locations, and dates of his ventures:

Reunion (Jasper County, Missouri): 1868-71.
Friendship Community (Dallas County, Missouri): 1872-77.
Principia (Polk County, Missouri): ca. 1880
Mutual Aid Community (Bollinger County, Missouri): 1883-87
Altruist Community (Jefferson County, Missouri): 1907-09.

Some material on the Longley communities is in the American Communities Collection at Syracuse University.

Survey work: Albertson (item 27), 419; Liefmann (item 125), 22-3; Okugawa (item 139), 203, 205.

*Community periodicals*

1920. *Altruist*. 1885-1917. Edited by Alcander Longley. Continuation of *The Communist* (item 1921, below).

1921. *Communist*. 1868-85. Edited by Alcander Longley. Official publication of various Longley communities; publication began before the first community was formally organized. A complete run of the paper is located at the State Historical Society of Wisconsin.

*Works by the community leader*

1922. Longley, Alcander. *Communism, the Right Way, and the Best Way, for All to Live*. An Essay on the Principles,

Organization, and Practical Details of Liberal
Communism.  Also Containing a Complete System of
Simple Phonography or Rapid Writing.  With Several
Communist Songs, Printed in a New System of Phonetic
Figure Music. St. Louis: n.p., 1880.  108 pp.

1923. ———. *For the Homestead Fund.* [St. Louis: n.p.,
189-?]

1924. ———. *Phonetic Songster, and Simple Phonography.*
St. Louis: n.p., [188-?].
Songs with phonetic spelling of words.

1925. ———. *Reunion; or, The True Family.  A Guide to
Practical Communism.*  St. Louis: n.p., 1867.  31 pp.

1926. ———. *What Is Communism? A Narrative of the Relief
Community.*   St.  Louis:  Altruist  Community,  1890.
Repr., New York: AMS Press, 1976.
A novel about people who theorize about communes and
then found one.  A lengthy book-within-the-book (pp.
173-278)  is  a  treatise  on  the  strengths  of  communal
living.   An  appendix  contains  the  actual  Articles  of
Agreement of the Altruist Community (pp. 414-9).

*Secondary works*

1927. Albertson, Ralph.   "Altruist Community."   "Survey of
Mutualistic  Communities  in  America"  (cited  above  as
item 27), 406-7.
Brief  sketch  of  the  history  and  philosophy  of  the
community.

1928. Bliss, W.D.P.   "Altruist Community."   *New Encyclopedia
of  Social  Reform*  (cited  above  as  item  35),  29.
Provides a brief characterization of the community.

* Bushee, Frederick.   "Communistic Societies in the United
States" (cited above as item 35), 639-40.
A  sketch  of  Longley's  life  and  commune-founding
ventures.

* Carroll, H.K.   *Religious Forces of the United States*
(cited above as item 40), 116.
Provides  a  copy  of  the  community's  statement  of

principles.

* Fogarty, Robert S. "American Communes, 1865-1914" (cited above as item 74), 153.
Contains a list of Longley's several communities.

1929. ———. "Longley, Alcander." *Dictionary of American Communal and Utopian History* (cited above as item 76), 69-70.
Biographical dictionary entry.

1930. Grant, H. Roger. "Alcander Longley and the Friendship Community: An 1872 Account." *Missouri Historical Society Bulletin* 31 (January, 1975): 79-90.
An edited presentation of an account of a visit to Friendship, published in the Buffalo *Reflex* in 1872. Provides a brief account of Longley's earlier relations with William H. Bennett; presents Longley's optimisic views about the future of his community. Also presents Longley's response to the news story as published.

* Grant, H. Roger. "New Communitarianism" (cited above as item 86), 65.
Provides an overview of the Friendship Community.

1931. Hinds, William Alfred. "Altruist Community." *American Communities and Co-operative Colonies* (cited above as item 95), 486-7.
Outlines Longley's plans for his new community.

* Lauer, Robert H., and Jeanette C. Lauer. *Spirit and the Flesh* (cited above as item 120), 192-3, 203.
Describes a threat of mob action which forced the Friendship Community to relocate; tell of internal conflict within the Reunion Colony over traditional marriage and fidelity.

1932. Kent, Alexander. "Altruist Community of St. Louis, Mo." "Cooperative Communities in the United States" (cited above as item 117), 634-5.
Outlines the philosophy of the Altruist Community and Longley's goals for its future.

1933. Sears, Hal D. "Alcander Longley, Missouri Communist: A History of Reunion Community and a Study of the Constitutions of Reunion and Friendship." *Bulletin of*

*the Missouri Historical Society* 25 (January, 1969): 123-37.
Contains a biography of Longley and a history of the Reunion Community, along with a brief note on the Friendship Community.

1934.    ———. *Sex Radicals*. Lawrence: Regents' Press of Kansas, 1977.
Contains information on Longley's ideas about sexuality; he eventually rejected tinkering with tradition and became a strong advocate of conventional marriage.

1935.    Solis, Miguel J. "Friendship Community." *American Utopias* (cited above as item 20), 51.
Provides a brief description of the community plus a bibliographical entry.

1936.    Taylor, R. Bruce. "Altruist Community." "Communistic Societies of America" (cited above as item 163), 787.
Contains a brief overview description of the community.

*        Yarmolinsky, Avraham. *Russian's American Dream* (cited above as item 363), 14-21.
Describes the association of the William Frey family with Reunion Community and the life of the community at that time. When the community failed in 1870, the Freys and Stephen Briggs set out to establish a new community, ending up in Cedar Vale, Kansas, where they founded the Progressive Community.

# LXXXVIII. LOPEZ ISLAND COLONY

A colony was founded on Lopez Island in northwest Washington in 1912 by some 150 Pentecostalists seeking to escape the temptations of modern society. They built homes and several other buildings, including a power plant. Income came from wood sold to a sawmill and from outside employment on the part of some members. The group was weakened during World War I when Thomas Gourley, its leader, opposed the war and encouraged his young men to shun the draft. Gourley was evicted in 1916 amid rumors of misappropriated funds; thereafter the community began to break up.

Survey work:  Curl (item 52), 40; Okugawa (item 139), 230.

*Secondary works*

1937.  LeWarne, Charles P.    "'And Be Ye Separate': The Lopez
       Island Colony of Thomas Gourley."    *Communal Societies*
       1 (Autumn, 1981): 19-35.    Previously published in *Puget
       Soundings* (November, 1979) and *Pacific Northwest
       Themes* (edited by James W. Scott.    Bellingham,
       Washington: Center for Pacific Northwest Studies,
       Western Washington University, 1978).
          Provides an overview history of the colony.    Well
       documented from primary sources.

*          ————.    "Communitarian Experiments in Western   Wash-
       ington, 1885-1915" (cited above as item 122), 532-3.
          Provides a brief historical sketch, including essentially
       the same material found in the author's published book
       (following item).

*          ————.    *Utopias on Puget Sound* (cited above as    item
       124), 227-8.
          Provides a brief historical sketch of the colony.

1938.  Marshall, Margaret.    "Solitary Settler at Hunter's Bay:
       'Grandpa' Wilson Is Last Remaining Resident of Lopez
       Island Religious Colony."    Seattle *Times*, December 4,
       1944, magazine section, p. 11.
          Describes the colony and Lee Wilson, who with his
       wife stayed on Lopez after the breakup of the colony.

# LXXXIX.  THE LORD'S FARM

   Mason T. Huntsman, who took the name Paul Blaudin
Mnason and was known to participants in this commune as the
"New Christ," was the motive personality at the Lord's Farm,
started at Woodcliff, New Jersey, in 1889.    No private property
was held by anyone; the commune was open to all and
undertook to feed anyone who showed up at its door.    The
commune's economy, such as it was, was agricultural,
specializing in the growing of fruit on the Farm's 23 1/2 acres.
Problems soon were legion:    the authorities repeatedly
intervened in community life; freeloaders and outright robbers

plagued the group; many cranks showed up to live there.   40 members were reported in 1906.   Accusations by neighbors that some members practiced nudity provided more headaches and legal problems.   The dissolution came when Mnason was evicted from the property.

Survey work: Okugawa (item 139), 215.

*Secondary works*

1939. Albertson, Ralph.   "Lord's Farm."   "Survey of Mutualistic Communities in America" (cited above as item 27), 392-3.
         Provides a sketch of the movement, emphasizing its anarchy.

1940. Cohen, David Steven.   "Angel Dancers."   *New Jersey History* 95 (Spring, 1977): 5-20.
         Provides a history of the group; tracks the rumors of nudity and promiscuity which haunted the group, concluding that they were probably without foundation. Documented extensively with local materials not cited here.

1941. Fogarty, Robert S.   "Huntsman, Mason T."   *Dictionary of American Communal and Utopian History* (cited above as item 76), 57.
         Biographical dictionary entry.

1942. Hinds, Alfred.   "Lord's Farm."   *American Communities and Co-operative Colonies* (cited above as item 95), 442-3.
         Provides a brief sketch of the community.

1943. Kent, Alexander.   "Lord's Farm."   "Cooperative Communities in the United States" (cited above as item 117), 635-6.
         Provides a characterization of the oddities of the colony, noting that members advocated such causes as wearing long hair, vegetarianism, avoiding medicine, and drinking only water.

1944. Schroeder, Theodore.   "Anarchism and the Lord's Farm." *Open Court* 33 (October, 1919): 589-607.
         Provides a somewhat hostile sketch of life at the

commune.

1945. ———. "Psychology of One Pantheist." *Psychoanalytic Review* 8 (July, 1921): 314-28.
Describes Mnason's behavior and ideas, and makes a sort of psychological assessment of him.

1946. ———. "Unique Blasphemy Case." *Truth Seeker* 47 (March 13, 1920): 170-1.
Declares Mnason's conviction and punishment on a blasphemy charge based on the "new Christ" claim to be only the latest in a long line of heresy hunts perpetrated by the established clergy.

* Strachey, Ray, and Hannah Whitall Smith. *Group Movements of the Past and Experiments in Guidance* (cited above as item 161), 145-6.
Provides a brief and not entirely reliable history of the Lord's Farm. Characterizes it as lasting from 1877 well into the 20th century, much longer than most accounts give it.

1947. Wooster, Ernest S. "Lord's Farm." *Communities of the Past and Present* (cited above as item 175), 66-70.
Provides an overview of the community, the information coming principally from Schroeder's article (item 1944).

# XC. MACEDONIA COOPERATIVE COMMUNITY

The Macedonia Cooperative Community was founded in 1937 by Morris Mitchell (1895-1976), a liberal southern educator. Between 1935 and 1937 he purchased land (ultimately 1100 acres) near Clarkesville in northeastern Georgia and began to develop it into an intentional community named after the nearby Macedonia Baptist Church. By 1939 four families were living there. The first major problems arose when the community's pacifism was unpopular during World War II. Things improved somewhat after the war (the population reached 47 in 1952), but other problems (especially a damaging fire) occurred during the early 1950s. After 1953 the community had considerable contact with the Bruderhof, and began moving toward a more explicitly religious center. Late in 1957, some members became novices in the Bruderhof and moved to its communities; others dispersed. The property was sold in 1958.

The papers of the community are housed in the Swarthmore College Peace Collection. The Morris R. Mitchell papers are in the Southern Historical Collection, University of North Carolina Library, Chapel Hill.

## Primary work

1948. *Macedonia    Cooperative    Community:    Report—1948.*    Glen Gardner, New Jersey: Libertarian Press, 1948.    20 pp.
Provides a survey of the community's history and its guiding principles, along with a description of its current status, including its balance sheet.    Copies are located at Swarthmore College and at Community Service, Inc.

## Works by the community leader

1949. Mitchell, Morris R.    "Conserving Values in Group Living." *Childhood    Education*  20  (February,  1944):  247-9.
Argues that children need to be educated to work at finding creative solutions to problems, to cooperate, to avoid conflict.

1950. ———.    "Habersham    County    in  the  Awakening  South." *Progressive    Education*  17  (December,  1940):  517-23.
Provides an overview of community life and history in a very upbeat fashion.

## Secondary works

1951. Ball, Lamar O.    "Hard Labor Is Foundation of Utopia." Altanta *Constitution*, July 23, 1939, p. 3.

1952. Eaton, Joseph W.    "Macedonia Co-operative Community." *Exploring Tomorrow's Agriculture* (cited above as item 59), 204-6.
Tells, with an optimistic tone, the story of the founding and development of the community.

* Gladstone, Arthur.    "Cooperative Communities Today II"

(cited above as item 82), 15.
Describes the industries of the community, including the dairy and timber businesses, as well as the nursery and preschool.

1953. Infield, Henrick. "Macedonia in Georgia, U.S.A." *Utopia and Experiment* (cited above as item 108), 226-231.
Contains a basic overview of the progress made at Macedonia.

1954. ———. "Macedonia, the Case of a 'Clean Bill of Health.'" *American Intentional Communities* (cited above as item 104), 39-72.
Provides a basic overview of the community's history and development, including a late update from the author's recent visit to the community. Also discloses the results of sociological testing of the community.

1955. ———. "Macedonia, the Case of the 'Clean Bill of Health.'" *Cooperative Living* 6 (Winter, 1954-5): 1-12.
Presents the findings of a sociological study of the community, conducted through individual testing of members. Concludes that the community is very healthy and is overcoming the enormous problems associated with its founding. Contains much statistical information similar to that in item 1954, above, but in abbreviated form.

1956. ———. "Matador and Macedonia: A Veterans' and Conscientious Objectors' Community." *Cooperative Group Living* (cited above as item 109), 192-223.
A comparative study of the Matador colony (in Saskatchewan) and Macedonia. Provides demographic data, plus several charts and sociograms.

1957. Kramer, Wendell B. "Macedonia Co-op Community." "Criteria for the Intentional Community" (cited above as item 118), 68-71.
Provides a historical sketch of the community.

1958. Newton, David. "Macedonia Community." *Politics* 5 (Winter, 1948): 27-30. Reprinted under the title "Problems of the Co-operative Colony." *Introduction to Social Science.* Edited by Arthur Naftalin et al. Chicago: Lippincott, 1953, book 3, pp. 318-23.

Pictures a meager but satisfying life in the community shortly after World War II. Written by an active member of the community.

1959. Orser, W. Edward. "Macedonia Coooperative Community (1937-58) and the Quest for a Communal Center." *Prospects: An Annual of American Cultural Studies* 4 (1979): 365-87.
Stresses the hope the community provides to idealists looking for decentralized economic alternatives during the depression and World War II; also discusses the criticism that colonists were escapist, leveled by other pacifists and intellectuals.

1960. ———. "Morris R. Mitchell (1895-1976): Social and Educational Visionary." *Appalachian Journal* 4 (Winter, 1977): 100-4.
Provides a biographical sketch of Mitchell and an overview history of Macedonia. Illustrated with a photograph of Mitchell late in life.

1961. ———. *Searching for a Viable Alternative: The Macedonia Cooperative Community, 1937-58.* New York: Burt Franklin and Co., 1981.
The principal monograph on the community.

1962. Wiser, Art. "Macedonia Community." *Cooperative Group Living* (cited above as item 109), 13-21.
Describes the community, its founder, its economic enterprises, and its physical facilities.

# XCI. MANKIND UNITED

In 1934 a book entitled *Mankind United* appeared in California. It told of a plot to enslave the world, and of a heroic countereffort which had been in place since 1875. Now those leading the countereffort were going public with their actions, and a man of mystery, later identified as Arthur L. Bell, was their public representative. The book predicted that Mankind United, working for the forces of good, would eventually effect an earthly paradise for its members, featuring great prosperity and leisure. At its peak the group had many thousands of followers; some have claimed counts as high as

250,000. In 1943 Bell established Christ's Church of the Golden Rule, the communal part of the movement. Persons who joined it gave all they owned to the movement and were assigned to communal living quarters. They lived Spartan lives under a stringent code of conduct. Bell disappeared in 1951 and the group dwindled.

## Community periodical

1963. *Weekly Message*. Newspaper of the movement.

## Primary works

Mankind United published many pamphlets which are not listed here. Some of them have been collected at the Institute for the Study of American Religion.

1964. *Mankind United*. N.p.: International Registration Bureau, 1934.
The manifesto of the organization. Features a visionary description of an ideal, socialized world to come; provides a scenario for the overthrow of the "hidden rulers" of the world.

## Secondary works

1965. Dohrman, H.T. *California Cult: The Story of "Mankind United."* Boston: Beacon, 1958. 163 pp.
The basic monograph and sociological study of the group.

* Faris, Robert E.L. *Social Disorganization* (cited above as item 66), 415-6 (second edition, pp. 578-80).
Provides a brief history of the movement.

* McWilliams, Carey. *Southern California Country* (cited above as item 126), 265-8.
Describes Arthur Bell and his promises, his demands on the movement's members, and the seeming resemblance of the movement and its ideas to the earlier I AM movement.

1966. "Mankind United." *Un-American Activities in California:*

*Report of the Joint Fact-Finding Committee on Un-American Activities in California.* Sacramento: State Printer, 1943, pp. 353-82.
The proceedings of a government investigation into the movement, primarily featuring the testimony of witnesses.

1967. Mathison, Richard. "Mankind United." *Faiths, Cults and Sects of America: From Atheism to Zen* (cited above as item 127), 196-202.
Characterizes Arthur Bell and the growth of the group; provides a detailed account of its decline and demise.

1968. "Profit's Prophet." *Time*, May 21, 1945, pp. 20-1.
Depicts Bell as a swifty who has purchased much real estate and has built an empire on the labor of his unpaid followers.

# XCII. MAY VALLEY COOPERATIVE

Several Seattle-area residents began looking toward developing a housing co-operative in the years following World War II, and after several years of meetings and planning, purchased 37 acres near Renton in the 1950s. At first lots were individually owned, but gradually the community moved toward mutual ownership. The first members moved onto the site in 1957. The community was deliberately racially integrated from the beginning, and was reported to be thriving in the mid-1970s.

*Community periodicals*

1969. *MVC Bulletin.* In publication in 1972.

1970. *Together.* Newsletter. In publication in the 1950s.

*Works by a community leader*

1971. Affolter, John. "Land Planning: May Valley Cooperative Community." *Communities* no. 16 (September/October, 1975): 42-4.
Chronicles the lengthy land planning activities of the community.

1972. ———. "May Valley Co-op." *Communities* no. 6 (December 1973-January 1974): 14-7.
An account of the development of the community by one of its founding members. Covers the first stirrings of persons interested in community in 1949, the galvanizing encounter with representatives of the Bruderhof in 1953, the purchase of the land, and the gradual movement toward fuller community.

## Secondary works

\* Bouvard, Marguerite. *Intentional Community Movement* (cited above as item 37), 91, 100.
Makes brief references to the community, attributing its origin to the ideas of Ralph Borsodi and Mildred Loomis.

1973. "May Valley Co-op Community." *Intentional Communities: the 1959 Yearbook of the Fellowship of Intentional Communities* (cited above as item 807), 33-4.
Contains a description of the May Valley project.

# XCIII. MODJESKA'S COLONY

In the winter of 1875 a group of Poles began talking about moving to warm California, where land was said to be fertile and cheap, and founding a Polish version of Brook Farm. Among those interested in the project was Helena Modjeska, the leading Polish actress of the day and the wife of Karol Bozenta Chlapowski, a nobleman. Anaheim, California, was chosen as the location where they would settle; at first they rented a small house there, and in 1876 Chlapowski bought a 40-acre farm. One member of the community was Henryk Sienkiewicz, who later wrote the best seller *Quo Vadis?* Modjeska soon left to take a theatrical tour, and a bad drought in 1877 destroyed the farm's agricultural prospects. Moreover, some of the Poles got homesick and returned to Poland. The community broke up; Modjeska went on to enjoy a successful career on the American stage, living in Orange County between tours.

Many biographical accounts of Modjeska touch on the community, but those which do so only in passing are not listed here.

Modjeska's scrapbook is in the New York Public Library Theatre Collection.

Survey work: Okugawa (item 139), 207.

### Work by the community leader

1974. Modjeska, Helena.    *Memories and Impressions of Helena Modjeska.*    New York: Macmillan, 1910.    571 pp. Illustrated.
Modjeska's memoirs, including much anecdotal material about the colony.    Most of the material on the colony is found in chapters 34-6, pp. 283-305.

### Secondary works

1975. Albertson, Ralph.    "Modjeska Colony."    "Survey of Mutualistic Communities in America" (cited above as item 27), 407.
Provides a brief sketch of the colony, calling it "misguided."

1976. Altemus, Jameson.    *Helena Modjeska.*    New York: J.S. Ogilvie, 1883.  217 pp.

1977. Coleman, Arthur Prudden, and Marion Moore Coleman. *Wanderers Twain: Modjeska and Sienkiewicz.*    Cheshire, Connecticut: Cherry Hill-Books, 1964.    111 pp.
Contains scattered references to and anecdotes about the colony, especially in chapter 9 (pp. 57-64).

1978. Coleman, Marion Moore.    *Fair Rosalind: The American Career of Helena Modjeska.*    Cheshire, Connecticut: Cherry Hill Books, 1969.  1019 pp.
An exhaustive biography which mentions the Anaheim colony frequently.    The most concentrated material on the colony is in chapters 6 and 7, pp. 41-56.    The account is well documented, much of the documentation coming from letters and contemporary press notices of Modjeska's acting career.

1979. ———.    "Modjeska and That 'Colony' in California." *Straz* (Scranton, Pennsylvania), October 28, 1976. Argues that the Modjeska farm really wasn't much of a commune, especially because of its brief life span.

1980. Cook, Mabel (Collins). *Story of Helena Modjeska.* London: W.H. Allen and Co., 1883. 296 pp.

1981. Fogarty, Robert S. "Modjeska, Helena." *Dictionary of American Communal and Utopian History* (cited above as item 76), 77-8.
Biographical dictionary entry.

1982. Hinds, William Alfred. "Polish Brook-Farm." *American Communities and Co-operative Colonies* (cited above as item 95), 444-51.
Primarily a reproduction of an account of the colony from a Los Angeles newspaper, ca. 1901.

\* Hine, Robert V. *California's Utopian Colonies* (cited above as item 98), 137-140.
Contains a scholarly account of the history of the community.

1983. Kosberg, Milton L. *Polish Colony of California 1876-1914.* San Francisco: R & E Research Associates, 1971, pp. 18-41.
Originally an M.A. thesis at the University of Southern California (1952). Describes Modjeska's life in Poland, the move to California, the cultural life of the colony, and the scattering of its inhabitants when it closed.

1984. Kowalik, Jan. *Modjeska Bibliography.* San Jose: American-Polish Documentation Studio, 1977. 51 pp.
A comprehensive bibliography of Modjeska (the majority of the citations are to articles in Polish). Lists many articles which refer briefly to the colony; the more important ones are also cited in this list.

1985. Lee, Ellen K. "Helena Modjeska: the California Years." *Polish Americans in California 1827-1927 and Who's Who.* Edited by Jacek Przygoda. Los Angeles: Polish American Historical Association—California Chapter, n.d. (ca. 1977).

\* McWilliams, Carey. *Southern California Country* (cited above as item 126), 139-41.
Provides a brief account of the founding of the colony and the rationale for its location (primarily the climate

and the proximity of German-speaking people).

1986. "Modjeska." *Scribners Monthly Magazine* 17 (March, 1879): 665-71.
Focuses primarily on Modjeska's stage career.

1987. "Modjeska-Land." *Westways*, September, 1939, pp. 24-5.
Provides a few anecdotes of life at the colony, plus information on other legacies of Modjeska's life in Orange County.

1988. "Modjeska's Life in California." *Overland Monthly* 57 (February, 1911): 117-85.
Discusses the selection of the colony's site and facilities on the property; provides anecdotes of group life, and describes the decline of the colony when its novelty wore off. Illustrated with photographs of Modjeska in her later years in California, but none of the pictures comes from the communal era.

1989. Morley, Charles. Foreword to "Chinese in California" by Henryk Sienkiewicz. *California Historical Society Quarterly* 34 (December, 1955): 301-2.
Provides an overview of the colony and of the American career of Sienkiewicz.

1990. Payne, Theodore. *Life on the Modjeska Ranch in the Gay Nineties.* Los Angeles: Kruckeberg Press, 1962, pp. 18-9.
Provides a brief discussion of the commune. Says that Modjeska and her husband dropped quite a bit of money on the venture, enough that by the end of 1876 they were in financial trouble.

1991. Rubin, Maude. "Modjeska's American Arden." *Rawhide and Orange Blossoms* (cited above as item 147), 139-54.
Discusses the planning process which led the group to America; recreates, in semifictional form, slices of colony life.

1992. Solis, Miguel J. "Modjeska Colony." *American Utopias* (cited above as item 20), 92-3.
Contains a brief description of the enterprise plus three bibliographical entries.

1993. Stephenson, Terry E. *Shadows of Old Saddleback.* Santa

Ana: Fine Arts Press, 1948, pp. 21-38.
Contains material on Modjeska and the geographical setting of her home. The period dealt with primarily is one later than the communal one, but the commune is mentioned briefly.

\* Strachey, Ray, and Hannah Whitall Smith. *Group Movements of the Past and Experiments in Guidance* (cited above as item 161), 85-6.
Contains a brief characterization of the colony, saying that it had one happy year before it broke up.

1994. Wooster, Ernest S. "Mme. Modjeska's Colony." *Communities of the Past and Present* (cited above as item 175), 65.
Portrays the colony as having failed soon after its establishment due to a lack of practical knowledge and skills by its members.

# XCIV. THE MOLOKANS

The Molokans split from the Doukhobors in Russia in the eighteenth century, some groups of them taking up communal living there. In 1904 the first group of them settled in America, in East Los Angeles; other centers developed soon thereafter, most of them with a strong sense of ethnic identity and, frequently, cooperative economic institutions such as grocery stores. Several rural experiments with cooperative or communal structures were started; the most perfectly communal was located in Glendale, Arizona, in 1911, with over 100 families. The group grew cotton, but a sudden drop in cotton prices in 1921 wiped them out.

*Secondary works*

1995. Berokoff, John K. *Molokans in America.* Los Angeles: Stockton-Doty, 1969, pp. 40-3, 56-62.
Provides a history of the Molokan colony in the Guadalupe Valley in Baja California and of the Arizona commune; also provides brief descriptions of several other Molokan colonies in California, Washington, Utah, and Oregon.

1996. Conybeare, Frederick C. *Russian Dissenters.* New York: Russell and Russell, 1962, pp. 289-330. Originally published in 1921.
Contains no American material, but provides a clear exposition of Molokan history, teachings, and practices in Russia, including information on the "communists," a subsect practicing community of goods.

1997. Moore, Willard B. "Communal Experiments as Resolution of Sectarian Identity Crises." *International Review of Modern Sociology* 6 (Spring, 1976): 85-102.
Sketches the history of the Molokans in Russia and America, focusing on their cooperative and communal projects in the United States.

1998. Moore, William Haas. "Prisoners in the Promised Land." *Journal of Arizona History* 14 (Winter, 1973): 281-302.
Describes the resistance of the Arizona Molokans to draft registration in World War I, a course which led many of them to go to prison. Based on the author's M.A. thesis, "Prisoners in the Promised Land: The Story of the Molokans in World War I" (Arizona State University, 1972).

1999. Schmieder, Oscar. "Russian Colony of Guadalupe Valley." *University of California Publications in Geography* 2 (1928): 409-34.
Describes the Molokan community in Baja California, depicting the area's geography and the Molokan adaptation to it.

2000. Young, Pauline V. *Pilgrims of Russian-Town.* Chicago: University of Chicago Press, 1932. 296 pp.
Describes the attempts of the Molokans in Los Angeles to maintain a tight, noncompetitive community in modern urban America. Contains an extensive bibliography on the Molokans.

# XCV (A). MORMON COMMUNALISM

The first Mormon experimentation with communitarianism came in the early 1830s, just after the founding of the church. However, the major communal undertaking came in Utah in the meddle 1870s, and the Mormons are therefore included in this volume. Since the three bibliographies of this series are keeping their communal "families" intact, all Mormon-derived communalism is included here, even though some of it took place prior to 1860.

In 1874 Brigham Young, the president of the Mormon church, urged members to organize themselves into local outposts of the United Order of Enoch, as the communal way of life was known. Although the majority of Mormons, including Young, never joined the United Order groups, several groups enjoyed varying degrees of success. The most successful of all was Orderville, in southern Utah, which operated on a fully communal basis from 1874 to 1884, with a peak membership of over 600.

Some of the earlier Mormon communitarian projects took place in Kirtland, Ohio, and Independence, Missouri. Another communal project was begun at San Bernardino, California, in 1851; the colony soon became an important grain and cattle supplier to Salt Lake City. The economy was communal; settlers lived in private homes. By 1856, 200 persons lived there. However, growing internal dissent had put the colony on the verge of abandonment when Brigham Young recalled all outlying settlers to Salt Lake in 1857.

A few years before Mormon communitarianism started in earnest in 1874, a model which should be followed later was undertaken in northern Utah at Brigham City. A cooperative general store was founded in 1864; several cooperative industries led to growth and prosperity. In the late 1870's following the death of Brigham Young and amid the general decline of the United Order, the town drifted toward privatization. Although communalism was gone by the 1880's, Mormon cooperative economic ventures have continued to the present.

Much manuscript material is in Salt Lake City and in various stake and ward headquarters. See Leonard Arrington et al., *Building the City of God* (item 2014, below), for bibliographical notes on such items.

Survey work: Okugawa (item 139), 206

### Primary works

2001. *Book of Mormon*, Mosiah, chapter 4. Provides some of the scriptural basis for Mormon communitarianism.

2002. *United Order.* Articles of Association. Salt Lake City: n.p., 187-? 19 pp.

2003.  *United Order.*  Instructions for Members of the United
       Order. N.p.: 1874? 32 pp.


                              *Secondary works*

2004.  Albertson, Ralph.  "Mormon Communities."  "Survey of
       Mutualistic Communities in America" (cited above as
       item 27), 382-4.
       Outlines the history of the *United Order* at
       Independence and in Utah; also provides a brief history
       of the Thompsonite Mormons.

2005.  Allen, Edward J.  *Second United Order Among the
       Mormons.*  New York: Columbia University Press, 1936.
       Repr., New York: AMS Press, 1967.

2006.  Anderson, Nels.  *Desert Saints: The Mormon Frontier in
       Utah.*  Chicago: University of Chicago Press, 1942.
       Discusses the United Order from the time of Joseph
       Smith's alleged revelations about it onward, including the
       early efforts to establish it in Independence and
       occasional flurries of interest in it from that time until
       the major push in the 1870's.  Includes an extended
       discussion and analysis of the Utah phase, pp. 300-2 and
       361-89.

2007.  Arndt, Karl J.  "Harmonists and the Mormons." *American-
       German Review* 10 (June, 1944): 6-9.
       Argues that the model on which much of Mormonism
       was based was the Harmony Society of George Rapp.

2008.  Arrington, Leonard J.  *Brigham Young: American Moses.*
       New York: Knopf, 1985, pp. 376-81.
       Discusses Young's crucial and formative role in the
       development of the United Order in Utah.

2009.  ———.  "Cooperative Community in the North: Brigham
       City, Utah." *Utah Historical Quarterly* 33 (Summer,
       1965): 198-217.
       Describes the cooperative store and industries which
       made the town a forerunner of the United Order.
       Illustrated.

2010.  ———.  "Early Mormon Communitarianism: The Law of
       Consecration and Stewardship." *Western Humanities*

*Review* 7 (Autumn, 1953): 341-69.
Discusses the beginnings of communal sentiment among the Mormons as early as 1831; analyzes the contribution thinking made to the growth of Mormon communitarian thinking by Sidney Rigdon, whose communal group "The Family" was already established when they joined the Mormons as a body; discusses the first brief attempt to establish a United Order community in Ohio, and the similar attempt shortly thereafter at Independence and elsewhere in Missouri; and describes the suspension, at Nauvoo, of the "law" commanding the development of communalism. An important source for the early period of Mormon communalism.

2011. ———. Great Basin Kingdom. Cambridge: Harvard University Press, 1958, pp. 321-49.
Provides a history of the United Order, describing the Brigham City cooperative, the origins of the United Order in southern Utah, and its eventual decline and replacement with Zion's Central Board of Trade. Argues that there were four kinds of United Orders in various localities, ranging from fully communal towns to cooperative businesses operated by local Mormon churches. Other references to the United Order are scattered throughout the book.

2012. ———. Orderville, Utah: A Pioneer Mormon Experiment in Economic Organization. *Logan: Utah State Agricultural College Monograph Series* 1 (March, 1954).

2013. Arrington, Leonard J., and Davis Bitton. *Mormon Experience*. New York: Knopf, 1979, pp. 125-6, 331.
Provides a brief sketch of Mormon cooperative and communal projects. Describes Carol Lynn Pearson's play about Orderville (item 2050) as exemplifying Mormonism's new, broader outlook.

2014. Arrington, Leonard J., Feramorz Y. Fox, and Dean L. May. *Building the City of God: Community and Cooperation Among the Mormons*. Salt Lake City: Desert Book Co., 1976. 497 pp.
An in-depth study of Mormon communitarianism. Surveys community and cooperation from the beginnings to the present-day Mormon welfare system. Provides substantial information on specific Mormon United Order experiments, including Orderville, St. George, and several

others. Nine appendicies contain primary documents and lists of United Order experiments. Extensive references in endnotes.

2015. Bassett, T.D. Seymour, Donald Drew Egbert, and Stow Persons. "Early Religious Communism." *Socialism and American Life* (cited above as item 3), vol. 2, p. 182.
Provides a bibliographic overview of Mormon communitarianism.

\*        Beadle, John Hanson. *Life in Utah or, Mysteries and Crimes of Mormonism* (cited below as item 2071), 405-6.
Contains a brief historical sketch of the San Bernardino community.

2016. Calverton, Victor F. "Mormon Dream." *Where Angels Dared to Tread* (cited below as item 39), 127-73.
Provides a basic history of the Mormons and information about their early cooperative schemes; describes Mormon cooperative projects in Utah and the ideals and organization of the United Order.

2017. Carter, Kate, ed. "United Order." *Heart Throbs of the West*. Salt Lake City: Daughters of Utah Pioneers, 1947, v. 1, pp. 50-71.
Describes the founding of the United Order and the life at Order communities of Orderville and Glenwood. Pp. 53-6 contain rare information on the United Order of Northern Utah. Also reproduces United Order Articles of Association and Bylaws, instructions for members of the Order, and "Rules that Should Be Observed by Members of the United Order."

2018. Creer, Leland H. "Mormonism." *Encyclopedia of the Social Sciences*. Edited by Edwin R.A. Seligman. New York: Macmillian, 1933, v. 11, pp. 14-7.
Argues that Sidney Rigdon's interest in the work of Robert Owen led the Mormons to found the first United Order. Mentions communal ownership of land and canals, along with the development of cooperative commercial institutions in Utah.

2019. Davies, J. Kenneth. *Mormon Gold: The Story of California's Mormon Argonauts*. Salt Lake City: Olympus, 1984, pp. 303-17.
Describes the founding and development of the San

Bernardino colony, emphasizing its role in helping Mormons working in the gold country and the Sierra Nevada. Illustrated with one photograph.

2020. DePillis, Mario S. "Development of Mormon Communitarianism, 1826-1846." Ph.D. dissertation, Yale University, 1960. 391 pp.
A history of the earliest phase of Mormon communitarianism, with an examination of its sources in the lives and minds of Joseph Smith and his associates.

2021. ———. "Early Mormon Communitarianism." Communities no. 68 (Winter, 1985): 39-42.
Describes the early Mormon plan for a series of Cities of Zion, ideal communal settlements.

2022. *Doctrine and Covenants.* Salt Lake City: Church of Jesus Christ of Latter-day Saints, 1949.
Chapter 42 is the original law of consecration and stewardship, which sets forth the principle of community of goods. Also pertinent to the topic of the United Order are parts of chapters 38, 45, 51, 57-61, 78, 82, and 104.

2023. Ely, Richard T. "Economic Aspects of Mormonism." Harper's Monthly Magazine 106 (April, 1903): 667-78.
Concerns Mormon economic cooperation in a broad sense, covering more than just one United Order. Also contains general information on Mormonism. Illustrated with photographs.

2024. Ericksen, Ephraim E. *Psychological and Ethical Aspects of Mormon Group Life.* Chicago: University of Chicago Press, 1922, pp. 49-55.
Discusses the United Order and particularly the role of Zion's Cooperative Mercantile Institution in providing exchange among the various United Order colonies. Argues that increased interest in communalism came at a time of increasing industrialization in Utah, shortly after the arrival of the railroad in 1870.

2025. Evans, David W., ed. *Journal of Discourses.* Liverpool: Albert Carrington, 1875. Repr., Los Angeles: Gartner Printing and Lithographing Co., 1956.
Texts of speeches by Mormon leaders, including many, chiefly by Brigham Young, pushing the United Order.

2026.  Fielding, R. Kent.    "Mormon Economy in Kirtland, Ohio."
       *Utah Historical Quarterly* 27 (October, 1959): 331-56.
       Describes the earliest functioning of the United Order
       in Kirkland, among other topics.

2027.  Fox, Feramorz Y.    "Experiment in Utopia: The United
       Order of Richfield, 1874-1877."    *Utah Historical
       Quarterly* (Fall, 1964): 355-80.
       Describes the settlement of this southern Utah area
       and the establishment of the United Order there under
       Joseph A. Young, son of Brigham.    Depicts the basic goal
       of economic equality, management and labor policies, the
       economics of the Order, and its dissolution in the late
       1870's.

2028.  Gardner, Hamilton.    "Communism Among the Mormons."
       *Quarterly Journal of Economics* 37 (1922-3): 134-74.
       Discusses the original concept of the United Order, of
       which all Mormons would be members.    Provides an
       overview of United Order activities in Missouri and Utah

2029.  Gates, Susa Young.    *Life Story of Brigham Young.*    New
       York: Macmillan, 1930, pp. 156-62.
       Describes the early revelations on communitarianism
       claimed by Joseph Smith, the beginnings of community in
       Kirtland an Missouri, and the efforts made by Brigham
       Young to institute it in Utah; provides a hagiographic
       presentation of the ideals of Young on cooperation and
       self-reliance.

2030.  Geddes, Joseph A.    *United Order Among the Mormons
       (Missouri Phase).*    Salt Lake City: Deseret News Press,
       1924.
       Provides a detailed examination of an early phase of
       Mormon communalism.

2031.  Hayden, Dolores.    "Eden Versus Jerusalem."    *Seven
       American Utopias* (cited above as item 90), 104-47.
       Portrays the city-building and utopian dreams of the
       Mormons, especially at Nauvoo, Illinois.    Heavily
       illustrated with photographs, mas, and diagrams.

*      Hine, Robert V.    *California's Utopian Colonies* (cited
       above as item 98), 132-7.
       Describes the San Bernardino Mormon settlement of
       1851, one of the first Mormon communal projects.    It

predated the Utah United Order colonies by over two decades.

\* ———. *Community on the American Frontier* (cited above as item 99), 210-3, 216.
Provides a historical sketch of Mormon colonies in Utah, focusing on Orderville.

2032. Houston, Flora Belle. "Mormons in California, 1846-1857." M.A. thesis, University of California, Berkeley, 1929. 106 pp.

2033. Israelson, L. Dwight. "Economic Analysis of the United Order." *Brigham Young University Studies* 18 (Summer, 1978): 536-62.
Enumerates hypotheses describing the economic situations of various United Orders. Lists all known United Order communities. Contains statistical tables and graphs.

2034. Jenson, Andrew. *Encyclopedic History of the Church of Jesus Christ of Latter-Day Saints.* Salt Lake City: Deseret News Publishing Co., 1941. 976 pp.
A dictionary of Mormon history with entries on Mormon localities, including United Order groups, and Mormon sectarian movements.

2035. ———. "Orderville: An Experiment on a Communistic System, Called the 'United Order.'" *Utah Genealogical and Historical Magazine,* July, 1916: 128-41.
Provides an extensive excerpt from a manuscript on Orderville history written by Edward M. Webb, secretary of the United Order there; reproduces the text of the Rules and Regulations of the Orderville United Order; furnishes extracts from letters and newspaper articles describing the town, its economic system, its philosophy, and its dissolution.

2036. ———. "Orderville Ward." *Encyclopedic History of the Church of the Church of Jesus Christ of Latter-Day Saints* (cited above as item 2034): 621-2.
Encyclopedia entry providing a brief history of Orderville and its United Order.

2037. ———. "San Bernardino, California." *Encyclopedic History of the Church of Jesus Christ of Latter-Day*

*Saints* (cited above as item 2034): 766-8.
Provides an outline history of the San Bernardino
Mormon colony.

2038. Larson, Gustive O.    *Prelude to the Kingdom: Mormon
      Desert Conquest.*    Francestown, New Hampshire:
      Marshall Jones Co., 1947.
      An account of the gathering of the Mormons in Utah,
      with several scattered references to the United Order
      and other cooperative work.

2039. Leone, Mark P.    "Evolution of Mormon Culture in
      Eastern Arizona."    *Utah Historical Quarterly* 40
      (Spring, 1972): 122-41.
      A history of the United Order in northeastern Arizona,
      on the Little Colorado River, from 1876 until about 1885.

2040. Lum, Dyer D.    *Social Problems of Today, or The Mormon
      Question in Its Economic Aspects; a Study of
      Cooperation and Arbitration in Mormandom, from the
      Standpoint of a Wage-Worker.*    Port Jervis, New York:
      D.D. Lum and Co., 1886.
      A sympathetic account of Mormon cooperation,
      including the United Order experiment.

2041. McBrian, Dean D.    "The Economic Content of Early
      Mormon Doctrine."    *Southwestern Political and Social
      Science Quarterly* 6 (September, 1925): 179-91.
      Argues that understanding Mormonism requires the
      study of its economics as well as its doctrine and
      history.    Outlines Joseph Smith's economic system and
      his indictment of the prevailing economic system in the
      larger society.    Describes some Mormon efforts to
      implement their system within their own society.

2042. McNiff, W.J.    *Heaven on Earth: A Planned Mormon
      Society.*    Oxford, Ohio: Mississippi Valley Press, 1940.
      Repr., New York: AMS Press, 1974. 261 pp.
      A social history of the Utah phase of Mormonism, with
      general information on the United Order.    Contains a
      useful bibliography.

2043. May, Dean L.    "Towards a Dependent Commonwealth."
      *Utah's History.*    Edited by Richard D. Poll.    Provo:
      Brigham Young University Press, 1978, pp. 230-4.
      Discusses the idea of Mormon economic communism,

particularly as it related to larger economic issues in Utah.

2044. Midgley, J[oshua] H. *United Order.* Salt Lake City: n.p., n.d. 73 pp.
A manifesto for a communal economy, one which incorporates many elements of the Mormon plan, but never specifically calls itself Mormon.

2045. Muir, Leo J. *Century of Mormon Activities in California.* Salt Lake City: Desert News Press, n.d. Two volumes, 512 and 471 pp.
Volume I tells in some detail of Mormon colonizing in California, focusing on San Bernardino on pp. 78-86 with a detailed account of the origins of the colony, specific information about its erection, and the recall of the colonists to Utah in 1857. Provides many names, dates, and genealogies. Volume II provides, on pp. 61-8, biographical sketches of leaders of the colony, including Charles J. Hunt, Amasa M. Lyman, and Charles C. Rich.

2046. Nelson, Lowry. *Mormon Village: A Study in Social Origins.* Provo: Brigham University Press, 1930. Reprinted from *Proceedings of the Utah Academy of Sciences* 7 (1930): 11-37.
Contains much specific information on layout of the original Mormon plan for the City of Zion, the ideal Mormon communal town. Also discusses cooperation in the Mormon towns. Illustrated with maps.

2047. O'Dea, Thomas F. *Mormons.* Chicago: University of Chicago Press, 1957, pp. 186-221 plus other scattered references.
Summarizes the *Law of Consecration* and the relationship of public and private holdings in Utah. Describes life at Orderville and the later church welfare plan.

2048. Palmer, William R. "United Order in Utah." *Improvement Era* 45 (December, 1942): 788-9, 820; 46 (January, 1943): 24-5; 46 (February, 1943); 86-7, 116.
Part 1: Distinguishes between the United Order and socialism/communism; explains the meaning of the original United Order (in pre-Utah times). Part 2: Describes the founding of the United Order in Utah, showing how it differed from the earlier projects. Part 3: Describes the workings of the Untied Order; provides a sketch of life

at Orderville; provides a copy of the bylaws of the United Order of Cedar City; explains the decline of the movement.

2049.  Patton, Annaleone D.   *California Mormons by Sail and Trail.*   Salt Lake City: Deseret Book Co., 1961, pp. 133-48.
Tells the story of the founding and development of the community and the fort, the gradual broadening of the community as nonmormons settled in the area, and the shock of the recall of the Mormons to Salt Lake City. Contains an extensive biography of primary sources and pieces from the contemporary popular press.

2050.  Pearson, Carol Lynn.   *Order is Love.*   Provo, Utah: Trilogy Arts, 1971.  96 pp.
A play about the United Order set in Orderville.   Not seen.

2051.  Pendleton, Mark A.   "Orderville United Order of Zion." *Utah Historical Quarterly* 7 (October, 1939): 141-59.
Describes the exploration and earliest settlement of the Orderville area, the beginnings of the town and its United Order, colony life, and the decline which set in after the U.S. government cracked down on polygamy. Contains a copy of the application from prospective members had to complete.

2052.  Peterson, Charles S.   *Take up your Mission: Mormon Colonizing Along the Little Colorado River 1870-1900.* Tuscon: University of Arizona Press, 1973.  309 pp.
Describes several United Order colonies in Arizona; tells of internal problems in the communities as well as problems with water, Indians, and Arizona politics.

2053.  Raup, Hallock Floy.   *San Bernardino, California: Settlement and Growth of a Pass-Site City.*   Berkeley and Los Angeles: University of California Publications in Geography 8, University of California Press, 1940, pp. 1-63.
Discusses the Mormon decision to locate a colony at San Bernardino, the settling of the colony, its communal economy, and the closing of the colony in 1857. Illustrated with several maps.

2054.  Reilly, P.T.   "Kanab United Order: The President's

Nephew and the Bishop." *Utah Historical Quarterly* 42 (Spring, 1974): 144-64.
Describes the origins of the United Order in St. George, focusing on the role of John R Young in developing the United Order of Kanab and other small towns in southern Utah.

2055. Roberts, B.H. *Comprehensive History of the Church of Jesus Christ of Latter-Day Saints.* Salt Lake City: Deseret News, 1930. Six volumes.
Tells of Joseph Smith's disapproval of the communalism of the followers of Sidney Rigdon and their consequent disbanding after joining the Mormons (v. 1, p. 243). Discusses the earliest "law of consecration" as it was introduced in Ohio in 1831; it was then largely a system of sharing one's surplus with others (v. 1, pp. 246-7). Chronicles the rise of the United Order in Utah from the first efforts of Brigham Young to establish it in 1874 through the backing away from it under President John Taylor in 1882; discusses problems which kept the United Order from being universal in Mormonism (v. 5, pp. 484-98).

2056. Robinson, Phil. *Sinners and Saints.* Boston: Roberts Brothers, 1883, pp. 208-15; 219-34. Section on Orderville reprinted under the title "Orderville Brethren" in *Among the Mormons: Historic Accounts by Contemporary Observers.* Edited by William Mulder and A. Russell Mortensen. New York: Knopf, 1958, pp. 393-8.
A traveler's view of Mormon life in Utah, with specific material on the United Order experiments at Orderville and Kingston.

2057. Sataty, Nechama. "Utopian Visions and Their Critics: Press Reactions to American Utopias in the Ante-Bellum Era." Ph.D. dissertation, University of Pennsylvania, 1986. 749 pp.

2058. Seegmiller, Emma Carroll. "Personal Memories of the United Order." *Utah Historical Quarterly* 7 (October, 1939): 159-200.
A personal memoir of Orderville life, rich in color and anecdote. Contains some specific information, such as a list of the 94 persons who initiated the experiment. Contains parts of letters and other original documents;

reproduces the "United Order Song."

2059.  Smith, Joseph F.   "Truth About Mormonism."   *Out West* 23 (September, 1905): 239-55.
       A response, by the President of the Mormon Church, to criticisms being leveled against his movement.   Pp. 244-8 focus on the United Order, describing the original communal ideals of Joseph Smith, Jr., the early activities trying to put those ideals into practice, and the Mormon tithing system.

2060.  Solis, Miguel J.   "Mormons."   *American Utopias* (cited above as item 20), 93-102.
       Contains a brief overview of Mormon history plus 41 bibliographical entries, not all of them primarily concerned with the communal phase of Mormonism.

2061.  Stegner, Wallace.   *Mormon Country*.   New York: Bonanza Books, 1942, pp. 108-27.
       Provides a good overview of the Orderville community.

2062.  Talmage, James E.   *Articles of Faith*.   Salt Lake City: Church of Jesus Christ of Latter-Day Saints, 1959, pp. 435-41.
       Provides an official doctrinal statement on stewardship and the ultimate rightness of the United Order.

2063.  Wagner, Gordon E.   "Consecration and Stewardship: A Socially Efficient System of Justice."   Ph.D. dissertation, Cornell University, 1977.  233 pp.
       Provides an analysis of the Law of Consecration and Stewardship as a theoretical system which was never fully implemented; concludes that the Law is rooted in the Mormon view of social justice and is a method of trying to attain the goals of the Mormon social contract.

2064.  Warner, Amos G.   "Cooperation Among Mormons." *History of Cooperation in the United States* (cited above as item 26), 427-39.
       Almost identical to Warner's work the previous year by the same title (item 2065).

2065.  ———.   "Cooperation Among Mormons."   Part 3 of "Three Phases of Cooperation in the West." Publications of the *American Economic Association* 2 (March, 1887): 106-19.

Provides basic information on Zion's Cooperative Mercantile Institution and other cooperative projects.

2066. Werner, M.R. *Brigham Young*. New York: Harcourt, Brace and Co., 1925, pp. 418-50.
Discusses Mormon mechanisms for community maintenance, including the United Order. Contains an extensive bibliography.

2067. West, Ray B., Jr. *Kingdom of the Saints.* New York: Viking, 1957, pp. 311-5.
Gives a brief overview of the United Order, and then discusses Orderville's physical layout, work credit system, economic success, and methods of coping with problems. Attributes part of the decline of the community to antipolygamy raids by federal agents.

2068. Wilson, A.E. "Gemeinwirtschaft und Unternehmungsformen in Mormonstaat." *Jahrbuch fuer Gesetzgebung Verwaltung und Volkswirtschaft* 31 (1907): 1003-1056.
Traces the abandonment of cooperative ventures in Utah. In German.

2069. Young, Brigham. *Discourses of Brigham Young.* Edited by John A. Widtsoe. Salt Lake City: Deseret Book Co., 1925.
This book is a digest of recorded speeches of Brigham Young. Several chapters touch on the United Order; chapter 15, "Tithing; the United Order" (pp. 269-81, and chapter 25, "Unity and Cooperation" (pp, 433-45), present Young's position that communalism represented the will of God and deserved support from all Mormons.

# XCV(B). SECTARIAN LATTER-DAY SAINTS COMMUNALISM

Splinter groups departed from the main body of the Mormons even while founder Joseph Smith was alive, and many such groups were formed during the power struggle which followed his death in 1844. Still more developed in subsequent years. Several of them entered communal living and economic arrangements, and many, especially in rural Utah, practiced polygamy. Note: some of these groups predate the scope of this volume; they are included here because Mormon (main Utah body) communalism did not begin in earnest until after 1860, and the Mormon communal family is presented here as a whole. The customary practice of referring to Mormon splinter groups by the names of their leaders is followed here.

A substantial collection of material on sectarian Latter-Day Saint groups has been collected at the archives of the Reorganized Church of Jesus Christ of Latter Day Saints in Independence, Missouri.

### Secondary works on communal Mormon sectarianism generally

2070. Anderson, J. Max. *Polygamy Story: Fiction and Fact.* Salt Lake City: Publishers Press, 1979. 166 pp.

2071. Beadle, John Hanson. *Life in Utah; or Mysteries and Crimes of Mormonism.* Philadelphia: National Publishing Co., 1870, pp. 402-34.
    A chapter on "Recusant Sects of Mormonism" provides sketches of the groups led by Rigdon, Strang, Wight, and Morris, along with information of the San Bernardino Mormon colony and Heaven Colony.

2072. Melton, J. Gordon. *Encyclopedic Handbook of Cults in America.* New York: Garland, 1986, pp. 39-44.
    Provides overviews of several prominent Mormon fundamentalist groups, including three families of groups practicing communalism as well as polygamy. The groups covered are those founded by Joseph, LeBaron, and Wooley.

2073. Merril, Melissa. *Polygamist's Wife.* Salt Lake City: Olympus, 1975. 167 pp.

2074. Morgan, Dale Lowell. Bibliography of the Churches of the Dispersion. *Western Humanities Review*, 1953. (Introduction published in *Western Humanities Review* 7 [Summer, 1953]: 255-66; introduction plus body of bibliography published at the same time as a separate pamphlet.)
    An introduction to sectarian Mormonism, followed by a 61-page bibliography. The more important accessible items are listed in the appropriate sections below; the bibliography also cites many old and rare items in various church archives. Communal Latter-Day Saints

bodies covered include those led by Rigdon, Wight, Brewster, Thompson, and Cutler.

2075. Religious Bodies: 1936. Washington: Department of Commerce, Bureau of the Census, 1941, v. 2, part 2, pp. 828-39.
Provides statistics and other basic information on the Bickertonites, Cutlerites, and Strangites.

2076. Shields, Steven L. *Divergent Paths of the Restoration: A History of the Latter Day Saint Movement.* Provo, Utah: author, 1975. 282 pp. Third edition, Bountiful, Utah: author, 1982. 282 pp.
Provides brief histories of over 125 Latter-Day Saints groups, including several communal groups. Among the groups presented are the Bickertonites, Cutlerites, Glendenningites, LeBaronites, Morrisites, Rigdonites, Strangites, and Thompsonites. There is also a general discussion of the Mormon fundamentalists on pp. 104-6, and information on several marginal groups not listed in this bibliography.

2077. ———. Latter Day Saint Churches: An Annotated Bibliography. New York: Garland, 1987. 281 pp.
A bibliography covering many different Latter-Day Saints groups. Movements covered include those founded by Bautista, Bickerton, Brewster, Cutler, Glendenning, Gudmundsen, Joseph, Kilgore, LeBaron, Morris, Peterson, Strang, Thompson, Wight, and Zahnd, along with splinters from several of them. Also includes material on LDS factions which may or may not have had communal phases.

# XCV(C). BAUTISTA

Margarito Bautista led the Church of Jesus Christ of Latter Day Saints (Bautista) away from a Mormon group known as the Third Convention in the mid-1930's. Bautista advocated communalism and polygamy; some of his followers believed him to be the expected prophet known as "the one mighty and strong."

*Secondary work*

2078. Shields, Steven L. "Church of Jesus Christ of Latter Day

Saints (Bautista)." *Latter Day Saints Churches* (cited above as item 2077), 144.
Provides an overview of the movement plus three primary bibliographical entries.

2079. ———. "Church of Jesus Christ of Latter Day Saints (Margarito Bautista)." *Divergent Paths of the Restoration* (cited above as item 2076), 142.
Describes the schism which gave rise to this group, its establishment of a colony in Mexico, and its practice of polygamy.

# XCV(D). BICKERTON

William Bickerton was originally a follower of Sidney Rigdon. He broke with Rigdon to found his own group, which was established in 1862. In 1874 the Bickertonites settled near St. John, Kansas. Later some of them withdrew to follow William H. Cadman in a separate community. Bickerton died at St. John about 1903. His followers regrouped and survived although not communally; today their group is headquartered in Monongahela, Pennsylvania.

## Community periodicals

2080. *Gospel News.* Monongahela, Pennsylvania. Published sporadically after 1938 or earlier; monthly, 1945-.

2081. *Gospel Reflector.* Roscoe, Pennsylvania. 1905-10. Monthly.

## Secondary works

2082. Cadman, William H. *History of the Church of Jesus Christ, Organized at Green Oak, Pennsylvania, U.S.A....* Monongahela, Pennsylvania: Church of Jesus Christ, 1945. 413 pp.

2083. Jenson, Andrew. "Bickertonites." *Encyclopedic History of the Church of Jesus Christ of Latter-Day Saints* (cited above as item 2034): 61-2.
Encyclopedia entry on the Bickertonites.

2084. Lovalvo, V. James. *It is Written Truth Shall Spring Out of the Earth.* Fresno: Mid-Cal Publishers, 1980. 325 pp.
The author is one of the twelve apostles of the Bickertonite church.

2085. Melton, J. Gordon. "Church of Jesus Christ (Bickertonite)" and "Primitive Church of Jesus Christ (Bickertonite)." *Encyclopedia of American Religions* (cited above as item 130), 492-4.
Provides historical sketches of the Bickertonite church and a splinter group it spawned.

2086. Morgon, Dale Lowell. "Bibliography of the Church of Jesus Christ." *Western Humanities Review* 4 (Winter, 1949-50): 42-70.
Provides a brief history of the Bickertonite Mormons plus a 55-item annotated bibliography. Also contains a 5-item bibliography of the Re-organized Church of Jesus Christ, a Bickerton splinter.

\* *Religious Bodies: 1936* (cited above as item 2075), v. 2, part 2, pp. 828-33.
Provides statistics and basic information on the history, doctrine, and organization of the Bickertonites.

2087. Shields, Steven L. "Church of Jesus Christ (William Bickerton)." *Divergent Paths of the Restoration* (cited above as item 2076), 89-98.
Describes the ideas, history, and leadership of the movement.

2088. ———. "Church of Jesus Christ (William Bickerton)." *Latter Day Saint Churches* (cited above as item 2077), 229-39.
Contains an introduction and 53 bibliographical entries on the Bickertonites, as well as introductions and brief bibliographies on two Bickerton splinter groups.

# XCV(E). BREWSTER

James C. Brewster established one of the churches of the Mormon dispersion; he had displayed schismatic tendencies even during the lifetime of Joseph Smith. His church was to be communal, but the commune never got very far off the ground, and the church itself collapsed in the early 1850s. The colony which existed briefly in the Rio Grande valley was called Colonia.

## Community periodical

2089. *Olive Branch, or, Herald of Peace and Truth to All Saints.* Kirtland, Ohio; later Springfield, Illinois. 1848-52.

## Works by the community leader

2090. Brewster, James Collins. *Address to the Church of Christ, and Latter Day Saints.* [Springfield, Illinois: author, 1848]. 24 pp.

2091. ———. *Very Important! To the Mormon Money Diggers.* Why Do the Mormons Rage . . . ? . . . [Springfield, Illinois: n.p., 1843]. 12 pp.

2092. ———. *Warning to the Latter Day Saints Generally Called Mormons.* An Abridgment of the Ninth Book of Esdras. Springfield, Illinois: author, 1845. 16 pp.

2093. ———. *Words of Righteousness to All Men, Written from One of the Books of Esaras [sic], Which Was Written by the Five Ready Writers. . . .* Springfield, Illinois: Ballad and Roberts, 1842. 48 pp.

## Secondary works

2094. Jenson, Andrew. "Brewsterites." *Encyclopedic History of the Church of Jesus Christ of Latter-Day Saints* (cited above as item 2034), 85.
Encyclopedia entry on the Brewsterites.

2095. Morgan, Dale Lowell. "Church of Jesus Christ of Latter Day Saints (Brewsterite)." "Bibliography of Churches of the Dispersion" (cited above as item 2074), 141-6.
Provides an introduction to the group plus an eight-item bibliography.

2096. Shields, Steven L. "Church of Christ." *Latter Day Saint Churches* (cited above as item 2077), 37-8.
Provides an introduction to the movement and a brief bibliography including some items not cited here.

2097. ———. "Church of Christ (James Colin Brewster)." *Divergent Paths of the Restoration* (cited above as item 2076), 55-6.
Provides an overview of the movement.

# XCV(F). CUTLER

Alpheus Cutler was the leader of a schismatic group which broke with Brigham Young and settled first in Manti, Iowa, in 1853. After Cutler's death in 1864 the group established the small settlement of Clitherall, Minnesota, in 1865. In their early years they held all property in common; all worked for the church and did not hold outside jobs. A slow decline took place throughout much of the 20th century. In the 1920s an outpost was established in Independence, Missouri.

*Primary work*

2098. *Book of Commandments and Covenants: God's Revelations Through His Holy Prophets.* Independence, Missouri: Church of Jesus Christ, 1978. 604 pp.
Reproduces the original 1835 edition of the Doctrine and Covenants along with additional theological writings.

*Secondary works*

2099. Fletcher, Daisy Whiting. *Alpheus Cutler and the Church of Jesus Christ.* Independence, Mo.: author, 1970. 56 pp.
Provides a biography of Cutler, a sketch of early Mormon history, and a treatise on the organization and history of the Cutlerites.

2100. Fletcher, Rupert J. *Scattered Children of Zion.* Independence, Mo.: author, 1959. 90 pp.

2101. Fletcher, Rupert J., and Daisy Whiting Fletcher. *Alpheus Cutler and the Church of Jesus Christ.* [Independence,

Mo.: Church of Jesus Christ, 1974]. 350 pp.

2102. Jenson, Andrew. "Cutlerites." *Encyclopedic History of the Church of Jesus Christ of Latter-Day Saints* (cited above as item 2034): 168.
Encyclopedia entry on the Cutlerites.

2103. Melton, J. Gordon. "Church of Jesus Christ (Cutlerite)." *Encyclopedia of American Religions* (cited above as item 130), 493.
Provides a brief history of the group.

2104. Morgan, Dale Lowell. "Church of Jesus Christ (Cutlerite)." "Bibliography of the Churches of the Dispersion" (cited above as item 2074), 178-9.
Provides a brief history of the Cutlerites plus one bibliographical entry.

* *Religious Bodies: 1936* (cited above as item 2075), v. 2, part 2, 834-5.
Provides statistics and information on the history and organization of the Cutlerites.

2105. Shields, Steven L. "Church of Jesus Christ (Alpheus Cutler)." *Divergent Paths of the Restoration* (cited above as item 2076), 60-5.
Provides a sketch of Cutlerite history and life.

2106. ———. "Church of Jesus Christ (Alpheus Cutler)." *Latter Day Saint Churches* (cited above as item 2077), 185-9.
Provides introductory material and bibliographies, including items not cited here, for the main body of Cutlerites plus one splinter group.

2107. Young, Biloine W. "Minnesota Mormons: The Cutlerites." *Courage* (Lamoni, Iowa) 3; reprinted in *Restoration* 2 (July, 1983): 1, 5-12.
Provides an overview history of the movement. The author is descended from Cutlerites.

# XCV(G). GLENDENNING

Maurice and Helen Glendenning joined the LDS Church in 1929. However, after Maurice began receiving alleged revelations, they were excommunicated. They began to gather followers, and officially organized their sect, which they called the Aaronic Order, in 1943. They also called themselves "Levites." They founded the community of Partoun in 1949; it had a population of about 60 by 1955. This patriarchal, millennial group has congregations in Salt Lake City and Springville as well as the rural cooperative communities in rural Utah.

### Community periodicals

2108. *Aaron's Star.* Salt Lake City; later New Haven, Indiana. In publication from at least the 1960s through the 1980s.
Newsletter.

2109. *Newsletter of the Order of Aaron.* In publication in the 1950s.

### Primary works

2110. *Book of Elias; or, the Record of John.* . . . Salt Lake City: Aaronic Order, 1944. 101 pp.

2111. *Schematic Chart and Its Explanation of the Order of Aaron and the True Church of God, the Church of Christ, the Church of the Firstborn.* No imprint. 7 pp. mimeographed.
A circular organizational chart centered on the office of the chief high priest, with explanatory notes. At Community Service, Inc., and the Institute for the Study of American Religion.

2112. *Office of the Corporation of the President of the Order of Aaron: a Letter.* Colorado Springs: n.p., February, 1950. 7 pp.
A form letter used to answer inquiries about the movement. Tells the story of the goals of the group, focusing on its theology and ideas. At Community

Service, Inc., and the Institute for the Study of American Religion.

*Work by a community leader*

2113.  Glendenning, Maurice L.  *Church of the First-Born, the Church of Christ, the Church of Jesus Christ, the Church of God: A Treatise.*  Salt Lake City: Corporation of the President of the Aaronic Order, 1955. 119 pp.

*Secondary works*

2114.  Baer, Hans A.  "Aaronic Order: The Development of a Modern Mormon Sect." *Dialogue* 12 (1979): 57-71.
Describes the group's expulsions of members thought to be leaning excessively toward fundamentalist Protestantism, which led to a major schism about 1975. Not seen.

2115.  ———.  "Field Perspective of Religious Conversion: The Levites of Utah." *Review of Religious Research* 19 (Spring, 1978): 279-94.
Studies 35 conversions to the movement, finding that the most consistent factor in conversion was a sense of ethical, economic, social, or psychic deprivation.

2116.  ———.  "Levites of Utah." *Proceedings of the Central States Anthropological Society, Selected Papers* 3 (1977): 9-16.
Describes the early development of the group and its communities and the interest many members had in the Koyle Relief Mine; analyzes the group's growth as it moved away from Mormonism toward Protestant fundamentalism.

2117.  ———.  *Levites of Utah: The Development of and Conversion to a Small Millenarian Sect.*  Ph.D. dissertation, University of Utah, 1976. 357 pp.
Provides an ethnography of the group, a recounting of its origin and development, and an examination of conversions to it, including factors which predisposed individuals to join the group.

2118. ———. *Recreating Utopia in the Desert: A Sectarian Challenge to Modern Mormonism.* Albany: State University of New York Press, 1988. 225 pp.
Provides a historical and anthropological study of the group, covering such topics as conversion, community, and relations with orthodox Mormons. Contains a substantial bibliography.

2119. ———. "Sex Roles in a Mormon Schismatic Group: The Levites of Utah." *Sex Roles in Contemporary American Communes* (cited above as item 167), 111-54.
Provides a brief description of the movement and finds that women are limited in power and authority in this patriarchal community. A bibliography cites several publications of the movement.

2120. Beeston, Blanch W. *Now My Servant: A Brief Biography of a Firstborn Son of Aaron.* Caldwell, Idaho: Caxton Printers, 1957. 216 pp.
A biography of Glendenning. Not seen

2121. ———. *Purified as Gold and Silver.* Caldwell, Idaho: Caxton Printers, 1966. 315 pp.

2122. Buchanan, Frederick S., and Larry W. Stott. "The EskDale Commune: Desert Alternative to Secular Schools." *Intellect* (January, 1974).
Describes the Order of Aaron's private communal school.

2123. Erickson, Ralph D. "History and Doctrinal Development of the Order of Aaron." M.A. thesis, Brigham Young University, 1969. 159 pp.

2124. Melton, J. Gordon. "Aaronic Order." *Encyclopedia of American Religions* (cited above as item 130), 481-2.
Provides an overview of the history, organization, and teachings of the group.

2125. "Order of Aaron." *Intentional Communities: 1959 Yearbook of the Fellowship of Intentional Communities* (cited above as item 807), 481-2.
Provides a brief introduction to the Glendenningites.

2126. Shields, Steven L. "Order of Aaron." *Latter Day Saints Churches* (cited above as item 2077), 144-7.

Provides an introduction to the movement and a bibliography of 24 items, many of them primary materials not cited here.

2127. ———. "Order of Aaron (Maurice L. Glendenning)." *Divergent Paths of the Restoration* (cited above as item 2076), 146-52.
Presents the history, beliefs, and leadership of the movement.

## XCV(H). GUDMUNDSEN

Moses Gudmundsen and his brother filed for homesteads at West Tintic, Utah, in 1918; he encouraged friends to do the same, and eventually developed a colony of about 60 members. At first the group adhered to the main Mormon church, but Gudmundsen's claim of a new revelation soon separated his followers from the main church. The colony disbanded in 1921.

*Secondary works*

2128. Culmsee, Carlton. *Modern Moses at West Tintic*. Logan: Utah State University Press, 1967. 40 pp.

2129. Shields, Steven L. "Moses Gudmundsen." *Divergent Paths of the Restoration* (cited above as item 2076), 117-8.
Provides a brief historical sketch of the group.

2130. ———. "Moses Gudmundsen." *Latter Day Saint Churches* (cited above as item 2077), 143.
Provides a historical sketch of the group and a single bibliographic entry.

## XCV(I). JOSEPH

Alexander Joseph founded a polygamous colony now located at Big Water, Utah, in 1974, known as the Church of Jesus Christ of Solemn Assembly. Joseph had previously been involved in Mormon fundamentalism under Rulon Allred.

Work by the community leader

2131. Joseph, Alexander. *Dry Bones: A Resurrection of Ancient Understandings.* Glen Canyon City, Utah: University of the Great Spirit Press, 1979. 208 pp.

*Secondary works*

2132. Melton, J. Gordon. "Church of Jesus Christ in Solemn Assembly." *Encyclopedia of American Religions* (cited above as item 130), 484-5.
Provides a brief statement of the group's history, organization, and teachings.

2133. ———. "Church of Jesus Christ in Solemn Assembly." *Encyclopedic Handbook of Cults in America* (cited above as item 2072), 41.
Provides a brief historical sketch of the group.

2134. Riesen, Phil. *Nickel's Worth: Channel 4 Television Interview with Polygamist A. Joseph.* Salt Lake City: Dennis R. Short, [1977?] 36 pp.

2135. Shields, Steven L. "Church of Jesus Christ on Solemn Assembly." *Latter Day Saint Churches* (cited above as item 2077), 170-1.
Provides an introduction to the group plus two bibliographical entries.

2136. ———. "Church of Jesus Christ of Solemn Assembly (Alexander Joseph)." *Divergent Paths of the Restoration* (cited above as item 2076), 197.
Outlines the history, doctrine, and publications of the movement.

# XCV(J). KILGORE

Founded in Phoenix in 1951, Zion's Order soon moved to a site near Mansfield, Missouri. The founder, Marl V. Kilgore, a former member of the Glendenningite Aaronic Order, claimed to have received hundreds of revelations providing direction for his group. The group has been active in missionary work among the Navajo.

Secondary work

2137. Shields, Steven L.    "Zion's Order of the Sons of Levi."
      *Divergent Paths of the Restoration* (cited above as
      item 2076), 155-8.
      Provides a brief overview of the group.

2138. ———.    "Zion's Order of the Sons of Levi."    *Latter
      Day Saint Churches.* (cited above as item 2077), 147-8.
      Provides a brief sketch of the group and nine primary
      bibliographical entries.

# XCV(K).  LEBARON

Alma Dayer LeBaron started a dissident communal Mormon
church, the Church of the Firstborn of the Fulness of Times,
in the early 20th century, and various of his sons took up the
cause, founding several offshoot groups in the process.
Feuding among the LeBaron brothers culminated in the death of
one of them, Joel, at the instigation of another, Ervill.   Ervill
later died in prison.    The largest part of the church is located
in Galeana, Chihuahua, Mexico.    Several groups have split from
the original one; they are combined in a single listing here.

*Community periodical*

2139. *Ensign.*    Official LeBaronite publication.    El Paso.    1961-
      mid-1960s. Monthly.

2140. *Ensign News.* 1984-5.

*Primary works*

2141. *Economic Reformation Begins: The Preservation of
      American Liberty.*  No imprint. 8 pp.
      Argues that we must separate ourselves from the
      economic bondage we suffer by joining separatist groups.
      At the Institute for the Study of American Religion.

2142. *Law of Consecration.*  Not imprint. 10 pp.
      An exposition of the LeBaronite view of the Law of

Consecration, the United Order, and tithing. At the Institute for the Study of American Religion.

## Works by community leaders

2143. [LeBaron, Ervil] *Priesthood Expounded.* Colonia LeBaron, Mexico: Mexican Mission of the Church of the Firstborn of the Fulness of Times, 1956. 56 pp.
Describes the leadership and priesthood of the LeBaronite church; also contains some information on the history of the church and the LeBaron family.

2144. LeBaron, Joel F., and Siegfried J. Widmar. *Thus Joel Taught.* Colonia LeBaron: Church of the Firstborn of the Fulness of Times, 1984. 105 pp.

2145. LeBaron, Ross W. *Church of the Firstborn.* LeBaron, Mexico: Church of the Firstborn, [1962?]. 32 pp.
Contains the author's purported revelations. Not seen.

2146. LeBaron, Verlan M. "Economic Democracy Under Eternal Law—The Economic Government of God." *Ensign* 3 (June and July, 1963).
A treatise on LeBaronite economic ideas, including information on its version of the United Order.

2147. ———. *LeBaron Story.* Lubbock, Texas: author, 1981. 316 pp.
An insider version of the LeBaron story, heavily documented from primary sources.

## Secondary works

2148. Bradlee, Ben Jr. "Mormon Manson." *New Times*, March 6, 1978, pp. 38-43.
A historical account of the LeBaron movement, focusing on the family's best-known member, Ervil, known for his homicidal ways as well as for his leadership of a polygamous commune.

2149. Bradlee, Ben Jr., and Dale Van Atta. *Prophets of Blood: the Untold Story of Ervil LeBaron and the Lambs of God.* New York: G.P. Putnam's Sons, 1981.
An account of Ervil LeBaron, his group, and the

murders they have been accused of.

2150. Butchereit, John G. *Priesthood and Prophecy: Comprehensive Issues of Our Time Treated in an Open Letter to the Fundamentalists.* Salt Lake City: Church of the Firstborn of the Fulness of Times, 1962. 68 pp.

2151. Collier, Fred C. *Priesthood and the Law of Succession.* N.p.: 1978.

2152. Jensen, Earl L. "Abuse of the Rights of Religious Liberty: Crime of the Age." *Ensign* 3 (August, 1963): 1-8.
Vigorously denounces the LDS Church for its errors and its alleged abuse of the LeBaronites religious liberty. Argues that the LeBaron church is the true repository of Mormon practice.

2153. Liddiard, Thomas J. *Government of the Church of God: A Sufficient Answer to Henry Richards and the LDS Church.* LeBaron, Mexico: Church of the Firstborn of the Fulness of Times, 1968. 261 pp.

2154. Melton, J. Gordon. "Church of the First Born," "Church of the First Born of the Fulness of Times," "Church of the Lamb of God," and "Millennial Church of Jesus Christ." *Encyclopedia of American Religions* (cited above as item 130), 485-6.
Provides a brief historical sketch of the main body, with a briefer item on Ervil LeBaron's violence.

2155. ———. "Church of the First Born of the Fullness of Times." *Encyclopedic Handbook of Cults in America* (cited above as item 2072), 41-3.
Provides a good synopsis of the complex history of the LeBaron clan.

2156. Richards, Henry W. Reply to "The Church of the Firstborn of the Fullness of Times." Salt Lake City: Deseret News Press, 1965. 159 pp.
A rebuttal of LeBaronite priesthood claims in the form of a letter to Stephen M. Silver, a member of the LeBaronite church. Contains photocopies of early LeBaronite documents.

2157. Shields, Steven L. "Benjamin T. LeBaron," "Church of

the Firstborn of the Fulness of Times (Joel F. LeBaron)," "Church of the Lamb of God (Ervil M. LeBaron)." *Divergent Paths of the Restoration* (cited above as item 2076), 142-3, 159-63, 189-90.
Traces the history and ideas of several parts of the LeBaron movement.

2158. ———. "Church of the Firstborn," "Church of the Firstborn of the Fulness of Times," and "Church of the Lamb of God." *Latter Day Saint Churches* (cited above as item 2077), 150-61, 167-9.
Provides overviews of the main branches of the LeBaron movement and substantial, largely primary, bibliographies for each, listing many works not cited here.

2159. Shore, David T. "Gathering of the Saints." *Ensign* 4 (November, 1964): 1-8.
Describes the LeBaronite gathering of persons to participate in a re-established United Order.

2160. Silver, Stephen M. "Priesthood and Presidency: An Answer to Henry W. Richards." *Ensign* 2 (January, 1963): 1-127.
A statement of LeBaronite ideas on the priesthood; part of an ongoing debate between Richards and Silver.

2161. Stubbs, Lawrence Ritchie. *Freedom from Economic Bondage: The Blessings of Eternal Life: Zion's Redemption.* No imprint. 45 pp.
A LeBaronite tract urging the living of the United Order. At the Institute for the Study of American Religion.

2162. Tucker, William P. *In Reply to Bruce R. McConkie.* Galeana, Chihuahua, Mexico: Colonia LeBaron, 1963. 38 pp.
A vigorous reply to an LDS critic of the LeBaron movement, focusing primarily on issues relating to the priesthood. At the Institute for the Study of American Religion.

2163. Widmar, Siegfried. *Kingdom.* [N.p.: Church of the Firstborn of the Fulness of Times, 1975]. 77 pp. At the Institute for the Study of American Religion.

2164. ———. *Political Kingdom of God is at Hand.* El Paso: author, 1975. 107 pp.
    Presents the LeBaronite argument for religious liberty, which includes the freedom to practice polygamy and communal living.

2165. Wright, Lyle O. "Origins and Development of the Church of the Firstborn of the Fulness of Times." M.S. thesis, Brigham Young University, 1963. 268 pp.


# XCV(L). MORRIS

Joseph Morris was converted to Mormonism in his native Britain by missionaries in 1848. He soon thereafter moved to the United States and ended up at Salt Lake City in 1854. He had already claimed to have had revelations at that time, and they persisted in Utah. In 1861 he organized a communal settlement of followers along the bank of the Weber River within thirty miles of Salt Lake City; by 1862, its population was in the hundreds. In June, 1862, the settlement was overrun by a territorial posse of Mormons following as armed battle, and Morris and others were killed. Other believers scattered. Several new prophets came forward to claim Morris's mantle, but few had notable success. Some Morrisite factions were still in existence as late as the 1950s.


*Works by the community leader*

2166. Morris, Joseph. *Spirit Prevails: Containing the Revelations, Articles, and Letters.* San Francisco: George S. Dove, 1886. 684 pp.


*Secondary works*

2167. Anderson, C. LeRoy. *For Christ Will Come Tomorrow: The Sage of the Morrisites.* Logan: Utah State University Press, 1981. Revised edition (with illustrations) entitles Joseph Morris and the Saga of the Morrisites, 1988. 263 pp.
    The major monograph on the Morrisites. Contains a good bibliography of primary and secondary materials.

2168. ———. "Scattered Morrisites." *Montana: The Magazine of Western History* 26 (October, 1976): 50-69.
Traces the careers of leaders of various Morrisite factions after the 1862 battle down to the death of the last leader, George Johnson, in 1954. Illustrated with photographs. Documentation contains many rcfcrcnccs to primary sources, most of them in manuscript.

2169. Anderson, C. LeRoy, and Larry J. Halford. "Mormons and the Morrisite War." *Montana: the Magazine of Western History* 24 (Autumn, 1974): 42-53.
Provides a history of Morris and his movement. Presents various historical and psychological analyses of the episode. Illustrated with photographs and engravings.

2170. Banks, John. "Document History of the Morrisites in Utah." B.A. thesis, University of Utah, 1909. 94 pp.

\* Beadle, John Hanson. *Life in Utah; of Mysteries and Crimes of Mormonism* (cited above as item 2071), 413-27.
Describes the revelations claimed by Morris and his excommunication from the Mormon church; provides a detailed account of the "Morrisite War" and its aftermath.

2171. Cannon, M. Hamlin. "Morrisite War." *American West* 7 (November, 1970): 4-9, 62.
Describes the 1862 battle and events leading up to it; tells of the fate of the followers in the dispersion which followed the fighting, especially in regard to legal proceedings against surviving Morrisites. Illustrated with photographs and drawings.

2172. Dove, George S. *Voice from the West to the Scattered People of Weber and All the Seed of Abraham.* San Francisco: Dove, 1879. 39 pp.

2173. Halford, Larry J. "Mormons and Morrisites: A Study in the Sociology of Conflict." Ph.D. dissertation, University of Montana, 1972. 140 pp.

2174. Howard, G.M. "Men, Motives, and Misunderstandings: A New Look at the Morrisite War of 1862." *Utah Historical Quarterly* 44 (Spring, 1976): 112-32.
Provides a biography of Morris, an account of his

claimed revelations, the origins of the Morrisite church in 1861, a detailed account of the armed conflict, and an analysis of Morris's appeal to his followers. Illustrated with photographs; documentation includes several references to manuscript sources.

2175. Jenson, Andrew. "Morrisites" and "Morristown." *Encyclopedic History of the Church of Jesus Christ of Latter-Day Saints* (cited above as item 2034): 540-1.
Encyclopedia entries on the Morrisites and on the town in Idaho where some believers settled after the Morrisite war.

2176. Shields, Steven L. "Church of Jesus Christ of Latter Day Saints or Church of the First Born (Joseph Morris)." *Divergent Paths of the Restoration* (cited above as item 2076), 86-8.
Recounts the history and ideas of the Morrisites.

2177. ————. "Church of Jesus Christ of Latter Day Saints of Church of the First Born (Morris)" and "Church of the First Born (Dove)." *Latter Day Saint Churches* (cited above as item 2077), 124-5, 127-8.
Provides an introduction to and bibliography of the Morrisites, plus introductory and bibliographical materials for a group led by George S. Dove, who gathered many of the scattered Morrisites following the death of Morris.

2178. Young, Richard W. "Morrisite War." *Contributor* (Salt Lake City) 11 (June, 1890): 281-4.
Provides much color on life in the Morrisite camp, which was suffused with an expectation of an imminent Second Coming of Christ. Lists the names of the 142 sworn members of the Morrisite military force.

# XCV(M). PETERSON

The United Order of Equality was founded by Ephraim Peterson and others around the turn of the century in Independence, Missouri. It never achieved a large following.

*Works by the community leader*

2179. Peterson, Ephraim. *Ideal City for Ideal People.* [Independence, Missouri: author, 1905.] 134 pp.

2180. ———. *Redemption.* Independence, Missouri: author, [1909]. 140 pp.

*Secondary work*

2181. Shields, Steven L. "United Order of Equality." *Latter Day Saint Churches* (cited above as item 2077), 140-1.
Provides a brief introduction to the group plus four bibliographical references.

# XCV(N) RIGDON

Sidney Rigdon was a Protestant minister with a following who had been interested in communalism before he and his congregation converted to Mormonism in 1832. He tried to assume the leadership of the Mormons after the death of Joseph Smith, but was excommunicated by Brigham Young in September, 1844. Rigdon ended up at Friendship, New York; various of his congregations continued to work toward communalism, although no greatly successful groups emerged.

*Secondary works*

* Beadle, John Hanson. *Life in Utah; or, Mysteries and Crimes of Mormonism* (cited above as item 2071), 403.
Provides a brief sketch of the Rigdonites.

2182. Bowden, Henry Warner. "Rigdon, Sidney." *Dictionary of American Religious Biography* (cited above as item 709), 380-1.
Biographical dictionary entry.

2183. Fogarty, Robert S. "Kirtland Community" and "Rigdon, Sidney." *Dictionary of American Communal and Utopian History* (cited above as item 76), 149-50 and 98, respectively.
Dictionary entries providing an overview of Rigdon's

communal activity both before and after he joined the Mormons.

2184. Gregory, Thomas J. "Sidney Rigdon: Post Nauvoo." *Brigham Young University Studies* 21 (Winter, 1981): 51-67.
Provides a sketch of the Rigdonite movement from Rigdon's excommunication in 1844 through his death in 1876. Provides extensive documentation in footnotes.

2185. McKiernan, F. Mark. "Conversion of Sidney Rigdon to Mormonism." *Dialogue* 5 (Summer, 1970): 71-8.
Describes Rigdon's early life as a revival preacher with an interest in communitarianism, and his conversion and early contributions to Mormonism.

2186. ———. *Voice of One Crying in the Wilderness: Sidney Rigdon, Religious Reformer 1793-1876.* Lawrence, Kansas: Coronado Press, 1971.
A biography of Rigdon.

2187. McKinley, Kenneth William. "Guide to the Communistic Communities of Ohio." *Ohio State Archaeological and Historical Quarterly* 46 (January, 1937): 5-6.
Contains material on over a dozen Ohio communities, including the Rigdonites.

2188. Morgan, Dale Lowell. "Church of Jesus Christ (Rigdonite)" and "Splinter Churches (Rigdonite)." "Bibliography of the Churches of the Dispersion" (cited above as item 2074), 124-31.
A bibliography of early primary Rigdonite literature, including material from groups which splintered from the Rigdonites.

2189. Shields, Steven L. "Church of Jesus Christ of the Children of Zion (Sidney Rigdon)." *Divergent Paths of the Restoration* (cited above as item 2076), 36-9.
Presents the ideas and basic history of the Rigdonites.
Service, Inc., and the Institute for the Study of American Religion.

# XCV(0). STRANG

The Strangites constituted one of the most important early splinter groups. James J. Strang claimed to have received a revelation designating him the successor of the slain Joseph Smith, but his leadership was quickly rejected by the main body of the Mormons. He gathered some followers and established a headquarters in Voree, Wisconsin, where he claimed to dig some character-laden metal plates (the "Voree Plates") from the ground in much the fashion that Joseph Smith had allegedly done a few years earlier. The Voree colony may have had as many as 2,000 members at its peak. In 1847, seeking greater isolation, the group moved to Beaver Island in Northern Lake Michigan. There they survived fairly prosperously for several years; Strang at one point became a Michigan state legislator, and at another time had himself crowned "king" of his little domain. His slaying in 1856 signalled the effective end of the movement, although a few Strangites remain today. Watson Wingfield was the chief leader of the group in the late nineteenth and early twentieth century.

The largest body of Strangite manuscript materials is in the Beinecke Library at Yale University. Other collections are in the Detroit Public Library, and Clarke Historical Library at Central Michigan University. For a list of additional libraries and archives with Strangite manuscripts see Van Noord (item 2287, below), p. 325.

For a more detailed bibliography, especially of primary materials, see Steven L. Shields, "Church of Jesus Christ of Latter Day Saints (Strangite)," in *Latter Day Saint Churches* (item 2278, below).

Survey work: Okugawa (item 139), 191, 195.

### Community periodicals

2190. *Chronicles of Voree.* Burlington, Wisconsin. 1879-?

2191. *Gospel Herald.* Voree, Wisconsin. 1847-50. Revived in the 1940s and ca. 1969-80.

2192. *Latter Day Precept.* Kansas City, Missouri. 1919-20.

2193. *Northern   Islander.*   St.   James,   Michigan.   1850-6.
Weekly; sometimes daily.

2194. *Star in the East.* 1846.

2195. *Voree Herald.* Voree, Wisconsin. 1846.

2196. *Zion's   Reveille* (or   *Voree   Reveille.*   Voree,   Wisconsin.
1846-7.
*Zion's   Reveille,*   the   *Voree   Herald,*   and   the   Gospel
Herald   were   essentially   the   same   publication   with
changing names.  Publication was monthly and weekly.

### *Works by community leaders*

Citations   of   a   few   shorter   Strang   works   and   many   other
editions   of   the   works   listed   here   are   in   the   National   Union
Catalog.

2197. Strang, James J.   *Ancient   and   Modern   Michilimackinac,*
*Including   an   Account   of   the   Controversy   Between*
*Mackinac   and   the   Mormons*   St.   James,   Michigan:
Cooper   and   Chidester,   1854.   48 pp.   Reprinted,   with
new   notes   and   introduction   by   George   S.   May,
Mackinac   Island,   Michigan:   W.   Stewart   Woodfill,   1959.
100 pp.
Contains   a   historical   sketch   of   the   area,   an   account   of
the   history   of   the   colony   to   1854,   and   the   story   of
Strang's election to the Michigan legislature.

2198. ———.   "Beaver   Island   Mormons."   *New   York   Tribune,*
July 2, 1853.
Lengthy   letter   from   Strang   defending   his   movement   in
response   to   press   reports   of   illegal   behavior;   argues   that
his   followers   have   worked   diligently   to   build   their
society and industries and asks for fair treatment.

2199. ———.   *Book   of   the   Law   of   the   Lord.*   St.   James,
Michigan: Royal Press, 1856.
Basic   Strangite   special   scripture,   covering   religion   and
the   conduct   of   life   and   disclosing   God's   framework   for   a
divine government.

2200. ———.   *Catholic   Discussion.*   Voree,   Wisconsin:   Gospel
Herald, 1848.  60 pp.

A tract criticizing the Roman Catholic Church.

2201. ———. *Diamond: Being the Law of Prophetic Succession and the Defense of the Calling of James J. Strang and Successor to Joseph Smith.* Voree, Wisconsin: Gospel Herald, 1848. 19 pp.

2202. ———. *Diary of James J. Strang, Deciphered, Transcribed, Introduced and Annotated.* edited by Mark A. Strand. East Lansing: Michigan State University Press, 1961. 78 pp.
Also contains biographical information on Strang by Russel Nye as well as a lengthy introduction by Mark Strang. This is a diary James Strang kept from 1831 to 1836. Mark Strang has supplied a comprehensive annotated bibliography.

2203. ———. *Few Historical Facts Concerning the Murderous Assault at Pine River; Also the Life, Ministry, Ancestry and Childhood of James J. Strang.* Edited by Charles J. Strang. [Lansing, Michigan: n.p., 1892.]
Written by James Strang about 1855 as the beginning of his autobiography.

2204. ———. *Prophetic Controversy.* St. James, Michigan: Cooper and Chidester, 1856.
Strang's defense of his claim to be the successor to Joseph Smith.

2205. ———. *Revelations of James J. Strang.* Boyne, Michigan: Watson, 1885. Compiled by Wingfield Watson.

2206. ———. "Some Remarks on the Natural History of Beaver Islands, Michigan." Smithsonian Institution. Ninth Annual Report, 1854. Washington: Beverly Tucker, Senate Printer, 1855.
A catalog of the wildlife of the Beaver Islands, focusing principally on fish, especially on the best means of catching them.

2207. Watson, Wingfield. *Book of Mormon: An Essay on Its Claims and Prophecies.* [Burlington? Wisconsin: n.p., 1899.]

2208. ———. *Catholic Discussion.* [Burlington, Wisconsin? n.p., 1902.]

2209. *Friendly Admonition.* [Nauvoo: Rustler Printing, 1913?]

2210.  ———.  *Latter    Day    Signs.*    [Burlington?, Wisconsin: n.p., 1897.]

2211.  ———.  *One    Mighty    and    Strong.*    [Burlington?, Wisconsin: n.p., 1915.]

2212.  ———.  *Open   Letter   to   B.H.   Roberts,   Salt   Lake   City, Utah.* [Burlington? Wisconsin: n.p., 1896.]

2213.  ———.  *Prophetic    Controversy.*    Various    locations, 1887-1918.  A series of pamphlets in defense of Strang.

2214.  ———.  *Watson-Blair   Debate.*    Galien,    Michigan:    W.J. Smith, 1892.

## Secondary works

2215.  Adams,  George  J.    *True   History   of   the   Rise   of   the Church   of   Jesus    Christ    of    Latter    Day    Saints—the Restoration   of   the   Holy   Priesthood.*    Baltimore: Hoffman, [1846?] 44 pp.
Contains    stories    of    alleged    ancient    records    of prehistoric  America,  plus  an  argument  for  the  claim Strang  made  to  be  the  proper  successor  to  Joseph  Smith, Jr.

2216.  Austin,  H.  Russell.    *Wisconsin    Story.*    Milwaukee: Milwaukee Journal, 1948, pp. 102-7.
Provides  a  good  overview  of  the  movement,  covering Strang's  entry  into  Mormonism,  the  establishment  of  his original  community  at  Voree,  the  founding  and development  of  the  Beaver  Island  colony,  Strang's coronation,  and  his  death  and  the  scattering  of  the members.  Illustrated with photographs.

2217.  Backus,  Charles  K.    "American  King."    *Harper's Monthly*  64  (March,  1882): 553-9.    Reprinted  as  King  of Beaver  Island,  with  foreward,  notes,  and  bibliography by  Paul  Bailey.    Los  Angeles:  Westernlore  Press,  [1955]. 43 pp.
Describes  the  origins  of  the  Strangites,  life  on  Beaver Island,  and  the  death  of  Strang.    Illustrated  with  pictures of Strang and of the Voree plates.

2218.  Bates,  George  C.    "Trail  in  This  City  of  King  Strang."

Detroit Advertiser and Tribune, July 12, 1877. Reprinted as "Beaver Island Prophet." *Michigan Pioneer and Historical Collections* 32 (1903): 225-35.

A sharply partisan account of the arrest and trial of Strang on charges of trespassing on public lands in 1851. (Strang was acquitted.) Bates was the prosecuting attorney (who lost) in the case.

\* Beadle, John Hanson. *Life in Utah; or, Mysteries and Crimes of Mormonism* (cited above as item 2071), 403-3.
Provides a brief historical overview of the Strangites.

2219. Bringhurst, Newell G. "Forgotten Mormon Perspectives: Slavery, Race, and the Black Man as Issues Among Non-Utah Latter-Day Saints, 1844-1873." *Michigan History* 61 (Winter, 1977): 351-70.
Argues that Strang had a much more progressive attitude toward blacks than the Utah church did; compares his outlook with that of Charles B. Thompson, another Mormon sectarian. Illustrated with photographs.

2220. Burgess, Charles O. "Green Bay and the Mormons of Beaver Island." *Wisconsin Magazine of History* 42 (Autumn, 1958): 39-49.
Describes the varying coverage given the Beaver Island doings by the papers of Green Bay, especially the *Green Bay Advocate.* Describes the coverage of the Strangites as a combination of truths, half-truths, and myths which were the basis for later misunderstandings of the movement.

2221. Collar, Helen. "Mormon Land Policy on Beaver Island." *Michigan History* 56 (Summer, 1972): 87-118.
Describes the conflict between Mormons and Gentiles on Beaver Island by analyzing land transactions. Finds that the Mormons never secured lawful title to their land.

2222. *Collection of Sacred Hymns; Adapted to the Faith and Views of the Church of Jesus Christ of Latter Day Saints.* Voree, Wisconsin: Gospel Press, 1849. 172 pp.

2223. Couch, Edward T. *Prophetic Office.* Boyne City, Michigan: n.p., 1908. 67 pp.
Several other titles by this author are also listed in the National Union Catalog.

2224. Cowdery, Oliver. *Epistles of Oliver Cowdery on the Bringing in of a New Dispensation.* St. James, Michigan: Cooper and Childester, 1854. 56 pp.
Contains Cowdrey's letters plus commentary by Strang. Not Seen.

2225. Cronyn, Margaret, and John Kenny. *Saga of Beaver Island.* Ann Arbor: Braun and Brumfield, 1958, pp. 31-63.
Contains an informally written history of the Strangites on beaver Island richly laced with local anecdotes and lore.

2226. Cumming, John. "Lorenzo Dow Hickey: The Last of the Twelve." *Michigan History* 50 (March, 1966): 50-75.
Provides a biographical sketch of Hickey, an independent-minded follower of Strang who was a major leader in the movement in the late ninteenth century.

2227. ———. "Wingfield Watson: The Loyal Disciple of James J. Strang." *Michigan History* 47 (December, 1963): 312-20.
Provides a biographical sketch of Watson, who lived at the Beaver Island colony from 1852 to 1856 and became a major leader of the Strangites until his death in 1922.

2228. Curwood, James Oliver. *Courage of Captain Plum.* New York: McKinlay, Stone and Mackenzie, 1912. 320 pp.
A novel about the Beaver Island community and the murder of Strang.

2229. Davis, Marion M. "Stories of Saint Helena Island." *Michigan History Magazine* 10 (1926): 411-46.
Tells of the breaking away of the Strangites from the Mormons and their subsequent settlement on Beaver Island.

2230. Eaton, Conan Bryant. "King Sleeps in Wisconsin." *Wisconsin magazine of History* 40 (Winter, 1956-7): 107-12.
An overview history of Strang and his movement.

2231. Eberstadt, Charles. "Letters That Founded a Kingdom." *Autograph Collectors Journal* 3 (October, 1950): 3-5, 32
Finds that the letter from Joseph Smith to Strang allegedly passing leadership to the latter was not actually

signed by Smith, but that its postmark, which was attacked as fraudulent by Brigham Young and others, was genuine, even though the letter was mailed (from Nauvoo, Illinois) while Strang was in Wisconsin.

* Federal Writers Project. *Michigan: A Guide to the Wolverine State* (cited above as item 68), 603-5.
Provides a historical sketch of the Beaver Island colony, describing daily life in the colony and the death of Strang and dispersal of his followers.

2232. Fitzpatrick, Doyle C. *King Strang Story: A Vindication of James J. Strang, the Beaver Island Mormon King.* Lansing, Michigan: National Heritage, 1970.
A narrative of Strangite history and a refutation of published anti-Strangite materials. Strongly partisan presentation of the position of the contemporary Strangites.

2233. Flanders, Bruce B. "In Defense of James J. Strang." *Restoration* 2 (October, 1983): 13-5.
A rejoinder to the alleged errors contained in Lawrence Foster's article on Strang (item 2237, below).

2234. ———. "Introduction to the Church of Jesus Christ of Latter Day Saints (Strangite)." *Restoration* 1 (July, 1982): 6-7.
A basic account of the Strangite movement, emphasizing its fidelity to original LDS beliefs.

2235. Fogarty, Robert S. "Strang, James Jesse." *Dictionary of American Communal and Utopian History* (cited above as item 76), 109-10.
Biographical dictionary entry.

2236. Forster, John H. "Reminiscences of the Survey of the Northwestern Lakes." *Michigan Pioneer and Historical Collections* 9 ([1886]; repr., 1908): 100-7.
The material on the Strangites is on pp. 106-7. Describes the town of St. James, including the interior of Strang's house. Implies that Strang was wont to drink with visitors and become talkative about life in his movement.

2237. Foster, Lawrence. "James J. Strang: The Prophet Who Failed." *Church History* 50 (June, 1981): 182-92.

Reprinted in *Restoration* 1 (October, 1982): 9-13.
Finds Strang to be the archetype of the failed prophet, a complex and powerful figure whose motivations and ideals have never been fully understood.

2238. ———. *Religion and Sexuality.* New York: Oxford University Press, 1981, pp. 190-5.
Traces the career of Strang, focusing on his rationale for introducing polygamy into his community.

2239. Fulton, Antoinette Meinhardt. "Adventures in Old Voree." *Wisconsin Magazine of History* 33 (June, 1950): 391-402.
Describes activities of the Strangite Mormons at Voree, the digging up of the Voree Plates, and the development of the religious community there; also describes twentieth-century historical preservation work done at the site.

2240. Gregg, Thomas. *Prophet of Palmyra.* New York: John B. Alden, 1880, pp. 312-9.
Contains information on the Strangite movement, with special emphasis on the Voree Plates.

2241. Hanson, Klaus. "Making of King Strang: A Re-examination." *Michigan History* 46 (September, 1962): 201-19.
Focuses on Mormon ideas about theocratic government which influenced Strang. Describes the royal claims of Strang at the time of his coronation.

2242. ———. Quest for Empire. East Lansing, Michigan: Michigan State University Press, 1967, pp. 96-104.
Argues that the Strangite movement failed because Strang's vision was too much like that of Brigham Young, and he therefore failed to rally the many who were unhappy with the political and corporate nature the LDS movement had assumed.

2243. Hickey, Lorenzo Dow. *Card to the Kind and Brave People of utah.* No imprint. 8 pp.

2244. ———. *Card to the Public, Defending Honorable James J. Strang.* [Monte Vista? Colorado: n.p., 1896?] 4 pp.

2245. ———. *Who Was the Successor of Joseph Smith?*

[Coldwater, Michigan? n.p., 1891?] 5 pp.

2246. Holbrook, Stewart. "Rise and Fall of King Strang." *Woman's Day*, April 1955, 36, 94, 96.
Provides a basic account of the Strangites, with a few errors, including an incorrect account of Strang's death.

2247. Holmes, Fred L. *Badger Saints and Sinners*. Milwaukee: E.M. Hale, 1939, pp. 107-20.
Provides a biographical sketch of Strang, focusing on the Wisconsin portions of his career, including the beginnings of his community at Voree.

2248. Horton, Thomas. *True History of the Rise of the Church of Jesus Christ of Latter Day Saints*. Geneva, New York: Gazette, [184-?]. 47 pp.
One of the earliest works depicting Strang as Joseph Smith's proper successor.

2249. Hutchins, James. *Outline Sketch of the Travels of James Hutchins*. Black River Falls, Wisconsin: n.p., 1871. 123 pp.
The National Union Catalog lists several other titles by Hutchins, who was a member of the Strangite Quorum of Twelve at the time of Strang's death.

2250. Jenson, Andrew. "Strangites." *Encyclopedic History of the Church of Jesus Christ of Latter-Day Saints* (cited above as item 1877): 839-40.
Encyclopedia entry on the Strangites.

2251. Kennedy, J.H. *Early Days of Mormonism*. London: Reeves and Turner, 1888, pp. 254-64.
Recounts the history of the Strangites, quoting extensively from the research of F.D. Leslie (item 2256, below).

2252. Leach, Morgan Lewis. "History of the Grand Traverse Region." *Michigan Pioneer and Historical Collections* 32 (1903): 98-138. Facsimile reprint, Mt. Pleasant, Michigan: Central Michigan University Press, 1964.
Principally relates tales of Strangite Mormon depradations—murder, thievery, denial of civil rights to their own people and to others, and so forth; describes local opposition to the group in some detail.

2253. Legler, Henry E.    "King of Beaver Island."  *Chautauquan*
31 (May, 1900): 133-7.
Emphasizes the royal claims and coronation of Strang.
Illustrated with photographs of Beaver Island buildings
and the Voree Plates.

2254.  ———.   "King    Strang's    Press:    A    Bibliographical
Narrative." *Literary Collector* 8 (1904): 33-40.
Describes Strang's publishing house and its prodigious
output of pamphlets, books, and newspapers; discusses the
origins and development of the Strangite movement;
provides an excerpt from the *Book of the Law of the
Lord*.   Contains a facsimile of a page from the *Gospel
Herald*.

2255.  ———.   "Moses    of    the    Mormons."   *Michigan Pioneer
and Historical Collections* 32 (1903): 180-224.
Provides a narrative biography of Strang, plus four
pages of Strang's autobiography, together with other
accounts and memoirs of the Strangites, including other
quotes from Strang's works and a description of the
characters on the Voree Plates.   Contains a bibliography
of Strangite and secondary publications, including
several specialized items not included here.

2256. Leslie, F.D.    "American Kingdon of Mormons."  *Magazine
of Western History* 3 (April, 1886): 645-51.
Tells the story of the Strangites; protests the
persecution they suffered.

2257. Lewis, David Rich.    "'For Life, the Resurrection , and
the Life Everlasting': James J. Strang and Strangite
Mormon Polygamy, 1849-1856."  *Wisconsin Magazine of
History* 66 (Summer, 1983): 274-91.   Reprinted in
*Restoration* 4 (April, 1985): 1, 10-14, 19-20.
Outlines the development of polygamy under a leader
who had criticized the practice of it by the main body of
Mormons a few years earlier.   Illustrated with
photographs.

2258. Mathison, Richard.    "King James I."   *Faiths, Cults and
Sects of America: From Atheism to Zen* (cited above as
item 127), 95-103.
Provides an overview of the movement.

2259. Melton, J. Gordon.    "Church of Jesus Christ of Latter-

Day Saints (Strangite)." *Encyclopedia of American Religions* (cited above as item 130), 494.
Provides a brief historical sketch of the movement.

2260. Miller, Reuben. *Defense of the Claims of James J. Strang to the Authority Now Usurped by the Twelve...* [Keokuk, Iowa: author, 1846]. 16 pp.

2261. ———. *James J. Strang, Weighed in the Balance of Truth and Found Wanting....* [Burlington, Wisconsin: n.p.], 1846. 26 pp.

2262. Morgan, Dale L. "Bibliography of the Church of Jesus Christ of Latter-Day Saints (Strangite)." *Western Humanities Review* 5 (Winter, 1950-51): 49-114.
Brief history of the Strangites plus a 112-item annotated bibliography of the movement, including many references to primary sources from the early years of the movement not cited here.

\* Muncy, Raymond Lee. *Sex and Marriage in Utopian Communities* (cited above as item 135), 150-4.
Discusses the Strangite movement, especially in regard to its claims to authority, its move from Voree to Beaver Island, and its practice of polygamy.

2263. Nichols, Reuben T. *Ministerial Labors of Reuben T. Nichols in the Church of Jesus Christ of Latter Day Saints.* N.p.: 1886? 11 pp.

2264. Nye, Russel B. *Baker's Dozen: Thirteen Unusual Americans.* Lansing: Michigan State University Press, 1963, pp. 162-82.
Describes the separation of the Strangites from the main body of the Mormons, the establishment of the original Strangite colony at Voree, the move to Beaver Island, the development of polygamy, and the murder of Strang and downfall of the movement.

2265. Orrmont, Arthur. "James J. Strang: The King of Beaver Island." *Love Cults and Faith Healers* (cited above as item 141), 51-74.
Sketches Strang's early life, his early days as an orthodox Mormon, life at Beaver Island.

2266. Poling, James. "King of the Beaver Islands." *Treasury*

*of True.* Edited by Charles N. Barnard. Greenwich, Connecticut: Fawcett Publications, 1958, pp. 276-319.
A telling of the story of the Strangites, with some dramatic emphasis which fictionalizes the account slightly.

2267. Poppleton, Orrin. "Tales and Traditions of Northern Michigan, Mackinac Island, King Strang the Mormon and O'Malley the Irish Dragon." *Michigan Pioneer and Historical Collections* 18 ([1891]; repr., 1911): 623-6.
Describes conflicts between Strang and Charles O'Malley, a justice of the peace at Mackinac.

2268. Post, Warren, and Edward Chidester. "James J. Strang." *Journal of History* (published by the Reorganized Church of Jesus Christ of Latter Day Saints) 3 (January, 1910): 72-9.
Contains Post's account of the murder of Strang and his eyewitness report on the mob violence against Strang's followers, along with a brief sketch of Strang's childhood; reproduces Chidester's eyewitness account of Strang's death and burial.

2269. Quaife, Milo M. *Kingdom of St. James: A Narrative of the Mormons.* New Have: Yale University Press, 1930.
A basic monograph on the Strangites. Thoroughly documented, with many references to Strangite periodicals. Appendices reproduce several primary Strangite documents.

2270. ———. "Polygamy at Beaver Island." *Michigan History Magazine* 5 (1921): 333-55.
Debunks the Bates account (item 2218, above) of the arrest of Strang in 1856; details the history of Strangite polygamy, with accounts of the wives and progeny of Strang and what happened to them after the fall of the Beaver Island colony. Based largely on interviews with former members of the colony.

2271. ———. "Utopia—Nineteenth-Century Model." *Lake Michigan* (cited above as item 146), 231-47.
Provides an overview history of the Strangites.

2272. Randolph, Vance. "Beaver Island Kingdom." *Americans Who Thought They Were Gods* (cited above as item 149), 3-7.
Discusses the founding of the Strangites, the

behavioral rules of the movement, the Voree Plates, and the killing of Strang.

\* Religious Bodies: 1936 (cited above as item 2075), v 2, part 2, pp. 836-9.

Provides statistics plus an overview of the history, doctrine, organization, and work of the Strangites.

2273. Riegel, O.W. *Crown of Glory: The Life of James J. Strang, Moses of the Mormons.* New Haven: Yale University Press, 1935.

Puts the Strangite saga into the form of a novel, with consequent factual shortcomings.

2274. Russel, Oland D. "King James I of Michigan." *American Mercury* 46 (March, 1939): 273-81.

Tells the Strang story, emphasizing the strict behavioral rules laid down by the leader.

2275. Russel, William D. "King James Strang: Joseph Smith's Successor?" *Restoration Movement: Essays in Mormon History.* Edited by F. Mark McKiernan, Alma R. Blair, and Paul M. Edwards. Lawrence, Kansas: Coronado Press, 1973, pp. 231-56.

Depicts the early life of Strang, his Mormon years, and the movement he founded. Contains the text of the purported "Letter of Appointment" in which Joseph Smith appointed Strang his successor.

2276. St. Bernard, Alexander. "Murder of King Strang." *Michigan Pioneer and Historical Collections* 18 ([1891]; repr., 1911): 626-7. Reprinted from the *Detroit Free Press*, June 30, 1889.

An eyewitness account of the killing of Strang, provided by Alexander St. Bernard, an officer on the ship which had come to arrest Strang at the time of the murder.

2277. Shepard, William, Donna Falk, and Thelma Lewis, eds. *James J. Strang: Teachings of an American Prophet.* N.p.: Church of Jesus Christ of Latter Day Saints (Strangite), 1977.

A compendium of Strang's writings, with a few notes by his contemporary followers.

2278. Shields, Steven L. "Church of Jesus Christ of Latter Day

Saints (Strangite)." *Divergent Paths of the Restoration* (cited above as item 2076), 40-6.
Presents the history and principles of the Strangite movement.

2279. ———. "Church of Jesus Christ of Latter Day Saints (Strangite)," plus six ensuing articles. *Latter Day Saint Churches* (cited above as item 2077), 41-70.
Provides introductory materials and extensive bibliographical information on the Strangites and six splinters from the movement.

2280. Solis, Miguel J. "Kingdom of St. James." *American Utopian* (cited above as item 20), 90-1.
Provides a brief description of the colony plus one bibliographical entry.

2281. Somers, A.N. "American King." *National Magazine* 14 (May, 1901): 115-21.
Provides an overview history of the movement. Contains pictures of Strang and of hte Voree Plates, as well as a translation of the Plates.

2282. Strang, Charles J. "Beaver Island and Its Mormon Kingdom." *Little Traverse Bay Souvenir* (Lansing, Michigan: n.p., 1895). Also printed in *The Ottawan*. Edited by John C. Wright. Lansing: Robert Smith and Co., 1895, 63-8.
A basic account of the Strangites, told by Strang's son.

2283. ———. "King of the Saints." *New York Times*, September 3, 1882. Reprinted under the title "Michigan Monarchy." *Michigan Pioneer and Historical Collections* 18 ([1891]; repr., 1911): 628-38.
Strang's history of his father's movement, based on information furnished by his mother.

2284. Strang, Clement J. "Why I Am Not a Strangite." *Michigan History* 26 (1942): 457-79.
James Strang's son lists some of his father's good qualities, but expresses disagreement on polygamy, royal government, and other things, and suggests that James Strang was not entirely sincere in his religious teachings. Includes autobiographical information about the author and his family after 1856. Also reproduces a letter from

Eugenia Strang Phillips, daughter of James Strang, providing reminiscences.

2285. Titus, W.A. "Voree." *Wisconsin Magazine of History* 9 (1925-6): 435-41.
Provides a history of the Voree years of the Strangites, outlining Strang's conversion to Mormonism, his acquisition of 105 acres for the original Voree commune, the growth of the Voree community, and the move to Beaver Island. Illustrated with a photograph of a Strangite house.

2286. Utley, Henry M., and Byron M. Cutcheon. *Michigan as a Province, Territory, and State.* New York: Publishing Society of Michigan, 1906, v. 3, pp. 299-310.
Describes the geography of the Beaver Islands; provides a biographical sketch of Strang; details the settlement at Beaver and the internal dissent which led to Strang's murder. Describes the mob action which forced the believers off the island shortly thereafter, calling it "the most disgraceful day in Michigan history."

2287. Van Noord, Roger. *King of Beaver Island: The Life and Assassination of James Jesse Strang.* Urbana: University of Illinois Press, 1988. 335 pp.
The definitive biography of Strang and history of his movement. Meticulously documented. Illustrated with photographs and maps.

2288. Waldron, Webb. "Beavers." *We Explore the Great Lakes* (cited above as item 1033), 291-9.
Contains a brief recounting of the Strang story and accounts of conversations about Strang with two later Beaver Island residents who knew local lore about him.

2289. Webber, Everett. "King Jimmy and His Saints." *Escape to Utopia* (cited above as item 168), 238-73.
Provides a general history of the Strangite movement from a gently skeptical point of view.

2290. Weeks, Robert P. "For His Was the Kingdom, and the Power, and the Glory . . . Briefly." *American Heritage* 21 (June, 1970): 4-7, 78-86.
Provides a biographical sketch of Strang and an account of the movement. Illustrated with photographs, including pictures of two of Strang's plural wives.

2291.  ———.   *King Strang: A   Biography   of   James   Jesse Strang*.  Ann Arbor: Five Wives Press, 1971.
Provides  a  history  of  the  movement  and  an  analysis  of the life and writings of Strang.

2292.  ———.   "Utopian   Kingdom   in   the   American   Grain." *Wisconsin Magazine of History* 61 (Autumn, 1977): 3-20.
Argues  that  Strang  embodies  quintessential  American attitudes,   such   as   experimentalism,   utopianism,   and enthusiasm,  and  thus  was  not  a  lunatic,  but  a  product  of his   extraordinary   times.      Thus   argues   that   his   movement was an important part of our national experience.

2293.  Williams,  Elizabeth  Whitney.   *Child  of  the  Sea;  and  Life Among  the  Mormons*.   St. James, Michigan: Henry Allen Family, 1900.  229 pp.  Reprinted in several editions.
A  memoir  of  a  woman  who  grew  up  on  St.  Helena Island,  near  Beaver.   Much  of  the  material  is  based  on stories  she  as  a  child  heard  told  by  adults.   An unreliable source with substantial misinformation.

# XCV(P).  THOMPSON

Charles   B.   Thompson   joined   the   Mormons   in   1835   at Kirtland,  Ohio.   After  the  death  of  Joseph  Smith  in  1844,  he, like  many  other  Mormons,  claimed  to  have  visions  (in  his  case, through   a   spirit   named   Baneemy)   which   declared   that   he   was the  proper  leader  for  the  Mormons.   He  began  to  organize  his own  group  about  1850.   In  1853,  he  and  his  followers  founded "Preparation,"  a  communal  settlement  in  Monona  County,  Iowa. Thompson  was  incessant  in  his  demands  for  the  money  and possessions  of  his  followers,  and  the  colony  split  up  amid lawsuits  in  1858.   The  property  was  divided  by  the  courts. Thompson's  later  attempts  to  found  another  movement  were unsuccessful.

*Community periodicals*

2294.  *Harbinger  and  Organ*.   Preparation,  Iowa.   1853-?   Three times a year.

2295.  *Nachashlogian*.  St. Louis.  1860?
Probably  only  lasted  for  one  issue.   Promoted Thompson's racist ideas.

2296. *Preparation News.* Preparation, Iowa. 1854-5.

2297. *Preparation News and Ephraims' Messenger.* Preparation, Iowa. 1855-?

2298. *Western Nucleus and Democratic Echo.* Preparation, Iowa. 1856-?

2299. *Zion's Haringer and Baneemy'y Organ.* 1849-55. Monthly. Called *Baneemy's Organ and Zion's Harbinger*, 1855.

### Works by the community leader

2300. Thompson, Charles B. *Evidences on Proof of the Book of Mormon.* Batavia, N.Y.: D.D. Waite, 1841. 256 pp.

2301. ――――. *Great Divine Charter and Sacred Constitution of Iabba's Universal and Everlasting Kingdom.* Philadelphia: n.p., 1873. 64 pp.

2302. ――――. *Laws and Covenants of Israel, written to Ephraim, from Jehovah, the Mighty God of Jacob.* Preparation, Iowa: Zion's Presbytery, 1857. 208 pp.

2303. ――――. *Nachash Origin of the Black and Mixed Races.* St. Louis: Knapp, 1860. 84 pp.

2304. ――――. *Voice of Him! That Crieth in the Wilderness: Prepare Ye the Way of the Lord!!!* St. Louis: n.p., 1848.

### Secondary works

2305. Aumann, F.R. "Minor Prophet in Iowa." *Palompsest* 8 (July, 1927): 253-60.
Provides a history of the Thompsonite colony of Preparation from its founding through Thompson's downfall.

* Bringhurst, Newell G. "Forgotten Mormon Perspectives: Slavery, Race, and the Black Man as Issues Among

Non-Utah Latter-Day Saints, 1844-1873" (cited above as item 2219).
Shows that Thompson, unlike James Strang, had an attitude toward blacks much like that of the Utah church, and that over time his anti-black convictions grew stronger. Illustrated with photographs.

2306. Hall, John R. *Gone from the Promised Land: Jonestown in American Cultural History.* New Brunswick, N.J.: Transaction Books, 1987, p. 34.
Judges Thompson to be virtually an "outright charlatan" whose main work was to defraud followers of their property and who finally fled when his misdeeds caught up with him.

2307. Marks, Constant R. "Monona County, Iowa, Mormons." *Annals of Iowa* series 3, v. 7 (April, 1906): 321-46.
A history of the group from its birth in the aftermath of the murder of Joseph Smith in 1844 to its end in 1858. Describes the group's publications and Thompson's visions.

2308. Morgan, Dale Lowell. "Jehovah's Presbytery of Zion" and "Thompsonite Dissenters." "Bibliography of the Churches of the Dispersion" (cited above as item 2074): 147-57.
Lists early Thompsonite and Thompsonite splinter group works, most of them by Thompson himself.

2309. Shields, Steven L. "Congregation of Jehovah's Presbytery of Zion (Charles B. Thompson)." *Divergent Paths of the Restoration* (cited above as item 2076), 51-3.
Provides an overview of the history of the movement.

2310. ———. "Jehovah's Presbytery of Zion." *Latter Day Saint Churches* (cited above as item 2077), 35-7.
Provides an introduction to the movement and a bibliography of ten items, including some not cited here.

2311. Solis, Miguel J. "Preparation." *American Utopias* (cited above as item 20), 144.
Provides a brief description of the community plus one bibliographical entry.

* Weisbrod, Carol. *Boundaries of Utopia* (cited above as item 170), 159-61.

Discusses a legal issue encountered by the Thompsonites: what property rights do persons retain after they have conveyed property to a leader who later proves unworthy?

# XCV(Q). TICKHILL

A group called the Church of Jesus Christ established a colony under the leadership of Charles Tickhill (and later A.B. Cadman) in the southeastern part of Commanche County, Kansas, in the fall of 1909. The group purchased 1,920 acres of ranch land in the hope of providing missions to Indians in nearby Oklahoma Territory. The group built at least two dwellings and raised grain and livestock. Over 80 persons participated in the colony overall, although no more than 50 were ever there at any one time. A series of dissatisfactions and misfortunes led to the closing of the colony in 1928.

### Secondary work

2312. "Religious Colonies." Commanche County History. Coldwater, Kansas: Commanche County Historical Society, 1981, p. 164.
Briefly recounts the story of the colony.

# XCV(R). WIGHT

A Mormon United Order was established near Austin, Texas, in 1846 and moved to a site on the Pedernales River near Fredericksburg the following year. The colony was called Zodiac. One of its leaders, Lyman Wight, eventually was excommunicated for his independent ways; the colony under his leadership prospered, its economy based on its grist mill. When Wight died in 1858 the colonists scattered.

### Secondary works

* Beadle, John Hanson. *Life in Utah; or, Mysteries and Crimes of Mormonism* (cited above as item 2071), 405.
Provides a brief historical overview of the group.

2313. Fischer, Ernest G. "Mills of the Mormons." *Marxists and Utopias in Texas.* Burnet, Texas: Eakin Press, 1908, pp. 89-121.
Provides a basic historical account of the Wight colony. Much of the documentation refers to manuscripts not cited here.

2314. Hunter, John Marvin. *Lyman Wight Colony in Texas Came to Bandera in 1854.* Bandera, Texas: Bandera Bulletin, [1950]. 37 pp.

2315. Morgan, Dale Lowell. "Church of Jesus Christ of Latter Day Saints (Wightite)." *Bibliography of the Churches of the Dispersion*" (cited above as item 2074), 138-9.
Provides a brief history of the Wight movement plus one bibliographical entry.

2316. Shields, Steven L. "Church of Jesus Christ of Latter Day Saints." *Divergent Paths of the Restoration* (cited above as item 2076), 46-8.
Provides a sketch of the movement's history, doctrine, and publication.

2317. ———. "Church of Jesus Christ of Latter Day Saints." *Latter Day Saint Churches* (cited above as item 2077), 38-9.
Provides an introduction to Wight's movement plus three bibliographical entries, including one primary item not cited here.

2318. Wight, Levi Lamoni. *Reminiscence and Civil War Letters of Levi Lamoni Wight: Life in a Mormon Splinter Colony on the Texas Frontier.* Edited by Davis Bitton. Salt Lake City: University of Utah Press, 1970. 191 pp.
Contains Lyman Wight's son's stories of life at the colony.

# XCV(S). WOOLLEY

The United Order Effort was founded by Lorin C. Woolly in 1929 as a haven for Mormon communal polygamists. Woolly claimed to have been commissioned for the project by Mormon Church President John P. Taylor in 1886. Short Creek,

Arizona, located in a remote location near the Utah border, became the colony's site in the 1920s. A major raid in the arrests of many for polygamy. LeRoy Johnson assumed the leadership of the group in 1951. Short Creek has since been renamed Colorado City.

## Community periodicals

2319. *Star of Truth*. Murray, Utah. 1954-6.

2320. *Truth*. In publication in the 1940s.

## Secondary works

2321. Fessier, Michael, Jr. "Jessica's Story." *New West* 4 (December 31, 1979): 17-43.
    Describes in some detail the raid on Short Creek on July 26, 1953.

2322. Maloney, Wiley S. "Short Creek Story." *American West* 11 (March, 1974): 16-23, 60-2.
    A journalist's account of the Short Creek raid. Well illustrated with photographs taken during the raid.

2323. Melton, J. Gordon. "United Order Effort." *Encyclopedia of American Religions* (cited above as item 130), 487-8.
    Describes the origins of the group, the rise of the Short Creek community, and its life under LeRoy Johnson since the 1950s.

2324. ———. "United Order Effort." *Encyclopedia Handbook of Cults in America* (cited above as item 2072), 40.
    Provides a brief sketch of the Short Creek/Colorado City group from 1936 onward.

2325. Taylor, Samuel W. *Family Kingdom*. London: Hodder and Stoughton, 1951. 320 pp.
    An account of the polygamous (six wives) life of John W. Taylor, son of Mormon President John Taylor. The author was John W. Taylor's son; the author's mother was the cousin of Lorin Woolley. Provides good background on the Woolley movement.

2326. Turner, Wallace. *Mormon Establishment*. Boston:

Houghton Mifflin, pp. 209-12.
Provides a historical sketch of Short Creek.

# XCV(T). ZAHND

John Zahnd withdrew from the Reorganized Church of Jesus Christ of Latter Day Saints about 1918, seeking to live in Mormon communal fashion. He founded a Kansas City-based group which lasted for less than a decade.

### Community periodical

2327. *Order of Zion.*

### Works by the Community leader

2328. Zahnd, John. *All Things Common.* Kansas City: Church of Christ/Order of Zion, [1920?]. 68 pp.
A prospectus for the community. Not seen.

2329. ———. *Old Paths.* Kansas City: n.p., 1920. 27 pp.

2330. ———. *Order of Zion.* [Kansas City: Order of Zion, 1920]. 89 pp.

### Secondary works

2331. Shields, Steven L. "Church of Christ, the Order of Zion." *Divergent Paths of the Restoration* (cited above as item 2076), 118-20.
Provides an overview of the history and doctrines of the group.

2332. ———. "Church of Christ, the Order of Zion." *Latter Day Saint Churches* (cited above as item 2077), 221.
Provides a brief introduction to the group and a bibliography including specialized items not cited here.

# XCVI. NEHALEM VALLEY COOPERATIVE COLONY

Also known as the Columbia Cooperative Colony. The group was organized at Mist, Oregon, in 1886. Its goal was to provide homes and employment for its members. It was reported to have had 50 members in the late nineteenth century. Its economy was based on lumbering. The colony finally failed because of continuing opposition from its neighbors and ongoing financial problems.

Survey work: Albertson (item 27), 419-20; Okugawa (item 139), 214.

*Secondary work*

2333. Kent, Alexander. "Nehalem Valley Cooperative Colony." "Cooperative Communities in the United States" (cited above as item 117), 642.
Provides a sketch of the colony's history.

# XCVII. NEVADA COLONY

The Nevada Colony was begun at Fallon, Nevada, as a branch of the still-new Llano del Rio colony in 1916. C.V. Eggleston was instrumental in promoting it, but he soon had a falling out with Llano's Job Harriman, and the organizations separated. The Nevada Colony reached its peak size early in 1918, with about 200 members. Grand plans were unveiled, but relatively little was accomplished; although some businesses and industries were established, none fared particularly well. Legal disputes and other internal problems in the summer of 1918 helped speed the colony toward its dissolution.

Survey works: Albertson (item 27), 421; Okugawa (item 139), 232-3.

2334.  *Co-operative Colonist.* 1916-8. Monthly.


*Secondary works*

2335.  Fairfield, Dick.  "Nevada Cooperative Colony."
       "Communes U.S.A." (cited above as item 63), 40.
       Provides a brief sketch of the colony, arguing that it
       failed in part because it could not satisfy the enormous
       aspirations of its members.

2336.  Fogarty, Robert S.  "Bray, R.E." and "Eggleston, C.V."
       *Dictionary of American Communal and Utopian History*
       (cited above as item 76), 18, 35.  Biographical
       dictionary entry.

2337.  Shepperson, Wilbur S.  *Retreat to Nevada: A Socialist
       Colony of World War I.*  Reno: University of Nevada
       Press, 1966.
       Describes the career of Job Harriman, the launching of
       Llano del Rio, and the founding of the Nevada Colony as
       a Llano satellite in 1916.  Provides information about the
       life of the colony and its demise two years after its
       founding.

2338.  ———.  "Socialist Pacifism in the American West During
       World War I.  A Case Study."  *Historian* 29 (August,
       1967): 619-33.
       Describes the founding and promoting of the colony,
       its ill-advised industrial projects, and its decline and
       aftermath.

2339.  Wooster, Ernest S.  "Nevada Colony."  *Communities of
       the Past and Present* (cited above as item 175), 70-4.
       Describes the founding of the colony as a branch of
       Llano; focuses on the disputes which hastened its demise.

# XCVIII.  NEW CLAIRVAUX

Edward Pearson Pressey, a Christian socialist, tried to
revive local craftwork while a Unitarian minister in Rowe,
Massachusetts, about 1897, but met with little success,
whereupon he moved to Montague, Massachusetts, and started a
community of artisans which supported itself through

subsistence farming and a small printing press, as well as the craftwork of community members. Pressey was contemptuous of intellectuals, but eventually opened a school which sought to reorient upper-class urban children. The colony closed in 1909.

### Community periodical

2340. *Country Time and Tide.* Montague, Massachusetts. 1902-9.

### Secondary works

\*     Lears, T.J. Jackson. *No Place of Grace* (cited above as item 121), 67-96.
       Characterizes the ideas of Pressey and the life and activities of the community.

2341. "New Clairvaux." *Country Time and Tide* 1 (January, 1902): 9-19.
      Describes, in idealized fashion, Pressey's goals, and the organization and physical facilities of the community.

2342. "New Clairvaux: Training School, Industries and Settlement." *Country Time and Tide* 3 (February, 1903): 121-31.
      Provides a historical sketch of the community; describes the school, the industries proposed for the future, and the community as a whole.

2343. "Village Industries: One Year's Work of New Clairvaux." *Country Time and Tide* 2 (October, 1902): 1-13.
      Provides a balance sheet for the community nine months after its opening; describes the press, farm, and artistic enterprises of the community. Provides a chronology of major community events to date.

## XCIX.  NEW JERUSALEM

Cyrus Spragg was an early Mormon who was expelled from that movement. Later he founded a small nudist commune in Michigan, which outraged neighbors managed to close down. Moving to Cairo, Illinois, he built an ark to ride out a large flood which he predicted was coming. Finally he founded New Jerusalem, also in Illinois, where he oversaw the building of an eight-sided temple with no windows and a single door, as well as an "ecclesiastical palace" to house his large family. Eventually Spragg disappeared into the temple; only virgins were allowed to enter to serve him. Finally an attempt was made to murder him; the community thought he survived, but apparently his two sons took over his secret role in the dark temple. When they were exposed, the community collapsed.

## Secondary works

2344. Bromfield, Louis. *Strange Case of Miss Annie Spragg.* New York: Frederick A. Stokes Co., 1928, pp. 47-65. This book, although in the form of a novel, contains apparently accurate material about Spragg's community. Also includes a lengthy account of the later life of Annie Spragg, Cyrus Spragg's daughter.

* Muncy, Raymond Lee. *Sex and Marriage in Utopian Communities* (cited above as item 135), 212-3. Provides an outline history of Spragg and his movement.

2345. Randolph, Vance. "God Works in Illinois." *Americans Who Thought They Were Gods* (cited above as item 149), 7-8. Contains a recounting of the Spragg story as told by Bromfield, with assurances that oral confirmations of the material had been secured from "many elderly people in Illinois."

* Webber, Everett. *Escape to Utopia* (cited above as item 168), 346-8. Tells of the activities in the mysterious temple.

# C. OLIVENHAIN

Colony Olivenhain was founded in 1884 as a German speaking community which mixed public and private ownership of land and equipment. Land was purchased near Encinitas, north of San Diego, in 1884; 67 settlers were there at the outset, a number which grew to around 300 the next year but soon thereafter declined. Originally the group planned to buy 4431 acres, but after a battle with the sellers they ended up with only 442. Land was owned in common; members paid a fee which entitled them to use of an acreage. Work horses, fruit processing equipment, and the like were owned in common, and colonists were instructed as to what crops to grow. By the end of the century the colony had evolved into a group of private farms; by the 1970s it had become part of the Southern California suburbs.

*Secondary work*

2346. Bumann, Richard. *Colony Olivenhain.* N.p.: author, 1981. 106 pp.
    Provides a history of the colony. Heavily illustrated with photographs and reproductions of documents and maps.

# CI. ORA LABORA

Emil Gottlieb Baur began to promote a colony for German Methodists, based on the Methodist Discipline, in 1862. The colony which was eventually founded by the Christian German Agricultural and Benevolent Society (usually called simply Ora Labora) attracted several dozen families at and soon after its opening in 1863. It was located in the thumb of Michigan near the present town of Bay Port and owned 3000 acres, farming part of it, raising livestock, and opening several small industries. Financial problems were bad by 1865; the colony was dissolved in 1868. The Harmony Society (Rappites) helped finance the colony with a $20,000 loan, most of which it lost.

Survey work: Okugawa (item 139), 201-2.

*Secondary works*

\*    Arndt, Karl J.R. *George Rapp's Successors and Material Heirs, 1847-1916* (cited above as item 1061), 93, 138-9. Characterizes relations between Ora Labora and the Harmony Society, especially detailing Harmonist financial involvement in the Ora Labora project.

\*       Federal Writers' Project.   *Michigan: A Guide to the Wolverine State* (cited above as item 68), 455-6. Describes the site in 1941, but provides incorrect information on the founding date of the colony and the number of persons involved.

2347.   Wittke, Carl.   "Ora et Labora: A German Methodist Utopia."   *Ohio Historical Quarterly* 67 (April, 1958): 129-40.
        Provides a general history of the colony.


# CII. PARISHFIELD

Parishfield was founded in 1948 near Brighton, Michigan, on 38 acres and was operated by three families living communally, sharing a common purse, as an Episcopal church training center.


## *Secondary work*

2348.   Kramer, Wendell B.   "Parishfield."   "Criteria for the Intentional Community" (cited above as item 118), 95.


# CIII. PENN-CRAFT

Penn-Craft was developed near Uniontown, Pennsylvania, as a resettlement program for unemployed coal miners.   Funding was provided by Friends' Service, Inc., a Quaker group, and the first families moved in 1937.   Houses were built, cooperatively, of native materials.   A cooperative store was opened, and a knitting mill was the first community industry.


## *Secondary works*

2349.   Infield, Henrik.   "Penn-Craft Community."   *Utopia and Experiment* (cited above as item 108), 66-70.
        Provides a five-page overview of the project.

\*       Phillips, Jack.   *Directory of Some Persons Planning to Live in Small Communities* (cited above as item 836),

31.
Provides a description of the community, focusing on housing and commercial ventures.

2350. *Progress Report on Development of Penn-Craft Community, 1937-1940.* Philadelphia: American Friends Service Committee, 1941.

2351. Richardson, Frederick L.W., Jr. "Community Resettlement in a Depressed Coal Region." *Journal of Applied Anthropology* 1 (October-December, 1941): 24-53.
Describes the charitable corporation established to help unemployed coal miners and the corporation's efforts to establish a cooperative village for them.

2352. ———. "Community Resettlement in a Depressed Coal Region II: Economic Problems of the New Community." *Applied Anthropology* 1 (April-June, 1942): 32-61.
Continues Richardson's earlier article (item 2351, above), describing efforts to introduce an economic basis other than mining to the poor families served by the project, as well as problems the project encountered.

# CIV. PEOPLE OF THE LIVING GOD

This community was founded in 1932 by Harry Miller in the Garden District of New Orleans. A Pentecostal group, it featured a communal economy, communal dining, and classes in ministry; it sent missionaries out to spread its message. In 1971 it had about 85 members. In 1985 the group moved to rural McMinnville, Tennessee.

### Community periodical

2353. *Marturion.* 1942-. Monthly.

### Primary works

These pamphlets were issued at various times by the movement. Many of them have been collected at the Institute for the Study of American Religion.

2354.  *Community: A Way of Life.*

2355.  *Dilemma of the Sectarian System.*

2356.  *Enchantments.*

2357.  *Expose of the Cult Called Christian.*

2358.  *Gifted but Not Godly.*

2359.  *Gospel of the Kingdom.*

2360.  *Is the Sabbath Perpetual?*

2361.  *Man of Like Passions.*

2362.  *Mystery of God.*

2363.  *Outside the Door.*

2364.  *Pentecostalism and the Devil's Revival.*

2365.  *Redeemer.*

2366.  *Sacred Names?*

2367.  *Three Days and Three Nights.*

### Works by the community leader

2368.  Miller, Harry R.   *Christianity: What Is It?*   New Orleans:
        People of the Living God, n.d.  20 pp.
        At the Institute for the Study of American Religion.

2369.  ———.      *Millennium.*    Chickasaw,   Alabama:   The   Biblicist
        Press, 1957.

### Secondary work

2370.  Melton,   J.   Gordon.      "People   of   the   Living   God."
        *Encyclopedia   of   American   Religions*   (cited   above   as
        item 130), 501- 2.
        Provides a brief overview of the movement.

# CV. PISGAH GRANDE

Pisgah Grande was a fundamentalist/charismatic Christian community in which all goods were held in common. Finis Yoakum, a physician, claimed to have been divinely healed following a bad accident in Denver. He founded Pisgah Home in Los Angeles to serve the down and out, as well as Pisgah Store, which gave free necessities to the poor, and other such charitable ventures. In 1914 he purchased a 3200-acre ranch outside Los Angeles; it became the base for several service enterprises. Following Yoakum's death in 1920, at which time there were 75 members, the organization began to deteriorate, and the commune was closed the next year. However, a remnant of the movement was still in operation in 1974 in Pikeville, Tennessee, where it had moved under the leadership of James and Amanda Cheek, and at that time the original Pisgah Home had also been reactivated as an evangelical Christian center. Many original buildings at Pisgah Grande were still standing in the 1960s.

Survey work: Curl (item 52), 40; Okugawa (item 139), 232.

### Community periodicals

2371. *Herald of Hope* Los Angeles.

2372. *Pisgah*. 1909-21.

### Works by community leaders

2373. Cheek, Amanda (Mrs. James). *Cherished Memories, or, the Life of a Tennessee Girl.* [Los Angeles?]: Bedrock Press, [194-?].

2374. Cheek, James. *Footprints of a Human Life: An Autobiographical of the Life of James Cheek.* Los Angeles: Christ Faith Mission, 1949.

### Secondary works

*    Hine, Robert V. *California's Utopian Colonies* (cited

above as item 98), 153-4.
Provides a brief sketch of the community.

2375. Kagan, Paul. "Pisgah Grande." *New World Utopias* (cited above as item 115), 138-57.
Well illustrated history of Pisgah Grande, including several photographs of the remaining buildings in the 1970s.

2376. Lea, Beverly. "Pisgah Grande." *Ventura County Historical Society Quarterly* 9 (May, 1964): 22-8.
Retells the history of the colony and revisits the colony property in the 1960s. Well illustrated with photographs of buildings.

2377. Melton, J. Gordon. "Christ Faith Mission." *Encyclopedia of American Religions* (cited above as item 130), 356.
Sketches the history of Pisgah Grande as well as the renewal of Yoakum's urban work at the Pisgah Home site under James Cheek. Describes the 1972 merger of the Tennessee and California branches of the Pisgah movement.

# CVI. PORT ROYAL

Port Royal was located on the South Carolina Sea Islands. In 1861 the islands fell to Union forces, and many slaves from the area fled there to freedom. By early 1862 thousands of them were living there and working on plantations. A somewhat communal economic and residential experiment was conducted first by the federal government and later by private citizens.

*Secondary works*

2378. Billington, Ray A. "Social Experiment: The Port Royal Journal of Charlotte L. Forten, 1862-1863." *Journal of Negro History* 35 (July, 1950): 233-64.
Discusses and summarizes the observations made by Forten, a schoolteacher at Port Royal, in her journal (see item 2381, below).

2379. Botume, Elizabeth Hyde. *First Days Among the*

*Contrabands*. Boston: Lee and Shepard, 1893.

Botume was a schoolteacher on the Sea Islands; this memoir argues that she and her colleagues made an important contribution to the education of the freed slaves there.

2380. Doig, Ivan. "Black Utopia: The Port Royal Experiment." *Utopian America: Dreams and Realities* (cited above as item 55), 58-65.

Provides an introduction to the colony and an excerpt from Pease and Pease, *Black Utopia* (item 2387).

2381. Forten, Charlotte. "Life on the Sea Islands." *Atlantic Monthly* 103 (May, 1864): 587-96; 103 (June, 1864): 666-76.

A physical and cultural description of Port Royal by a black northern schoolteacher who went there to help with the project. She found the environment alien, but her work essential.

2382. [Gannett, W.C.] "Freedmen at Port Royal." *North American Review* 101 (July, 1865): 1-28.

Takes a pessimistic view about the possibility that the emancipated slaves will make quick progress in society, using Port Royal as a yardstick.

2383. Hoffman, Edwin D. "From Slavery to Self-Reliance." *Journal of Negro History* 41 (January, 1956): 8-42.

Focuses on the adjustments the Sea Islanders had to make by living in freedom after the war. Contains much documentation from primary sources.

2384. Johnson, Guion Griffis. *Social History of the Sea Islands*. Chapel Hill: University of North Carolina Press, 1930. Repr., New York: Negro Universities Press, 1969.

Discusses the Port Royal experiment briefly at several points. See especially chapter 8, "Contraband of War."

2385. Pearson, Elizabeth Ware, ed. *Letters from Port Royal Written at the Time of the Civil War*. Boston: W.B. Clarke Co., 1906. Repr., New York: Arno, 1969, as *Letters from Port Royal 1862-1868*.

Reproduces letters, arranged chronologically, from the war years; provides good eyewitness information on Port Royal.

2386. Pease, William H.   "Three Years Among the Freedmen: William C. Gannett and the Port Royal Experiment." *Journal of Negro History* 42 (April, 1957): 98-117. Provides a basic overview of the history of the Port Royal project.   Provides references to many manuscripts and newspaper articles on Port Royal.

2387. Pease, William H., and Jane Pease.   *Black Utopia: Negro Communal Experiments in America.*   Madison: State Historical Society of Wisconsin, 1963.   204 pp. Discusses several black colonization projects, all but Port Royal having taken place prior to the Civil War. Provides a good overview history of the Port Royal project.   Includes an extensive bibliography with many references to primary sources.

2388. Pierce, Edward L.   "Freedmen at Port Royal." *Enfranchisement and Citizenship: Addresses and Papers by Edward L. Pierce.*   Edited by A. W. Stevens. Boston: Roberts Brothers, 1896. Pierce was assigned by Treasury Secretary Salmon P. Chase to report on progress being made at Port Royal; his two reports, made in 1862 (item 2390, below), and his Atlantic Monthly article of September, 1863 (item 2389, below), are reproduced here.

2389. ———.   "Freedmen at Port Royal."   *Atlantic Monthly* 102 (September, 1863): 291-315. An upbeat account which depicts the freed slaves at Port Royal as possessing industry, respect for law, interest in religion, desire for knowledge, and the like. Written for a northern audience during the war.

2390. ———.   "Second Report."   *Rebellion Record: A Diary of American Events, with Documents, Narratives, Illustrative Incidents, Poetry, Etc.*   Edited by Frank Moore.   New York: G.P. Putnam and Henry Holt, 1864, supplement I, pp. 315-23. Reproduces Pierce's summary report on Port Royal upon his departure from the site.   His evaluation and prognosis are largely positive.

2391. Rose, Willie Lee.   *Rehearsal for Reconstruction: The Port Royal Experiment.*   New York: Oxford University Press, 1964. 442 pp. The basic monograph on Port Royal.   Tells the story of the experiment which made determined progress in the face of major problems. Bibliography lists many manuscripts and much ephemeral material.

2391. Rose, Willie Lee. *Rehearsal for Reconstruction: the Port Royal Experiment.* New York: Oxford University Press, 1964. 442 pp.
    The basic monograph on Port Royal. Tells the story of the experiment which made determined progress in the face of major problems. Bibliography lists many manuscripts and much ephemeral material.

2392. Towne, Laura M. *Letters and Diary of Laura M. Towne, Written from the Sea Islands of South Carolina, 1862-84.* Edited by Rupert S. Holland. Cambridge, Massachusetts: Riverside Press, 1912.
    A collection of first-hand experiences of life among the ex-slaves on the Sea Islands from one who taught school there for nearly 40 years. Much of the material concerns the weather and details of daily life, but contains a number of amusing and thought-provoking anecdotes as well.

# CVII. PRESTON

Emily Preston, a spiritual healer in San Francisco, moved to Preston, near Cloverdale, California, with her husband in 1872. People began to journey there for healing, and eventually some settled there, building simple dwellings. The community provided running water, a school, and other amenities for all who lived there. Mrs. Preston preached her "Religion of Inspiration" in a church built there for her. In 1909 she died, and the colony, sometimes called "Free Pilgrims Covenant," soon largely dissolved. A few faithful, however, were still having meditation services in the church in the 1940s. Later an artists' colony developed in the buildings. Most of the colony buildings burned in 1988.

### Secondary works

2393. "Flames All But Destroy Historic Northern California Community." Los Angeles *Times*, June 29, 1988.
    Provides a brief sketch of the colony and of the fire

which destroyed the buildings.

2394.  Votruba, M.J.    "The Preston Story."    1971.    Manuscript at
       the Institute  for  the  Study  of  American  Religion.    40
       pp.
       Provides  a  history  of  the  colony  based  on  manuscript
       materials and interviews.


# CVIII.  PUGET SOUND
# CO-OPERATIVE COLONY

The  colony  was  incorporated  and  issued  a  prospectus  in
1887.    The  response  was  strong,  and  $50,000  was  soon  raised  as
initial  capital.    Land  was  purchased  at  Port  Angeles,
Washington,  and  several  colony  businesses  were  started,
including  a  lumber  mill,  timber  cutting,  and  potato  farming.
Soon  an  agent  was  sent  to  get  a  loan  from  outside  sources;
while  the  agent  was  gone,  disputes  and  financial  problems
arose.    The  property  was  finally  sold  in  1895.    Many  residents,
however, continued to live in the vicinity.

Survey  works:    Albertson  (item  27),  420;  Curl  (item  52),  30;
Okugawa (item 139), 214.


*Community periodical*

2395.  *Model Commonwealth*. 1886-9. Weekly.


*Primary work*

2396.  *Puget  Sound  Co-operative  Colony:  Town  Site  Lands  and
       Fine  Harbor  on  Puget  Sound,  Washington  Territory.*
       Milwaukee:  Ellery  W.  Ellis,  [1886?].      Facsimile  reprint,
       Seattle: Shorey Book Store, 1965. 32 pp.
       The  manifesto  of  the  colony,  providing  a  glowing
       description  of  the  site,  the  proposed  organization  of  the
       colony,  rules  governing  land  use,  colony  capital  stock,
       work  and  money,  equality  of  women,  colony  philosophy,
       and instructions for joining.

*Work by a community leader*

2397. Smith, George Venable. *Co-operative Plan for Securing Homes and Occupations at Port Angeles, Washington.* Port Angeles: Tribune-Times Job Printing, 1893. Facsimile reprint, Seattle: Shorey Book Store, 1965. 16 pp.

*Secondary works*

2398. Cloud, Barbara. "Cooperation and Printer's Ink." *Rendezvous* 19 (1983): 33-42.
Describes the founding of the colony and its newspaper in the context of political controversies of the day in western Washington. Finds that the paper was an efficient means of informing colonists about the progress of the project and of making them proud of their accomplishments.

2399. Fogarty, Robert S. "Smith, George Venable." *Dictionary of American Communal and Utopian History* (cited above as item 76), 104-5.
Biographical dictionary entry.

* Holbrook, Stewart H. *Far Corner* (cited above as item 101), 145-9.
Provides an informal history of the colony and descriptions of its economy, its financial problems, and its demise in bankruptcy.

2400. Lauridsen, Gregers Marius, and A.A. Smith. *Story of Port Angeles, Clallam County, Washington: An Historical Symposium.* Seattle: Lowman and Hanford Co., 1937, part 3, pp. 45-63.
Provides information on the business side of the colony. Contains information from an interview with an early member and quotes from the *Model Commonwealth*.

2401. LeWarne, Charles P. "Imogen Cunningham in Utopia." *Pacific Northwest Quarterly* 74 (April, 1983): 88-9.
Depicts Cunningham's memories of the colony, where she spent a few years of her childhood.

2402. ———. "Puget Sound Co-operative Colony: The Model Commonwealth of the Olympic Peninsula." "Communitarian Experiments in Western Washington, 1885-1915" (cited above as item 122), 31-126.

Provides the most comprehensive history available of the colony. Extensively documented, including references to specialized materials not cited here.

2403. ———. "Puget Sound Co-operative Colony: The Model Commonwealth of the Olympic Peninsula." *Utopias on Puget Sound* (cited above as item 124), 15-54.
Provides a standard history of the community, covering the organization of the colony, its government and internal politicking, daily life, education, industries and economy, problems, and dissolution. Heavily documented; includes many references to specialized material not cited here.

2404. McCallum, John, and Lorraine Wilcox Ross. *Port Angeles, U.S.A.* Seattle: Wood and Reber, 1961, pp. 56-62.
Provides a history of the colony based on primary documents and first-person memoirs. Contains a photograph of part of the original colony and of the site in 1961, then occupied by a paper mill.

* Meany, Edmond S. *History of the State of Washington* (cited above as item 129), 320-1.
Provides an overview history of the colony.

* Oved, Yaacov. *Two Hundred Years of American Communes* (cited above as item 142), 257-8.
Provides a brief overview of the colony.

2405. Welsh, William D. *Brief History of Port Angeles*. Port Angeles: Port Angeles Chamber of Commerce, 1941. 24 pp.
A local booster booklet which tells of the incorporation of the colony, its early prosperity, and its decline.

# CIX. QUEST

Quest was organized in 1950 near Royal Oak, Michigan. Families lived in proximity in houses built and owned by the community. The group performed joint work tasks on Saturdays and shared a common meal and worship services each week. Incomes were pooled. Many members were of Methodist background, and weekly worship services were held. In 1953 the community consisted of four families.

*Secondary works*

\*    Gladstone, Arthur. "Cooperative Communities Today II" (cited above as item 82), 15.
Provides a basic overview of the community.

2406.  Kramer, Wendell B. "Quest." "Criteria for the Intentional Community" (cited above as item 118), 96.

## CX. REBA PLACE FELLOWSHIP

Reba Place was founded in Evanston, Illinois, in 1957 by young Mennonite idealists looking for a radical, evangelical Christian community. One couple purchased a house, and the community developed from that base, naming itself after the street on which that first house was located (several other communal dwellings were developed later). Members worked at outside jobs and pooled their incomes, each receiving a small allowance. The community has spent much of its income helping the underprivileged. The group was reported to have 160 members in 1974 and over 400 in the late 1980s. Over the years it has spawned several similar, related communities in other towns.

Archives covering the early days of Reba Place are located at Goshen Seminary, Goshen, Indiana. Later archives are kept at Reba Place.

*Work by a community leader*

2407.  Miller, John W. *Christian Way: A Guide to the Christian Life Based on the Sermon on the Mount.* Scottdale, Pennsylvania: Herald Press, 1969.
A theological and ethical discussion of the Sermon on the Mount, containing a closely reasoned analysis of the sermon and an appendix suggesting methods in which to apply the teachings in the sermon to daily life. This book is the most important work, apart from the Bible, used by Reba Place as a guide to decision-making, and was written by one of the founders of the community.

*Secondary works*

2408. Belser, Julius H. "Reba Place Fellowship." *Brethren Encyclopedia* (cited above as item 57), v. 2, pp. 1084-5. Provides an overview of the community. Illustrated with a photograph of members at worship.

*       Bloesch, Donald G. *Wellsprings of Renewal* (cited above as item 35), 81-2. Provides a brief description of Reba Place.

2409. Bouvard, Marguerite. "Reba Place Fellowship." *Intentional Community Movement* (cited above as item 37), 67-76. Describes the founding of the community, its "complete sharing" of goods and property, and the many outside jobs which support it.

2410. "Community at Evanston." *Intentional Communities: 1959 Yearbook of the Fellowship of Intentional Communities* (cited above as item 807), 32. Provides a brief note on the community, at this time so new that it has not yet been formally named.

2411. Fretz, J. Winfield. "Newly Emerging Communes in Mennonite Communities." *International Review of Modern Sociology* 6 (Spring, 1976): 103-12. Charts the growth of Mennonite communities in the U.S. and Canada; finds 24 of them, all except Reba Place founded after 1960.

*       *Intentional Community Handbook* (cited above as item 808), unpaginated. Provides a brief description of Reba Place.

2412. Jackson, Dave. "Appendix B: Reba Place Fellowship." *Coming Together* (cited above as item 111), unpaginated (at end of book). Provides basic information on the group in question-and-answer form. Illustrated.

2413. Jackson, David, and Neta Jackson. *Glimpses of Glory: Thirty Years of Community: The Story of Reba Place Fellowship*. Elgin, Illinois: Brethren Press, 1987. A history of Reba Place written by long-time members of the group. Illustrated with photographs.

2414. ———. "Reba Place Fellowship." *Living Together in a World Falling Apart* (cited above as item 112), 36-9.
Provides a brief history and description of Reba Place.

2415. Melton, J. Gordon. "Reba Place Fellowship and Associated Communities." *Encyclopedia of American Religions* (cited above as item 130), 508-9.
Provides a historical sketch of Reba Place and other communities it has spawned.

2416. "Reba—A Fellowship That Works." Evanston *Review*, December 15, 1977, pp. 29A-30A.
A feature article based on interviews with members of the community. Heavily illustrated.

2417. Redekop, Calvin. "Social Ecology of Communal Socialization." *International Review of Modern Sociology* 6 (Spring, 1976): 113-25.
Provides a comparative analysis of the socialization practices of two Mennonite communes, Reba Place and the Old Colony Mennonites.

* Redekop, Calvin, and William Shaffir. "Communal Organization and Secular Education: Hutterite and Hassidic Comparisons" (cited above as item 1360), 342-57.
Compares and contrasts the Hutterites and Reba Place in regard to their organizational structures and their educational systems.

2418. Roberts, Ron E. "Urban Commune—Reba Place Fellowship." *New Communes: Coming Together in America* (cited above as item 153): 65-8.
Describes the origins and development, economy, and social reform projects of the community.

2419. Shenk, Sarah Wenger. *Why Not Celebrate?* Intercourse, Pennsylvania: Good Books, 1987. 188 pp.
A collection of Reba Place celebrations and rituals. Not seen.

2420. Zeik, Michael. "Family of Families: Reba Place Fellowship." *New Christian Communities.* Williston Park, New York: Roth Publishing, 1973, pp. 173-99.
A look at the ideas and workings of Reba Place, primarily in the form of a transcript of a group

interview with members.

# CXI. ROSE VALLEY

Horace Traubel, a leader in the Arts and Crafts Movement, founded Rose Valley on 80 acres near Philadelphia in 1903 with two associates, Will Price and Hawley McLanahan. The colony supported itself through subsistence agriculture and arts-oriented cottage industries. Proclaiming work to be worship, Traubel attracted as many as 60 residents to the community at its peak. In finally folded in financial distress in 1908.

*Community periodical*

2421.  *Artsman.* Philadelphia. 1903-7.

*Works by community leaders*

2422.  McLanahan, Hawley.    "Rose    Valley    in    Particular."
        *Artsman* 1 (October, 1903): 13-21.
        Outlines the founding of the community and proclaims its devotion to manual labor; describes the government of the community and the ongoing plans for the property.

2423.  Price, Will.    "Is Rose Valley Worth While?"    *Artsman* 1
        (October, 1903): 5-11.
        Argues that Rose Valley will help promote the onward progress of truth.

2424.  ————.    "Rose   Valley   Fact   and   Spirit."    *Artsman* 2
        (January, 1905): 129-35.
        Argues that Rose Valley and its vision will succeed, at least in improving the human prospect.

2425.  Traubel, Horace.    "Rose   Valley   in   General."    *Artsman* 1
        (October, 1903): 23-30.
        Provides a manifesto for the community, emphasizing its exaltation of work.

## Secondary works

2426. Karsner, David. *Horace Traubel.* New York: Egmont Arens, 1919, pp. 78-83.
Provides a brief sketch of the ideals behind the community, quoting extensively from the writings of Traubel, Price, and McLanahan in the *Artsman.*

\* Lears, T.J. Jackson. *No Place of Grace* (cited above as item 121), 67-96.
Provides an overview of Traubel's ideas and the history of the community.

2427. Noyes, Carleton. "A Glimpse of Rose Valley from the Outside." *Artsman* 1 (February, 1904): 159-64.
A visitor's description of the colony and its ideals and goals.

2428. Wentworth, Franklin. "Beautiful Rose Valley Where Art and Life Are One." *Artsman* 3 (October, 1905): 5-22.
Tells the story of the founding of Rose Valley and describes the relationships among the resident artists.

# CXII. THE ROYCROFTERS

The Roycrofters were a community of artisans founded by Elbert Hubbard at East Aurora, New York, about 1900; their name honored Samuel and Thomas Roycroft, makers of beautiful books in 17th century London, and indicates that they thought their crafts worthy of royalty. They produced fine books and other craft works. All worked in the community industries; Hubbard's large lecture fees helped underwrite the project. The personality of Hubbard dominated Roycroft, and it was probably as much an enlightened private enterprise (residents were paid salaries by the Hubbard family corporation, and also received shares in the corporation) as it was a communal society. It reportedly had 800 residents at its peak in the early 20th century; decline set in following Hubbard's death (he went down with the Lusitania) in 1915.

Some material on the Roycrofters is located in the American Communities Collection at Syracuse University.

Survey work: Okugawa (item 139), 226.

*Community periodicals*

2429.  *Fra.* 1908-1917.  Monthly.

2430.  *Philistine: A Periodical of Protest.*    1895-1915.    Monthly.
       A small-format literary magazine.

2431.  *Roycroft.* 1917-1926.

2432.  *Roycroft Quarterly.* 1896.

2433.  *Roycrofter.* 1926-1932.


*Works by the community leader*

The listing of Elbert Hubbard's works occupies 33 pages in
the National Union Catalog.    The only Hubbard works cited
here are those with a direct bearing on the community and/or
its ideas.

2434.  Hubbard, Elbert.    *Book of Business.*    East Aurora, N.Y.:
       Roycrofters, 1913.  163 pp.
       Consists of aphorisms about conducting good, honest
       business, the kind of philosophy purportedly undergirding
       the businesses of the Roycrofters themselves.

2435.  ———.  Note Book of  Elbert  Hubbard.    New   York:
       William H. Wise, 1927.
       Aphorisms and short  essays  collected  by  Hubbard's
       friends after his death.

2436.  ———.  *Philosophy  of  Elbert  Hubbard.*    New   York:
       William H. Wise, 1930.  181 pp.
       A collection of  Hubbard's  ideas,  edited  by  his  son
       Elbert Hubbard II.

2437.  ———.  *Roycroft Shop: A History.*    East   Aurora,   N.Y.:
       Roycroft Shop, 1908.
       An  exposition  of  Hubbard's  Roycroft  philosophy  with
       some  information  about  the  history  and  life  of  the
       movement.

2438.  ———.  "Social      and      Industrial      Experiment."
       *Cosmopolitan* 32 (January, 1902): 309-20.
       Hubbard's  own  account  of  life  among  the  Roycrofters.
       Illustrated with photographs.

2439. Hubbard, Elbert, and Francis and Abigail Farrar. *Book of the Roycrofters*. East Aurora, N.Y.: Roycrofters, 1907. 17 pp.
Part one, by Hubbard, is an essay urging people to live consecrated lives; part two, by the Farrars, provides a description of the community's work and economy.

## Secondary works

2440. Allen, Frederick Lewis. "Elbert Hubbard." *Scribner's Magazine* 104 (September, 1938): 12-4, 49-51.
A biographical sketch; argues that Roycroft was perhaps less communal than Hubbard liked to depict it, but that Hubbard was at least progressive in his handling of his employees. Depicts Hubbard as an opportunist who succeeded largely because he figured out how to make big money by writing pro-business essays and epigrams.

2441. Balch, David Arnold. *Elbert Hubbard: Genius of Roycroft*. New York: Frederick A. Stokes Co., 1940. 320 pp.

2442. Beisner, Robert L. "'Commune' in East Aurora." *American Heritage* 22 (February, 1971): 72-7, 106-9.
Provides a biographical sketch of Hubbard, emphasizing his paradoxes in being communalist and capitalist, radical and traditionalist, elitist and commoner. Illustrated with photographs of Hubbard and reproductions of some of his graphic work.

2443. Bliss, W.D.P. "Hubbard, Elbert." *New Encyclopedia of Social Reform* (cited above as item 35), 586.
Paints a picture of worker ownership of the business at Roycroft.

2444. Champney, Freeman. *Art and Glory: The Story of Elbert Hubbard*. New York: Crown, 1968. 248 pp.
The standard biography of Hubbard and chronicle of the development of Roycroft. Bibliography includes many specialized references not cited here.

2445. "Elbert Hubbard's Price." *Harper's Weekly* 60 (January 30, 1915): 112.
Reproduces Hubbard's correspondence with John D.

Rockefeller, Jr., showing how Hubbard tried to peddle his antilabor analysis of a strike against a Rockefeller company.

2446. Federal Writers' Project. *New York: A Guide to the Empire State.* New York: Oxford University Press, 1940, p. 443.
Provides a sketch of the development of the Roycroft community and its crafts.

2447. Heath, Mary Hubbard. *Elbert Hubbard I Knew.* East Aurora, N.Y.: Roycrofters, 1929. 221 pp.
The author was Hubbard's sister.

2448. Hinds, William A. "Roycrofters." *American Communities and Co-operative Colonies* (cited above as item 95), 513-21.
Provides an overview history and sketch of community life.

2449. Hubbard, Elbert II. *Impressions.* East Aurora, N.Y.: Roycrofters, 1921. Reminiscences of Hubbard's son. Not seen.

2450. Kemp, Harry. *Tramping on Life.* New York: Boni and Liveright, 1922, pp. 188-208.
A lightly disguised memoir of Kemp's sojourn at Roycroft, in which he was given a job there but was gradually disillusioned with the situation, which turned out to be less utopian than its reputation. Hubbard is here called "Roderick Spalton" and Roycroft is the "Eos Artwork Studios."

2451. Koch, Robert. "Elbert Hubbard's Roycrofters as Artist-Craftsmen." *Winterthur Portfolio* 3 (1967): 67-82.
Describes the career of Hubbard and the development of the Roycrofters. Well illustrated with photographs of Roycroft's buildings, crafts, and books.

2452. Lambourne, Lionel. *Utopian Craftsmen.* Salt Lake City: Peregrine Smith, 1980, pp. 152-7.
Describes the products and promotions of the Roycrofters. Illustrated.

2453. Lane, Albert. *Elbert Hubbard and His Work.* Worcester, Massachusetts: Blanchard Press, 1901. 154 pp.

An early, largely uncritical, biography published soon after Hubbard had become famous for *Message to Garcia*. Contains a compilation of Hubbard epigrams, a bibliography of Hubbard's works, a bibliography of books published by the Roycrofters, and a partial bibliography of Hubbard's articles in the *Philistine*. Illustrated with photographs of Roycroft.

\*     Lears, T.J. Jackson. *No Place of Grace* (cited above as item 121), 86 and other scattered references.
Argues that although Hubbard once proclaimed himself a socialist, he operated Roycroft as a work of "enlightened capitalism."

2454.   Mott, Frank Luther. *A History of American Magazines, 1885-1905.* Cambridge, Massachusetts: Belknap/Harvard University Press, 1957, pp. 639-48.
Provides a history of the *Philistine* and its role in the development of the Roycrofters.

2455.   Reedy, William Marion, Harold Bolce, Ben DeCasseres, and Brainard L. Bates. *Feather Duster; or, Is He Sincere?* East Aurora, N.Y.: Roycrofters, 1912.

2456.   Scheller, William G. "East Aurora Roycrofters." *National Geographic Traveler* 4 (Spring, 1987): 10.
Describes the Roycroft Inn, still taking visitors, and the museum of the Roycrofters which has preserved the Roycroft crafts and books.

2457.   Shay, Felix. *Elbert Hubbard of East Aurora.* New York: William H. Wise and Co., 1926. 554 pp.
A sympathetic memoir of Hubbard and Roycroft by a onetime Roycrofter. A string of anecdotes, not a full biography.

2458.   Sinclair, Upton. *Brass Check.* Pasadena: author, 1931, pp. 314-7.
A diatribe against Hubbard for trying to sell himself to John D. Rockefeller, Jr; essentially a rehash of "Elbert Hubbard's Price" (cited above as item 2445).

2459.   Solis, Miguel J. "Roycroft Shop." *American Utopias* (cited above as item 20), 146.
Provides a brief description of the project plus three bibliographical entries.

2460. Tassin, Algernon.   *Magazine in America.*   New York: Dodd, Mead, 1916, pp. 356-8.
Sets the *Philistine* among the little magazines as an earnest, iconoclastic voice.

2461. Thorne, Bonnie Ruth Baker.   "Elbert Hubbard and the Publications of the Roycroft Shop."   Ph.D. dissertation, Texas Woman's University, 1975. 303 pp.
Provides detailed information on Roycroft book publishing. Not seen.

2462. Walle, Alf, and M.L. Brimo.   "Elbert Hubbard, the Arts and Crafts Movement, and the Commercialization of Folk Art."   *New York Folklore* 10 (Summer-Fall, 1984): 46-63.
Finds that Roycroft prospered only during the heyday of the Arts and Crafts movement, and that it died because it could not accommodate changing tastes.

2463. "Writer Who Made America Think."   *Current Opinion* 74 (April, 1923): 419-21.
A testimony to the genius of Hubbard on the occasion of the appearance of a memorial series of his collected writings.

# CXIII.  RUSKIN

Ruskin was founded by the prominent socialist J.A. Wayland, publisher of the *Coming Nation.*   It was named for John Ruskin.   Wayland originally purchased 1000 acres of Tennessee land, and moved the newspaper there with the colony in 1894.   After serious and chronic internal dissent, the Tennessee colony broke up; a majority (about 250) of its members then (in 1899) moved to Duke, Georgia, and merged with the American Settlers' Colony there.   However, more dissension occurred, along with disease and hunger, and the Georgia colony soon broke up as well.

The Ruskin Community Papers are in the University of Georgia library.   Some material on Ruskin is in the American Communities Collection at Syracuse University.

Survey works: Curl (item 52), 34; Liefmann (item 125), 21-2; Okugawa (item 139), 217, 223.

## Community periodical

2464. *Coming Nation.*
Begun by Wayland elsewhere; moved to Ruskin when the colony opened. Issues during the colony years contain much basic information on the experiment.

## Secondary works

2465. Albertson, Ralph. "Ruskin Cooperative Association and the Ruskin Commonwealth." "Survey of Mutualistic Communities in America" (cited above as item 27), 413.
Provides an overview of the colony, emphasizing its problems and discord; describes the move to Georgia and the colony that developed there.

2466. Bell, Daniel. "Background and Development of Marxian Socialism in the United States." *Socialism and American Life* (cited above as item 3), v. 1, p. 259.
Provides a sketch of Wayland, covering his early acquisition of wealth, his two major socialist papers, and the founding of the colony.

2467. Bliss, W.D.P. "Ruskin Cooperative Colony." *New Encyclopedia of Social Reform* (cited above as item 35), 1079.
Describes the founding of the colony, the disputes between Wayland and other colonists, the later disputes between charter members and later arrivals, the dissolution of the Tennessee colony, and the move to Georgia. An excellent overview history.

2468. Braam, J.W. "Ruskin Co-operative Colony." *American Journal of Sociology* 8 (1903): 667-80.
A good overview of the colony by one who spent five months there. Covers the roots of the colony in Wayland's propagandizing in his paper, the communal economy at Ruskin, daily life, family relationships, organizational structure, education, the arts, and religion and moral ideas. Tells of problems the community encountered and provides an analysis of what went wrong, notably the inability of its members to manage its business affairs well.

2469.  Broome, Isaac.  *Last Days of the Ruskin Cooperative Association*.  Chicago: Charles H. Kerr, 1902.
       Attempts to persuade readers to cease trying to build "miniature Utopias" and instead to devote their efforts to building up the international socialist movement. Discusses the physical site of the colony, its founding, Wayland's paper the *Coming Nation*, food, education, anarchy and free love at the colony, and internal conflict, especially that between socialists and anarchists. Chronicles the events leading to the breakup of the colony.  The book is an angry polemic written by one who had lived there.

*      Bushee, Frederick A.  "Communistic Societies in the United States" (cited above as item 38), 632-5.
       Provides good general information on the colony; special attention is paid to its internal dissension, financial problems, and breakup.

2470.  Butler, Francelia.  "Ruskin Commonwealth: A Unique Experiment in Marxian Socialism."  *Tennessee Historical Quarterly* 23 (December, 1964): 333-42.
       Describes the founding of the colony, its economic system, the fears harbored by its neighbors, and the internal problems which led to its dissolution.

2471.  Casson, Herbert N.  "Ruskin Co-operative Colony." *Independent* 51 (January 19, 1899): 192-5.
       Provides an overview of the colony, including a description of its two caves.  Written by a Ruskin resident, the editor of the *Coming Nation*, it provides a highly optimistic appraisal of the colony's prospects.

2472.  Corlew, Robert E.  *History of Dickson County, Tennessee*. Nashville: Tennessee Historical Commission and Dickson County Historical Society, 1956, pp. 137-52.
       Contains a readable narrative history of the colony, making heavy use of local Tennessee publications and Wayland's *Coming Nation*.

2473.  Davis, Walter G.  "Failure of the Ruskin Colony." *Gunton's Magazine* 21 (December, 1901): 530-7.
       Relates facts about the colony's history and decline; concludes that lazy, noncontributing members caused the demise of the community.

2474. Douglas, Dorothy W., and Katharine Du Pre Lumpkin. "Communistic Settlements" (cited above as item 56), 100.
Emphasizes the colony's anarchism.

2475. Egerton, John. "Ruskin: Julius Wayland and 'The Cooperative Commonwealth.'" *Visions of Utopia* (cited above as item 60), 64-86.
Contains a history of the colony. Illustrated with photographs.

\* Federal Writers' Project. *Tennessee: A Guide to the State* (cited above as item 70), 455-7.
Depicts Ruskin's industries, the hour-check system used in place of money, and the internal disputes which closed the colony.

2476. Fogarty, Robert S. "Ruskin Cooperative Association" and "Wayland, Julius." *Dictionary of American Communal and Utopian History* (cited above as item 76), 161-2 and 117, respectively.
Dictionary entries on the colony.

2477. Ghent, William J. "Appeal and Its Influence." *Survey* 26 (April 1, 1911): 24-8.
Discusses and analyzes Wayland and the *Appeal to Reason*; briefly recounts the story of Ruskin and tells how Wayland's earlier paper, the *Coming Nation*, went down with the colony.

2478. Hinds, William Alfred. "Ruskin Commonwealths." *American Communities and Co-operative Colonies* (cited above as item 95), 488-99.
Provides a general history of Ruskin, much of it quoted from Isaac Broome (item 2469, above).

2479. Kegel, Charles H., ed. "Earl Miller's Recollections of the Ruskin Cooperative Association." *Tennessee Historical Quarterly* 17 (March, 1958): 45-69.
Reproduces personal recollections of Ruskin containing much information on daily life at the colony and on the people who lived there.

2489. ———. "Ruskin's St. George in America." *American Quarterly* 9 (Winter, 1957): 412-20.
Finds that despite its name, the colony's organization

was influenced more by the ideas of Edward Bellamy than by those of John Ruskin; concludes that leading colonists tried to follow the spirit but not the letter of Ruskin's agrarian communitarian vision.

2481.   Kent, Alexander.   "Ruskin Commonwealth."   "Cooperative Communities in the United States" (cited above as item 117), 604-12.
Provides an overview of the history, financing, publishing activities, and internal conflicts of the community.   Describes the move to Georgia and characterizes colony life there.   Reproduces the "Covenant of Faith," a statement of goals, and "Agreement," a contract covering living and working conditions.

*       Lauer, Robert H., and Jeanette C. Lauer.   *Spirit and the Flesh* (cited above as item 120), 36-7, 126-7, 203-4.
Reproduces a statement of the goals of the community and describes its internal workings; reproduces a member's description of the commitment of some members to free love; describes the split in the community over free love and anarchy.

2482.   Lynd, Staughton.   "Can Men Live as Brothers?" *Liberation* 2 (February, 1958): 12-4.
Describes Ruskin's history, economy, and labor system; blames the decline of the colony on "personality clashes and petty squabbles."   Based largely on accounts in the *Coming Nation.*   Argues that political ideals are not enough to sustain a community, that ultimate metaphysical assumptions also need to be addressed.

2483.   McDill, H.C.   "Why Ruskin Colony Failed."   *Gunton's Magazine* 22 (May, 1902): 434-43.
A colony member's reply to Davis's earlier article in *Gunton's* (item 2473, above) lamenting the failure of Ruskin, describing little disputes which fostered resentment in the community, and telling of the move to Georgia, which, however, took place after the colony's unity had already been destroyed and thus was doomed to failure.

2484.   Miller, Ernest I.   "Ruskin Colony."   *Some Tennessee Utopias* (cited above as item 133), 58-71.
Outlines the history, businesses, monetary innovation,

social change programs, educational programs, and religious ideas of the colony. Finds that the colony suffered from insufficient control and direction, that it needed a dictator to make it succeed. Documentation cites specialized sources including some not cited here.

\* Muncy, Raymond Lee. *Sex and Marriage in Utopian Communities* (cited above as item 135), 117-9.
Tells the story of Wayland and the founding of Ruskin, its rapid growth, its unconventional ideas (especially the fact that some of its members preached free love), and its move to Georgia.

2485. Neet, Sharon E. "J.A. Wayland, Founding Editor and Publisher of the Appeal to Reason." *Little Balkans Review* 4 (Fall, 1983): 44-9.
Provides a biographical sketch of Wayland and a description of the diverse population which made up Ruskin. Describes the contradiction which fanned dissent at the colony: Wayland retained sole ownership of the *Coming Nation*, his paper which was the colony's chief source of income—yet the colony was supposedly a socialist venture. Discusses Wayland's departure from the colony in 1895 and his subsequent life.

2486. Oved, Yaacov. "Ruskin: the Communitarian Settlement in Tennessee." *Two Hundred Years of American Communes* (cited above as item 142), 247-56.
Provides a history of Wayland and the *Coming Nation*; describes the founding and structure of the colony, with its mix of communal and cooperative features; characterizes the development and physical facilities of the colony; chronicles the growing dissension among the members and the move to Georgia.

2487. Pomeroy, Eltweed. "Sketch of the Socialist Colony in Tennessee." *American Fabian* 3 (April, 1897): 1-3.
Describes the financial condition of the colony, its property holdings, its industries, its farms, its four caves, its people, its government, its free schooling and medical care, and its living arrangements (separate houses, but common dining facilities). An upbeat, positive article based on the author's visit to Ruskin and certain community documents.

2488. Quint, Howard H. "Julius A. Wayland, Pioneer Socialist

Propagandist." *Mississippi Valley Historical Review* 35 (March, 1949): 585-606.
Discusses Wayland's life and career, his purchase of 1000 acres in Tennessee and his moving there with 125 fellow socialists, the building of houses and the print shop, the bickering and problems of the community, and Wayland's later life and influence as a prominent socialist.

2489. ———. "Wayland Plants Grass Roots Socialism." *Forging of American Socialism* (cited above as item 148), 175-209.
Provides a good, concise history of Ruskin, with an emphasis on Wayland's role, along with broader material on Wayland's propagandizing.

2490. "Ruskin: Its Secret History." *Coming Nation* no. 410 (April 6, 1901): 2-4.
Provides a detailed, partisan account of the conflict which broke up both colonies, in Tennessee and Georgia. Blames the breakup on colonists, arriving after the colony had already been started, who wanted free stock in the enterprise.

2491. Shepstone, H.J. "Modern Utopia." *Wide World Magazine* 3 (June, 1899): 261-8.
Describes the purchase of the property, the call for settlers, the process of joining, daily life, the labor-credit system used in place of money, the colony's social life, and the two large caves. Well illustrated.

2492. Shore, Elliott. "Talkin' Socialism: Julius A. Wayland, Fred D. Warren and Radical Publishing, 1890-1914." Ph.D. dissertation, Bryn Mawr College, 1984. 264 pp.

2493. Skinner, Charles M. "Ruskin Socialists." *American Communes* (cited above as item 156), 3-6.
Describes the setting, the community, its economic system, and its organization. Provides an upbeat appraisal of the community's potential. Illustrated with photographs and line drawings, including a photograph of Ruskin, Georgia.

2494. Solis, Miguel J. "Ruskin Cooperative Association." *American Utopias* (cited above as item 20), 147-8.
Provides a brief description of the community plus one

bibliographical entry.

2495. Southworth, John.   "Cooperative Colony at Ruskin."
   *American Review of Reviews* 16 (November, 1897):
   606-7.
   Provides a synopsis of a longer article appearing in the
   October, 1897, issue of the *Home Magazine.*
   Characterizes the businesses of the colony, the
   labor-check system of payment, common ownership of the
   colony and its businesses, and services provided to
   members.

2496. Stone, Grace.   "Ruskin Colony."   "Tennessee: Social and
   Economic Laboratory" (cited above as item 160),
   312-26.
   Epitomizes Wayland and the *Coming Nation,* the
   founding of the colony, its industries, its ideas, and the
   problems which led to its demise.

2497. "Subterranean Industrial Plant."   *Scientific American* 81
   (August 5, 1899): 89.
   Describes the Grand Cave at Ruskin and the uses to
   which it was put by the community.   Provides a brief
   description of the Stalactite Cave, the second cavern on
   the property.  Illustrated with photographs of the caves.

2498. Taylor, R. Bruce.   "Ruskin Commonwealths."
   "Communistic Societies of America" (cited above as
   item 163), 787.
   Notes Wayland's role in the community's prosperity and
   describes the move to Georgia.

2499. "Why All 'Ruskin Colonies' Fail."   *Gunton's Magazine* 22
   (May, 1902): 444-51.
   A reply to the article of McDill (item 2483, above),
   arguing that human nature is not sufficiently advanced
   for humans to form colonies such as Ruskin.

2500. Wooster, Ernest S.   "Ruskin Commonwealth" and
   "Individualistic 'Colonies.'"   *Communities of the Past
   and Present* (cited above as item 175), 44-5, 146-7.
   Describes the rise and brief flowering of the colony,
   the dissent which caused its downfall in Tennessee, the
   effort to restart it in Georgia, and J.A. Wayland's
   disappointment at the colony's failure.   Concludes that
   Ruskin died because it overly respected individual

freedom and lost its sense of community.

# CXIV.  ST. LOUIS-WESTERN COLONY

This colony, originally called the Western Colony, was organized in Ayres Point, Illinois, by Andrew C. Todd, a Reformed Presbyterian minister, and settled near Greeley, Colorado, in 1871. Although the group had about 500 members initially, Union (at Greeley) proved the only colony in the area with staying power, and the St. Louis-Western Colony was dissolved in 1872.

Survey work: Okugawa (139), 204-5.

*Secondary work*

2501.  Willard, James F., and Colin B. Goodykoontz, eds.  "St. Louis-Western Colony."  *Experiments in Colorado Colonization* (cited above as item 173), 331-96.
Provides basic documents of and newspaper accounts about the colony.

# CXV.  SALINE VALLEY FARMS

In 1931 and 1932, Harold Studley Gray purchased 596 acres of Michigan farmland and began to add improvements. By 1940 the land had 16 dwellings housing presumably as many families; by 1944, the community was operating in the black. It was food-oriented; main businesses included the raising of fruits and vegetables, eggs and dairy products, swine and poultry, and canning some of the farm's products. The cooperative features of the project eventually disappeared.

*Secondary works*

2502.  Dickinson, Z. Clark, and Joseph W. Eaton.  "Saline Valley Farms."  *Cooperative Group Living* (cited above as item 109), 22- 35.
Provides an overview of the project.

2503. Eaton, Joseph W. "Saline Valley Farm." *Exploring Tomorrow's Agriculture* (cited above as item 59), 196-8. Provides an overview of the project.

2504. Kramer, Wendell B. "Saline Valley Cooperative Farms, Inc." "Criteria for the Intentional Community" (cited above as item 118), 86-7.
Supplies a sketch of the agricultural operations and facilities of the farm; claims that its cooperative features are essentially defunct and that many farm facilities now sit idle.

# CXVI. SALVATION ARMY COLONIES

In 1898 the Salvation Army founded three colonies in an attempt to provide a livelihood for the urban poor outside what it considered the corrupt, unhealthy cities. The colonies were known as Fort Amity, Colorado, Fort Romie, California, and Fort Herrick, Ohio. Amity was the largest (1820 acres, peak population reported to be 450) and the longest-lived, surviving until 1909. Herrick was never successful, usually with fewer than a dozen families, and in 1903 it became a drying-out home for inebriates. Romie, on 520 acres near Soledad, reportedly had 24 families resident in 1904. The colonies were agricultural in economic base; Fort Amity also operated an orphanage.

Survey work: Okugawa (item 139), 223.

*Community periodicals*

2505. *Amity Observer*. 1905.

2506. *Amity Optimist*. 1903-5. Weekly.

2507. *Amity Sentinal*. 1902-3. Weekly.

*Works by community leaders*

2508. Booth, William. *In Darkest England and the Way Out.* Chicago: Charles H. Sergel, 1890.
Proposes farm colonies, among other projects, as a

solution to the bleak life of the poor in England.

2509.  Booth-Tucker, Frederick.  *Back to the Land!  Or the Ten-Acre Farms of the Salvation Army.*  N.p.: Salvation Army, 1898.  16 pp.
Booth-Tucker helped spearhead the founding and support of the farm colonies.

2510.  ———.  "Farm Colonies of the Salvation Army."  *Forum* 23 (August, 1897): 750-60.
Outlines the farm colony plan, arguing that it is a very inexpensive way to help the poor.

2511.  ———.  *Farm Colonies of the Salvation Army.*  New York: Salvation Army Printing and Engraving Department, 1898.  40 pp.

2512.  ———.  "Farm Colonies of the Salvation Army." *Bulletin of the Department of Labor* 8 (1903): 983-1005. Reprinted in *Salvation Army in America: Selected Reports, 1899-1903.*  New York: Arno, 1972.
Describes the history, goals, and current situation of the three colonies.  Describes the state of colony finances and the status of irrigation projects.  Also discusses farm colonies in other countries.

2513.  ———.  *Prairie Homes for City Poor.*  New York: n.p., 190-?  45 pp.

2514.  ———.  *Review of the Salvation Army Land Colony in California.*  New York: Salvation Army Press, 1903.  26 pp.

*Secondary works*

2515.  Antalek, Marie.  "Amity Colony."  M.A. thesis, Kansas State Teachers College, 1968.  91 pp.

2516.  "Colonization and Irrigation."  *American Monthly Review of Reviews* 28 (November, 1903): 610-l.
Proposes, on the basis of the apparent success to date of Amity, methods for settling poor urban families on rural land.

2517.  Fogarty, Robert S.  "Amity Colony."  *Dictionary of*

*American Communal and Utopian History* (cited above as item 76), 128-9.
Provides a brief overview of the colony.

2518. Haggard, H. Rider. *Poor and the Land*. London: Longmans, Green and Co., 1905. 157 pp.
Haggard made a tour of the three American and one British colonies (the latter at Hadleigh, England); this book is his report. It is primarily a collection of documents, including letters, notes taken by Haggard during colony visits, reports of interviews he made, and statements provided by colonists. Contains many charts, tables, and statistics with a wealth of specific data. Illustrated with photographs.

2519. Kellogg, R.S. "Interesting Experiment." *Jayhawker* (Manhattan, Kansas) 2 (January 15, 1904): 100-1.
Describes the five-year-old Amity colony, telling of irrigation, roads, homes, and telephones. Depicts an economy based on sugar beets and alfalfa. Includes a photograph of a large colony building.

2520. McKinley, Edward H. *Marching to Glory: The History of the Salvation Army in the United States of America, 1880-1980*. San Francisco: Harper and Row, 1980, pp. 89-93.
Provides an overview history of the colonies.

2521. "Making Successful Farmers of City Failures." *World's Work* 6 (September, 1903): 3929-30.
Describes several individuals who have left virtual destitution in cities and have prospered at Amity, providing facts and figures on their former and current situations.

2522. Murdoch, Norman H. "Anglo-American Salvation Army Farm Colonies, 1890-1910." *Communal Societies* 3 (1983): 111-9.
Characterizes the thinking of William Booth which underlay the colony project and the planning of the American colonies by Frederick Booth-Tucker. Provides sketches of the American colonies.

2523. Roberts, Dorothy. "Fort Amity, the Salvation Army Colony in Colorado." *Colorado Magazine* 17 (September, 1940): 168-74.

Provides a general historical sketch, including an overview of the settlement and physical building of the colony.

2524. Shaw, Albert. "Successful Farm Colony in the Irrigation Country." *American Monthly Review of Reviews* 26 (November, 1902): 561-6.
An upbeat article describing the origins of Amity colony, its settlement and development, and its finances. Provides an optimistic appraisal of its future. Heavily illustrated with photographs and a map.

2525. Solis, Miguel J. "Salvation Army Colonies." *American Utopias* (cited above as item 20), 149.
Provides a brief description of the colonies plus three bibliographical entries.

2526. Spence, Clark C. "Landless Man and the Manless Land." *Western Historical Quarterly* 16 (October, 1985): 397-412.
Describes the founding of the colonies; depicts the types of settlers involved in the project; evaluates the overall success of the farm colonies. Extensively documented with specialized materials not cited here.

2527. ———. *Salvation Army Farm Colonies*. Tucson: University of Arizona Press, 1985. 151 pp.
The standard monograph on the colonies. Contains a detailed bibliographical essay.

2528. *What Others Think of the Salvation Army Colony at Amity, Powers County, Colorado: A Few Letters from Neighbors, Residents and Visitors*. New York: Salvation Army, 1904. 31 pp.

2529. Whelpley, J.D. "Salvation Army Colonies." *Harper's Weekly* 45 (September 7, 1901): 902-3.
Provides a historical sketch of Fort Amity, finding it prospering with a population of 250. Says that the Salvation Army headquarters in New York has over 1,000 applications on file from persons wanting to move into the colonies.

2530. Wisbey, Herbert A., Jr. *Soldiers without Swords: A History of the Salvation Army in the United States*. New York: Macmillan, 1956, pp. 128-33.

Provides a general sketch of the colonies, principally Fort Amity and Fort Romie.

# CXVII. SAN FERNANDO FARM

San Fernando Farm, located 25 miles north of Los Angeles, was founded in 1943 by families of men who served together in Civilian Public Service camps during World War II. They sought a semirural life; government was by consensus.

### Secondary work

2531. Kramer, Wendell B. "San Fernando Farm." "Criteria for the Intentional Community" (cited above as item 118), 78-9.
Provides a brief sketch of the community's goal and farm operations.

# CXVIII. SCHOOL OF LIVING/ HEATHCOTE CENTER

In the 1920s and 1930s, Ralph Borsodi emerged as a strong critic of American culture, advocating decentralization and self-sufficiency as ways to solve growing problems of industrial society. One of his early projects, in the 1930s, was Dayton Homesteads, which was founded when he was invited by the City of Dayton to work on a small-plot, self-sufficiency-oriented decentralized housing project as a means of dealing with the city's huge unemployment problem. In 1936 Borsodi and friends organized the School of Living in Suffern, New York. Sixteen families occupied two-acre plots; there was also common land. Title to the land remained with the School, not with individual families; cooperative labor and cooperative financing of homes were stressed. The property was sold in 1945 and the School's work was transferred to the Loomis Lane's End Homestead near Brookville, Ohio. Later it moved to Deep Run Farm Center, near York, Pennsylvania, and finally to Heathcote Mill at Freeland, Maryland, which became the headquarters of the school and of an intentional community, one more fully communal that any previous School of Living project had been.    Following the death of Heathcote's leader Mildred Loomis in 1986, Deep Run Farm was sold, the money going into a land trust fund.    Heathcote Center about that time lost most of its members; the School of Living became a land trust with board members from several intentional communities.

## Community periodicals

2532.  *Balanced Living.* 1958-62. Edited by Mildred Loomis.

2533.  *Decentralist.* Suffern, N.Y. 1942-6.
        Published by the School of Living.

2534.  *Free America: A Magazine to Promote Independence.*
        New York. 1937-47.
        Edited by Herbert Agar, Ralph Borsodi, B.B. Fowler, and others.

2535.  *Green Revolution.* 1968-.
        Edited by Larry Lack, 1971-74; later edited by a committee.

2536.  *Inter Community Newsletter.* 1975-.

2537.  *Seeds of Change.* In publication in the 1970s.

2538.  *A Way Out.* 1963-7.
        Edited by Robert Anton Wilson, Herbert Rosemann, and others. Continuation of *Balanced Living* (item 2532).

## Works by and about Ralph Borsodi

2539.  Borsodi, Ralph.    *Education and Living.*    Suffern, New
        York: School of Living, 1948.
        Presents a decentralist program for dealing with contemporary social problems.

2540.  ———.    *Flight from the City.*    New York:    Harper    and
        Row, 1933.
        The story of the Borsodi family's venture into "creative living on the land" in which they tried to achieve self-sufficiency in Ohio.    That venture led to the creation of Dayton Homesteads, in which settlers were provided with

small plots on which to do self-sufficient farming. The latter project was just beginning when this book was written.

2541. ———. *This Ugly Civilization.* New York: Simon and Schuster, 1929. Repr., New York: Porcupine Press, 1975.
Contains a stinging critique of American society and its factory-based economy.

2542. Dorn, Jacob H. "Subsistence Homesteading in Dayton, Ohio, 1933-1935." *Ohio History* 78 (1969): 75-93.

2543. Fogarty, Robert S. "Borsodi, Ralph." *Dictionary of American Communal and Utopian History* (cited above as item 76), 17-8.
Biographical dictionary entry.

2544. Loomis, Mildred. "Man for Our Time." *Gandhi Marg* 20 (1976): 187-96.
Compares Borsodi's ideas with those of Gandhi. Not seen.

2545. Norris, Richard Patrick. "Back to the Land: The Post-Industrial Agrarianism of Ralph Borsodi and Austin Tappan Wright." Ph.D. dissertation, University of Minnesota, 1976. 258 pp.

*Works by a community leader*

2546. Loomis, Mildred. *Alternative Americas.* New York: Universe Books, 1982. 175 pp.
Provides biographical material on Ralph Borsodi and historical information on the School of Living and Heathcote Center.

2547. ———. *Go Ahead and Live!* New York: Philosophical Library, 1965. 196 pp.
Provides an overview of School of Living ideas and urges that such schools be founded throughout the country.

2548. ———. "Ralph Borsodi and the School of Living." *Moving into the Front Ranks of Social Change.* Edited by Mildred Loomis. Hinsdale, Illinois: Sol Press, 1974,

pp. 42-50.
This article (in a volume of conference proceedings)
contains a brief history of the School of Living.


*Secondary works*

2549. Bouvard, Marguerite.   "Decentralism  and   the  Social
      Thought  of  Ralph  Borsodi,"  "The  Green  Revolution,"
      and  "Heathcote  Center."   *Intentional  Community
      Movement* (cited above as item 37), 90-9.
      Contains  a  description  of  Borsodi's  critique  of  modern
      American  culture  and  his  attempt  to  found  homesteading
      communities  for  the  unemployed.     Follows  Borsodi
      through  the  founding  of  the  School  for  Living  at  Suffern.
      Sketches  the  School  of  Living's  transition  in  the  1940s  to
      the  leadership  of  Mildred  and  John  Loomis,  and  their
      eventual founding of the Heathcote Center in Maryland.

*       "Communes  Report"  (cited  above  as  item  46),  41-3.
        Provides  an  overview  of  the  projects  and  life  of  the
        community.

2550. Fairfield,  Dick.   "School  of  Living"  and  "Heathcote
      Center."    "Communes  U.S.A."  (cited  above  as  item  63),
      42-7.
      Provides  basic  information  on  Borsodi,  Loomis,  and  the
      history of the School of Living.

2551. ———— (Richard     Fairfield).    "School     of     Living."
      *Communes  USA:  A  Personal  Tour* (cited  above  as  item
      69): 24-38.
      Describes  Borsodi's  experiments  in  self-sufficiency  and
      the  School  of  Living  projects  at  Lane's  End  and
      Heathcote.    Contains  a  sketch  of  Heathcote  by  Mildred
      Loomis,  who  includes  an  analysis  of  the  group's  problems
      as well as stories of successes.

2552. Fogarty,  Robert  S.    "Subsistence  Farming."   *American
      Utopianism* (cited above as item 75), 133.
      A  brief  overview  of  the  Dayton  Homesteads  project  and
      the  ideas  and  work  of  Ralph  Borsodi.    Followed  by  a
      selection  from  Borsodi's  *Flight  from  the  City* (item  2540,
      above), 134-9.

2553. Issel,  William  H.    "Ralph  Borsodi  and  the  Agrarian

Response to Modern America." *Agricultural History* 41 (April, 1967): 155-66.
Provides a sketch of Borsodi's career and of some of his projects promoting self-sufficiency. Footnotes contain many references to publications concerning Borsodi and his ideas not cited here.

2554. Katz, Elia. *Armed Love.* New York: Holt, Rinehart and Winston, 1971, pp. 37-46.
Provides an account of the author's visit to Heathcote; he depicts the residents as obsessive and hypocritical.

# CXIX. SHALAM

Shalam operated from 1884 to 1901 near Dona Ana, New Mexico. John B. Newbrough was a visionary and spiritualist whose long tract *Oahspe* (reportedly meaning "spiritual record of heaven and earth"), written by him under alleged inspiration, was regarded as scripture by his followers. Newbrough joined forces with Andrew Howland, a wealthy man with high humanitarian ideals. With Newbrough's ideas and Howland's money they built a commune on 930 acres near Las Cruces on the Rio Grande. A large building was built for members to live in; another was a large orphanage. Newbrough's authoritarianism led to problems in the colony, and problems increased after his death in 1891. Howland and his wife Jane Howland stayed on for some time; the colony was abandoned in 1901. There were several other Oahspe colonies as well, none large. The first preceded the Dona Ana commune, but quickly failed; the others were founded in later years, at least into the second half of the twentieth century. The most successful of them was the Essenes of Kosmon community, led by Wing Anderson, incorporated in 1932 in Los Angeles, which in 1947 purchased 150 acres near Montrose, Colorado, and established a new Shalam there, even adopting some children. Later the property was sold and the "old faithful" members moved to Palisade, Colorado.
Some material on Shalam is in the American Communities Collection at Syracuse University.

Survey works: Liefmann (item 125), 23; Okugawa (item 139), 213.

*Works by community leaders*

2555.  Anderson, Wing.  *Health, Wealth and Happiness While You Sleep.*  Los Angeles: Kosmon Press, 1948.  64 pp.

2556.  ———, ed.  *Light of Kosmon.*  Los Angeles: Kosmon Press, 1939.  Unpaginated.
Presents selections from *Oahspe*, comprising a bit more than 10% of the original.  Contains a glossary.

2557.  ———.  *Next Nine Years: An Analysis and a Prophecy.*  Los Angeles: Kosmon Press, 1938.  48 pp.

2558.  ———.  *1952: The Year of Crisis.*  Los Angeles: Kosmon Industries, 1952.  80 pp.

2559.  ———.  *Peace and Plenty for You: Revealing a New Vision of a Life of Abundance for You.*  Los Angeles: Kosmon Press, 1941.  155 pp.

2560.  ———.  *Prophetic Years, 1947-1953.*  Los Angeles: Kosmon Press, 1946.  234 pp.
A compendium of predictions of disaster in the near future.

2561.  ———.  *Seven Years That Change the World, 1941-1948.*  Los Angeles: Kosmon Press, 1940.  269 pp.

2562.  ———.  *War's End.*  Los Angeles: Kosmon Press, 1944.  64 pp.

2563.  Newbrough, John B.  *Oahspe: A New Bible in the Words of Jehovih and His Angel Ambassadors.*  New York and London: Oahspe Publishing Association, 1882.
The special scripture of the movement.  Provides a fanciful cosmogony, history of the last 24,000 years, and new divine commandments for modern life.  A massive work, with some editions running over 900 pages.

*Secondary works*

2564.  Albertson, Ralph.  "Shalam Community, the Children's Land."  "Survey of Mutualistic Communities in America" (cited above as item 27), 391-2.
Provides an overview of the community's history.

2565.  Anderson, George Baker.  "Land of Shalam."  *Out West*

25 (November, 1906): 414-24.
Describes the colony, the ideas of Newbrough, the content of *Oahspe*, and the ongoing presence of Andrew Howland and his wife at the site after the dissolution of the colony. Illustrated.

2566. Barda, Leon. "Fate of the Original Oahspe Colony." In *Land of Shalam* (cited below as item 2575), 14-6. Originally published in *Search* (Amherst, Wisconsin).
Reproduces a newspaper clipping, attributed to the *San Antonio* Express of Las Cruces, New Mexico, entitled "Old Shalam Colony Gone." Apparently written shortly after the death of the colony, it tells the story of Newbrough and Oahspe and discloses the recent sale of the communal property.

2567. Dennon, James L. *Oahspe Story.* Seaside, Oregon: author, 1965. 34 pp.
Provides an overview of Oahspe, a biography of Newbrough, and a major account of the colony. Especially important for its information on individuals involved in the original Oahspe group and on the various strands of the movement which seemed to multiply for decades after the colony broke up.

\* Fogarty, Robert S. "American Communes, 1865-1914" (cited above as item 74), 155.
Contains a two-paragraph overview of Shalam.

2568. ———. "Newbrough, John Ballou." *Dictionary of American Communal and Utopian History* (cited above as item 76), 80-1.
Biographical dictionary entry.

\* Gladstone, Arthur. "Cooperative Communities Today II" (cited above as item 82), 14.
Describes the community of the Essenes of Kosmon at Montrose, Colorado. The group is said to own a 150 acre communal farm, where meals are taken in common and a monthly magazine is published, based on teachings in *Oahspe.* As of May, 1954, the group was reported to have eight members.

2569. Hinds, William Alfred. "Shalam, or the Children's Land." *American Communities and Co-operative Colonies* (cited above as item 95), 452-5.

Provides a brief sketch of the community and quotes from community writings.

*       Hine, Robert V.   *Community on the American Frontier*
        (cited above as item 99), 205-6.
        Provides a brief historical sketch of the colony.

2570.   Horst, Laura.   *Condensed Version of Oahspe*.   Amherst,
        Wisconsin: Palmer Publications, 1977.   256 pp.
        Contains a digest of Oahspe, plus a seven-page
        synopsis of that book and several introductory articles
        on Newbrough, Oahspe, and Shalam.

2571.   Howland, Jane (writing under the pseudonym "Jone
        Howlind").   "Shalam: Facts Versus Fiction."   *New
        Mexico Historical Review* 20 (October, 1945): 281-309.
        Provides a substantial history of Shalam from the
        perspective of a core member of the colony.   Takes
        strong exception to what the author says are the "wild
        statements and prevarications" of Julia Keleher in her
        article on Shalam (item 2573, below).

2572.   Johnson, Samuel G., ed. *Land of Shalam*. 17 pp.
        Pamphlet containing "Land of Shalam" (item 2575,
        below) and articles by Barda and Priestley (items 2566
        and 2577). At the Albuquerque Public Library.

2573.   Keleher, Julia.   "Land of Shalam: Utopia in New Mexico."
        *New Mexico Historical Review* 19 (April, 1944): 123-34.
        Provides a basic history of the colony, from the
        spiritual teachings of Newbrough through the decline of
        the organization.   A seemingly informative article, but
        one hotly contested by a Shalam veteran (see item 2571,
        above).

2574.   Kramer, Wendell B.   "Essenes of Kosmon."   "Criteria for
        the Intentional Community" (cited above as item 118),
        89-90.
        Provides a brief description of the Essenes' commune
        and its goals.

2575.   "Land of Shalam."   *History of New Mexico: Its Resources
        and People*.   Los Angeles: Pacific States Publishing
        Company, 1907, v. 1, pp. 511-8.
        A basic account of Newbrough, Howland, and the
        founding, life, and demise of their colony.   The

perspective is critical to the point of ridicule. Provides some local, anecdotal information. No references or bibliography.

2576. "Oahspe Circle." *Search* (Amherst, Wisc.) no. 141 (Winter, 1979-80): 23-5.
Describes a new Shalam colony near Orlando, Florida. Illustrated with photographs. (A column called "Oahspe Circle" was a regular feature in *Search* in this era.)

2577. Priestley, Lee. "Shalam—'Land of Children.'" *New Mexico Magazine* 39 (November-December, 1961): 20-3, 46.
Tells the story of Newbrough and the development of his religious enterprise; describes the building of the colony in terms of structures and agricultural projects; details the reasons for the decline of the experiment.

2578. Simundson, Daniel. "Strangers in the Valley: The Rio Grande Republican and Shalam, 1884-1891." *New Mexico Historical Review* 45 (July, 1970): 197-208.
Documents the shift in newspaper coverage of the colony as it shifted from favorable to antagonistic. Illustrated with photographs.

2579. Stoes, K.D. "Land of Shalam." *New Mexico Historical Review* 33. Part I: January, 1958, pp. 1-23. Part II: April, 1958, pp. 103-27.
Part I provides an overview of the life of Newbrough, the creation of *Oahspe*, and the founding of the colony. Part II describes the physical development of the colony, including the construction of the orphanage, and life at the colony after the death of Newbrough in 1891. Follows the decline of the colony until its abandonment in 1901, and tells of the life of Howland until his death in 1917.

2580. Wooster, Ernest S. "Shalam, or the Children's Colony." *Communities of the Past and Present* (cited above as item 175), 65.
Contains a one-paragraph account of Shalam.

# CXX. SHILOH FARMS

Shiloh Farms (also known as Shiloh Trust) was founded by
Eugene Crosby Monroe (1880-1961) in Chautauqua County, New
York, in 1941.    Monroe had been influenced by the
perfectionism of John Humphrey Noyes.    In 1968 the group
moved to northwest Arkansas pursuant to a revelation.    In 1977
the group reportedly had 102 members.    The movement is
Pentecostal and is involved in health food distribution.

*Secondary works*

2581.  Mathieu, Barbara.    "Shiloh Farms Community: A Case of
       Complementarity in Sex-Role Dualism."    *Sex Roles in
       Contemporary American Communes* (cited above as item
       167), 155-71.
       Provides a history of the community and concludes that
       while sexual equality is taught as a community ideal, sex
       roles within the community are not identical.

2582.  Melton, J. Gordon.    "Shiloh Trust."    *Encyclopedia of
       American Religions* (cited above as item 130), 502.
       Provides a brief historical sketch of the group.

2583.  "Monroe, the Reverend Eugene Crosby."    *Encyclopedia of
       American Biography* 37 (New York and West Palm
       Beach: American Historical Society, 1970): 227-8.
       Provides a biography of Monroe and a brief history of
       the community. Illustrated with a photograph of Monroe.

# CXXI. SILKVILLE

Ernest Valeton de Boissiere made a fortune in France but
was forced into exile by political conditions there in 1852.    He
met Charles Sears, of the late North American Phalanx, in
1856, and the two began to conceive of a new Fourierist
phalanx.    In 1869 de Boissiere purchased 3,500 acres in
Franklin County, Kansas, and began to develop the new
community, erecting several buildings, including a large
communal dwelling, early on.    De Boissiere called his
community Prairie Home, but the local monicker "Silkville"

quickly caught on. Silk was to be the economic mainstay of the community; many mulberry trees were planted to feed the silkworms. However, the panic of 1873 hurt the community's recruitment of new members, and it turned out that cheap labor made Chinese and Japanese silk cheaper than American silk could ever be. Formal dissolution of Silkville came in 1892; de Boissiere donated the property to the Odd Fellows for use as an orphanage.

Some correspondence between Charles Sears and E.P. Grant (1871) is located in the E. P. Grant papers at the University of Chicago. A small amount of primary material is located at the Kansas State Historical Society, Topeka.

Survey work: Okugawa (item 139), 203-4.

## Secondary works

2584. *Address of the Trustees of the De Boissiere Odd Fellows' Home and Industrial School Association.* Ottawa, Kansas: n.p., 1892. 3 pp.
Provides a brief history of Silkville, along with an account of the conflicts between the International Order of Odd Fellows and the estate of Charles Sears, when Sears claimed an interest in the property which de Boissiere had apparently given to the Odd Fellows. At the Kansas State Historical Society.

2585. Albertson, Ralph. "Silkville or the Prairie Home Colony." "Survey of Mutualistic Communities in America" (cited above as item 27), 410-l.
Provides a brief sketch of the community.

2586. Bestor, Arthur Eugene, Jr. "American Phalanxes." Ph.D. dissertation, Yale University, 1938, v. 2, pp. 68-72.
Includes a bibliography of Silkville containing some items not listed here.

2587. Blackmar, Frank W. "Silk Culture." *Kansas: A Cyclopedia of State History* (cited above as item 34), v. 2, pp. 694-6.
Describes the silk industry introduced to Kansas by de Boissiere, and traces the spread of that industry to other places in the state.

2588. Bracke, William B. *Wheat Country.* New York: Duell,

Sloan and Pearce, 1950, pp. 62-5.
Claims that the colony abolished marriage and
practiced free love, that de Boissiere was a publicly
avowed infidel, and that neighbors assiduously shunned
the community. None of Bracke's claims have any
apparent basis in fact.

2589. "Brisbane in Kansas." *Circular* (Oneida), n.s., 5 (March
15, 1869): 412-3. Reprinted from the *Communist* of
Alcander Longley.
Criticizes the Articles of Association of Silkville,
arguing that they set up a cooperative project, not a
true community.

2590. Carpenter, Garrett R. "Silkville: A Kansas Attempt in
the History of Fourierist Utopias, 1869-1892." *Emporia
State Research Studies* 3 (December, 1954): 3-29.
The most complete monograph on Silkville, covering
the life and career of de Boissiere, the founding and
building of Silkville, and the demise of the community
and its aftermath. Illustrated.

2591. "Communism in Kansas." *Circular* (Oneida), n.s., 7
(December 26, 1870): 322-3.
Reproduces an article from the New York *Herald*
setting forth de Boissiere's goals and detailing the
progress made so far in preparing the community for full
occupancy.

2592. "Co-operative Farm in Kansas." *Kansas Weekly
Commonwealth* (Topeka), June 9, 1870, p. 1.
Describes the purchase of the acreage and the
beginning of the physical development of the colony.
Quotes de Boissiere at some length on the early progress
of the colony.

2593. Fogarty, Robert S. "Brisbane, Albert," "De Boissiere,
Ernest Valeton," and "Silkville Colony, or Prairie
Home." *Dictionary of American Communal and Utopian
History* (cited above as item 76), 19-20, 29-30, 164-5.
Dictionary articles providing basic information on the
colony.

2594. Grant, E.P. *Co-Operation; or, Sketch of the Conditions
of Attractive Industry; and Outline of a Plan for the
Organization of Labor. With a Notice of the Kansas*

*Co-Operative Farm of M. Ernest V. de Boissiere.* New York: American News Co., 1870. 89 pp.
An essay on communalism and the Fourierist theory of attractive industry, with an appendix which provides a favorable portrayal of Silkville.

2595. Harner, J. "History of Silkville." Topeka *Daily Capital*, August 19, 1886, p. 2.
A letter recounting information gained from a member of the colony, focusing on successes experienced there, especially in the raising of silk, and reflecting on the community's problems, especially in the reeling of the silk.

* Hinds, William Alfred. *American Communities* (cited above as item 94), 157.
Characterizes the goals of de Boissiere and describes the early progress made in erecting buildings and starting industries.

2596. Huron, George A. "Ernest Valeton Boissiere." *Kansas Historical Collections* 7 (1901-2): 552-64.
Provides a history of Silkville from its origins through its aftermath, plus a biography of de Bossiere from his early years until his death.

2597. "Kansas Cooperative Farm." *Circular* (Oneida), n.s., 6 (July 12, 1869): 135-6.
Discusses the progress of the project to date, emphasizing that it is not intended to be fully communal, but rather to be cooperative in its economy.

2598. Kent, Alexander. "Prairie Home, or Silkville." "Cooperative Communities in the United States" (cited above as item 117), 641.
Provides a brief sketch of de Boissiere's plan and of the disposition of the property after the experiment had ended.

2599. Keroher, Grace Cable. "Silkville: Colony of Dreams." *Common Ground* 5 (Summer, 1944): 86-91.
Describes de Boissiere's innovative enterprises in France and New Orleans which made him wealthy; provides an overview history of Silkville.

2600. Long, Paul F. "Silkville: The Dream that Failed."

Ellsworth (Kansas) *Reporter,* March 29, 1979, pp. 6-7 of "The Best" feature supplement.
An illustrated newspaper feature story giving a concise, generally accurate history of the colony.

2601. "M. de Boissiere's Co-operative Farm in Kansas." *Circular* (Oneida), n.s., 7 (May 28, 1870): 78-9.
Describes de Boissiere's efforts to date and reproduces a letter from him telling of the project's current status.

2602. Nordhoff, Charles. "Prairie Home." *Communistic Societies of the United States* (cited above as item 138), 375-82.
Quotes extensively from de Boissiere's circular of March, 1874, but provides little other information.

2603. Raymond, W.M. "Silkville Commune." *Seminary Notes* 2 (May, 1893): 162-8. Published by the University of Kansas.
Provides a sketch of the community shortly after its dissolution. Reproduces the text of the 1873 circular by which de Boissiere sought to attract settlers.

2604. *Report of the Board of Trustees of the De Boissiere Odd Fellows Orphans' Home and Industrial School Association of Kansas.* Silkville: n.p., 1894. 29 pp.
Provides some details about the problems concerning the title to the property after de Boissiere's departure. At the Kansas State Historical Society.

2605. Richards, W.M. "Silkville: The Town Which Had No Sound Economic Basis." *Heritage of Kansas* 5 (February, 1961): 6-9, 27-9.
Provides a historical sketch of the colony and of the Kansas silk industry. Also reproduces de Boissiere's 1872 report to the Secretary of the Franklin County Agricultural Society, giving details about the silk operation, and an excerpt from de Boissiere's prospectus for the community. Illustrated with photographs.

2606. Sears, Charles. "Co-operation in Kansas. Development of Silk Culture." *Circular* (Oneida), n.s., 8 (January 6, 1876): 3.
Proudly describes the progress made at Silkville in its first four years, focusing on buildings, mulberry trees, and other improvements.

2607. ———. "Silk Culture in Kansas." *Brown's Industrial Gazetteer and Hand-book of the AT&SFRR.* Edited by George Lee Brown. Topeka: author, 1881, 12-6.
Provides general information on silk culture together with specific advice on how to undertake such a venture.

\* Waldron, Nell Blythe. *Colonization in Kansas from 1861 to 1890* (cited above as item 533), 72-5.
Provides a good overview history of the community.

2608. Watson, John. "Kansas Town Originally Utopian Colony." Wichita *Eagle*, June 3, 1955, p. 16A.
Feature article on Silkville. Contains photographs of the mulberry trees and of a former cocoonery, now a horse barn.

2609. Weeks, Vickie D. "Silkville." *Late Nineteenth Century Kansas Utopian Communities* (cited above as item 169), 40-9.
Provides a history of deBoissiere and his project; portrays the colony as having had good relations with its neighbors, so good that the outflow of members into the surrounding community helped cause Silkville to fail.

# CXXII. SINGLE TAX COLONIES

Some ten colonies were founded in the late nineteenth and early twentieth centuries as a means of demonstrating the utility of the single-tax philosophy of Henry George. They approximated George's proposal for a single tax on the value of unimproved land by dividing up a colony's property tax bill according to unimproved land value, thus not directly taxing homes or other improvements. By far the most successful and famous of the enclaves was Fairhope, founded in 1895, which still exists in somewhat altered form in Alabama. Its guiding figure was Ernest B. Gaston. Some attention was also focused on the enclave of Free Acres, New Jersey, founded in 1910, and that of Arden, Delaware, founded in 1900 (both are also still in existence as organized groups). The remaining colonies have received scant attention.

The other colonies and dates of founding were as follows:

Tahanto; Massachusetts; 1909
Halidon; Maine; 1911
Shakerton; Massachusetts; 1921
Ardentown; Delaware; 1922
Gilpin's Point; Maryland; 1926
Trapelo; Massachusetts; 1927
Wall Hill; Mississippi; 1932

Other independent experiments also tried versions of the single-tax system.

The Fairhope Single Tax Corporation maintains extensive archives at the site. Some other material on Fairhope is in the American Communities Collection at Syracuse University.

Survey works: Curl (item 52), 31; Okugawa (item 139), 219-20, 225, 229, 230.

### Single-tax periodicals relating to the colonies

Most single-tax periodicals carried news and comment concerning the colonies. Some of the more important ones were the following:

2610. *National Single Taxer.* Minneapolis. 1896-8; New York. 1898-1901.

2611. *Public.* Chicago. 1898-1916; New York. 1917-9.

2612. *Single Tax Review.* New York. 1901-23.

### Fairhope community periodicals

2613. *Fairhope Courier.*
First issue (August 1, 1894) published at Des Moines; issues from November 15, 1894 published at Battles Wharf, Alabama; issues from September 1, 1895, published at Fairhope. Published by the Fairhope Industrial Association until 1937, and thereafter under other auspices. Ernest B. Gaston was the editor through much of the paper's life.

2614. *Fairhope Monitor.*

2615. *Liberty Bell.*

### Arden community periodical

2616.  *Arden Leaves.*

### Primary works

2617.  *Arden Book.* Arden, Delaware: Community Planning Committee, 1973. 29 pp.

2618.  *Constitution of Fairhope Single Tax Corporation, Fairhope, Alabama.* Fairhope: Fairhope Courier Print, 1911. 16 pp.

2619.  *Fairhope, Alabama: Single Tax Colony on Mobile Bay.* Fairhope: Fairhope Courier Print, 1904. 29 pp. Descriptive pamphlet aimed at stimulating investment and colonization. Illustrated.

2620.  *Twenty-sixth Anniversary, Fairhope Single Tax Colony: Addresses, Messages, History, Songs.* [Fairhope]: Fairhope Courier, 1921. 24 pp.

### Works by a community leader

2621.  Gaston, Ernest B. "Fairhope, the Home of the Single Tax and the Referendum." *Independent* 55 (July 16, 1903): 1670-7. Describes Fairhope from a highly favorable perspective. Well illustrated with photographs.

2622.  ———. *Quarter Centennial History of Fairhope Single Tax Colony.* [Fairhope: 1920.] A brief manuscript history in the New York Public Library.

### Secondary works

2623.  Albertson, Ralph. "Fairhope Industrial Association." "Survey of Mutualistic Communities in America" (cited above as item 27), 414. Provides a brief overview of the colony's history and development.

2624.  Alyea, Paul E., and Blanche Alyea.  *Fairhope 1894-1954*.
       Tuscaloosa: University of Alabama Press, 1956.
       The most complete work on Fairhope.  Most references
       are to colony records and publications, especially the
       *Fairhope Courier*.  Contains copies of original and revised
       constitutions.

2625.  Bellangee, James.  "Fairhope: Its Problems and Its
       Future."  *Single Tax Review* 13 (May-June, 1913):
       17-27.
       Muses about the future of the colony, now nearly 20
       years old.  Provides a description of the motivations of
       the founders of the colony and chides the current
       management for not being democratic enough from the
       perspective of a member of the resident loyal opposition.

2626.  ———.  "Fairhope the Forerunner."  *Twentieth Century
       Magazine* 4 (September, 1911): 483-92.
       Explains George's single-tax theory and the version of
       it in effect at Fairhope.  Illustrated with photographs of
       colony buildings and other structures.

2627.  Bennett, Helen C.  "Fairhope—A Single-Tax Colony
       Which Has Made Good."  *Collier's* 49 (September 14,
       1912): 24, 44-6.
       Describes the development of Fairhope, its industries,
       its version of single-tax economics, and the alternative
       school there.  Illustrated.

2628.  Bercovici, Konrad.  "Colonies, Campfires, and Theories."
       *New York Times Magazine*, October 21, 1923, p. 6.
       Describes the single-tax theory and the diverse group
       that lived at Free Acres, noting that hostility from
       neighbors faded with time.  Also describes two nearby
       back-to-nature colonies which met heavy local opposition.

2629.  ———.  *It's the Gypsy in Me*.  New York: Prentice-
       Hall, 1941.  337 pp.
       Contains scattered references to Arden and other
       single-tax colonies; a good source for the flavor of life
       in the colonies.

2630.  Bierbaum, Martin A.  "Bolton Hall's Free Acres
       Experiment: The Single Tax and Anarchism in New
       Jersey."  *Communal Societies* 6 (1986): 61-83.
       Describes the founding of Free Acres by Bolton Hall in

1910 and traces its evolution. The colony still exists under common ownership, although residents now have long-term leases on the land they inhabit.

2631.  ———. "Free Acres: Bolton Hall's Single-Tax Experimental Community." *New Jersey History* 102 (Spring/Summer 1984): 37-63.
Describes the life of Hall, the founding of Free Acres, community life over the years, suburban encroachment, and the community still surviving in the 1980s. Illustrated with photographs.

2632.  Bliss, W.D.P. "Fairhope Colony." *New Encyclopedia of Social Reform* (cited above as item 35), 475-6.
Discusses the colony, its life, its history, dissension within it, and the single tax policy.

*       Douglas, Dorothy W., and Katharine Du Pre Lumpkin. "Communistic Settlements" (cited above as item 56), 101.
Describes the property leasing system used in the single tax enclaves.

2633.  Dudden, Arthur P. *Joseph Fels and the Single-Tax Movement.* Philadelphia: Temple University Press, 1971. 308 pp.
Documents the important role of Fels, a successful capitalist who wanted to abolish the system which had made him rich, as the chief financial angel of Fairhope.

2634.  "Fairhope Colony." *Arena* 40 (July, 1908): 108-9.
Quotes the text of resolutions recently adopted at Fairhope providing for initiative and referendum and for proportional representation in governmental bodies.

2635.  Federal Writers' Project. *Alabama: A Guide to the Deep South.* New York: Hastings House, 1941, pp. 397-8.
Provides a brief note on the history of Fairhope and on the Organic School; also includes a description of tourist facilities there.

2636.  Fogarty, Robert S. "Bellangee, James," and "Fairhope." *Dictionary of American Communal and Utopian History* (cited above as item 76), 13-4, 139-40.
Dictionary entries providing basic information on Fairhope.

2637.   Garvin, F.   "Arden, a Social Experiment."   *American City*
        (Town and Country Edition) 15 (July, 1916): 23-6.

2638.   Gaskine, J.W.   "Arden, a Modern 'As You Like It.'"
        *Independent* 71 (August 10, 1911): 299-304.
        Provides an enthusiastic overview of this single-tax
        colony of 70 acres nineteen miles from Philadelphia in
        northern Delaware. Illustrated with photographs.

2639.   Gaston, Paul M.   "Gaston, Ernest Berry."   *American
        Reformers* (cited above as item 172), 342-3.
        Provides a biographical sketch and a description of
        Gaston's theories which led to Fairhope, along with an
        account of the founding and development of the colony,
        emphasizing its experimental, innovative nature.

2640.   ———.   "Irony in Utopia: The Discovery of Nancy
        Lewis."   *Virginia Quarterly Review* 60 (Summer, 1984):
        473-87.
        Nancy Lewis was a black woman living on land
        purchased by Fairhope; she was required to leave rather
        than invited to join the colony.  This essay examines the
        ways in which race has been a stumbling block to
        utopian social reformers.

2641.   ———.   *Women of Fair Hope.*   Athens: University of
        Georgia Press, 1984.  143 pp.
        The story of the roles of three prominent women in
        the history of Fairhope: Nancy Lewis, Marie Howland,
        and Marietta Johnson.   Contains biographical material on
        each plus a discussion of each's role in the colony.

2642.   Geiger, George R.   *Philosophy of Henry George.*   New
        York: Macmillan, 1933, pp. 441-4.
        Describes the economic system of the single-tax
        colonies which made rent correspond to taxes under a
        single-tax system.   Provides brief information on all the
        American colonies.

2643.   George, Henry.   *Progress and Poverty.*   New York: J.W.
        Lovell Co., 1879, plus many other editions.
        The most important work of the prophet of the single
        tax.

2644.   Hall, Bolton.   *Little Land and a Living.*   New York:
        Arcadia Press, 1908.  292 pp.

A manifesto for small cooperative farming, much of it a manual for growing specific garden crops in innovative ways. Contains a bibliography of books on farming and gardening. (Bolton Hall published extensively on the single tax and other topics; his works cited here are those which have a direct bearing on cooperative farming. Hall founded the single tax colony Free Acres in New Jersey; his writings also influenced William Smythe, founder of the Little Landers colonies.)

2645. ———. *Money Making in Free America.* New York: Arcadia Press, 1909. 315 pp.
A treatise on wealth and financial security; advocates small-scale farming and collective enterprise.

2646. ———. *New Thrift.* New York: B.W. Huebsch, 1923. 247 pp.
A back-to-the-land tract, advocating intensive cultivation of small tracts in cooperative situations.

2647. ———. *Things as They Are.* New York: Arcadia Press, 1909, pp. 123-34.
Presents Hall's philosophy about getting back to the land and cultivating small acreages.

2648. ———. *Three Acres and Liberty.* New York: Macmillan, 1907. 435 pp.
A guide to making a living by going back to the land.

2649. ———. *Thrift.* New York: Huebsch, 1916. 247 pp.
Argues in favor of personal thrift; finds small cultivation an ideal way to practice thrift.

2650. Hinds, William Alfred. "Fairhope Industrial Association." *American Communities and Co-operative Colonies* (cited above as item 95), 505-12.
Provides a historical sketch and an overview of Fairhope's current condition; provides quotes on community goals from a Fairhope brochure.

2651. Horgan, Edward R. *Shaker Holy Land.* Harvard, Massachusetts: Harvard Common Press, 1982, pp. 152-5.
Discusses the history of the single-tax colony of Tahanto, Massachusetts, from the first purchase of land which would be the colony's in 1909 until the dissolution at the death of Fiske Warren, the founder and guiding

light, in 1938.    Focus is on the connections of the single
tax colony to the Shakers, whose land Warren had
bought for his colony.

2652.  Huntington, Charles White, ed.    *Enclaves of Economic
       Rent.*  Harvard, Massachusetts: Fiske Warren.
       At least thirteen annual volumes were published in this
       series, beginning in 1921.  150 to 338 pp. per volume.
       Reproduces basic documents of the single-tax colonies,
       such as constitutions, deeds of trust, and incorporation
       papers.    Also provides narrative histories of each colony.
       Covers foreign as well as domestic colonies.

2653.  Johnson, Marietta.    *Thirty Years with an Idea.*
       University, Alabama: University of Alabama Press, 1974.
       142 pp.
       Provides a history of the Fairhope Organic School.

2654.  Luther, D.S.    "Fairhope, Alabama."    *Public* (Chicago) 9
       (June 23, 1906): 271-4.
       Describes the founding of the Fairhope Industrial
       Association and the workings of its version of the single
       tax.    Characterizes Fairhope's geography and climate and
       describes improvements made to the town.

2655.  Montoliu, C.    "Fairhope: A Single-Tax Colony."    *Garden
       Cities and Town Planning* 11 (1919): 162-6.
       Outlines the enclave method of simulating the single
       tax; discusses town planning for Fairhope.    Illustrated
       with photographs and a planning map of Fairhope.

2656.  Petrie, George.    "Social Experiment: The Alabama Single
       Tax Colony."    *Book Lover's Magazine* 2 (1903): 416-8.
       Describes the organization of Fairhope; argues that the
       setting of proper rents is a major problem for the
       colony.

2657.  Sawyer, Rollin Alger.    *Henry George and the Single Tax.*
       New York: New York Public Library, 1926.  90 pp.
       A catalog of New York Public Library works on George
       and the single tax, including a number of works about
       the colonies.    Includes some specialized references not
       cited here.

2658.  "Single Tax Community."    *Current Literature* 35
       (November, 1903): 601.

Describes Fairhope's use of the "Guernsey Market House Plan" to build community facilities, using negotiable scrip to pay workers when money was not available.

2659. Solis, Miguel J. "Fairhope Single Tax Corporation." *American Utopias* (cited above as item 20), 50-1. Provides a brief description of the project plus three bibliographical entries on the single tax.

2660. Stewart, G.T. "Economic and Legal Aspects of the Single Tax Colony." *Journal of the Alabama Academy of Science* 41 (January, 1970): 9-16. Concludes that Fairhope residents benefit economically by the single-tax setup, but that they are frustrated in their inability to buy land. Based on questionnaires; includes tabulation of responses.

2661. Trenchard, P. "Only Single-Tax Colony in the World." *World Today* 11 (November, 1906): 1211-3.

2662. Trillin, Calvin. "U.S. Journal: Fairhope, Alabama." *New Yorker* 55 (June 11, 1979): 80-7, 90-1. Provides a look at comtemporary Fairhope in light of its history; focuses on an ongoing dispute over control of the library between the city council and the library board.

2663. Tucker, Gardiner L. "Single Tax Community." *Nation* 62 (April 2, 1896): 269. A letter to the editor providing a glowing description of Fairhope after it had existed for a year.

* Veysey, Laurence. *Communal Experience* (cited above as item 166), 115. Briefly characterizes Fellowship Farm, a single-tax colony near New Brunswick, New Jersey. The largely German-speaking community is pictured as "unusually strait-laced and moralistic," and some of its members therefore left it for the more freewheeling Ferrer Colony just down the road.

2664. Warren, Fiske. "Single Tax Enclaves." *Single Tax Year Book: The History, Principles, and Application of the Single Tax Philosophy.* Edited by Joseph Dana Miller. New York: Single Tax Review Publishing Co., 1917, pp.

66-80.
Describes several enclaves where land is rented to residents but no tax is levied on improvements. Includes material on the history and development of Fairhope and Arden, with briefer notes on Tahanto (Massachusetts), Halidon (Maine), and Free Acres (New Jersey).

2665.  Young, Arthur N. *Single Tax Movement in the United States.* Princeton: Princeton University Press, 1916, pp. 250-6.
Contains an account of the development of Fairhope, including the unsuccessful suit brought by disgruntled residents in 1914 to dissolve the corporation, along with brief a note on Arden.

# CXXIII.  SKYVIEW ACRES

Skyview Acres was founded at Pomona, New York, in 1946 to provide democratic, interracial housing in a semirural setting. It featured many cooperative services, from child care to car pools. It had 37 member families in the early 1950s.

## *Community periodical*

2666.  *Skyviews.* Monthly.

## *Secondary work*

2667.  Kramer, Wendell B. "Skyview Acres." "Criteria for the Intentional Community (cited above as item 118), 79-81. Provides a brief introduction to the community.

# CXXIV.  SOCIAL FREEDOM COMMUNITY

The Social Freedom Community was founded in 1874 in Chesterfield County, Virginia, on 333 acres. Soon after its founding it was reported to have six full and nine probationary members. It was disbanded in 1880.

Survey works: Albertson (item 27), 408; Okugawa (item 139), 205.

*Secondary works*

2668.   Nordhoff, Charles.   "Social Freedom Community."
*Communistic Societies of the United States* (cited
above as item 138), 357.
Quotes from a letter from members of the community
to the author describing the community shortly after its
founding.

*       Strachey, Ray, and Hannah Whitall Smith.   *Group
Movements of the Past and Experiments in Guidance*
(cited above as item 161), 85.
Contains a brief characterization of the community,
which is described as anarchical, with no religion, no
bylaws, and no concept of original sin.


# CXXV.  SOCIETAS FRATERNIA

In 1876 George Hinde purchased 23 acres near Fullerton,
California; in 1878 a spiritualist, Dr. Louis Schlesinger, arrived.
A community was founded on the property; it centered on
spiritualism, raw food, and group marriage.    Schlesinger left
amid controversy in 1882; Hinde vanished in 1883.    Walter
Lockwood, the next leader, presided peacefully until his death
in 1921.    The colony was dissolved soon thereafter.    Some
accounts spell the last name of the colony "Fraterna."

Survey work: Okugawa (item 139), 209.


*Secondary works*

2669.   Colman, Fern.   "Vegetarian Health Seekers of Orange
County."   *Rawhide and Orange Blossoms* (cited above as
item 147), 227-31.
Provides a brief history of the colony, emphasizing its
role in developing the subtropical fruit and vegetable
industries of southern California.    Contains a line
drawing of the colony's dwelling.

*       Hine, Robert V.   *California's Utopian Colonies* (cited

above as item 98), 142.
Contains a brief note on the colony's diet and provides
a bibliographical reference which I could not confirm.

2670.   Wilson, John Albert.   *History of Los Angeles County,*
        *California.*   Oakland: Thompson and West, 1880.   Repr.,
        Berkeley: Howell-North, 1966, p. 159.
        Reproduces an article from the May 10, 1879, Anaheim
        *Gazette* reporting the editor's visit to the group.
        Describes the founding of the movement, the unusual
        mansion which housed it, the raw-food diet, sexual
        attitudes, and the claim of psychic powers made by
        members.


# CXXVI.  SOUTHWESTERN COLONY

This colony was founded in the heyday of Colorado
colonization in the early 1870s, when several groups tried to
imitate the apparent success of Union Colony. This one was
located at Green City, 30 miles from Greeley, and was headed
by Davis S. Green of Memphis. It appears to have been as
much a scheme to sell real estate as a real colony, but at least
superficially tried to promote cooperative ideals.


*Secondary works*

*       Baker, James H., ed.   *History of Colorado* (cited above as
        item 30), v. 2, p. 451.
        Provides a brief historical note on the colony.

2671.   Willard, James F., and Colin B. Goodykoontz, eds.
        "Southwestern Colony."   *Experiments in Colorado*
        *Colonization, 1869-1872* (cited above as item 173),
        397-421.
        Provides basic documents of and newspaper articles
        about the colony.


# CXXVII.  SPIRIT FRUIT SOCIETY

Jacob Beilhart began his religious career working for the
Seventh-Day Adventists. He became interested in other

religions, however, and eventually formed the Spirit Fruit Society in about 1899. The community was originally located in Lisbon, Ohio; later it moved to Ingleside, Illinois (simultaneously maintaining a Chicago branch), and still later to a rural landholding near Santa Cruz, California. Although Beilhart died before the move to California, the society managed to stay together, at least minimally, for many years thereafter. It was finally dissolved in 1930.

Some material on the Society is in the American Communities Collection at Syracuse University. Other material is at the Ohio Historical Society in Columbus.

Survey work: Okugawa (item 139), 224.

### Community periodicals

2672. *Spirit Fruit.* 1899-1908. The organ of the movement in its early years in Lisbon and Ingleside; later reprinted at Roscoe, California.

2673. *Spirit's Voice.* 1900-1908. Second publication of the society.

### Primary work

2674. Henry, Leroy ("Freedom Hill Henry"), ed. *Jacob Beilhart: Life and Teachings.* Burbank, California: Freedom Hill Pressery, 1925. Second edition entitled *Life of Jacob Beilhart.* Roscoe, California: Freedom Hill Henry, 1930. 207 pp.
Compiled from the society's publications *Spirit Fruit* and *Spirit's Voice.* Illustrated.

### Works by the community leader

2675. Beilhart, Jacob. *Anarchy, Its Cause, and a Suggestion for Its Cure.* [Ingleside, Illinois: n.p., 1908]. 4 pp.

2676. ———. *Fruit of Spirit.* Ingleside, Illinois: Spirit Fruit Society, 1908. 25 pp.
At the Ohio Historical Society.

2677. ———. *Love Letters from Spirit to You.* Roscoe,

California: Freedom Hill Henry [Leroy Henry], 1929.
Purports to be a series of letters to God's beloved
from the spirit of love.

2678.  ―――.  *My Life and Teachings.*  Compiled by Freedom
Hill Henry [Leroy Henry].   Geneva, Switzerland: Quo
Vadis?, 1932.
Provides autobiographical information and messages
from the voice of the spirit.   At the Institute for the
Study of American Religion.

2679.  ―――.   *Spirit Fruit and Voice.*   Roscoe, California:
Freedom Hill Pressery, 1926.
Compiled from Beilhart's writing in two of the
society's publications, *Spirit Fruit* and *Spirit's Voice,* by
Leroy Henry ("Freedom Hill Henry").

2680.  ―――.   *Utopia Is Possible.*   Ingleside, Illinois: Spirit
Fruit Society, n.d.  20 pp.
At the Ohio Historical Society.

2681.  ―――.   *Very Personal.*   Ingleside, Illinois: Spirit Fruit
Society, 1908.  50 pp.


### Secondary works

2682.  Fogarty, Robert S.   "Beilhart, Jacob."   *Dictionary of
American Communal and Utopian History* (cited above
as item 76), 11.
Biographical dictionary entry.

2683.  Fogarty, Robert S., and H. Roger Grant.   "Free Love in
Ohio: Jacob Beilhart and the Spirit Fruit Colony."
*Ohio History* 89 (Spring, 1980): 206-21.
Tells the history of Beilhart and the Society, beginning
with Beilhart's work for the Seventh-Day Adventists.
Discusses allegations of free love levelled against the
community after Beilhart's sister had a child out of
wedlock around 1903.   Describes the colony's move from
Lisbon, Ohio, to Ingleside, Illinois, and its teachings in
the Chicago area.

2684.  Grant, H. Roger.   "Gentle Utopia: The California Years of
the Spirit Fruit Society, 1914-1930."   *Pacific Historian*
30 (Fall, 1986): 55-70.

Provides a historical sketch emphasizing the group's California years. Illustrated with photographs.

2685. ———. "Idahoan Experiences Utopia: Irvin E. Rockwell and the Spirit Fruit Society." *Idaho Yesterdays* 29 (Spring, 1985): 24-32.

Details the support which the wealthy Rockwell gave to the Society over many years after being spiritually healed of major ailments by Beilhart.

2686. ———. "Prairie State Utopia: The Spirit Fruit Society of Chicago and Ingleside." *Chicago History* 12 (Spring, 1983): 28-35.

An illustrated history of the society. Very similar to the author's article, "The Spirit Fruit Society: A Perfectionist Utopia in the Old Northwest" (item 2689, below).

2687. ———. *Spirit Fruit: A Gentle Utopia.* DeKalb, Illinois: Northern Illinois Press, 1988. 203 pp.

The standard monograph on the movement.

2688. ———. "Spirit Fruit: 'Jacob's' Ohio Utopia." *Timeline* (December, 1985-January, 1986): 18-27.

A popular account of the society, focusing on its unconventional ideas about sex and marriage and the spiritual search of Beilhart. Includes a brief account of what happened to the group after it moved to Illinois, but mainly deals with the early years in Ohio.

2689. ———. "Spirit Fruit Society: A Perfectionist Utopia in the Old Northwest, 1899-1915." *Old Northwest* 9 (Spring, 1983): 23-36.

Provides the basic story of the Spirit Fruit Society, particularly in the Chicago area phase of its history. Illustrated.

2690. Hinds, William Alfred. "Spirit Fruit Society." *American Communities and Co-operative Colonies* (cited above as item 90), 556-62.

Describes the development of Beilhart's ideas; reproduces a letter from Beilhart giving a brief sketch of the community as of March, 1907.

\* Lauer, Robert H., and Jeanette C. Lauer. *Spirit and the Flesh* (cited above as item 120), 125-6, 205-6.

Characterizes Beilhart's concept of love as a way to freedom; tells of a threat of mob violence which made the community move to Chicago.

# CXXVIII. STRAIGHT EDGE COMMUNITY

This social gospel-era movement was begun in New York City in 1899 as a project in which the teachings of Jesus would be applied to business and society generally. It began with Mr. and Mrs. Wilbur F. Copeland's turning their home into a center for the study of social and industrial problems. They started their weekly newspaper and several industries, including a farm on Staten Island, teaching trades to persons in need of jobs. The group's communal living arrangements were to end in due course, the persons involved achieving economic independence. Day care and education were provided. 12 members were reported in 1901.

Some information on the community is in the American Communities Collection at Syracuse University.

Survey works: Albertson (item 27), 420; Okugawa (item 139), 223-4.

### Community periodical

2691. *Straight Edge*. 1899-1921. Weekly/monthly.

### Work by a community leader

2692. Copeland, Wilbur F. "Straight Edge Industrial Settlement." *New Encyclopedia of Social Reform* (cited above as item 35), 1164.
    Describes the community's purpose, organization, and economy. Lists the grading criteria on which salaries were based.

### Secondary works

2693. Fogarty, Robert S. "Copeland, Wilbur F." and "Straight Edge Industrial Settlement." *Dictionary of American Communal and Utopian History* (cited above as item

76), 26 and 167, respectively.
Provides a brief overview of the community.

2694. Hinds, William Alfred. "Straight-Edgers." *American Communities and Co-operative Colonies* (cited above as item 95), 548-55.
Provides a historical overview and a description of the group's principles and procedures.

2695. Kent, Alexander. "Straight Edge People." "Cooperative Communities in the United States" (cited above as item 117), 626-8.
Describes the community's industries, newspaper, and goals for the future.

# CXXIX. SUNNYSIDE

Samuel Donnelly began working the Copper Glance Mine in the Huachuca Mountains of Arizona in 1887; it turned out to be a good producer of silver and copper. In 1890 Donnely founded a commune there; it attracted mainly Holiness-oriented Methodists. At its peak the community had 50 to 80 members. The group scattered after Donnelly's death on 1901.

*Secondary work*

2696. Szasz, Ferenc Morton. *Protestant Clergy in the Great Plains and Mountain West, 1865-1915.* Albuquerque: University of New Mexico Press, 1988, p. 90.
Provides a brief sketch of the community. Endnotes provide citations of other sources I was not able to verify.

# CXXX. SUNRISE

Joseph J. Cohen, the founder of Sunrise, had been involved in operating the Ferrer Colony in New Jersey. In the fall and winter of 1932 he promoted his new communal vision mostly among urban Jewish immigrants; finally, working in conjunction with Eli Greenblatt, he purchased a 9000-acre farm near Alicia, Michigan, in 1933. The colony attracted a great many settlers—including many anarchists and radicals—quickly, reaching 300 members by its first autumn. There were problems and progress for several years; finally the property was sold to the Resettlement Administration at the end of 1936. Although some conflicts lingered, many members moved to a new 642-acre communal site in Virginia. That successor colony was also plagued by interpersonal and financial problems. Cohen left the Virginia site in 1938, and the property was sold in 1940.

Collections of Sunrise materials are located at the Hoyt Public Library, Saginaw, Michigan, and in two separate parts of the University of Michigan library system: the Bentley Historical Library and the Department of Rare Books and Special Collections (Labadie Collection).

### Community periodicals

2697.  *Children's Work*. 1935-6.
Written by Sunrise elementary schoolchildren.

2698.  *High School Review*. 1934-5.
Newspaper published by Sunrise High School students.

2699.  *Orb*. 1934.
Sunrise High School literary magazine.

2700.  *Our Opinion*. 1934.
Commentary written by Sunrise High School students.

2701.  *Out at Sunrise*. 1936. Daily (irregular) newsletter.
Collected at Hoyt Public Library, Saginaw.

2702.  *Sunrise News*. 1934-1935. Weekly, later monthly, periodical of the colony.
Collected at Hoyt Public Library, Saginaw.

2703.  *Voice of Sunrise Youth*. 1933.
A newspaper written and published by Sunrise High School students.

### Works by a community leader

2704.  Cohen, Joseph J. "Community Origins." *American Utopianism* (cited above as item 75), 140-4.

An excerpt from founder Cohen's writings on Sunrise.

2705. ———. *House Stood Forlorn.* N.p.: privately published, 1954. 175 pp.
An autobiography of early life in Russia in the late 19th century.

2706. ———. *In Quest of Heaven: The Story of the Sunrise Co-operative Farm Community.* New York: Sunrise History Publishing Committee, 1957. Repr., Philadelphia: Porcupine Press, 1975.
Provides some background on other communes (Harmony, Brook Farm, and others); tells the story of Sunrise beginning with the background of the author, who founded the community. Describes the oversupply of settlers in relation to facilities, community crises (such as several fires), and internal conflicts. Very personally and engagingly told; author's perspective seems fair, despite his deep involvement in the subject. Cohen's original typescript of this book (located in the Labadie Collection at the University of Michigan Library) is markedly different from the published version.

2707. ———. *Jewish Anarchist Movement in the United States: A Historical Review and Personal Reminiscences.* Philadelphia: Workmen's Circle, 1905. 557 pp.
In Yiddish.

2708. ———. "Sunrise Cooperative Farm Community." *Freedom* (New York) n.s., v. 1 (June, 1933): 6.
Outlines the plans for the community, which is to take possession of its land on June 15. Details the resources of the farm, its projected industries, its communal economy, and its anticipated cultural and educational programs.

*Secondary works*

2709. Albertson, Ralph. "Sunrise Cooperative Community." "Survey of Mutualistic Communities in America" (cited above as item 27), 419.
Provides a sketch of the colony.

* Avrich, Paul. *Modern School Movement* (cited above as item 839), 179-82.

Provides a biographical sketch of Joseph Cohen, who is depicted as a dedicated worker but a cold and distant person.

* Federal Writers' Project. *Michigan: A Guide to the Wolverine State* (cited above as item 68), 446. Characterizes the founding and dissolution of the community, paying special attention to describing the community's buildings and levees.

2710. Fogarty, Robert S. "Cohen, Joseph B.[sic]" and "Sunrise Community." *Dictionary of American Communal and Utopian History* (cited above as item 76), 23-4, 167-8. Dictionary entries providing basic information on the community.

2711. ————. "Sunrise Community." *American Utopianism* (cited above as item 75), 140. A brief introduction to the Sunrise endeavor; written as an introduction to "Community Origins" (item 2704, above).

2712. Infield, Henrik. "Sunrise Community." *Cooperative Communities at Work* (cited above as item 105), 53-62. Provides a good overview of the community, its founding, its life, and its problems.

2713. Lemieux, Christina M. "From Sunrise to Sunset: Seeds of Destruction in the Sunrise Cooperative Farm Community." Typescript. At the Center for Communal Studies.

2714. ————. "Michigan Utopia: The Sunrise Cooperative Farm Community." *Chronicle* (Historical Society of Michigan) 23 (March-April, 1988): 4-8. A good general history of the colony covering its origins, problems, relocation, and aftermath. Illustrated with photographs and a map.

2715. ————. "Sunrise in Virginia: The Final Experiment." Typescript. At the Center for Communal Studies.

2716. "Michigan Colony Denies Plan Has Russian Backing." New Orleans *Times-Picayune*, July 6, 1933, p. 4. Quotes Cohen as denying local allegations that he has

Soviet backing; provides an on-the-scene look at the colony, quoting residents on their experiences there.

2717. Oved, Yaacov. "Sunrise and Anarchist Communities." *Two Hundred Years of American Communes* (cited above as item 142), 311-31 (see especially pp. 315-30). Describes the purchase of the farm and its early development, the rise of internal conflict, agricultural problems, the sale of the property to the government in 1936, and the abortive move to Virginia.

2718. Shor, Francis. "American Kibbutz? The Sunrise Colony and the Utopian Problematics in Comparative Perspective." *Communal Life: An International Perspective* (cited above as item 84), 174- 83. Similar to the author's article "Utopian Project" (item 2719, below).

\* ———. "Cultural Identity and Americanization: The Life History of a Jewish Anarchist" (cited above as item 855), 324-46. Provides a biographical sketch of Cohen, including accounts of his involvement in Ferrer Colony and Sunrise.

2719. ———. "Utopian Project in a Communal Experiment of the 1930's: The Sunrise Colony in Historical and Comparative Perspective." *Communal Societies* 7 (1987): 82-94. Furnishes a history of the colony in light of utopian thought prevalent in the 1930's, examining its leadership, work patterns, and educational program; provides a comparative analysis of Sunrise and the kibbutzim of Israel. Provides an excellent overview of disputes and problems in the group.

2720. Singer, Richard E. "Sunrise Cooperative Farm Community." *American Jew in Agriculture* (cited above as item 1504), 638-9. Provides a brief history of the community.

2721. Trupin, Philip. "Epilogue: Sunrise in Virginia." Unpublished typescript, 1959. 7 pp. At the Bentley Historical Library, University of Michigan.

## CXXXI. SUNRISE COOPERATIVE FARMS

In the early 1930s, a group of Jewish philanthropists raised money to buy 1,000 acres of land in Monmouth County, New Jersey. The aim was to resettle poor urban Jewish families there; the first were to be needle workers from the garment district in New York. Each family would have a house and a one-acre tract for personal gardening; all other garden, dairy, and industrial work was to be done by the community. The colony was never very large or successful; it was formally dissolved in the mid-1930s.

Some of the Sunrise papers are at the New York Public Library.

### Secondary works

2722. Albertson, Ralph. "Sunrise Cooperative Farms." "Survey of Mutualistic Communities in America" (cited above as item 27), 418-9.
    Provides an overview of the community, noting that after its dissolution it became the site of a federal Resettlement Administration colony.

2733. "Jews Here to Open Community Farm." New York *Times*, November 29, 1933, p. 17.
    Describes the land purchase and the prospect of moving 200 families there soon, with industry to follow.

2744. "Needle Workers Get Farm Homes." New York *Times*, December 23, 1933, p. 20.
    Provides an update on the plan, explaining that the 200 initial families are to move in soon.

## CXXXII. TANGUY HOMESTEADS

This residential community was founded in 1945 near Glen Mills, Pennsylvania, on cooperative principles, seeking to stimulate work for the common good. Its population was reported as 85 in the early 1950s; it was still operating in the late 1980s.

*Secondary works*

\*   Bouvard, Marguerite. *Intentional Community Movement* (cited above as item 37), 100.
    Provides a brief characterization of the project.

2725.   Kramer, Wendell B. "Fellowship Co-op Homestead, Inc.--Tanguy." "Criteria for the Intentional Community" (cited above as item 118), 77-8.
    Outlines the goals and group process of the community.

2726.   "Tanguy Homesteads." *Intentional Communities: 1959 Yearbook of the Fellowship of Intentional Communities* (cited above as item 807), 27-8.
    Provides a basic history of the community.

# CXXXIII. TEMPLE OF THE GOSPEL OF THE KINGDOM

Around 1900 a Virginian named Warien Roberson claimed mystical revelations which led him to found a communal society of black Jews. The group, centered in Harlem after about 1917, had "kingdoms" for urban members as well as farms in rural New Jersey, including, allegedly, a farm where pregnant women—presumably bearing Roberson's children, since celibacy was the rule for other members—were housed. Roberson taught that his followers would achieve immortality; therefore outsiders following the movement dubbed it the "Live Ever, Die Never" society.

*Secondary works*

2727.   Landes, Ruth. "Negro Jews in Harlem." *Jewish Journal of Sociology* 9 (1967): 175-89.
    Provides an overview of black Judaism in Harlem, with a characterization of Roberson and his flock, its communal economy, and the "baby farm" in New Jersey. Also contains information on noncommunal black Jewish groups.

2728.   Reid, Ira De A. "Let Us Prey!" *Opportunity: A Journal*

*of Negro Life* 4 (September, 1926): 274-8.
Describes the sexual misconduct of Roberson and depicts the group as robbing the public.

# CXXXIV. THELEMIC MAGIC COMMUNITY AT PASADENA

In 1939 Jack Parsons and Wilfred Smith rented a mansion in Pasadena to serve as home for a Thelemic Magic commune, one with connections to Aleister Crowley. Changes in sex-magic partners led to tensions, and internal difficulties resulted. The community ended in the 1950s, when a mysterious explosion in the house killed Parsons.

*Secondary works*

2729. Grant, Kenneth. *Magical Revival.* New York: Samuel Weiser, 1973, pp. 107, 157-60.
Contains brief references to the Pasadena Lodge of the Ordo Templi Orientis, along with biographical material on Jack Parsons and Wilfred Smith.

2730. Melton, J. Gordon. "Thelemic Magic in America." *Alternatives to American Mainline Churches.* Edited by Joseph H. Fichter. New York: Rose of Sharon Press, 1983, pp. 67-87.
An exposition of the Thelemic magical tradition in America, including a brief history of its communal phase in Pasadena.

# CXXXIV(A). THEOSOPHICAL COMMUNES

The Theosophical Society was founded in the 1870s by Helena P. Blavatsky. Following her death in 1891, the movement divided, one faction following the old Blavatsky associate William Quan Judge, the other following the newer leader Annie Besant. Two major communes emerged from the Judge branch. The more important was the Point Loma community near San Diego, led by Katherine Tingley. The other was the Temple of the People, originally the Syracuse,

New York, chapter of the Theosophical Society, which moved to Halcyon, California, and established a community there in 1903. The Besant branch of the movement also produced a major community, known as Krotona, originally based in Hollywood, and later with two branches, at Ojai, California, and Wheaton, Illinois. Later another Theosophical commune was founded; it was known as Camphill Village and was based on the ideas of Rudolph Steiner, the leader of the German branch of the movement, which became known as Anthroposophy.

There is an enormous literature on Theosophy, and specifically on its communal phase. This list, therefore, represents only selections of material. See the National Union Catalog for many more entries, especially for ephemera and short items.

Survey work: Curl (item 52), 40.

### *Secondary works on Theosophical communalism in general*

\* Faris, Robert E.L. *Social Disorganization* (cited above as item 66), 413-4 (second edition, pp. 576-7).
Provides a brief historical sketch of Point Loma and Krotona.

2731. Fogarty, Robert S. "Willard, Cyrus Field." *Dictionary of American Communal and Utopian History* (cited above as item 76), 120-1.
Biographical dictionary entry.

2732. Hine, Robert V. "Cult and Occult in California." *Pacific Spectator* 8 (Summer, 1954): 196-203.
Discusses Hinduistic religious movements in California, including Theosophy, Vedanta, the Self-Realization Fellowship, and several others. Includes a brief discussion of the communal projects at Point Loma, Halcyon, and Ojai.

2733. ------. "Theosophical Colonies in California: Point Loma and Temple Home." *California's Utopian Colonies* (cited above as item 98), 33-57.
Contains informative accounts of the history of Point Loma and Temple Home (Temple of the People), plus a note on Krotona.

2734. Kagan, Paul. "Theosophist Communes in California."

*New World Utopias* (cited above as item 115), 48-83.
A readable, heavily illustrated history of all of the major California Theosophical utopian communities.

2735.   McWilliams, Carey.   "Purple Mother."   *Southern California Country* (cited above as item 126), 252-8.
Describes the development of the Point Loma' community, its conflicts with its neighbors, and the development of Krotona in Hollywood and its subsequent move of Ojai.

2736.   Mathison, Richard.   "Annie Besant, Katherine Tingley and Krishnamurti."   *Faiths, Cults and Sects of America: From Atheism to Zen* (cited above as item 127), 148-59.
Sketches the histories of Point Loma and Krotona; describes the conflicts between the two branches of the Theosophical movement.

# CXXXV(B).  AQUARIAN FOUNDATION

Edward Arthur Wilson developed a following in England for his claims that he was "Brother XII," in touch with a secret brotherhood of theosophical masters.   In 1927 he moved to Vancouver Island with some 200 followers.   Internal dissension appeared quickly; the movement expired in violence and the disappearance of Brother XII in 1933.   Some followers regrouped and continued the movement.   The writer Will Levington Comfort was at one time the most prominent member of the group.

### Community periodicals

2737.   *Chalice.*

2738.   *Beehive.*   Edited by Will Levington Comfort.

### Primary work

2739.   *Three Truths: A Simple Statement of the Fundamental Philosophy of Life as Declared and Shown to "Brother XII."*   Akron, Ohio: Sun Publishing Co., 1927.   49 pp.

*Secondary works*

2740. Berton, Pierre. *My Country.* Toronto: McClelland and Stewart, 1976, pp. 100-21.
Provides the only reasonably reliable history of the movement, from its early days in England through the scandal and disappearance of Brother XII. Illustrated with photographs and a reproduction of the front page of an issue of the *Chalice.*

2741. Wilson, Herbert Emmerson. *Canada's False Prophet: The Notorious Brother Twelve.* Richmond Hill, Ontario: Simon and Schuster, 1967. 144 pp.
Purportedly written by Brother XII's brother, never a part of the movement, this book is a sensationalized history of the group which claims to be based in part on letters written by XII to his brother. Herbert Wilson characterizes his guru brother as a fraud. However, the author's claim to be the brother of the prophet is itself fraudulent; while some of the book's content is factual, some is not.

# CXXXV(C). CAMPHILL

The Camphill Community was initiated in Scotland in the 1940s, dedicated to the philosophy of Rudolf Steiner. The community's "industry" and reason for existence was assisting and teaching handicapped and retarded children. When the American community was established at Copake, New York, in 1961 by Carlo Pietzner and others, these activities were expanded and intensified. The community has grown considerably from its original 200 acres and two buildings. A second Camphill community known as Beaver Run was opened later at Glenmoore, Pennsylvania; it specialized in the treatment of mentally retarded children.

*Community periodicals*

2742. *Camphill Village USA Newsletter.* In publication in the 1960s. Monthly.

2743. *Cresset: Journal of the Camphill Movement.* In publication in the 1960s.

2744. *Friends of the Camphill Movement USA Newsletter.*
1973-.

### Primary works

2745. *Camphill Movement.* Copake, New York: n.p., n.d.   14
pp.
A pamphlet describing the life and philosophy of the
community. At Community Service, Inc.

2746. *Project: A Village Community for Mentally Retarded
Children.* Copake, New York: Camphill Village, n.d.
A pamphlet explaining the community's work.   At
Community Service, Inc.

### Secondary works

2747. Fairfield, Dick.   "Camphill Village."   "Communes U.S.A."
(cited above as item 63), 161.
Provides a brief characterization of Camphill.

2748. Fairfield, Richard.   "Camphill Village."   *Communes USA:
A Personal Tour* (cited above as item 64), 332-3.
Describes the founding of and services provided by
Camphill at both of its locations; discusses the
organization and standards of the group.

* *Intentional Community Handbook* (cited above as item
808). Unpaginated.
Contains a report on and description of the community,
including a statement on the work of the community in
helping handicapped and retarded children.

2749. Raz, Jon.   "Camphill Village."   *Communities* no. 1
(December, 1972): 17-23.
Describes the founding and growth of the community,
emphasizing its role in serving the handicapped.

## CXXXV(D). KROTONA

One of the Theosophical splinters after Blavatsky's death
was headed by Annie Besant.   She founded Krotona in
Hollywood in the early twentieth century; a communal group

developed there for several years. In 1924 Krotona moved to Ojai, California, to be close to J. Krishnamurti, whom the Krotonans regarded as the World Teacher.

Survey work: Okugawa (item 139), 230.

### Community periodical

2750. *Messenger*. Published 1913-. Official journal of the Besant wing of the Theosophical movement.

### Secondary works

2751. Comfort, Jane Levington, writing under the pseudonym Jane Annixter. *From These Beginnings*. New York: Dutton, 1937.
Tells the story of Krotona in the form of a novel.

2752. Ranson, Josephine. *Short History of the Theosophical Society*. Adyar, India: Theosophical Publishing House, 1938. 589 pp.
Describes the origins of Krotona in Hollywood, problems within the movement there, and the development of the communities at Wheaton and Ojai.

# CXXXV(E).  POINT LOMA

Theosophy was again fragmented after the death of William Quan Judge, successor to Helena P. Blavatsky; Katherine Tingley emerged as the leader of one group, which in 1897 bought land at Point Loma, across the harbor from San Diego, and began to build buildings. Eventually a strong community was established; it featured educational activities, a vigorous publishing and printing program, and classical drama, among other things. Following Tingley's death in 1929, the community slowly declined; finally the property was sold in 1942 and the group moved to Pasadena.

The Bancroft Library at the University of California, Berkeley, has a number of pamphlets from Point Loma. The American Communities Collection at Syracuse University also has material on the community.

Survey works: Liefmann (item 125), 23-5; Okugawa (item 139), 222.

## Community periodicals

The following periodicals are cited either in the Union List of Serials or in Greenwalt (item 2788, below).

2753. *Century Path.* New York and San Diego. 1907-11. Weekly.

2754. *Lotus Circle Messenger.* Point Loma. 1930-5. Children's monthly.

2755. *Lucifer.* Point Loma. 1930-51. Monthly.

2756. *New Century.* New York and San Diego. 1897-1903. Weekly.

2757. *New Century Path.* New York and San Diego. 1903-7. Weekly.

2758. *New Way.* Point Loma. 1911-26. Monthly for prisoners.

2759. *Raja-Yoga Messenger.* Point Loma. 1904-29. Monthly.

2760. *Searchlight.* Point Loma. 1898-1911. Irregular.

2761. *Theosophical Forum.* Point Loma. 1929-51. Monthly.

2762. *Theosophical Path.* Point Loma. 1911-35. Monthly.

2763. *Universal Brotherhood.* Point Loma. 1897-9. Monthly.

2764. *Universal Brotherhood Path.* Point Loma. 1900-3. Monthly.

## Primary works

2765. *Katherine Tingley's Raja-Yoga System of Education, Its Aims and Achievements.* Point Loma: Aryan Theosophical Press, [1922]. 31 pp.

2766. *Theosophical Leaflets.* [Point Loma: Aryan Theosophical

Press, 1890?] 13 volumes in one. Contains Theosophical tracts written by many authors.

2767. *Theosophical Manuals.* Point Loma: Aryan Theosophical Press, 1907-10. Eighteen volumes.

2768. *Theosophical Society, Its Nature and Objectives.* Point Loma: Theosophical University Press, 1940. 20 pp.

2769. Theosophical Society, Point Loma, California. *Constitution.* Point Loma: n.p., 193-? 11 pp.
Listed in the National Union Catalog under "Theosophical Society, Pasadena, California."

*Works by a community leader*

2770. Tingley, Katherine A. *Brief Sketch of the History and Work of the Original Theosophical Society, Founded 1875, Reorganized 1898, Now Known as the Universal Brotherhood and Theosophical Society.* Point Loma: Aryan Theosophical Press, ca. 1915. 24 pp.

2771. ———. *Gods Await.* Point Loma: Woman's International Theosophical League, [1926]. 186 pp.

2772. ———. *Helena Petrovna Blavatsky, foundress of the original Theosophical Society in New York, 1875, the International Headquarters of Which Are Now at Point Loma, California.* Point Loma: Woman's International Theosophical League, [1921]. 81 pp.

2773. ———. *Life at Point Loma. Some Notes by Katherine Tingley, Leader and Official Head of the Universal Brotherhood and Theosophical Society.* Point Loma: Aryan Theosophical Press, 1908. 18 pp.

2774. ———. *Mysteries of the Heart Doctrine, Prepared by Kathering Tingley and Her Pupils.* Point Loma: Theosophical Publishing Co., [1902]. 350 pp.

2775. ———. *Nosegay of Everlastings from Katherine Tingley's Garden of Helpful Thoughts.* Point Loma: Students of the Raja Yoga College, 1914.

2776. ———. *Pith and Marrow of Some Sacred Writings.*

Point Loma: T.P. Co., 1905.

2777. ———. *Readjustment of the Human Race Through Theosophy.* Point Loma: Woman's International Theosophical League, [1924]. 29 pp.

2778. ———. *Theosophy, the Path of the Mystic.* Compiled by Grace Knoche. Point Loma: Woman's International Theosophical League, [1922]. 185 pp.
Aphorisms and observations.

2779. ———. *Travail of the Soul.* Point Loma: Woman's International Theosophical League, [1927]. 291 pp.

2780. ———. *Voice of the Soul.* Point Loma: Woman's International Theosophical League, [1928]. 308 pp.

2781. ———. *Wine of Life.* Point Loma: Woman's International Theosophical League, 1925.

*Secondary works*

2782. Baker, Ray Stannard. "Extraordinary Experiment in Brotherhood." *American Magazine* 63 (January, 1907): 227-40.
A favorable survey of the colony, sketching its physical setting, people, care of children, family life, culture, and relations with neighbors. Heavily illustrated with photographs.

2783. Brown, Lauren R. *Point Loma Theosophical Society: A List of Publications, 1898-1942.* La Jolla: Friends of the University of California at San Diego Library, 1977. 132 pp.
A comprehensive list covering all aspects of Point Loma plus the most important primary materials on Theosophy generally. Illustrated with photographs taken at Point Loma.

2784. Campbell, Bruce F. *Ancient Wisdom Revived: A History of the Theosophical Movement.* Berkeley: University of California Press, 1980, pp. 131-42.
Describes the rise of Katherine Tingley, the development of the Point Loma comminnty, the Raja Yoga system, the community's rich cultural life, and the

group's eventual decline. The book as a whole provides a concise history of the whole theosophical movement.

2785. Fogarty, Robert S. "Point Loma or the Universal Brotherhood and Theosophical Society" and "Tingley, Katherine." *Dictionary of American Communal and Utopian History* (cited above as item 76), 158 and 112, respectively.
Dictionary entries providing basic information on the community.

2786. Fussell, Joseph Hall. *Incidents in the History of the Theosophical Movement Founded in New York in 1875 by H.P. Blavatsky, Continued under William Q. Judge, and Now under the Direction of Their Successor, Katherine Tingley.* Point Loma: Aryan Theosophical Press, 1910 (plus later revised editions). 32 pp.

2787. Greenwalt, Emmett Alwyn. "Point Loma Community in California, 1897-1942." Ph.D. dissertation, University of California at Los Angeles, 1949. 129 pp.

2788. ———. *Point Loma Community in California, 1897-1942: A Theosophical Experiment.* Berkeley: University of California Press, 1955. Revised edition, *California Utopia: Point Loma: 1897-1942.* San Diego: Point Loma Publications, 1978.
A comprehensive history of the Point Loma Theosophists. Illustrated with photographs. Extensive bibliography contains citations of many primary sources not cited here.

2789. Harris, Iverson L. "Reminiscences of Lomaland." *Journal of San Diego History* 20 (Summer, 1974): 11-32.
An interview with a lifelong Theosophist who lived many years at Point Loma. Contains many anecdotes and details about life at the community.

2790. ———. *Theosophy Under Fire: A Miniature "Key to Theosophy" As Recorded in a Legal Deposition.* San Diego: author, 1970. 88 pp.
Provides informationa about the Theosophical Society from the man who was chairman of the Cabinet of the Society in 1945. Reproduces the questions and answers of a legal deposition from a case in which a will was being contested. Provides many scattered bits of

information about Point Loma and Katherine Tingley.

2791.   Hinds, William Alfred.    "Universal Brotherhood at Point
        Loma, Cal."    *American Communities and Co-operative
        Colonies* (cited above as item 95), 464-70.
        Provides an overview of the community, quoting
        community leaders and documents extensively.

2792.   Kagan, Paul, and Marilyn Ziebarth.    "Eastern Thought on
        a Western Shore: Point Loma Community."    *California
        Historical Quarterly* 52 (Spring, 1973): 3-15.
        Describes the origins of the colony; provides an
        overview of the Tingley years; describes the abandonment
        of Point Loma during World War II.    Heavily illustrated
        with photographs.

2793.   Knobe, Bertha Damaris.    "Point Loma Community."
        *Munsey's Magazine* 29 (June, 1903): 357-63.
        Provides an overview of the community, describing its
        physical plant, its educational program, and some of the
        basic concepts in Theosophy.    Heavily illustrated with
        photographs.

2794.   Koch, Felix J.    "With the Theosophists at Point Loma."
        *Overland Monthly* 62 (October, 1913): 340-44.
        Recounts a visit to Point Loma, quoting from
        conversations with members and describing the colony
        and its life.    Emphasizes the physical facilities of the
        community and the role of Tingley.

2795.   *Loma-Land, a Delightful Place for Rest or Residence.*
        Point Loma: Theosophical Publishing Co., 1901.  36 pp.

2796.   Lummis, Charles F.    "Those Terrible Mysteries."    *Out
        West* 18 (January, 1903): 35-48.
        Describes the arrival of Cuban children at Point Loma
        and decries rumors circulating about the community.
        Avers that the colonists are normal persons who neither
        eat children, worship purple dogs, nor have orgies.
        Heavily illustrated with photographs.

*       Pourade, Richard F.    *History of San Diego: Gold in the
        Sun* (cited above as item 1865) v. 5, pp. 18, 21, 24-8,
        34, 88, 140, 235.
        Contains scattered brief references to the colony, plus
        a more detailed account of attacks on the theosophists

by ministers and newspapers in California, investigations by various government agencies and citizens' groups, and Tingley's successful libel suit against the Los Angeles *Times*.

2797. Ryan, Charles J. *H.P. Blavatsky and the Theosophical Movement.* Pasadena: Theosophical University Press, 1937.
An overview history of Theosophy in America, including a sympathetic account of the founding of the Point Loma commune.

2798. Small, W. Emmett, ed. *Wisdom of the Heart: Katherine Tingley Speaks.* San Diego: Point Loma Publications, Inc., 1978.

2799. Smythe, William E. *History of San Diego, 1542-1908.* San Diego: History Co., 1908, v. I, pp. 715-7.
Provides a historical sketch of the Point Loma Community, listing the various branches of the movement and characterizing cultural activities at Point Loma.

2800. Solis, Miguel J. "Universal Brotherhood and Theosophical Society." *American Utopias* (cited above as item 20), 167-70.
Provides a brief historical sketch of Point Loma plus 12 bibliographical entries, many of them referring to works on theosophy not dealing specifically with its communal phase.

2801. Von Wiegand, Karl H. "Mystics, Babies and Bloom." *Sunset* 23 (August, 1909): 115-26.
Describes the community campus and its environs, the group's day care and educational programs, its organization, and its basic ideals and purpose. Illustrated with photographs of Point Loma and its members.

\*        Webber, Everett. *Escape to Utopia* (cited above as item 168), 344-5.
Depicts a colorful colony ruled by a leader with "a whim of iron."

# CXXXV(F).  TEMPLE OF THE PEOPLE

The Syracuse chapter of the Theosophical Society early achieved considerable strength.    After the breakup of the Theosophical Society following the death of William Quan Judge, the chapter moved to Halcyon, California, in 1903, where it founded a community known as the Temple of the People. The community is still alive and well at this writing.

Survey work: Okugawa (item 139), 227.

## Community periodical

2802.  *Temple Artisan*. 1900-. Monthly.

## Primary works

2803.  *From the Mountaintop*.    Halcyon, California: Temple of the People, 1914, 1975, 1985.  Three volumes.

2804.  *Teachings of the Temple*.    Halcyon, California: Temple of the People, 1925, 1985.  Three volumes.

2805.  *Temple Messages*.    Halcyon, California: Temple of the People, 1983.

2806.  *Theogenesis*.    Halcyon, California: Temple of the People, 1981.

## Secondary works

2807.  Hinds, William Alfred.    "Temple Home Association." *American Communities and Co-operative Colonies* (cited above as item 95), 577-80.
        Provides an overview of the state of the community; quotes a community booklet's list of the group's goals.

2808.  Melton, J. Gordon.    "Temple of the People." *Encyclopedia of American Religions* (cited above as item 130), 604-5.
        Provides a historical sketch of the group plus an

outline of its distinctive theosophical doctrines.

# CXXXVI. THOMPSON COLONY

Elizabeth Rowell Thompson, a wealthy widow, sponsored many social reform projects, including several communes, in the late nineteenth century. This colony, founded in 1880, was among those she helped. It was located near Salina, Kansas. Colonists were given separate homes and land; they worked large fields jointly and were required to devote time to major colony projects. Colony profits were divided among members.

Survey work: Okugawa (item 139), 210.

*Secondary works*

2809. Fogarty, Robert S. "Thompson, Elizabeth Rowell." *Dictionary of American Communal and Utopian History* (cited above as item 76), 111-2.
Biographical dictionary entry.

2810. Holyoake, George Jacob. *Among the Americans, and A Stranger in America.* Chicago: Belford Clarke and Co., 1881; repr., Westport, Connecticut: Greenwood Press, 1970, pp. 232-3.
Contains a discussion of the involvement of Elizabeth Thompson in the Co-operative Colony Aid Association, which was established to buy land, design colonies, set up basic institutions on colony grounds, and provide initial sustenance of new communities.

2811. Miller, Howard S. "Elizabeth Rowell Thompson." *Notable American Women 1607-1950.* Edited by Edward T. James et al. Cambridge, Massachusetts: Belknap Press, 1971, v. 3, pp. 452-4.
Provides a brief biographical sketch of Thompson, a wealthy benefactress to several cooperative colonies, including the Chicago-Colorado Colony at Longmont, near Burlington, Colorado, and the Thompson Colony, which was named for her.

2812. "New Colonization Plan." New York *Times*, June 6, 1879, p. 2.

Discusses the formation of the Co-operative Colony Aid Society, emphasizing the role of Thompson.

2813.  Zornow, William F. *Kansas: A History of the Jayhawk State.* Norman: University of Oklahoma Press, 1957, p. 180.
Tells of reports in 1869 that a French emigrant company has purchased 91,000 acres for the founding of Thompson Colony, but can find no further information about the venture.

# CXXXVII. TOPOLOBAMPO

In the early 1870s, Albert Kimsey Owen concluded that a railroad from the U.S. to the Pacific should most efficiently run to a port in Mexico; having the Pacific terminus at the Mexican port of Topolobampo would cut 400 to 600 miles off the American cross-country distance, and would thus look very attractive to shippers. He first explored Topolobampo Bay in 1872; later he proposed that a commune be developed along with the railroad. Work on the railroad began in the 1880s, and in 1886 permanent settlement at the Bay was begun. By 1894, 1189 persons were reported to have arrived, although the population was never that high at any one time. The railroad was never finished; meanwhile, two factions developed amid disputes over land and water rights, among other things. Litigation led to evictions and dispossessions from land. Some of the Americans married Mexicans and remained there, but most returned home in or shortly after 1894.

Credit foncier, a term intimately connected to the movement, referred to fixed real estate, as opposed to credit mobilier, credit based on movable property, such as railroad rolling stock. The point was that security is based on one's home.

Most of the primary pamphlet and periodical material listed here is at the Kansas Collection of the Spencer Research Library at the University of Kansas. Some other material is in the American Communities Collection at Syracuse University. Much manuscript, ephemeral, and other early material is at the California State University, Fresno, library. Other primary materials are at the Huntington Library, San Marino, California.

Notes constituting a substantial bibliography of works in Spanish on Topolobampo are located in the article by Bennett Lowenthal (item 2879, below).

## Community periodicals

2814. *Credit Foncier of Sinaloa.* Hammonton, New Jersey, 1885-1888; Topolobampo, Sinaloa, Mexico, 1888-1895. Usually weekly or biweekly.
The University of Kansas libraries have four volumes covering most of the run of the paper.

2815. *Integral Co-operator.* Enterprise, Kansas. 1889-94. Weekly (later semimonthly) American organ of the Credit Foncier. Edited by C.B. Hoffman.
The journal of the Kansas Sinaloa Investment Company, a group of Americans contributing to further land purchases at the colony site. A basic primary document for the study of Topolobampo, containing correspondence to and from the colony, aids to those who would join the movement and move to Mexico, and general articles on the theory and practice of communal living.

2816. *Jeffersonian.* Topeka, Kansas. 1889-90.
For a brief period, this periodical was the "Credit Foncier organ of the U.S."

2817. *New City.* New York. 1892-4. Biweekly. Edited by A.K. Owen.
Official organ of the Credit Foncier Co. The University of Kansas libraries hold two volumes covering the life of the paper.

2818. *Pacific Wave.* Topolobampo. 1895.
An apparently short-lived Topolobampo periodical. Copies for May 1 and May 9, 1895 (each 2 pp.) are in *Pamphlets on the Credit Foncier Co., volume 2* (item 2820, below).


## Primary works

Most of the items listed in this section are contained in two bound volumes of pamphlets at the University of Kansas libraries:

2819. *Pamphlets on the Credit Foncier Company, volume 1: 1874-1892.* Hereafter cited as *Pamphlets, 1.*
Contains 22 pamphlets and leaflets.

2820. *Pamphlets on the Credit Foncier Company, volume 2: 1886-1893.* Hereafter cited as *Pamphlets, 2.*
Contains 14 pamphlets and leaflets plus five large maps and drawings.

## Individual pamphlets

2821. *By-Laws of the Credit Foncier Co., to Which Is Added the New Colonization Contract of February 28, 1890.* New York: Credit Foncier Co., 1890. 38 pp. In *Pamphlets, 1.*

2822. Clerco, D. *De Socialistische Kolonie te Sinaloa.* No imprint. 28 pp. In Dutch. In *Pamphlets, 1.*

2823. *Concessions for "The Topolobampo-Texas, Limited" with Pacific City and Colony.* New York: n.p., 1890. 32 pp. In *Pamphlets, 1.*
Provides the text of the detailed and ambitious agreement Owen reached with the Mexican government.

2824. *Credit Foncier Company: Its Charter, Constitution, Pledge, By-Laws (First Draft).* New York: Credit Foncier Co., 1892. 46 pp. In *Pamphlets, 1.*

2825. *Credit Foncier Company. Our Principles. N.p., 1886.* 7 pp. In *Pamphlets, 1.*
A 37-point statement of principles.

2826. *Credit Foncier Company, Sinaloa, Mexico.* Chicago: n.p., 1892.
A prospectus for would-be investors in or settlers at Topolobampo, containing a description of the work accomplished to date.

2827. *Credit Foncier Company: The Topolobampo Colonists.* No imprint. 16 pp. In *Pamphlets, 2.*
A portfolio of illustrations of the colony.

2828. *Credit Foncier of Sinaloa: Circular of Information.* N.p., [ca. 1891]. 3 pp. text, 5 pp. illustrations. In *Pamphlets, 2.*

2829. *Great Southern Trans-Oceanic and Inter-National Air-Line, Asia to Europe via Mexico and the Southern*

    *States.*    9    pp.     Supplement   to   the   above   item.     In *Pamphlets, 1.*

2830. *Homes and How to Obtain Them: Integral Cooperation the Solution of the Problem.*    Topeka:   W.II.T.   Wakefield, 1890. 104 pp. In *Pamphlets, 1.*
Information for prospective colonists.

2831. *Integral Co-operation at Work.*    New    York:   John    W. Lovell Co., 1890. 135 pp. In *Pamphlets, 1.*
Contains several articles on cooperation and on the Topolobampo project.

2832. List of articles shipped to colonists.    No imprint.    2   pp. In *Pamphlets, 1.*

2833. Lovell, John W.    *Co-operative City, and the Credit Foncier of Sinaloa.*    New   York:   Credit   Foncier   Co., 1886. 18 pp. In *Pamphlets, 1.*
Condensed version of an optimistic speech about the project.

2834. *Memoranda.* No imprint. 3 pp. In *Pamphlets, 2.*

2835. *Memoranda of Agreement.*    N.p.,   March   16,   1892.    1   p. In *Pamphlets, 2.*

2836. Muller, William H.    *New Departure: A Description of Pacific Colony.*    New   York:   Credit   Foncier   Co.,   1886. 23 pp. In *Pamphlets, 1.*
A discussion of the proposed project.

2837. ———.    *New    Departure:    A    Description    of    Pacific Colony.*    New   York:   Credit   Foncier   Co.,   1890.    67   pp. In *Pamphlets, 1.*
An expanded version of Muller's previous work of the same title.

2838. "New and Strange Yankee Colony in Mexico."    Newspaper clipping dated January 23, 1887. 1 p. In *Pamphlets, 2.*

2839. *Principles and By-Laws of The Credit Foncier Company, to Which Is Added "The Colonization Contract".*    New York: Credit Foncier Co., 1886.    31   pp.    In *Pamphlets, 1*; another copy is bound separately at the University of Kansas libraries.

Contains list of personnel, 31-point statement of principles, bylaws, and the colonization contract between the government of Mexico and the Texas, Topolobampo and Pacific Railroad and Telegraph Co.

2840.  *Proposed Form of Incorporation and By-Laws.*   N.p., [ca. 1893]. 4 pp. In *Pamphlets, 2.*

2841.  Reports to stockholders.   March 16, 1887, 8 pp.   May 14, 1887, 4 pp. In *Pamphlets, 2.*

2842.  Schellhous, E.J.   *Topolobampo Colony: Its Principles Outlined, and the Country of Its Adoption Described.* San Francisco: n.p., n.d. 7 pp. In *Pamphlets, 1.*

2843.  *Sinaloa Intelligence.* No imprint. 4 pp.
Tells how the Kansas-Sinaloa Investment Company has been formed to help Topolobampo by getting Americans to help fund land purchases in Mexico.   Provides some basic information on the organization of the K-SIC as well as the Credit Foncier Co.   At the Kansas State Historical Society.

2844.  *Some Late Letters.* No imprint. 1 p. In *Pamphlets, 2.*

2845.  *Statement to Accompany the Call of Treasurer John W. Lovell for the Payment of the Second Assessment on the Stock of The Credit Foncier Company, and for Placing the Equipment Bonds for the Railroad Line from Topolobampo Harbor to the Rio Fuerte Valley.* N.p., 1887. 4 pp. In *Pamphlets, 2.*

2846.  *Subscriptions.   The Pacific Investment Company.*   No imprint. 3 pp. In *Pamphlets, 2.*

2847.  *Topolobampo Colonists: What Is Said of Them.*   N.p., 1892. 10 pp. In *Pamphlets, 1.*

2848.  *Topolobampo: Projector Owen Denounced as an Unspeakable Fraud.*   No imprint.   1 p.   In *Pamphlets, 2.*

### Works by a community leader

2849.  Owen, Albert Kimsey.   *Austin-Topolovampo Pacific Survey*

[sic]. Philadelphia: H.C. Baird and Co., 1877.

2850. ———. *Credit Foncier of Sinaloa.* No imprint. 1 p.
In *Pamphlets, 1.*
Circular.

2851. ———. *Credit Foncier of Sinaloa: A Social Study.*
[New York: n.p., 1885?] 64 pp.

2852. ———. *Dream of an Ideal City.* London: Murdoch and
Co., 1897.
Owen's vision of Topolobampo as an ideal community,
with such features as fulfilling work, an absence of vice
and crime, a quiet and attractive environment, good
educational opportunities, good, cooperative people, great
architecture, and an absence of poverty. Each paragraph
begins with the words "I love to dream."

2853. ———, ed. *Extracts from Newspapers, Explanatory of
the Credit Foncier Company.* New York: Credit
Foncier Co., 1887. 52 pp. In *Pamphlets, 1.*
Includes articles from the New York *Sun*, New York
*Tribune*, New York *Herald*, San Diego *Union*, and several
other papers.

2854. ———. *Great Southern Trans-Oceanic and International
Air Line.* Asia to Europe, via Mexico and the Southern
States. Philadelphia: Rowley and Chew, 1873. 4 pp.
In *Pamphlets, 1.*
A.K. Owen's letter to Congress proposing the project.

2855. ———. *Integral Co-operation at Work, #2.* New York:
United States Book Co., 1891.

2856. ———. *Integral Co-operation: Its Practical Application.* New York: J.W. Lovell Co., [1884].
The most complete exposition of Owen's ideas and
manifesto for Topolobampo he ever published. The first
quarter of the book explains Owen's vision and plans; the
balance contains appendices with diverse kinds of
materials directly and indirectly related to the
Topolobampo project. Contains many foldout maps.

2857. ———. *Interesting Data Concerning the Harbor of
Topolobampo and the State of Sinaloa, Mexico.*
Washington: Gibson Brothers, 1883.
One of Owen's earliest writings specifically promoting

Topolobampo.

2858.    ———.    *Leaflet*.    N.p., 1892.    36 pp.    In *Pamphlets, 1.*
         Contains six articles by Owen.

2859.    ———.    "Let Us Have Evolution, Not Revolution."    New
         York *American*, February 11, 1885.
         A manifesto by Owen arguing for the need for
         attractive labor, describing the organization of the Credit
         Foncier and urging the construction of better homes for
         workers.

2860.    ———.    *Pacific City Studies*.    [Boston: n.p., 1892.]

2861.    ———.    *Problems of the Hour*.    New York:    Humboldt
         Library, 1897.    37 pp.

2862.    ———.    *Texcoco-Huehuetoca Canal*.    Philadelphia:    H.C.
         Baird and Co., 1880.

2863.    ———.    Untitled report.    September 25, 1888.    12 pp.
         In *Pamphlets, 1.*


                            Secondary works

2864.    Albertson, Ralph.    "Topolobampo."    "Survey of Mutualistic
         Communities in America" (cited above as item 27), 412.
         Provides an overview of the colony's history.

  *      Arndt.    Karl J.R.    "Koreshanity, Topolobampo, Olombia,
         and the Harmonist Millions" (cited above as item 1762).
         Describes the efforts of these three later movements to
         get their hands on the millions of dollars belonging to
         the nearly defunct Harmonists.

2865.    Bernard, L.L., and Jessie Bernard.    *Origins of American
         Sociology*.    New York:    Thomas Y. Crowell, 1943, pp.
         359-71.
         Covers Albert Kimsey Owen, his new version of
         associationism/ Fourierism, his ideas on such topics as
         women's rights and economics, the nature of the
         Topolobampo project, and the failure of the experiment.
         Much of the rest of the book covers earlier communal
         ideas and projects, especially those related to Fourierism.

2866. Bruce, J. Campbell. "Prosperity Comes to Topolobampo." *Catholic Digest* 17 (March, 1953): 31-5.

Concerns the revival of the town of Topolobampo and the rehabilitation of the railroad in the 1940s. The railroad brought the village access to markets and thus made it a major center of shrimp fishing. Contains only a brief reference to the colony, but provides a valuable glimpse of later occurences there.

2867. Carnahan, Arthur L. "Orient." *Southwestern Historical Quarterly* 53 (April, 1950): 479-81.

Provides an account of the actual building of the various sections of the railroad after the chartering of the private Kansas City, Mexico and Orient Railway Co. in 1900.

\* Douglas, Dorothy W., and Katharine Du Pre Lumpkin. "Communistic Settlements" (cited above as item 56), 100-1.

Provides a brief description of Topolobampo's financial arrangements.

2868. "Fateful Sinaloa." Dickinson County (Kansas) *Daily Reflector*, July 29, 1891.

Describes the return of several colonists from Topolobampo, recounting their tales of exotic, fatal fevers, greedy colony bosses, and a failing economy there.

2869. Felt, W. Sherman. "Credit Foncier of Sinaloa." *Nationalist* 3 (February, 1891): 433-8.

Tells the story of the founding and development of the colony and of the contract Owen made with the Mexican government; provides an optimistic appraisal of the future of the colony.

\* Fogarty, Robert S. "American Communes, 1865-1914" (cited above as item 74), 155-7.

Contains a good, concise history of the project.

2870. ———. "Hoffman, Christian Balzac," "Howland, Edward," "Howland, Marie Stevens," "Owen, Albert Kimsey," and "Topolobampo Bay Colony." *Dictionary of American Communal and Utopian History* (cited above as item 76), pp. 52-6, 88, 168-9.

Dictionary entries providing a general overview of the

project.

2871. Hinds, William Alfred. "Topolobampo." *American Communities and Co-operative Colonies* (cited above as item 95), 456-63.
Provides an overview history of the colony with a critical analysis of its demise.

2872. Hope, Derrill. "Topolobampo." *Social Gospel no. 36* (February, 1901): 3-14.
An upbeat review of the colony, admitting that it is experiencing problems but arguing that nevertheless it is a major boon to the communitarian movement.

2873. "Kansas Colony." Topeka *Daily Capital*, June 16, 1889, p. 8.
An optimistic article about preparations for the colony. Tells of the colonists' hope that eventually their territory will be annexed by the United States.

2874. Katscher, Leopold. "Owen's Topolobampo Colony, Mexico." *American Journal of Sociology* 12 (September, 1906): 145-75.
Provides a narrative history of the colony, including Owen's efforts to get Theodor Hertzka to merge his new Freeland with Topolobampo in Mexico. Provides a good exposition of Owen's physical plans for the colony and his proposed social policy. Reproduces the constitution of the community, along with a statement of its ideals.

2875. Kent, Alexander. "Topolobampo." "Cooperative Communities in the United States" (cited above as item 117), 640-1.
Sketches the ideas of Owen, the Mexican railroad concession, the Golden Rule idealism of Owen and the other founders, the organization of the Credit Foncier Co., and the community's problems and failure.

2876. Kerr, John L. *Destination Topolobampo: The Kansas City, Mexican and Orient Railway*. San Marino, California: Golden West Books, 1968. 270 pp.
Provides an account of the efforts of Owen and Arthur Stilwell to build the railroad. Focus is on the romance of early railroading.

2877. Lindstrom, C.T. "Brief History of Topolobampo."

*Integral Co-operator* 4-5 (December 1, 1893-October 1, 1894).
A lengthy history of Topolobampo in fourteen installments written from the point of view of a disillusioned member

2878. Lovell, John W. *Co-operative City, and the Credit Foncier of Sinaloa.* New York: Credit Foncier Co., [1886]. 18 pp.

2879. Lowenthal, Bennett. "Topolobampo Colony in the Context of Porfirian Mexico." *Communal Societies* 7 (1987): 47-66.
Provides an overview of the surge of colonization in Mexico between 1877 and 1910, including a list of the major colonies founded by Americans. Describes Owen's ideals and development plans for the colony. Characterizes the rise of factionalism and decline of the colony, the Mexican reaction to the American presence there, and the city of Topolobampo today. Footnotes contain references to many books and articles in Spanish on Topolobampo.

2880. McCarty, F.M. *Chihuahua Al Pacific.* Amarillo: author, 1968. 63 pp.
Provides a history of the original railroad project and an illustrated diary of an actual trip on the railroad taken in 1963.

2881. Michaelis, Patricia. "C.B. Hoffman, Kansas Socialist." *Kansas Historical Quarterly* 41 (Summer, 1975): 166-82.
Provides a biography of Hoffman and describes the work of the Kansas-Sinaloa Investment Co., which Hoffman quit when he was accused of being a profiteer from the project. Well documented. Illustrated.

2882. Moore, Charles W. "Paradise at Topolobampo." *Journal of Arizona History* 16 (Spring, 1975): 1-28.
Moore, a member of the community, wrote this memoir in 1944. It contains much information on persons involved in the colony and on daily life there. Illustrated with photographs.

2883. Mosk, Sanford A. "Railroad to Utopia." *Southwestern Social Science Quarterly* 20 (December, 1939): 243-59.
Provides a narrative history of the project, focusing on

the railroad.

2884.  Nelson,  Edward.   *Company  and  the  Community*.
       Lawrence,  Kansas:  University  of  Kansas  School  of
       Business, 1956, pp. 356-71.
       Provides  information  on  the  Hoffman  family  of
       Enterprise,  Kansas,  including  the  activities  of  C.B.
       Hoffman,  "the  millionaire  socialist,"  who  was  a  major
       stateside backer of Topolobampo.

2885.  Pletcher,  David.   *Rails,  Mines,  and  Progress:  Seven
       American  Promoters  in  Mexico,  1867-1911*.   Ithaca:
       Cornell University Press, 1958, pp. 106-48.
       Provides  a  detailed  examination  of  Owen's  career,
       focusing  on  Topolobampo.   Includes  details  of  the
       planning  of  the  community,  its  proposed  financing,  early
       settlement,  problems  and  controversies  at  the  site,  and
       the  dissolution  of  the  project  amid  controversy  over
       Owen and the railroad project.

2886.  Reynolds,  Ray.   *Cat'spaw  Utopia*.   El  Cajon,  California:
       author,  1972.    171  pp.  plus  many  more  unpaginated
       pages of pictures and documents.
       Contains  a  great  deal  of  information  about
       Topolobampo,  including  a  biography  of  Owen,  the  ideas
       behind  the  project,  the  role  of  Marie  Howland,  the
       founding  of  the  colony,  problems  which  developed,  and
       the  aftermath  through  the  death  of  the  last  colonist  who
       remained  at  the  original  site  in  1967.   Heavily  illustrated;
       many  basic  documents  of  the  colony  are  reproduced.
       Contains  an  extensive  primary  and  secondary
       bibliography,  including  many  items  not  listed  here,
       especially  regarding  railway  development  in  Mexico  at  the
       time of the project.

2887.  Robertson,  Thomas  A.    *Southwestern  Utopia*.   Los
       Angeles: Ward Ritchie Press, 1964.
       A  memoir  and  history  of  Topolobampo  by  one  who
       grew  up  there.   Covers  the  whole  history  of  the  project,
       from  Owen's  theorizing  and  propagandizing  through  the
       end,  with  a  balanced  appraisal  of  the  internal  friction
       which hastened the colony's demise.

2888.  "Sinaloa  Colony:  Experiences  of  a  Kansas  Woman  at
       Topolobampo."   *Republican  Record*  (Erie,  Kansas),
       November 28, 1890, p. 1.

Quotes a Dickinson County, Kansas, woman on life at the colony, painting a grim picture of conditions there.

2889. Texas, Topolobampo, and Pacific Railroad and Telegraph Co. *Reports of George W. Simmons, Jr., Dr. B.R. Carman, and John E. Price, Esq., upon the Route of the Railroad from Topolobampo Bay, on the Gulf of California, to Piedras Negras, on the Rio Grande.* Boston: Press of Rockwell and Churchill, 1881. 48 pp.

2890. ———. *Text of Contract and Concession for the Construction and Operation of the Railroad and Telegraph Line from Piedras Negras to Topolobampo, with Branches to Alamos, Mazatlan, and Presidio del Norte.* Boston: n.p., 1881. 41 pp.

2891. "Topolobampo Colony." *Harper's Weekly* 31 (July 2, 1887): 475, 478.
Says that there are now over 300 colonists at two town sites; provides a grand account of the progress of the colony to date, praising the planning which has gone into it and describing the exchange of labor which is being used in place of money. A drawing of the main colony site shows mainly tent dwellings.

2892. "Topolobampo Folly to Be Revived: Reincarnation of a Scheme Which Cost Kansans Much." Topeka *Daily Capital*, December 21, 1901, p. 8.
Describes an attempt to revive the bankrupt colony using money provided by British investors.

2893. "Topolobampo Scheme Ends." Topeka *Daily Capital*, September 24, 1901, p. 5.
Tells of the abandonment of the colony by its settlers and the purchase of the land by a company proposing to turn it into a sugar plantation.

2894. "Topolobampo: the Site of a Colony Trying Bellamy's Plan." Topeka *Daily Capital*, May 10, 1890, p. 5.
A glowing article telling of great success at the colony. Lists officers of the Kansas-Sinaloa Investment Company.

2895. Valades, Jose C. *Topolobampo: La Metropoli Socialista de Occidente.* Mexico: Fordo de Cultura Economica, 1939. In Spanish.

2896.  Wooster, Ernest S.    "Topolobampo Colony."    *Communities
       of the Past and Present* (cited above as item 175),
       40-44.
           Provides a general history of the project, quoting
       extensively from letters of former members.


# CXXXVIII.  TUOLUMNE CO-OPERATIVE FARM

       Tuolumne Co-operative Farm was founded in the fall of
1945 along the Tuolumne River in the Central Valley of
California.    Its purpose was to provide a community for those
living there, as well as to house a training center for those
who would live cooperatively elsewhere.    155 acres were
purchased; much work was done to put the land into
production.    Cows and goats were raised, along with crops.
Resources were distributed to members on the basis of need.
Members lived in proximity, taking some (but usually not all)
meals in common.    In February, 1954, the group was reported
to have 19 members, including 9 children.


### *Community periodicals*

2897.  *Creative Living.* In publication in the 1950s.

2898.  *Interdependence.* 1951-?
           Contains news on communities, especially those on the
       west coast.


### *Secondary works*

*      Gladstone, Arthur.    "Cooperative Communities Today II"
       (cited above as item 82), 15.
           Describes the cooperative features and the living
       patterns of the community.

*      Hine, Robert V.    *California's Utopian Colonies* (cited
       above as item 98), 157-9.
           Provides a brief overview of the colony.

2899.  Kramer, Wendell B.    "Tuolumne Cooperative Farms."
       *Cooperative Living* 4 (Fall, 1952): 13-4.
           Provides a brief but substantial account of community

life to date.

2900. ———. "Tuolumne Cooperative Farms, Inc." "Criteria for the Intentional Community" (cited above as item 118), 71-4.
Describes the history and goals of the community, detailing its farming operation.

2901. "Tuolumne Cooperative Farm." *Intentional Communities: 1959 Yearbook of the Fellowship of Intentional Communities* (cited above as item 807), 32-3.
Contains a basic description of the community.

# CXXXIX. UNION COLONY

Union Colony was conceived by Nathan C. Meeker, who published a letter seeking fellow colonists in the New York *Tribune* in 1869. Late that year prospective colonists began to meet to lay plans. In 1870 a "locating committee" headed west; a site north of Denver was chosen, and development began. By October 800 settlers were reported to have arrived. The colony named its town to honor Horace Greeley, who enthusiastically promoted the colony in his New York *Tribune*. Among other things, the colony was noted for its dedication to total abstinence from liquor; alcohol was long illegal in Greeley. The cooperative colony lasted only until 1872, but many like-minded persons remained at Greeley, which continued to grow and prosper as a town. W.A. Hinds reported a population of 4,000 in 1878. Meeker became an Indian agent and is usually described as bigoted and insensitive in his dealing with Indians. He was killed in an attack by Ute Indians in 1879.

Survey work: Okugawa (item 139), 203.

*Community periodical*

2902. Greeley *Tribune*.
The town newspaper, originally published by Meeker and named for Horace Greeley's famous newspaper.

*Work by the community leader*

2903. Meeker, N.C.    "Western    Colony."    New    York    *Tribune*,
      December 4, 1869, p. 11.
      A   letter   providing   the   colony's   manifesto   and   urging
      people to join.


*Secondary works*

2904. Albertson,    Ralph.    "Union    Colony."    "Survey    of
      Mutualistic    Communities    in    America"    (cited    above    as
      item 27), 411.
      Provides   a   sketch   of   the   colony,   focusing   on   land
      distribution arrangements.

2905. Arnold,    C.P.    *Joe    Rankin's    Record    Run.*    Douglas,
      Wyoming: n.p., 1929. 7 pp.
      Describes the killing of Meeker. Not seen.

*        Baker, James H., ed.    *History of Colorado* (cited above as
         item 30), v. 2, pp. 448-9, 597-9.
         Provides   a   historical   sketch   including   a   passage   from   a
         settler's   description   of   hardships   in   the   early   days   of   the
         colony;   argues   that   the   founders   of   Union   were   persons
         of   great   ability.    Relates   the   role   of   the   irrigation   work
         at   Union   to   later   irrigation   and   agricultural   developments
         in Colorado.

2906. Baumunk, Lowell.    "Nathan   Cook   Meeker,   Colonist."    M.A.
      thesis,   Colorado   State   College   of   Education,   1949.    135
      pp.
      A   biography   of   the   founder   of   Union   Colony,   from
      Meeker's   involvement   in   Fourierism   from   the   late   1830s
      through   the   Union   Colony   period   to   the   aftermath   of   his
      death.    Contains   a   24-page   annotated   bibliography   of
      books,   newspaper   articles,   letters,   magazine   articles,
      manuscripts, and colony documents.

2907. Boyd, David.    *History: Greeley   and   the   Union   Colony   of
      Colorado.*    Greeley:   Greeley   Tribune   Press,   1890.
      Provides   excellent   early   information   on   Meeker's   ideas
      and   work   toward   the   founding   of   the   colony,   together
      with   a   fairly   detailed   history   of   the   town   to   1890.
      Three   appendices   provide   lists   of   names,   rainfall   charts,
      and other specialized information.

2908. Clark, James Maxwell. *Colonial Days.* Denver: Smith-Brooks, 1902. 148 pp.
Provides historical information on the colony based on files of the Greeley *Tribune.* Not seen.

2909. "Colonization." *Report of the Commissioner of Agriculture for the Year 1870.* Washington: Government Printing Office, 1871, pp. 569-72.
Characterizes the goals, site selection process, and beginnings of the colony; finds it currently prospering.

2910. Ely, Richard T. "Study of a 'Decreed' Town." *Harper's Monthly Magazine* 106 (February, 1903): 390-401.
A favorable account of Greeley, focusing on the post-communal period. The author finds economic cooperation still active, and prohibition still intact. Illustrated with photographs.

\* Federal Writers' Project. *Colorado: A Guide to the Highest State* (cited above as item 67), 162-5.
Details the propagandizing for the colony conducted by Horace Greeley, the settlement of the site, the development of buildings and industries, and the later growth of Greeley as a city.

2911. Flynn, Mary E. "Economic Development of Union Colony." M.A. thesis, Colorado State Teachers College, 1928. 121 pp.
Describes the natural resources of Colorado and the Greeley area, the irrigation projects of the colony, the colony's agricultural enterprises, and the economy of Greeley in the years after the end of the colonization experiment. Contains "A Western Colony," Meeker's manifesto for Union (originally published in 1869), the constitution and bylaws of the colony, and the official certificate of incorporation.

2912. Fogarty, Robert S. "Meeker, Nathaniel C." and "Union Colony." *Dictionary of American Communal and Utopian History* (cited above as item 76), 75, 170-1.
Dictionary entries providing a general picture of the colony.

2913. Geffs, Mary L. *Under Ten Flags: A History of Weld County, Colorado.* Greeley: McVey Printery, 1938.
Makes scattered references to Union Colony, especially

in chapter 2, pp. 25-49.

\*     Hafen, LeRoy R., ed.   *Colorado and its People* (cited above as item 88), v. 1, pp. 328-31.
Sketches the early history of Union, depicting it as a great success which made it a model for many later colonies.

\*     Hall, Frank.   *History of the State of Colorado* (cited above as item 89), v. 1, pp. 531-42.
Describes the site selection for the colony, the settling of the land, the rise of dissent, including a conflict over the sale of liquor, and the cherished visit of Horace Greeley in October, 1870. V. 2, pp. 495-502, contains a description of the Indian massacre (and the situation leading up to it) which killed Meeker.

2914.  Harvey, Mark W.T.   "Misguided Reformer: Nathan Meeker among the Ute."   *Colorado Heritage* 1 (1982): 36-44.
Argues that Meeker was not simply tactless and insensitive to the Utes, as has often been alleged, but that he wanted the Utes to make radical changes in their way of life to cope with an encroaching civilization. Illustrated with engravings, a photograph, and a map.

2915.  Hayden, Dolores.   "Disintegration of Association."  *Seven American Utopias* (cited above as item 90), 260-87.
A history of Greeley and Union Colony, with a focus on architecture. Heavily illustrated. Endnotes contain references to several important newspaper articles not cited here.

\*     Hinds, William Alfred.   *American Communities* (cited above as item 94), 156-7.
Portrays the eight year old community as prospering with a cooperative organization based on agriculture.

\*     Hine, Robert V.   *Community on the American Frontier* (cited above as item 94), 214-9.
Provides a brief historical sketch of the colony, emphasizing its prohibitionism.

2916.  Smith, Barbara.   *First Hundred Years: Greeley, Colorado, 1870-1970.*   Greeley: Greater Greeley Centennial Commission, 1970. 96 pp.

\*     Smythe, William E. "Real Utopias in the Arid West" (cited above as item 1854), 599-604.
Depicts Union Colony as highly successful, and especially notable for bringing irrigation to the high plains.

2917.   Solis, Miguel J. "Union Colony of Colorado." *American Utopias* (cited above as item 20), 165-7.
Provides a brief description of the colony plus five bibliographical entries.

2918.   Sprague, Marshall. "Bloody End of Meeker's Utopia." *American Heritage* 8 (October, 1957): 36-9, 90-4.
Provides a sketch of the colony and its financial problems; argues that Meeker, in dying, helped people to see that Indians were human beings and that he thus made a valuable contribution to his country.

2919.   ————. *Massacre: The Tragedy at White River.* Boston: Little, Brown, 1957, pp. 19-27 (plus other scattered references).
Describes the development of Meeker's ideas about a colony, the selection of a site, problems and disappointments there, and the split of colonists into factions. Describes at some length the events leading up to and following the death of Meeker.

2920.   Willard, James F. *Union Colony at Greeley, Colorado, 1869-1871.* Boulder: University of Colorado Press, 1918. 412 pp.
Introduction provides an overview history of the colony; the balance of the book reproduces original documents, such as minutes, financial records, circulars, membership lists, correspondence, newspaper accounts of the project, and miscellaneous documents. The largest section contains reproduced newspaper articles.

# CXL. UNITED COOPERATIVE INDUSTRIES

United Cooperative Industries was founded in 1923 in Los Angeles as a producers' cooperative, with democratic, worker-owned industries, but by the 1950s it was moving toward becoming a communal society. It operated several businesses related to the film industry. As of February, 1954, it had nine members.

*Community periodical*

2921.  *UCOPIA.*
       Newsletter containing primarily in-house news, but
       some news of other communities as well.


*Secondary works*

\*      Gladstone, Arthur.    "Cooperative Communities Today III"
       (cited above as item 82), 10.
       Describes the situation of the cooperative as it tried
       to become a commune.

2922.  Wooster, Ernest S.    "United Co-operative Industries."
       *Communities of the Past and Present* (cited above as
       item 175), 144-5.
       Provides a brief characterization of the group.


# CXLI.  THE VALE

The Vale was founded outside Yellow Springs, Ohio, in 1960
by a group of Quakers which included Jane and Griscom
Morgan.    The 30 acres of the Vale are owned in common;
homes are private.    The residents seek spiritual fellowship and
individual freedom.
    Correspondence and manuscripts from the Vale are at
Community Service, Inc.


*Secondary works*

\*      *Intentional Community Handbook* (cited above as item
       808), unpaginated.
       Contains a brief description of the community.

2923.  Kramer, Wendell B.    "Vale."    "Criteria for the Intentional
       Community" (cited above as item 118), 97-8.
       Provides a brief overview of the community's goals and
       activities.

2924.  Roberts, Ron E.    "Quaker Experiments: The Vale."    *New
       Communes: Coming Together in America* (cited above as
       item 153), 71-5.

Discusses the Vale's attempt to provide both community and privacy, its pacifism, and the ideas of Griscom Morgan.

2925. "Vale." *Intentional Communities: 1959 Yearbook of the Fellowship of Intentional Communities* (cited above as item 807), 20-1.
Provides a brief introduction to the community.

2926. "Vale Evolves." Dayton *Journal-Herald*, November 25, 1971, pp. 1A, 2A.

# CXLII. VEDANTA COMMUNALISM

The Vedanta Society was established in the wake of the success of Swami Vivekananda in speaking at the World's Parliament of Religions in Chicago in 1893. As early as the summer of 1895, a group of Society members had established a communal residence. In 1900 a 160-acre ashram was established near San Jose, California; in 1906 a monastery was established on the top floor of the new San Francisco temple under the leadership of Swami Trigunatita. A women's convent was established in a rented house nearby, and a short-lived rural communal unit was established at Concord, California. A 375-acre ashram was established in the Berkshires of Connecticut in 1907, and another community was built on 140 acres outside Los Angeles in 1923. Other ventures continued over the years.

*Secondary works*

2927. Avyaktananda, Swami. *Spiritual Communism*. Bath, England: Vedanta Movement, 1970.
A theological and programmatic treatise on community.

2928. Fogarty, Robert S. "Heard, Henry Fitzgerald" and "Paramananda, Swami." *Dictionary of American Communal and Utopian History* (cited above as item 76), 48, 90.
Biographical dictionary entries.

2929. Gambhirananda, Swami. *History of the Ramakrishna Math and Mission*. Calcutta: Advaita Ashrama, 1957.

Describes early communalism in the Vedanta movement, beginning with the construction of a Hindu temple in San Francisco in 1905.

2930. Veysey, Laurence. "Vedanta Monasteries." *Communal Experience* (cited above as item 166), 207-278.
Provides a solid history of Vedanta communalism, including information on history, daily life, and personalities in the movement.

# CXLIII. WASHINGTON COLONY

Washington Colony was organized in Kansas under the leadership of Alexander McPherson, who worked out an arrangement for land to be provided for a settlement on Bellingham Bay in Washington. Some 25 families of colonists arrived by prairie schooner in 1881 and 1882. Its main industry was a sawmill which for a time thrived. However, the colony had problems with the title to its land (part of which was tied up in an estate) and personality conflicts. A creditor finally forced a sale of community assets, bringing the venture to an end in 1884.

Survey work: Okugawa (item 139), 210.

## Secondary works

2931. Edson, Lelah Jackson. *Fourth Corner*. Bellingham, Washington: Whatcom Museum of History and Art, 1968, pp. 204-10.
Provides a history of the colony, focusing on the land title and personality conflicts.

* LeWarne, Charles P. "Communitarian Experiments in Western Washington, 1885-1915" (cited above as item 122), 21-2.
Provides a brief historical sketch of the colony.

* LeWarne, Charles P. *Utopias on Puget Sound* (cited above as item 124), 13.
Contains a brief historical note on the colony, based on information from the author's dissertation (preceding item).

*     Meany, Edmond S.    *History of the State of Washington*
      (cited above as item 129), 320.
      Provides an overview history of the colony.

2932.  Roth, Lottie Roeder.    *History of Whatcom County*.
       Chicago and Seattle: Pioneer Historical Publishing Co.,
       1926, v. 1, pp. 221-33, 245-6.
       Provides a history of the colony, specifying in detail
       the dispute over title to the land.    Illustrated with a
       photograph of the colony mill.

# CXLIV.  WAYNE PRODUCE ASSOCATION

The Wayne Produce Assocation was founded in 1921 at
McKinnon, Georgia, as a community of ethnic Finns engaged
largely in truck gardening.    It was reported to have about 75
members at its peak; most were recruited from the ranks of
Communists or Wobblies.  The group owned some 800 acres.

Survey work:  Albertson (item 27), 421.

*Secondary work*

2933.  Wooster, Ernest S.    "Colony of Finns."    *Communities of
       the Past and Present* (cited above as item 175), 140-2.
       Provides a sketch of the history and organization of
       the colony.

# CXLV.  WESTMINSTER COLONY

Westminster was founded by Lemuel P. Webber, a
Presbyterian clergyman, in 1869.    The following year he came
into control of 6500 acres at Anaheim, California, and began to
build his town.    Land was privately owned, but owners had a
buy-and-sell agreement with the colony.    The major commercial
institution in the town was a cooperative store.    The economy
of Westminster appears to have been largely private, although
land was controlled by the colony and there were several
cooperative enterprises.    The cooperative features of the colony
declined in the late 1870s, and the experiment came to an end
in 1879.

*Secondary work*

2934. Bollman, Ivana Freeman. *Westminster Colony, California 1869-1879*. Santa Ana, California: Friis-Pioneer Press, 1983. 151 pp. Illustrated.
Provides a basic history of the colony.

# CXLVI. WFLK FOUNTAIN OF THE WORLD

Francis H. Pencovic founded this movement, renaming himself Krishna Venta, in the late 1940s. His ideas were influenced by the Book of Mormon. His communal center was located on 16 acres in Box Canyon in the Santa Susanna mountains near Los Angeles. Krishna Venta's alleged sexual promiscuity caused him problems; finally two of his followers set off an explosion which killed him, them, and several others in 1958.

*Secondary works*

2935. Beam, Maurice. "God in a Station Wagon." *Cults of America* (cited above as item 216), 76-90.
Provides an informal look at the group, picturing Krishna Venta as an inept leader.

2936. Mathison, Richard. "Krishna Venta." *Faiths, Cults, and Sects of America* (cited above as item 127), 212-9.
Provides a brief overview of the movement, including information on how it operated after Krishna Venta's death.

2937. Melton, J. Gordon. "WFLK Fountain of the World." *Encyclopedia of American Religions* (cited above as item 130), 504.
Provides a brief history of the community.

2938. Orrmont, Arthur. "Krishna Venta: Mystic with the Mostest." *Love Cults and Faith Healers* (cited above as item 141), 172-90.
Outlines Krishna Venta's early life, including his scrapes with the law, and the development of his religious ideas. Provides an overview of the colony in Box Canyon and of the controversies over the leader's

lifestyle excesses. Describes the fatal explosion and its aftermath.

# CXLVII. WILLARD CO-OPERATIVE COLONY

Willard was a small prohibitionist colony founded by William C. Damon in 1895. Originally organized at Harriman, Tennessee, the colony was finally established near Andrews, Cherokee County, North Carolina. Its economy was to be based primarily on farming; a gold mine and a marble quarry were also to be developed. The colony featured a union Protestant church, a disavowal of competition, a declared aversion to trusts, and ardent prohibitionism. When the colony disbanded in 1896, some members joined the Christian Commonwealth Colony.

Survey work: Okugawa (item 139), 219.

*Secondary works*

2939.  Albertson, Ralph. "Willard Cooperative Colony." "Survey of Mutualistic Communities in America" (cited above as item 27), 414.
Provides a brief sketch of the colony.

\*  Dombrowski, James. *Early Days of Christian Socialism in America* (cited above as item 404), 134.
Provides brief, basic information about the colony.

2940.  Earhart, Mary. *Frances Willard: From Prayers to Politics*. Chicago: University of Chicago Press, 1944, p. 291.
Describes the ideals and early history of the colony.

\*  Fish, John O. "Christian Commonwealth Colony: A Georgia Experiment, 1896-1900" (cited above as item 405), 215.
Provides a brief description of the closing of Willard Colony.

2941.  Kent, Alexander. "Willard Cooperative Colony." "Cooperative Communities in the United States" (cited above as item 117), 639.

Describes the organization, ideals and goals, and disbanding of the community.

2942. "Willard Colony." *Appleton's Annual Cyclopedia, third series, 1896.* New York: D. Appleton and Co., 1897, v. 1, pp. 535-6.
Describes the opening of the colony, the industries it has established, its physical plant, and its eleemosynary institutions.

# CXLVIII. WINTERS ISLAND

Erastus Kelsey of Oakland owned this island in Suisun Bay (in the upper reaches of San Francisco Bay). In 1893 he and Kate Lockwood Nevins organized the colony. The island needed levees to protect against flood to make the land tillable; much work for that purpose was completed. However, the depression which began in 1893 hurt the project. By the late 1890s few of the settlers were left, although Nevins stayed on alone into the 1930s.

Survey work: Okugawa (item 139), 216.

*Community periodical*

2943. *Co-operator.* 1895-7.

*Secondary work*

*        Hine, Robert V. *California's Utopian Colonies* (cited above as item 98), 142-4.
Provides an overview history of the colony.

# CXLIX. WOMAN'S COMMONWEALTH

In the 1860s, Martha White McWhirter of Belton, Texas, founded a new Sunday School in opposition to the existing Methodist institution there; she had come to subscribe to the doctrine of sanctification, which her church rejected. She attracted a following; gradually the group came to be composed primarily (and eventually entirely) of women. In 1879 they began to pool money to help sisters in need, and began to develop industries for self-support. In 1886 they opened a hotel, which was very successful and became a financial mainstay. Membership peaked around 1880 at about 50. Eventually the group moved to Washington, D.C., and lived prosperously, gradually dying out in the early years of the twentieth century.

Some material on the community is in the American Communities Collection at Syracuse University.

Survey work: Okugawa (item 139), 206.

### Secondary works

2944. Albertson, Ralph. "Women's Commonwealth." "Survey of Mutualistic Communnities in America" (cited above as item 27), 407.
Provides a brief sketch of the colony.

2945. Andreadis, A. Harriette. "Woman's Commonwealth: A Study in the Coalescence of Social Forms." *Frontiers* 7 (1984): 79-86.
Sees the group as a synthesis of women's reform societies, Wesleyan perfectionism, and utopian experimentation. Argues that the group did not flout convention so much as seek independence through available social channels.

2946. Atkinson, Bertha. "History of Bell County, Texas." M.A. thesis, University of Texas, 1929, pp. 140-2.
Argues that members of the "Sanctified Band" were largely women unhappy in marriage; that they did not believe in medicine, and that therefore a small child died without medical attention; and that the group was "composed of some of the best people in town." Based largely on interviews with Belton residents.

2947. Bennett, A.L. "Sanctified Sisters." *Sunny Slopes of Long Ago.* Edited by Wilson M. Hudson and Allen Maxwell. Dallas: Southern Methodist University Press, 1966, pp. 136-45.
Focuses on McWhirter's religious experiences and the role special revelation played in her work.

2948. Fischer, Ernest G. "Sanctified Sisters." *Marxists and Utopias in Texas* (cited above as item 2313), 159-76.
Provides a somewhat anecdotal history of the group's Texas years, based largely on contemporary newspaper accounts.

\*      Fogarty, Robert S. "American Communes, 1865-1914" (cited above as item 74), 152.
Contains a one-paragraph history of the group plus a quotation from its constitution.

2949. ———. "McWhirter, Martha" and "Women's Commonwealth, or the Sanctificationists." *Dictionary of American Communal and Utopian History* (cited above as item 76), pp. 72-3 and 171.
Dictionary articles providing a basic overview of the community.

2950. Friend, Llerena. "Texas Communism or Socialism—Early Style." *Library Chronicle of the University of Texas* 7 (Summer, 1963): 33-7.
Provides background information on George Garrison, who wrote an early and important article on the colony (item 2951, below). Also contains brief notes on several pre-1860 Texas colonies.

2951. Garrison, George P. "Woman's Community in Texas." *Charities Review* 3 (November, 1893): 28-46.
Probably the best extant history of the community. Discusses the background and ideas of McWhirter, the development of the community and its relations with the other citizens of Belton, and details of community life, all prior to the move to Washington.

2952. Gerry, Margarita Spalding. "Woman's Commonwealth of Washington." *Ainslee's Magazine* 10 (September, 1902): 133-41.
Describes the group's Belton years, focusing on the successful businesses which brought prosperity, and its way of life in its new quarters in Washington.

2953. Hinds, William Alfred. "Woman's Commonwealth." *American Communities and Co-operative Colonies* (cited above as item 95), 435-41.
Describes the origins of the community and its history through the move to Washington. Provides excerpts from

community documents.

*    Hinc, Robert V.   *Community on the American Frontier*
     (cited above as item 99), 219-20.
     Provides   a   very   brief   characterization   of   the
     community.

2954.  James,  Eleanor.   "Martha  White  McWhirter  (1827-1904)."
       *Women  in  Early  Texas.*   Edited  by  Evelyn  M.
       Carrington.   Austin:  Jenkins  Publishing  Co.,  1975,  pp.
       180-90.
       Details  McWhirter's  development  of  her  distinctive
       ideas  about  sanctification,  the  growth  of  her  following,
       the  group's  financial  success,  and  the  move  to
       Washington.

2955.  ———.   "Sanctificationists  of  Belton."   *American  West*  2
       (Summer, 1965): 65-73.

2956.  Kent,   Alexander.    "Woman's   Commonwealth."
       "Cooperative  Communities  in  the  United  States"  (cited
       above as item 117), 602-4.
       Provides a sympathetic historical sketch of the group.

*    Kitch,  Sally  L.   "Body  of  Her  Own:  Female  Celibacy  in
     Three   Nineteenth-Century   American   Utopian
     Communities" (cited above as item 1784).
     Argues  that  the  choice  of  celibacy  by  the  Shakers,  the
     Koreshans,  and  the  Woman's  Commonwealth  enabled
     female  members  to  reach  higher  than  usual  political,
     economic, and spiritual status.

*    Lauer,  Robert  H.,  and  Jeanette  C.  Lauer.   *Spirit  and  the
     Flesh* (cited above as item 120), 189.
     Describes  the  situation  in  which  two  male  members
     were  allowed  to  join  the  society,  only  to  be  attacked  by
     a mob in Belton.

*    Muncy,  Raymond  Lee.   *Sex  and  Marriage  in  Utopian
     Communities* (cited above as item 135), 34.
     Provides a brief overview history of the community.

2957.  Sokolow,  Jayme,  and  Mary  Ann  Lamanna.   "Women  and
       Utopia:  The  Woman's  Commonwealth  of  Belton,  Texas."
       *Southwestern  Historical  Quarterly*  87  (April,  1984):
       371-92.

Examines the group in light of prevailing ideas about
the proper role of women in the late nineteenth century.
Argues that the Woman's Commonwealth was the most
successful female commune in the nineteenth century,
providing members with business and leadership
experience.

* Strachey, Ray, and Hannah Whitall Smith, *Group
Movements of the Past and Experiments in Guidance*
(cited above as item 161), 143-4.
Provides a history of the community, emphasizing the
social divisiveness it engendered.

2958. Taylor, R. Bruce.     "Woman's Commonwealth."
"Communistic Societies of America" (cited above as
item 163), 787.
Describes the community as small but successful after
its move to Washington.

2959. Tyler, George W.   *History of Bell County.*   San Antonio:
Naylor Co., 1936, pp. 391-5.
Provides a biography of Martha McWhirter, a
description of the growth of the movement, and an
account of the development of the commune in Belton
and Washington. Portrays the movement's members as
honest and sincere, although they were unpopular among
the men of Belton.

2960. Wooster, Ernest S.     "Women's Commonwealth."
*Communities of the Past and Present* (cited above as
item 175), 39.
Provides a brief history of the community,
characterizing it as one of the most successful American
communes.

2961. Wright, Gwendolyn.     "Woman's Commonwealth."
*Architectural Association Quarterly* 6 (1974): 36-43;
*Heresies* 11 (1981): 24-27.
Two versions, essentially, of one article.   Sketches the
history of the movement and its ideas, emphasizing the
way in which the community's use of space expressed its
ideas.   Illustrated with photographs and a diagram.   *AAQ*
much more heavily illustrated.

# CL.  ZION CITY

John Alexander Dowie, a native of Australia, founded Zion City (a community site for his Christian Catholic Church in Zion) in 1901 as a model of what heaven would be like.  He stressed Christian cooperation in business affairs (although Zion City's economy retained some private elements), clean living, and faith healing; he also preached racial equality.  The community was founded in 1901, and soon had industries (including a lace factory), schools, and a large tabernacle. 5000 to 6000 persons may have lived there at one time or another; 2000 blacks had settled there by 1906.  Dowie's guiding hand eventually faltered.  A massive crusade in New York in 1903 failed; by 1904 Dowie was often absent, and he increasingly came to see himself as the prophet Elijah III.  In April, 1906, while he was in Mexico, he was deposed by his lieutenants.  Wilbur Glenn Voliva became the new theocrat, holding the community together fairly well until the depression. Voliva was perhaps best known for his belief in a flat-earth theory.

Dowie and Zion City produced much literature; this listing represents selections only.  See the National Union Catalog for many more items, primarily booklets and pamphlets.  Some materials on the community are in the American Communities Collection at Syracuse Univesity.

Survey works:  Liefmann (item 125), 23; Okugawa (item 139), 226-7.


*Community periodicals*

2962.  *Divine Healing Series.*
    Zion City serial.

2963.  *Final Warning.* Zion City. 1934-1938.
    Replaced *Leaves of Healing* (item 2965, below) during a four-year suspension of publication of that periodical.

2964.  *Herald of the Kingdom.* Zion City.
    Replaced *Leaves of Healing* for two issues.

2965.  *Leaves of Healing.*  1894-1934 and 1938-.  Published at Chicago through 1902; thereafter at Zion City.

2966.  *Theocrat.*   In   publication   from   the   1910's   at   least   into
       the 1930's.

2967.  *Voice   from   Zion.*     1897-1904.     Published   at   Chicago
       through part of 1902; thereafter at Zion City.

2968.  *Zion Banner.*

### Primary work

2969.  *American   First-Fruits:   Being   a   Brief   Record   of   One
       Year's   Divine   Healing   Missions   in   the   State   of
       California   by   the   Rev.   John   Alexander   and   Mrs.   Dowie.*
       San Francisco: Leaves of Healing, 1890.  175 pp.

### Works by a community leader

2970.  Dowie,   John   Alexander.     *Gospel   of   Divine   Healing   and
       How   I   Came   to   Preach   It.*     Zion   City:     n.p.,   n.d.
       Pamphlet. "Divine Healing Series #7."

2971.  ———.     *Personal   Letters   of   John   Alexander   Dowie.*
       Compiled   by   Edna   Sheldrake.     Zion   City:   W.G.   Voliva,
       [1912].

2972.  ———.     *Sermons   of   John   Alexander   Dowie,   Champion   of
       the   Faith.*     Edited   by   Gordon   Lindsay.     N.p.:   Voice   of
       Healing Publishing Co., [1951].  125 pp.

2973.  ———.     *"Times   of   the   Restoration   of   All   Things,"   Elijah
       the   Restorer—Malachi   4:5;   Illustrated   in   the   Life   and
       Work   of   John   Alexander   Dowie.*     Edited   by   John   A.
       Lewis. Zion City: John A. Lewis, 1917.  36 pp.

2974.  ———.     *Voice   from   Zion:   Sermons   and   Addresses.*
       Chicago:   Zion   Printing   and   Publishing   Co.,   1897-1904.
       Eight volumes.

2975.  ———.     *Zion's   Conflict   with   Methodist   Apostasy
       Especially   in   Connection   with   Freemasonry.*     Chicago:
       Zion Publishing House, 1900.  204 pp.

2976.  ———.     *Zion's   Holy   War   Against   the   Hosts   of   Hell   in
       Chicago.*     Chicago:   Zion   Publishing   House,   1900.     330

pp.
A Collection of addresses.

2977. ————. *Zion's Second Feast of Tabernacles Field [sic] in Shiloh Tabernacle, Zion City, Illinois, July 12 to 22, 1902.* Chicago: Zion Printing and Publishing HOuse, 1903. 316 pp.

### Secondary works

2978. Abbott, Ernest. "Religious Life in America: New Sects and Old." *Outlook* 72 (September 13, 1902): 122-8.
This survey of current dissenting religious movements includes, on pp. 124-6, an account of the author's visit to a Dowie worship service; he found the people a "fold of submissive sheep."

2979. "America's Model Community." *National Business Review* 7 (February 15, 1928): 5.
A brief puff depicting Zion City as an ideal community and Voliva as a brilliant leader.

2980. Barton, William E. "Dream of Dowie—and the Awakening of Zion." *Independent* 60 (April 19, 1906): 915-7.
An unsympathetic account by a Protestant minister of Dowie's claiming to be king and prophet; reflects on changes implied by the recent takeover by Voliva.

2981. Blumhofer, Edith. "Pentecostal Branch Grows in Dowie's Zion." *Assemblies of God Heritage* 6 (Fall, 1986): 3-5.
Describes Charles Parham's Pentecostal preaching mission to Zion City and his enthusiastic reception by the Zionites; argues that many in Zion City found Pentecostalism to be a fulfillment of Dowie's teachings. Illustrated.

2982. Bovard, Freeman D. "Dowie's Story of the Pacific Coast." *Christian Advocate* 78 (December 10, 1903): 2001-2.
Argues that Dowie's healings do not actually occur; recounts an incident in which Dowie was treated by doctors for a dislocated shoulder.

2983. Buckley, James M. "Dowie, Analyzed and Classified." *Century Magazine* 64 (October, 1902): 928-32.

Discusses Dowie under several headings: personage, ecclesiastic, healer, and the like. Finds much failure in him, but notes that shortcomings seem not to discourage Dowie's followers. Illustrated.

2984. Calverton, Victor. "Zion City." *Where Angels Dared to Tread* (cited above as item 39), 311-27.
Describes Dowie's early life, the development of the movement, Dowie's excesses and weaknesses, and the movement's decline.

2985. "Church and State in America." *Outlook* 83 (August 4, 1906): 779-80.
Provides a favorable account of a court's intervention into the financial affairs of Zion City.

2986. "City Built on Lace." *Illustrated World* 35 (June, 1921): 659.
Provides a description of the lace factory at Zion City, emphasizing the huge size of the machines and the skill needed to operate them. Illustrated with two photographs of lace machines.

2987. Clark, Elmer T. "Christian Catholic Church." *Small Sects in America* (cited above as item 43), 154-6.
Sketches the history of Dowie and the church, Dowie's downfall, and the rise of Voliva.

2988. Cook, Philip L. *Zion City, Illinois: John Alexander Dowie's Theocracy.* Zion, Illinois: Zion Historical Society, 1970. 20 pp.
Provides a biography of Dowie and a history of the development of Zion City through the rise of Voliva.

2989. ———. "Zion City, Illinois—The Kingdom of Heaven and Race." *Illinois Quarterly* 38 (Winter, 1975): 50-62.
Provides a good historical overview of the community, including a biographical sketch of Dowie, the founding of the colony, and the deposing of Dowie and rise to leadership of Voliva.

2990. ———. "Zion City, Illinois: Twentieth Century Utopia." Ph.D. dissertation, University of Colorado, 1965. 443 pp.
A detailed study of the movement and its context in American social history from the beginning through the

deposing of Dowie and the decline of the community. Contains a 16-page bibliography listing primary sources, contemporary news stories, and theses not cited here.

2991.   Darms, Anton.  *Life and Works of John Alexander Dowie, 1847-1907.*  Zion, Illinois: Christian Catholic Church, 191-?  16 pp.

2992.   Davenport, Walter.  "They Call Me a Flathead."  *Collier's* 79 (May 14, 1927): 30-1.
Conveys Voliva's ideas on fundamentalism, the flat-earth theory, and the rapture.  Illustrated with photographs of Dowie and Voliva.

2993.   "Dowie and Dowieism."  *American Monthly Review of Reviews* 28 (November, 1903): 611-3.
Provides a sketch of Dowie's rapid rise to prominence.

2994.   "Dowie and His Troubles in New York."  *Literary Digest* 27 (October 31, 1903): 572.
Reviews hostile press coverage of Dowie's New York crusade.  Illustrated with several acerbic cartoons from newspapers.

2995.   "Dowie Bankrupt."  *Literary Digest* 27 (December 12, 1903): 820-1.
Reviews press coverage of serious financial problems afflicting Zion City; most accounts suggest that Zion City faces hard times, but will probably survive.

2996.   "Dowie Financial Embarrassments."  *Outlook* 72 (November 8, 1902): 574-5.
Reports on financial problems looming in the Dowie empire.

2997.   "Dowie Host in New York City."  *Outlook* 75 (October 24, 1903): 430-1.
Reflects on the New York crusade, concluding that Dowie plays on human weaknesses, bribing followers with promises of healing and joy in the afterlife.

2998.   "Dowie Movement in Chicago."  *Outlook* 68 (June 22, 1901): 429-30.
Describes the recent substantial growth of Dowieism in Chicago and the movement's claim of many miraculous healings.

2999. "Dowie's Coming Invasion of New York." *Literary Digest* 26 (March 21, 1903): 429-30.
Reviews press reactions to the news that Dowie will hold a crusade in New York; most papers expect him to have a good chance of success at making converts.

3000. Duis, Perry R., and Glen E. Holt.    "God in Illinois." *Chicago* 28 (March, 1979): 116-9.
A feature story recounting the history of Zion City. Illustrated with photographs of Dowie and his wife, Voliva, Zion City buildings, and members of the movement.

3001. Dwyer, James L.    "Elijah the Third."    *American Mercury* 11 (July, 1927): 291-9.
Recounts the life and career of Dowie.    Focuses on his personal shortcomings and more extravagant claims.

3002. "End of a Sect Maker."    *Outlook* 85 (March 16, 1907): 593.
A brief characterization of Dowie and his followers at the time of his death.

3003. Federal Writers' Project.    *Illinois: A Descriptive and Historical Guide.*    Chicago: A.C. McClurg, 1939, pp. 407-8.
Describes the origins and early growth of the town, the roller-coaster economy of the years after Dowie's demise, the distinctive buildings in Zion City, and the prevalence of stringent blue laws.

3004. Felton, Bruce, and Mark Fowler.    "Wilbur Glenn Voliva." *Felton and Fowler's Famous Americans You Never Knew Existed* (cited above as item 72), 253-4.
Details Voliva's flat-earth theory.

3005. "Flat Voliva."    *Literary Digest* 121 (May 23, 1936): 32-3.
Describes the decline of Zion City under Voliva, with depression-era financial problems and the increasing population of non-Dowieites who were beginning to dominate Zion's political scene.

3006. Fogarty, Robert S.    "Dowie, John Alexander."    *Dictionary of American Communal and Utopian History* (cited above as item 76), 32.
Biographical dictionary entry.

3007. Friedman, I.K. "John Alexander Dowie." *Everybody's Magazine* 9 (November, 1903): 567-75. Excerpted in "Dowie and Dowieism." *American Monthly Review of Reviews* 28 (November, 1903): 611-3.
A flattering personality profile of Dowie; provides a brief history of Dowie and his movement. Heavily illustrated with pictures of Zion City.

3008. Gadd, Laurence D. "Flat Earth." *Second Book of the Strange* (cited above as item 1780), 235-6.
Provides notes on the history of the flat-earth theory; describes Voliva's version of it and his promotion of the concept from his base in Zion City.

\* Gardner, Martin. "Flat and Hollow" (cited above as item 1781), 16-9.
Describes and ridicules Voliva's flat-earth theory.

3009. Gilchrist, H.H. *Dr. Dowie Before the Court of Public Opinion.* Topeka: Crane and Co., 1899. 109 pp.

3010. "Giving Out That Himself Was Some Great One." *Christian Advocate* 78 (October 22, 1903): 1695-6.
Refutes the claims of Dowie of his prophetic powers; exposes false statements Dowie has made.

3011. Halsey, John J. "Genesis of a Modern Prophet." *American Journal of Sociology* 9 (November, 1903): 311-28.
Describes the life of Dowie, the development of his work, his conflicts with the medical establishment and with the law, and the financing and land purchases for Zion City. Focuses on conferences in early 1896 at which Dowie organized his church; contains several pages of quotes in which Dowie outlines his ideas, the organization of the movement, and the rules by which members would have to live.

3012. ———. *History of Lake County, Illinois.* Chicago: Roy S. Bates, 1912, pp. 214-8, 251-3, 740-77.
Provides a general history of Zion City and an analysis of its economic failure, a detailed account of the money and property involved in the receivership decreed by a court in 1907, a summary of the religious and moral precepts of Zion City (by Theodore Forby), a discussion of the political and commercial history of the city (by

Judge V.V. Barnes), and a biography of Dowie to 1903.

3013.  Harlan, Rolvix.  *John Alexander Dowie and the Christian Catholic Apostolic Church in Zion.*  Evansville, Wisconsin: Robert M. Antes, 1906.  204 pp.  Originally a Ph.D. dissertation at the University of Chicago. Describes Dowie's life, healing, publicity, theology, and followers; portrays Dowie as a religious imposter of low character.  Quotes frequently from Dowieite literature and reproduces texts of several of Dowie's tracts.

*       Hayden, Dolores.  *Seven American Utopias* (cited above as item 90), 18, 48, 54.
        Provides brief information on Zion City's planning and architecture.  Contains a picture of the hotel at Zion City.

3014.  Heath, Alden R.  "Apostle in Zion."  *Journal of the Illinois State Historical Society* 70 (May, 1977): 98-113. Describes Dowie's early life, the growth of the tales of healing and of the movement, the establishment of Zion City, and later events in the movement.  Illustrated with photographs and graphics from the movement.

3015.  "Heresy of Over-Faith."  *Independent* 60 (April 5, 1906): 814-5.
        Tells of the deposing of Dowie; expresses hope that Zion City will prosper under new leadership.

3016.  Holland, Robert T.  "Ethical Phase of the Zion City Movement."  M.A. thesis, Northwestern University, 1911.  77 pp.
        Analyzes the activities and behaviors of the movement (including healing, abstinence from alcohol and tobacco, and community-building) as expressions of its ethical stance.

3017.  "John Alexander Dowie."  *Current Literature* 35 (November, 1902): 539-40.
        Biographical sketch and note on Dowie's empire at the onset of his New York crusade.  Illustrated with a photograph of Dowie.

3018.  Kneitel, Tom.  "WCBD, the 'Flat Earth' Radio Station." *Popular Communications*, June, 1986, pp. 31-4.
        Provides a brief characterization of Zion City and of

the founding of Voliva's radio station there; describes Voliva's flat-earth theory. Illustrated with photographs.

3019. Kusch, Monica H. "Zion, Illinois: An Attempt at a Theocentric City." Ph.D. dissertation, University of California at Los Angeles, 1954. 286 pp.
Tells the history of Zion City and analyzes its political and economic stagnation after Dowie's time. Concludes that the religious circumstances of the founding of the city have left a lasting mark on its land use and social, political, and economic development. Illustrated with photographs and maps of Zion City in various periods. Includes three appendices, comprising biographies of Dowie and Voliva and summarizing the teachings of the church.

3020. Lindsay, Gordon. *Life of John Alexander Dowie, Whose Trials, Tragedies, and Triumphs are the Most Fascinating Object Lesson of Christian History.* Shreveport: Voice of Healing Publishing Co., 1951. 275 pp.

3021. McDermott, William F. "Zion City Comes Down to Earth." *Coronet*, June 1943, 49-52.
Describes the flamboyant career of Dowie, the rule of Voliva in Zion, and the normalization of public life there after the decline of Voliva's power in the 1930s.

3022. Mayer, F.E. "Christian Catholic Church in Zion." *Religious Bodies of America* (cited above as item 128), 446.
Contains three paragraphs of basic information on Dowie and his organization, delineating the differences between Dowie and Voliva regarding interpretation of scriptures.

3023. Mehling, Harold. *Scandalous Scamps.* New York: Henry Holt, 1959, pp. 108-31.
Provides a skeptical overview of Dowie's career, depicting him as combining "sanctimoniousness, sexual thievery, and the profit motive."

3024. Napes, John A. "John Alexander Dowie and His Zions." *Independent* 53 (August 1, 1901): 1786-91.
Describes the various Dowie buildings and enterprises in Chicago, the new city being built, and a recent

worship service in Chicago. Illustrated with pictures of
the movement's Chicago buildings and the first few new,
modest buildings at Zion City.

3025. Newcomb, Arthur. *Dowie: Anointed of the Lord.* New
York: Century, 1930. 403 pp.
Provides a skeptical but informed history of the
Chicago and Zion City years of Dowie and his movement,
written in the form of a novel focusing on a movement
leader close to Dowie.

3026. Orrmont, Arthur. "John Dowie: The Great Restorer."
*Love Cults and Faith Healers* (cited above as item 141),
75-91.
Provides a biographical sketch of Dowie and an outline
history of the movement, emphasizing the centralization
of power in Dowie; describes the New York debacle and
the decline of the movement.

3027. "Our Own Times." *Reader Magazine* 8 (July, 1906): 100-1.
Characterizes Dowie, following his stroke and loss of
leadership position, as a "faker," and now a "blubbering,
shuddering, irascible, noisy old man."

3028. Parham, Sarah E. (Mrs. Charles F. Parham). *Life of
Charles F. Parham.* Joplin, Missouri: Tri-State Printing
Co., 1930, pp. 155-77.
Describes Parham's Pentecostal revival in Zion City in
1906, after the fall (but before the death) of Dowie;
criticizes Dowie for losing his once-great power by
achieving great popularity and wealth.

3029. Pokin, F.N. "Zion: City of the White Dove." M.A.
thesis, University of Chicago, 1967. 178 pp.
A comprehensive account of Dowie and the movement
through the rise of Voliva. Compares Zion City to the
planned city of Pullman, Illinois. Includes a substantial
bibliography listing many theses, dissertations, pamphlets,
and special materials, including some not cited here.

3030. Prowitt, Alfred E. "Croesus at the Altar." *American
Mercury* 19 (April, 1930): 398-405.
Profiles Voliva from his childhood through his work for
Dowie and his achievement of total power at Zion City;
focuses on his dominant, combative personality.

3031. Randolph, Vance. "Elijah the Restorer." *Americans Who Thought They Were Gods* (cited above as item 149), 8-9. A brief account of the history of the community, focusing on the special prophetic claims of Dowie.

3032. Reinders, Robert C. "Trianinng for a Prophet: The West Coast Missions of John Alexander Dowie, 1888-1890." *Pacific Historian* 30 (Spring, 1986): 3-14. Describes Dowie's variety of faith healing and his early healing revivals in California. Illustrated with photographs.

3033. "Religious Comment on the Dowie Crusade." *Literary Digest* 27 (October 31, 1903): 585-6. Recounts comments by religious leaders critical of the Dowie crusade in New York, especially by those taking offense at Dowie's assaults on the intelligence and outlook of the clergy.

3034. "Rise and Fall of Dowieism." *Current Literature* 42 (February, 1907): 206-7. Argues that the Christian Catholic Church was a personality cult which would not long outlast Dowie, who was now incapacitated.

3035. Seldes, Gilbert. *Stammering Century*. New York: John Day, 1928, pp. 389-401. Provides a skeptical but balanced overview history of Dowie and Zion City.

3036. "Some Reflections Suggested by the Dowie Crusade." *Literary Digest* 27 (October 24, 1903): 547-8. Contains a digest of reactions to Dowie by Stephen Bonsal, who finds that people seeking truth are attracted to all kinds of religious movements, and therefore Dowie's success should not be surprising.

3037. "Spectator." *Outlook* 75 (October 31, 1903): 486-8. Provides accounts of visits to two Dowie crusade sessions in New York.

3038. Swain, John. "John Alexander Dowie: The Prophet and His Profits." *Century Magazine* 64 (October, 1902): 933-44. Describes the personality and style of Dowie, the lifestyle rules for followers, the growth of his empire, and the development of his anti-medical ideas; concludes that Dowie was sincere but that he used poor methods in his work. Illustrated with drawings.

3039.  "Third Elijah." *Independent* 62 (March 14, 1907): 626-8.
       Recalls Dowie's strengths and weaknesses at his death; expresses the hope that Zion City will prosper under new, more rational leadership.

3040.  "They Stand Out from the Crowd." *Literary Digest* 117 (May 12, 1934): 11.
       Notes that Voliva's flock seems to be deserting him and that Zion is becoming secularized.

3041.  Thompson, Charles A., Jr. "Social, Economic and Political Development of Zion, Illinois." M.A. thesis, Northern Illinois University, 1963. 110 pp.
       Provides a biographical sketch of Dowie and a history of the church and community, including much material on the community after Dowie's death. Especially useful for its outlining of the detailed regulations which governed daily life in Zion City, and for its description of the local Theocratic Party and Zion City politics.

3042.  Townshend, Grover. "City of the Plains." *Munsey's Magazine* 27 (September, 1902): 843-5.
       Describes the first six months of development at Zion City. Well illustrated with photographs, including some of the city under construction.

3043.  Underwood, Henry. "Downfall of a Prophet." *Harper's Weekly* 50 (December 22, 1906): 1857.
       Pinpoints the debacle of the New York crusade of 1903 as the beginning of the end for Dowie; includes an account of one of the services during that episode.

3044.  Wacker, Grant. "Marching to Zion: Religion in a Modern Utopian Community." *Church History* 54 (December, 1985): 496-511. Reprinted in revised version, *Assemblies of God Heritage* 6 (Summer and Fall, 1986): 7-9, 7-10.
       Finds that Zion City was created not so much by Dowie as by the deeply religious convictions of the people in the movement whose energies Dowie mobilized; argues that explanations of Zion City which overlook its perfectionist religiosity fail to explain why so many

people joined such an improbable movement. Illustrated.

3045. Wallace, Irving. *Square Pegs: Some Americans Who Dared to Be Different.* New York: Knopf, 1957. 315 pp.
The first part of chapter 1 (pp. 3-9) contains the author's childhood recollections of Zion City and recounts Voliva's flat-earth theory as described personally to the author by Voliva many years earlier.

* Webber, Everett. *Escape to Utopia* (cited above as item 168), 346.
Contains a brief characterization of Dowie and Voliva.

3046. "What is Dowie?" *Independent* 55 (October 22, 1903): 2528-30.
Appraises the state of Dowie's empire at the time of his New York crusade; speculates that the movement will decline quickly after the death of its leader.

3047. "When Dowie Invades New York." *Munsey's Magazine* 29 (April, 1903): 42-7.
A lighthearted joshing of Dowie and his movement on the eve of their visit to New York. Illustrated with a full-page formal portrait of Dowie.

3048. "Where the Rules of the Church Are Law." *Christian Century* 49 (August 17, 1932): 997-8.
Describes disputes in Zion City, which now has a substantial nonmember population, especially focusing on a fracas caused by city officials' ordering interstate buses not to stop in the city on Sundays.

3049. White, Roy. "Play—That Saved a City." *Christian Herald* 61 (March, 1951): 6, 87-8, 90.
Depicts the Zion City passion play as a rallying point which stands against Zion City's divided and confused past. Includes accounts of conversations with actors in the play.

3050. "Zion City." *Engineering News and American Railway Journal* 44 (August 16, 1900): 101.
Brief news item describing the topographic survey of the townsite, early planning for the city, and the sizes and specifications of buildings.

3051. "Zion in a Ferment."    *Outlook* 82 (April 14, 1906): 825.
      Describes financial and personal problems boiling over
      at Zion City.

This index refers to entries by item number, not by page number. Items listed more than once in the bibliography are cited in each appearance after the first by an asterisk (*), not by number; this index does not include terms used in items listed by asterisk. Similarly it does not include terms used in the introduction or in section introductions.